FIFTH EDITION

E-MARKETING

Judy Strauss

Associate Professor of Marketing

University of Nevada, Reno

Raymond Frost

Professor of Management Information Systems

Ohio University

Pearson Education International

Editorial Director: Sally Yagan
Acquisitions Editor: James Heine
Product Development Manager: Ashley Santora
Editorial Project Manager: Melissa Pellerano
Editorial Assistant: Karin Williams
Media Project Manager: Denise Vaughn
Director of Marketing: Patrice Lumumba Jones
Senior Marketing Manager: Anne Fahlgren
Marketing Assistant: Susan Osterlitz
Permissions Project Manager: Charles Morris
Production Project Manager: Renata Butera
Senior Managing Editor: Judy Leale
Operations Specialist: Renata Butera

Art Director: Jayne Conte
Cover Designer: Bruce Kenselaar

Director, Image Resource Center: Melinda Patelli
Manager, Rights and Permissions: Zina Arabia
Manager, Visual Research: Beth Brenzel
Image Permission Coordinator: Kathy Gavilanes
Manager, Cover Visual Research & Permissions: Karen Sanatar
Full-Service Project Management / Composition: Integra Software Services, Ltd.
Printer/Binder: Bind-Rite, Robbinsville/Command Web
Typeface: 10/12 Minion

Credits and acknowledgments borrowed from other sources and reproduced, with permission, in this textbook appear on appropriate page within the text.

Pearson Education LTD., London
Pearson Education Australia PTY, Limited
Pearson Education Singapore, Pte. Ltd
Pearson Education North Asia Ltd
Pearson Education Canada, Inc.
Pearson Educación de Mexico, S.A. de C.V.
Pearson Education -- Japan
Pearson Education Malaysia, Pte. Ltd
Pearson Education, Upper Saddle River, New Jersey

Prentice Hall
is an imprint of

PEARSON
Prentice
Hall

www.pearsonhighered.com

10 9 8 7 6 5 4 3 2 1
ISBN 13: 978-0-13-246184-9
ISBN 10: 0-13-246184-6

This book is dedicated to Cyndi and Malia
Raymond Jr., Luke, and David

BRIEF CONTENTS

CONTENTS

PREFACE

The internet, combined with other information technologies, has created many interesting and innovative ways to provide customer value since its inception in 1969. Web sites for marketing communication and customer support; one-to-one communication to many different receiving devices; consumer behavior insights based on off-line and online data combination; inventory optimization through CRM–SCM integration; a single-minded focus on ROI and associated performance metrics were all on the cutting edge of e-marketing when the fourth edition of this textbook was published and they continue to develop as important strategies.

As internet adoption matured at 70 percent–75 percent in the United States in the past few years, we thought things would be pretty quiet on the internet frontier. Then the social media appeared, holding marketers to their holy grail that customer needs and wants are paramount. High-readership blogs, social networks (such as Facebook and LinkedIn), and online communities (such as YouTube and Second Life) gave consumers the opportunity to be heard in large numbers. We've also discovered that consumers trust each other more than they trust companies, fueling the growth of social media. Further, search engines have become reputation engines, ranking Web sites partially according to popularity and relevancy. A simple brand misstep can appear as an online video showing a product malfunction or in the thousands of words posted by disgruntled customers. Conversely, marketers can use the Web, e-mail, and social media to build stellar brand images online and increase sales both online and offline. To do this, marketers must now learn how to engage the citizen journalists, listen to them, and use what they learn to improve their offerings. This book uniquely tells how to do this.

The book you have in your hands is the fifth edition of *E-Marketing* (the first edition was named *Marketing on the Internet*). We added a new chapter on the social media for this edition and discuss many perspectives on these new media throughout other chapters—for example, in the chapter "E-Marketing Research" , we describe RSS feeds and other means of monitoring social media for chatter about a company and its brands, and in the chapter on consumer behavior online, we added a section on user-generated content. This textbook is also different in the following important ways:

- We wrote the first edition of this book in 1996, providing a long-term perspective on e-marketing not available in any other book.
- We explain electronic marketing not simply as a list of ideas, strategies, and techniques, but as part of a larger set of concepts and theories in the marketing discipline. In writing the book, we discovered that most new terminology could be put into traditional marketing frameworks for greater understanding.
- The text focuses on **cutting-edge business strategies** that generate revenue while delivering customer value. As well, we reflect current practice by devoting many pages to **performance metrics** that monitor the success of those strategies.
- We highly recommend that **marketers learn a bit about the technology** behind the internet, something most of us are not drawn to naturally. Although it is not necessary to be able to set up e-commerce servers, knowledge of the possibilities for their use will give savvy marketers an advantage in the marketplace. This book attempts to educate marketers gently in important technology issues, showing the relevance of each concept.

- This book describes e-marketing practices in the United States, but it also takes a **global perspective** in describing market developments in both emerging and developed nations. Much can be learned from other industrialized nations that lead in certain technologies, such as wireless internet access.
- Most e-marketing books do not devote much space to **law and ethics**: we devote an entire chapter to this, contributed by a practicing attorney.

WHAT'S NEW IN THIS EDITION

Following the fourth edition, this book elaborates on the e-marketing planning and marketing mix topics from a strategic perspective. Part I begins with setting the context for marketing planning. Part II discusses legal and global environments. Part III begins the e-marketing strategy discussion in depth, and Part IV continues with marketing mix and customer relationship management strategy and implementation issues.

This edition focuses more on e-marketing strategy and less on principles of marketing refresher material. Statistics about internet use and strategy effectiveness were extensively updated throughout every chapter. This edition also features seven new chapter-opening vignettes, many new screen images, and updated "Let's Get Technical" boxes. Significantly covered new topics include Web analytics, engagement metrics, virtual worlds, location marketing online, and an entire new chapter and appendix on the social media (including search marketing). We also propose a new way of looking at physical and digital media and suggest that the terms *off-line/online* and *traditional/non-traditional* media no longer work. The following table highlights additions and significant revisions for the fifth edition.

Chapter	Opening Vignette	Chapter Content (subject areas that were added or expanded)
1	New: Dell Starts Listening	• A largely re-written chapter • Web 1.0: E-marketing's past and history timeline • Web 2.0: E-marketing today and what strategies are working • Web 3.0: The future, with customers gaining control, appliances converging, traditional and social media losing their distinction, wireless networking increasing, and the semantic Web
2	The Amazon Story (updated)	• Updated e-business models to prune the less successful and add others such as social networking • New metrics sections for Web analytics (e.g., server logs and page tags) and user engagement (e.g., time spent on page) • Revised balanced scorecard to reflect currently used internet metrics
3	New: The Second Life Story	• Updated cost figures within the general framework for e-marketing strategy

Chapter	Opening Vignette	Chapter Content (subject areas that were added or expanded)
4	New: *Idol* Goes Global	• Updated all internet adoption statistics and global practices in emerging economies • New stories from Ethiopia, Nepal, Egypt, and Lithuania, and an extensive update on China, the rising star in the internet world • New table showing that internet growth occurs in countries with low computer adoption
5	Software Infringement (updated)	• Revised by an attorney specializing in trademark, patent, and copyright law to include up-to-date legal concerns
6	The Purina Story	• New sections on monitoring the social media using Google alerts, RSS feeds, or special software • Removed less-used research techniques online and added more on survey research, especially panel data • Presented 12 channels for online reputation monitoring • Added data about Wikipedia's proven quality
7	New: The Customer's Story (how they use the social media)	• New findings on consumers trusting each other more than companies or anyone else except doctors • Data showing that internet adoption is at the maturity phase of life cycle • Expanded the previous four desired outcomes to five—connect, create, enjoy, learn, trade—explaining the trend of content uploading on blogs, YouTube, and more
8	The 1–800-Flowers Story (updated)	• New local marketing section as part of geographic segmentation • New kids segment and lengthy explanation of the Webkinz virtual world for social networking • New social media engagement segments from Forrester Research, from "Inactives" at the bottom rung to "Creators" at the topmost rung
9	The J. Peterman Story	• Examples of e-mail addresses that build trust in companies • New section on how to invite user-generated content as a differentiation strategy (e.g., blog visitor comments and space for images/videos) • Presented the idea of trusting, listening, responding, and learning from customers • Included a product differentiation comparison of MSN, Yahoo! and Google

(continued)

Chapter	Opening Vignette	Chapter Content (subject areas that were added or expanded)
10	The Google Story (updated)	• Added much more on customer product codesign and how companies solicit product improvement ideas using blogs and RSS feeds • Reflections from the Interbrand 100 global brands in 2007 about what makes a great global brand (including several internet pure plays)
11	New: The VideoEgg Story	• Added a price comparison for a book at MySimon • Introduced a new section on online payment options, such as PayPal and other e-money options • Discussed yield management in the context of dynamic pricing • Included a new section on the trend toward renting software (e.g., Salesforce.com)
12	The Dell Direct Model (updated)	• Expanded the discussion on multichannel marketing and consumer friction for online shopping, such as shopping cart abandonment • Introduced the long tail concept from the book by Chris Anderson • Major chapter reorganization, cutting lots of basic marketing principles and putting the e-marketing models first • Added more information on B2B markets and content sponsorship • Included a discussion about online retailer conversion rates and industry benchmarks
13	New: Will it Blend?	• Discussed many emerging trends such as consumer-generated ads, mobile SMS/location-based ads and lots of new rich media formats (e.g., gadgets and widgets) • New sections: how to build a buzz online, rules for e-mail marketing success, and personal selling online using live chat • Added podcasts and MP3 players to the discussion • Expanded material about the Web site as a doorway to the site • Moved all the media discussion to the new Chapter 14
14 (new chapter)	New: Halo 3 Launch	• Introduced a new way of looking at media to replace traditional/nontraditional and off-line/online: physical/digital and paid/unpaid (Exhibit 14.1) • Most of the chapter is about the social media, with sections on search engines (with natural, paid, and vertical search strategies), online communities, blogs, and social networks • Brought the media discussion and metrics from Chapter 13

Chapter	Opening Vignette	Chapter Content (subject areas that were added or expanded)
15	The Cisco Story (updated)	• Included more about marketing automation from SAS • Added information about Sales Force Automation (SFA) from Salesforce.com • Discussed behavioral targeting • Added more on RSS feeds in the technology section

PEDAGOGICAL FEATURES

We included many features in *E-Marketing* to enhance learning. Based on our cumulative years of teaching experience, we've identified the best practices in university teaching and integrated items that work well for us and from which we've had positive faculty adopter responses.

- **Marketing concept grounding:** In each chapter we structure material around a principle of marketing framework and then tell how the internet changed the structure or practices. This technique provides a bridge from previously learned material and presents it in a framework for easier learning. In addition, as things change on the internet, students will understand the new ideas based on underlying concepts.
- **Learning objectives:** Each chapter begins with a list of objectives that, after studying the chapter, students should be able to accomplish. Given our active learning preference, the objectives are behavioral in nature.
- **Best practices from real companies:** A company success story starts each chapter. Students will find these to be exciting introductions to the material. Numerous new case histories for this edition offer current examples of firms that do it right.
- **Graphical frameworks in each chapter:** We created unique e-marketing visual models to show how each chapter fits among other chapters in the entire part. In addition, several chapters feature models for within-chapter understanding.
- **Chapter summaries:** Each chapter ends with a summary of its contents. Although these summaries capsulate the chapter guts, they were not created so that students can read them in lieu of the chapter content.
- **Key terms:** These terms are set in bold text within the chapter to signal their importance.
- **Review and discussion questions:** Questions at the chapter end are aimed at both knowledge-level learning and higher levels of application, synthesis, and evaluation.
- **Web activities:** When students become actively engaged in the material, learning is enhanced. To this end we included several activities and internet exercises at the end of each chapter.
- **Appendices:** Most people don't brag about an appendix, but we included four important ones: internet adoption statistics, 50 social media sites, a thorough glossary, and book references.

INSTRUCTOR SUPPORT MATERIALS

This book is a fifth edition text about a moving target. No one has quite laid out the territory the way we have in *E-Marketing*. To assist in developing courses, Prentice Hall offers an online Instructor's Resource Center with various support materials.

Web site location: www.pearsonhighered.com/strauss

1. **Instructor's Manual:** On the site are traditional instructor's manual items as well as class assignments, links to internet marketing syllabi, and other materials to enhance teaching from this book. Contact your Prentice Hall representative to gain password access to the site.
2. **Test bank:** An electronic test bank is available to faculty adopting this textbook. Question items focus on chapter learning objectives and other important material. They include items at all levels of learning from knowledge through application and evaluation.
3. **PowerPoint Slides:** The Web site holds files containing improved slides for lectures to accompany each chapter. This aid is for those who want to present book material in class lectures.
4. **E-mail the authors:** We encourage e-mail from faculty using this textbook. Send questions, suggestions for improving the text, and ideas about teaching the class jstrauss@unr.edu.

ACKNOWLEDGMENTS

The most pleasant task in this project is expressing our appreciation to the many individuals who helped us create this work. We are always amazed that the scope of the job requires us to request, plead, cajole, and charm a number of folks into helping us. Our gratitude is enormous.

First, we would like to thank our students over the years. We teach primarily because we love working with our students. They inspire us, teach us, and keep us on our toes.

Next we want to thank Prentice Hall for giving us a place to showcase our ideas. Charles Morris was especially responsive with copyright permission questions. We want to thank Sally Yagan, our Editorial Director and acting Editor, as well as Melissa Pellerano, who served as our Editorial Project Manager, and Judy Leale, who led the way in production. We also appreciate the many reviewers who gave us excellent suggestions for improving the fourth edition—we've used nearly all of them in writing the fifth edition. We could not have written this book without the support of our institutions, the University of Nevada, Reno and Ohio University.

Other individuals contributed significantly to this book's content. Brian O'Connell contributed the interesting and timely "Ethical and Legal Issues" chapter for the fourth edition, and Brett J. Trout, Esq., revised it for this edition. Al Rosenbloom wrote the fascinating chapter on "A World of E-Marketing Opportunities." Special thanks to Adel I. El-Ansary at the University of North Florida for his expert assistance on the third and fourth editions of this book. Cyndi Jakus single-handedly obtained permission to reprint all the screen images in the book. Ching-Chu Huang provided tremendous help with research, references, and the glossary. We would also like to acknowledge the contribution of Jacqueline Pike to the "Let's Get Technical" boxes.

Finally, support and encouragement to accomplish a major piece of work come from friends and family. To them we are indebted beyond words.

ABOUT THE AUTHORS

Judy Strauss and Raymond Frost have collaborated on Web development, academic papers, practitioner seminars, and three books in eleven editions since 1995. They also developed a new course in 1996, "Marketing in Cyberspace." This book grew out of that course and has significantly evolved along with changes in e-marketing.

Judy Strauss is Associate Professor of Marketing at the University of Nevada, Reno. She is an award-winning author of 12 books and numerous academic papers in internet marketing, advertising, and marketing education. Strauss is co-author of the trade book *Radically Transparent: Monitoring and Managing Reputations Online*, and textbooks *Building Effective Web Sites* and the *E-Marketing Guide*. She has had many years of professional experience in marketing, serving as entrepreneur as well as marketing director of two firms. She currently teaches undergraduate and M.B.A. courses in marketing communications, internet marketing, and marketing management and has won two college-wide teaching awards. Strauss earned a doctorate in marketing at Southern Illinois University and a finance M.B.A. and marketing B.B.A. at the University of North Texas. Contact: jstrauss@unr.edu.

Raymond Frost is Professor of Management Information Systems at Ohio University. He has published scholarly papers in the information systems and marketing fields and is an associate editor of *The Journal of Database Management*. Frost is co-author of *Building Effective Web Sites* and the *E-Marketing Guide*. Dr. Frost teaches database, electronic commerce, and information design courses. He has received Ohio University's Presidential, University Professor, College of Business, and Senior Class teaching awards. Dr. Frost is working on publications in data modeling and database pedagogy. He is co-author of a forthcoming book, *A Visual Introduction to Database: An E-Business Perspective*. Dr. Frost earned a doctorate in business administration and an M.S. in computer science at the University of Miami (Florida) and received his B.A. in philosophy at Swarthmore College.

PART ONE

E-Marketing in Context

CHAPTER 1

Past, Present, and Future

The old message, market, and medium *have been replaced by* conversation, community and connection.

—Sonia Simone, CEO, Remarkable Communication

We're living through a wholesale change, but all most of us can do is worry about the color of the links on our blogs.

—Seth Godin, author

Chapter Outline

E-Marketing Landscape
    What Works?
    Internet 101
    E-Marketing is Bigger Than the Web
    E-Marketing is Bigger Than Technology
        Individuals
        Communities
        Businesses
        Societies

E-Marketing's Past: Web 1.0
    The "E" Drops from E-Marketing
    Marketing Implications of Internet Technologies

E-Marketing Today: Web 2.0

The Future: Web 3.0
    Consumers in Control—But Not Complete Control

The key objective of this chapter is to develop an understanding of the background, current state, and future potential of e-marketing. You will learn about e-marketing's important role in the firm's overall integrated marketing strategy.

After reading this chapter, you will be able to:

- Explain how the internet and information technology advances offer benefits and challenges to consumers, businesses, marketers, and society.

- Distinguish between e-business and e-marketing.

- Explain how increasing buyer control is changing the marketing landscape.

- Understand the distinction between information or entertainment as data and the information-receiving appliance used to view or hear it.

- Identify several trends that may shape the future of e-marketing.

Dell Starts Listening

Dell Computer has always been America's darling with its high quality equipment, direct distribution model, and great customer service. Yet, in June 2005, Dell was brought to its knees by a single blogger—Jeff Jarvis of BuzzMachine.com:

> I just got a new Dell laptop and paid a fortune for the four-year, in-home service. . . . The machine is a lemon and the service is a lie . . . DELL SUCKS. DELL LIES. Put that in your Google and smoke it, Dell.

This post brought a hailstorm of similar customer service complaints that lasted for nearly two years, and this issue has come to be known as "Dell's Hell." What happened?

Dell held 28.2 percent of U.S. computer market share in 2004, according to the global market intelligence firm IDC. Wanting to pare costs, Dell followed a current trend and outsourced its technical customer service to a firm in India in the early 2000s. Things looked great as costs dropped and market share increased to 28.8 percent the following year. However, complaints about the customer service also increased: Better Business Bureau complaints rose 23 percent and Dell's customer satisfaction declined 6.3 percent, according to a University of Michigan survey. A 2005 Google search for "dell customer service problems" returned nearly 3 million links. Clearly the outsourcing strategy was not having the desired effect.

Like many firms, Dell decided to sit tight for a year and wait for the online complaint storm to pass. When it didn't stop, Dell appointed a digital media manager to "deal" with the internet chatter. Lional Menchaca initiated

(*continued*)

(*continued*)

several Dell blogs in multiple languages as mechanisms for handling customer complaints and ideas and to have conversations with stakeholders about the problems and Dell's actions to fix them. IdeaStorm.com is a notable blog and social network where users post ideas and vote on them, with the best percolating to the top.

Dell responds to the ideas, makes changes in the company, and reports on the progress. In the first three months, IdeaStorm gathered 5,000 ideas, over 20,000 comments, and more than 350,000 idea endorsements. These resulted in over 20 changes to the company (see Beal and Strauss, 2008, for more on "Dell's Hell").

E-MARKETING LANDSCAPE

Dell learned the hard way that companies must listen to individual customers online or pay a dear price. Listening was only a start—Dell found that a company can benefit by truly engaging stakeholders in conversation and using what it learned to improve the company. This example also shows that some marketing principles never change. Companies must meet the needs of their customers. Further, markets always welcome good products and demand good customer service. Customers trust well-respected brands and talk to others about them. What is new is that these classic concepts are tested and enhanced on blogs, databases, wireless mobile devices, and other internet technologies.

What Works?

The rapid growth of the Web, the subsequent bursting of the dot-com bubble, and mainstreaming of the internet and related technologies created today's climate: the comprehensive integration of e-marketing and traditional marketing to create seamless strategies and tactics. This provides plenty of profitable strategies, as below. This is just a sampling of what you'll find in later chapters.

- **E-commerce** shipments by U.S. manufacturers were 27 percent of all commerce in 2005. Fifteen percent of service revenue and 18 percent of all wholesaler trade sales used online technologies, according to the U.S. Census Bureau.
- **Advertising online** has finally become an important part of advertiser media budgets, with a growth rate of 25 percent from 2006 to 2007 (totaling over $20 billion).

- **Search engine advertising** (i.e., purchasing ads on a search engine results page) yielded 35 percent of new customers for online retailers, while 29 percent came from natural search (i.e., tactics to land a firm's link high on a search engine results page), according to Morgan Stanley research.
- **User-generated content** is now a huge part of online content. This includes everything from consumer-created commercials to YouTube videos, Flickr photos, iTunes podcasts, as well as all the text on blogs and user review sites (such as the Amazon.com book reviews).
- **Online communities** gather users with like-minded interests for conversation and networking. This includes social networking sites such as LinkedIn and Facebook, social media Wikipedia, Yahoo! Answers, and more. Marketers use these sites to build brands and create a buzz.
- **Personalization** on Web site recommendation engines such as Amazon and Yahoo! Music helps marketers target individuals based on their online behaviors.
- **Internet communications** such as instant messaging, e-mail marketing, and telephony (VoIP) are here to stay. For example, Skype (the free internet telephony service) is available in 28 languages and has over 100 million registered users.
- **Mobile internet access.** There are 3.25 billion mobile phone subscriptions worldwide. When added to mobile computing, the wireless internet offers users anytime, anywhere access.
- **Local marketing** efforts work well online, thanks to Google local search, eBay classifieds

(with 19 million visitors in the second quarter of 2006), and the hugely popular Craigslist. eBay and Craigslist also showed that charging a **transaction fee** works well online.

- **Online aggregators** are sites that bring together users and information, such as Squidoo.com (entertainment), Monster.com (jobs), Wikipedia.com, and Meebo.com (instant messaging portal).
- **Infrastructure processing** allows supply chains to save costs by moving products, information, and financing data quickly, accurately, and automatically.

Internet 101

Technically speaking, the **internet** is a global network of interconnected networks. This includes millions of corporate, government, organizational, and private networks. Many of the computers in these networks hold files, such as Web pages and videos, that can be accessed by all other networked computers. Every computer, cell phone, or other networked device can send and receive data in the form of e-mail or digital files over the internet. These data move over phone lines, cables, and satellites from sender to receiver. One way to understand this process is to consider the internet as having three technical roles: (1) content providers who create information, entertainment, and so forth that reside on computers with network access, (2) users (also known as *client* computers) who access content and send e-mail and other data over the network, and (3) a technology infrastructure to move, create, and view or listen to the content (the software and hardware). Note that individuals can be both users and content providers at various times. Incidentally, with this edition of *E-Marketing*, we stopped capitalizing the word *internet*. Following *Wired Magazine*'s suggestion, we agree that the internet is not a place (requiring a proper noun's capitalization) but a medium, similar to radio and television.

There are two special uses of the internet:

1. **Intranet**—A network that runs internally in a corporation but uses internet standards such as HTML and browsers. Thus, an intranet is like a mini-internet but with password protection for internal corporate consumption.

2. **Extranet**—Two or more proprietary networks that are joined for the purpose of sharing information. If two companies, or a company and its suppliers or customers, link their intranets, they would have an extranet. The access is normally only partial.

E-business, e-marketing, and e-commerce are internet applications. **E-business** is the continuous optimization of a firm's business activities through digital technology (according to the Gartner Group). Digital technologies are things such as computers and the internet, which allow the storage and transmission of data in digital formats (1s and 0s). In this book, we use the terms *digital technology* and *information technology* interchangeably. E-business involves attracting and retaining the right customers and business partners. It permeates business processes, such as product buying and selling. It includes digital communication, e-commerce, and online research, and it is used in every business discipline. **E-commerce** is the subset of e-business focused on transactions.

E-marketing is only one part of an organization's e-business activities. **E-marketing** is the *use of information technology* in the processes of creating, communicating, and delivering value to customers and for managing customer relationships in ways that benefit the organization and its stakeholders. More simply defined, e-marketing is the result of information technology applied to traditional marketing. E-marketing affects traditional marketing in two ways. First, it increases efficiency and effectiveness in traditional marketing functions. Second, the technology of e-marketing transforms many marketing strategies, as shown in the Dell example. This transformation also results in new business models that add customer value and/or increase company profitability, such as the highly successful Craigslist and Google Ad Sense advertising models (see Chapter 2).

However, e-marketing involves much more than these basic technologies and applications.

E-Marketing Is Bigger Than the Web

The **Web** is the portion of the internet that supports a graphical user interface for hypertext navigation with a browser such as Internet

Explorer. The Web is what most people think about when they think of the internet. Electronic marketing reaches far beyond the Web. First, many e-marketing technologies exist without the Web, including software and hardware used in customer relationship management, supply chain management, and electronic data interchange arrangements pre-dating the Web. Second, non-Web internet communications such as e-mail, internet telephony, and text messaging are effective avenues for marketing. Some of these services can also use the Web, such as Web-based e-mail; however, most professionals do not use the Web for e-mail (preferring software such as Microsoft Outlook). Third, the internet delivers text, video, audio, and graphics to many more information-receiving appliances than simply personal computers (PCs). As shown in Exhibit 1.1, these forms of digital content also go over the internet infrastructure to the television, personal digital assistants, cell phones, and even the refrigerator or automobile. Finally, offline electronic data-collection devices, such as bar code scanners and databases, receive and send data about customers and products over an intranet.

It is helpful to think of it this way: Content providers create digital text, video, audio, and graphics to send over the internet infrastructure to users who receive it as information, entertainment, or communication on many types of appliances. As marketers think outside of the Web, they find many new possibilities for creating products that provide value and communicate in ways that build relationships with customers.

E-Marketing Is Bigger Than Technology

The internet is like a watering hole for humans. We come for easy, inexpensive, and quick access to digital information and entertainment, and in turn it transforms individuals, businesses, economies, and societies. This book focuses on the union of technology and marketing; however, a brief overview of the big picture is useful for understanding e-marketing's impact.

INDIVIDUALS The internet provides individual users with convenient and continuous access to information, entertainment, and communication. If "information is power," individuals have more power than ever before, as Dell experienced. Consumers compare product features and prices using search engines and read product reviews from other consumers at www.epinions.com and other sites. Further, consumers use the internet to bring music, movies, and other types of entertainment directly to their PCs and televisions—on their schedule and preferred receiving device, not that of the medium distributor. Finally, the internet enables multimedia one-to-one communication through e-mail, internet-based telephone services, collaborative software such as NetMeeting, and more. The internet continues to affect the way many individuals work, communicate, and consume, and marketers scramble to provide value and earn a piece of the profits.

COMMUNITIES Strangers in countries worldwide form online communities to discuss a variety of

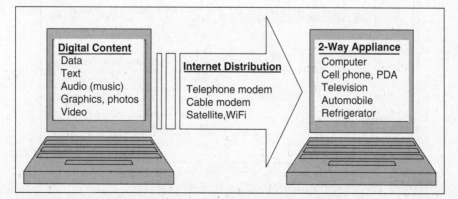

EXHIBIT 1.1 The Web Is Only One Aspect of E-Marketing

things because of the internet. Consumers pay monthly fees to compete in highly engaging multimedia games and virtual worlds online, such as Second Life. Communities form around shared photos (Flickr), videos (YouTube), and individual or company profiles (FaceBook). One of the biggest trends in community building centers on Web logs (blogs). **Blogs** are online diaries, or journals, frequently updated on Web pages. Search engine Technorati.com follows over 112 million blogs and notes that there are over 175,000 new blogs every day (Exhibit 1.2). Micro sites, such as tumblr.com and twitter.com allow individuals to follow each other's short posts and link uploads. Business communities also abound online, especially around shared industries or professions. Another example of online communities is auctions in both business and consumer markets. Finally, independent communities have formed around peer-to-peer networking in the music industry. Individuals download music files from one person's PC to another's using software such as that offered by KaZaA. The internet brings together business partners and consumers from faraway geographic locations to communicate and collaborate online.

BUSINESSES The digital environment enhances business processes and activities across the entire organization. Disciplines work together in cross-functional teams worldwide using computer networks to share and apply knowledge for increased efficiency and profitability. Financial experts communicate shareholder information and file required government statements online. Human resources personnel use the internet for electronic recruiting and training—in fact, 78 percent of recruiters use search engines to learn more about candidates and 35 percent have eliminated prospects based on what they found (according to recruiting firm ExecuNet). Production and operation managers adjust manufacturing based on the internet's ability to give immediate sales feedback—resulting in just-in-time inventory and building products to order.

Strategists at top corporate levels leverage computer networks to apply the firm's knowledge in building and maintaining a competitive edge. Digital tools allow executives easy access to data from their desktops and show results of the firm's strategies at the click of a mouse.

SOCIETIES Digital information enhances economies through more efficient markets, more jobs, information access, communication globalization, lower barriers to foreign trade and investment, and more. The internet's impact is not evenly

EXHIBIT 1.2   Technorati.com Follows the Blogosphere
Source: Courtesy of Technorati (www.technorati.com).

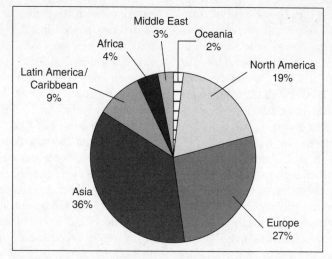

EXHIBIT 1.3 Proportion of Global Internet Users in Various Regions
Source: www.internetworldstats.com.

distributed across the globe, as shown in Exhibit 1.3. The approximately 1.24 billion users connected to the internet worldwide represent just 18.9 percent of the global population (see www.internetworldstats.com). The top 10 nations account for 61 percent of all usage (see Exhibit 4.2). There were about 215.0 million U.S. internet users in 2007, representing 71.4 percent of the population—as compared with China, the second largest market with 162.0 million users, and Norway, with the highest percentage of internet penetration (88.0%). At the same time, stories abound about indigenous peoples in remote locations gaining health, legal, and other advice or selling native products using the internet. Clearly, the internet is having a huge, but unequal, worldwide impact.

A networked world creates effects that some see as undesirable. Societies change as global communities based on interests form, and worldwide information access slowly decreases cultural and language differences. Some say that the existence of a truly global village will have the effect of removing cultural differences, which is seen as negative. As well, many in the United States are concerned by the high degree of technology outsourcing. This inevitable result of a global economy, greased by the internet, means there will be big changes in many countries.

Easy computer networking on mobile devices from any location means that work and home boundaries are blurring. Although this option makes working more convenient, it may encourage more workaholism and less time with family. Yet another issue is the digital divide—the idea that internet adoption occurs when folks have enough money to buy a computer, the literacy to read what is on Web pages, and the education to be motivated to do it. Internet critics are justifiably concerned that class divisions will grow, preventing the upward mobility of people on lower socioeconomic levels and even entire developing countries. Meantime, governments are working to solve some of these problems, but they have other important worries, such as how to collect taxes and tariffs when transactions occur in cyberspace in a borderless world. Finally, the problems of **spam** (unsolicited e-mail), online fraud, and computer viruses slow down the positive impact of the internet and e-marketing practices. These kinds of problems are the unavoidable results of all new technologies.

E-MARKETING'S PAST: WEB 1.0

The internet is nearly 40 years old. Started in 1969 as the ARPANET, it was commissioned by U.S. Department of Defense's Advanced Research Projects Agency (ARPA) as a network for academic and military use. The first online community, the USENET, began 10 years later and over 800 million messages are now archived in Google Groups. The first Web pages and internet browsers appeared in 1993 and that was the internet's tipping point. This was Web 1.0. Companies, media, and users flocked to this new Web and it grew more quickly than had radio, television, or any previous medium (Exhibit 1.4).

This first generation of e-business was like a gold rush. New start-ups and well-established businesses alike created a Web presence and experimented plenty. Many companies quickly attracted huge sales and market shares, but only a handful brought anything to the bottom line. In early 2000, one estimate listed 21 firms with 12-month sales growth between 100 percent and 500 percent—but all had negative profits. Between early 2000 and 2002, however, more than 500 internet firms shut down in the United States alone—the so-called dot-com bust. After the bust dust had settled, almost 60 percent of the public dot-com companies making it through hard times were profitable by the fourth quarter of 2003.

Brick-and-mortar retailers, such as the bookseller Barnes & Noble and Wall Street investment firms, may have felt relief as their online competitors were failing, but quickly noted that internet technologies had fundamentally changed the structure of theirs and several other industries. In what *BusinessWeek* called the "first wave of internet disruption," firms such as Amazon, Expedia,

---

1969 ARPANET commissioned by U.S. Department of Defense for academic and military use.

1975 First mailing list for the new computer network (first e-mail sent in 1965).

1979 USENET established to host discussions. First post in 1981. Later managed by GoogleGroups (800 million archived messages as of 2008).

1984 Number of connected computer hosts reaches 1000.

1987 Number of connected computer hosts reaches 10,000. First e-mail connection with China.

1988 First virus, affects 10% of the 60,000 hosts.

1993 Early Web sites appear and business and media take notice.

1994 First banner ads appear on hotwired.com. "Jerry and David's Guide to the World Wide Web" appears (later named Yahoo!).

1995 eBay opens its doors and disrupts the classified advertising business.

2000 Napster.com shows the world that peer-to-peer networking can work. Businesses show that e-commerce doesn't always work (the dot-com crash).

2002 Running your own blog is now considered hip. Power begins to shift to users.

2003 Recording Industry Association of America (RIAA) sues 261 people for illegal music downloading.

2004 16% of the world's population uses the Internet. Businesses figure out how to be profitable with e-business models.

2007 19% of the world's population is online. Internet usage in industrialized nations reaches maturity.

EXHIBIT 1.4 Internet Timeline for Interesting and Amusing Facts

Source: Some of this information from Hobbes' Internet Timeline (available at www.zakon.org). Internet adoption rates from www.worldinternetstats.com.

E*TRADE, and the former CDNow (purchased by Amazon) transformed the way books, travel, investments, and music were sold ("E-Biz Strikes Again!" 2004). Disrupted industries in the first wave generally offered tangible products that were easily compared online and purchased for the lowest price.

Having gone through the boom and the bust in developed nations (the internet is still booming in many emerging economies), businesses then entered what Gartner Group called the *plateau of profitability* (Exhibit 1.5). It was a time when marketers returned to their traditional roots, relying on well-grounded strategy and sound marketing practices, but using information technology in ways that increased the firm's profit—no more throwing money at ideas that don't return a desired amount on investment. During the dot-com shakeout from 2000 to 2002, the industry experienced much consolidation. Some firms, such as Levi Strauss, stopped selling online both because it was not efficient and because it created *channel conflict* with Sears Roebuck and Company and other long-time retail customers. Other firms merged, with the stronger firms acquiring smaller ones, although in at least one case an e-business firm took over a traditional firm: AOL purchased Time Warner (as of this writing that union is about to break up). All of this activity is typical in a maturing market environment.

The "E" Drops from E-Marketing

Gartner Group predicted that the "e" would drop, making electronic business just part of the way things are done (refer to Exhibit 1.5). This means that e-business is just business, and e-marketing is just marketing. We believe that this is now true; however, e-business will always have its unique models, concepts, and practices. Markets and traditional marketing practices continue to change, sometimes in fundamental ways, due to information technology. For instance, the concept of online search is intrinsic to e-marketing, continues to evolve, and has important implications that marketers must understand. However, most marketing processes stand the test of time—technology has

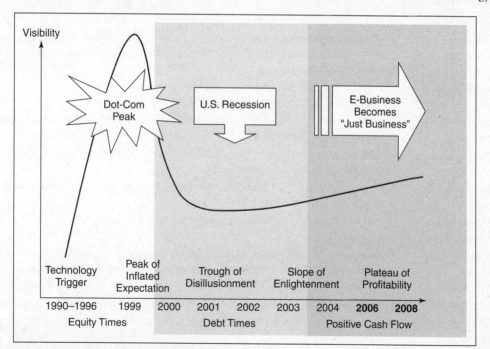

EXHIBIT 1.5 E-Business Just Business?

Source: Courtesy of Reinier Evers (www.trendwatching.com).

just given them a new twist. Marketing research is greatly enhanced with online data collection, but the process of identifying research problems, collecting data, and using the results to make marketing decisions will never change. In short, marketers must stay well grounded in the discipline and simultaneously be current on new information technologies and changing e-marketing concepts to remain competitive. This is necessary because the moment marketers feel comfortable about the "e" dropping, new technologies will challenge traditional practices. For example, the e-marketing landscape is now changing rapidly due to consumer-generated content and social networking.

An example of a firm that has already gone through Gartner's entire cycle is Charles Schwab, which allowed e.Schwab.com to cannibalize the larger brick-and-mortar securities firm in 1998. Dubbed "eat your own DNA" by former CEO Jack Welch of General Electric, Schwab astutely pitted the online and offline business models against each other and allowed the most profitable methods to win. The e.Schwab model resulted in lower prices, incorporation of successful e-marketing strategies, and faster-growing accounts and assets. For this brokerage firm, e-business is just business.

Marketing Implications of Internet Technologies

Early marketers who grasped what internet technologies could do were better poised to integrate information technology into marketing practice (Exhibit 1.6). Compare these properties to those of the telephone. The telephone is a mediating technology, has global reach, and has network externality. In contrast, the internet has properties that create opportunities beyond those possible

Property	Marketing Implications
Bits, not atoms	Information, products, and communication in digital form can be stored, sent, and received nearly instantaneously. Text, audio, video, graphics, and photos can all be digitized, but digital products cannot be touched, tasted, or smelled.
Mediating technology	Peer-to-peer relationships, such as auctions and music file sharing, and business partnerships can be formed regardless of geographic location. Technology allows timely communication and data sharing, such as with businesses in a supply chain.
Global reach	Opens new markets and allows for worldwide partnerships, employee collaboration, and salesperson telecommuting.
Network externality	Businesses can reach more of their markets with automated communication, and consumers can disseminate brand attitudes worldwide in an instant.
Time moderator	Consumers hold higher expectations about communication with companies and faster work processes within companies.
Information equalizer	Firms employ mass customization of communication, and consumers have more access to product information and pricing.
Scalable capacity	Firms pay for only as much data storage or server space as needed and can store huge amounts of data.
Open standard	Companies can access each other's databases for smooth supply chain and customer relationship management, which equalizes large and small firms.
Market deconstruction	Many distribution channel functions are performed by nontraditional firms (e.g., Edmunds.com and online travel agents) and new industries emerged (e.g., ISPs).
Task automation	Self-service online lowers costs and makes automated transactions, payment, and fulfillment possible.

EXHIBIT 1.6   Internet Properties and Marketing Implications

Source: Properties adapted from Allan Afuah and Christopher Tucci, *Internet Business Models and Strategies* (New York: McGraw-Hill/Irwin, 2001).

with the telephone, television, postal mail, or other communication media. It is these differences that excited early marketers and had them wondering how to best capitalize on them.

These internet properties not only allow for more effective and efficient marketing strategy and tactical implementation but also actually changed the way marketing is conducted. For example, the fundamental idea of digitizing data (bits, not atoms) has transformed media and software delivery methods, as well as created a new transaction channel. Also, the internet as information equalizer has shifted the balance of power from marketer to consumer.

Marketers must understand internet technology to harness its power. They do not have to personally develop the technologies, but they need to know enough to select appropriate suppliers and direct technology professionals.

Biz/ed, the Web site for educators, summarized e-business and e-marketing opportunities flowing from the internet's unique properties:

- Reduce costs of production by reducing overheads—for example, not having a retail outlet in a busy high street location with high rents, and reducing stock costs.
- Increase sales.
- Access new markets across the globe.
- Target market segments more effectively.
- Provide more accurate information and improve the customer service experience.
- Improve the efficiency of the supply chain.
- Improve employee motivation through more flexible working methods.
- Allow 24/7 access to the firm's products and services.

(The Benefits of e-Business and Marketing, 2006)

E-MARKETING TODAY: WEB 2.0

The unique properties and strengths of internet technologies provided a springboard from the first to the second generation (Web 2.0), as described by NetLingo:

The components of Web 2.0 sites (and the popularity of blogs and social networking) exist because of the ability to offer mini-homepages, a gig of storage, your own e-mail, a music player and photo, video and bookmark sharing . . . all of which are initially "first-generation" technologies.

(www.netlingo.com)

However, technology only opens the window of opportunity. Marketers and their markets create the hot new products that capitalize on Web 2.0 technologies. Whereas Web 1.0 connected people to computer networks, Web 2.0 connected people with machines and also with each other in social networks. Collectively called **social media**, these are Web pages allowing social networking and are primarily authored by internet users (also called user-generated media [UGM] or consumer-generated media [CGM]). Social media sites are increasing in number and attracting users more quickly than are traditional media sites (such as CNN.com).

Today, the internet has matured in industrialized nations. High adoption rates and heavy Web and e-mail use are commonplace. User-generated media are the norm. Let's examine some of the key elements of today's Web 2.0 landscape.

- **Power shift from sellers to buyers.** Both individual and business buyers are more demanding than ever because they are just one click away from a plethora of global competitors, all vying for their business. As well, consumers have more control than ever, shaping brand images with their every online post. In this environment, buyer attention is a scarce commodity and customer relationship capital a valued asset, and companies are learning to engage and listen to customers (as Dell discovered).
- **Search engines are now reputation engines.** Relevance is one of Google's search algorithm variables. The more high-traffic, similar-topic Web pages that point to a site, the higher it appears on search engine results pages (SERP) for specific key words—meaning it is more relevant to the user. Popularity, as measured by incoming links, improves brand exposure, awareness, image, site traffic, and

ultimately sales. Search marketing is now a key part of online marketer budgets.

- **Market and media fragmentation.** The mass market has been slowly disappearing since about 1992, as evidenced by the decline in prime-time television ratings (Bianco, 2004), growth of cable television, and increasing number of special-interest magazines. The internet put finality to this trend by extending it to its ultimate—a market size of one customer—and prompted marketers to create products and communication to small target groups.
- **Content is still king online.** Marketers must now be agile and flexible for blog posting and responding to consumer-generated media. In this environment, corporate one-way spin is yielding to corporate and stakeholder conversation. Content changes rapidly and moves around to blogs and other pages in a flash.
- **Connections are critical.** Social networking is the name of the game today. Job recruiters scour social networks for job candidates, and business deals are made among LinkedIn members who have never met in person. It is about who you know online and what they say about you.
- **Improved online and offline strategy integration.** This integration is especially evident in **multichannel marketing**—offering customers more than one way to buy something, such as a Web site, retail store, and catalog. Retailers manage customers via databases accessible by all employees. In a media example, NBC allows its 13.5 million online users to subscribe to the site content; download widgets; add content to wikis, message boards, and the corporate blog; and view video clips through their site, as well as through iTunes and YouTube.
- **Marketing investment is moving online.** As previously mentioned, both advertising and e-commerce dollars have jumped dramatically in the last two years. Although the number of U.S. internet users has remained stable for years, now there are more dollars chasing them and profits are improving.

- **High broadband adoption at home (57%).** Fast internet connectivity allows consumers to enjoy entertainment on demand. They can record television programs on digital video recorders and send to their PCs or iPods for viewing on the airplane, for example. Just as important, fast internet connectivity allows consumers to upload their own videos and other content to social media Web sites.
- **Refined metrics.** The internet allows for tracking every mouse click, and marketers now have well-established measures for online tactics. For instance, many use **customer acquisition cost (CAC)**—the cost of acquiring a new customer—and most monitor Web site visitor numbers, conversions to sales, and return on online investment. Of course, as the social media change the scene, marketers are experimenting with new metrics.
- **Intellectual capital rules.** Imagination, creativity, and entrepreneurship are more important resources than financial capital. This was true of the first-generation internet and continues to this day. The difference today is that marketers now know how to use solid marketing and business principles to monetize creative ideas.
- **The long tail.** Made famous by Chris Anderson's book, this refers to the economy of abundance and explains how cheap computing and storage make it possible to increase revenue by selling small quantities of a large number of products online. For example, in 2004, Amazon.com had 2.3 million books in inventory as compared to 130,000 at a typical Barnes & Noble brick-and-mortar store. Amazon is able to sell a large variety of hard-to-find books in smaller quantities, and the sale of products not available in offline bookstores comprises 57 percent of Amazon's total sales. This idea has turned economic models upside down.

Many of these changes made traditional marketing more efficient and effective in reaching and selling to markets. However, some truly changed traditional marketing in fundamental and critical ways.

THE FUTURE: WEB 3.0

Marketers are in a "new age of engagement, participation, and co-creation," according to Nielsen Media ("Super Buzz or Super Blues?" 2008). These budding trends will help to define the next few years in the internet's evolution. **Engagement** involves turning on a prospect to a brand idea enhanced by the surrounding context, according to the Advertising Research Foundation. Turning on a prospect means to connect with her emotionally and cognitively. Online engagement is analogous to offline experience marketing, such as the famous Build-A-Bear retailers or Disney theme parks. Online, marketers engage users by enticing them to participate—upload videos or photos, post comments on a blog, and so forth. Co-creation occurs when users help marketers create products or advertising. For example, Doritos held a contest where users created 30-second televison commercials. Site visitors voted on the finalists and the winner's ad was shown during the 2007 SuperBowl game. Software developers use co-creation when they ask users to test beta versions of Web sites or next version software and suggest improvements.

Nowhere is user engagement more intense than in online gaming. From Second Life (SL) to World of Warcraft, and the Webkinz World for 6- to 13-year-old kids, 15 million players worldwide spent over $1 billion in USD revenues in 2006. SL avatars create their own world and wander or teleport around it to meet others, buy products, listen to academic lectures, and just hang out. Virtual worlds, such as SL, will continue to grow in popularity and may become the place for business networking (see the opening story in Chapter 3).

A challenge for marketers involves developing new metrics to monitor the success of social media tactics. The standard measurement of number of site visitors does not measure site engagement well. Nielsen Media and others are now measuring length of time spent on a site, number of comments posted, time spent watching a video, and other metrics to determine site engagement. These metrics will evolve further in the near future.

Plenty of other exciting new opportunities lie ahead, but firms move with caution, watching the results of every goal, strategy, and tactic for signs of effectiveness. In the following sections, we describe several important trends that will further solidify in the near future and some that may take 10 to 15 years.

Consumers in Control—But Not Complete Control

Another lesson from Dell's experience in the chapter-opening story is that the internet provides a communication platform where individual comments can spread like wildfire in a short time and quickly damage a brand image. "Marketers of all sorts are now being urged to give up the steering wheel to a new breed of consumers who want more control over the ways products are peddled to them," according to Stuart Elliott, a *New York Times* columnist. Consumer and business customer word-of-mouth has long been a powerful market force, but now individuals are not limited to their friends, colleagues, and families. The internet allows a disgruntled customer to tell a few thousand friends with one mouse click. This phenomenon is only one part of a trend that has been working for years because of the internet—we believe that the power balance has finally shifted from companies to individuals, as shown in Exhibit 1.7. How did this happen?

It started with consumer control of both the television remote control and the computer mouse. This meant that marketers could no longer hold an individual captive for 30 seconds in front of a TV screen or even for 10 seconds in front of a computer screen. With **digital video recorders (DVR)**, consumers can easily pause, rewind, or record up to 160 hours of live television programming for later viewing—fast-forwarding through commercials. DVRs enjoy only 17 percent penetration but their use is growing rapidly. Another new service, Akimbo, maintains a library of over 10,000 programs and gives customers access via the internet to the television or other appliance

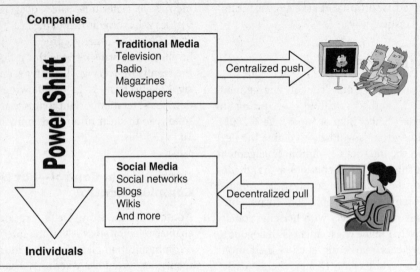

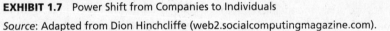

EXHIBIT 1.7   Power Shift from Companies to Individuals

Source: Adapted from Dion Hinchcliffe (web2.socialcomputingmagazine.com).

(see www.akimbo.com). Consumers can now get entertainment and information on demand, anytime, anywhere. See the "Let's Get Technical" box for details on the TiVo DVR.

One reason that consumers are not watching marketing ads with glee is that they don't trust companies or advertising much anymore. In its 2007 Trust Barometer, public relations firm Edelman asked survey respondents in developed nations who they thought provided the most credible information. Fifty-two percent (52%) said they find "a person like yourself" to be most trustworthy—equal only to the trust in doctors and higher than for any other type of communicator. Trust in a company's CEO (26%) and PR professional (14%) fell to the bottom of the list. A "person like yourself" is someone who shares values and interests. For example, the Tripadvisor.com site allows travellers to review hotels worldwide, and other travellers rely upon it to pick hotels for upcoming trips—they trust it more than the corporate pitch they see at the hotel Web sites.

One hundred years of exposure to marketing strategies have made consumers more demanding and more sophisticated, and marketers will have to become better at delivering customer value. Marketers need to ask permission to deliver communication if they want it to be attended and generally give customers what they want when they want it. Further, they need to listen to customers and respond to their needs, as did Dell. Marketers have practically lost control of brand images due to blogs, online bulletin boards, and other online communications, but they still have the opportunity to guide brand messages if they do it honestly and openly online. Marketers are leaving the world of corporate spin and entering the world of radical transparency online. Be honest or be exposed online.

Appliance Convergence

Digital media are simply data that can be sent to viewers a number of ways as seen in Exhibit 1.1. Television programs, radio shows, news, movies, books, and photos are sent by their creators in electronic form via satellite, telephone wires, or cable and then viewed by the audience on receiving appliances such as televisions, computers, radios, cell phones, PDAs, and others. Contrary to popular terminology usage, the receiving appliance is separate from the media type. In other words, watching a television set doesn't mean one must be viewing television programming. Computers can receive digital radio and television transmissions, and

LET'S GET TECHNICAL

DVR vs. Internet TV

It is Saturday night at 7:50 P.M. Your friends want you to go with them to the 8:30 showing of the latest movie, and you know that your favorite actor is the lead. However, you also do not want to miss the season finale of your favorite reality show, which airs at 8:00 P.M. With little time to get ready, programming your VCR is not an option. The thought of missing the show truly annoys you because you have seen all 13 episodes leading up to it. If only you had asked for a digital video recorder for your birthday last month . . .

DVR

Founded in 1997, TiVo provides today's television viewer what he or she has long wished for: ultimate control. TiVo is a provider of television services for the digital video recorder (DVR)—which is a growing category of consumer electronics. In its most basic form, a DVR allows TV viewers to record programs and play them back later. According to the company's Web site, the TiVo philosophy is "Watch what you want, when you want."

Now a public company, TiVo was a pioneer in television services for DVRs. The company quickly beat out its competition in the United States and recorded one of the fastest adoption rates in the history of consumer electronics. According to surveys conducted by TiVo in 2003, 98 percent of TiVo subscribers said they could not live without the TiVo service and more than 40 percent said they would choose to disconnect their cell phone over "unplugging" TiVo.

TiVo's target market consists of technologically comfortable 25- to 45-year-olds who are married and have an average yearly income of $70,000 to $100,000.

In order to have TiVo, five elements are required: a television, the TiVo DVR, a phone line or Internet connection, a TiVo subscription plan, and a television programming source. TiVo is compatible with nearly any television, VCR, and DVD player, and all equipment needed comes with the TiVo DVR. The programming source may be either an antenna, satellite dish, or cable TV.

Similar technology and services are offered by competitor ReplayTV and cable companies, such as Time Warner. Most offer the following benefits:

- *Season Pass*: Automatically records all episodes of a show for the entire season.
- *WishList*: Records any program containing a specified keyword, such as actor's name.
- *Smart Recording*: Detects changes in programming schedules and changes recording time accordingly.
- *Parental Controls*: Allows parents to establish limits on programs available to children.

With the control over programming in the hands of the TV viewer, television marketers are faced with additional challenges. For example, when playing back an episode of a sitcom that aired an hour before, the viewer has the option to skip the commercials. However, the commercials provide the revenue needed to pay for the sitcom. The commercials' producers and purchasers are paying for the contact with the potential consumers, who are bypassing the contact. This has led to an enormous increase in product placement—100,000 product placements by the networks (ABC, CBS, NBC, FOX, UPN, WB) alone in the 2004–2005 season, according to PQ Media. That represents $2 billion in product placement.

In the short time since TiVo's invention, it has received a frenzy of attention. The word *tivo* has even become a verb in popular media—"Did you tivo that football game on Sunday?" On the popular talk show *Live with Regis and Kelly,* host Kelly Ripa frequently discusses how she uses and loves her TiVo.

Internet TV—Watch Anything, Anytime, Anywhere, or Any Device

Although TiVo has revolutionized the way that television is watched, TV over the internet is the future. The internet, which in the past was used

(continued)

(*continued*)

solely through the PC, may provide viewers with the opportunity to sidestep traditional cable and satellite services. According to SRG, the number of Americans who watched one of their favorite TV shows online almost doubled to 43 percent between fall 2006 and fall 2007.

One huge advantage for advertisers is that commercials cannot be skipped online. In fact, ads can even run around the window where the content appears. It is small wonder then that the networks promote online viewing even during their broadcast episodes.

The great advantage of internet TV for consumers is the ability to watch anything, anytime, anywhere, on any device. Unlike using a DVR, the consumer does not have to remember to program the show in advance. Just find it online and watch it on the platform of choice to match your lifestyle—whether that be an iPod, iPhone, laptop, or even a regular old TV.

---

television sets can receive the Web and satellite radio. Some appliances, such as radio and fax machines, have limited receiving capabilities, while others are more flexible.

The idea of separating the medium from the appliance is both mind-boggling and exciting because of the business opportunities. It opens the door to new types of receiving appliances that are also "smart," allowing for saving, editing, and sending transmissions. For instance, LG Electronics currently sells an internet refrigerator (www.lginternetfamily.co.uk). Consumers can view television programs, movies, family photos, and Web pages on its 15.1-inch touch screen; read e-mail and handwritten or typed messages entered by the family; listen to downloaded music and recorded messages from the family; track the food inventory in the refrigerator; and also keep food cold.

The LG internet refrigerator is a good example of receiving-appliance convergence—many digital appliances in one. Another example is the convergence of PDA, cell phone, and digital camera. Finally, consider the automobile. The Lincoln LS owner can watch a movie, use the telephone, listen to music on disk or from radio station transmission, view the time, and communicate using a global positioning system (GPS). If the car is in an accident or needs repair, it will automatically send a message to the nearest Lincoln dealer via the internet. So, next time you think of television programming, remember that by U.S. law it is all simply digitized video that can be sent through several ways to a number of receiving devices. This convergence trend is far from over and has extreme implications, as discussed next.

Traditional and Social Media Lose Their Distinction

Marketers currently allocate advertising budgets by media type such as newspaper, television, or internet. Conversely, the audience doesn't discriminate between the same video advertising it sees on the NBC broadcast news, the MSNBC cable news, the MSNBC. msn.com Web site news, and on YouTube. Similarly, the newspaper classifieds are equivalent to those on Craigslist.org, and magazine ads can be found as display ads on the magazine's or other Web sites. Individuals record television commercials, manipulate them using video software, and upload to video-posting or their own Web sites. Media editorial already appears both online and offline, paralleling the blurring of media advertising. Appliance convergence means that both editorial and advertising content is already viewed on a myriad of mobile and stationary devices. What does this mean for marketers? In the future, marketers will begin to realize that the medium and the appliance are no longer the defining way to reach customers (i.e., the words *television commercial* will lose their meaning). Instead, marketers will create multimedia communication for distribution to audience members anytime, anywhere, to any device—on demand by the user. In this light, social media and traditional media become simply media.

Wireless Networking Increases

GPRS (General Packet Radio Service) is close to being a third-generation Web device. Also known as 3G (third generation) mobile phone technology, it supports a wide range of bandwidths for receiving and sending e-mail and large amounts of data, and for Web browsing in many different countries. GPRS may well be the first indication of Web 3.0. Using cell phones, PDAs, and PCs, customers check e-mail at Starbucks in Shanghai, receive flight information in the smallest airport, and catch the latest sports scores while at the Gare du Nord train station in France (Exhibit 1.8). Wireless nodes are multiplying like rabbits. Consider the following (see www.trendwatching.com for more):

- Both Virgin Atlantic and American Airlines plan to offer internet connections on airplanes.
- Autonet Mobile offers an in-car router and service that turns an automobile into a WiFi hot spot.
- Coffee drinkers listening to music in Starbucks can instantly find the artist, track, and album on their iPods or iPhones via the iTunes WiFi Music Store.
- There are over 100,000 WiFi access points worldwide. The top three cities in 2006 were Seoul, Tokyo, and London, according to JiWire WiFi provider (www.jiwire.com).

The rapid growth of wireless access points, when coupled with the 41 percent of individuals worldwide owning cell phones and the huge numbers owning PDAs or notebook computers, indicates a continuing growth in wireless networking. As this trend plays out, customers will demand information, entertainment, and communication whenever and however they desire and in small file sizes for fast downloading.

Semantic Web

Conceptualizing the media as data that are separate from the receiving appliance is one way that marketers can give customers exactly what they want when and where they want it. Travelers want current flight information on demand via their cell phones or PDAs, and the airlines today dish it out as a few words of text. Customers of nightclubs in Germany want to know which performers will play on Friday night, and the club sends it to their cell phones as a few words of text (along with a bit of music).

Sir Tim Berners-Lee, the Web's co-inventor, has been working with many others over the past several years on the technology to organize the Web's data for greater user convenience. His idea, the **semantic Web**, is an extension of the current Web, in which information is given well-defined meaning through HTML-like tags. The current Web carries text documents, photos, graphics, audio, and video files embedded in Web pages that search engines struggle to catalog for users to find. The semantic Web will make it easier by providing a standard definition protocol so that users can easily find information based on its type, such as a person (e.g., <person> in the HTMLcode), the next available appointment for a particular doctor (found by searching the doctor's database), details on an upcoming concert, the hours of the library, the menu at the local restaurant, and so forth (for

EXHIBIT 1.8 WiFi at the Gare du Nord Train Station in France

Source: www.trendwatching.com

more information, see Berners-Lee, Hendler, and Lassila, 2001 and www.w3.org).

The value of the semantic Web is truly information on demand. Using an analogy, think for a minute about the development of time-telling devices. All clocks before 1929 required user effort to find the time. The sundial took a lot of user effort to go look at the time and reposition the instrument as the sun position changed. Later, mechanical, wind-up clocks displayed time only if the user wound the watch or clock pendulum to keep it running (Exhibit 1.9). In 1929, the quartz crystal changed things dramatically. From that point, the piece of data called *time* was pushed to users on demand with no effort on their part, a fundamental change from user finding or pulling the time to automated delivery of the time data. Afterward, time appeared in lots of devices, controlling lawn sprinklers, microwave ovens, manufacturing processes, and so forth. Individuals have come to depend upon that piece of data arriving reliably when and where they want it.

Now, think of the text, video, and audio available via the internet. Users must go find what they want, and it is not easy: They must spend effort searching, just as with early clocks. We believe that the internet is awaiting the next big technological leap, similar to the quartz crystal. Imagine the information on the Web arriving just as reliably as time, on demand. Consumers will define tasks for their personal digital agents, which will search for pieces of data and return them as movies to the television set, appointments to the PDA, contact information to the address book, and more. The semantic Web holds the promise of being this next huge advance: worldwide access to data on demand without effort. Get ready for the internet's "quartz crystal" and the next wave of disruption.

What Will Characterize Web 3.0?

The semantic Web is only one view of the future. Others predict that it will be higher bandwidth, faster connection speeds, artificial intelligence, seamless social networking, or modular Web applications eliminating the need for software on individual PCs. The following are predictions by industry experts:

> People keep asking what Web 3.0 is. I think maybe when you've got an overlay of scalable vector graphics [i.e., images containing hyperlinks]—everything rippling and folding and looking misty—on Web 2.0 and access to a semantic Web integrated across a huge space of data, you'll have access to an unbelievable data resource.
>
> SIR TIM BERNERS-LEE

Web 1.0 was dial-up, 50 K average bandwidth, Web 2.0 is an average 1 megabit

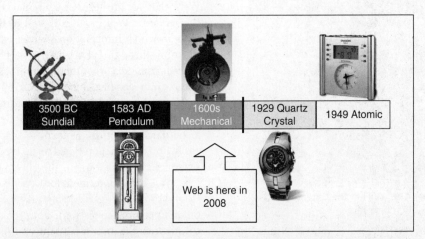

EXHIBIT 1.9 Internet–Time Analogy: Awaiting the Next Technological Breakthrough

of bandwidth and Web 3.0 will be 10 megabits of bandwidth all the time, which will be the full video Web, and that will feel like Web 3.0.

REED HASTINGS,
Founder and CEO of Netflix

My prediction would be that Web 3.0 will ultimately be seen as applications which are pieced together. There are a number of characteristics: the applications are relatively small, the data is in the cloud, the applications can run on any device, PC or mobile phone, the applications are very fast and they're very customizable. Furthermore, the applications are distributed virtually: literally by social networks, by email. You won't go to the store and purchase them . . . That's a very different application model than we've ever seen in computing.

ERIC SCHMIDT,
CEO of Google

READ ON

This book follows the structure of traditional marketing processes but discusses effective and efficient e-marketing concepts and practices. Technology is an important aspect of the e-marketing environment, and because it is critical for marketers to understand it, we integrate "Let's Get Technical" boxes throughout the text to help marketers understand some of the basics. *E-Marketing* is organized into four parts.

1. "E-Marketing in Context" (Chapters 1–3) introduces strategic e-marketing and the e-marketing plan. The discussions include e-business models, performance metrics for measuring e-marketing success, and the steps involved in an e-marketing plan.
2. "E-Marketing Environment" (Chapters 4 and 5) explains the legal and global environments that are critical to the success of any e-marketing effort. We place special emphasis on the next frontier: emerging markets, such as China, and their barriers to internet adoption.
3. "E-Marketing Strategy" (Chapters 6–9) deals with e-strategy formulation, including the marketing knowledge base and customer behavior data needed for designing what we call tier 1 strategies: segmentation, targeting, differentiation, and positioning.
4. "E-Marketing Management" (Chapters 10–15) covers tier 2 strategies: the marketing mix and customer relationship management best practices.

Chapter Summary

E-business is the continuous optimization of a firm's business activities through digital technology. E-commerce is the subset of e-business focused on transactions. E-marketing is the *use of information technology* in the processes of creating, communicating, and delivering value to customers and for managing customer relationships in ways that benefit the organization and its stakeholders. It is the application of information technology to traditional marketing practices.

The dynamic e-marketing environment offers opportunities to develop new products, new markets, new media, and new channels. Individual buyers have more power because of the television remote control, the computer mouse, the ability to compare products and pricing online, and the ability to upload content that affects brand images. Web 2.0 communities form online to discuss products, share files, and more, and this activity is out of marketers' control. Most businesses in developed nations have adopted at least some information technologies; however, they continue to strive for effective and efficient IT use to entice and sell to buyers. The internet deeply affects the citizens of many countries.

The internet consists of computers with data, users who send and receive the data files on a myriad of receiving appliances, and a technology infrastructure to move, create, and view or listen to the content. An intranet is a network that runs internally in a corporation using internet standards. An extranet is an intranet to which value chain partners are admitted for strategic reasons. The Web is the part of the internet that supports a graphical user interface for hypertext navigation with a browser. The internet's properties allow for more effective and efficient marketing strategy and tactical implementation and are changing marketing in the Web 2.0 by shifting power from sellers to buyers; empowering search engines as reputation engines; increasing market and media fragmentation, and improving online and offline strategy integration (especially multichannel marketing). Content is still king online, but connections are critical in this climate and intellectual capital rules. Finally, the long tail theory showed that the economy has changed from one of scarcity to one of abundance.

In the future, Web 3.0 will be a time of engagement, participation, and co-creation where consumer control, increased wireless networking, receiving-appliance convergence, merging of traditional and social media, refined engagement metrics, and the semantic Web will change the marketing landscape. It is essential for marketers to realize that television programs, radio shows, news, movies, books, and photos are simply digital data sent by their creators in electronic form via satellite, telephone wires, or cable and then viewed by the audience on receiving appliances such as televisions, computers, radios, cell phones, PDAs, and others. This understanding opens the door for many new product opportunities that provide value to demanding customers of the future. Web 3.0 will be defined by better technology and Web applications, and possibly artificial intelligence.

Exercises

REVIEW QUESTIONS

1. Define e-business and e-marketing.
2. What are metrics and why are they important?
3. How does technology change traditional marketing?
4. As a technology, how does the internet compare with the telephone?
5. What are some of the marketing implications of internet technologies?
6. In the context of e-marketing, what does "the medium is not the appliance" mean?
7. Describe the important internet properties that affect marketing.
8. What fundamental changes has the internet brought to marketing?
9. What are the key elements of Web 2.0?

DISCUSSION QUESTIONS

10. What are the implications of the declining U.S. share of worldwide internet adoption?
11. As a consumer, are you likely to benefit if e-business becomes "just business"? Explain your answer.
12. Some economists suggest that the increase in e-commerce within the B2B market will lead to greater competition and more goods and services becoming commodities, meaning they will compete solely on price. How do you think this competition is likely to affect buyers within the B2B market? How would it affect sellers?
13. What concerns about consumer privacy are raised by the increased use of wireless computing and handheld devices outside the home or workplace?
14. As a consumer, how will your life change when the semantic Web becomes a reality?
15. How will social media and consumer-generated content change the way marketers operate? Explain.

WEB ACTIVITIES

16. See if you can find the portion of your university's Web site that is for students and employees only (intranet). What information is contained on those pages? Should outsiders be excluded from accessing the pages? Why or why not?
17. Visit the McDonald's Web site. List each stakeholder it reaches and tell what basic content is targeted to each stakeholder.
18. Visit MySpace.com and find a company profile (such as Aquafina). How many friends does it have? Why would MySpace customers want to befriend a company, especially in light of the Edelman Trust Barometer findings?

CHAPTER 2

Strategic E-Marketing and Performance Metrics

We have the right model for the Internet age . . . [including] a partnership of trust and communication among our people, our customers, and our suppliers.

—MICHAEL DELL

What you measure is what you get: The performance measures you use affect the behavior of your managers and employees.

—DAVID NORTON AND ROBERT KAPLAN, HARVARD BUSINESS SCHOOL

Chapter Outline

The main goal of this chapter is to understand strategic planning and the way companies seek to achieve their objectives through strategies involving e-business and e-marketing. You will become familiar with common e-business models implemented at different organizational levels and with the application of performance metrics to monitor progress toward objectives.

After reading this chapter, you will be able to:

- Explain the importance of strategic planning, strategy, e-business strategy, and e-marketing strategy.

- Identify the main e-business models at the activity, business process, and enterprise levels.

- Discuss the use of performance metrics and the Balanced Scorecard to measure e-business and e-marketing performance.

The Amazon Story

After opening its virtual doors in 1995, Amazon.com finally proved that the online retailing business model can be profitable, reporting its first-ever net profit in the fourth quarter of 2001 on $3.1 billion in net sales. Now a Fortune 500 company, Amazon.com announced $14.8 billion in net sales and $476 million in net income for 2007—an impressive growth rate. "Amazon.com strives to be the Earth's most customer-centric company where people can find and discover virtually anything they want to buy online," according to Amazon, and this strategy has paid off big time (see the www.amazon.com press room pages).

Amazon, a dot-com survivor, is quite adept at leveraging its competencies into many different e-business models. It started as the world's biggest bookstore, but soon branched out into the everything store. First is its core business—online retailing. Sales of books, music, and DVDs account for the majority of Amazon's sales, but nonmedia sales now comprise 34 percent of all sales (toys, tools, health and beauty aids, prescription drugs, home furnishing, electronics, apparel, and more). A truly global firm, 45 percent of these sales occur outside of North America.

Second are Amazon's e-commerce partnerships with Target, Macy's, and others. These

(continued)

(*continued*)

partnerships bring revenue through differing commitments, but they typically involve Amazon earning fixed fees, sales commissions, or per-unit activity fees by offering third party merchandise on the Amazon.com Web site. Customers can purchase items in dozens of product categories and complete the transaction in one checkout process. Amazon also offers to undertake marketing, customer service, and product fulfillment services (inventory storage and delivery) on behalf of its partners. This partnership business model can be more profitable than the pure retailing model because Amazon earns a fee by leveraging its automated services, e-commerce experience, and huge customer base.

Amazon has evolved from online retailer, to e-commerce partner, and now to developer service provider. It sells ten different Web services and space for computing, storing, and retrieving data from anywhere on the Web through its Amazon Web Services (AWS) business. This new business serves over 240,000 registered software developers and is quite profitable.

Amazon also uses another important e-business model. Amazon created the first affiliate program (called Amazon Associates), giving hundreds of thousands of Web site owners a 10-percent commission for referring customers who purchase at Amazon. These partners can now integrate merchandise seamlessly into their Web sites via Amazon's Associate program. It is like having lots of sales people all over the world.

According to Jeff Bezos, CEO, Amazon is not interested in expanding to the physical world because it cannot differentiate Amazon-branded brick and mortar stores from well-established physical bookstores in a meaningful way. Amazon's success is based on selection, lower prices, better availability, solid and innovative technology, and better product information. Amazon's use of customer product reviews and product suggestions based on collective purchasing behavior also puts it a cut above other retailers. It wins with low capital and high return business models. Amazon's future success seems certain because it knows how to capitalize on its unique capabilities through strategic planning and with careful management of its existing business models.

STRATEGIC PLANNING

Amazon, like every other marketer, uses strategic planning for a profitable and sustainable business future. **Strategic planning** is the "managerial process of developing and maintaining a viable fit between the organization's objectives, skills, and resources and its changing market opportunities" (Kotler and Keller 2006). Part of this process is to identify the firm's goals, such as the following:

- **Growth.** How much can the firm reasonably expect to grow in terms of revenues, and how fast? The answer to these questions involves a thorough understanding of the competition, product life cycles, and market factors.
- **Competitive position.** How should the firm position itself against other firms in the industry? Viable positions are industry leader (Google), price leader (Priceline), quality leader (Mercedes), niche firm (Technorati), best customer service (Dell), and so forth.
- **Geographic scope.** Where should the firm serve its customers on the continuum of local to multinational?
- **Other objectives.** Companies often set objectives for the number of industries they will enter, the range of products they will offer, the types of channels they will use, and so on.

For example, Facebook switched strategic direction in 2007, choosing to open its network to third party developers—expanding customer benefits in the process.

Environment, Strategy, and Performance

The e-marketing plan is often a part of its overall marketing plan, flowing from the organization's overall goals and strategies. As depicted in Exhibit 2.1, it starts with the business environment, where legal, ethical, technological, competitive, market-related, and other environmental factors external to the firm create both opportunities and threats. Organizations perform SWOT analyses to discover what strengths and weaknesses they have to deploy against threats and opportunities, leading to e-business and e-marketing strategy. Firms select e-business models, and then marketers formulate strategy and create marketing plans that will help the firm accomplish its overall goals. The final step is to determine the success of the strategies and plans by measuring results. **Performance metrics** are specific measures designed to evaluate the effectiveness and efficiency of the e-business and e-marketing operations.

The environment-strategy-performance (ESP) model might just as easily depict a brick-and-mortar business process—by removing a few Es. It underscores the idea that businesses are not only built on sound practices and proven processes but with important technology transformations and e-marketing practices, as discussed in this book.

This chapter and Chapter 3 describe e-business and e-marketing strategies, the e-marketing plan, and performance metrics. Chapters 4 and 5 explore environmental factors particularly important for e-marketing and leading to the SWOT analysis.

Strategy

The term *strategy* has been used to describe everything from "the course we chart, the journey we imagine and, at the same time, the course we steer, and the trip we actually make" (Nickols, 2000, p. 6). Although the term is used in many different contexts to mean many different things, most strategists agree that **strategy** is the means to achieve a goal. It is concerned with how the firm will achieve its *objectives*, not what its goals are. Interestingly, strategy has its roots in military action. For example, the country's objective is to win the war, its strategy is to deploy troops to a particular country, and its tactics are to land a particular battalion in a specific location at a specified day and time. This process translates well to business strategy because the firm sets its growth and other objectives, then decides which strategies it will use to accomplish them. The tactics are detailed plans to implement the strategies.

It is important to note that objectives, strategies, and tactics can exist at many different

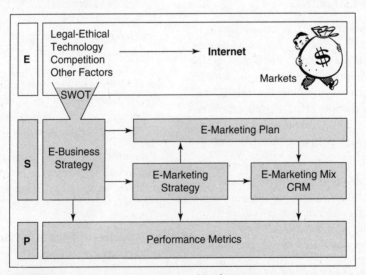

EXHIBIT 2.1   Focusing on Strategy and Performance

levels in a firm. Thus far, we've been discussing high-level corporate strategic planning. Functional areas within a firm also develop goals, strategies, and tactics to support corporate-level objectives. If a firm wants to grow by 10 percent in the coming year, the marketing function may set supporting goals to introduce new products and increase market share. Similarly, finance, human resources, and other functional areas set goals to help achieve the firm's overall objectives.

FROM STRATEGY TO ELECTRONIC STRATEGY

How does traditional strategy differ from e-business strategy? **E-business strategy** is the deployment of enterprise resources to capitalize on technologies for reaching specified objectives that ultimately improve performance and create sustainable competitive advantage. Thus, when corporate-level (also called *enterprise-level*) business strategies include information technology components (internet, digital data, databases, and so forth), they become e-business strategies. As an example, Tchibo, the German retailer, has two key strategies for reaching its growth goals: First is the corporate-level business strategy of building new retail stores in selected European cities, and second is the e-business strategy of selling products on its Web site. Using strategic planning, Tchibo elects to use an e-business strategy only after careful analysis of its internal capabilities and the needs of its customers, retail competitors, and other environmental issues.

In a parallel fashion, marketing strategy becomes e-marketing strategy when marketers use digital technology to implement the strategy. **E-marketing strategy** is the design of marketing strategy that capitalizes on the organization's electronic or information technology capabilities to reach specified objectives. In essence, e-marketing strategy is where technology strategy and marketing strategy wed.

For example, Sharper Image, a specialty retailer, maintains a customer database available to all employees. Regardless of whether a customer buys from the store, the catalog, or the Web site, or whether contact is made by phone, in person, through e-mail, or by postal mail, employees can access the computerized database for up-to-date account activity and information when dealing with customers. This responsive service keeps customers happy and supports Sharper Image's customer relationship management e-marketing strategy—ultimately supporting the corporate growth strategy.

Most strategic plans explain the rationale for the chosen objectives and strategies. They are especially important for a single e-business project trying to win its share of corporate resources and top-management support. Kalakota and Robinson (1999) suggest four appropriate types of rationale:

1. Strategic justification shows how the strategy fits with the firm's overall mission and business objectives, and where it will take the firm if successfully accomplished.
2. Operational justification identifies and quantifies the specific process improvements that will result from the strategy. For example, if CRM (customer relationship management) software is proposed, how will that translate to increased customer retention and higher revenues?
3. Technical justification shows how the technology will fit and provide synergy with current information technology capabilities. For example, is there interoperability along the currently integrated supply chain?
4. Financial justification examines cost/benefit analysis and uses standard measures such as return on investment (ROI) and net income.

FROM BUSINESS MODELS TO E-BUSINESS MODELS

One more piece of this puzzle needs to be explained before we get into the really interesting content of e-business and e-marketing strategies. The term *business model* is often mentioned in print and by executives. Based on current use of the term, we suggest that a **business model** is a method by which the organization sustains itself in the long term and includes its value proposition for partners and customers as well as its revenue streams.

A business model does not exist in a vacuum. It relates to strategy in that a firm will select one or more business models as strategies to accomplish enterprise goals. For instance, if the firm's goal is to position itself as a high-tech, innovative company, it might decide to use the internet to connect and communicate with its suppliers and customers, as does Dell Computer (see opening quote).

Presented with many opportunities, how does a firm select the best business models? The authors of *Internet Business Models and Strategies* suggest the following components as critical to appraising the fit of a business model for the company and its environment (Afuah and Tucci, 2001):

- **Customer value.** Does the model create value through its product offerings that is differentiated in some way from that of its competitors?
- **Scope.** Which markets does the firm serve, and are they growing? Are these markets currently served by the firm, or will they be higher-risk new markets?
- **Price.** Are the firm's products priced to appeal to markets and also achieve company share and profit objectives?
- **Revenue sources.** Where is the money coming from? Is it plentiful enough to sustain growth and profit objectives over time? Many dot-com failures, for example, overlooked this element.
- **Connected activities.** What activities will the firm need to perform to create the value described in the model? Does the firm have these capabilities? For example, if 24/7 customer service is part of the value, the firm must be prepared to deliver it.
- **Implementation.** The company must have the ability to actually make it happen, which involves the firm's systems, people, culture, and so on.
- **Capabilities.** Does the firm have the resources (financial, core competencies, etc.) to make the selected models work?

- **Sustainability.** The e-business model is particularly appropriate if it will create a competitive advantage over time. Will it be difficult to imitate, and will the environment be attractive for maintaining the model over time?

E-BUSINESS MODELS

Traditional business models such as retailing, selling advertising, and auctions have been around ever since the first business set up shop. What makes a business model an e-business model is the use of information technology. Thus, an **e-business model** is a method by which the organization sustains itself in the long term using information technology, which includes its value proposition for partners and customers as well as its revenue streams. For example, the internet allows education, music, and software firms to deliver their products over the internet, thus creating a new distribution model that cuts costs and increases value. E-business models successfully take advantage of the internet properties described in Chapter 1 (i.e., global reach, time moderator, and so forth).

E-business models can capitalize on digital data collection and distribution techniques without using the internet. For example, when retailers scan products and customer cards at the checkout, these data can become a rich source of knowledge for inventory management and promo-tional offers—e-marketing without the internet. Similarly, when these data are available through the firm's proprietary computer network (intranet), the firm is applying e-marketing without the internet. For simplicity, we use the term *e-business models* to include both internet and offline digital models throughout the rest of our discussion.

Value and Revenue

As part of its e-business model, an organization describes the ways in which it creates value for customers and partners. This description is in line with the **marketing concept**, which suggests that the social and economic justification for an organization's existence is the satisfaction of customer wants and needs while meeting organizational objectives. Business partners might include supply chain members such as suppliers, wholesalers, and retailers, or firms with which the company joins forces to create new brands (such as the Microsoft and NBC alliance to create MSNBC). Firms deliver stakeholder value through e-business models by using digital products and processes. Whether online or offline, the value proposition involves knowing what is important to the customer or partner and delivering it better than other firms. **Value** encompasses the customer's perceptions of the product's benefits, specifically its attributes, brand name, and support services. Subtracted from benefits are the costs involved in acquiring the product, such as monetary, time, energy, and psychic costs. Like customers, partners evaluate value by determining whether the partnership provides more benefits than costs. This concept is shown as follows:

$$\text{Value} = \text{Benefits} - \text{Costs}$$

Information technology usually, but not always, increases benefits and lowers costs to stakeholders. Conversely, it can decrease value when Web sites are complex, information is hard to locate, and technical difficulties interrupt data access or shopping transactions.

As shown in Exhibit 2.2, e-business strategies help firms to decrease internal costs, often improving the value proposition for customers and partners. They can also increase the enterprise revenue stream, an important part of the e-business model.

Menu of Strategic E-Business Models

A key element in setting strategic objectives is to take stock of the company's current situation and decide the level of commitment to e-business in general and e-marketing in particular. The possible levels of commitment fall along a continuum that is appropriately represented as a pyramid

---

E-Marketing Increases Benefits

- Online mass customization (different products and messages to different stakeholders)
- Personalization (giving stakeholders relevant information)
- 24/7 convenience
- Self-service ordering and tracking
- One-stop shopping
- Learning from customers on social networking sites

E-Marketing Decreases Costs

- Low-cost distribution of communication messages (e.g., e-mail)
- Low-cost distribution channel for digital products
- Lowers costs for transaction processing
- Lowers costs for knowledge acquisition (e.g., research and customer feedback)
- Creates efficiencies in supply chain (through communication and inventory optimization)
- Decreases the cost of customer service

E-Marketing Increases Revenues

- Online transaction revenues such as product, information, advertising, and subscription fees; or commission/fee on a transaction or referral
- Adds value to products/services and increase prices (e.g., online FAQ and customer support)
- Increases customer base by reaching new markets
- Builds customer relationships and, thus, increases current customer spending (share of wallet)

EXHIBIT 2.2   E-Marketing Contributes to the E-Business Model

because fewer businesses occupy the top position (Exhibit 2.3). As a general rule, the higher the firm travels up the pyramid, the greater its level of commitment to e-business, the more its strategies are integrated with information technology, and the greater the impact on the organization. Also, the more strategic moves are at the top, while the more tactical activities are at lower levels; as a result, higher levels carry more risk than lower levels for most firms.

Bear in mind that one firm's activity may be another's enterprise-level strategy. For example, electronic transaction order processing (e.g., selling products on a Web site) may be a small activity for a ski shop with 1 percent of its business from the online channel, but it is an enterprise-level activity for FedEx, the package delivery service.

It is also important to note that the lowest level of commitment—not shown on the pyramid—is no e-business involvement at all. Research shows that many small local retailers and other small businesses are at this level and should remain there because of their capabilities. For example, it is unlikely that the local independently owned dry cleaner could benefit much from e-business strategies.

In consulting with CEOs worldwide, the Gartner Group suggests the following questions organizations must ask prior to embarking on any e-business strategies:

1. *Are the business models likely to change in my industry?* If they are not, a company will find no reason to get involved. If they are, answering this question suggests a strategic direction for the firm.
2. *What does the answer to question 1 mean to my company?* The answers vary by size, industry, location, and more.
3. *When do I need to be ready?* This issue involves thoughtful competitive analysis.
4. *How do I get there from here?* This point is where e-business strategy enters.

Each level of the pyramid in Exhibit 2.3 indicates a number of opportunities for the firm to provide stakeholder value and generate revenue streams using information technology. Because no single, comprehensive, ideal taxonomy of e-business models is available, we categorize the most commonly used models based on the firm's level of commitment (Exhibit 2.4). This scheme is not perfect either, because the level of commitment for each model varies by firm, as previously mentioned. Also, the activity-level items generally add value by shaving costs but may not generate a direct revenue stream. Nonetheless, we present it as a good menu

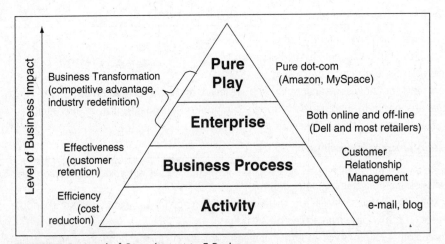

EXHIBIT 2.3   Level of Commitment to E-Business

Source: Adapted from www.mohansawhney.com

Activity Level	Business Process Level	Enterprise Level

1. Order processing
2. Online purchasing
3. E-mail
4. Content publishing
5. Business intelligence (BI)
6. Online advertising and public relations
7. Online sales promotions
8. Dynamic pricing strategies online
	1. Customer relationship management (CRM)
	2. Knowledge management (KM)
	3. Supply chain management (SCM)
	4. Community building online
	5. Database marketing
	6. Enterprise resource planning (ERP)
	7. Mass customization
		1. E-commerce, direct selling, content sponsorship
		2. Portal
		3. Social networking
		4. Broker models
		  • Online exchange, hub
		  • Online auction
		5. Agent models
		  • Manufacturer's/selling agents
		  • Shopping agent
		  • Reverse auction

EXHIBIT 2.4   E-Business Model Classification

of strategic opportunities, arranged by level of commitment to e-business, focusing primarily on models that involve e-marketing. We'll briefly describe many models here and expand upon them in later chapters.

Although we are discussing individual e-business models, many firms combine two or more e-business models. For example, Yahoo! is both an online retailer and content publisher. It also uses many processes and activities listed in the exhibit, such as e-mail and customer relationship management.

ACTIVITY-LEVEL E-BUSINESS MODELS The lowest level of the pyramid affects individual business activities that can save the firm money if automated using information technology or the internet. In this low-risk area, the firm realizes cost reductions through e-business efficiencies (e.g., order processing, competitive intelligence, or surveys online). The following is a brief description of activity-level models:

1. **Online purchasing.** Firms can use the Web to place orders with suppliers, thus automating the activity. Normally this activity is not a marketing function, but when retailers such as Wal-Mart created automated order processing throughout the supply chain, it had a huge impact on marketing.

2. **Order processing.** This model occurs when online retailers automate internet transactions created by customers.

3. **E-mail.** When organizations send e-mail communications to stakeholders, they save printing and mailing costs.

4. **Content publishing.** In this model, companies create valuable content or services on their Web sites, draw lots of traffic, and sell advertising. In another type of content publishing, the firm posts information about its offerings on a Web site, thus saving printing costs. See the "Let's Get Technical" box for streaming audio as subscription-based content.

5. **Business intelligence** (BI). This activity refers to the low-cost online gathering of secondary and primary information about competitors, markets, customers, and more.

6. **Online advertising and public relations** (PR). As an activity, the firm buys advertising on someone else's e-mail or Web site. When the firm sells advertising, it is engaging in content sponsorship, a higher-level process. Online PR includes a firm's own Web site, as well as online press releases, and more.

7. **Online sales promotions.** Companies use the internet to send samples of digital products (e.g., music or software) or to run sweepstakes, among other tactics.

LET'S GET TECHNICAL

Streaming Audio

You are at the office and, well, a little bored. A little music would really spice up your day. A colleague told you about a new group that really rocks. You're wishing about now that you had the CD to run on your computer's speakers. Suddenly you remember that your folks gave you a subscription to a streaming music service for your birthday. You log on and play the album. Unfortunately, it isn't that good. Relieved that you didn't spend $15 for the CD, you start to stream music from another group—and this one is awesome.

Streaming music is a service which allows listening to music while it is still being downloaded. In other words, you don't have to wait for the entire track to download before it begins playing. Streaming music services are ideal for users who are nearly always near a computer or an iPhone, like to experiment with different kinds of music, and prefer the try-before-you-buy model.

The services offer hundreds of thousands of tracks for a monthly subscription fee of about $10. Some services also offer the ability to burn tracks to a CD for an additional $1 fee per track. The services require three technologies—a music server, a high-speed internet connection (wired or wireless), and security software to prevent unauthorized access and duplication of the music.

The music server is where the music is actually stored. At the user's request, the music begins to stream to the user's computer. When enough of the track has arrived (the music gets buffered in memory), it begins to play while the rest of it continues to stream. If the internet connection slows down, the song may actually catch up to the stream and briefly stop until more has been buffered.

The user installs jukebox software on his or her computer to connect with the music server. The jukebox provides searching by artist, album, track, or genre. It also allows the user to store custom playlists. Some services also offer mini reviews and music suggestions based on listening preferences. The usability and slickness of the interface are key differentiators.

Because of the buffering issue, streaming music is only advisable over a high-speed internet connection. However, mobile users can even stream to an iPhone on the fast 3G cell phone network.

Security with streaming music is important to the record companies who do not want unauthorized duplication of their music. Most streaming music services do not allow a user to log in from two computers simultaneously. Additionally, security software will not allow the music to be permanently captured on the user's computer without paying the additional $1 fee per track.

From a user's perspective, the major limiting factor used to be the restriction of nearness to a computer. However, some add-on technologies allow a computer to wirelessly send its music data to remote speakers located in another room. Furthermore, expect more streaming music to iPhone-type devices.

8. **Pricing strategies.** With dynamic pricing, a firm presents different prices to various groups of customers, even at the individual level. Online negotiation through auctions is one type of dynamic pricing initiated by the buyer instead of the seller. Technology allows this activity to be automated.

BUSINESS PROCESS–LEVEL E-BUSINESS MODELS

The next level of the pyramid changes business processes to increase the firm's effectiveness.

Customer relationship management (CRM) involves retaining and growing business and individual customers through strategies that ensure their satisfaction with the firm and its products. CRM seeks to keep customers for the long term and to increase the number and frequency of their transactions with the firm. In the context of e-business, CRM uses digital processes and integrates customer information collected at every customer "touch point." Customers interact with firms in person at retail stores or company offices, by mail, via telephone, or over the internet. The results of interactions at all these touch points are integrated to build a complete picture of customer characteristics, behavior, and preferences—all stored in electronic databases.

Knowledge management (KM) is a combination of a firm's database contents, the technology used to create the system, and the transformation of data into useful information and knowledge. KM systems create a storehouse of reports, customer account information, product sales, and other valuable information managers can use to make decisions.

Supply chain management (SCM) involves coordination of the distribution channel to deliver products more effectively and efficiently to customers. For example, when a user orders from certain Web sites, FedEx's computers receive the instruction to pick up product from a warehouse and deliver it quickly to the customer. Similarly, when consumers buy a product at the grocery store, the bar code scanner at the checkout tells the store's computer to reduce the inventory count by one and then automatically orders more cases of the product from warehouses or suppliers if inventory in the back room is low.

With **community building**, firms build Web sites to draw groups of special interest users. In this model, firms invite users to chat and post comments on their Web sites or blogs with the purpose of building a buzz online and attracting potential customers to the site (**Blogs** are Web pages where entries are listed in reverse chronological order). Firms often contribute content on community and networking sites that their customers frequent. Through community building, marketers can create social bonds that enhance customer relationships while building their images as experts in specific knowledge areas.

Affiliate programs occur when firms put a link to someone else's retail Web site and earn a commission on all purchases by referred customers. Amazon.com pioneered this e-business model. When viewed from an Amazon affiliate's perspective, it is operating as a selling agent for Amazon's products.

Database marketing involves collecting, analyzing, and disseminating electronic information about customers, prospects, and products to increase profits. It is one of the oldest and most important strategies for e-marketers. Database marketing systems can be a part of the firm's overall knowledge management system.

Enterprise resource planning (ERP) refers to a back-office system for order entry, purchasing, invoicing, and inventory control. ERP systems allow organizations to optimize business processes while lowering costs. Many ERP systems predate the Web. ERP is not a marketing function, but it is so important that it must be included in this list.

Mass customization refers to the internet's unique ability to customize marketing mixes electronically and automatically to the individual level. Firms use this practice when they collect information from customers and prospects, and use it to customize products and communication on an individual basis for a large number of people.

ENTERPRISE-LEVEL E-BUSINESS MODELS At the enterprise level of the pyramid, the firm automates many business processes in a unified system—demonstrating a significant commitment to e-business. Firms relying heavily on these models (such as Dell Computer, Google, and CNN) believe that their future will depend on e-business activities.

E-commerce refers to online transactions: selling goods and services on the internet, either in one transaction or over time with an ongoing subscription price (e.g., Wall Street Journal Online). Online retailers are firms that buy products and resell them online. One type of online retailer sells physical products and uses traditional transportation methods to deliver them. The other type sells digital products such as information, software, and music and delivers them via the internet (and usually ground transportation too). Many online retailers maintain brick-and-mortar stores as well. **Virtual worlds** often create revenue through subscriptions—these are sites where users can take the form of avatars and socialize in an online space of their own making. Second Life is the most well known of these; however,

Webkinz and the Penguin Club are very popular with children.

Direct distribution refers to a type of e-commerce in which manufacturers sell directly to consumers, eliminating intermediaries such as retailers (the Dell model). **Content sponsorship** online is a form of e-commerce in which companies sell advertising either on their Web sites or through their e-mail. It is called content sponsorship because this model sprang from the media, which depend on advertising sales to pay for editorial content. Today, many sites use consumer-generated content to build their sites, such as Yahoo's Flickr—the digital photo hosting site.

A **portal** is a point of entry to the internet, such as the Yahoo! and AOL Web sites. They are portals because they provide many services in addition to search capabilities. They include destinations for news, games, maps, shopping, mail, and so forth in addition to being jump-off points for content provided by others. AOL uses its portal to communicate with members, help them find other Web sites, offer entertaining content, and conduct e-commerce—driving tens of billions of dollars in sales per year to partner merchants. Some portals focus on vertical industries, such as Edmunds.com for automobiles and theKnot.com for couples planning a wedding.

Social networking sites are those that bring users together to share interests and personal or professional profiles. They use the community-building model previously described, but social networks are communities with the purpose of connecting like-minded individuals for friendship or business—such as LinkedIn for professionals and FaceBook for friends and family. Social networking site owners monetize the model by selling advertising, charging recruiters for searching profiles, or by partnering with third party developers for adding valuable applications to benefit users.

Online brokers are intermediaries who assist in the purchase negotiations without actually representing either buyers or sellers. The revenue stream in these models is commission or fee based. Examples of firms using the brokerage model are E*TRADE (**online exchange**), Guru.com (exchange for freelancers looking to connect with project managers), and eBay (**online auction**). Brokers usually create a market space for exchanges to occur, taking a piece of the action. A **B2B exchange** is a special place because it allows buyers and sellers in a specific industry to quickly get connected. Online auctions occur in both B2B and B2C markets, with the online broker providing the Web site and technology in exchange for a commission on all sales.

Unlike brokers, **online agents** tend to represent either the buyer or the seller and earn a commission for their work. **Selling agents** help a seller move product. Many selling agents work in the B2B market. In the B2C market, affiliate programs, discussed earlier, are also an example of the selling agent model.

Manufacturer's agents represent more than one seller. In traditional marketing, they often represent manufacturing firms that sell complementary products to avoid conflicts of interest. However, in the virtual world, they generally create Web sites to help an entire industry sell product. For example, Travelocity.com, the online travel agent, is a manufacturer's agent in the travel industry.

Purchasing agents represent buyers. In traditional marketing, they often forge long-term relationships with one or more firms; on the internet, however, they represent any number of buyers, often anonymously. For example, **shopping agents** help individual consumers find specific products and the best prices online (e.g., www.bizrate.com). Another model, the **reverse auction**, allows individual buyers to enter the price they will pay for particular items at the purchasing agent's Web site, and sellers can agree or not (e.g., Priceline.com). Purchasing agents often help buyers form cooperatives online for the purpose of buying in larger quantities to reduce prices.

PURE PLAY The final level of the pyramid is comprised of internet pure plays. **Pure plays** are businesses that began on the internet, even if they subsequently added a brick-and-mortar presence. We do not include pure plays in Exhibit 2.4 because they start right at the top of the pyramid rather than progressing upward as do traditional brick-and-mortar firms. For example, E*TRADE is a pure play, beginning with only online trading. Interestingly, E*TRADE has several retail storefronts in major cities worldwide. Amazon and Newegg are pure plays that ranked first and tenth in sales among all online retailers in 2005, according to Morgan Stanley (Office Depot was second).

Pure plays face significant challenges: They must compete as new brands and take customers away from established brick-and-mortar businesses. The successful ones have been able to do so by industry redefinition (i.e., changing the rules of the game) (Modahl, 2000). One way to change the rules is to invent a new e-business model, as Yahoo!, MySpace, and eBay did. In fact, some observers believe that eBay has the only truly viable pure play model in existence. The key to pure play success is offering greater customer value. For example, Buy.com increases customer value by utilizing a content sponsorship model combined with direct sales. The ad inventory sold on the site helps to subsidize prices for the consumer.

PERFORMANCE METRICS

The only way to know whether a company has reached its objectives is to measure its results. **Performance metrics** are specific measures designed to evaluate the effectiveness and efficiency of an organization's operations. For example, if the company wants 30 percent of its sales to come from the online channel, it needs to continually measure revenue from various channels to determine whether it is achieving the goal. Armed with this information, the company can make corrections to make sure it accomplishes the goal. For instance, Skechers USA, the trendy shoe producer, discovered many problems by using special software to track visitors on its Web site. As a result, it changed the site to offer faster access to product photos and require fewer clicks to view and purchase products. The result was a 70 percent increase in sales ($227.5 million) from the first quarter in 2000 to the same period in 2001 (Jarvis, 2001).

Because strategy is the means to the end—the way of accomplishing objectives—performance metrics should be defined along with the strategy formulation so that the entire organization will know what results constitute successful performance. (Refer to Exhibit 2.1 for the role of performance.) Nickols (2000) put it well:

> Strategy, then, has no existence apart from the ends sought. It is a general framework that provides guidance for actions to be taken and, at the same time, is shaped by the actions taken. This means that the necessary precondition for formulating strategy is a clear and widespread understanding of the ends to be obtained. Without these ends in view, action is purely tactical and can quickly degenerate into nothing more than a flailing about. (p. 6)

When a company designates the performance metrics it will use to measure strategy effectiveness, it does four important things:

1. It translates its vision, strategy, or e-business model into components with measurable outcomes. Some e-marketing goals needing metrics include attracting visitors to the Web site for selling more advertising or converting them to sales and building visitor loyalty to the site.

2. The performance metrics must be easy to understand and use. They should be accessible to employees using them for decision making. It is difficult to choose from among all the available data, so firms often settle on Key Performance Indicators (KPI) to monitor progress toward important goals.

3. Metrics must be actionable. Companies use benchmarking and last year's metrics to decide where they are and then can set metric goals for the future (such as increase the amount of time visitors spend on the site from 5 minutes to 10 minutes per session).

4. Finally, when employee evaluations are tied to the metrics, people will be motivated to make decisions that lead to the desired outcomes. Even though the metrics are usually set by top management, successful firms

collect employee input throughout the process so that the measurements are relevant and the organization gains consensus on their importance. Thus, the adage, "What you measure is what you get."

Two important types of performance metrics include Web analytics and user-engagement metrics, two important types of performance metrics for Web site user behavior analysis (next sections). Throughout this book we expand this chapter and present many more very specific metrics for each type of tactic.

Web Analytics

Web analytics is the study of user behavior on Web pages. Companies collect data as users click through pages and use it to optimize their online investments. Commonly collected metrics include which tactics generated the site traffic (e.g., click throughs from online advertising), which pages are viewed most often, what patterns visitors use in clicking through the site, and how long they stay on various pages. Of course, a key metric involves conversions to sales or other desired behaviors, such as registering at the site. Finally, organizations want to know which of their new tactics are working well—things such as a new one day shipping price or special promotion on the site to increase sales. These data for Web analytics are collected in several ways:

- Web site server logs record the user's IP (internet protocol) address, which browser he is using, his location before arriving at the company site, the time of the day, and every user click through the site. The IP address helps companies understand where users live (e.g., .jp for Japan).
- Cookie files are small data files written to a user's hard drive when visiting a site. They are necessary for using shopping carts and other operations at a site. When customers return, the cookie file data are retrieved and used to understand how many visitors are returning and more. Amazon.com uses cookie file data to display the user name on its home page instantaneously.

- **Page tags** are one pixel on a page that is invisible to users (a pixel is one dot of light on a computer screen). Page tags activate a special script when users are on the page, providing information such as when items are removed from a shopping cart. Tags can also be activated based on cookie files on the visitor's hard drive from a previous visit—creating data about the return visit and what the user did.

Web analytics software helps companies analyze all these data on server logs to uncover usage patterns.

Social Engagement Metrics

Web 2.0 technologies have rendered the page view metric nearly useless (one visitor viewing one Web page). Online measurement giant Nielsen//NetRatings recently announced it will soon abandon the page view in its online media measurement system. The reason for this is that when internet users view an online video, for example, they might spend four minutes viewing it, but this only counts as one page view. This underestimates the user activity online and is especially important for a site like YouTube when it sells advertising. Today, marketers want to know how visitors participate on the site rather than simply measuring whether or not they landed on the page.

Participation can be measured by some of the following social engagement metrics:

- Time spent viewing a video, playing a game, or listening to music.
- Downloading a white paper, MP3 music file, ring tone, or other content.
- Bookmarking a Web site at a social bookmarking site such as Del.ic.ious.com.
- Uploading a user-created video, photo, or other multimedia content to a Web site.
- Writing a comment on a blog or other Web page.
- Rating a book or online retailer by leaving a review or other type of rating measure.
- Subscribing to a blog or Web site using an RSS feed.

Customer Perspective		Internal Business Perspective		Learning and Growth Perspective		Financial Perspective	
Goals	Measures	Goals	Measures	Goals	Measures	Goals	Measures

EXHIBIT 2.5   The Four Perspectives of the Balanced Scorecard

Some of these activies are difficult to measure, but the page tag is one way companies can tell if visitors do things such as change the color of an automobile graphic at a Web site or rotate a product to view it from different angles. Companies also can tell if a visitor stops a video in the middle or restarts. There are many complexities to social engagement measurement, and marketers are just beginning to find robust ways for collecting these important Web 2.0 metrics.

THE BALANCED SCORECARD

Several well-known performance metrics systems include these metrics in dashboards individualized to an organization's needs. The Balanced Scorecard is a good framework for understanding e-marketing metrics; thus, we present it to bring together important performance metrics.

For years, firms valued financial performance or market share as the most important success measure. The large firms fostered competition among their brand groups or retail outlets and measured success by the bottom line (profits). Many still do so. During the mid- to late-1990s, the dot-com firms ignored financial measures and focused on growth, much to their dismay. These approaches are narrowly focused and place more weight on short-term results rather than on addressing the firm's long-term sustainability.

These weaknesses paved the way for enterprise performance management systems that measure many aspects of a firm's achievements. The **Balanced Scorecard**, developed by two Harvard Business School professors in 1990, is one such system with a huge adoption rate (57% to 64% of all global companies, according to

various estimates). The scorecard approach links strategy to measurement by asking firms to consider their vision, critical success factors for accomplishing it, and subsequent performance metrics in four areas: customer, internal, learning and growth, and financial (Exhibit 2.5). In the following sections we describe the typical goals and e-business metrics in each perspective. However, it is important to remember that each firm defines the specific measures for each box—the system is very flexible.

Four Perspectives

The customer perspective uses measures of the value delivered to customers. These metrics tend to fall into four areas: time, quality, performance and service, and cost. They also include measures such as time from order to delivery, customer satisfaction levels with product performance, amount of sales from new products, and industry-specific metrics such as equipment up-time percentage or number of service calls.

The internal perspective evaluates a company's success at meeting customer expectations through its internal processes. The items with greatest impact in this area include cycle time (how long it takes to make the product), manufacturing quality, and employee skills and productivity. Information systems are a critical component of the internal perspective for e-business firms.

The learning and growth perspective, sometimes called the growth perspective, is one of the Balanced Scorecard's unique contributions. Here, companies place value on continuous improvement to existing products and services as well as on innovation in new products. These activities take employees away from their daily work of selling products, asking them to pay attention to factors critical to the firm's long-term sustainability, which is especially important for e-business firms. Measures in this area include number of new products and the percentage of sales attributable to each, penetration of new markets, and the improvement of processes such as CRM or SCM initiatives.

If the projected outcomes result from the previous perspectives and performance metrics, the financial perspective will be on target too. Financial measures include income and expense metrics as well as return on investment, sales, and market share growth. Companies must be careful to relate measurements from the first three perspectives to the financial area whenever possible.

Each firm will select metrics for the four perspectives based on its objectives, business model, strategies, industry, and so forth. The point is to understand what the company wants to accomplish and devise performance metrics to monitor the progress and see that the goals are reached.

A regional U.S. airline developed a Balanced Scorecard to build and sustain its unique position as a high-frequency, short-haul carrier (see www.balancedscorecard.org case studies). Consider the performance metrics goals it associated with each goal:

- **Customer perspective.** On-time flights, more customers, and lower prices. Metrics included being the first in the industry according to FAA on-time arrival ratings, customer satisfaction rankings of 98 percent, and a healthy percent change in number of customers.

- **Internal perspective.** Improve turnaround time as measured by on-ground time of less than 25 minutes and 93 percent accurate departure time.

- **Learning and growth perspective.** Align ground crews better with company goals, measured by percent of ground crew trained and percent of ground crew who are stockholders. The airline wanted 70 percent of 1-year employees, 90 percent of 4-year employees, and all of 6-year employees to own the company's stock.

- **Financial perspective.** Profitability increase of 25 percent per year, lower costs, and increased revenue (based on market value, seat revenue, and plane lease cost).

Applying the Balanced Scorecard to E-Business and E-Marketing

E-business firms are swimming in data. They have databases full of customer information, Web site logs that automatically record every click of every page visitor and how long the user stays, customer service records, sales data from many different channels, and so forth. One service firm manager reported: "Since I've got all these things to measure, I'm paralyzed by all the opportunities." In spite of these difficulties, measurement is vital to success. When Forrester Research surveyed executives at 51 companies, 63 percent said measurement is extremely or very important today versus only 24 percent in 2000. Sixty-one percent of the executives further stated that today they are focusing more on return on investment (ROI) as a measure (Cutler, 2001).

METRICS FOR THE CUSTOMER PERSPECTIVE

The most important of these metrics measure customer loyalty and lifetime value. However, many other metrics can help a firm optimize customer value: for example, customer perceptions of product value, appropriateness of selected targets, and customer buying patterns. The firm must also measure value created for partners and other supply chain members because many can easily partner elsewhere if they are not satisfied. Customer engagement online is an important emerging metric involving the number of comments, photos, videos, or other user-generated content posted to a site, among other things. As an example, Exhibit 2.6 displays several possible measures for some customer goals of a firm employing e-business models.

METRICS FOR THE INTERNAL PERSPECTIVE

The internal perspective is critical to a successful e-business. Many goals in this perspective affect human resources, information technology, and

Customer Perspective	
Example Goals	**Possible Measures**
Build awareness of a new Web site service	Survey target awareness of service
	Number of visitors to the site
Engage customers on a site	Number of comments, photos, or videos posted
Increase number of software downloads from the Web site	Number from Web site log
High customer satisfaction with Web site	Survey of target at Web site
	Number of visits and activity at site
High customer satisfaction with value of online purchasing	Number of complaints (e-mail, phone)
	Number of abandoned shopping carts
	Sales of online versus off-line for same products
Increase the amount or frequency of online sales from current customers	Mine the database for change in frequency of purchases over time
Build customer relationships	Number of purchases per customer over time (using cookie data)
	Customer retention percentage
Appropriate target markets	Data mining to find purchase patterns by targeting criteria
Buy-to-delivery time faster than competition	Number of days from order to delivery
	Competition delivery times
Increased visits from sweepstake offers	Number who enter
Build communities on the site	Number of registrations to community
	Amount of content uploaded to user profiles
Value for Business Partners	
Increase number of affiliates in program	Number of affiliates over time
Cross-sell to partner sites	Number of visitors to partner site from our site

EXHIBIT 2.6   Customer Perspective Scorecard for E-Business Firm

other areas that directly and indirectly affect marketing. Of particular note is that the entire supply chain is considered *internal* in this analysis. Obviously the manufacturing firm cannot control the employees of its online retailers. At the same time, neither business customers nor consumers differentiate among firms in a supply chain—they just want quality products on demand. Thus, recent work on the Balanced Scorecard includes measures for the entire supply chain. See Exhibit 2.7 for example goals and measures in the internal perspective.

METRICS FOR THE LEARNING AND GROWTH PERSPECTIVE   The learning and growth perspective typically falls under the human resources umbrella. Two exceptions include product innovation and continuous improvement of marketing processes, both of which are important for e-business firms due to rapid changes in technology. Exhibit 2.8 includes a few sample goals and measures affecting e-marketers.

METRICS FOR THE FINANCIAL PERSPECTIVE
Marketing strategies clearly drive revenues, online

Internal Perspective	
Example Goals	**Possible Measures**
Improve the quality of online service	Target market survey
	Number of customers who use the service
	Time to run the service software from Web site
Quality online technical help	Amount of time to answer customer e-mail
	Number of contacts to solve a problem
	Number of problems covered by Web site FAQ
	Customer follow-up survey
High product quality for online service	Product test statistics on specific performance measures
Web server size adequate and operational 24/7	Number of actual simultaneous Web page requests ÷ maximum possible
	Percentage of up-time for server
	Number of mirrored or backup sites
Optimized number of customer service reps responding to online help	Number of inquiries to customer service rep ratio
Superior Web site content management	Number of updates per day
	Web site log traffic pattern statistics
Optimized inventory levels	Average number of items in warehouse
	Inventory turnover
	Supplier speed to deliver product
Supply Chain Value to Firm	
High supplier satisfaction	Supplier profits from our firm's orders
Partner value	Number of visitors from partner site to ours and number who purchase
	Partner contribution to product design

EXHIBIT 2.7   Internal Perspective Scorecard for E-Business Firm

and offline. They can affect profits as well, but other operational factors enter the equation when figuring company expenses. Nevertheless, marketers who manage brands have responsibility for their profits. When marketers propose new products or online services, they must forecast the potential sales over time, estimate the expenses to deliver that level of sales, and project the amount of time needed to break even (create enough revenues to cover expenses and start-up investments). In most cases, the product or internal project with the fastest break-even period or best potential for meeting the firm's return on investment hurdle will get funded.

Two of the most frequently used metrics are profits and return on investment. This section will outline basic ideas without considering taxes and other details. Net profits are revenues minus expenses. Revenues are the actual amount of dollars customers give the firm in exchange for products. Expenses include many things, most commonly the variable costs for producing the product, the selling costs (advertising, free product giveaways, and other customer acquisition costs), delivery, customer support, and other administrative costs.

Return on investment (ROI) is calculated by dividing net profit by total assets (fixed plus current). Marketers often evaluate ROI for specific

Learning and Growth Perspective	
Example Goals	**Possible Measures**
Online service innovation	Number of new service products to market in a year
	Number of new service features not offered by competitive offerings
	Percent of sales from new services
Continuous improvement in CRM system	Number of employee suggestions
	Number/type of improvements over time
High Internet lead-to-sales conversion	Revenue per sales employee from Internet leads
	Number of conversions from online leads
Increased value in knowledge management system	Number of accesses by employees
	Number of knowledge contributions by employees
Successful penetration of new markets	Percentage of the firm's sales in each new market

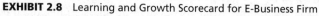

EXHIBIT 2.8   Learning and Growth Scorecard for E-Business Firm

e-business projects by dividing the project's profits by its investment dollars, such as the research, development, and the testing funds needed to introduce the new service. As an example, a firm might invest $100,000 in software to analyze Web traffic patterns, use the results, change the Web site for better usability, and realize an additional $75,000 in e-commerce revenues: a 75 percent ROI.

The financial perspective scorecard relies heavily on sales, profit, and return figures. Exhibit 2.9 presents some common performance metrics used by e-marketers.

Financial Perspective	
Example Goals	**Possible Measures**
Increase market share for online products	Market share percentage (firm's sales as percentage of industry sales)
Double-digit sales growth	Dollar volume of sales from one time period to the next
Target 10% ROI within one year for each new product	ROI
Lower customer acquisition costs (CAC) in online channel	CAC (costs for advertising, and so forth, divided by number of customers)
Increase conversion rates at Web site	Number of orders divided by number of visitors to site
Increase individual customer profit	Average order value
	Profit contribution over time less CAC
Achieve at least a 10% net profit in first year of new product	Net profit as percentage of sales

EXHIBIT 2.9   Financial Perspective Scorecard for E-Business Firm

Balanced Scorecard for Raytheon's E-Business

To see the Balanced Scorecard in action, consider how Raytheon applied it to the company's e-business. "It works for Raytheon; I don't see why it can't work for everyone" (Melymuka, 2001, p. 1). Following are many of the measures Raytheon established for its Web site business:

- **Customer perspective**
  - *Loyalty*. Percentage of visitors who return to the site within a year; time between visits; duration of visit; conversion rate; percentage who give personal information; percentage of e-mail addresses collected out of all traffic.
  - *Transactions*. Unique visitors each month; online sales abandoned; percentage of correct orders; time to respond to a customer; percentage of orders filled on time.
- **Internal perspective**
  - *Web site*. Time to load a Web page; network up-time and scalability.
  - *Supply chain excellence*. Inventory levels; inventory turns; order confirmation time; percentage of products built to order.
  - *Complementary channels*. Percentage of total revenue generated online.
- **Learning and growth perspective**. Average time from concept to start; speed to match a rival's site; speed at which the competition will match the site; time between relaunches.
- **Financial perspective**. Return on invested capital; market capitalization migration (changing value).

Although performance metrics affect the entire firm, this book focuses on e-marketing metrics. Many of the measures mentioned earlier will be described in more detail in later chapters.

In the next chapter, we move to the e-marketing plan and discuss how this plan flows from corporate e-business strategies, and how the marketing mix and CRM enter the picture. The e-marketing plan is a management guide and road map that paves the way to achieving performance goals.

Chapter Summary

A business or e-business needs strategic planning to develop and maintain the proper fit between the organization's objectives, skills, and resources and its ever-changing market opportunities. Key goals for growth, competitive position, geographic scope, and other areas must be determined.

Strategy is defined as the means to achieve a goal. E-business strategy is the deployment of enterprise resources to capitalize on technologies for reaching specified objectives that ultimately improve performance and create sustainable competitive advantage. E-marketing strategy is the design of marketing strategy that capitalizes on the organization's electronic or information technology capabilities to reach specified objectives.

An e-business model is a method by which the organization sustains itself in the long term using information technology, including its value proposition for partners and customers as well as its revenue streams. Firms deliver value by providing more benefits in relation to costs, as perceived by customers and partners. E-marketing improves the value proposition by increasing benefits, decreasing costs, and increasing revenues.

Companies can become involved in e-business at the activity level, business process level, enterprise level, or through a pure play. Commitment and risk are lower at the activity level and rise with each level. The main e-business models at the activity level include online purchasing, order processing, e-mail, content publishing, business intelligence, online advertising, online sales promotion, and dynamic pricing strategies. The main e-business models at the business process level are customer relationship management, knowledge management, supply chain management, community building online, database marketing, enterprise resource planning, and mass customization. The main e-business models at the enterprise level are e-commerce, portal, social networking, online broker (online exchange and online auction), and online agent (manufacturer's agent, shopping agent, and reverse auction).

Performance metrics are specific measures designed to evaluate the effectiveness and efficiency of an organization's operations. Web analytics analyzes user behavior on a Web site by using server logs, cookie files, and page tags. Social media engagement metrics are important for measuring user participation on a Web site, such as time spent viewing a video.

The Balanced Scorecard links strategy to measurement by asking firms to consider their vision, critical success factors for accomplishing it, and subsequent performance metrics in four areas: customer, internal, learning and growth, and financial. The customer perspective uses measures of the value delivered to customers. The internal perspective evaluates a company's success at meeting customer expectations through its internal processes. The learning and growth perspective looks at continuous improvement to existing products and services as well as innovation in new products. The financial perspective looks at income and expense metrics as well as return on investment, sales, and market share growth. Each firm selects metrics for the four perspectives based on its objectives, business model, strategies, industry, and so forth. In this way, the firm can measure progress toward achieving its objectives.

Exercises

REVIEW QUESTIONS

1. What is strategic planning and why do companies prepare a SWOT analysis during the strategic planning process?
2. How does e-business strategy relate to strategy on the corporate level?
3. Define e-marketing strategy and explain how it is used.
4. Give examples of e-business models.
5. What is the formula for determining value?
6. What are the four levels of commitment to e-business and give some examples of each?
7. What is customer relationship management (CRM), and why do companies create strategies in this area?
8. How is e-commerce defined?
9. What is an internet pure play, and what are some examples?
10. What are three ways of collecting Web analytics?
11. Name several types of social media engagement metrics?
12. What is the Balanced Scorecard, and how do companies use it in e-business?

DISCUSSION QUESTIONS

13. Why is it important for an e-business model to create value in a way that is differentiated from the way competitors' models create value?

14. Based on the opening vignette and your examination of the Amazon.com site (or your experience as a customer), what strategic objectives do you think are appropriate for this e-business? What performance metrics would you use to measure progress toward achieving these objectives—and why?
15. The Balanced Scorecard helps e-businesses examine results from four perspectives. Would you recommend that e-businesses also look at results from a societal perspective? Explain your response.
16. Should e-businesses strive to build community with noncustomers as well as customers? Why or why not?
17. Do you agree or disagree that the page view metric is nearly useless in the Web 2.0 environment?

WEB ACTIVITIES

18. Visit www.Dell.com. Write down what you think the firm's goals are for its Web site. Then make a list recommending relevant performance metrics from each of the four perspectives.
19. Visit the shopping agent MySimon at www.MySimon.com. Do a search for this book (*E-Marketing*). What is the lowest price available for the book? The highest? Compare these prices with those found at the brick-and-mortar sites Border's and Barnes & Noble. Check out used bookstore site www.half.com (partnered with eBay.) Explain in terms of value why customers might buy the book at a higher price.

CHAPTER 3

The E-Marketing Plan

If I had one hour to chop down a tree, I'd spend the first 30 minutes sharpening the axe.

—ABRAHAM LINCOLN (COMMONLY ATTRIBUTED)

It's not the strongest or most intelligent that survive, but the ones most responsive to change.

—CHARLES DARWIN

Chapter Outline

The primary goal of this chapter is to explain the importance of creating an e-marketing plan and present the seven steps in the e-marketing planning process. You will see how marketers incorporate information technology in plans for effectively and efficiently achieving e-business objectives such as increasing revenues and slashing costs.

After reading this chapter, you will be able to:

- Discuss the nature and importance of an e-marketing plan and outline its seven steps.
- Show the form of an e-marketing objective and explain the use of an objective–strategy matrix.
- Describe the tasks that marketers complete in tiers 1 and 2 as they create e-marketing strategies.
- List some key revenues and costs identified during the budgeting step of the e-marketing planning process.

The E-Marketing Plan

The Second Life Story

How would you like to dress as a huge spider or rock star and take a class in a virtual world? There are over 115 universities hosting classes in Second Life, according to Wikipedia.com. U.S. faculty from Harvard and Penn State join those from Italian, Thai, German, and other international schools to offer everything from physics to digital media classes in world.

Second Life (SL) is a 3-D virtual world entirely created by its residents. Opened to the public in 1999, SL had 2.3 million residents in 2008, with close to 500,000 logging in during a seven-day period. Residents can get a basic account for free and receive an avatar to represent their virtual selves. They dress the avatar and teleport or walk to any location within the millions of square meters of SL property. Second Life residents create the world by constructing buildings, trading Linden dollars (which can be exchanged for U.S. dollars), and by chatting and hanging out with other avatars. A few residents even make real money by accepting jobs in-world or selling cool outfits and other virtual world merchandise. One guy even got a real job by visiting an SL job fair hosted by recruiting firm TMP Worldwide.

Second Life is a massively multiplayer online role-playing game (MMORPG): "a genre of online role-playing video games (RPGs) in which a large number of players interact with one another in a virtual world . . . which continues to

(continued)

(continued)

exist and evolve while the player is away from the game (www.wikipedia.com)" Fifteen million players worldwide spent over $1 billion in USD revenues in 2006 in games such as SL, World of Warcraft, and the Webkinz world for 6- to 13-year-old kids.

Over 50,000 businesses have a presence in SL, including Adidas, Sun Microsystems, Pontiac, IBM, *Wired* magazine, and Toyota. Their strategies include brand building, introducing new products, creating a buzz, and simply connecting with the younger demographic who are big SL inhabitants. *Wired* uses the space to let writers chat with each other.

In-world advertising revenue in the United States was $186 million in 2005, according to Yankee Group.

Research firm Gartner Group believes that 80 percent of active online users will join a virtual world by 2010. Google is rumored to be working on a virtual world for business networking. Second Life has a steep learning curve for players, but if Google and others follow the Webkinz and other simpler models, virtual worlds may soon appear in many business strategic plans. For now, get yourself an avatar and take a class—the time you invest may just put you in the front of this rapidly growing trend.

OVERVIEW OF THE E-MARKETING PLANNING PROCESS

How can information technologies assist marketers in building revenues and market sharing or lowering costs? How can firms identify a sustainable competitive advantage with the internet when the landscape is constantly changing? The answer lies in determining how to apply digital data and information technologies both effectively and efficiently. The best firms have clear visions that they translate, through the marketing process, from e-business objectives and strategies into e-marketing goals and well-executed strategies and tactics for achieving those goals. This marketing process entails three steps: marketing plan creation, plan implementation, and plan evaluation/corrective action (using performance metrics, as discussed in Chapter 2). This chapter examines the first of these steps: the e-marketing plan.

CREATING AN E-MARKETING PLAN

The e-marketing plan is a blueprint for e-marketing strategy formulation and implementation. It is a guiding, dynamic document that links the firm's e-business strategy (e-business models) with technology-driven marketing strategies and lays out details for plan implementation through marketing management. It is often combined with the firm's overall marketing plan. The marketing plan guides delivery of the desired results measured by performance metrics according to the specifications of the e-business model imbedded in the firm's e-business strategy. Exhibit 3.1 shows where the e-marketing plan fits in the process.

The e-marketing plan also serves as a road map to guide the direction of the firm, allocate resources, and make tough decisions at critical junctures (Kalakota and Robinson, 1999). Many companies short-circuit this process and develop strategies ad hoc. Some of them are successful, but many more fail. The Gartner Group correctly predicted that up to 75 percent of all e-business projects prior to 2002 would fail due to fundamental flaws in planning. Nonetheless, some of the best firms discover successful e-commerce tactics accidentally and then use those experiences to build a bottom-up plan. Such was the case with eSchwab, the online stock trading firm, which allowed its online channel successes to change the entire brick-and-mortar firm. Whether the result of top-down or bottom-up planning, firms must plan for long-term sustainability.

This chapter is structured around a seven-step traditional marketing plan. It presents a generic plan that includes a menu of tasks from which marketers can select activities relevant to their firm, industry, brands, and internal

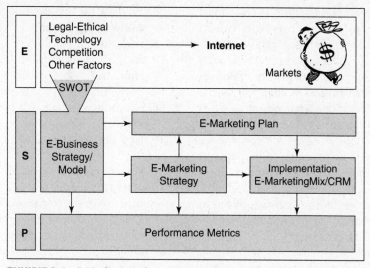

EXHIBIT 3.1 E-Marketing Plan—Strategy Formulation and Implementation

processes. It assumes that a higher-level corporate plan is already in place, outlining the firm's goals, e-business strategies, and selected enterprise-level e-business models. If such a plan has not already been formulated, marketers must go through the environmental scan and SWOT analyses prior to creating the plan. Two common types of e-marketing plans are the napkin plan and the venture capital plan, discussed next.

The Napkin Plan

In what one marketer calls the *napkin plan*, many entrepreneurs simply jot their ideas on a napkin over lunch or cocktails and then run off to find financing. The big-company version of this process is the just-do-it, activity-based, bottom-up plan. As an example, Kevin Rose of Digg.com had an idea about how to set up a Web site to host the most liked stories of the day, and he just built this now hugely successful site. In another example, an e-marketing student who works for a local ski shop approached the owner, asking for $500 for software and $50 a month for Web hosting to start an experimental e-commerce site. He placed a few pictures of skis on the site and included information about how to call the store to order. The site brought in several orders a week, quickly paying off the investment. These ad hoc plans sometimes

work and are sometimes even necessary given a stodgy corporate culture, but they are not recommended when substantial resources are involved. Sound planning and thoughtful implementation are needed for long-term success in business and e-business—a principle that became increasingly evident during the dot-com shakeout.

The Venture Capital E-Marketing Plan

Small to mid-sized firms and entrepreneurs with start-up ideas usually begin with a *napkin plan* and do not initially go through the entire traditional marketing planning process. One reason is that one or two leaders generally plan the whole venture, intuitively understanding the marketing environment and how their hot new idea is positioned for success. Such was the case for Jerry Yang and Dave Filo when in 1994 they started *Jerry's Guide to the World Wide Web*—later named Yahoo! However, as the company grew and needed capital, Jerry and Dave had to put together a comprehensive e-marketing plan. Without an emphasis on strategic planning, Yahoo! would not be an internet survivor.

Where does an entrepreneur go for capital? Some of it is debt financed through bank loans, though most of it is equity financed. Start-up companies tap private funds (friends and family), angel investors, and venture capitalists (VCs). Angel investors provide funds with fewer requirements than those of venture capitalists. In general, friends and family are the smallest sources of capital; angel investors invest hundreds of thousands of dollars; and venture capitalists invest millions of dollars. Even banks, corporations, and consulting firms have established venture capital branches to finance internet start-ups. Some VCs even finance companies operated out of college dorm rooms.

Plenty of money is available to e-business entrepreneurs, and 2007 saw an increasing number of e-businesses venture funded—largely due to the social media boom. The conventional wisdom is that money is scarce, when talent is really the scarce resource. Obviously, investors aren't stupid. They are looking for a well-composed business plan, and more importantly, a good team to implement it. Two quotes from a well-known venture capitalist, Arthur Rock, who helped to finance Intel, Apple, and Teledyne, say it best:

> I invest in people, not ideas. . . . If you can find good people, if they're wrong about the product, they'll make a switch, so what good is it to understand the product that they're talking about in the first place?

This kind of thinking relieves some of the planning pressure on entrepreneurs—but does not eliminate the need for planning to maximize organizational resources. The plan prepared by entrepreneurs for VCs should be about 8–10 pages long and contain enough data and logic to prove that (1) the e-business idea is solid and (2) the entrepreneur has some idea of how to run the business. William Sahlman of Harvard University identifies nine questions that every business plan should answer:

1. Who is the new venture's customer?
2. How does the customer make decisions about buying this product or service?
3. To what degree is the product or service a compelling purchase for the customer?
4. How will the product or service be priced?

5. How will the venture reach all the identified customer segments?
6. How much does it cost (in time and resources) to acquire a customer?
7. How much does it cost to produce and deliver the product or service?
8. How much does it cost to support a customer?
9. How easy is it to retain a customer?

Venture capitalists typically look for an exit plan—a way to get their money and profits out of the venture within a few years. The golden exit plan is to go public and issue stock in an initial public offering (IPO). As soon as the stock price rises sufficiently, the VC cashes out and moves on to another investment. VCs don't even pretend that all their investments will be successful. But even if one out of 20 is an Amazon.com or eBay.com, the risk was well worth the reward. The employees of these start-ups typically work for very low wages—deferring their compensation in stock options. Of particular interest to investors are projects that tap new markets with high margins. First came a boom in B2C investments and then B2B investments and now social networking investments. As soon as observers feel that the markets are becoming saturated, another opportunity arises. Some think it is the virtual world market that is about to take off (refer to the opening story on Second Life).

A SEVEN-STEP E-MARKETING PLAN

Seven key planning elements include a situation analysis, e-marketing strategic planning, the plan objectives, e-marketing strategy, an implementation plan, the budget, and a plan for evaluating success (Exhibit 3.2). We cannot overemphasize the need to include feedback mechanisms to assess the plan's success and to use in making course corrections along the way, especially in the fast-paced e-business environment. In fact, some marketers recommend contingency plans and "trigger points" that if reached will invoke strategy refinement.

A good way to think about the marketing plan is through the analogy of preparing for a

Step	Tasks
1 Situation analysis	Review the firm's environmental and SWOT analyses.
	Review the existing marketing plan and any other information that can be obtained about the company and its brands.
	Review the firm's e-business objectives, strategies, and performance metrics.
2 E-marketing strategic planning	Determine the fit between the organization and its strategic planning changing market opportunities. Perform marketing opportunity analysis, demand and supply analyses, and segment analysis.
	Tier 1 Strategies • Segmentation • Targeting • Differentiation • Positioning
3 Objectives	Identify general goals flowing from e-business strategy.
4 E-marketing strategy	Identify revenue streams suggested by e-business models.
	Tier 2 Strategies Design the offer, value, distribution, communication, and market/partner relationship management strategies. Modify objectives as warranted.
5 Implementation plan	Design e-marketing mix tactics: • product/service offering • pricing/valuation • distribution/supply chain • integrated communication mix Design relationship management tactics. Design information gathering tactics. Design organizational structures for implementing the plan.
6 Budget	Forecast revenues. Evaluate costs to reach goals.
7 Evaluation plan	Identify appropriate performance metrics.

EXHIBIT 3.2   E-Marketing Plan Process

football game. While reviewing game films, a situation analysis reveals each team's strengths and weaknesses (e.g., the home team has a good passing game, the visitors have an excellent run defense). A likely objective would then be to win the game by throwing the ball. Strategies are developed to meet this objective (e.g., use play action to draw in the coverage; throw deep). Next, tactics implement the strategies (e.g., use a play action pass on first down; run on second down to keep them honest, pass on

third down). Finally, Monday morning quarterbacking provides the postgame evaluation.

STEP 1—SITUATION ANALYSIS

Some people feel that planning for e-marketing means starting from scratch. Nothing could be further from the truth. Working with existing business, e-business, and marketing plans is an excellent place to start.

The marketing environment is ever chang-ing, providing plenty of opportunities to develop new products, new markets, and new media to communicate with customers, plus new channels to reach business partners. At the same time, the environment poses competitive, economic, and other threats. Three key environmental factors that affect e-marketing and are part of any situa-tion analysis include legal, technological, and market-related factors. They are covered in depth in Chapters 4, 5, and 7, as well as the technology boxes throughout the text.

The **SWOT** analysis (strengths, weak-nesses, opportunities, and threats) flows from a situation analysis that examines the company's internal strengths and weaknesses with respect to the environment and the competition, and looks at external opportunities and threats. Opportunities may help to define a target mar-ket or identify new product opportunities, while threats are areas of exposure. For example, when Amazon.com seized the opportunity to sell online, it had no significant competition. Its biggest threat was a full-scale push by one of the large bookstore chains to claim the online mar-ket. The company's greatest weakness was that it had no experience selling books or even process-ing credit card transactions. What's more, it had no experience boxing books for shipment and originally packed them on the floor until a visiting carpenter suggested building packing tables (Spector, 2000). The company's greatest strength was a smart and talented team that stayed focused and learned what it didn't know. Fortunately for Amazon, the big stores were caught napping. The delay by the bookstore chains gave Amazon the opportunity to establish its brand online. Barnes & Noble (www.bn.com) did not fight back until Amazon was on the eve of a stock offering. By then it was too late. Further proving Amazon's strategy skills, CEO Jeff Bezos states that the company will not open brick-and-mortar stores because it has no way to differentiate itself from the current players.

Bear in mind that a company's strengths and weaknesses in the online world may be some-what different from its strengths and weaknesses in the brick-and-mortar world. Exhibit 3.3 dis-plays a few of the key capabilities needed by e-business firms. Barnes & Noble has enormous strengths in the brick-and-mortar world, but they do not necessarily translate into strengths in the online world. Barnes & Noble can easily find itself in the unfortunate position of channel conflict—having to explain to channel partners why customers can purchase for less online than in the store. However, Amazon has no potential channel conflict because it only sells online.

Internal Capability	Examples
Customer interactions	E-commerce, customer service, distribution channels
Production and fulfillment	SCM, production scheduling, inventory management
People	Culture, skills, knowledge management, leadership, and commitment to e-business
Change management	Culture, business intelligence, ability to move quickly as conditions change
Technology	ERP systems, legacy applications, networks, Web site, security, IT skills
Performance measurement	Ability to measure the right things, take corrective action
Core infrastructure	Financial systems, R&D, HR

EXHIBIT 3.3   Key Internal Capabilities for E-Business

Source: Adapted from Kalakota and Robinson (1999) and 2008 at www.ebstrategy.com.

STEP 2—E-MARKETING STRATEGIC PLANNING

After reviewing the situation analysis and currently used marketing plans, marketers engage in strategic planning. As you recall from Chapter 2, the strategic planning process involves determining the fit between the organization's objectives, skills, and resources and its changing market opportunities. For clarification throughout the book, we present these tasks as *tier 1 strategies*, including segmentation, targeting, differentiation, and positioning. During this phase, marketers uncover opportunities that help formulate the e-marketing objectives.

Marketers conduct a **market opportunity analysis (MOA)**, including both demand and supply analyses, for *segmenting* and *targeting*. The demand analysis portion includes market segmentation analyses to describe and evaluate the potential profitability, sustainability, accessibility, and size of various potential segments. Segment analysis in the B2C market uses descriptors such as demographic characteristics, geographic location, selected psychographic characteristics (such as attitude toward technology and wireless communication device ownership), and past behavior toward the product (such as purchasing patterns online and off-line). B2B descriptors include firm location, size, industry, type of need, and more. These descriptors help firms identify potentially attractive markets. Firms must also understand segment trends—are they growing or declining in absolute size and product use?

Firms use traditional segmentation analyses when they enter new markets through the online channel; however, if the firm plans to serve current markets online, it will delve more deeply into these customers' needs. Which of the firm's customers will want to use the internet? How do the needs of customers using the firm's Web site differ from those of other customers? For example, most internet users expect e-mails to be answered within 24 hours but will be satisfied if a postal letter is answered within weeks. In addition, firms often discover new markets as these customers find their way to the Web site.

Marketers can use cookies, database analyses, and other techniques to discover how best to serve these new markets.

The purpose of a supply analysis is to assist in forecasting segment profitability as well as to find competitive advantages to exploit in the online market. Only by carefully analyzing competitive strengths and weaknesses can a firm find its own performance advantages. Therefore, firms should review the competition, their e-marketing initiatives, and their strengths and weaknesses prior to developing e-marketing initiatives. Firms must also try to identify future industry changes—which new firms might appear online, and which will drop away? For example, iGo's competitive advantage is a huge database of battery information. This firm knows which battery goes with every appliance and can ship it to customers within hours.

With a thorough MOA, the company can select its target market and understand its characteristics, behavior, and desires in the firm's product category. Furthermore, firms will want to understand the value proposition for each market. In our next example (Exhibit 3.4), marketers might decide to target several Hispanic markets.

Another tier 1 step in e-marketing strategic planning includes identifying brand *differentiation* variables and *positioning* strategies. Based on an understanding of both the competition and the target(s), marketers must decide how to differentiate their products from competitors' products in a way that provides benefits perceived as important by the target. In Facebook's case, management opted to add third-party applications to differentiate the site from its competitor, MySpace. Flowing from this differentiation is the positioning statement: the desired image for the brand relative to the competition. If this positioning strategy was already decided upon in the traditional marketing plan, e-marketers must decide whether it will be effective online as well. If planning for a new brand or market, e-marketers must decide on branding strategies of differentiation and positioning at this point in the process.

Opportunities	Threats
1. Hispanic markets growing and untapped in our industry.	1. Pending security law means costly software upgrades.
2. Save postage costs through e-mail marketing.	2. Competitor X is aggressively using e-commerce.
Strengths	**Weaknesses**
1. Strong customer service department.	1. Low-tech corporate culture.
2. Excellent Web site and database system.	2. Seasonal business: Peak is summer months.
E-Marketing Objective: $500,000 in revenues from e-commerce in one year.	

EXHIBIT 3.4   SWOT Analysis Leading to E-Marketing Objective

STEP 3—OBJECTIVES

In general, an objective in an e-marketing plan takes a form that includes the following aspects:

- Task (what is to be accomplished).
- Measurable quantity (how much).
- Time frame (by when).

Assume that Pontiac wants to increase the number of avatar visitors to its Motari Island property in Second Life (SL) from 5,000 to 6,000 in one year. This type of objective is easy to evaluate and a critical part of the e-marketing plan. The plan will often include the rationale for setting each objective—why each is desirable and achievable given the situation analysis findings, e-marketing, and e-business strategy.

Even though e-commerce transactions are an exciting dimension of an e-business presence, other objectives are also worthwhile, especially when the firm is using technology only to create internal efficiencies such as target market communication. In fact, most e-marketing plans aim to accomplish multiple objectives such as the following:

- Increase market share.
- Increase the number of comments left on a blog.
- Increase sales revenue (measured in dollars or units).
- Reduce costs (such as distribution or promotion costs).
- Achieve branding goals (such as increasing brand awareness).
- Increase database size.

- Achieve customer relationship management (CRM) goals (such as increasing customer satisfaction, frequency of purchases, or customer retention rates).
- Improve supply chain management (such as by enhancing member coordination, adding partners, or optimizing inventory levels).

An important part of the planning process is to define potential revenue streams. In the SL example, the firm selected e-commerce as one goal, selling premium memberships at $9.95 per month. The organizational e-business plan might contain a SWOT analysis similar to the example depicted in Exhibit 3.4, leading to the firm adopting an e-business model of e-commerce. E-marketers take over from here, setting a measurable objective of generating $500,000 from e-commerce sales within the first year.

STEP 4—E-MARKETING STRATEGIES

Next, marketers craft strategies regarding the 4 Ps and relationship management to achieve plan objectives regarding the offer (product), value (pricing), distribution (place), and communication (promotion). Further, marketers design customer and partner relationship management strategies (CRM/PRM). For clarification, we call these *tier 2 strategies* throughout the book. In practice, tier 1 and 2 strategies are interrelated (Exhibit 3.5). For example, marketers select the best target market and identify a competitive product position, which dictates the ideal type of advertising, pricing, and so forth. Steps 2, 3, and 4 are an iterative process

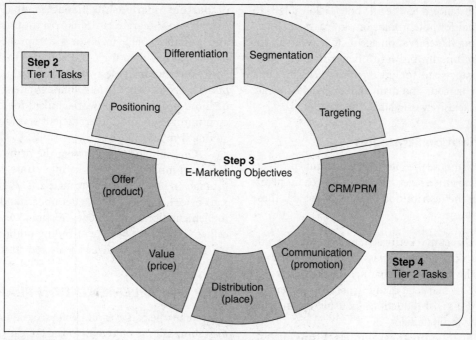

EXHIBIT 3.5   Steps 2, 3, and 4 of the E-Marketing Plan

because it is difficult to know what the brand position should be without understanding the offer that comprises the brand promise (i.e., the benefits the firm promises to customers). Following are some of the tier 2 strategies covered in detail in subsequent chapters.

The Offer: Product Strategies

The organization can sell merchandise, services, or advertising on the Web site. It can adopt one of the e-business models discussed in Chapter 2, such as online auctions, to generate a revenue stream. The firm can create new brands for the online market or simply sell selected current or enhanced products in that channel. Obviously, the previous analyses will reveal many options. If the firm offers current brands online, it will need to solve many different problems, such as the way colors appear differently on a computer screen than in print. The most astute firms take advantage of information technology capabilities to alter their online offerings. For example, Dell Computer allows product customization in a jiffy: Customers configure the computer they want to

buy using an online form, and the database returns a page that includes current information about the computer and its price.

The Value: Pricing Strategies

A firm must decide how online product prices will compare with off-line equivalents. To make these decisions, firms consider the differing costs of sorting and delivering products to individuals through the online channel as well as competitive and market concerns. Two particularly important online pricing trends include the following:

- **Dynamic pricing.** This strategy applies different price levels for different customers or situations. For example, a first-time buyer or someone who hasn't purchased for many months may receive discounted prices to motivate purchase, or prices may drop during low demand periods. The internet allows firms to price items automatically and "on the fly" while users view pages.
- **Online bidding.** This approach presents a way to optimize inventory management. For

instance, a few Seattle hotels allow guests to bid for hotel rooms on slow days, instructing its reservation agents to accept various minimum bid levels depending on occupancy rates for any given day. Priceline.com, eBay.com, and many B2B exchanges operate exclusively using this strategy.

Distribution Strategies

Many firms use the internet to distribute products or create efficiencies among supply chain members in the distribution channel. Consider these examples:

- **Direct marketing.** Many firms sell directly to customers, bypassing intermediaries in the traditional channel for some sales. In B2B markets, many firms realize tremendous cost reductions by using the internet to facilitate sales.
- **Agent e-business models.** Firms such as eBay and E*TRADE bring buyers and sellers together and earn a fee for the transaction.

Marketing Communication Strategies

The internet spawned a multitude of new marketing communication strategies, both to draw customers to a Web site and to interact with brick-and-mortar customers. Firms use Web pages, blogs, and e-mail to communicate with their target markets and business partners. Companies build brand images, create awareness of new products, and position products using online content. Database marketing is key to maintaining records about the needs, preferences, and behavior of individual customers so companies can send relevant and personalized information and persuasive communication at strategic times.

Relationship Management Strategies

Many e-marketing communication strategies also help build relationships with a firm's partners, supply chain members, or customers. However, some firms up the ante by using CRM or **partner relationship management (PRM)** software to integrate customer communication and purchase behavior into a comprehensive database. They then use CRM software to retain customers and increase average order values and lifetime value. Other firms build extranets—two or more proprietary networks linked for better communication and more efficient transactions among firms as in PRM.

One simple way to present the firm's goals and accompanying e-marketing strategies is through an objective–strategy matrix. This graphical device helps marketers better understand their implementation requirements (Exhibit 3.6). Each cell contains a *yes* or *no*, depending on how the marketer will link particular goals and strategies.

STEP 5—IMPLEMENTATION PLAN

Now comes the part everyone enjoys: deciding how to accomplish the objectives through creative and effective tactics. Marketers select the marketing mix (4 Ps), relationship management tactics, and other tactics to achieve the plan objectives and then devise detailed plans for implementation (the action plans). They also check to be sure the right marketing organization is in place for implementation (i.e., staff, department structure, application service providers, and other outside firms). The right combination of tactics will help the firm meet its objectives effectively and efficiently.

E-marketers pay special attention to information-gathering tactics because information technologies are especially adept at automating these processes. Web site forms, cookies, feedback e-mail, and online surveys are just some of the tactics firms use to collect information about customers, prospects, and other stakeholders. Other important tactics include the following:

- Web site log analysis software helps firms review user behavior at the site and make changes to better meet the needs of users.
- Business intelligence uses the internet for secondary research, assisting firms in understanding competitors and other market forces.

	Online Goals	Online Strategies			
	Online Advertising	Database Marketing	Direct E-Mail	Online Sales	Viral Marketing
Increase blog comments	Yes	No	Yes	No	Yes
Gather customer information	No	Yes	Yes	Yes	Yes
Improve customer service	No	Yes	Yes	Yes	No
Increase brand name awareness	Yes	Yes	Yes	Yes	Yes
Sell goods or services	Yes	Yes	Yes	Yes	Yes
Enhance company image	Possibly	Yes	Yes	Yes	Yes
Engage in suggestive selling	Possibly	Yes	Yes	Yes	Yes
Generate sales leads	No	No	Yes	Yes	Yes

EXHIBIT 3.6 E-Marketing Objective–Strategy Matrix
Source: Adapted from Embellix eMarketing Suite.

STEP 6—BUDGET

A key part of any strategic plan is to identify the expected returns from an investment. These returns can then be matched against costs to develop a cost/benefit analysis, for ROI calculation, or for calculating internal rate of return (IRR), which management uses to determine whether the effort is worthwhile. Marketers today are especially concerned with adequate return on marketing investment (ROMI). During plan implementation, marketers will closely monitor actual revenues and costs to see that results are on track for accomplishing the objectives. The internet is terrific for monitoring results because technology records a visitor's every click. The following sections describe some of the revenues and costs associated with e-marketing initiatives.

Revenue Forecast

In this budget section, the firm uses an established sales forecasting method for estimating the site revenues in the short, intermediate, and long term. The firm's historical data, industry reports, and competitive actions are all inputs to this process. An important part of forecasting is to estimate the level of Web site traffic over time, because this number affects the amount of revenue a firm can expect to generate from its site. Revenue streams that produce internet profits come mainly from Web site direct sales, advertising sales, subscription fees, affiliate referrals, sales at partner sites, commissions, and other fees. Companies usually summarize this analysis in a spreadsheet showing expected revenues over time and accompanying rationale.

INTANGIBLE BENEFITS The intangible benefits of e-marketing strategies are much more difficult to establish, as are intangible benefits in the brick-and-mortar world. How much brand equity is created, for example, through an American Airlines program in which customers receive periodic e-mail messages about their frequent-flyer account balances? What is the value of increased brand awareness from a Web site? Putting a financial figure on such benefits is challenging but essential for e-marketers.

COST SAVINGS Money saved through internet efficiencies is considered soft revenue for a firm. For example, if the distribution channel linking a producer with its customers contains a wholesaler, distributor, and retailer, each intermediary will take a profit. A typical markup scheme is 10 percent from manufacturer to the wholesaler, 100 percent from wholesaler to the retailer, and 50 percent to the consumer. Thus, if a producer sells the product to a wholesaler for $50, the consumer ultimately pays $165. If the producer cuts out the intermediaries (disintermediation) and sells its product online directly to the consumer, it can price the product at $85 and increase revenue by $30. Whether this approach translates into profits depends on the cost of getting the product to the consumer. Other examples include the $5,000 a marketer might save in printing and postage for a direct-mail piece costing $1.00 per piece to 5,000 consumers, or the $270 million Cisco actually saved in one year on handling costs for its online computer system sales.

E-Marketing Costs

E-marketing entails many costs, including costs for employees, hardware, software, programming, and more. In addition, some traditional marketing costs may creep into the e-marketing budget—for example, the cost of off-line advertising to draw traffic to the Web site. For simplicity, this section will discuss technology-related cost items only. See the "Let's Get Technical" box for the steps required to build a Web site. Consider that the cost of a Web site (except the most basic or a blog) can range from $5,000 to $50 million. Following are just a few of the costs site developers incur:

- **Technology costs.** These costs include software, hardware, internet access or hosting services, educational materials and training, and other site operation and maintenance costs.
- **Site design.** Web sites need graphic designers to create appealing page layouts, graphics, and photos.

- **Salaries.** All personnel who work on Web site development and maintenance are budget items.
- **Other site development expenses.** Expenses not included in the technology or salary categories will fall here—things such as registering multiple domain names and hiring consultants to write content or perform other development and design activities.
- **Marketing communication.** All advertising, public relations, and promotions activities, both online and off-line, that directly relate to drawing site traffic and enticing them to return and purchase are pegged here. Other costs include search engine optimization (SEO), online directory costs, e-mail list rental, prizes for contests, and more.
- **Miscellaneous.** Other typical project costs might fall here—expenses such as travel, telephone, stationery printing to add the new URL, and more.

STEP 7—EVALUATION PLAN

Once the e-marketing plan is implemented, its success depends on continuous evaluation. This type of evaluation means e-marketers must have tracking systems in place before the electronic doors open. What should be measured? The answer depends on the plan objectives. Review the balanced scorecard for e-business (in Chapter 2) to see how various metrics relate to specific plan goals.

In general, today's firms are quite ROI driven. As a result, e-marketers must show how their intangible goals, such as brand building or CRM, will lead to higher revenue down the road. Also, they must present accurate and timely metrics to justify their initial and ongoing e-marketing expenditures throughout the period covered by the plan. For example, the huge German chemical company, BASF, must provide an ROI measure for its global search engine advertising. It is very difficult to follow lead activity because Web site leads are sent to sales people worldwide who take many months to close the deals.

LET'S GET TECHNICAL

Building a Web Site

You have been added to the team charged with redesigning your company's Web site. You have heard that colleagues in graphic design and information systems will also be on the team. You are not quite sure who is responsible for what function or even what all the issues are. You would like to appear articulate and informed in the meetings.

How are Web sites actually built? The process is similar in some ways to building a home. In home building, an architect works with clients to determine their needs, draws up a design to meet those requirements, and then hands that design over to a developer who builds the home. The sequence moves from requirements to design to development. Similarly, the marketing department draws up a creative brief that specifies in detail the requirements for the site and specific design elements (e.g., fonts and colors that will go into the site). The next step is to create a mockup of the homepage and a few interior pages in a design tool such as Adobe Photoshop. Mastery of Photoshop and of design theory in general requires training and practice. In a large shop, the marketing department would look to the visual communication or graphic design team to produce the design. The design is run past the client and adjustments are made. Once the design is finalized, the development team takes over. The development team takes the design and makes it functional. The development team has five major goals for the site. The site should be:

1. ***Easy to update.*** Content changes should be easy to implement. Ideally an input screen should allow an authorized user to type or paste content directly into the site without technical assistance. Any continuous updates such as stock feeds or weather updates should be programmed to take place automatically without human intervention.
2. ***Optimized for quick download.*** Each page on the site should load on the user's computer within 10 seconds even over a slow modem connection. Research shows that users will not wait longer than 10 seconds. Optimizing involves compressing the graphic elements on the page as either GIF or JPEG files. GIF files are used for line art that has areas of flat color (e.g., a corporate logo).

JPEG is used for continuous tone images such as photographs. The increasingly popular flash technology allows for animation and movies but rarely meets the 10 second threshold. Flash is targeted more for users who will be viewing over a high-speed connection. It is one reason why many sites offer the option to skip the Flash introduction. Text does not require compression because it loads quickly.

3. ***Easy to find.*** The site should be easy for search engines to index and find. This accessibility involves the careful placement of keyword terms in locations that the search engines will rate highly.
4. ***Interactive.*** Simple interactivity is generated by including hyperlinks to link the pages together. However, more complex interactivity can require some sophisticated programming. Examples of complex interactivity include the following:
   - A search box on the site.
   - Validation of user input (e.g., checking to see that the e-mail address contains an @ symbol or that a credit card number is valid).
   - Processing of transactions such as completing a purchase.
   - User login for sites requiring high security such as bank or stock accounts.
   - Connection to backend databases, which could be public databases such as sports scores, news feeds, stock tickers, and weather updates. They could also be private databases containing sensitive company or personal account information.

   Interactivity is accomplished using development tools such as Macromedia Dream weaver or Microsoft Visual Web Developer. These tools develop computer code in HTML, Javascript, Java, Flash, and a variety of other computer languages. Mastery of these tools requires a considerable degree of training and practice.
5. ***Secure.*** In this age of hackers and viruses, the site needs to be protected against malicious attack. Oftentimes, organizations attempt to quantify the dollar value of their exposure to attack to determine whether to even continue with development.

Chapter Summary

The e-marketing plan is a guiding, dynamic document for e-marketing strategy formulation and implementation. The purpose is to help the firm achieve its desired results as measured by performance metrics according to the specifications of the e-business model and e-business strategy. Although some entrepreneurs use a napkin plan to informally sketch out their ideas, a venture capital e-marketing plan will help show that the e-business idea is solid and the entrepreneur has an idea of how to run it.

Creating an e-marketing plan requires seven steps. The first is to conduct a situation analysis by reviewing environmental and SWOT analyses, existing marketing plans and company/brand information, and e-business objectives, strategies, and performance metrics. In the second step, e-marketers perform strategic planning, which includes a marketing opportunity analysis to develop segmentation, targeting, differentiation, and positioning strategies (tier 1 strategies). Next,

e-marketers formulate objectives, usually setting multiple objectives; they may use an objective–strategy matrix to guide implementation. In the fourth step, e-marketers design e-marketing strategies for the 4 Ps and relationship management (tier 2 strategies).

In the fifth step, e-marketers develop an implementation plan with a suitable 4 Ps marketing mix, select appropriate relationship management tactics, design information-gathering tactics, and select other tactics to achieve their objectives. They must also devise detailed implementation plans during this step in the process. In the next step, e-marketers prepare a revenue forecast to estimate the expected returns from the plan's investment and detail the e-marketing costs to come up with a calculation that management can use to determine whether the effort is worthwhile. In the final step of the plan, e-marketers use tracking systems to measure results and evaluate the plan's success on a continuous basis.

Exercises

REVIEW QUESTIONS

1. What are the seven steps in an e-marketing plan?
2. Why do entrepreneurs seeking funding need a venture capital e-marketing plan rather than a napkin plan?
3. What is the purpose of the marketing opportunity analysis and the segment analysis?
4. What four elements in tier 1 and five elements in tier 2 are devised for e-marketing strategy?
5. What is the purpose of an e-marketing objective–strategy matrix?
6. How do managers use budgeting within the e-marketing planning process?
7. Why do e-marketing plans need an evaluation component?

DISCUSSION QUESTIONS

8. If you had money to invest, what would you look for in a venture capital e-marketing plan?
9. What kinds of questions should a firm ask in developing an e-marketing plan to serve customers in current markets through an online channel?

10. Why is it important for e-marketers to specify not only the task but also the measurable quantity and time frame for accomplishing an objective?
11. Why would the management of American Airlines expect its e-marketers to estimate the financial impact of intangible benefits such as building brand equity through e-mail messages to frequent flyers?

WEB ACTIVITIES

12. Consider a local business that you know about and sketch a bare-bones e-marketing plan for it.
13. Find the Web site for a firm that offers Web site building services. What steps does it recommend? What does it charge to develop a Web site?
14. Go to the Web site for your university and describe how well you think the site fulfills the marketing objectives of the university. Suggest improvements.

PART TWO

E-Marketing Environment

CHAPTER 4

A World of E-Marketing Opportunities

The internet is becoming the town square for the global village of tomorrow.

—BILL GATES

On the internet, you can listen to a poem in Quechua with a translation . . . or get an update on the fight by the Ogiek people to keep their homes in the Mau Forest of Kenya where they have lived for centuries.

—UNESCO, PUBLIC SERVICE APPLICATIONS OF THE INTERNET
IN DEVELOPING COUNTRIES

Chapter Outline

The primary objective of this chapter is to gain an understanding of the main country-by-country differences in internet access and usage as a foundation for segmenting and targeting specific markets. You will learn about some of the barriers to internet adoption and e-commerce in emerging economies and see how these barriers are being addressed. You will learn how consumer behavior and attitudes, payment methods, technological issues, and both economic and technological disparities within nations can influence e-marketing in less developed countries.

After reading this chapter, you will be able to:

- Discuss overall trends in internet access, usage, and purchasing around the world.
- Define emerging economies and explain the vital role of information technology in economic development.
- Outline how e-marketers apply market similarity and analyze online purchase and payment behaviors in planning market entry opportunities.
- Describe how e-marketing strategy is influenced by computer and telephone access, credit card availability, attitudes toward internet use, slow connection speeds, Web site design, and electricity problems.
- Review the special challenges of e-marketing on the wireless internet in the context of emerging economies.
- Discuss the controversy related to the digital divide.
- Explain why China is becoming a major market for e-marketing innovation and competition.

Idol Goes Global

The names Simon Cowell, Randy Jackson, and Paul Abdul, along with singers Carry Underwood, Clay Aiken, Kelly Clarkson, and Jennifer Hudson, are well known in America. Even the name Sanjaya is known. These are all individuals connected with the American TV program *American Idol*. But what about Prashant Tamang, Jessica Mauboy, or Žanamari Lalić These are also well-known names, but to TV viewers, internet surfers, and text messaging devotees in India, Australia, and Croatia, respectively. All these individuals are winners of local versions of the *"American Idol"* franchise in countries outside the United States, or as it is known in Germany, *Deutschland sucht den Superstar. American Idol* is broadcast in over 100 countries, often 48 hours after the original show airs in the United States. The success of

(*continued*)

(*continued*)

American Idol spawned 39 national versions in countries like Ethiopia, the Philippines, Russia, and even Kazakhstan.

Bulgarians can follow the rise (or fall) of that season's music contestants by logging onto http://musicidol.btv.bg/news/6. Although the show is called *Music Idol* in Bulgaria, the blue logo with its curvy neon letters that greets each viewer on the homepage brands the Web page as connected with *American Idol*. Ethiopians living anywhere in the world can stay current by logging onto Jump TV (http://www2.jumptv.com/seo/Ethiopian_Idols/Ethiopian_Idols.htm) to see rebroadcasts of *Ethiopian Idol*. *Ethiopian Idol* also has Feleke Hailu, a straightforward, sometimes rude judge in the mold of Simon Cowell. Feleke alternates between his catchphrase "alta fakedem," or "you didn't make it" in Amharic, and blunt judgments like, "You sing like a donkey."

In Poland, where the program is simply known as *Idol*, the home page (http://idol.interia.pl/) has a link for cell phones and phone cards, for the obligatory voting to keep or eliminate a contestant. SMS is very popular in India. Indian viewers not only vote for singers (30 million SMS messages were sent in the run-up to a final show), but can also apply to be a contestant on *Indian Idol* through SMS by typing the keyword "IDOL" into their handset when they call Sony Entertainment TV Asia, the cable system that carries *Indian Idol* (http://sify.com/indianidol/). Tensions can run high in the Middle East, where the Arabic-language version of *Idol* is called

Super Star ($$$) (http://www.futuresuperstar.com/). *Super Star* includes contestants from across the Middle East. National loyalties can be fierce. As a semifinal show drew near, an ice cream shop in Amman, Jordan, offered free ice cream to anyone who voted for the Jordanian contestant, Diana Karzon. In Syria, a mobile phone company hung posters in the streets urging people to vote for the Syrian singer Rowaida Attiyeh, and "Give your vote to Syria." When a popular Lebanese singer was eliminated in the semifinals, Lebanese audience members threw chairs and anything else they could find. In that mayhem, the two remaining singers fainted. In the end, free ice cream might have made the difference: Diana Karzon won.

From Israel (http://www.keshet-tv.com/starborn4/default.aspx) to Iceland (http://idol.visir.is/) and from Kenya (http://www.mnetafrica.com/idols/) to Kazakhstan (http://superstarkz.net/superstarkz/), the *American Idol* franchise is big business. It is estimated that Freemantle Media, the company that markets *American Idol* abroad, generates over $1 billion a year from advertising, license fees, merchandising, co-branding, and recording. The convergence of TV, internet, mobile phones, and short message services, when added to the unpredictability of what will happen on each show, keeps global and national audiences tuning in each week. As a cynic said, probably the only place in the world that *Idol* does not have a franchise is Antarctica—at least not yet.

OVERVIEW OF GLOBAL E-MARKETING ISSUES

Picture this Accenture ad in your mind: The silhouette of a Chinese fisherman as he sits atop his small boat at twilight. The ad's right-hand corner has a headline that looks like it had been torn from a daily newspaper: "Chinese to be the number one internet language by the year 2007." Beneath that are the words, "Now it gets interesting." This and the global *Idol* example are indications of how the online marketplace is changing—users from other

countries, speaking languages other than English, will increasingly dominate the internet. Changing usage rates will have a significant influence on internet marketing. Geoffrey Ramsey, *eMarketer* statistician, noted: "The increasing number of non-U.S. internet users will have two important effects on the internet. The Web's content and language will become more diversified as internet companies catering to languages and tastes in other countries provide unique local content. At the same time, a truly global internet . . . is likely to accelerate the convergence of styles, tastes, and products" to create a more homogenous, global marketplace ("New eGlobal Report," 2000). Icann, the official body that assigns internet domain names, has recognized the internet's changing language and usage patterns. It is currently testing the direct entry of complete Web addresses in languages that do not use the 26 letters of the Roman alphabet. Until now, Web users whose native language was written with non-Roman characters (e.g., Russian, Hindi, Japanese, Greek, Hebrew, and Arabic) had to use keyboards that could type both Roman and local characters. As Paul Hoffman, the U.S.-based programmer who created these standards said, these new domain names are not for the Web's current, one-billion plus users, but for the next billion users who are now not on the Web (Rhoads, 2007).

How can marketers capitalize on these changing dynamics when planning e-marketing strategies? Foremost, global e-marketers must understand that a country's e-readiness profile significantly influences marketing strategy and tactics. It is important to differentiate between the industrialized nations of North America, Western Europe, and Japan that held 27 percent of all internet users in 2007 and the emerging economies of India, China, Russia, and Brazil that provide great promise in the future. We briefly introduce the global market context in this chapter, but focus primarily on emerging economies. E-marketing strategies and internet usage in industrialized nations are generally similar to those in the United States (and will be discussed extensively in the rest of the text), while those in emerging markets are not. This chapter is about what makes e-marketing in emerging economies different.

Global Markets

The *American Idol* example clearly reflects the global reach and impact of SMS messaging. Organizations can reach 19 percent of the world's population online and some regions and countries are excellent markets with high internet usage.

Finally, a company such as Haier might give a preview of not only global marketing but also global e-marketing in the twenty-first century. Haier is a Chinese company with one overriding ambition: It wants to be the first Chinese company to have a true, world-class global brand that is acknowledged as equal to (and Haier's CEO would say "better than") the best global brands from Japan, the United States, Germany, and South Korea. Haier is well on its way to achieving that goal. Indeed, some readers may already know the Haier brand name: Wal-Mart sells Haier's popular mini-fridge, which has developed a cult following among college students living in campus dorms. Domestically, Haier is China's leading manufacturer of refrigerators, washing machines, and air conditioners. Globally, Haier has offices or production facilities in more than 100 countries (including a $15 million headquarters in Manhattan). It is ranked fourth in the world in the white goods industry, right behind Whirlpool, Electrolux, and Bosch-Siemens ("Haier's Purpose," 2004). Haier's internet presence supports its global ambition. Log on to Haier's English-language home page (www.haier.com/english/) to see a map of the world highlighting Haier's Web presence in China, North America, Europe, and Oceania. Alternatively, one can log onto Haier's North American Web site directly at http://www.haieramerica.com/en/. Haier presents the face of a contemporary online retailer. Consumers can shop and register for products, subscribe to a Haier newsletter, access warranty information, locate after-sales support, inquire about becoming a Haier distributor, and find tips and hints for maintaining Haier products. Haier is poised to become a fierce global competitor in the twenty-first century and the continued development of its Web presence will help it achieve that goal.

As Haier, Dangdang, and the other companies profiled in this chapter suggest, e-marketing is flourishing around the world. Global e-marketers must be alert to the significant differences that influence e-marketing strategy wherever they occur. Savvy global e-marketers recognize that in most instances, successful e-marketing strategies are not about decisions to have either a strong wireless marketing campaign or a graphics-intensive Web design that takes advantage of high-speed internet access, but rather it is a decision to have both. When viewed from this perspective, the globe is literally a world of opportunities.

World Regions	2004 Internet Use (millions)	2007 Internet Use (millions)	User Growth (2004–2007) (%)	Percentage of Users Worldwide (2007) (%)	Estimated 2007 Population (millions)	Internet Usage as Percentage of Population (%)
North America	228.0	234.8	2.9	18.9	334.5	70.2
Europe	217.9	337.9		27.2	809.6	41.7
Asia	243.6	459.5	55.1	36.9	3,712.5	12.4
Latin America/Caribbean	51.1	115.8	126.6	9.3	556.6	20.8
Africa	12.3	44.0	257.7	3.5	993.4	4.7
Middle East	16.8	33.5	99.4	2.7	193.5	17.3
Oceania	16.0	19.0	18.6	1.5	34.5	55.2
Worldwide Total	785.7	1,244.4	58.4	100.0	6,574.7	18.9

EXHIBIT 4.1 Worldwide Internet Usage and Population Statistics

Source: Adapted from "Internet Usage Statistics—The Big Picture" at www.internetworldstats.com/stats.htm.

Exhibit 4.1 shows that worldwide internet usage increased more than 55 percent between 2004 and 2007. In 2007, the internet had a little less than one-and-a-quarter billion users worldwide. Yet absolute numbers and rates of growth vary considerably by continent. Africa saw the greatest growth in internet use, with an increase of more than 250 percent in three years. Asia has the most internet users, with slightly more than 459 million users. This figure seems reasonable since Asia is home to China and India. Both countries have populations greater than 1 billion and both countries are experiencing significant economic growth. Yet when internet penetration rates (internet use divided by population) are determined, a different global picture emerges. North America has the highest internet penetration rate, with almost 70 percent. Asia, in contrast, has an internet penetration rate of only 12.4 percent; and in Africa, the world's second most populous continent, internet penetration is still less than 5 percent, even with its 250 percent increase between 2004 and 2007.

Most e-marketers prefer to evaluate individual countries for online-strategy profitability.

Internet use varies greatly from country to country. Country size and population have little bearing on internet penetration. This distinction is important because the countries with highest internet usage may not contain a large population. In 2007, the world's largest online market was the United States, with 210.6 million users, yet the Untied States is the third most populous country in the world. Japan, on the other hand, had the third largest number of internet users, with 86.3 million, yet ranks 10th in terms of world population. The top 10 countries in 2007, in terms of absolute number of users, account for 763 million internet users (70% of all global users). Even though these countries represent huge markets, some smaller countries, such as Norway, the Netherlands, and Iceland enjoyed 88 percent, 87 percent, and 85 percent internet penetration in their populations, respectively (see Exhibit 4.2). Obviously, internet penetration is not the sole factor in developing country markets. E-marketers must carefully research each country's current market conditions and environmental factors before selecting specific targets for entry. See Appendix A for a table of internet penetration for all countries in 2008.

Rank	Country	Number of Internet Users (millions)	Country	Percentage of Population Internet Users
1	United States	215.0	Norway	88.0
2	China	162.0	The Netherlands	87.8
3	Japan	87.5	Iceland	85.4
4	India	60.0	Sweden	77.3
5	Germany	53.2	Australia	72.9
6	Brazil	42.6	United States	71.7
7	United Kingdom	40.4	South Korea	70.2
8	South Korea	34.4	Switzerland	69.2
9	France	34.9	Denmark	68.8
10	Italy	33.1	Japan	68.7
Total		763.1		

EXHIBIT 4.2   Top 10 Countries in Number or Percentage of Internet Usage

Source: Data compiled from www.worldinternetstats.com.

These brief country profiles suggest that as internet access and use accelerates around the world, so, too, will e-marketing opportunities. Bhutan, a small country in the Himalayan Mountains, is a good example. Bhutan was literally excluded from the internet revolution until 1999. In June 1999, the king of Bhutan inaugurated Druk.net, the first and still only internet service provider (ISP) in the country (Long, 2000). The Bhutanese can now send e-mail, surf the Web, play online games, and establish online businesses just like citizens in other countries (see Exhibit 4.3). The internet has literally connected them to the rest of the world, as buyers, sellers, and surfers.

Yet we believe the greatest challenges for the global e-marketer lie in countries with emerging economies—countries such as Russia, India, Nepal, Hungary, and China—which present different and sometimes difficult e-marketing decisions.

Emerging Economies

Countries vary in their level of economic development. Some countries, such as the United States, Canada, Japan, Australia, Great Britain, and Germany, have high levels of economic development. Economists classify these countries as *developed*. Developed countries include all of Western Europe, North America, Japan, Australia, and New Zealand (Case and Fair, 2001). These countries are highly industrialized, use technology to increase their production efficiency, and, as a result, have a high gross domestic product (GDP) per capita. A high GDP means that citizens have enough discretionary income to buy items that will make their lives easier, richer, and fuller. Developed countries are, therefore, ideally suited for the broad range of e-marketing activities discussed throughout the text.

It is difficult to find a single label to describe the rest of the world's economies. Rapid economic growth has brought some countries, such as South Korea and Chile, much closer to developed economies. Yet most countries are struggling with—and working toward—improved standards of living for their citizens. We call this broad, diversified group of countries **emerging economies**—those with low levels of GDP per capita that are experiencing rapid growth.

EXHIBIT 4.3   Bhutanese Children Playing an Online Game in Tsongas, Bhutan

Source: Photo by Al Rosenbloom.

Countries with emerging economies can be found on every continent. In North America, Mexico has an emerging economy. All of the Central and South American countries have emerging economies. In Europe, all the countries in the former Baltic States (Latvia, Estonia, and Lithuania) and in Eastern Europe (Poland, Hungary, the Czech Republic, Slovakia, Romania, Bulgaria, and all the states that made up the former Yugoslavia) have emerging economies. Russia, Belarus, and the Ukraine also have emerging economies, as do all the countries in Africa and in Central Asia (Afghanistan, Tajikistan, Kazakhstan, and Uzbekistan), South Asia (India, Pakistan, Bangladesh, Nepal, and Bhutan), and Southeast Asia (Thailand, Vietnam, Cambodia, Myanmar, and Laos). Finally, China, the world's most populous country, has an emerging economy.

Importance of Information Technology

Every country can improve its level of economic development through increased efficiencies in the production, distribution, and sale of goods and services. For countries with emerging economies, technology plays an especially important role. Although technology can, in general, boost a nation's overall production capacity and efficiency, it is through the application of information technology that countries with emerging economies can really open up new, exciting, global markets. As is often noted, "The internet accelerates the process of economic growth by speeding up the diffusion of new technologies to emerging economies" (Cateora and Graham, 2007, p. 251). In the past, decades passed before many developing countries could benefit from railroads, electricity, and telephones.

Today, the internet, along with its supporting information technologies, can jump-start many national economies. India is a prime example of such efforts.

Until recently, Bangalore was a city well known in India mainly for its wonderful gardens and mild temperatures. Today, Bangalore is globally famous as the center of India's explosive growth in software and IT services. The epicenter of all this activity is a sprawling 330-acre industrial park called Electronic City. In Electronic City, one will find the corporate headquarters of Wipro and Infosys, two global giants that are leaders in this Indian information revolution. In addition, Electronic City is home to both well-known American companies (Motorola and H-P) and European companies (Siemens) that are outsourcing call center operations, medical transcription, and even income tax processing to India. The internet allows businesses in emerging economies to instantaneously tap a global marketplace. Successful marketing on the internet can leapfrog a company from *nowhere to somewhere* overnight.

E-marketers from countries with emerging economies face a double challenge. Not only must they confront all the marketing issues and decisions described throughout this text, but they must also address some unique challenges related to the conditions of operating within a still developing nation. Some of the internet marketing differences between developed and still developing countries are fewer computer users, limited credit card use, lack of secure online payment methods, and unexpected power failures. We will now look at these challenges in more detail.

COUNTRY AND MARKET OPPORTUNITY ANALYSIS

As noted in Chapter 3, an e-marketing plan guides the marketer through the process of identifying and analyzing potential markets. Astute global e-marketers must carefully balance two different analytical approaches. **Market differences** are ways in which two markets exhibit dissimilar characteristics, such as different languages, cultural behaviors, buying behaviors, and so forth. **Market similarity** refers to ways in which two markets exhibit similar characteristics. Applying this concept, if a firm is based in an emerging economy and wants to market to its home (domestic) target market, then the marketer must identify market differences within the population. The same is true when a firm operates in a developed economy and wants to target groups in an emerging economy—it must look for differences between home and target country markets. Conversely, marketers in emerging economies must find market similarities in order to be successful in selling products in developed economies (see Exhibit 4.4).

Market Similarity

According to the concept of market similarity, marketers often choose foreign markets that have characteristics similar to their home market for initial market entry (Jeanette and Hennessy, 2002). Thus, a U.S.-based company would first target countries such as Canada, the United Kingdom, and Australia before targeting France, Japan, or Germany. Amazon.com used this strategy as it expanded globally. It has international Web sites in the United Kingdom (www.amazon.co.uk), Canada (www.amazon.com.ca), France (www.amazon.fr), Germany (www.amazon.de), and Japan (www.amazon.com.jp). Even though three markets (the United States, Canada, and the United Kingdom) share a common language (English), deeper similarities exist across each foreign market: All these countries have high literacy rates, high internet usage rates, and clearly defined market segments willing to shop for books (and other products) online; in each country credit cards are widely used for purchases; each country has secure, trusted online payment mechanisms; and each country has efficient package delivery services. For Amazon.com, market similarity not only reduces (without eliminating) the risk of entry into foreign markets but also helps explain why it targeted these countries in the first place.

Globalization helps explain the increased migration of individuals from one country to another. When a large number of people leave their home country and live together in a common

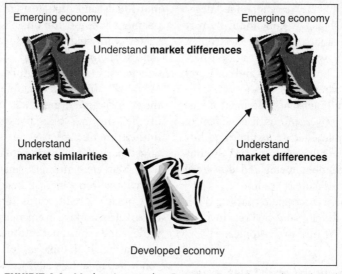

EXHIBIT 4.4   Market Approaches Between Emerging and Developed Economies

neighborhood or city abroad, they become part of a diaspora community. **Diaspora communities** often want to maintain a relationship with their homeland. E-businesses in countries with emerging markets use market similarity to target their own diaspora communities living aborad. For example, Tortas Peru (www.tortasperu.com.pe) specifically targets the Peruvian diaspora community who would like to surprise friends and family living in Peru with homemade, traditional Peruvian cakes. All of the cakes are made in Peru for delivery to a Peruvian home market. Peruvian homemakers who need a second income to help support their families do all the baking. A similar Web site, www.muncha.com, offers a wide range of products that Nepalis living overseas can send to individuals back home. This site is presented online as a traditional retailer, which is appropriate because Muncha House is a famous department store in the main shopping center of Kathmandu.

Market similarity can be seen in the phenomenon called "market convergence," that is, "the process by which markets become increasingly similar over time" (Pennings and Puranam, 2000, p. 1). The Czech Republic is an excellent example of how consumers have matured into accepting online marketing and appear to have online shopping preferences and attitudes mirroring those of consumers in developed countries. In 2001, one survey found that an astonishing 75 percent of Czech consumers said that it was more secure buying goods and services in a store than online. Sixty-five percent said it was both easier and more fun to buy goods and services in a store, and 61 percent said one of their prime concerns about online shopping was "You don't know what you get." Finally, 42 percent said they didn't trust online brands (Taylor Nelson Sofres, 2001). By 2007, however, 97 percent of Czech consumers who used the internet said they were aware of online shopping. Sixty-two percent said that they either "loved" or "liked" the online shopping experience. When asked what motivated their online shopping , respondents said that it saved them money (29%), saved them time (24%), allowed them to shop for the best quality products (17%), and was just a pleasant way to spend time (16%). Like consumers in many developed countries, Czech consumers said the internet was their preferred way to obtain information about travel services, phones and GSM accessories, domestic appliances, photo equipment, computer hardware, and cinema tickets (Gemius, 2007a). With a product list this long, it is not surprising that the Czech Republic has several online "mega" online retailers, such as www.obchodni-dum.cz (a specialist in appliances, consumer electronics, and mobile phones), www.vltava.cz (a site where users can buy music, books, videos, and software) and www.alza.cz (where one can shop for consumer electronics in English and German, as well as Czech). Market convergence is also evident in Web sites that enable Czech consumers to buy flowers (www.bohemiaflowers.com) and also buy music from independent metal and deadhead rock bands (www.czechcore.cz) online.

One area where emerging e-markets differ significantly from developed e-markets involves online purchasing. We turn to this topic next.

E-Commerce Payment and Trust Issues

E-commerce in emerging markets is often hampered by the limited use of credit cards and the lack of trust in safely conducting online transactions. Nepal, for example, is at the early stage of credit card adoption; it is still predominantly a cash-based economy. Credit cards are scarce and are available only to the rich and the elite. This is evident when making a purchase on the Muncha site (www.muncha.com). For individuals living outside Nepal, all major credit cards are accepted for payment. But for local Nepalis, only Visa, Mastercard, and Himalayan Bank cards are accepted. As noted on the payment details Web page (http://www.muncha.com/paymentdetails.asp), for Nepali citizens, Visa and Mastercard must be issued by a Nepali bank. Individuals with credit cards issued in Nepal face one more hurdle: Their credit card can be used in only two countries—Nepal and India (Minges, 2000).

The situation is similar in Bolivia, one of the poorest nations in South America. Fewer than 200,000 credit cards are in circulation within a country with a population of 8.3 million people. Only 2.3 percent of all Bolivians have a credit card (ITU, 2000). An even more extreme example is Ethiopia. In this country of more than 76 million people, credit card use is virtually nonexistent. Few Ethiopians have credit cards—cash and check are the preferred payment methods between

individuals, and a letter of credit is the preferred payment method for businesses. International visitors with credit cards issued by foreign banks can use them only in a five-star hotel and a few selected stores in Addis Abba, the capital. As of May 2007, there was only one ATM machine in the entire country, and it was located in the lobby of the country's only five-star hotel. Clearly, limited credit card use can severely restrict a target market's purchasing ability.

Marketers must also analyze relevant buyer behavior within a market. In addition to knowing how many credit cards are in circulation, e-marketers working in emerging economies should understand consumer attitudes toward online purchasing. In Lithuania, for example, research conducted in January 2007 found that 51 percent of current internet users had not made a purchase online because they thought it was too risky. When probed, 40 percent said they were afraid of sending their credit card information over the internet, while 39 percent were afraid of making personal information available. See "Let's Get Technical" for more details concerning online security. Lithuanians, it appears, still liked to shop in brick-and-mortar stores as 59 percent agreed with the statement, "I like to see the product and evaluate its quality," and 49 precent agreed with the statement, "I am used to traditional shops." Real or perceived transaction security is an important issue in emerging markets (Gemius, 2007b). Global e-marketers understand and accept these differences.

One innovative solution to the credit card and online payment dilemma is eBanka (www.ebanka.com) in the Czech Republic. Established in 1998, eBanka is the oldest purely internet bank in Central and Eastern Europe. The bank issues credit cards (Eurocard, Visa, and MasterCard) and handles secure and efficient online money transfer accounts for online purchases. A customer simply opens an eBanka account, deposits money, uses that money to make online purchases, and deposits more money when the account balance is low. It is the Czech version of digital cash. Because of eBanka's success, in July 2006 Raiffeisen International (RI), an Austrian bank, bought eBanka for €130 million.

LET'S GET TECHNICAL

Transaction Security

You've been asked to launch a Web site in Brazil. Upon investigating you find that the Brazilians tend to be wary of internet credit card transactions. That wariness is understandable because until a few years ago Brazilians were liable for all transactions made with a stolen credit card number. Because your company prefers to take credit transactions, you are worried. You need to educate consumers that credit transactions on your site are secure. But how? You are not sure that you understand much about it yourself.

Is concern over transaction security a legitimate concern? Are users afraid of the unknown or are their fears the result of media hype? As shown in Exhibit 4.5, the answer is yes. Ironically, transactions are probably much more secure on the internet than in the brick-and-mortar world. To understand why requires exploring the technology behind transaction security.

Credit Card Number Theft

A credit card number could potentially be stolen in three different places on the internet. It could be stolen from a user's home or business computer; it could be stolen in transit from the user's computer to the merchant's Web site; or it could be stolen once it reaches the merchant's site. How likely is each of these scenarios?

1. **Stolen from the user's computer:** Unlikely unless users store credit card numbers on their computers.
2. **Stolen in transit:** Almost impossible and in fact this situation has never been reported as long as vendors use a secure internet connection (https). Encryption algorithms (described later) make this possibility remote.
3. **Stolen at the merchant's site:** Probably the most legitimate user concern given the following possibilities:
   - The merchant may be fraudulent.
   - The merchant may be honest but have a dishonest employee.
   - The merchant may be honest but fails to protect its database of credit card numbers from hackers.

One way e-marketers are addressing transaction security is through the use of encryption algorithms.

Encryption Algorithms

Encryption algorithms cannot stop dishonest merchants or employees, but they are designed to protect transaction information in transit. Try to read the following encrypted phrase:

JCRRA JQNKFCAU

Issue	Extremely Concerned or Very Concerned
Security of credit card transactions	86%
Protecting privacy	75%
Censorship	72%
Hate group Web sites	47%
Depiction of violence	38%
Pornography	30%

EXHIBIT 4.5 Top Issues for Online Users

Source: Data from www.lycos.com.

(continued)

(continued)

You may have guessed that the key to decrypt this message is 2. All letters have been shifted two characters to the right in the alphabet.

A-B-C-D-E-F-G-H-I-J-K-L-M-N-O-P-Q-
R-S-T-U-V-W-X-Y-Z

To decrypt we shift back two letters to the left.

J becomes **H**

C becomes **A**

R becomes **P**

R becomes **P**

A becomes **Y**

Continuing to decrypt reveals the message "HAPPY HOLIDAYS." Encryption on the internet works in a similar fashion except that the key is a big number, which is almost impossible to guess, and the encryption scheme is a good deal more sophisticated than shifting along the alphabet. In fact the industry standard RSA encryption scheme (named after the inventors Rivest, Shamir, and Adleman) has never been broken outside of university laboratories, and then only with weeks of effort by high-speed computers. This level of sophistication means a user's information is quite secure in transit.

When two computers on the internet communicate in secure mode, the messages are encrypted in both directions. The user's browser encrypts the credit card number and then sends it to the merchant; the merchant in turn encrypts confidential information sent back to the user. Each side uses a key to decrypt the other's message.

But how does the user get the merchant's key? If the merchant sends the key unencrypted, it could be stolen in transit. As amazing as it may seem, it is not a problem. In fact, merchants willingly give out what is known as a **public key**. However, the encryption algorithms are so clever that while the public key can encrypt the message, the same key cannot decrypt it. Only a complementary **private key**, which the merchant does not distribute, can decrypt the message, a process involving complex polynomial calculations and extremely large prime numbers.

Encryption protects the transaction while it is in transit between the user's computer and the retailer. Sometimes, however, the retailer does not adequately protect the records stored on its computer. In one security breach years ago, the online storefronts of ESPN SportsZone and NBA.com were "broken into." The hacker stole the credit card numbers and e-mail addresses of hundreds of customers. As proof, he then sent each person an e-mail message containing his or her card number.

How does this sort of theft happen? Most Web servers are secure if properly installed and maintained following best practices. But in the rush to get things done, information system professionals sometimes get sloppy: Passwords are set to easily guessed names, passwords are loosely shared, or some accounts are enabled without passwords. Hackers usually begin by obtaining access to an account with limited access to protected computer resources. Using that account they compromise an account with a bit more access. They continue to work their way up from account to account until they have sufficient access to compromise the system.

Merchants can protect themselves by trying to break into their own systems or hiring professionals to do so. Professionals are able to recognize flaws in the security system of the merchant's computer and suggest remedies to make it more secure. Computer programs such as NESSUS, SARA, and SAINT are available for merchants to use to attack their own sites. And, of course, corresponding intrusion detection systems, such as Snort, Bro, Prelude, and OSSEC can notify the merchant of an actual attack by recognizing the digital signatures of these attack programs. These software systems experience short but sweet product life cycles: First, a new attack program comes along, then a detection program is upgraded to counteract it, then a new attack program is designed, and the cycle continues with increasing sophistication.

TECHNOLOGICAL READINESS INFLUENCES MARKETING

Solving credit card payment and trust issues are only two of several marketing challenges in emerging economies. E-marketers must also deal with daunting issues of basic technology: limited access to and limited use of computers and telephones, high internet connection costs, slow internet connection speeds, and unpredictable power supplies.

Computers and Telephones

Clearly, customers must have a mechanism for connecting to the internet. In industrialized countries, connections are made, historically and predominantly, with desktop computers and an internet service provider (ISP). For e-businesses operating in developed countries, connecting to the internet is generally not a problem. Individuals can use desk and laptop computers at home, at work, at school, or at libraries and other community institutions. For consumers in emerging economies, however, computer access is a big problem. Countries vary in the number of personal computers privately owned. Exhibit 4.6 shows the percentage of computer ownership in selected countries around the world in 2007. Interestingly, Kuwait and Sweden had higher computer ownership rates than the United States. Eighty-four percent of Kuwaitis and 81 percent of Swedes said they owned computers. This compares with 76 percent of Americans who said they owned a personal computer. Contrasts in computer ownership can be found in most regions of the world. Asia, for example, is home to the country with the highest reported computer ownership (South Korea has 93 percent of its citizens owning a computer) and to a country with one of the lowest ownership rates (Bangladesh, with only 2 percent individual ownership). In Latin America, Venezuela had the highest computer ownership rate, with 43 percent, while Mexico had 22 percent. The Middle East also had striking contrasts. Seventy-seven percent of Israelis own computers, while only 11 percent

of Moroccans did. Not surprisingly, Africa had some of the lowest computer ownership rates: 27 percent in South Africa, 16 percent in Nigeria, 6 percent in Ivory Coast, 5 percent in Senegal, and 2 percent in Uganda.

E-marketers should never underestimate the influence of limited computer access on internet marketing. It frequently limits market size. Exhibit 4.6 suggests that e-marketing faces

Country	Percentage of Surveyed Individuals Owning a Personal Computer
Bangladesh	2
Brazil	34
Bulgaria	29
Egypt	18
Ghana	6
Indonesia	6
Israel	77
Italy	43
Jordan	44
Kenya	3
Kuwait	84
Mali	6
Mexico	22
Morocco	11
Nigeria	16
Pakistan	11
Peru	17
Russia	30
Senegal	5
South Africa	27
Turkey	20
Uganda	2
Ukraine	21
United States	77

EXHIBIT 4.6 Computer Ownership in Selected Countries

Source: Adapted from *National Pew Global Attitudes Survey* (2007).

some of its most basic challenges in countries such as Pakistan, Nigeria, Bangladesh, Turkey, and Mexico.

Low rates of computer ownership create opportunities for local, small business entrepreneurs, and e-marketers. While many individuals in the world may not own a computer, this does not necessarily limit access to and use of online content. Exhibit 4.7 illustrates the difference between ownership and use in countries with emerging markets. Telecenters—small shops with three to ten computers that offer internet connections to the general public in simply furnished settings—are the most popular means for accessing the Web in many countries. Peru, where the telecenters are called "cabinas publicas," has one of the highest usage rates of telecenters in the world. A 2005 study estimated that 6,000 cabinas were available in the capital city, Lima, with another 4,000 cabinas scattered throughout the rest of Peru (Exhibits 4.8 and 4.9) (cited in Curioso et al., 2007). The Peruvian Institute of Marketing found that 35 percent of cabinas users went there to check their e-mail, 25 percent went to do online chatting, and 20 percent went to surf the World Wide Web. This same study found that 62 percent of all cabinas users were online for two hours every time they logged on (Palacios, 2002).

Owning or having access to a computer is only the first hurdle for e-marketing in countries with emerging markets. Individuals and businesses need to be connected to the internet in some way. Historically, connections have been made through telephone lines, although internet connection patterns are changing rapidly. Fixed-line telephones are a common and prevalent commodity in developed countries such as the United States, the United Kingdom, Germany, and France. With the explosive rise of mobile phones, however, having a fixed-line telephone to connect to the internet may become less important, as seen with the worldwide SMS voting for American and other country Idols.

In countries with emerging economies, however, fixed-line telephones can be both scarce and expensive. A startling statistic comes from Indonesia, the world's largest Muslim country. Muslims pray in mosques five times a day. In Indonesia, "Indonesians are closer to mosques than public phones" (ITU, 2002, p. 13). In other words, 80 percent of all Indonesians are less than 1 kilometer (0.6 mile) away from a mosque; only slightly more than 20 percent are that close to a single telephone. Forty percent of all Indonesians are more than 5 kilometers (3 miles) from a telephone (ITU, 2000). Data from *The World*

	Individuals using computers (%)	Individuals owning computers (%)
Egypt	28	.18
Ethiopia	27	7
Ghana	20	6
India	28	14
Ivory Coast	41	6
Mali	38	6
Mexico	32	22
Morocco	23	11
Nigeria	37	16
Senegal	39	17

EXHIBIT 4.7 Computer Ownership Compared to Computer Use

EXHIBIT 4.8   Entrance to a Typical Cabinas in Lima, Peru

Telecommunication/ICT Development Report 2006 indicated that Indonesia had 4.4 fixed-line phones for every 100 individuals. The same report found that India had 4.0 fixed-line phones per 100 people, Bangladesh had .06 fixed-line phones per 100 people, Rwanda had 0.2, Tajikistan 3.6, Nicaragua 3.8, Iraq 4.0, Cuba 6.8, and Madagascar 0.3 (ITU, 2006a). Finally, consider Thailand. The official Thai 2000 census reported that 91.5 percent of all Thais owned a television, but only 27.7 percent owned a phone. More than twice as many Thais own motorcycles (64.5%) as own telephones (27.7%) (Minges,

2001). In emerging economies, fixed-line telephone access follows a different pattern than in developed countries. Online firms can't market to someone who has no computer or no means of connecting to the internet, which leads to the next topic: internet connection costs.

Internet Connection Costs

Countries with emerging economies often have higher internet-related business costs—a concern because internet access is essential for every e-business. In the past, a dial-up connection was

EXHIBIT 4.9   Inside a Typical Cabinas in Chivay, Peru

Source: Photo by Al Rosenbloom.

the most common way that individuals connected to the internet worldwide. Dial-up connections use telephone lines, as does a digital subscriber line (DSL). Although increased competition and improved technology have greatly lowered fixed-line phone costs around the world, dial-up connection costs can still vary quite considerably in emerging economies. Exhibit 4.10 compares the total access costs in various Central American countries. The total price for only 20 hours of internet service was quite large in some countries. In Belize, for example, 20 hours of home service cost just over $75 per month; in Guatemala and Nicaragua, it cost more than $50; and in Honduras, it is slightly more than $35 for 20 hours of service.

This situation illustrates one of the inescapable ironies of emerging economies. Although labor costs may be quite low, technology

and other business costs can be quite high. Why? Two major explanations include government-owned telephone monopolies and limited competition among ISPs—although the latter is improving. Consumers and e-marketers both will benefit if the situation improves. Consumers will have cheaper and better ways to access the internet, while e-marketers will have access to expanding domestic and global markets.

Egypt is an interesting example of how innovative strategies can increase internet access in a country with a developing economy. The Egyptian government's overall approach has been to encourage private sector competition within its domestic telecommunication markets. From only two ISPs, when the internet was introduced in Egypt in 1993, there were more than 100 ISPs competing in the market by the end of 2006. The number of internet users has skyrocketed,

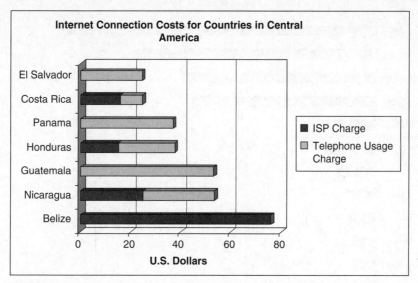

Internet Connection Costs for Countries in Central America

ISP Charge

Telephone Usage Charge

U.S. Dollars

EXHIBIT 4.10   Total Internet Connection Costs in Central America

Source: Adapted from ITU (2006a). *World Telecommunication/ICT Development Report 2006.*

from about 1.35 million in 2002 to 6 million by December 2006 (American Chamber of Commerce in Egypt, 2007). Two government programs have helped fuel this increase. The first was the government's decision in 2002 to end ISP surcharges. This meant that Egyptians could surf for an unlimited amount of time for only the cost of one phone call, or about 15 cents per hour ("Egyptians Flock to New Net Plan," 2002). The second initiative was a program called "A PC for Every Home." This program's goal was to enable every Egyptian household to purchase a desktop computer. Families would purchase their desktop on an installment plan, using their telephone bill as collateral. More than 100,000 personal computers (PCs) have been sold with this plan (Esmat, n.d.).

Broadband is also changing the global telecommunication landscape. The number of countries having broadband has increased from 88 in 2002 to 166 in 2006 (Ponder, 2006). In 2004, South Korea, Hong Kong, the Netherlands, Denmark, and Iceland were the five countries that had the greatest percentage of broadband users. The United States ranked 16th in the world (ITU, 2006b). Exhibit 4.11 indicates that broadband

connections are still expensive in most countries throughout the world. For example, it costs around $980 per month in Mozambique for low-speed broadband. In Yemen it costs $750 per month, in Pakistan $600 per month, and in Benin $560 per month for low-speed broadband access. Even in a modernized country like Singapore, low-speed broadband access can be relatively expensive, at around $90 per month. Two of the world's cheapest countries for broadband are the Netherlands and Brazil (around $12 per month and $18 per month, respectively). This conclusion is inescapable: Connecting to the internet through landlines, whether dial-up or broadband, can still be expensive.

Connection Speeds and Web Site Design: Broadband's Influence

Another key issue for e-marketers in emerging economies is the relationship between connection speed and Web site design. High-speed internet access is gaining momentum worldwide. The global e-marketer understands, however, that many consumers, especially those in the developing world, still do not use broadband to access the internet.

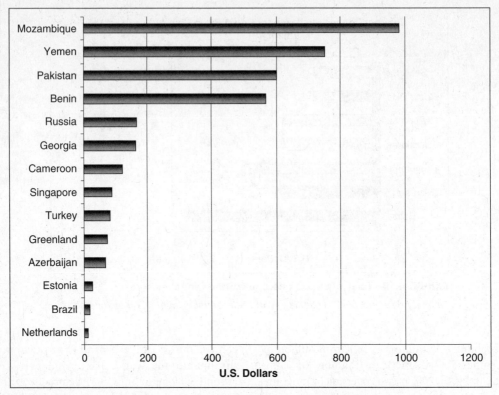

EXHIBIT 4.11 Broadband Subscription Costs per Month in Selected Countries

Source: Adapted from Table 7 in ITU (2006b). *ITU Internet Report 2006: Digital.Life.*

When dial-up connections *are* used, telephone lines still limit the speed at which data can be sent and received. These limitations have significant implications for Web site design, especially the extent to which graphics are used.

The Web is quintessentially a visual medium, and users expect to see pictures, particularly complicated graphics and pictures that move, swirl, and morph into usual shapes. Web sites may also have sound. Yet, each of these elements slows down the download rate, especially for home pages that attempt to *wow* the user. In countries with emerging economies, where connections speeds are low and a user may be paying by the minute, download speed is a major consideration. Two points are important here. First, every e-marketer needs to understand how connection speeds influence download rates. Second, just because graphic designers *can* do something cutting edge on Web sites doesn't mean they *should*. In other words, just because a Web site *can* use flash graphics and incorporate lots of pictures doesn't mean that it should—especially when targeting emerging markets.

E-marketers must see the world from their target market's perspective. In the world of e-marketing, e-marketers need to understand the target market's total experience with a Web site. E-marketers are always selling an experience along with the site content. E-marketers and Web site developers who live in countries where high-speed internet access is common might mistakenly infer that their target market's experience is consistent across global markets. It is not. A graphics-intensive Web site with an introductory Flash graphic that is optimized for quick download in Canada may not work well in Cameroon or Kazakhstan. Google, the world's leading search engine, understands this fact. Google's simple, clean, text-only format supports rapid download times anywhere in the world, with any kind of internet connection. In developing countries, slow downloads are still common. Consider one professor's experience while teaching in India: He wanted his students to explore the Amazon.com site, but each student had to wait more than five minutes for the home page to download! Multiply that connection time by every hyperlink and query, and e-marketers can begin to understand the consequence of slow download speeds coupled with graphic-intensive Web page design. To avoid this problem, e-marketers need to understand the target market; consider the country's overall bandwidth; keep graphics simple; and limit the number of pictures, optimizing the site for speedy and smooth downloads.

Electricity Problems

Countries with emerging economies pose another challenge for e-marketers: sporadic electricity. Nepal is a good example. One of the poorest countries in the world, with an annual per capita income of less than $250, Nepal is rich in many natural resources, including water. Through the efforts of the United Nations and other international aid organizations, Nepal has built a series of hydroelectric dams throughout the country. Nepal needs these dams because only 15 percent of all households in Nepal have electricity. Most people living in Nepal's major cities of Kathmandu, Pokhara, and Nepalgunj have electricity. Even so, households and businesses in these major cities are sometimes without electricity during the summer months when frequent rolling blackouts occur across the entire country. Consumers living in Kathamandu experienced 6–12 hours of blackout every day between November 2007 and January 2008. The Nepal Electrical Authority (NEA) simply could not generate enough electricity for the entire country. A similar situation is common in Brazil, Vietnam, South Africa, and Zimbabwe. In 2004, several regions in China experienced blackouts. But with major infrastructure improvements as preparation for the 2008 Summer Olympics, China seems to have resolved its electricity problem. When lack of electricity forces an e-business offline, the business is effectively closed. Running an e-business in countries with electricity shortages can be challenging, to say the least.

WIRELESS INTERNET ACCESS

Until recently, the technological problems previously noted (i.e., fewer fixed-line telephone connections, higher ISP fees, and costly dial-up connections) limited e-marketing activities in countries with emerging economies. With the explosive growth and diffusion of cellular telephones throughout the world, the face of e-marketing worldwide is changing dramatically. In fact, in an interesting reversal of the relationships just described, countries with emerging economies, instead of developed economies, are *the* global market leaders in cellular technology use. John Tysoe, cofounder of the British mobile phone company The Mobile World, made this statement, "[The cellular industry] took over 20 years to connect the first billion subscribers, but only 40 months to connect the second billion. The three billion milestone will be passed in July 2007" (Ridley, 2007). Tysoe was on target. It is estimated that at the end of 2007 there will be 3.25 billion mobile phone subscriptions worldwide. The top countries for volume of new connections were in China, India, Russia, USA, Pakistan, Ukraine, Brazil, Indonesia, Nigeria, and Bangladesh. Among them, they accounted for over half of the growth in the global mobile market in 2007.

The rapid diffusion of cell phones in the world is shown in Exhibit 4.12. This exhibit also shows how countries with emerging economies have leapfrogged industrialized countries in terms of mobile phone usage. Nowhere is this more evident than in Africa, the most underserved continent in the world by traditional measures of connectivity (number of landline phones and number of internet users). The number of African mobile phone subscribers skyrocketed from 16 million in 2000 to 198 million in 2006. By the

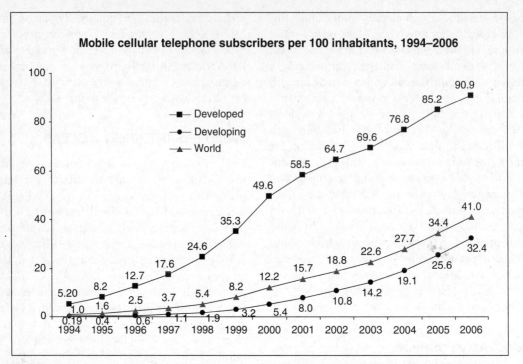

EXHIBIT 4.12   Comparison of Mobile Phone Subscribers in Developed versus Developing Countries
Source: ITU Telecommunication Indicators Database. Reproduced with the kind permission of ITU.

end of 2007, it was estimated that Africa will have 258 million cell phone users. The island nation of the Seychelles, which has a total population of 81 million, has 70.3 million mobile phone users (or 86.5 phones per 100 people). Tunisia has 71.88 mobile phone subscribers per 100 individuals, Algeria has 62.95 per 100, Botswana has 55.68 per 100, and Gabon has 54.39 cell phone subscribers per 100 individuals ("The ICT Picture in Africa," 2007; Baez, 2004).

Cambodia is a country that does not receive much attention outside of Southeast Asia. But in 1993, Cambodia became the first country in the world to have more mobile telephone subscribers than fixed-line telephone subscribers. Why? Price is part of the answer. Even in 1993, cell phones and the accompanying technology for mobile networks were less expensive than fixed-line telephones. But country history also provides a clue. Part of Cambodia's recent political history includes a long and

violent civil war (the movie *The Killing Fields* is about this war). During this conflict, the Khmer Rouge, one of the warring political parties, planted land mines throughout the country. The U.S. State Department estimates that "As a result of more than two decades of war . . . Cambodia has 4 to 6 million land mines in the ground" (U.S. State Department, 1998). The country is still littered with landmines, so digging up the ground to lay telephone cable is simply too risky. As a result, mobile phones and mobile phone networks found and satisfied a large, unmet need in Cambodia. The case of Cambodia reminds international e-marketers that understanding country *history* is an important element in assessing foreign markets. "Executives often underestimate the value of appreciating a country's history. Many developments that appear to be of a short-term political nature are driven by the longer-term historical experiences of a country" (Jeanette and Hennessy, 2002, p. 269).

Just having a cell phone, however, does not eliminate the challenges of wireless e-marketing. E-marketers must still determine how to modify existing Web site content for the smaller screens on cell phone displays; how to resolve potentially cumbersome text entry using tiny keypads; how to develop new content that consumers will want; how to price services; and how to develop easy, secure payment methods. E-marketers must also understand that consumer behavior with the mobile internet differs from consumer behavior with stationary desktop computers or even laptop computers.

Text messaging is a good example. On PCs, a user can write e-mail and send instant messages. E-mail length is not a problem with PCs. It is, however, a problem with mobile phones. The mobile phone counterpart to e-mail is short messaging service (SMS). As the name implies, SMS is the ability to send short messages (up to 160 characters) to and from mobile devices (pagers, phones, PDAs, etc.). In 2006, China became the world's leader in text messaging (displacing the Philippines). Chinese cell phone users sent 429 billion messages that year. Wise e-marketers must not only look at the magnitude of these numbers but also at the consumer behavior that stands behind them. A comparison between the cell phone behavior of the mainland Chinese and Chinese living in Hong Kong SAR makes this point. Cell phone users in Hong Kong tend to be wealthy, sophisticated, and young. It would be easy (and incorrect) to think that they are constantly texting one another. The average Hong Kong cell phone user sends only 20 SMS messages a month. The average mainland Chinese cell phone user, on the other hand, sends more than 85. The underlying reason for this difference is that in Hong Kong many cell phone packages include around 1,000 minutes of use per month, and while it is cheaper to send a short message, it is only marginally so. Mobile phone subscribers in Hong Kong prefer to pick up the phone and talk. On the mainland, a mobile phone subscriber can send up to eight SMS messages for the price of a minute-long phone call. Thus

for the mainland Chinese, SMS substitutes for e-mail and some voice calls (ITU, 2006b).

Given its rising popularity, e-marketers must be creative in their use of SMS. Taking content developed for a Web browser and attempting to squeeze it onto the small screens of mobile phones will not work. To give a sense of just how short a message 160 characters can convey, this complete sentence contains 154 characters, including the spaces between words. New content and new marketing strategies must be developed for wireless internet access.

During the 2002 World Cup finals, McDonald's developed a special SMS promotion for the Chinese market. China is the world's largest mobile telephone market, with more than 160 million subscribers. McDonald's sent an SMS alert to selected mobile phone subscribers explaining how to download coupons for free ice cream, how to get a special McSmilie icon for their mobile phones, and how to download a McDonald's theme song as a special phone ringer. As a result, store sales increased because the free ice cream required the purchase of other food items. Also, every mobile phone with a McDonald's phone ringer promoted McDonald's every time the subscriber received an incoming phone call. In addition, McDonald's developed a special game for mobile phone subscribers during the 2002 World Cup. A couple of hours before certain matches, registered subscribers received an SMS asking them to predict the winning team for that match. Gamers earned points toward winning cash or soccer-related merchandise (Bolande, 2002). This success story shows how McDonald's identified and capitalized on an e-marketing opportunity by merging the anytime, anywhere capability of mobile phones with China's interest in soccer and its rapidly growing consumer economy.

THE DIGITAL DIVIDE

In addition to the technical challenges they must overcome, e-marketers have to consider the social environment in which their e-businesses operate. Nations with emerging economies may be in different stages of economic development, which affects their social climate. The United Nations had developed a classification system to rank the economic development of countries. **Least developed countries (LDCs)** are those countries with the world's poorest economies. As the term implies, LDCs are economically underdeveloped. They also share one other common characteristic: excruciating poverty. Rather than use gross national product or gross domestic product as a way to describe the economic situation, Exhibit 4.13 lists the percentage of a country's population earning less than $2 per day. In these, the world's poorest countries, life is literally a war waged for survival.

Case and Fair (2001) describe the reality behind the numbers in Exhibit 4.13. In the least developed countries:

> Meager incomes provide only the basic necessities. Most meals are the same, consisting of the region's food staple— rice, wheat, or corn. Shelter is primitive. Many people share a small room, usually with an earthen floor and no sanitary facilities. The great major of the population lives in rural areas where agricultural work is hard and extremely time-consuming. Productivity . . . is low because household plots are small and only the crudest of farm implements are available. Low productivity means farm output per person is barely sufficient to feed a farmer's own family, with nothing left to sell to others. School-age children may receive some formal education, but illiteracy remains chronic for young and old. Infant mortality runs 10 times higher than in the United States. Although parasitic infections are common and debilitating, there is only one physician per 5,000 people (pp. 434–435).

Life in an LDC is lived at its most basic and starkest level: survival. Of course, not every individual in these countries is poor. In fact, LDCs often contain population segments with much higher income levels, dividing the country into *haves* and *have-nots,* a division that creates a dual economy. In practical terms it means that wealth is concentrated in a country's largest city, usually the capital. Capital cities look surprisingly the same everywhere in the world. Country capitals all have jet airports, world-class hotels, banks, department stores, movie theaters, new factories, and a middle and upper class. Outside the capital, life is similar to what Case and Fair described in the preceding quote. Two completely different economies exist side-by-side in an LDC. Although they may be geographically close to each other, these two economies are centuries apart in terms of economic and technological development.

Country	Percentage of Population Earning Less Than $2 a Day
Bangladesh	82.8
Benin	73.7
Botswana	50.3
Cambodia	77.7
Central African Republic	84.0
Colombia	17.8
Ecuador	37.2
El Salvador	40.5
Guatemala	31.9
Haiti	78.0
Kazakhstan	16.0
Laos	74.1
Madagascar	85.1
Moldova	63.7
Pakistan	73.6
Rwanda	83.7
Yemen	45.2
Zambia	94.1

EXHIBIT 4.13 International Poverty Lines for Selected Countries

Source: Adapted from Table 2, World Bank (2007).

This disparity, especially as it concerns the ability of technology to raise both a person's and a whole country's standard of living, is called the **digital divide**. The Bridges Organizations (www.bridges.org) interprets *digital divide* to mean "that between countries and between different groups of people within countries, there is a wide division between those who have real access to information and communications technology and are using it effectively, and those who don't." The digital divide is illustrated in this statistic: There are more than five times as many internet users in the United States and two times as many internet users in Japan than on the entire continent of Africa. As we have noted, the rapid diffusion of mobile phones throughout the developing world, along with creativity in developing small-scale, affordable, income-generating projects for low income consumers, suggests that the digital divide is narrowing. As a percentage of total income monthly, though, internet access for individuals in the least developed countries can still be quite expensive. The ITU estimated that in 2006, 10 hours of peak-time internet use and 10 hours of off-peak time used 0.9 percent of the average person's monthly income in high-income, Westernized countries, but used 172 percent of the average person's monthly income in low-income countries (ITU, 2007).

The digital divide raises challenging questions for global policy makers, international businesses, and local entrepreneurs. What responsibilities, if any, do these different groups have for narrowing the gap between those that have and those that don't have access to technology? Should an e-business in Calcutta, India, be competitive with an e-business in Calumet City, Illinois? Global policy makers at the United Nations, the World Bank, and the G8 (leaders of the world's eight wealthiest countries who meet regularly to discuss common economic problems) believe the answer is yes. Numerous initiatives around the world work to bring internet technology and e-commerce capabilities to LDCs.

One such effort is the One Laptop per Child campaign spearheaded by Nicholas Negroponte. Negroponte's goal was to design a portable laptop for children living in least developed countries that would cost around $100. Some innovations in Negroponte's laptop were using Linux as the laptop's operating system, having a sunlight-readable screen so that children can use it outdoors, and building in a hand crank to generate power. The laptop does not need electricity to work. Exhibit 4.14 shows a picture of the bright green laptop, which began production in November, 2007. Further information can be found at http://laptop.org/.

Some e-marketers are successfully helping to close the digital divide. One example is the e-marketing effort in Robib, Cambodia, a group of six small villages in an inaccessible part of the country where only 128 families live. As might be expected, most of Robib's families are subsistence farmers and have no running water, electricity, or telephones. Annual family income is less than $40 per year. The village, though, has a Web site (www.villageleap.com) through which village women successfully market traditional Cambodian silk weavings to overseas buyers. Money earned from the internet sales is reinvested in the local pig farm, the main form of livelihood for the villagers. Additionally, the communications linkages that make Robib's internet site possible also allow villagers to send and receive medical information. This capability has greatly reduced the number of two-hour, bone-jarring trips, on deeply rutted roads, that villagers must take to the nearest hospital (Chandrasekaran, 2001; Chon, 2001). One may wonder why the name "villageleap" and why the URL is .com and not .org. Both questions are answered simply and elegantly by clicking on the hyperlink marked "Introduction" on Villageleap's Web site:

The internet now offers leapfrogging opportunities to take such villages out of their isolation and poverty into our

EXHIBIT 4.14   The "$100" or XO Laptop

Source: **One Laptop per Child. (Used with permission).**

global village. Thus, the name of this site: villageleap.com.

Why com and not org? Because, though this project aims to show that a small village such as Robib has tremendous untapped assets and potential skills to fulfill computer-generated assignments, to produce and market hand-made products, to access information, to communicate its views to anywhere in the world and to enjoy better health care via the internet, one

of the aims is to help the people of Robib prosper through cyber commerce. . . . This hopefully will become a model for villages all over the world which can watch Robib and learn how to adapt some of its leapfrogs in its race toward a better life.

As this example shows, internet technology has substantially improved the quality of life for villagers in Robib. The success of Robib gives hope for closing the digital divide.

CHINA: A VIEW OF THE FUTURE

"Big" is a word frequently associated with China. China is big both in terms of population (1.3 billion inhabitants) and in terms of economic power. China is, in fact, the world's largest emerging market, and there are estimates that if China's annual growth continues at its current rate of 8–9 percent per year, China will be the largest economy in the world by 2015 (Hill, 2008). This helps explain the intense interest from world trade organizations, global corporations, global investment firms, national governments, and even individual entrepreneurs. In many ways, China summarizes both the promise as well as the challenge of e-marketing in emerging market economies.

A *BusinessWeek* cover story (March 15, 2004, International edition) correctly saw the future. The cover read: "China.Net: Why China's internet is growing so fast—and how it could soon dominate cyberspace." As we have seen in this chapter, China already leads the world in cell phone users and SMS. It is even on the verge of surpassing the United States in terms of total Internet users. The 20th Statistical Survey of Internet Use in China stated that as of June 2007 internet users in the People's Republic of China numbered 162 million. Only the United States had more users. The 20th Statistical Survey also noted that 31.6 million Chinese accessed the internet through dial-up, while 55.6 million gained access through their mobile phones and 122.4 million used broadband (CNNIC, 2007, p. 12). Exhibit 4.15 provides the age structure of Chinese internet users. Following early adoption patterns in every country, Chinese internet users are predominately young. Fully, a third are between 18 and 24 years old. An amazing 70 percent of all Chinese internet users are under the age of 30. They will form the next generation of Chinese e-consumers.

Market convergence can be seen in China as well. Exhibit 4.16 lists some well-known, high traffic Chinese Web sites. The exhibit includes sites that would be familiar to online users in any e-ready country: search engines (e.g., Baidu),

Age	Percentage of Users
Under 18	17.7
18–24	33.5
25–30	19.4
31–35	10.1
36–40	8.4
41–50	7.2
51–60	2.7
Over 60	1.0
Total	100

EXHIBIT 4.15 Profile of Chinese Internet Users

Source: Adapted from CNNIC (2007). 20th Statistical Survey Report on the Internet in China.

gaming portals (NetEase), travel reservation sites (Ctrip), job recruitment sites (51job), and even a highly successful B2B auction site (Alibaba). Market convergence is leading the luxury goods retailer, Louis Vuitton, to China as well. Louis Vuitton already has 18 stores in China and is expected to open ten more stores by the end of 2008. Sales in Beijing and Shanghai were said to be comparable to those in other fashion centers of the world, such as New York, Rome, and Paris (Newman, 2007). To better serve its growing Chinese market, LouisVuitton also has a Chinese-language version of its Web site: http://www.louisvuitton.com/ (first and second language from the bottom on the right-hand side of the page).

Although China has a vibrant, growing online market, adaptation is essential for success in some product categories. Consider, for example, Dangdang (www.dangdang.com). Dangdang is a vigorous online retailer and aspires to be the Amazon.com of China. Like Amazon.com, Dangdang sells books, CDs, DVDs, and computer games online. But unlike Amazon.com, Dangdang has a ready fleet of couriers on bicycles who zip around China's major cities, delivering packages and collecting

Name	URL	Comments
Sohu	www.sohu.com	Leading internet portal; has China's first search engine "search fox"
NetEase	www.163.com	Leading gaming portal with 166 million users; domestic game, Westward Journey, extremely popular
Tom Online	www.tom.com	Leading mobile internet portal; delivers SMS, MMS products
Ctrip	english.ctrip.com	English language version of major online travel company; unlike Expedia and Travelocity, 70 percent of Ctrip's business comes through offline call centers
3721 (Yahoo!)	www.3721.com	Chinese language search engine; users can enter Chinese language characters directly into address bar
51job	www.51job.com	Online recruitment, similar to monster.com
Alibaba	www.alibaba.com	B2B portal; all-English site; mirror site in Chinese is china.alibaba.com
Baidu	www.baidu.com	Chinese language search engine; offers pay-per-click ads and MP3; Google is investment partner
Yaolan	www.yaolan.com	Provides infant care information on nutrition, educational toys, parenting; has direct sales staff to support product purchases
Dangdang	www.dangdang.com	Online retailer selling books, CDs, DVDs; delivers products through bicycle riders in major cities; accepts payment on delivery
KongZhong	www.kongzhong.com	Specialized provider of services to mobile phones: SMS, ringtones, games, weather; provides #1 mobile game in 2003 "Bai Bao Xiang"
Taobao	www.taobao.com	Consumer trading site
SouFun	house.focus.cn	Real estate portal; English website at http://world.soufun.com
21CN	*www.21cn.com*	*Aspires to be China's leading broadband portal; has videos on demand and China's largest MP3 collection*

EXHIBIT 4.16   Selected Popular Web Sites in China

cash. This innovation is necessary because the Chinese postal system is unreliable and credit card use is still low. China is still a cash-driven economy. E-marketers at Dangdang know that brand names are important. Dangdang is the short form of the Chinese word *xiangdangdang* meaning "worthy" or "resounding." More importantly, though, the name carries for the Chinese a similar connotation as the American slang word *cha-ching*, meaning cash register. Dandang's success ultimately caught the attention of Amazon.com founder Jeff Bezos. In 2004, Amazon.com bought Joyo.com, an e-commerce site selling books, videos, and music. In June, 2007, the Joyo site was rebranded with the URL http://www.amazon.cn/.

E-marketers are also looking for ways to drive traffic to their Web sites. In Shanghai, a local taxi company has its Web site address stenciled on the door of every cab. Customers can log onto www.96822.com and preorder a cab. (See Exhibit 4.17.)

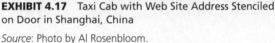

EXHIBIT 4.17   Taxi Cab with Web Site Address Stenciled on Door in Shanghai, China

Source: Photo by Al Rosenbloom.

Chapter Summary

Within a worldwide B2C market of 1.2 billion consumers, some countries have higher penetration of internet access, usage, and shopping. Among the many factors affecting internet penetration are income, infrastructure, computer ownership, telecommunication availability and pricing, social and cultural traditions, business attitudes, and wireless Web access. E-marketers must carefully research each country's current market conditions and environmental factors before selecting specific targets for entry.

Internet usage is growing so rapidly outside the United States that users from other countries will increasingly dominate the internet. This growth is creating opportunities and challenges for e-marketers to target or operate in countries that are less developed than the most highly industrialized nations. Emerging economies are

those with low levels of GDP per capita that are experiencing rapid growth. Not only can technology generally boost a nation's overall production capacity and efficiency, but also information technology can help countries with emerging economies open up promising global markets.

In the course of analyzing country and market opportunities, e-marketers in emerging economies that target markets in developed countries must understand market similarity. E-marketers in emerging economies that market within their own countries or those in developed economies that want to target groups in an emerging economy must understand market differences. In general, e-marketers that target emerging economies must deal with a variety of challenges, including limited credit card use, lack of secure online payment methods, consumer attitudes toward online purchasing and payment, limited computer and telephone access, slow connection speeds that affect Web page download rates, and unexpected power failures. Enterprising e-marketers have reacted to these challenges with innovative solutions.

Many countries, including those with emerging economies, have more mobile telephone subscribers than fixed-line telephone subscribers. As a result, e-marketers must consider how to modify Web site content for small cell phone displays; how to handle text entry using tiny keypads; how to develop appropriate content for wireless Web users; how to price services; and how to develop appropriate payment methods. E-marketers also must understand how consumers behave with the mobile internet.

Nations with emerging economies may be in different stages of economic development, which affects their social climate. Least developed countries (LDCs) have the poorest economies and, in many cases, a dual economy because the population has both higher-income citizens and poorer citizens. Capital cities in LDCs may have both a middle and an upper class, while the areas outside these cities are underdeveloped economically and technologically. This disparity, especially as it concerns the ability of technology to raise both a person's and an entire nation's standard of living, is called the digital divide. Many organizations and e-marketers are working to close this digital divide by bringing internet technology and e-commerce capabilities to LDCs.

China is the largest emerging economy in the world. China's rapid economic growth has made it an attractive market. China will soon have more internet users, mobile phone subscribers, and broadband customers than any other nation on earth. Chinese-language Web sites are developing rapidly to reach this expanding domestic market. Adaptation is a necessary feature for domestic e-marketing, because China still lags behind industrialized nations in terms of its infrastructure. Some Chinese companies are also using the Web to create a global brand presence.

Exercises

REVIEW QUESTIONS

1. What is an emerging economy?
2. What use can countries with emerging economies make of information technology?
3. What is the concept of market similarity and how does it apply to companies that target foreign markets?
4. Why is credit card payment a conundrum in emerging economies?
5. How do computer and telephone ownership affect e-marketing in emerging economies?
6. Why must Web site designers consider connection speeds in emerging economies?
7. What are some of the electricity problems faced by e-marketers in emerging economies?
8. How is wireless internet access likely to influence e-marketing around the world?
9. What is the digital divide, and what does it mean for e-marketers?

DISCUSSION QUESTIONS

10. Do you agree with the observation that the global internet will drive styles, tastes, and products to converge and create a more homogenous global marketplace? Why or why not?
11. Knowing that many consumers in emerging economies are wary of buying online, what would you do, as an e-marketer, to encourage them to change their attitudes and behavior?
12. What are the advantages and disadvantages of e-marketers creating fast-loading, low-graphics versions of their Web sites to accommodate slower connection speeds in emerging economies?
13. What responsibility do you think e-marketers should assume for helping to close the digital divide? Do you think consumers and governments should assume some responsibility as well? Explain your answers.
14. How serious is the online threat from Chinese companies? Are some product or service categories

more likely for Chinese companies to succeed in globally than others? Explain your answer.

WEB ACTIVITIES

15. Visit the Internet Usage Statistics at www.internet worldstats.com/. According to this site, what percentage of the world is currently online? How has that changed since this book was written? Divided by region, which areas of the world show the highest percentage for online usage? In comparison to the United States, what are the usage patterns of those in Europe and Asia? What trends in internet adoption and usage do you think will occur as the internet continues to mature?

16. Visit the UPS Web site at www.ups.com. If you wanted to deliver a package to Paris, France, what steps would you have to take to complete the transaction? How has UPS made the process easier? What languages other than English are available to UPS customers? What difficulties might you run into when delivering to an address that doesn't use English characters? How does UPS address these issues?

17. More Web sites are providing pages in languages other than English. Visit Google.com and select language tools. What types of services does Google provide for specific languages and countries? Try translating an entire Web page into a different language and view the results. What languages are compatible with these feature sets? What efforts is Google making to translate sites from languages that are currently unavailable?

This chapter was contributed by Al Rosenbloom, Associate Professor of Marketing at Dominican University in Illinois (arosenbloom@dom.edu). In 2001, Rosenbloom was a Fulbright Scholar and taught internet marketing to MBA students in Nepal. This chapter is based on his experiences in a number of emerging economies with particular emphasis on Far Eastern nations, including Nepal, India, and China.

CHAPTER 5

Ethical and Legal Issues

The biggest infraction of privacy actually occurs when people post their own e-mail addresses in public places on the Net.

—Patricia Seybold, Customers.com

Dave Bowman: "Open the pod bay doors, Hal."
HAL 9000 (computer): "I'm sorry, Dave. I'm afraid I can't do that."

—Arthur C. Clarke, *2001: A Space Odyssey*

Chapter Outline

The main goal of this chapter is to explore the ethical and legal issues that e-businesses face in marketing online. You will learn about the current and emerging issues that have caused concern among a variety of stakeholders, including e-businesses and consumers.

After reading this chapter, you will be able to:

- Compare and contrast ethics and law.
- Discuss the implications of ethical codes and self-regulation.
- Identify some of the main privacy concerns within traditional and digital contexts.
- Explain some of the important patent, copyright, trademark, and data ownership issues related to the internet.
- Highlight key ethical and legal concerns related to online expression.

Software Infringement

Have you ever broken the law while sitting at your computer? Most people would probably say no—not recalling the times they installed computer software that they did not purchase (known as software **piracy**). Infringement of the copyright in software occurs when people loan software CDs to others or companies install computer software for which they have no software licenses. Counterfeiting occurs when illegally copied software is duplicated and distributed on a large scale. Both infringement and counterfeiting violate U.S. copyright laws and are illegal.

So what is the big deal? Suppose you spent months writing a best-selling novel and then learned that thousands of people were copying it instead of buying it. That copying would cut into your income and reduce your enthusiasm for writing more novels. Infringement of the copyright in software creates a similar situation. The firms creating the software use the income to pay for innovative upgrades and new products; they cannot do as much if they lose income. Also, software marketers must raise the price paid by legitimate buyers to replace income lost to infringement.

This cause and effect relationship between protection and innovation plays out around the globe. The United States, Japan, and most of the countries in Europe are examples of countries producing and protecting trillions of dollars worth of new software every year. In stark contrast, Asia-Pacific countries with very weak software copyright enforcement, like China, India, Singapore, and Vietnam, produce little in the way of valuable software, but every year cost software owners billions of dollars in lost revenue. The United States has the lowest rate of software infringement in the world. Globally, however, over a third of the software sold is an infringing version. Cutting this number by even a third would create millions of jobs and generate

(continued)

(*continued*)

hundreds of billions in new economic growth around the world.

What can companies do? Microsoft, one of the main victims of software infringement, uses several methods: It proposes intellectual property legislation, files civil lawsuits, and creates noninfringement technologies such as digital rights management (DRM) security programs embedded in software CDs. Critics have argued that while security measures like DRM do little to stop sophisticated international counterfeiters, such systems make legal use of the software more difficult for the average user. A few years ago, Microsoft tried a system of sniffing out users' hard drives while they were online, but privacy advocates objected. In the end, Microsoft believes that education is the best weapon. Many people who use infringing software do not know they are stealing, and it is not against the law or out of the cultural norms in many countries. For example, executives in some countries believe that if they buy one copy of the software, they can use it as they please, as with other products. To support its educational goal, Microsoft created a Web site about software infringement which, like the campaigns of many other large copyright holders, refers to software infringement as "piracy" (www.microsoft.com/piracy). Infringement and counterfeiting remain huge problems for the software industry—problems that are unlikely to be solved for a long time.

OVERVIEW OF ETHICS AND LEGAL ISSUES

Scholars often treat ethical and legal issues as separate, even unrelated, subjects. In reality, ethics and law are integrally related. As we will see, **ethics** frequently concerns the values and practices of professionals and others who have expert knowledge of a specific field. Ethics is also a general endeavor that takes into account the concerns and values of society as a whole.

Law is similar to ethics in the sense that it, too, is an expression of values, but while ethics may be directed toward individual or group endeavors, laws are normally created for broader purposes, with the goal of addressing national, or sometimes international, populations. In the Anglo-American tradition, law is made by legislatures such as Congress or Parliament, enforced by executives or agencies, and interpreted by the courts. In all these instances, it is a public endeavor, which is reflected in the fact that law is often the result of political and social compromise. Additionally, law attempts to be consistent in both time and place so that citizens will be familiar with their rights and obligations.

Because law results from combinations of interests, beliefs, and goals, the processes that lead up to the making of laws are often slow and complex. Unfair laws, a common by-product of one-sided lobbying efforts, overly generous political contributions, and other special influences have been the focus of criticism and calls for reform. The problem has become so unwieldy that it prompted one of the world's premier copyright scholars, Lawrence Lessig, to consider a bid for Congress, running primarily on the platform of reducing political corruption.

Even in a perfect world of no political corruption, new laws cannot anticipate every nuance of how people and companies will push the proverbial legal envelope months, or years, down the road. New laws regulating the internet are at a particular disadvantage. Given the speed with which the internet landscape changes and the slowness with which laws are enacted, some laws are nearly obsolete by the time they are passed. Similarly troubling, even when Congress passes "good" laws, many questions remain concerning the meaning of the law itself, or about how the law is to be enforced. Thus, aggrieved parties file lawsuits demanding courts interpret these laws and determine their impact on particular conflicts. Administrative agencies such as the Federal Trade Commission (FTC) also promulgate rules and opinions governing online activity. Given the complexity of the task, efforts to tame online transactions can be slow, particularly within the new and often unfamiliar context of digital communication.

Ethics make important contributions to legal developments, influencing lobbyists, legislators, and eventually judges. The filtering that takes place as an ethical tenet moves from idea, to law, to enforcement interferes with what would ideally be a seamless legal enforcement of an ethical precept. As a result of this imperfect system, laws do not correlate directly with ethics. The debates and compromises which end up dictating the metes and bounds of a resulting law provide at least some assurance that most laws pass at least some ethical muster. Problems like legislators' weak grasp of complex information technology issues, biased lobbying efforts, and the large time lag between online innovations and laws that govern them, however, mandate that the law itself be merely the beginning, and not the end, of the ethical inquiry.

Laws lag far behind online innovations. The ethical debates surrounding these innovations, however, happen in real time. It is critical that lawmakers understand these issues clearly before trying to mold them into laws. Digital marketers play a crucial role in assisting legislators. Legislators seeking insight into the complex ethics of a particular online issue look to experts and real-world entities for guidance. Impressions from the trenches are lawmakers' most unvarnished source of information concerning the ongoing ethical debate.

Ethics and Ethical Codes

The study of ethics has been in existence for more than 2,500 years. The central focus of this study is the analysis and description of such basic concepts as right and wrong and how we judge the difference. An important dimension of this investigation concerns the types of conduct that comprise ethical behavior. These tasks necessarily involve the examination of rights, responsibilities, and obligations. Ethical inquiry is not limited to purely theoretical boundaries.

Rather, questions are studied at all levels of human interaction and often appear as political, legal, and commercial issues. Consequently, the scope of ethics is virtually as wide as its subject matter. Similarly, many types of ethical positions compete against each other for acceptance.

A particularly important aspect of ethical inquiry involves the study of professional activities. Traditionally, groups of individuals possessing special skills or knowledge have established codes and systems of fair practice. A classical example is the Hippocratic Oath of physicians. Ethical standards work both externally and internally. They help to communicate consistency and trustworthiness to the community at large, while also assisting in maintaining stability and integrity within the profession. In these ways, ethics are both pragmatic tools and essential elements of professional identity.

Documents such as the American Marketing Association's (AMA) Code of Ethics [1] reflect the recognition of a commitment to the exercise of honesty, integrity, and fairness within all professional transactions. In addition to articulating overall values, professional codes provide members with guidelines that are specific to their pursuits. They are often products of the combined experiences of practitioners, scholars, and the public that are passed along to the entire membership and eventually published. Historically, codes have been interpreted or revised to respond to changed circumstances and new issues. In the past, these processes have been relatively gradual, with modifications often coming in conservative degrees. Today, this situation is changed.

Modern technology presents a radical challenge to marketing ethics as well as to those of other professions. The extent of this demand is perhaps best reflected in the revolutionary features of the computer itself. When compared with other major technical advances such as the printing press, telephone, or automobile, digital media is arguably unique in its capacity for speed, ubiquity, and versatility. Computers serve as data collectors, compilers, and disseminators. They represent the fastest-growing form of communication and, through the internet and similar systems, forge global links of unprecedented proportion.

These factors create vacuums in ethical policy. Although they do not directly challenge such general ideals as fairness or honesty, digital processes and potentialities are so new that ethics, like many other social endeavors, is only beginning to adapt itself to the computer revolution. Currently, a number of critical issues confront those who work within electronic environments, including the ownership of intangible data, often termed *intellectual property*; the role of privacy in a virtual world without walls, locks, or doors; the extent to which freedom of expression should be allowed; the uses of data, including methods of collection; and the special status of children who log on to digital networks.

Easy solutions are seldom achieved within ethics or law, and, in the electronic context, progress is complicated by a lack of comparative historical situations. Likewise, the ability to analogize computers to objects or institutions with which society has had greater experience is often questionable. Is the computer network more like a broadcast station or a printing press or a public library? Our current lack of experience in these matters makes it difficult to say for certain. Finally, the fact that electronic spaces are global in nature accentuates the earlier observation that ethical positions are by no means agreed upon. What is accepted in Europe may be rejected in Asia or America.

The seemingly limitless opportunities afforded by computers also suggest the need for the constant assessment of their implications. Each participant in electronic marketing is given not only the responsibility to adhere to professional codes but also, in a very real sense, the unique opportunity to contribute to these standards in a meaningful way.

The Problem of Self-Regulation

Although law and ethics are frequently directed toward the same goals and often provide mutual assistance in the examination of complex problems, one emerging area of conflict involves the role of formal law in the regulation of online conduct. Throughout their tenures, the Clinton and Bush administrations have expressed the position that the development of the internet should be largely left to the free operation of the market. Within such a system, rather than mandate behavior through legislation, ethical codes developed by trade associations, commercial standards groups, and various professional organizations dictate appropriate behavior of participants.

Supporters of the **self-regulation** model point to the private sector's ability to rapidly identify and resolve problems specific to its areas of competence, particularly when compared to the seemingly confusing, contradictory, and lengthy processes of the law. According to this view, problems encountered within technological environments are particularly amenable to the expertise possessed by market actors. Once consensus is reached, uniformity is achieved through members' compliance with ethical codes, as well as by ongoing education of providers and consumers. Although the law cannot normally force anyone to adhere to these codes, many believe that improved consumer confidence and, consequently, enhanced economic opportunities will ensure voluntary compliance.

Critics of self-regulation argue that its incentives are insufficiently compelling. They note that perpetrators of such activities as fraud and deception frequently benefit from schemes of short duration and are rarely interested in the long-term gains offered by adherence to ethical codes. On a broader level, it has been suggested that commercial self-interest and pressures to maximize profits compromise the private sector's ability to police itself and that, absent the type of sanctions only the law can provide, true deterrence cannot be achieved.

Although the resolution of this debate is far from over, recent policy-making activities indicate that governments are asserting themselves at least in the area of fraud prevention and in issues involving children's privacy. The Australian Bureau of Consumer Affairs has, for example, stated that a law enforcement role in the prevention of fraud is essential to consumer security. The FTC in the United States has likewise targeted detection and suppression of domestic and international fraud as a priority (Exhibit 5.1).

EXHIBIT 5.1   E-Commerce Consumer Protection on the FTC's *Next Tech-ade Blog*

Source: ftcblog.gov/techade/.

Even though heightened governmental involvement appears to be an increasing response to many online issues, it is significant to note that lawmakers in the United States and elsewhere have entered into a close dialogue with private entrepreneurs, public interest groups, and commercial associations. Such arguably unprecedented instances of cooperation and sharing of resources suggest that future regulations will take the form of "networked responsibility" among many participants.

PRIVACY

The concept of **privacy** encompasses both ethical and legal aspects. It is also relatively new to both disciplines. Perhaps more than any other legal or ethical issue, privacy is a product of the twentieth century. Although many cultures follow established customs of social boundaries, detailed consideration of this subject did not come about until 1890 when Samuel Warren and future Supreme Court Justice Louis Brandeis published an article that urged the recognition of a right to privacy within

American law. This protection was defined as the "right to be left alone."[2] Significantly, many of the justifications of this new idea were reactions to the phenomena of a maturing industrial and technological age, including the mass distribution of newspapers, the development of listening devices, and the widespread use of photography. In essence, privacy's young tradition has always been about information and the means of its delivery.

Although it has been the subject of constant debate since the Warren and Brandeis article, privacy has proven to be an elusive concept, both ethically and legally. One reason for legal confusion is the lack of any specific privacy provision within the Constitution. This situation was recognized in the U.S. Supreme Court's 1965 decision of *Griswold v. Connecticut*,[3] which held that privacy in the use of contraceptives could be inferred from a number of elaborated Constitutional rights, including those of association, freedom from illegal searches and seizures, self-incrimination, and the quartering of soldiers. Later, in the 1973 opinion of *Roe v. Wade*,[4] the Court found a privacy right in a woman's reproductive decision making. Through the Fourth Amendment to the U.S. Constitution, the privacy of the home has been established against governmental agencies, which are required to obtain warrants before entering upon and searching a dwelling. This provision is, however, only applicable to officials or those acting on their behalf and not against private individuals.

In addition to Constitutional developments, privacy has been addressed in the *common law*. This term refers to decisions, presumptions, and practices traditionally embraced by Anglo-American courts. The common law has established a series of privacy violations that, both individually and together, form the basis of invasion of privacy lawsuits. They are arranged into four categories: unreasonable intrusion into the seclusion of another, unreasonable publicity of another's private life, the appropriation of another's name or likeness, and the publication of another's personal information in a false light. These elements are codified in many state statutes and appear in the influential legal treatise Restatement of Torts.[5]

Despite these developments, much disagreement remains as to what privacy entails. Identified central attributes fall into three general areas. The first is the Warren and Brandeis concept of a right to be left alone, often referred to as the *seclusion* theory. Privacy within this perspective is the ability to remain isolated from society. This model encourages laws and ethical standards that are oriented toward maintaining personal distance and punishing those who cross the limits set by individuals. A second, intermediate theory, known as *access control,* does not presume isolation as a norm but places its emphasis upon laws and standards that enable persons to reasonably regulate the information that they are giving up. Expressions of this model can be found in laws and standards that empower individuals to protect personal material from unauthorized release.

Both seclusion and access control models provide measures of protection, but their focus is concerned more with how information is released and less with what actually constitutes private data. A third theory, known as the *autonomy* model, attempts to provide such a definition. It does so by

identifying private matters as those necessary for a person to make life decisions. This model entails freedom from the coercive use of personal information as well as the ability to be alone when reflection is necessary.

In addition to difficulties in definition and scope, privacy exists as one value among many. Within society, privacy interests routinely compete against concerns of personal and public safety, economics, and even the social and psychological need for association with others—a process that can require the divulging of sensitive information. The ways in which these interests are coordinated involve complex balances that can result in difficult choices. Often people are willing to give up personal information for benefits they perceive to be worthwhile—credit cards, frequent flyer mileage, and security precautions in airports are but a few examples. In such cases, ethics and law attempt to provide guidelines helpful in critically examining definitions, priorities, and implications.

Privacy Within Digital Contexts

Information plays a pivotal role in the concept of privacy, as well as that of marketing and electronic commerce. It is, therefore, not surprising that conflicts about how data should be collected and used have developed. A starting point for this discussion is the AMA Code of Ethics for Marketing on the internet. This code states that "information collected from customers should be confidential and used only for expressed purposes." This principle is concise and straightforward in general terms, but it must be applied to the internet's many information-gathering mechanisms.

In the spring of 2000, the attention of the media, the government, and the public was captured by reports that DoubleClick, an online advertising firm, was engaged in an effort to collect and compile large amounts of personal consumer information. Within the relatively theretofore brief history of internet marketing, DoubleClick achieved success by establishing a system of more than 11,000 Web sites with advertising that, when clicked, enabled users to visit product sites. The system also recorded the responses, known as **clickstreams**, within its own databases. Clickstream information was then available to form a user profile, allowing the transmission of individually targeted advertising. Users were not required to give their active consent to this collection. At the time, DoubleClick had reportedly accumulated 100,000 online profiles.

Although privacy advocates had already voiced concern about the system's potential for abuse, the controversy reached a new height when DoubleClick acquired a second company, Abacus-Direct, which specialized in the acquisition of off-line consumer data. Abacus-Direct had amassed an electronic list that included the names, addresses, and buying histories of a large percentage of American households. With the merger, plans were reportedly under way to integrate data, providing a premium subscription service that would, for the first time, link these real-life identities to DoubleClick's online personalities. Pursuant to this news, a coalition of privacy, civil rights, and consumer groups filed a complaint with the FTC in an effort to prevent the tying of the Abacus-Direct information to online profile data and to enjoin the registration of users to the new database without first obtaining each subject's consent.

The most common means by which this type of data is obtained is through the use of cookies. Cookies are packets of data created within the hard drive of a user in response to instructions received from a Web page. Once stored, cookies can be retransmitted from a user's computer to a pertinent Web site. Cookies serve many purposes. For example, they may handle online information, creating features like shopping baskets to hold purchases. They may recall stored sales information to remind users of items already ordered or to suggest new products. Significantly, cookies may collect other data, such as full name, e-mail and postal addresses, phone numbers, a computer's geographic location, and the time logged online.

Although cookies may be configured within a browser to run only with explicit permission, they are normally automatically executed without any user action. Cookie packets may be combined with other digital information and may be transferred between servers or sold on the open market. User tracking occurs when cookies are appended and examined in the course of a user's online travels. The result is an ability to pinpoint an individual's online behavior. With the integration of off-line data, such tracking takes on a more encompassing, and more troubling, dimension.

The DoubleClick controversy illustrates several significant aspects of the online privacy controversy. Perhaps the most basic reflects the unsettled nature of privacy itself. Many people value privacy as a closely guarded right unto itself. According to this view, the ability to remain secluded from unwelcome intrusion as well as the capability to control the disclosure of personal data is presumed. This position advocates policies that require individuals be explicitly informed of any data collection event and then to allow the individuals the opportunity to participate (opt-in) or decline (opt-out). Supporters of systems such as DoubleClick's argue an opposite presumption. They presume most users wish to receive the benefits of targeted advertising. This position reflects the view that privacy is only one of many values to be balanced. It generally supports an opt-out policy, which presumes that data collection will take place, but still allows users to withdraw consent by a variety of methods, including sending e-mail to collectors requesting removal from their databases.

Pro-privacy critics of opt-out presumptions point to the fact that most users have no significant knowledge of how computers operate or process data. They question whether the average person will take the steps necessary to withhold data and suggest that many opt-out routines are confusing and thus are unlikely to be successfully accomplished. Commercial proponents of opt-out solutions emphasize consumer surveys that reveal a preference for targeted advertising and argue that the data necessary to provide this service should be collected unless otherwise denied. Although several Congressional bills are pending, no law yet exists to resolve the debate. Similarly, industry has not developed a widely accepted solution to the challenge. Presently, many firms and associations are emphasizing notification as the best approach. Others, such as Real Media Corporation, have developed routines that do not allow the sharing of its visitors' information with other Web sites.

The DoubleClick matter was partially resolved by the withdrawing of the database integration plans within months of the initial announcement. Attention continued to be focused on the company until 2001, when, pursuant to an investigation, the FTC concluded that no privacy violations had been committed by the company. In the spring of 2002, a remaining group of state and federal class-action privacy suits were settled. The preliminary terms of this agreement provide a template for contemporary industry standards in consumer privacy. They include the obligation to provide clear notice of data collection, a ban on combining existing data with personal information unless explicit (opt-in) permission is obtained. Moreover, data obtained from cookies must be routinely deleted and new cookies be programmed to deactivate at five-year intervals. Finally, DoubleClick was forced to initiate an extensive program of consumer privacy education and submit to regular, independent audits. Critics of the settlement point to the relative brevity of its two-year term of enforcement and to the overly generous lifespan given to cookies.

While overt exploitation of personally identifiable information has decreased since the turn of the century, technology has increased the ways in which such information is collected. Accordingly, while the impact may not be as noticeable to consumers, the usage is more widespread. Adding to the problem is the confusion over what the Web sites do with the information they collect. Nearly every major Web site collects some type of personally identifiable information. Just over half, however, specify on the Web site exactly how the information will be used. For several years, the industry has recognized that privacy is a significant consumer concern. This realization has prompted a greater use of privacy policies, including a more extensive use of opt-in routines.[6] It remains to be seen, however, whether these outward expressions will translate into greater protection of private information, or

merely serve as a cover for greater, more widespread exploitation of personally identifiable information

In addition to issues of data collection, the problem of access to data is of fundamental significance within the context of online privacy. In this area, the status of sensitive information is not only a matter of hardware security but also one of administrative policy. A clear example of the problem arose in 1998 when, with only an informal request, the U.S. Navy was able to obtain from America Online (AOL) the personal user data of a serviceman who was suspected of violating military rules concerning homosexual conduct. The resulting prosecution was later terminated after a court found that the Navy's request had likely violated federal privacy law.[7] An apology and compensation from AOL resulted, but the incident illustrates the risks involved after data leaves the control of a user.

The majority of privacy-related debates focus on traditional methods of data processing and the recently developed, but already well-established, use of cookies. Beyond these technologies, cutting-edge applications promise to gain popularity and to raise additional issues.

Java is a Web-friendly programming language that allows the downloading and running of programs or *applets* on individual computers. These applications are increasingly used to provide such enhancements as dynamic animation, Web-based simulations, and other useful additions to plain hypertext. Java may also be used to design programs known as hostile applets, which can be used to surreptitiously access and transmit data on hard drives, including e-mail addresses, credit card records, and other account information.

Intelligent agents are a growing topic of interest within Web marketing and computer science research. The products of developments in artificial intelligence, **agents** are programs that, once released by a user, can function autonomously within the Web to make electronic decisions. Some potential tasks include the searching of sites or the buying of products that conform to an individual's tastes or interests. Critics of agents worry that the preferences they hold may be chosen or controlled by entities other than their "owner." Such a situation would limit the individual's ability to make autonomous decisions and could create an incentive to distribute personal information contained in the agent applications.

Cookies, Java applets, and intelligent agents are **ubiquitous applications**; that is, they are able to function in the course of nearly any online session, without a user's knowledge or control. The ease of their operation explains why some sites would not want to inform a user that data are being collected. This objectionable attitude places technological ease above ethical principles. Similarly, because much of the information is not of an explicitly confidential character, it may be tempting to disregard privacy implications. This argument ignores the fact that even apparently innocuous data may, when combined, result in very specific information.

In addition to application-based collection, sites may gather information through online forms and electronic mail, often in exchange for browsing privileges or other benefits with or without the full disclosure of the terms of use. Regardless of how it is elicited, the use of information as a form of currency has raised ethical questions, particularly when most average users (as well as information experts) are understandably uncertain of the ultimate value of the data. Although such valuation may indeed be unattainable at this stage of internet development, consumer education about all uses of revealed data has been suggested as a solution to help users make informed judgments in this area. Information may also be gathered through explicitly fraudulent methods—an approach that has unambiguous ethical and legal implications.

A particularly active area of study involves the collection of material from children. Back in 1998, a report of the FTC indicates that 89 percent of the children's sites surveyed collected identifiable user data and 46 percent of these sites did not reveal their policies of collection or use. Only 10 percent of the surveyed sites contained provisions for parental control.[8]

In response to research, reports of abuses, and lobbying from parents and other advocates, Congress passed the Children's Online Privacy Protection Act (COPPA).[9] In effect since 2000, the law requires that Web sites and other online media that knowingly collect information from children 12 years of age or under (1) provide notice to parents; (2) obtain verifiable parental consent prior to the collection, use, or disclosure of most information; (3) allow parents to view and correct this information; (4) enable parents to prevent further use or collection of data; (5) limit personal information collection for a child's participation in games, prize offers, or related activities; and (6) establish procedures that protect the "confidentiality, security, and integrity of the personal information collected." In addition, the FTC, as required by Congress, enacted specific rules to govern and enforce the act[10] and, in its second year of administration, instituted a total of six COPPA enforcement actions. One major change brought about by the act is the increasing presence of data collection policies at sites used by children and the provision of an active means, such as a click button, for parents to confirm their awareness of these practices. In some cases, sites previously open to children now restrict admission to users of certain ages.

While federal laws relating to internet privacy remain in debate, many explicit offenses can be addressed by conventional criminal statutes. Sanctions for misuse of consumer data are present in the Fair Credit Reporting Act[11] and the Electronic Communication Privacy Act (ECPA).[12] Additionally, organizations such as the Direct Marketing Association have developed comprehensive guidelines for Web privacy.[13] One troubling development within this area is a decision of a federal trial court to dismiss a class action suit that alleged breaches of privacy policies by an airline. The dismissal was based, in part, upon the court's finding that even though an allegedly violated privacy policy was posted at the airline's site, the plaintiffs did not claim to have read its contents and therefore had few actual privacy expectations.[14] Critics of this decision claim that requiring such a showing would impose an enormous burden upon those attempting to enforce Web privacy policies, essentially making those policies worthless.

The problem of privacy within electronic mail remains an unsettled aspect of online interaction. Under U.S. law, users who operate e-mail accounts on private services are generally assured of their legal privacy through service agreements with their internet service provider (ISP). In addition, the ECPA addresses the privacy of ISP clients, with certain exceptions that include situations in which e-mail is inadvertently discovered through system maintenance. The opposite condition applies to employees who use their organizations' computers or networks to communicate. Here, the current law generally extends no expectation of privacy to workers, particularly those employed by nongovernmental entities. Many companies emphasize this status in memoranda of policies, but even when such notices are absent, the employee's wisest course of action is to assume that all material that passes through workplace facilities is monitored. Ethical questions remain as to whether strict surveillance policies adequately reflect reasonable expectations or values of personal autonomy and integrity. Compare this to laws that prohibit unlimited monitoring of employer-owned phone systems or dressing rooms.

International Privacy Issues

On an international level, privacy issues have received close attention. On October 15, 1998, the European Union's (EU) Data Protection Directive[15] took effect, requiring its member states to enact national laws to protect "fundamental rights and freedoms of natural persons, and in particular their right to privacy with respect to the processing of personal data." The directive's provisions require that:

- Subjects be apprised of how their data are used and be given opportunities to review and correct information.
- Data use be restricted to the announced purpose.
- The origin of data be disclosed, if known.
- Procedures to punish illegal activities be established.
- Consumer data collection procedures contain opt-out capabilities.

- Sensitive data collection cannot be accomplished without explicit permission.
- Any international transfer of data be executed only with countries possessing adequate privacy protection laws.

In March 2000, after extensive negotiation, the U.S. Department of Commerce and the European Commission reached agreement that U.S. organizations would submit to a series of **safe harbor** provisions for the protection of EU citizen data. These provisions essentially reflect the directive's emphases upon notice about collection, purpose, and use; choice in ability to opt-out of disclosure and third-party dissemination—including a requirement of affirmative permission in matters involving sensitive personal data; third-party transfer protection; and provisions for security, data integrity, redress, and enforcement.[16] Companies participating in data transactions with the EU can fulfill the safe harbor provisions by allowing the U.S. government to monitor compliance, by affiliating with a self-regulatory group under FTC supervision, by reporting directly to EU data protection agencies, or if not currently online, by promising to work with an EU privacy panel. A criticism of this plan focuses on its reliance on private compliance. Critics are particularly worried that without active governmental supervision, the aims of the safe harbor plan may largely be unfulfilled. In 2002, the European Commission issued a report on the safe harbor agreement process, affirming the establishment of required procedures, but expressing concern that some U.S. corporate policies and dispute resolution processes failed to meet expectations.[17]

Although there is much debate over which privacy policies most evenly balance corporate and individual interests, the following norms identified by the FTC[18] represent a consensus regarding the minimum requirements in the ethical use of consumer information (Exhibit 5.2):

1. **Notice:** Users should be aware of a site's information policy *before* data is collected.
2. **Consent:** Users should be allowed to choose participation or exclusion from the collection.
3. **Access:** Users should have the ability to access their data and correct them if erroneous.

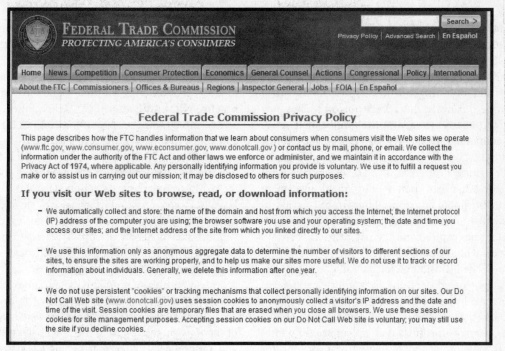

EXHIBIT 5.2 FTC Monitors Online Privacy

Source: www.ftc.gov/ftc/privacy.shtm

4. **Security:** Policies to ensure the integrity of data and the prevention of misuse should be in place.
5. **Enforcement:** Users should have effective means to hold data collectors to their policies.

DIGITAL PROPERTY

A primary function of law is to define ownership, but its consistency is currently being challenged by the mercurial nature of digital technology. Traditionally, the law protected intangible or intellectual property through three basic mechanisms. **Patent law** is centered upon inventions and the ability to reproduce or manufacture an inventor's product. **Copyright** addresses the realm of expression—specifically, the right to publish or duplicate expressions of ideas. **Trademark** is concerned with words or images used to identify products in the market. It is important to note that these categories have been flexible and often the boundaries between them have been modified by legislation and the courts. In addition, international treaties can redefine both distinctions and protections.

Computer-based communication poses particularly difficult problems for intellectual property. These communications may incorporate elements of patent, copyright, and trademark. The communication may embody a novel way of communicating covered by patent. The communication may contain text or pictures protected by copyright. The communication may also contain the proprietary images of a trademark.

Patents

The application of patent law to computing is an uncertain but developing field. Under conventional American law, patents are granted by the U.S. government for inventive processes or steps.[19] Grounded in English legal foundations and the heritage of conventional invention, the law is tailored toward industrial or mechanical concerns. In 1998, the case of *State Street Bank & Trust Co. v. Signature Financial Group, Inc.* held that a computer program could be patented. This ruling has since been expanded to include any method of doing business. Since *State Street* online businesses have been making use of its protections. A primary motivation for this preference may lie in the fact that unlike copyrights, patents prevent competitors from doing the same thing a different way. However, like copyright, American patent powers derive from Constitutional concerns. Thus, public access to patented material is assured after the term of the patent has expired and the patent itself is always on file with the government.

The inclusion of software under patent law is largely based upon the assertion that programs describe inventive processes. A contrary opinion holds that software at its root consists of algorithms—formulas that are generic in nature and, therefore, cannot be owned by anyone. A similar criticism states that programs are merely schemes or plans that machines actually execute. The details of both sides' arguments are complex and promise to be the subject of much future debate, litigation and, perhaps, Congressional action. An area of current internet focus centers on the use of *business patents* that describe such activities as marketing approaches and methods for conducting commerce. Patent protection has been claimed for reverse online auctions, secure credit card processing, and incentive-based methods for reading Web site advertising. When the Patent Office first started granting patents on business methods, the review process was less than vigorous. Many overly broad patents were issued in a short period of time. Opportunistic companies bought large numbers of these patents and began filing infringement lawsuits around the country. These patent trolls are still around, reaping millions of dollars in royalties every year for doing nothing but threatening to sue on somewhat suspect patents.

An example of the attempted enforcement of a software patent is found in the claim that secure digital time-stamping is a unique and protected process. Critics fear that if this assertion is upheld, the majority of online encryption routines will be affected. Similarly, in *Amazon.com v. Barnesandnoble.com*, the plaintiff relied upon a patent to allege that it alone had the ability to use *1-Click* ordering routines—a now-common practice within the internet.[20] The matter was settled in 2002, without final judicial resolution and with the details of the terms left undisclosed.

The U.S. Patent Office recently decided to increase the rigor with which it reviews applications for software-related protection (Exhibit 5.3). Likewise, both courts and Congress are being called upon to carefully examine whether historical data support the inclusion of software and business practices within a patent's ambit. Advocates of inclusion argue that the granting of patents in these areas will encourage productivity and innovation. Critics argue the opposite, stating that both the encryption matter as well as the unanswered issues of the *Amazon* case point to the potentially stifling and monopolistic effects of patent law's strong protections.

Copyright

At this comparatively early stage of online legal development, copyright appears to be established as the primary means of protecting most expression on the internet, including text and other data. In the conventional world, copyright has protected expressions of ideas in such formats as books, recordings, and film. Under American law, it is derived from the Constitution as a protection established for the benefit of the public, and within jurisprudence, it has been applied with certain limitations created for the public's benefit. Chief among these protections are the doctrines of fair use and of first sale. [21] Fair use consists of the ability to copy without cost reasonable portions of protected material for purposes relating to such public activities as education, news reporting, and editorial comment. Under conventional law, the doctrine of first sale limits the ability of a copyright holder to obtain profit from the sale of his or her work after the initial time at which the material is sold. Purchasers are subsequently given

EXHIBIT 5.3   United States Patent Office Reviews Patent Applications

Source: www.uspto.gov.

the ability to transfer or otherwise dispose of their copy. The first sale doctrine is viewed as benefiting such institutions as public libraries and can also increase access to intellectual material through discounts such as those offered by used bookstores.

In 1997, President Clinton signed the **No Electronic Theft (NET) Act**[22] into law. The NET Act confers copyright protection for computer content and imposes sanctions when infringement is committed for commercial or private financial gain, or by the reproduction or distribution, either commercial or noncommercial, of one or more copies of copyrighted works having $1,000 or more in retail value. Punishment under this provision may include criminal prosecution. While proponents believe that the NET Act will encourage innovation by protecting material placed on the internet, critics believe that the definition of *infringement* has been made problematically broad by shifting its traditional meaning, which is normally associated with permanent or semipermanent reproduction (known as fixing), to now include electronic distribution without reproduction. It is argued that such acts could include the mere perusal of digital material through a Web browser and, thus, make criminal activities of

what has been previously protected by the First Amendment. Additional criticism has been directed to the use of criminal sanctions, particularly at a time when there is great debate about the economic value of electronic material.

A related law, enacted in 1998, is the **Digital Millennium Copyright Act (DMCA)**.[23] The DMCA is a complex piece of legislation that contains several provisions. It grants ISPs protection from acts of user infringement as long as certain procedures are followed, including the prompt reporting and disabling of infringing material. Supporters of this legislation claim that the DMCA will free ISPs from liability for its users' illegal actions and, thus, encourage industry growth. Critics believe that the reporting and disabling requirements may cause innocent behavior to be presumed infringing and wrongfully censored.

The DMCA also criminalizes the circumvention of software protections and the development or distribution of circumvention products.[24] As with the NET Act, DMCA supporters believe that this law will increase commercial willingness to place material on the internet by deterring online infringement. Although some exceptions exist for educational and scientific activities, critics maintain that the DMCA goes well beyond this goal by banning the development of innocent and useful applications that may have minor circumvention capabilities, giving copyright holders a veto over any development that they perceive as a challenge to their profits.[25]

The DMCA was enacted in part to comply with the World Intellectual Property Organization's (WIPO) Copyright Treaty and the WIPO Performances and Phonograms Treaty.[26] These documents set forth international standards for copyrighted material and were recently ratified by the United States. Treaty proponents argue that in a global networked environment, international consensus regarding ownership, protection, and transfer of digital property is essential. As with the DMCA, critics argue that the specific laws required by the treaties unfairly favor copyright owners.

Trademarks

Trademark law is concerned with the ownership of intellectual property that identifies goods or services. Under the federal **Lanham Act**,[27] trademarks may be registered with the government. Registered or not, however, they may still be protected under the Act. To pursue an infringement case, claimants must prove that the trademark is *protectable.* Generally, the more distinctive the mark, the greater the strength of this claim. The Act also prohibits **dilution**—the use of famous trademarks in association with different goods or services in a manner likely to lead to dilution of the trademark.

Trademark law has recently been applied to the internet-naming system. Domains are unique configurations of letters or numbers that are used to route data. The most familiar examples of domains are addresses of Web sites, for example, www.someplace.com. In addition to designating Web sites, domain names are also used in e-mail addresses. As the primary means to reach commercial destinations, the significance of these identifiers is obvious.

Although the creative application of language provides for many distinctive names, it is inevitable that some similarity will occur.

For example, "General Signpost" can plausibly be thought to resemble "General Sign," but traditionally, trademark law has been able to allow such similarities because trademark protection is typically limited to a particular class or classes of goods or services. When enough dissimilarity of goods or services exists, a certain redundancy is permitted.

Another type of trademark violation is known as **cybersquatting**. This activity involves the registration of domain names that resemble or duplicate the names of existing corporations or other entities. The initial registrants are typically unrelated to the institution at issue. The domain name is then offered for sale at a price thousands of times higher than that originally paid. On November 29, 1999, President Clinton signed the Anticybersquatting Consumer Protection Act.[28] Under this law, a person is liable to suit if, in bad faith, he or she registers, traffics, or sells a domain bearing a name that is identical or confusingly similar to a protected trademark, or which would dilute the worth of the trademark. As a national law, the act makes it easier to place notoriously elusive cybersquatters under the control of the court system and allows for swift possession by a successful complainant of the disputed domain name. Heralded by trademark holders, the Act has received criticism similar to that lodged against the DCMA, specifically, that the swiftness of the transfer of contested domain names may unfairly deprive a defendant of a proper hearing and due process.

Metatags are HTML statements that describe a Web site's contents. They are not normally displayed by browsers. They allow search engines to identify sites relevant to topics of their inquiries. Accordingly, these tags can provide a valuable means of attracting users to a site. Because metatags are defined by HTML authors, it is possible to insert words or phrases that are calculated to provide optimal attractiveness, including material protected by trademark. In a matter involving Playboy Enterprises, Inc., the defendant included in its metatags the protected words *Playboy* and *Playmate.* In the subsequent suit, the court found that the intent of the site was to profit from a false association with Playboy and prohibited the inclusion, stating that dilution of the trademarks had occurred as a result.[29] This outcome should be contrasted with a more recent matter in which a former Playmate of the Year included similar terms within her site, albeit repeatedly noting that she was not presently associated with Playboy Enterprises. Here, the use was upheld as applied to the metatags, with the court holding that their presence was "nominative," meaning that the terms were simply descriptive and did not inaccurately imply an endorsement or make other misrepresentations. Significantly, the court did find that the repeated use of a trademarked term on the site's wallpaper did constitute an infringement and was unnecessary for the purposes of simple description.[30]

A variation of the metatag problem is found in the practice of assigning **keywords** within search engines. In one case, the cosmetic manufacturer, Estée Lauder, sued Excite and others, alleging that the entry of its trademarked name at the Excite Shopping Channel would direct users to the site of a specific, unlicensed dealer.[31] In addition to deception, Estée Lauder claimed that the practice diluted its trademark. The case was subsequently settled with Estée Lauder reacquiring control over its name. The selling of trademark-protected keywords has also been claimed to occur at other Web portals where these words or phrases trigger banner advertising that is not sanctioned by or directed to the trademark holder.

In addition to word appropriation, trademark has been implicated in matters involving use of hyperlinks. Although the Web has flourished with its abilities to seamlessly transfer information from site to site, some entities have become concerned that links that take users to areas other than their introductory page may cause confusion or deprive the target sites of revenue obtained through the selling of advertising. Such *deep linking* was the subject of litigation when Microsoft's Seattle Sidewalk created deep links to city-specific event sales within a site run by Ticketmaster. Here, Ticketmaster claimed that the practice diluted Ticketmaster trademarks and constituted unfair competition. Microsoft countered that the placement of any material within public areas

of the Web would make it open to access. These contrasting theoretical positions were never subjected to a final court ruling because the case was ultimately settled with Microsoft agreeing to link only to Ticketmaster's primary entry page.[32]

Related to linking is the practice of *framing*, a process in which a Web browser is instructed to divide itself into two or more partitions and load within a section material obtained from another Web site through the execution of an automatic link. In *Washington Post v. TotalNEWS, Inc.,* suit was filed over the use of a collage of frames, some linked to the *Post,* within a page dedicated to a sampling of news on the Web. Among other things, the *Post* alleged that the unattributed displays diluted trademarks, appropriated copyrighted material, and deprived the *Post* of advertising revenue.[33] The matter was settled before decision with TotalNEWS agreeing to use only nonframed, attributed textual links to the *Post.*

Licenses

An increasingly popular method of intellectual property protection involves the use of **licenses** (see the "Let's Get Technical" box). These instruments consist of contractual agreements made between consumers and software vendors, which allow the buyer to use the product but restrict duplication or distribution. Because laws related to licenses are derived from the commercially oriented law of contract, rather than through the constitutionally related realm of copyright or patent, public policy exceptions have traditionally played a less important role in its development. Moreover, because it is assumed that parties to contractual agreements bargain under conditions of informed self-interest, licenses may contain waivers of many protections normally found in consumer transactions.

Within the computer environment, a great deal of attention has been paid to the validity of licenses appearing upon or within software. Variations of this format are often known as shrinkwrap or *break-the-seal* licenses (when appearing outside of software) and clickwrap licenses when a user is required to click a button online or within a

LET'S GET TECHNICAL

Licensing Technology

Filename: LatestOperatingSystem.zip

Download Time: 10 hours and 34 minutes

Number of Files: 4215 files, 78 folders

Price: $0.00

Legality: 100% ILLEGAL

The feud between music fans and the music industry over the illegal distribution of albums and songs has been all over the media. As many already know, computer users with high-speed connections can download a client to get in on the trading—illegal trading, that is. Software is distributed through this medium as well. Just like copying music files to shared folders, users are copying the contents of installation CDs for such software as Microsoft Office, Macromedia Flash, and Adobe Photoshop.

However, when a user purchases software, he or she is most often just purchasing one license, or the right to install and run the software on one computer. When purchasing and installing the software, the user agrees to the end user license agreement (EULA). He or she agrees by selecting "I agree" or "I accept" in the installation process. The EULA also protects the software company from liability in case the software causes damage to the user's computer.

Breaking the agreement used to be simple. The user simply had to copy the CD and the CD's product key and distribute freely. Software companies then became more advanced in their quest to stop software piracy, or the illegal distribution of software, by instituting activation procedures. Upon installing the software, the computer user is allowed to either run the software for a certain number of days or open it a certain number of times. Once the user activates the software, either online or via telephone, the limitations are removed. The activation stops software piracy because it only allows the software associated with the product key to be activated once, and thus it can only be installed on one computer.

Also, this feature allows software companies to distribute trial versions of their software. Once the limit has been met, the software cannot be used without purchasing a full version. Other trial versions just offer limited features until a license is purchased.

Software piracy is often misunderstood, and it occurs in many different forms. Software piracy also includes fonts. Licenses can be issued for fonts, and using copyrighted fonts without a license is illegal. Whether using the software or font for business or personal purposes, using it without a license is illegal and punishable by law. Forms of software piracy include the illegal use of a software program over a network, distributing specialized education versions to unauthorized markets, and reporting an inaccurate number of users using software at a site. Even the possession of software that has been illegally copied is piracy.

Many organizations have been created to monitor software piracy and the illegal duplication of all copyrighted material worldwide. Examples include the Software & Information Industry Association's Anti-Piracy Division (www.siia.net/piracy) and the Business Software Alliance (www.bsa.org). The SIIA's Anti-Piracy Division conducts proactive campaigns to educate users about software piracy. The SIIA recently stated that software piracy cost the software industry $29 billion in sales in 2007. Software manufacturers, such as Microsoft and Adobe, have also set up Web sites to help determine whether users' software is legal and to report software piracy.

In the professional world, it is tempting to hand a CD and product key to one's coworker to install. However, if an audit is conducted by an outside source, that simple act can get the company in hot water. Software manufacturers can take such actions as warning, fining, or suing the company. In a professional setting, it is best to pursue a site license agreement (SLA) for the organization to use the software. An SLA, or site license, is simply a license to use the software within a certain facility. The license usually entails whether the software can be installed on all or specific computers or servers and if copies can be made and distributed within the facility.

program to acknowledge acceptance of terms. Although common to conventional business situations, the extent to which licenses with non-commercial purchasers will be enforced by the courts is not entirely clear, primarily due to the lack of bargaining that takes place between the user and the seller. Normally, a contract requires that an agreement can be demonstrated and it is not certain that average buyers agree to or even read the fine print that appears on their diskettes, boxes, installation routines, or software manuals.

The legal trend seems to favor enforcement of software licenses. Courts have upheld a shrinkwrap term that limited the vendor's liability for errors within the program.[34] At least one court also found enforceable a clickwrap term that dictated the state in which a suit against the vendor could be brought.[35]

A broad effort to enforce the terms of software licenses comes in the form of the **Uniform Computer Information Transactions Act (UCITA)**. If adopted by the states, this model would govern all legal agreements pertaining to software transactions, including sales. Supported by the majority of software manufacturers and publishers as a measure of legal uniformity, critics argue that UCITA will enforce license provisions including those restricting copying and resale of material, liability for damages incurred from defective software, and possibly the ability to criticize software performance. Because UCITA applies to any material in computer-readable form, including electronic books and other reading materials, librarians and educators fear it will effectively remove the public policy protections of copyright and patent, making online information expensive and restricted.

To date, only Virginia and Maryland have adopted UCITA. In 2001, the attorneys general of 32 states and two territories stated their opposition to the act, and in 2002 a task force of the American Bar Association issued a call for its redrafting. As the debate continues, it will be important to consider that, although intellectual property laws can act as incentives to create useful material, they can also work to restrict the data exchange that has contributed to the internet's popularity.

The achieving of a balance between both concerns will be an important and continuing task for digital law and ethics.

Trade Secrets

The field of trade secrecy has taken on new proportions with the advent of online technology. The federal Economic Espionage Act of 1996[36] was enacted in part to address digital advances and now makes it a criminal offense to divulge trade secrets, which are broadly defined to include such areas as commercial, scientific and technical endeavors. Trade secrets can include, but are not restricted to, formulas, market data, algorithms, programs, codes, and models. They may be stored online or in tangible formats. Significantly, computer-based disclosures such as e-mails, downloads, Web publications, and similar means are within the scope of the act.

Employees possessing trade secrets may be prohibited from engaging in similar businesses for a period of time. In one notable case, a court determined that an employee's particular skills in Web marketing were sufficiently protected under a noncompetition agreement with a former employer to prevent him from working for a competitor within a one-year period following his departure from a company.[37]

Data Ownership

It is not an overstatement to say that the online world runs on data. Not surprisingly, access and ownership questions relating to data and databases abound in current legal and ethical debate. As the electronic market becomes more competitive, attempts to obtain the advantages provided by control of information become more numerous.

Until recently, much data relating to such technical issues as Web site usage were easy to access and were often shared among site owners, marketing professionals, advertisers, and consumers. Currently, a new technology is being introduced that would make information collected from banner advertisements invisible to site owners and their clients. These *click data* have been important in determining such factors as site content and marketing strategy. Such protective technologies raise new issues concerning the ownership of information that is both a necessary element of online interaction and of extreme value in itself. A particularly significant question is whether the *fencing in* of data will achieve the same status as the more formal application of copyright, patent, trademark, or licensing laws. This process will challenge the model of cooperation that has been a characteristic of online dynamics and, arguably, a primary reason for the success of the interactive digital medium.

Another complex issue involving online data is an activity known as **spidering**. This process involves the use of software applications called *robots* to enter targeted Web sites and obtain data for the use of its owner. In a recent matter, the online auction site eBay instituted an action against Bidder's Edge, which operated a service that presented comparative auction information through spidering. The information collected from eBay was unprotected by copyright. Advocates of eBay claim that another's use of the data generated by their efforts constitutes unfair competition and dilutes the worth of their business. They also maintained that the spidering activity constituted a trespass to property, potentially impairing the eBay system. Proponents of Bidder's Edge expressed concern that if data are cordoned off from the rest of the online community, the presently information-rich internet will increasingly become a *gated community* where actions in trespass will become the predominant means of enforcing boundaries. The matter was settled before judgment on the merits, and the court sustained eBay's request for a preliminary injunction of Bidder's Edge activity based upon the trespass claim.[38]

A final area of consideration is that of the special protection of data relating to facts. As previously noted, U.S. copyright law protects *expressions* of ideas but not the ideas themselves. This distinction is due to the public policy emphasis of protecting the raw material of free expression and national learning. For similar reasons, copyright cannot be used to protect facts. Because electronic databases often contain arrangements of facts, a movement is growing within the law to protect specially compiled or *sui generis* data.

The Agreement on Trade Related Aspects of Intellectual Property Rights (TRIPs) of 1995 is part of the World Trade Organization's (WTO) program of international treaties. Provisions within this agreement set forth sui generis protection. The EU's Database Directive[39] also includes protection for compiled facts. Currently, the U.S. Congress has not adopted a sui generis law.

Arguments favoring sui generis protection revolve around the belief that this type of protection will afford an incentive for database vendors to create more of their products by assuring them of potential return on their investments and that their product will not be copied or diluted. In the long run, society will benefit from the increase, which would in turn help decrease the price of information.

Critics of these laws argue that no economic proof indicates that such incentives would produce an increase in databases or that, with an increase, prices would necessarily come down. Instead, they state that worries about copying and dilution can be addressed through encryption and similar methodologies. In the balance, they claim that sui generis protection could erect legal barriers that stifle innovation and lead to a monopolization of the basis for all education and learning. Another troubling fact is that many current proposals allow a virtually infinite term under which data could be kept out of the public domain. Under U.S. law, settling these issues will involve a close examination of the reasons underlying the constitutional aversion to the ownership of facts, and it will raise ethical questions about whether facts are merely commodities or are so valuable that exclusive control can never be granted to one individual.

ONLINE EXPRESSION

The mass distribution of unsolicited electronic mail or spam has been the subject of much complaint within the online world. The practice has been criticized on many levels. Internet service providers point to the burdens that spamming places upon network resources. Spam is, by definition, unrequested, and users complain of the unwanted intrusion into their affairs. Privacy-related worries are not restricted to transmission alone. Much spam is derived from mailing lists that are collected from e-mail addresses posted to such locations as Web bulletin boards or newsgroups without any intention to participate in mass mailings. Similarly, many users are disturbed to find that information given to individuals or entities for one purpose may be collected and sold for mass distribution. The frustration with spam is further compounded by the fact that often these messages are sent without valid return addresses or other contact information.

Although spam has been the subject of much justified criticism, its regulation must be approached with some caution. First, the topic implicates freedom of expression, which is a right protected under the First Amendment in the United States. A recent statement by the Direct Marketing Association's (DMA) president and CEO H. Robert Wientzen acknowledged that most reputable marketing professionals reject spam as an inappropriate means of consumer contact but also voiced concern that ill-conceived, blanket restrictions on bulk e-mail could pose a threat to expression and endanger the future of more sophisticated, responsibly targeted electronic messages.

The AMA Code of Ethics for Marketing on the internet also addresses the spam problem by stating that "the expressed wishes of others should be respected with regard to the receipt of unsolicited e-mail messages." Disagreement remains between those who believe that participation in mass e-mails should be restricted to those who voluntarily agree to receive mailings and those who advocate an opt-out-only approach. The DMA has established such an opt-out list for those who seek to avoid mass e-mail messages. Although it is certainly a progressive step, critics point out that only DMA members are obligated to respect this list and also worry that, like other opt-out systems, complexity and difficulty will prevent many average users from participation.

Within the law, spam has become a major issue. In the case of *Cyber Promotions, Inc. v. America Online, Inc.*,[40] the court held that a spam producer had no First Amendment right to send its product to AOL subscribers and that consequently the ISP could block its messaging activity. Similarly, a court ruled that spamming activity violated the federal Computer Fraud and Abuse Act.[41] Additionally, Congress passed, and President Bush signed, the Controlling the Assault of Non-Solicited Pornography and Marketing Act of 2003, better known as the CAN-SPAM Act.[42] The act creates a comprehensive, national framework for the use of marketing-directed e-mail. Although criticized by some consumer organizations as being more lenient than many state laws, the act permits federal and state authorities as well as ISPs to initiate both civil and criminal actions against advertising deemed to be conducted through spamming activities. Currently, the task of precise definition of illicit spamming is being determined by the FTC, but will include communications containing deceptive information, misleading statements, and false representations of an e-mail's content as displayed on the subject line. It will also require that e-mail headings reveal their commercial nature and that, in most circumstances, recipients are provided with clear instructions on how to terminate further contact. Finally, the use of autonomous data collection applications (such as spidering) will be prohibited. To many critics, a significant deficiency of the legislation is the absence of a private right to pursue actions against spammers.

Criticism of products or industries has also been addressed within and outside the spam context. In one case, a court prohibited an individual from sending mass e-mails to a corporation's employees complaining of employment violations. The trial court reasoned that corporate e-mail does not resemble traditional places of commentary and should, therefore, not be treated as a public forum, but instead, constituted private property, subject to trespass allegations. The decision was appealed to the California Supreme Court, which recently reversed the ruling, finding that because no impairment of the computer system or network occurred as a result of the mailings, a trespass action could not be maintained.[43] Less-specific mailings may also be restricted through terms of service agreements. A Canadian decision enforced such a contract that prohibited spam activity by the ISP's users.[44]

The inception of ISPs gave rise to a question about the liability of network owners for defamatory messages posted on bulletin boards or other public areas. Although most courts adopt the view that like publishers, ISPs are not normally susceptible to suit, Congress resolved the problem by placing this immunity within federal law.[45] The primary reason for this provision is a fear that if liability were at issue, a provider would be required to actively monitor and censor activity within its service, thus decreasing the level of free expression. The significance of this policy was demonstrated when a court determined that an ISP could not be held liable for negligently publishing anonymous, allegedly false and defamatory statements concerning an individual's profiteering from the Oklahoma City bombings.[46]

The issue of expression directed to children remains a highly visible issue within online law and ethics. In 1996, the federal Telecommunications Act of 1934 was amended to include the Computer Decency Act (CDA), which in relevant part made it a criminal act to send an "obscene or indecent" communication to a recipient who was known to the sender to be under 18 years of age. An additional provision made it an offense to use an interactive computer service to present material that "depicts or describes, in terms patently offensive, as measured by contemporary community standards, sexual or excretory organs" in a context available to minors. In 1997, in the case of *Reno v. American Civil Liberties Union*,[47] the U.S. Supreme Court found that these provisions were unconstitutionally vague, prohibiting, among other things, the exchange of information about such subjects as AIDS and reproductive decision making. It further noted that the provisions would hinder or *chill* adult speech through the placement of undue burdens.

Although the broad regulatory attempts of the CDA failed, a number of efforts are underway to provide more narrowly defined regulations for children's content. In addition, the use of filtering models has been considered. Perhaps the best known program is the Platform for Internet Content Selection Rules (PICS). This application allows the filtering of sites that are deemed inappropriate for minors. Advocates claim that PICS will place control into the hands of parents and schools. Some civil rights groups are concerned that this device, which works behind the scenes, presents a subtle but powerful means of censorship.

In December 2000, Congress passed the Children's Internet Protection Act (CIPA). The legislation links federal funding to libraries with the use of filtering software in public internet terminals. In May 2002, after hearing extensive evidence, a federal judicial panel invalidated the Act, stating that blocking software cannot adequately guarantee that only material harmful to minors would be screened. The decision was appealed to the U.S. Supreme Court, and on June 23, 2003, a plurality opinion reversed the lower court, holding that public funding can be made contingent upon the use of filters. Significantly, this declaration was effectively limited for, in the course of the proceedings, the government stated that libraries would retain the ability to remove filtering software if simply requested to do so by a patron. This concession was cited by two individual concurrences and likely played a determinative role in the outcome.[48]

These examples strongly suggest that the boundaries of expression will continue to be challenged by the internet. Although specific outcomes remain open to question, it appears that expression will be protected when the courts and the legislatures realize the purpose and importance of electronic communication. Education of all parties involved may prove to be the best security for the continued flourishing of online speech.

EMERGING ISSUES

Along with the more conventional problems of online dynamics, additional challenges are particularly unique to the internet at its current stage of development. The responses to these challenges will require the same levels of imagination and creativity demonstrated in the internet's creation.

Online Governance and ICANN

In 1998, the U.S. Department of Commerce called for the creation of a private, nonprofit regulatory body that would be responsible for the administration of the internet name and address system. In response, the **Internet Corporation for Assigned Names and Numbers (ICANN)** was formed. Ideally, the purpose of ICANN revolves around resolving the conflicts that arise in the assignment and possession of domains. Today, ICANN is comprised of a governing board that currently faces substantial criticism for operating under secrecy and for failing to represent the broad range of online users. Many of these problems may be attributed to the newness of this endeavor, but other questions concern the ability of any private regulatory organization to enforce its decisions within the online community. Along these lines, parties to serious disputes may attempt to bypass ICANN or other arbitration arrangements in favor of the conventional enforcement abilities of legal forums, through such vehicles as trademark infringement suits.

Jurisdiction

The establishment of ICANN reflects the growing awareness that online controversies transcend physical boundaries. **Jurisdiction** is the legal term that describes the authority of a court over a given party. Jurisdiction is traditionally based upon physical presence, which becomes an issue in the nonphysical nature of online world. Similarly, attempts to exercise jurisdiction within the geographic territories of other nations or states will most likely be rebuffed.

The majority of cases decided within the United States have focused upon the character and quality of contacts with the forum state; generally, the more active the involvement, the more likely that jurisdiction will be conferred. Thus, jurisdiction over online activity was found where the court determined that an out-of-state defendant had knowingly and purposefully done business within

the state of suit.[49] In contrast, another court found that mere advertising within a state will not, without more, subject the advertiser to jurisdiction.[50] A similar decision held that the ability to access a Web site within a particular state does not subject the site owner to jurisdiction.[51] As previously mentioned, digital licensing agreements that defined the jurisdiction in which suit may be brought have been upheld. Similarly, a recent state court decision indicated that such a selection may be contractually specified by digital means. In upholding the vendor's choice of forum, as disclosed through an internet hyperlink, the court noted that the use of hyperlinks to convey information has become an increasingly accepted practice and can validly designate a forum choice.[52]

In addition to conventional legal tribunals, such mediation-oriented programs as **Virtual Magistrate**[53] have been developed to resolve online disputes. These programs often attempt to tailor their procedures toward the special circumstances of the internet. Advocates of these approaches argue that their online orientation will encourage users to work out difficulties within a nonconfrontational framework. Critics voice concerns that online arbitration cannot adequately ensure enforcement or recognition of judgments.

The previously mentioned cases dealt exclusively with U.S. jurisdictional questions. Although difficult problems are presented, they are arguably less complex than those involving international disputes. One method aimed at achieving international cooperation is through the mediation of organizations. For example, the WIPO Arbitration and Mediation Center[54] exists to resolve commercial disputes relating to intellectual property.

Supranational organizations such as the EU may also regulate disputes between their members. Likewise, treaties may provide for international resolution and enforcement. The Model Law on Electronic Commerce by the United Nations Commission of International Trade Law (UNCITRAL) has been established to provide for global uniformity in digital commerce. This developing collection of laws addresses such matters as digital signatures, electronic documentation, sales of digital goods, contracts, exchanges of information, and credit records. The force of such model laws comes through their actual adoption or through the pressure that they can exert upon national legislatures and other organizations to conform to international standards. Although acceptance of jurisdiction cannot be forced upon noncooperating countries, the weight of international agreements concerning key questions favors the mutual enforcement of obligations.

Fraud

The use of deception and false claims to obtain profit is, of course, not unique to the internet. However, the nature of online dynamics introduces several factors that affect prevention efforts. The first general factor relates to the technical nature of networked communication. The average person is not in a position to understand exactly how information is displayed, transferred, or stored, and this lack of knowledge provides opportunities for novel deceptions. Included within this category is the use of e-mail or Web sites to impersonate individuals or corporations. This activity, known as **spoofing**, is often used to extract sensitive information by leading a user to believe that a request is coming from a reputable source, such as an ISP or credit card company. Other common swindles involve the use of programs that secretly dial long-distance locations for which the unknowing user pays the fees, or false login pages that record account information.

A second factor involves the psychology of digital environments. The media is full of stories concerning technological advances and opportunities for profit. Unfortunately, many people are unable to differentiate genuinely worthwhile endeavors from those presented by mere opportunists. Messages originating from the online world are likely to be viewed by some as having an air of authority, solely due to their association with the digital revolution. Many investment opportunities make use of this rhetoric, often promoting breakthrough technologies and applications.

The problem of consumer **fraud** is being addressed on several dimensions. Federal agencies such as the FTC and the FBI have increased their efforts to track and prosecute fraudulent conduct (Exhibit 5.4). Likewise, many state agencies have begun to prosecute criminal activity within their borders. The range of sanctions available includes stipulated lifetime bans in the conduct of internet commerce, civil judgments, forfeiture of property, and referrals for criminal prosecution. A recent FTC action report lists 301 cases pursued against companies and individuals involving the internet and other online services. [55] Similar initiatives have been undertaken by authorities of other countries.

The basis of fraud is usually incomplete or false information. Thus, a consumer's ability to evaluate online material is essential. Promotion and adherence to codes of ethics, such as those promulgated by the AMA, are one means of inspiring consumer confidence. Codes may include requirements that members refrain from doing business with questionable clients or third parties. Many online and real-world businesses, particularly those within the finance and credit industry, require that their licensees follow strict legal and ethical protocols and may withdraw affiliation in cases of violation.

Although the establishment and enforcement of laws are necessary responses to the problem of fraud, the internet's global reach continues to frustrate even the most comprehensive of enforcement plans. On the other hand, a weakness of purely private regulation is the potential for conflicts of interest or less than rigorous enforcement of rules. Recent revelations of unpunished violations by members of eTrust, the internet's largest nongovernmental privacy watchdog, have caused many to wonder whether industry-based enforcement is truly possible.

Even though law must frequently play a reactive role, the conditions of the online environment create unique opportunities for marketing professionals to educate potential victims of fraud. Professional associations have particular abilities to establish sites that outline and explain minimum standards and consumer protections. They may also serve as clearinghouses, reporting unethical or illegal conduct. Even within the information-rich environment of the internet, online knowledge continues to be a need without limits.

EXHIBIT 5.4   FBI Investigates Online Fraud

Source: http://www.fbi.gov/cyberinvest/websnare.htm.

Chapter Summary

Ethics is concerned with the values and practices of professionals and experts, as well as the concerns and values of society. Law is also an expression of values but created for the broader goal of addressing national or even global populations. Groups of individuals with special skills or knowledge have established ethical codes over the years. Differing views exist of the role of law and self-regulation in ethical online behavior.

The notion of privacy emerged during the twentieth century as a key ethical and legal concern. Key aspects include seclusion, access control, and autonomy. Online privacy issues in the United States and other countries relate to how data should be collected and used. U.S. firms can participate in a safe harbor plan to protect data from EU internet users. The FTC set forth five norms for ethical use of consumer information, including provisions for user notice, consent, access, security, and enforcement.

Intangible or intellectual property is protected through three basic legal mechanisms: patent law (covering inventions), copyright (covering the expression of ideas), and trademark (covering images, symbols, words, or other indicators associated with a product's market identity). A company can license its intellectual property, while restricting unauthorized duplication or distribution. Companies are concerned about legal protection for trade secrets and about the ownership of information such as Web site content, usage data, and facts. Online expression issues include concerns about spam, criticisms of products or industries, and expression directed to children. Three emerging legal and ethical issues are online governance, jurisdiction, and fraud.

Changes within the ethical and legal framework of networked communication are occurring with swiftness equal to the technical, economic, and social transformations this medium has brought about. As critical participants within the online world, marketing professionals will not only be required to remain well informed of regulations and accepted practices but also be increasingly called upon to contribute to the global dialogue on electronic spaces.

Note: Chapter footnotes appear at end of reference list in Appendix D.

Exercises

REVIEW QUESTIONS

1. Define ethics and law and show how they are different and similar.
2. What are some of the threats to internet user privacy?
3. According to the FTC, what are the minimum requirements for ethical use of consumer information?
4. How does copyright differ from patent and trademark law?
5. What does it mean to clickwrap a license?
6. What are the NET Act and the DMCA?
7. What is the doctrine of first sale? How should it be applied online?
8. What is the doctrine of fair use and how should it be applied online?
9. What are the EU safe harbor provisions and why are they important for U.S. companies doing business in Europe?

DISCUSSION QUESTIONS

10. Is it better to regulate industry via laws or let industry self-regulate? Support your claim.
11. Which is more ethically problematic: attacking a former employer via online discussion or making the same attack by e-mailing current employees?
12. Deep linking takes place regularly over the internet. Anytime you make a Web page that links to another site and bypasses the home page of that site, you are deep linking. Should this practice be allowed? Explain your position.
13. Framing takes place regularly over the internet. To see an example of framing, look up information at AskJeeves (www.ask.com). Should framing be allowed? Support your claim.
14. The CEO of Amazon publicly questioned the advisability of granting patents for business processes such as his company's 1-Click ordering process. Do such patents put a chilling effect on the expansion of e-commerce? Justify your position.
15. What court should have jurisdiction over the internet? Why?

WEB ACTIVITIES

16. Visit DoubleClick at www.doubleclick.com. Do you find any of its services ethically objectionable? Why or why not?
17. Visit the FTC site at www.ftc.gov. What cases is it currently reviewing that relate to the internet? Describe several and give your opinion about how the agency should rule.
18. The World Wide Web is a borderless medium that spans the globe. Check out the Internet Law and Policy Forum at www.ilpf.org. What attempts have been made to regulate the internet both domestically and overseas? What kind of problems may arise concerning jurisdiction and enforcement in a medium that spans the globe? Jurisdiction is typically based on the location of Web servers. What recourse do users have if they are wronged in activities such as gambling and if the servers are physically located outside the United States? What about spam outside the United States?
19. Visit www.epinions.com and www.amazon.com, and review their privacy policies. What sorts of things do they cover? Which one has a better policy in your opinion?

Portions of this chapter were contributed by Brett J. Trout, Esq. (Bretttrout.com). In 2006, Trout's popular blog BlawgIT.com was voted sixth best law blog in the world by Weblog Awards. His additions and edits are based on his experiences counseling internet-based clients on patent, copyright, and trademark issues. Trout is the author of several books on internet law, including Cyberlaw: A Legal Arsenal for Online Business.

PART THREE

E-Marketing Strategy

CHAPTER 6

E-Marketing Research

*Getting information off the internet is like taking a drink from
a fire hydrant.*

—MITCH KAPOR, CHAIR OF THE OPEN
SOURCE APPLICATIONS FOUNDATION

There's a long way from data to knowledge.

—CLIFFORD STOLL, AUTHOR

Chapter Outline

The main objective of this chapter is to develop an understanding of why and how e-marketers turn e-marketing research into marketing knowledge. You will learn about the three categories of internet data sources, consider the ethics of online research, discover ways to monitor social media, look at key database analysis techniques, and explore the use of knowledge management metrics.

After reading this chapter, you will be able to:

▪ Identify the three main sources of data that e-marketers use to address research problems.

▪ Discuss how and why e-marketers need to check the quality of research data gathered online.

▪ Explain why the internet is used as a contact method for primary research and describe the main internet-based approaches to primary research.

▪ Describe several ways to monitor the Web for gathering desired information.

▪ Contrast client-side data collection, server-side data collection, and real-space approaches to data collection.

▪ Highlight four important methods of analysis that e-marketers can apply to information in the data warehouse.

The Purina Story

Nestlé Purina PetCare Company knows with certainty that Purina Web sites and online advertising increase off-line buying. How? Through a carefully conducted study that integrated online and off-line behavioral data.

Switzerland-based Nestlé S.A. purchased the Ralston Purina Company in December, 2001, gaining a full line of dog- and cat-care brands such as Friskies, Alpo, Purina Dog Chow, and Fancy Feast. The firm manages more than 30

(continued)

(*continued*)

branded Web sites serving the following markets: consumers, veterinarians/veterinary schools, nutritionists/food scientists, and breeders/other enthusiasts. Nestlé started its inquiry with three research questions:

1. Are our buyers using our branded Web sites?
2. Should we invest beyond these branded Web sites in online advertising?
3. If so, where do we place that advertising?

Combining comScore Media Metrix's representative panel of 1.5 million internet consumers and the Knowledge Networks, Inc., frequent-grocery-shopper panel of 20 million households revealed 50,000 consumers belonging to both panels. Researchers created three experimental cells from survey panel members, two receiving Purina O.N.E. banner advertising as they naturally surfed the internet: a control cell (no ads), a low-exposure test cell (1 to 5 exposures), and a high-exposure test cell (6 to 20 exposures). Banner ads were randomly sent as exposure-cell subjects viewed Web pages anywhere on the internet. Next, the firm surveyed all cell members to assess Purina brand awareness, purchase intent, and advertising awareness. Finally, the researchers compared survey results with off-line buying, as measured in the Knowledge Networks panel.

Nestlé's marketers were very interested in the study's findings. First, banner click-through was low (0.06% on average). Second, when study participants were asked, "When thinking of dog food, what brand first comes to mind?" 31 percent of both exposure-cell subjects mentioned Purina. In contrast, only 22 percent of the no-exposure subjects mentioned the brand; this result clearly showed an advertising effect. Further, 7 percent more of the subjects in the high-exposure group mentioned the brand compared with those in the low-exposure group. Next, researchers reviewed the internet panel's Web site viewing habits for those who purchased Purina products and determined that home/health and living sites receive the most visits from these customers. This information helped the firm decide where to place banner ads. Among those, petsmart.com and about.com enjoy heavy usage and would be great ad buys.

DATA DRIVE STRATEGY

Organizations are drowning in data. Marketers spent about 1.5 billion in 2006 tracking consumers' online behavior, according to *Business 2.0*. This will buy a lot of data. Information overload is a reality for most consumers and marketers alike. It is an especially difficult problem for marketing decision makers as they gather survey results, product sales information, secondary data about competitors, and much more. The problem is compounded by automated data gathering at Web sites, brick-and-mortar points of purchase, and all other customer touch points. What to do with all the data? Purina marketers sorted through lots of consumer data to build a road map for their internet advertising strategy.

Exhibit 6.1 displays an overview of this process. Data are collected from a myriad of sources, filtered into databases, and turned into marketing knowledge that is then used to create marketing strategy. This chapter discusses internet data sources, describes important database analysis techniques, and most importantly, examines the purposes and payoffs for all this work. Most of these techniques are well grounded in marketing practice; however, new technology brings new applications that are both helpful and confusing for market researchers.

This chapter discusses the *source* and *databases* areas in Exhibit 6.1; Chapters 8 and 9 focus on tier 1 e-marketing strategies of segmentation, targeting, differentiation, and positioning. Tier 2 strategies are covered in Part IV; because performance metrics permeate each of these processes, the relevant metrics are described in most chapters.

Data growth rates are astounding, at about 80 percent a year, necessitating an increasing

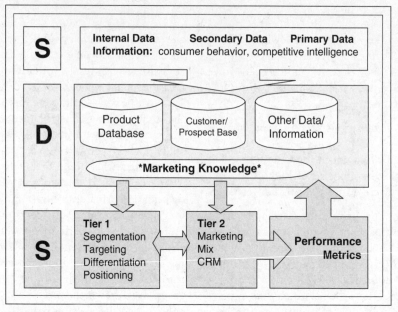

EXHIBIT 6.1 From Sources to Databases to Strategy (SDS model)

amount of storage hardware space (e.g., data ware-houses). This presents a problem for information technology managers, and e-marketers must deter-mine how to glean insights from these billions of bytes. In just the third quarter of 2007, the capacity of disk storage systems sold came to 1.3 exabytes, according to market intelligence firm IDC (one exabyte is a million terabytes). What does this mean? A character, such as the letter A, is 10 bits of data or 1 byte; a kilobyte (1 KB) of data is about

1,024 bytes; a megabyte (MB) is about 1 million bytes; a gigabyte is about 1 billion bytes; a terabyte is a thousand billion bytes (or 1,000 gigabytes); and an Exabytes are, well, a lot more data.

The Purina research vignette is a good example of how a firm sorts through hundreds of millions of pieces of data from about 21.5 million consumers, collects even more data, and makes decisions (Exhibit 6.2). Organizations must go through this process with all the data they collect,

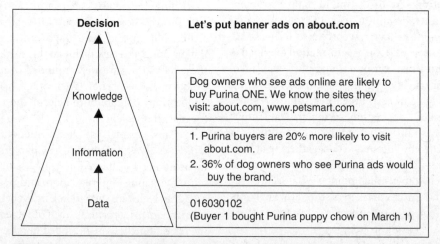

EXHIBIT 6.2 From Data to Decision at Nestle Purina PetCare Company

or their data will simply be an overwhelming bunch of facts and numbers.

Marketing insight occurs somewhere between information and knowledge. Knowledge is more than a collection of information but something that resides in the marketer, not the computer. It can be compared to the difference between teaching and learning. A professor might spout information in a lecture or from a textbook, but it is not usable unless the student ponders it, relates it to other pieces of information, and adds insights that result in acquired and useful knowledge. People, not the internet or computers, create knowledge; computers are simply learning enablers.

MARKETING KNOWLEDGE MANAGEMENT

Knowledge management is the process of managing the creation, use, and dissemination of knowledge. Thus, data, information, and knowledge are shared with internal marketing decision makers, partners, distribution channel members, and sometimes customers. When other stakeholders can access selected knowledge, the firm becomes a learning organization and is better able to reach desired ROI and other performance goals. Such was the case when Dell created its IdeaStorm blog (Chapter 1).

Marketing knowledge is the digitized "group mind" or "collective memory" of the marketing personnel and sometimes of consultants, partners, and former employees as well. Sometimes the knowledge management technology even allows marketing staff to chat in real time for problem solving, which is why the system also includes contact information. For example, a Context Integration consultant working on an e-commerce problem at the client's offices can enter a "911" help call into the Web page and immediately chat with other internal experts to solve the problem. A complete marketing knowledge database includes all the data about customers, prospects, and competitors, the analyses and outputs based on the data, and access to marketing experts, all available 24/7 through a number of digital

receiving appliances. Consider these examples, and those in Exhibit 6.3:

- An international technology firm uses Salesforce.com to manage the sales pipeline. When someone downloads a white paper from the Web site, registers online, or sends an e-mail inquiry, it goes into the Salesforce.com software for all salespeople and managers to view—and pick up contact information for e-mail or phone follow-up. The CEO gets a text message for each new lead.
- An insurance firm with 200 independent agents allows them access to claim data from more than 1 million customers. This access allows the agents to avoid high-risk customers as well as to compare claim data with their own database of customers.
- i-Go, a catalog marketer and online retailer, integrates incoming customer service calls with Web purchases, e-mail inquiries, and fax and postal orders, allowing customer service representatives to have up-to-date information when talking with customers.
- Context Integration maintains a $10 million knowledge management system that serves daily customized electronic newsletters to its 200 marketing consultants, provides a searchable database of previous projects and experts, and allows online chats with experts and employees.

The Electronic Marketing Information System

A **marketing information system (MIS)** is the process by which marketers manage knowledge. The MIS is a system of assessing information needs, gathering information, analyzing it, and disseminating it to marketing decision makers. The process begins when marketing managers have a problem that requires data to solve. The next step is to gather the data from internal sources, from secondary sources, or by conducting primary marketing research. The process is complete when these managers receive the needed information in a timely manner and usable form. For example, Web advertisers need audience statistics prior to

Use in the Telecom Industry	Representative Firm
Scanner Check-Out Data Analysis	AT&T
Call Volume Analysis	Ameritech
Equipment Sales Analysis	Belgacom
Customer Profitability Analysis	British Telecom
Cost and Inventory Analysis	Telestra Australia
Purchasing Leverage with Suppliers	Telecom Ireland
Frequent-Buyer Program Management	Telecom Italia
Use in the Retail Industry	**Representative Firm**
Scanner Check-Out Data Analysis	Wal-Mart
Sales Promotion Tracking	Kmart
Inventory Analysis and Deployment	Sears
Price Reduction Modeling	Osco/Savon Drugs
Negotiating Leverage with Suppliers	Casino Supermarkets
Frequent-Buyer Program Management	W. H. Smith Books
Profitability Analysis	Otto Versand Mail Order
Product Selection for Markets	Amazon.com

EXHIBIT 6.3 Uses of Knowledge Management in Two Industries

Source: Adapted from Ravi Kalakota and Marcia Robinson, *E-Business: Roadmap for Success* (Reading, MA: Addison-Wesley, 1999).

deciding where to purchase online display ad space (the problem). They want to know how many people in their target market view various Web sites to evaluate the value of Web ads versus TV and other media ads (information need). One way to get this information is through secondary sources such as comScore or Nielsen//NetRatings. Such firms rate Web sites by researching the internet usage habits of large panels of consumers. Web advertisers use the data to make effective and efficient Web media buys.

In the past, marketers needing answers asked information technology or information systems personnel what software they had on the shelf. Today, however, e-marketing actually drives technology change. E-marketing changed the MIS landscape in several ways. First, many firms store electronic marketing data in databases and **data warehouses**. These data warehouses enable marketers to obtain valuable, appropriate, and tailored information anytime—day or night. Second, marketers can receive database information in Web pages and e-mail on a number of appliances in addition to the desktop computer: pagers, fax machines, PDAs such as the Palm Treo, and even cellular phones. Third, customers also have access to portions of the database. For example, when consumers visit Amazon.com, they can query the product database for book titles and also receive information about their account status and past book purchases. Business customers, channel members, and partners often have access to customer sales data to facilitate product planning. Customer inquiries are usually automated, with personalized Web pages created instantaneously from customer databases. Finally, most firms recognize that data and information are useless unless turned into knowledge to increase profits. Therefore, cutting-edge firms make one employee's project reports, proposals, and data analyses available to other stakeholders in the MIS network. In sum, all the data, the output from their use, and stakeholders' contact information that are gathered via an MIS comprise a firm's marketing knowledge.

The internet and other technologies greatly facilitate marketing data collection. Internal records give marketing planners excellent insights about sales and inventory movement. **Secondary** data help marketers understand competitors, consumers, the economic environment, political and legal factors, technological forces, and other factors in the macroenvironment affecting an organization. Marketing planners use the internet, the telephone, product **bar code scanners**, and other technologies to collect **primary data** about consumers. Through online e-mail and Web surveys, online experiments, **focus groups**, and observation of internet user discussions, marketers learn about both current and prospective customers.

Exhibit 6.4 displays the most commonly used primary data collection methods, according to a MarketResearchCareers.com survey. **Syndicated research** is data collected regularly using a systematic process, such as the Nielsen Television Ratings. Companies purchase syndicated research as a part of their secondary data-gathering efforts. Scanner data are collected at the point of sale, such as a grocery store cash register with a universal product code scanner—you'll learn more about this in the "Real-Space Approaches" section later in this chapter. All of the approaches in this exhibit benefit from online methods except for focus group research.

Source 1: Internal Records

Internal records, such as sales data (Exhibit 6.4), comprise one important source of marketing knowledge. Accounting, finance, and production

personnel collect and analyze data that provide valuable information for marketing planning. The marketing department itself collects and maintains much relevant information about customer characteristics and activities. For example, logistics personnel use the internet to track product shipment through distribution channels, information that can help marketers improve the order-to-delivery and payment cycles.

SALES DATA Sales data come from accounting systems and the company Web site log. When a customer purchases online, this transaction is recorded in a database for access. Marketing managers review and analyze these data to determine conversion rates (proportion of visitors who purchase online) and to see if online ads and other communication are driving sales.

Sales information systems, often using sales force automation software (such as Salesforce.com), allow representatives to input results of sales calls to both prospects and current customers into the MIS. Many sales reps use their laptop computers to access the product and customer databases both for input and review of customer records while on the road. For example, one office products firm has salespeople from different divisions calling on the same large customer. When the customer has a complaint, the sales rep must enter it into the database and other reps review the customer record

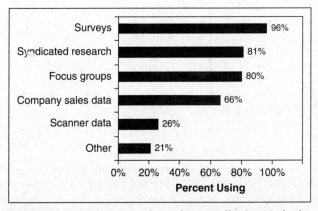

EXHIBIT 6.4 Most Commonly Used Data Collection Methods
Source: Data from MarketResearchCareers.com.

prior to making a visit to the same customer. This firm has a rule: If four reps record the same complaint, a warning is issued and they must immediately visit the customer as a team and solve the problem. Sales reps are also instrumental in entering competitive and industry information gained in the field. For a few cutting-edge firms, marketers enter proposals, reports, and papers written on various topics into the knowledge database.

CUSTOMER CHARACTERISTICS AND BEHAVIOR

Perhaps the most important internal marketing data involve individual customer activity. For instance, Exhibit 6.5 gives a hypothetical scenario for a computer company that collects data from its customers online and by telephone, and uses the information to improve products. At a minimum, database entries include an electronic list of customers and prospective customers, along with their addresses, phone numbers, and purchase behavior. Firms have used this technique for many years, but new storage and retrieval technologies, and the availability of large amounts of electronic

information, recently escalated its growth. For example, visitors to Expedia are asked to register before using its services. This firm has a large database that includes e-mail addresses, customer characteristics, and Web viewing and purchase behavior. Each customer file in a database might also include a record of calls made to customer service reps, product service records, specific problems or questions related to various products, and other data such as coupon and other promotional offer redemption. A complete customer record will include data from every customer touch point (contact with the company), including internet orders and e-mail interaction, and product purchases and coupon redemption at the grocery store. Data on in-store behavior are gathered through scanning **universal product codes (UPCs)**, or bar codes, on products. Firms use the data in customer databases to improve sales rep effectiveness, refine the product mix, identify optimum pricing for individual products, assess promotion effectiveness, and signal distribution opportunities. For example: Have you ever

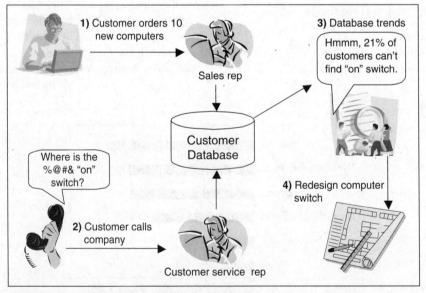

EXHIBIT 6.5 E-Marketers Learn from Customers

Source: Adaptation of ideas from Brain Caulfied (2001), "Facing up to CRM" at www.business2.com.

wondered why the local retailer asks for a ZIP code when you make a purchase? The retailer adds this information to the marketing database and uses it to decide whether a new store location might be profitable.

Many firms with Web sites track user movement through the pages and use these data to improve site effectiveness. By knowing how long users spend on each page, how long they are at the site, and what path they take through the site, Web developers can reorganize pages and content frequently and in a timely manner. In addition, firms can identify the Web site users visited immediately before and after the firm's site. This information provides competitive insights, especially if a user is reviewing particular products. These data are all generated automatically in the Web site logs and can be part of a firm's marketing databases. FedEx is especially adroit at gathering customer information automatically using electronic networks. Through its Web site, customers can dispatch a courier for package pickup, locate drop-off points, track shipments, obtain shipping rates, prepare shipping documents, and request a signature proof of delivery in many different languages. All this information can be analyzed by FedEx's marketers for planning purposes. FedEx maintains an extranet for frequent shippers, providing them with individualized rate books and other special services. In addition, FedEx maintains an intranet hub that serves over 20,000 visitors a month for human resources management and workplace and marketplace integration—a thorough system of internal data input for effective marketing knowledge management.

Source 2: Secondary Data

When faced with a need for specific information not available in company or partner databases, the e-marketer first looks for secondary data, which can be collected more quickly and less expensively than primary data—especially on the internet, where up-to-date information from more than 200 countries is available 24/7, from home or work, delivered in a matter of seconds.

Syndicated research is available via the internet with a credit card sign-up and password entry.

On the other hand, secondary data may not meet the e-marketer's information needs, because they were usually gathered for a different purpose than the one at hand. Another common problem is the quality of secondary data. Marketers have no control over data collection procedures, so they should always evaluate the quality of secondary data. Finally, secondary data are often out of date. The U.S. Census Bureau provides numerous population statistics; its heavy data collection periods occur only every 10 years, and results will not appear on the Web site until a year or two later. A marketer using data from www.census.gov must read the fine print to see when the data were collected (Exhibit 6.6).

Marketers continually scan the firm's macroenvironment for threats and opportunities. This procedure is commonly called **business intelligence**. What type of information do marketing managers need? An environmental scan seeks market information about the following:

- Demographic trends
- Competitors
- Technological forces
- Natural resources
- Social and cultural trends
- World and local economies
- Legal and political environments

For example, a firm wanting to understand the characteristics and behavior of the Generation Y demographic group can visit the U.S. Census Bureau site, read appropriate articles in online magazines and newspapers, and monitor Web sites such as MTV and www.gurl.com that target this group. The following sections present examples of public and private sources of data about the firm's macroenvironment.

PUBLICLY GENERATED DATA Most U.S. agencies provide online information in their respective areas. The U.S. Patent Office home page can explain how to apply for a patent and research pending trademarks. Many global organizations,

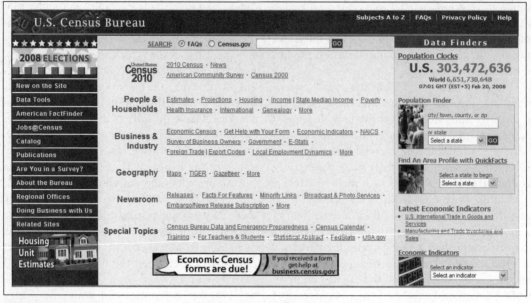

EXHIBIT 6.6 The Biggest Database of All: U.S. Census Bureau

Source: www.census.gov.

such as the International Monetary Fund (www.imf.org), are also good sources of data for environmental scans involving countries other than the United States. Generally speaking, however, U.S. agencies collect and disseminate a great deal more data than do governments in other countries. For example, the *CIA World Factbook* is an excellent source of information on internet adoption in every country. In the not-for-profit category, most universities provide extensive information through their libraries, and many faculty post their research results online. Finally, industry-or profession-specific information is available at the sites of professional associations such as the American Marketing Association (www.marketingpower.com).

Wikipedia, a social media database with over 9 million articles, is edited by some 75,000 contributors in 250 languages (see www.wikipedia.org). Many other wikis exist to provide specialized information, such as Wikihow.com, with 30,000 articles about how to do just about anything from building a workbench to making a voodoo doll. Most of this public information is free and available to all

internet users. A sampling of important public sites is displayed in Exhibit 6.7.

PRIVATELY GENERATED DATA Company Web sites provide a great overview of the firm's mission, products, partners, and current events. Individuals often maintain sites with useful information about companies as well. Politicians and other public figures create sites containing commentary about political issues. A growing source of current information and commentary comes from leading bloggers in various industries, such as well-known marketing author Seth Godin's blog (sethgodin.typepad.com/).

Another good resource is large research firms, such as comScore and Forrester Research, which put sample statistics and press releases on their sites as a way to entice users to purchase full research reports. Nielsen//NetRatings posts the top Web sites and advertisers in a survey period. Several large research firms now also offer e-mail newsletters that are sent automatically to subscriber desktops. For e-business information, free newsletters from the Interactive Advertising Bureau (www.iab.net) and

Web Site	Information
Stat-USA www.stat-usa.gov	U.S. Department of Commerce source of international trade data.
U.S. Patent Office www.uspto.gov	Provides trademark and patent data for businesses.
World Trade Organization www.wto.org	World trade data.
International Monetary Fund www.imf.org	Provides information on many social issues and projects.
Mohanbir Sawhney and Dave Chaffey www.mohansawhney.com http://www.davechaffey.com/	Academics who generously publish many e-marketing articles on their Web sites.
Securities and Exchange Commission www.sec.gov	Edgar database provides financial data on U.S. public corporations.
Small Business Administration www.sba.gov	Features information and links for small business owners.
University of Texas at Austin advertising.utexas.edu/world	Ad world with lots of links in the ad industry.
Federal Trade Commission www.ftc.gov	Shows regulations and decisions related to consumer protection and antitrust laws.
U.S. Census www.census.gov	Provides statistics and trends about the U.S. population.

EXHIBIT 6.7 Sample of Public Data Sources in the United States

ClickZ (www.clickz.com) are especially helpful. Although often incomplete, these tidbits of information are generally useful in an environmental scan and help marketers decide whether to purchase the full report.

Commercial online databases contain publicly available information that can be accessed via the internet. Thousands of databases are available online covering news, industry data, encyclopedias, airline routes and fares, Yellow Page directories, e-mail addresses, and much more. Marketers increasingly access syndicated data via the internet from well-respected firms such as the Nielsen Media television ratings, the Simmons annual survey of over 20,000 consumers, and the SRDS (Standard Rate and Data Service) listings of media advertising rates and specifications. Students access articles from a number of respected media via the university library databases from home—using the internet.

Note that many of these databases are not available on Web pages but are simply electronic versions of articles and other information ordinarily found in the library. Some databases are free but others charge a fee for access.

See Exhibit 6.8 for a sample of privately generated data sites.

COMPETITIVE INTELLIGENCE EXAMPLE Competitive intelligence (CI) involves analyzing the industries in which a firm operates as input to the firm's strategic positioning and to understand competitor vulnerabilities. According to Fuld & Co., 40 percent of all firms regularly conduct CI

Web Site	Information
ACNielsen Corporation www.acnielsen.com	Television audience, supermarket scanner data, and more.
The Gartner Group www.gartnergroup.com	Specializes in e-business and usually presents highlights of its latest findings on the Web site.
Information Resources, Inc. http://us.infores.com/	Supermarket scanner data and new-product purchasing data.
Arbitron www.arbitron.com	Local market and internet radio audience data.
The Commerce Business Daily cbdnet.access.gpo.gov	Lists of government requests for proposals online.
Simmons Market Research Bureau www.smrb.com	Media and ad spending data.
Dun & Bradstreet www.dnb.com	Database on more than 50 million companies worldwide.
LEXIS-NEXIS www.lexis-nexis.com	Articles from business, consumer, and marketing publications.
Hoovers Online www.hoovers.com	Business descriptions, financial overviews, and news about major companies worldwide.

EXHIBIT 6.8   Sampling of Privately Generated Data Sources in the United States

activities (www.fuld.com). Specialists at Fuld suggest the following intelligence cycle:

1. Define intelligence requirements.
2. Collect and organize information.
3. Analyze by applying information to the specific purpose and recommending action.
4. Report and inform others of the findings.
5. Evaluate the impact of intelligence use and suggest process improvements.

The Fuld & Co. Web site includes a thorough review of software to aid in CI activities as well as seminars on the topic. Astutely they note: "Technical tools without the right processes become shelfware!"

A few sources of CI include competitor press releases, new products, alliances and co-brands, trade show activity, and advertising strategies. The internet simplified CI. Firms can observe competitive marketing strategies right on competitors' Web sites and can sometimes catch announcements of

new products or price changes prior to media reports about them.

Marketers should be sure to check the Web sites linked to competitors' pages. For this activity, simply type *link:companyname.com* at Yahoo!, Google, or other search tools offering this protocol. The result is a list of links that may provide insight: Why are these sites linking to the competitor? Another technology-enabled CI activity involves analyzing a firm's Web site log to see which Web page users visited immediately prior to and after visiting the company's site. If, for example, Honda marketing managers noticed that a user visited the Toyota Matrix Web page prior to checking out Honda models, they would gain a consumer perspective on competitive shopping behavior. In a later section, we discuss online monitoring techniques in more detail.

Third-party, industry-specific sites can also provide timely information about competitive activities. An airline will monitor online travel agents to watch competitive pricing and route changes (e.g., Expedia and Travelocity) and social media sites such as Tripadvisor.com (where travelers post hotel reviews). Company profiles for public firms are available in the SEC's online EDGAR database as well as at many investment firm sites (e.g., E*TRADE).

Another valuable source of CI comes from user conversation, as will be discussed in the primary data collection section later—Google Groups offers Web access to more than 800,000 bulletin board postings by Web users, and firms can often find consumer conversation about competitive product strengths and weaknesses via keyword searches. Industry newsletters include comments from professionals in their industries, and combing through the many e-mail queries and responses can yield insights. A list called ELMAR, for instance, sends weekly edited e-mails from marketing educators discussing research, teaching, and job openings at universities worldwide.

INFORMATION QUALITY Secondary and primary data are subject to many limitations; thus, marketers should use all information with caution and with a full understanding of how the data were collected. It is advisable to be as objective as possible when reviewing data prior to using it for making marketing decisions—especially before using information on Web pages. Why? Because anyone can easily publish on the Web without being reviewed by a publisher or being screened for accuracy or appropriateness. Special care is needed when dealing with secondary data from international sources because of cultural and data collection differences.

E-marketers should not be seduced by good design: The best-designed sites may not be the most accurate or credible, and vice versa. For example, the Securities and Exchange Commission publishes reports filed by public companies in simple text, spending little taxpayer money to make them pretty. Two librarians at the University at Albany, SUNY (library.albany.edu/briggs/addiction.html), created a fake Web page to show just how easy it is to get fooled (Exhibit 6.9). Interestingly, this site was online for nearly 10 years before the authors had to take it down because so many people "misunderstood" its purpose, thinking it was a real site. The following

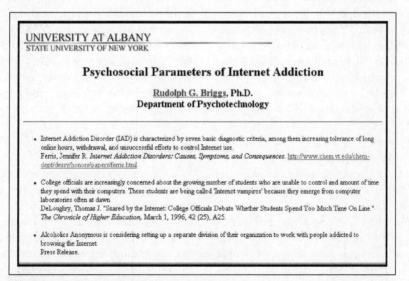

EXHIBIT 6.9   A Real Web Page?

Source: Laura B. Cohen and Trudi E. Jacobson at library.albany.edu/briggs/addiction.html.

steps can be taken to evaluate the quality of secondary data collected online (some of this information is from the Albany site):

- *Discover the Web site's author.* A site published by a government agency or well-known corporation has more credibility than one by an unknown author. Sometimes discerning the difference is quite tricky: For example, the same musical group usually has a number of sites—some official and some published by individual fans. A search in Google for "Rolling Stones" yielded more than 44 million results. Which of these sites are authorized by the group?
- *Try to determine whether the site author is an authority on the Web site topic.* For example, an economist from Harvard University or Merrill Lynch might have more credible information about interest rates than a politician. Furthermore, the university's Web site may be more objective than the financial firm's site.
- *Check to see when the site was last updated.* Many Web sites change every day, but some have not been maintained for years. Obviously, the more current the information is, the more useful it will be for decision making. Check the hyperlinks. Although many sites contain occasional broken links, a site with many inoperative links is a site that has not been updated recently.
- *Determine how comprehensive the site is.* Does it cover only one aspect of a topic, or does it consider the broader context?
- *Try to validate the research data by finding similar information at other sources on the internet or in hard copy at the library.* If the same statistics are not available elsewhere, look for other ways to validate the data. For example, one validation of the number of people with internet service providers might be to check the number of people with computers (the latter should be larger). In general it is also a good idea to compare sites that cover the same topic.
- *Check the site content for accuracy.* If it has lots of errors or if the numbers don't add

properly, it is a sign that the data cannot be trusted.

Don't stop looking when the first good screen full of hyperlinks appears. Remember that this site is only one of many potential sites to research, and the list of related hyperlinks is provided as a service—so these sites are not necessarily the best sources for the topic.

What about Wikipedia . . . is it accurate? Students like to use this site in their research, and many professors believe it is not accurate because all content is created and edited by **citizen journalists**—internet users who contribute their perspectives by posting content to online blogs, forums, and Web sites, usually without editorial review. *Nature*, an international science and medicine journal, conducted a study that compared articles from both Wikipedia and *Encyclopedia Britannica* for accuracy. *Nature* received 42 peer reviews from a preselected field of science experts and found that *Britannica* had 2.92 mistakes per article and Wikipedia had 3.86. However, Wikipedia articles were on average 2.6 times longer than the *Britannica* articles, indicating a lower error per word ratio in Wikipedia (Terdiman, 2005). Wikipedia is fairly accurate partially because there are 75,000 citizen journalists editing the articles and they keep each other from making too many errors. As with all Web pages, however, it is always better to check Wikipedia's original sources and validate the information by looking for similar work by other authors.

Source 3: Primary Data

When secondary data are not available to assist in marketing planning, marketing managers may decide to collect their own information. Primary data are information gathered for the first time to solve a particular problem. Gathering primary data is usually more expensive and time-consuming than it is to gather secondary data; on the other hand, the data are current and more relevant to the marketer's specific problem. In addition, primary data have the benefit of being proprietary and, thus, unavailable to competitors.

This section describes traditional approaches to primary data collection enhanced by the internet: experiments, focus groups, observation, and survey research. In-depth interviews (IDI) are another important form of primary data collection, but they are better done off-line because the questions tend to be less structured and more open-ended. A subsequent section discusses several other nontraditional primary data collection techniques only made possible by internet technologies. Whether collected on the internet or off-line, all electronic data gathered at any customer touch point (e.g., e-mail, telephone, Web site, grocery store purchase, and store kiosk) end up in a marketing database and become part of the marketing knowledge to be used for effective planning.

Each primary data collection method can provide important information, as long as e-marketers understand the limitations—one of which is that internet research can only collect information from people who use the internet, which leaves out nearly 30 percent of the U.S. population, and many more in other countries. As a review, we present the steps for conducting primary research and then discuss each approach along with its particular uses, strengths, and weaknesses.

PRIMARY RESEARCH STEPS A primary data collection project includes five steps (Exhibit 6.10).

1. **Research problem.** As with secondary data, specificity is vital. Exhibit 6.11 shows some typical e-marketing research problems that electronic data can help solve.
2. **Research plan.**
   - *Research approach.* On the basis of the information needed, researchers choose from among experiments, focus groups, observation techniques, and survey research, or nontraditional Web monitoring, real-time, and real-space techniques.
   - *Sample design.* At this stage researchers select the sample source and number of desired respondents.
   - *Contact method.* Ways to contact the sample include traditional methods such as the telephone, mail, and in person, as well as the internet and other technology-enabled approaches.
   - *Instrument design.* If a survey is planned, researchers develop a questionnaire. For other methods, researchers develop a protocol to guide the data collection.
3. **Data collection.** Researchers gather the information according to plan.
4. **Data analysis.** Researchers analyze the results in light of the original problem. This step includes using statistical software packages for traditional survey data analysis or data mining and other approaches to find patterns and test hypotheses in databases.
5. **Distribute findings/add to the database.** Research data might be placed in the marketing knowledge database and be presented in written or oral form to marketing managers.

INTERNET-BASED RESEARCH APPROACHES
The internet is fertile ground for primary data collection. One reason is declining cooperation from consumers when using traditional research approaches. Telephone survey refusal rates are between 40 and 60 percent, and an estimated 40 percent didn't answer the mailed 2000 U.S. Census. According to Fred Bove of Socratic Technologies, "Telemarketers ruined the telephone-interviewing enterprise" (Kasanoff and Thompson, 1999, p. 70). Conversely, with a large number of consumers online, conducting research using this inexpensive and quick method makes sense. According to a survey conducted by MarketResearchCareers.com, 29 percent of all market research dollars in 2007 were spent on

EXHIBIT 6.10   Primary Research Steps

Online Retailers	Web Sites
Improve online merchandising	Pages viewed most often
Forecast product demand	Increase time spent on site
Test new products	Increase number of comments posted to a blog
Test various price points	Path users take through the site
Test co-branding and partnership effectiveness	Site visit overall satisfaction efficient?
Measure affiliate program effectiveness	
Customers and Prospects	**Marketing Communication**
Identify new market segments	Test advertising copy
Measure loyalty among registered users	Test new promotions
Profile current customers	Number of white paper downloads
Test site-customization techniques	Measure display ad clickthrough

EXHIBIT 6.11   Typical Research Problems for E-Marketers

online methodologies (Exhibit 6.12). Another estimate puts online research at 17 percent of the $7.7 billion U.S. market research expenditures (Johnson, 2006). Here are three examples of successful online research:

- **Creative test.** Leo Burnett, the advertising agency, built a panel of 50 elementary schools for the purpose of testing advertising directed to the "kid" market. Burnett put some advertising posters online and sent e-mails directing students to the Web pages displaying the posters. After viewing the posters, students completed a survey to select the best one. In this test, more than 800 kids helped decide the best creative approach for the poster.
- **Customer satisfaction.** British Airways posted a questionnaire on its Web site to gather opinions of company services among Executive Club members. More than 9,000 people completed the questionnaire within nine months.
- **Product development.** The University of Nevada, Reno, posted a questionnaire on the marketing program Web site, inviting practitioners and academics to give opinions about what should be included in e-commerce programs at the university level; 140 respondents helped to shape new courses.

Marketers combine online and off-line data effectively and efficiently, as in the Purina example and as done by some brick-and-mortar retailers that also conduct e-commerce. This task involves merging data from older legacy systems, incoming call centers, retailer bar code scanners, government statistics, and many other places that are difficult to integrate. In one example, comScore Media Metrix installed PC meters on the computers of several thousand Information Resources, Inc. (IRI),

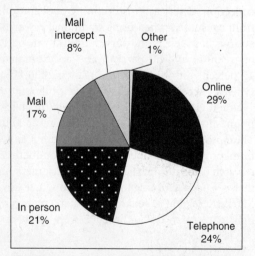

EXHIBIT 6.12   Proportion of Marketing Dollars Spent on Survey Research Methodologies

Source: Data from MarketResearchCareers.com.

Shoppers Hotline panel members. Web data include exposure to ads, sites visited, and purchasing frequency and patterns. These data are combined with off-line panel data: actual packaged goods purchased at brick-and-mortar grocery stores, as well as volume purchased, timing of purchases, promotional effectiveness, and brand loyalty.

In addition, primary data are collected online using experiments, focus groups, observations, in-depth interviews, and survey research, as discussed in the following sections.

Online Experiments Experimental research attempts to test cause-and-effect relationships, as in the Purina example. A researcher will select subjects, randomly put them into two or more groups, and then expose each group to different stimuli. The researcher then measures responses to the stimuli, usually in the form of a questionnaire, to determine whether differences exist among the groups. If the experiment has been carefully controlled (i.e., only the experimental stimuli have been varied), group differences can be attributed to the stimuli (cause and effect). Of course, these effects must be tested in other situations and with other subjects to determine their degree of generalizability.

Marketers can easily test alternative Web pages, display ads, and promotional offers online. For example, a firm might send e-mail notification of two different pricing offers, each to one half of its customer database. If a hyperlink to two different Web pages at the sponsoring firm's site is included in the e-mail, it will be quickly apparent which offer "pulls better."

Online Focus Groups Focus group research is a qualitative methodology that attempts to collect in-depth information from a small number of participants. Focus groups are often used to help marketers understand important feelings and behaviors prior to designing survey research. In the past many ad agencies tried to conduct group research online, but now qualitative research is just 1 percent of all online research spending (Johnson, 2006).

This contact method provides some advantages over traditional focus groups, where all participants are in one room. First, the internet can bring together people who do not live in the same geographic area, such as a focus group with consumers from five different countries discussing online shopping experiences. Second, because participants type their answers at the same time, they are not influenced as much by what others say (known as groupthink). Finally, by using the Web, researchers can show participants animated ads, demonstrate software, or use other multimedia stimuli to prompt group discussion.

Conversely, online focus groups can accommodate only four to eight participants at a time while traditional groups generally host 10 to 12. The reason behind the small group size is the difficulty in managing simultaneous, overlapping conversation online. Some researchers avoid this problem by using online bulletin boards and keeping focus groups going on for weeks. Also, nonverbal communication is lost online—in off-line groups facial expressions can be revealing in a way that typed smiley faces do not match. Another disadvantage of online groups is the authenticity problem. Without seeing people in person, it is difficult to be sure they are who they say they are. For example, it is quite common for children to pose as adults online. This dilemma can be solved by verifying respondent authenticity and requiring password entry to the group. Technical problems can also stall an online group. Finally, one study compared face-to-face, telephone, and online focus groups and found that subjects used stronger positive and negative words online than in other modalities—typing is different from speaking (Ponnaiya and Ponnaiya, 1999). These are the reasons for the decline in online focus group research.

King, Brown and Partners, a San Francisco research firm, conducts online focus groups for its clients (www.kingbrown.com) using this procedure:

- Contact potential participants via e-mail, asking them to go to a Web site and answer screening questions (e.g., the market may be teenagers in Europe who buy Levis).
- Send e-mail messages to qualified users, offering them money to participate in the group.

- Have clients and four to eight participants appear at an online site at the appointed time and day and have all greeted electronically by the moderator.
- Split the screen into two vertical portions: On the right, the moderator types questions and the participants type responses. Multimedia can also be presented on the right side. The left side is a "back room" where clients can communicate with each other and the moderator through their keyboards as the group progresses.

In another interesting example, Belgium research firm Synthetron, conducts simultaneous online focus groups with up to 200 participants each (www.synthetron.com). Participants type their opinions in response to questions, then everyone votes on the best responses, and collaborative filtering software sends these high-consensus views to another group working at the same time. The voting continues until the most agreed-with opinions percolate to the top and end up in the final report. This is the user four-step process:

1. Input your idea.
2. Read and evaluate the ideas of others (click on level of agreement).
3. React, bring nuance, depth and sharpness to the ideas you like by adding more opinion.
4. Click on a summary tab to reflect on all the best ideas generated thus far in the session.

Online Observation Observation research monitors people's behavior by watching them in relevant situations. For example, retailers videotape shoppers to see the pattern they choose in moving through the store and to monitor other shopping behaviors. Some researchers believe that actions speak louder than words, making customer observation stronger than surveys that record people's statements about what they believe and do. Of course, as a qualitative approach, observations of a small number of people cannot be used to describe how all people might act.

An interesting and important form of observational research, available only on the internet, involves monitoring consumer chatting and e-mail posting through chat rooms, bulletin boards, or mailing lists. One forum that predates the Web is the **Usenet**, consisting of more than 35,000 newsgroups, each a forum for public discussion on a specific topic—now hosted by Google Groups. People post articles to newsgroups for others to read. Discussions range from the meaningful to the absurd, but marketing planners can learn about products and industries by monitoring discussions. Companies can monitor the Google Groups to detect rumors circulating about them. This watchfulness enables the companies to quickly post a response and dispel rumors. To get an idea of the value of consumer observation, see Exhibit 6.13 for part of a discussion about the iPhone. Such information is extremely important for both Apple Computer and its competitors. Other ways to monitor customer chat are to provide space on the firm's Web site or to subscribe to e-mail lists on product-related topics.

Online Survey Research E-marketers conduct surveys by sending invitations to individuals via e-mail with a link to a survey form on the Web. Organizations draw a sample of e-mail addresses from its database, purchase a list, or simply present an invitation to visitors to the Web site. BizRate is a good example of a firm that has built its business using online survey research. BizRate presents Web questionnaires to a random sample of shoppers at client sites for the purpose of helping the sites improve marketing efforts. According to **MarketResearchCareers.com**, online survey research is now the most used methodology—drawing 29 percent of market research budgets.

Web Surveys Many companies post questionnaires on their Web pages. Respondents type answers into automated response mechanisms in the form of radio buttons (users click to indicate the response), drop-down menus, or blank areas for open-ended questions. One such Web survey was conducted to determine what topics should

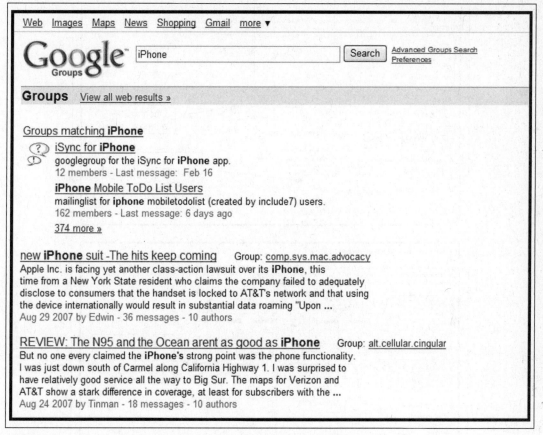

EXHIBIT 6.13   Consumers Discussing iPhones in Google Groups (formerly the Usenet)

Source: Courtesy of Google.com (www.groups.google.com).

be taught in e-commerce programs. Exhibit 6.14 displays question types from the Web survey. Sometimes the purpose of these questionnaires is to gather opinions from a site's visitors (e.g., Web site registration); sometimes it is a more formal survey research. For example, New Balance asks random Web site visitors to rate the importance and performance of various site features: customer service, navigation ease, product selection and prices, site security, and shopping. Through this process it learned that customers are willing to pay for shipping, which is why the firm added that element to the pricing structure.

Researchers will oftentimes post a Web survey and then send e-mail and use other forms of publicity to direct respondents to the Web site. The best response rates come from members of e-mail lists, such as customers and prospects, because they usually have a special interest in the topic. Advertising on electronic bulletin boards or via banner ads and links from other Web sites will also drive a small amount of traffic to a Web survey. For example, one firm placed a display ad on Yahoo! and received 1 percent click-through, which totaled 826 respondents. In general, response rates to online surveys are as good as or better than surveys using traditional approaches, sometimes reaching as much as 40 percent.

Online survey research has many advantages and disadvantages over traditional contact

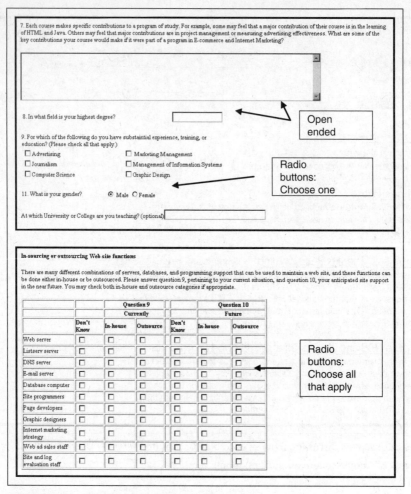

EXHIBIT 6.14 Mitchell and Strauss Web Survey

methods. Some are discussed in the next paragraphs; Exhibit 6.15 contains a more extensive list.

Online survey research is fast and inexpensive, especially when compared with traditional survey methodologies, perhaps its most important advantage. Questionnaires are delivered nearly instantaneously worldwide over the internet without paying for postage or an interviewer. Web surveys are converted to HTML files and do not need lengthy printing, collating, and mailing time. Those who complete the questionnaires generally do so in the first three days, making the entire process very quick. It is also easy to send multiple reminders if using e-mail invitations. Johnson

(2006) notes that "marketers historically have been able to cut costs 15 to 20 percent by moving from mail surveys to online and about 30 percent by shifting from phone surveys to online."

Some researchers believe that Web surveys reduce errors. For example, contingency questions are those that the computer automatically presents depending upon responses to previous questions. If a respondent answers "c" to question 9, the software can immediately skip three questions and present question 12. This technique reduces the complexity and time involved for respondents. In addition, respondents enter their answers, which eliminates data entry errors found in traditional

Advantages	Disadvantages
Fast and inexpensive	Sample selection/generalizability
Diverse, large group of internet users worldwide to small specialized niche	Measurement validity self-selection bias
Reduced researcher data entry errors because of respondent data entry	Respondent authenticity uncertain
Honest responses to sensitive questions	Frivolous or dishonest responses
Anyone-can-answer, invitation-only, or password protected	Duplicate submissions
Easy tabulation of electronic data	Declining response rates
Less interviewer bias	Perception that research solicitation is spam

EXHIBIT 6.15 Advantages and Disadvantages of Online Survey Research

methods when converting answers from paper questionnaires. In addition, some researchers have discovered that respondents will answer questions more honestly and openly on a computer than when an interviewer is present—and will answer sensitive questions about private matters over the internet. The reason may be that the computer is impersonal and no one is watching what the respondent types.

Sample representativeness and measurement validity are the biggest disadvantages of online surveys over their off-line counterparts (Miller, 2001). Marketers cannot draw a scientific probability sample because no list of internet users currently exists—unless the sample is only from a firm's customer list, they all use the internet, and the firm has all the e-mail addresses. In contrast, researchers employing in-person or mail contact methods have population lists and can draw probability samples. Although no public lists of all telephone numbers exists, random-digit-dialing technology solved the probability problem for this contact method. Without the ability to draw a random sample, researchers cannot generalize results to the entire population being studied. Therefore, researchers can send e-mail questionnaires to samples of respondents or put a Web survey online, but they must be careful when interpreting the results. What does it mean when 15,000 online survey participants click off the products they've shopped for online? How does the result relate to all Web users? This

problem is one of generalizability. Some firms, such as BizRate.com, compensate for sampling problems by offering the questionnaire to every *n*th visitor at a Web site. This technique works well if the firm wants information from a good sample of site visitors.

Online research entails several measurement issues. First, because of many different browsers, computer screen sizes, and resolution settings, researchers worry that colors will look different and measurement scales will not display properly online. On some computers, a scale from one to five might not have equidistant spaces between them, creating the image of different values. Second, a comparison study between telephone and online surveys found that online users were less likely to use the two extreme scale points on a five-point scale (i.e., the one and five were clicked less frequently) (Miller, 2001).

A majority of researchers is concerned about declining online research response rates and the quality of online survey data. To tackle this problem, MarketResearchCareers.com conducted a survey of research professionals in 2007. The 237 respondents supported the following solutions:

- "Limit the number of questions or time for survey completion (64%)
- Make surveys more engaging for respondents (63%)
- Better target surveys to respondents with an interest in the topic being researched (57%)

- Attempt to identify respondents providing insincere answers (45%)
- Increase the use of survey incentives (38%)
- Create a third party to identify and eliminate professional respondents from online panels (37%)
- Create engaged panels of highly compensated survey participants (33%)"

Some researchers believe that most differences among the various survey methodologies are due to demographic and other differences between online and off-line populations; although differences like these exist, researchers have not yet found proof to support this explanation. Weighting is one way of handling this and other survey sampling problems—the responses of underrepresented groups in the survey are multiplied by a specific number to bring it closer to the number in the overall population. Still, according to Andy Kohutt of the Pew Research Center, "The traditional corrections that we make in survey research adjust for small imbalances, not for large groups of people who have no chance to play the game" (Kasanoff and Thompson, 1999, p. 68). Some believe that the internet will not be a good vehicle for survey research until 80 percent of the population is online, but others believe that gaining large numbers of respondents, weighting, and comparing online and off-line results are enough. For example, Harris Interactive's Poll Online predicted the results of 21 out of 22 election races accurately in the United States in 1998, and Avon Products found mall intercept surveys in 17 cities to correlate highly with online surveys—so it dropped the mall methodology (Kasanoff and Thompson, 1999).

Another problem with Web surveys and questionnaires that are not password-protected is that the firm has no control over who responds. Whereas the person receiving an e-mail generally keeps it private and responds personally, anyone can answer a Web survey if the address is published. This possibility creates a self-selection bias that is difficult to measure.

A closely related concern is respondent authenticity. This problem affects any self-administered survey methodology, but it seems particularly acute on the internet. Surveys found that anywhere from 20 percent to 50 percent of Web users posed as the opposite sex on the internet, and children often pose as adults online. This situation is not easy to correct and obviously biases survey results. Many researchers are attempting to screen out illegitimate or flippant respondents. One way is to watch for frivolous results such as responses that form a pattern (e.g., each response is increased by one: 1, 2, 3, 4, and so on).

Another problem concerns duplicate responses to online surveys. GVU put e-mail address screening into its second user survey and found that 709 (3.8%) of its 18,503 completed questionnaires were multiple submissions from the same address. Some respondents simply make a mistake and submit a questionnaire more than once, and perhaps others want their opinion counted heavily! It is easy to remove duplicate responses from a database by just checking for identical responses submitted near the same time.

Finally, some researchers use e-mail to solicit responses to Web-based questionnaires. This e-mail may be perceived as spam unless the sample consists of a firm's customers.

Note that survey forms are not nearly as easy to create as most other types of Web pages. Also, in order to make the form interactive, developers must place a special program on the Web server (CGI or Perl script) that "tells" the server what to do with the respondent information. A few enterprising firms created software to assist in this process, such as the Web-based Survey Monkey.com. SurveySolutions software allows researchers to create a Web form survey nearly as simply as other Web page authoring tools or word processing software. Researchers then put the Web page on their site, and all the interactive work is done on the SurveySolutions server. Survey responses are e-mailed back to the researcher who uses the software to turn e-mails into data tables appropriate for analysis in spreadsheet or statistical software.

Online Panels Most researchers are using online panels to combat sampling and response problems. Also called **opt-in** communities, **online**

panels include a group of people who have agreed to be the subject of marketing research. Usually they are paid and often receive free products as well. Panel participants complete extensive questionnaires after being accepted, so that researchers have information about their characteristics and behavior. This way, when panel members are asked to test product, are given questionnaires to complete, or are sent coupons and other promotions, researchers can correlate results with already collected demographic data. In turn, the research firms can use shorter questionnaires, thus increasing response rates (i.e., no need for demographic questions). An advantage to large panels such those in the Purina opening story are that smaller groups of members can be targeted based on behavior or demographics. Firms with large online panels include America Consumer Opinion, Nielsen //NetRatings, NPD Group, Harris Interactive, and Digital Marketing Services (DMS).

In one interesting use of its 100,000-member panel, Nielsen//NetRatings tracked panel viewership of online advertising. It did this by asking the ad agency to place a tracking pixel in the ad. A **pixel** is one dot of light on a computer or television screen, so this was invisible to the ad viewer. Nielsen put a cookie on each panel member's computer that indicated when the pixel was viewed—that is, who was viewing the ad. After correlating the cookie information with panel demographics, Nielsen was able to build a complete profile of the online ad viewers (Bruner and Koegel, 2005).

On the downside, panel access is often more expensive for client firms than traditional methods of sample generation. Also, because research firms sometimes recruit panel members in nonscientific ways, the generalizability of survey results from panels is questionable. Large numbers of respondents and high response rates minimize this problem, however. One other problem with panels is that they are paid for their participation and sometimes cheat to get the participation money in three different ways:

1. Cheat by answering "yes" to questions they think will keep them from getting terminated mid-survey because of not using particular products or other screening criteria (they don't want to be terminated because they don't get paid).

2. Inattentive behavior so they can get through it quickly—for example, just clicking random answers without reading carefully, or "straight lining" (clicking all of one number for several questions in a row). Researchers check this by setting traps, such as oppositely worded questions that respondents must closely read without having inconsistent responses.

3. Closely related to inattention is speeding. Researchers detect this by timing how long it takes respondents to answer a survey, and if they took 5 minutes on a 15-minute questionnaire their responses are not counted.

ETHICS OF ONLINE RESEARCH Most companies conducting marketing research on the Web have considered its "gift culture" and decided to give something to respondents as appreciation for participating. With traditional research, respondents are frequently offered a nominal fee (e.g., $5) to complete a questionnaire, which increases the response rate. Some researchers draw names of those who submit responses, offering them free products or cash. Others donate money to charities selected by respondents (e.g., $3 to one of three charities listed on the Web page for each questionnaire submitted). Many post the entire results in downloadable form, and most provide at least some results on the Web sites after the survey period is completed.

Marketers face several other ethical concerns regarding survey research on the internet.

1. Respondents are increasingly upset at getting unsolicited e-mail requesting survey participation.

2. Some researchers "harvest" e-mail addresses from newsgroups without permission (e.g., from Google.com). Perhaps, this practice is analogous to gathering names from a telephone book, but some people object because consumers are not posting with the idea of being contacted by marketers.

3. Some companies conduct "surveys" for the purpose of building a database for later

solicitation. Ethical marketers clearly mark the difference between marketing research and marketing promotion and do not sell under the guise of research.

4. Privacy of user data is a huge issue in this medium, because it is relatively easy and profitable to send electronic data to others via the internet. Farhad Mohit, CEO at BizRate, notes that many others want the data they collect. According to Mohit, guarding respondent data privacy is central to the success of BizRate.

These and other concerns prompted ESOMAR®, the European Society for Opinion and Marketing Research, to include guidelines for internet research in its International Code of Marketing and Social Research Practice. ESOMAR has more than 4,500 members in 100 countries (www.esomar.org).

In spite of serious shortcomings, the internet is critical for conducting primary research and is an important tool for marketers. However, when using any primary or secondary data, marketers must evaluate their quality carefully and apply it accordingly.

MONITORING THE SOCIAL MEDIA

The citizen journalists post multimedia all over the social media, and companies must now monitor to see which of the 112 million blogs or 485 million photos at Flickr.com concern their brands or executives. This has become a huge problem because a quick Google search is no longer enough to catch a potentially damaging rumor or competitive announcement as it breaks. For example, an MSN.com reporter posted a story "Is Home Depot Shafting Shoppers?" and within one day he received 10,000 e-mails and 4,000 posts on MSN.com that told tales of poor customer service at Home Depot. The company needed automated tracking to catch something like this in time to make a response and control the crisis. This rapid spread of citizen journalist content is part of the reason that companies are losing control of their brand images. Sometimes they pay public relations firms or online reputation management firms to help (such as Weber Shandwick or Reputation

Defender.com). However, companies can easily set up an automated monitoring system on their own, using e-mail, RSS feeds, or special software.

Google offers e-mail alerts for any key words of the user's choice—such as a person's name, a brand name, a competitor's brand name, and so forth. Exhibit 6.16 shows a Google alert in the weekly incoming e-mail for one of the author's names. Users can set up an alert e-mail for the entire Web, blogs, news, videos, or groups and have them sent automatically as they happen, daily, or weekly. Technorati, the search engine that monitors over 112 million blogs, will also send e-mail alerts. It also helps marketers to subscribe to e-mail newsletters in their industry so they can watch for competitive and market announcements. See the "Let's Get Technical" box to learn how search engines work.

RSS (Really Simple Syndication) feeds are an XML format designed for sharing headlines and other Web content. When individuals subscribe to a blog or other social media site via RSS, the content goes to reader desktops as it is published. Customers can read the RSS feeds by downloading a free reader, such as the Google Reader (Exhibit 6.18). This is the way that most companies follow influential bloggers in their industry and watch for posts about their company and brands so they can add comments or react when crises hit.

Finally, special software allows companies to monitor social media conversations and disseminate them to affected personnel. *Copernic Tracker* is especially strong because it will track many Web sites that don't have RSS feeds, such as business profiles (e.g., at the Better Business Bureau), online forums, and competitor Web sites. One free offering comes from the World Bank, who designed it to monitor social media postings about its own projects and personnel. BuzzMonitor is available at buzzm.worldbank.com.

Where should companies look online for this conversation? Beal and Strauss (2008) offer these 12 channels for online reputation monitoring:

- Your own content channels—any blogs, comment sections on the company site, or other Web sites owned by the company that allow user posting.

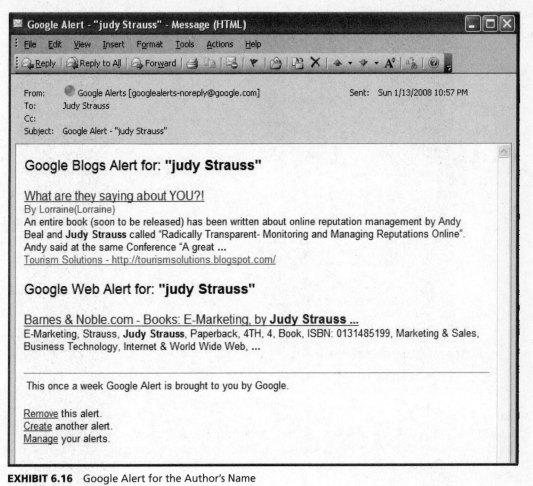

EXHIBIT 6.16 Google Alert for the Author's Name

Source: Author's e-mail.

LET'S GET TECHNICAL

Search Engines

You've just been hired as a junior executive in the marketing department. You'd like to make a good impression. Your manager hands you a study showing that most visitors to your company's Web site find the site using a search engine. She asks you to improve your site's ranking on the search engines. You have no idea where to begin and you are worried about looking bad. Fortunately, you've heard about services that help improve search engine rankings. If you could only remember what they are called and how they work . . .

The Web contains billions of pages. Realistically it would be impossible for the search engines to search the entire Web every time someone types in a search term. The task would take days to complete. Therefore, search engines actually do the searching up to a month in advance and store the results in a huge database. They send automatic programs called **spiders** out on the Web to go from site to site, page-by-page and word-by-word, as shown in Exhibit 6.17. These spiders build up a massive index or database of all the words found, where they were found, how many times they appear on each page, and so on.

(continued)

(continued)

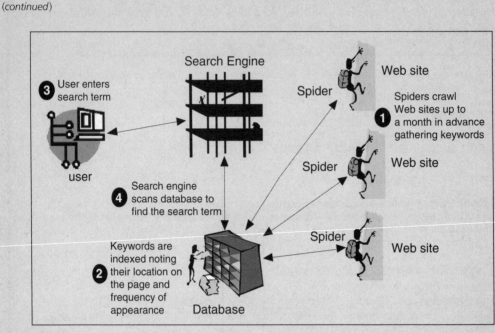

EXHIBIT 6.17   How Search Engines Work

When users type in a search term, they are actually querying this database. Because it is an indexed database, the query returns the results almost instantly. The results are generally returned in order of relevance with the most relevant site appearing first. But how does the search engine define relevance?

It is the search engine's job to figure out which sites are most likely to be relevant to the search term. Here the spider aids it. The spider does more than just count words. It also looks for the location of those words on the page and the frequency with which they appear. For example, if the word is in the title of a page, it is given a higher relevance value than a word appearing in the body text. A word appearing multiple times also earns a higher ranking.

So why not combine these ideas and repeat the keyword multiple times at the top of the page to fool the spider? The spiders are also trained to avoid sites that attempt to trick them by repeating words many times in a row. One technique is to ignore repeats that are not separated by at least, say, seven other words. This guards against someone loading a page with, for example, "Mazda, Mazda, and Mazda."

Search engines also take two other off-page considerations into account—how many sites link to a particular site and how many times users have clicked through to a site. Both links and click-throughs are indicators of a site's popularity.

So again why not just make a bunch of dummy sites that link to your site? Why not sign onto the search engine thousands of times and click through to your site to improve your ranking? The search engines are trained to spot both behaviors and compensate accordingly. The actual techniques used are becoming trade secrets because producing a search engine that returns truly useful results is actually a point of product differentiation and, therefore, provides a competitive advantage. Nonetheless, one Web site, SearchEngineWatch (www.searchenginewatch.com), reveals many of the secrets for each of the search engines.

E-marketers would like their sites to appear high in the search engine rankings—preferably on the first page—above the fold—meaning that they show without scrolling. One way to gain this placement is to purchase paid listings usually triggered by keywords in the search term. Another way is to hire a company that studies the search engines to determine their algorithms for ranking pages. The analysis provides information that can be used to redesign pages so they will rise in the rankings. Some of these companies have rather catchy names, such as Did-It, MoreVisibility, and SpiderBait.

EXHIBIT 6.18   Google Reader Aggregates RSS Feeds

Source: Courtesy of Google (www.google.com/reader).

- Social media and blogs using Technorati. com alerts and RSS feeds.
- Google's network of video, news, groups, and more.
- Industry news via e-mail newsletters or competitive site monitoring.
- Stakeholder conversations that occur at any other Web site not monitored in other ways.
- Social communities in the company's industry, such as Tripadvisor.com for the travel industry.
- Social bookmarking sites such as del.icio. us.com that allows users to tag Web sites for sharing with others.
- Multimedia content such as video at YouTube and photos at Flickr.
- Forums and message boards, both in Google Groups and Yahoo! Groups, and at any Web site in the company's industry that hosts them.
- Customer reviews at sites such as Amazon.com book reviews, BizRate.com or epinions.com—this is important for companies selling products online.
- Brand profiles at social networks such as LinkedIn.com and ZoomInfo.com
- Web analytics will help companies monitor the traffic coming to their own sites, the key words they used at Google to find them, and the sites they visited previously to landing at the company site.

OTHER TECHNOLOGY-ENABLED APPROACHES

The internet is an excellent place to observe user behavior because the technology automatically records actions in a format that can be easily, quickly, and mathematically manipulated for analysis. Computer client-side and server-side automated data collection are two nontraditional technology-enabled approaches deserving of special emphasis. Real-time profiling at Web sites is one particularly powerful server-side approach. These techniques are especially interesting and unusual because they did not exist prior to the internet, and because they allow marketers to make quick and responsive changes in Web pages, promotions, and pricing.

Client-Side Data Collection

Client-side data collection refers to collecting information about consumer click behavior right at the user's PC. One approach is to use cookies when a user visits a Web site. Cookie files are quite helpful, and even necessary, for e-commerce and other internet activities. Some cookies help marketers present appropriate promotions and Web pages to individual users using database information. Exhibit 6.19 displays an example of the sales funnel. It shows how cookie files and Web site logs can identify the number of visitors to a Web site that view desired pages and eventually purchase the product. As discussed in Chapter 2, these numbers are a result of Web analytics software.

One important client-side data collection method involves measuring user patterns by installing a PC meter on the computers of a panel of users and tracking the user **clickstream**. This approach is similar to the ACNielsen "people meter" used on TV sets to determine ratings for various programs. We discuss this technique more thoroughly in other chapters.

Server-Side Data Collection

Web analytics uses site log software to generate reports on numbers of users who view each page, the location of site visited prior to the firm's site, and what users buy at a site—fundamental elements in **server-side data collection**. For example, because of its online registration requirement, Expedia can track visitors' ticket purchases, browsing patterns, and how often they visit the site. It uses the information to send special offers to customers as well as to offer services such as the fare watcher. Amazon, through collaborative filtering software, keeps track of books ordered by customers and makes recommendations based on customer trends in its database. These observational data help firms improve online marketing strategies, sell advertising, and produce more effective Web sites. See Exhibit 6.20 for an example of the clickstream at FTC.gov that Web analytics software would help analyze. Armed with these data, the FTC can determine which pages are the most relevant to citizens and should remain as prominent banner links from its home page.

Increasingly firms use server-side data to make frequent changes in Web pages and promotional offers. **Real-time profiling** occurs when special software tracks a user's movements through a Web site, then compiles and reports on the data at

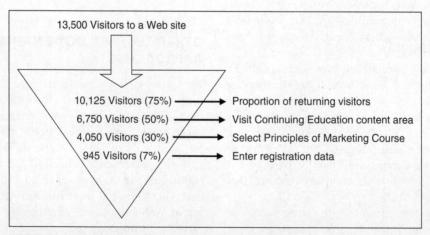

13,500 Visitors to a Web site

10,125 Visitors (75%) ——→ Proportion of returning visitors
6,750 Visitors (50%) ——→ Visit Continuing Education content area
4,050 Visitors (30%) ——→ Select Principles of Marketing Course
945 Visitors (7%) ——→ Enter registration data

EXHIBIT 6.19 Web Site Logs Assist in Sales Funnel Analysis

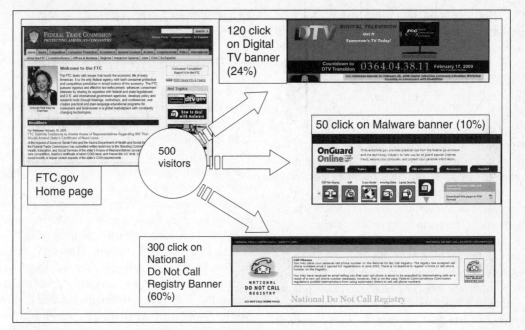

EXHIBIT 6.20 Following the Clickstream at FTC.gov

Source: www.ftc.gov.

a moment's notice. Also known as "tracking user clickstream in real time," this approach allows marketers to analyze consumer online behavior and make instantaneous adjustments to site promotional offers and Web pages. Real-time profiling is not cheap—one estimate puts the software at $150,000 to start and $10,000 a month thereafter. The ability to predict future behavior based on past behavior and, thus, offer customized Web pages to appropriate customers while they are visiting a Web site can pay off handsomely, however.

REAL-SPACE APPROACHES

Real-space primary data collection refers to technology-enabled approaches to gather information off-line that is subsequently stored and used in marketing databases. The most important real-space techniques are bar code scanners and credit card terminals at brick-and-mortar retail stores, although computer entry by customer service reps while talking on the telephone with customers might also be included here.

Real-space primary data collection occurs at off-line points of purchase. Off-line data collection is important for e-marketing because these data, when combined with online data, paint a complete picture of consumer behavior for individual retail firms. Smart card and credit card readers, interactive point of sale machines (iPOS), and bar code scanners are mechanisms for collecting real-space consumer data. Even though the universal product code (UPC), also known as the bar code, has been in grocery stores since 1974, its use has grown to the point where such codes are now scanned billions of times a day. Product sales data gathered by scanning the UPC at retail stores is currently used primarily for inventory management. As UPC data go from the cash register into the computer, the software reduces accounting inventory levels automatically and sends communication to suppliers for replenishment of physical goods. This immediate inventory updating is quite efficient for retailers, wholesalers, and manufacturers.

Catalina Marketing uses the UPC for promotional purposes. This firm places small machines next to the cash registers of grocery stores to generate coupons based on each customer's purchase. For example, if a customer buys Smucker's jam, the machine might spit out a $0.50 coupon for Knott's Berry jam. When the consumer redeems the Knott's coupon, the bar code scanner records it. In the process, Catalina Marketing and the retailer are building huge databases of customer purchases and responses to various offers. If consumers only redeem a small proportion of the Knott's coupons, Knott's Berry Farm might choose to increase the coupon size to $0.75. Although not common practice, it is now possible to combine data collected at the brick-and-mortar retail store with that of the online version of the store. The Sharper Image retailer amasses a huge amount of data by combining server-side data from its Web site with telephone and mail orders from the catalog and UPC real-space data from the brick-and-mortar stores. This data compilation gives its customer service representatives a complete customer record from the database whenever needed.

MARKETING DATABASES AND DATA WAREHOUSES

Regardless of whether data are collected online or off-line, they are moved to various marketing databases, as shown in Exhibit 6.1. Product databases hold information about product features, prices, and inventory levels; customer databases hold information about customer characteristics and behavior. Transaction processing databases are important for moving data from other databases into a data warehouse (Exhibit 6.21). Data warehouses are repositories for the entire organization's historical data (not just marketing data). They are designed specifically to support analyses necessary for decision-making. In other words, marketers cannot apply the data in product or consumer databases to marketing problems as well as they can apply information in a data warehouse. Sometimes the data in a warehouse are separated into more specific subject areas (called data marts) and indexed for easy use. These concepts are important to marketers because they use data warehouse information for planning purposes.

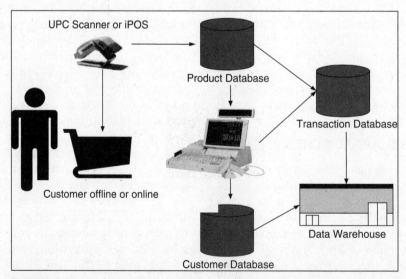

EXHIBIT 6.21　Real-Space Data Collection and Storage Example

Because Web sites are so complex, often including thousands of pages from or for many different corporate departments, content management is an important area. Many software vendors, including Microsoft, are attempting to solve the Web site maintenance problem with their software. These programs have features such as press release databases that automatically put the newest stories on a designated page and archive older stories, deleting them on a specified date.

DATA ANALYSIS AND DISTRIBUTION

Data collected from all customer touch points are stored in the data warehouse knowledge management system, ready for analysis and distribution to marketing decision makers. Four important types of analysis for marketing decision making include data mining, customer profiling, RFM analysis (recency, frequency, monetary value), and report generating.

Data mining involves the extraction of hidden predictive information in large databases through statistical analysis (see the "Let's Get Technical" box). Here, marketers don't need to approach the database with any hypotheses other than an interest in finding patterns among the data. For example, a marketer might want to know whether a product's heaviest users tend to purchase more during particular months, or whether most buy extended warranties. Patterns uncovered by marketers help them to refine marketing mix strategies, identify new-product opportunities, and predict consumer behavior. Using data mining helped Fingerhut, the $2 billion catalog retailer, discover that customers who move their residence triple their purchasing in the 12 weeks after the move. Data mining also revealed that movers tend to buy furniture, telephones, and decorations but not jewelry or home electronics. Fingerhut used this information to create a special "Mover's Catalog," selecting appropriate products from among the 15,000 items it sells. In addition, it stopped sending other specialty catalogs to movers during the 12-week window. Data mining also helped the

American Automobile Association (AAA) Mid-Atlantic office to streamline its marketing communication process, decreasing the amount mailed by 96 percent, from 1.2 million to 40,000 pieces per year. This reduced costs by 92 percent without a membership-enrollment decline.

Customer profiling uses data warehouse information to help marketers understand the characteristics and behavior of specific target groups. Through this process, marketers can really understand who buys particular products and how they react to promotional offers and pricing changes. Some additional uses of customer profiling include the following:

- Selecting target groups for promotional appeals
- Finding and keeping customers with a higher lifetime value to the firm
- Understanding the important characteristics of heavy product users
- Directing cross-selling activities to appropriate customers
- Reducing direct-mailing costs by targeting high-response customers

RFM analysis scans the database for three criteria. First, when did the customer last purchase (recency)? Second, how often has the customer purchased products (frequency)? Third, how much has the customer spent on product purchases (monetary value)? This process allows firms to target offers to the customers who are most responsive, saving promotional costs and increasing sales. For example, an online retailer might notice that the top customer segment pulled 32 percent of the sales with a $69 average order value (AOV), or $22 of sales per thousand exposures to a display ad on Yahoo! Now the retailer can estimate the value of this type of advertising and take steps to reach the top customer segment as directly as possible.

Individual marketing personnel can perform all data mining, customer profiling, and RFM analyses at any time through access to the data warehouse and distribute the results to other staff members involved in a particular decision.

LET'S GET TECHNICAL

Data Mining

You've just been hired to an entry-level position in marketing research. Your boss has asked you to find interesting cross-sell opportunities for the new iXT widget. He asks you to base your findings on the database of early adopters. You get the feeling that messing up this assignment could be bad, but you have no idea where to start. A friendly colleague suggests that you contact the data mining guru down the hall and recommends that you earn her good favor with a can of Coke. Rushing to the Coke machine you head off with a smile.

Data mining is the search for information hidden in large databases. It is much like scientific inquiry except that the subject of study is human-made data rather than nature. The larger the database, the more the need for specialized data mining tools to spot patterns and relationships in the data. The tools themselves are quite sophisticated and data miners tend to have advanced degrees—with special emphasis on statistical training.

The simplest forms of data mining utilize statistical packages such as SPSS and SAS. The investigator forms a hypothesis (e.g., advertising dollars are best spent on existing customers) and then uses a statistical technique such as regression to test the hypothesis. This process is the foundation of most academic research. However, it is somewhat slow and requires inventive hypothesis formation.

By contrast, much automated data mining involves fishing for relationships. One approach is to look at the strength of correlation between *every* combination of variables in the database, which is sometimes called factor analysis. However, factor analysis does not show the direction of dependence—which variable causes which. Nor does factor analysis incorporate subtle hypothesis variations to find just the right fit with the data.

More sophisticated still is a data mining technique called evolutionary programming. A computer program adopts the role of scientific investigator. The program forms and tests hypotheses. When it finds a hypothesis that looks promising, it varies it slightly, forming a series of daughter hypotheses. Each of these hypotheses is tested in turn looking for the best match with the data. After churning away for a while, the program reports back to the user on which hypotheses show interesting relationships in the data.

Tasks solved by data mining include predicting, classifying, detecting relationships, and market basket analysis (which goods sell well together). The packages themselves are becoming more user-friendly, which is good news for marketers. Companies such as Megaputer may one day make sophisticated data mining commonplace.

Report generators, on the other hand, automatically create easy-to-read, high-quality reports from data warehouse information on a regular basis. These reports may be placed in the marketing knowledge database on an intranet or extranet for all to access. Marketers can specify the particular information that should appear in these automatic reports and the time intervals for distribution, as in the earlier example of a retailer that sends online weekly sales reports to all managers. Back Web Technologies (www.backweb. com), HotOffice (www.hotoffice. com), and many similar firms provide collaborative software that automatically integrates data from both the firm's macroenvironment and its microenvironment.

For example, when a marketing manager working on a marketing plan saves the data, the system can automatically put the file on the server for other managers to access. Internal data are seamlessly integrated with the firm's Web site, external Web sites, newsgroups, and databases—all with search capabilities. Such software helps firms distribute the results of database analyses.

KNOWLEDGE MANAGEMENT METRICS

Marketing research is not cheap. Marketers often weigh the cost of gaining additional information against the value of potential opportunities or the risk of possible errors from decisions made with incomplete information. They are also concerned about the storage cost of all those terabytes of data coming from Web site logs, online surveys, Web registrations, and other real-time and real-space approaches. The good news is that data storage costs have declined steadily since 1998, from $0.40 to less than $0.05 per megabyte (Malik, 2003). Two metrics are currently in widespread use:

- **ROI.** Companies want to know why they should save all those data. How will they be used, and will the benefits in additional revenues or lowered costs return an acceptable rate on the storage space investment? For hardware storage space, ROI usually means total cost savings divided by total cost of the installation (Gruener, 2001). Notably, companies use ROI to justify the value of other knowledge management systems as well.
- **Total Cost of Ownership (TCO).** Largely a metric used by information technology managers, TCO includes not only the cost of hardware, software, and labor for data

storage but also other items such as cost savings by reducing Web server downtime and labor requirements.

For example, Galileo International offers travel reservations and maintains 102 terabytes of data—schedule, fare, and reservation information for 500 airlines, 47,000 hotels, and 37 car rental companies (Radding, 2001). The company booked 345 million reservations in 2000, sometimes handling 10,000 requests a second! Galileo's ROI is simple: According to its owner, Frank Auer, every bit of the firm's $1.6 billion in revenue is a return on its data storage system.

In another example, trucking company Schneider National had enough data to fill ten 53-foot trailers with floppy disks. But it still could not easily figure out why it cost $0.20 a pound to deliver cars to a Ford Dealership in Texas and only $0.17 elsewhere. The firm spent an estimated $2 million to purchase business intelligence software that allowed employees to get quick answers to marketing problems and realized a $2.5 million return on that investment within two years (25% ROI) (Brown, 2002).

Chapter Summary

E-marketers need data to guide decisions about creating and changing marketing mix elements. These data are collected from a myriad of sources, filtered into databases, and turned into marketing knowledge that is then used to develop marketing strategy. Knowledge management is the process of managing the creation, use, and dissemination of knowledge. A marketing information system (MIS) is the process by which marketers manage knowledge, using a system of assessing information needs, gathering information, analyzing it, and disseminating it to decision makers.

Marketers can tap three sources of marketing knowledge: (1) internal records (such as cash flow, sales force data, and customer data), (2) secondary data (publicly and privately generated, from online databases, and for competitive

intelligence), and (3) primary data (gathered for the first time to solve a particular problem). Competitive intelligence (CI) involves analyzing the industries in which a firm operates as input to the firm's strategic positioning and to understand competitor vulnerabilities. Marketers must evaluate the quality of data before relying on them to solve research problems.

Primary data is collected on the internet by over 90 percent of all companies. The steps to conduct primary research are (1) define the research problem, (2) develop a research plan, (3) collect data, (4) analyze the data, and (5) distribute results. Internet-based research may include any of the following activities conducted online: experiments, focus groups, observations, and surveys. Surveys may be conducted by e-mail invitation to a Web site. Advantages to online surveys are that they are fast and inexpensive, have broad reach, reduce errors, elicit honest responses, can be restricted to authorized participants, and are easy to tabulate. Disadvantages include poor generalizability of results due to poor sample selection, self-selection bias, inability to confirm the respondent's authenticity, frivolous or dishonest responses, and duplicate submissions.

Online panels are increasingly being used to combat sampling and response problems of online surveys. Although some of these panels are small, others contain millions of participants. Some ethical concerns of online research include unsolicited e-mail, harvesting e-mail addresses from newsgroups, selling under the guise of research, and lack of privacy of user data.

Companies must constantly monitor the social media and other Web sites to identify content about their brands and personnel that are posted by citizen journalists and other stakeholders. New technologies such as e-mail alerts, RSS feeds, and special software make this an easy and automated process.

Marketers use technology to observe user behavior on the user's computer (client side) via cookies and PC meters or the server (server side) via the use of log files and real-time profiling. Real-space data collection takes place at off-line points of purchase such as smart card and credit card readers, iPOS machines, and bar code scanners. The data can be used for inventory control and to target promotions.

Data warehouses are repositories for the organization's historical data. Data marts are subsections of the warehouse categorized by subject area. Data from all customer touch points are stored in the warehouse. Four types of analysis are conducted with the data: data mining, customer profiling, RFM (recency, frequency, monetary value) analysis, and report generation. Data mining extracts hidden predictive information from the warehouse via statistical analysis. Customer profiling helps marketers understand the characteristics and behavior of specific target groups. RFM analysis allows firms to target offers to customers who might be most responsive. Sophisticated report generation tools can automatically schedule and publish reports.

Exercises

REVIEW QUESTIONS

1. What are the three main sources of data for solving marketing research problems?
2. Contrast primary with secondary data and explain the advantages and disadvantages of each.
3. What is competitive intelligence, and what are some sources of online CI data?
4. Why and how do e-marketers evaluate the quality of information on a Web site?
5. What are the strengths and weaknesses of the internet for primary and secondary data collection?
6. How do marketers turn marketing data into marketing knowledge?
7. What is real-space data collection? Why is it important?
8. Is data mining possible without a data warehouse? Why or why not?
9. Give an example of how data mining uncovers new knowledge.

10. Identify the steps in a primary marketing research project.
11. What are the 12 channels for online reputation monitoring? Why are they important to a company?

DISCUSSION QUESTIONS

12. What online research method(s) would you use to test a new-product concept? Why?
13. What online research method(s) would you use to test the brand image of an existing product? Why?
14. Of the ethical issues mentioned in the chapter, which are you most concerned about as a consumer? Why?
15. Can you think of a marketing research technique that could not be supported online? Explain your answer.
16. What are the current limitations for undertaking market research on the general population on the

internet? How might these be overcome now and in the future?

17. Given that the cost of sending an e-mail questionnaire to 10,000 people is no higher than the cost of sending it to 10 people, why would market researchers bother devising samples if they were planning to undertake some research online?

18. What do you think a company should do if it receives a Google Alert or RSS feed showing that customers are speaking poorly about its products?

WEB ACTIVITIES

19. Join the American Consumer Opinion online panel and take a survey (www.acop.com). Did they screen for a particular type of respondent? What observations can you make about the client and research problem?

20. Look for the cookies file(s) on your hard drive (on a Microsoft PC, use the *find file* function and search for *cookie*). Do you see sites there that you have never visited? Is DoubleClick on the list? If so, visit the DoubleClick site to see why.

21. Find information on the U.S. Census and Nielsen TV ratings, either online or in the library. What methodology does each use? Evaluate their strengths and weaknesses based on what you've learned about research methods in this chapter.

22. Watch a friend surf for 10 minutes and record the clickstream. (Netscape records sites visited in its history list; Internet Explorer records sites visited using the drop-down arrow by the back button.) List each site, page within, and how long your friend spends on each page. Can you make any determination about your friend's attitudes, interests, and opinions based on the clickstream?

23. Toyota has asked you to test the effectiveness of its new banner ad using four primary research techniques. Design these tests.

CHAPTER 7

Consumer Behavior Online

Time is the only commodity worth anything anymore. Consumers will pay you to save them time. The internet saves people time.

—SCOTT REAMER, S.G. COWEN

Consumers are empowered in a way that's almost frightening.

—PETER WEEDFALD, SAMSUNG ELECTRONICS NORTH AMERICA

Contents Outline

The primary objective of this chapter is to develop a general understanding of the online consumer population. You will explore the context in which online consumer behavior occurs, the characteristics and resources of online consumers, and the outcomes of the online exchange process.

After reading this chapter, you will be able to:

- Discuss general statistics about the internet population.

- Describe the internet exchange process and the technological, social/cultural, and legal context in which consumers participate in this process.

- Outline the broad individual characteristics and consumer resources that consumers bring to the online exchange.

- Highlight the four main categories of outcomes that consumers seek from online exchanges.

The Customer's Story

This is the story of a typical one-hour adventure on a weekend afternoon in the life of a 25-year-old professional male, Justin. It begins when he tunes his iPod to the latest Diggnation podcast downloaded automatically the last time he connected it with his PC. Diggnation's Alex Albrecht and Kevin Rose chat about the weekly top stories on Digg.com, a social media site where users submit interesting news headlines and then site visitors vote by clicking that they "digg it." As our consumer watches the video podcast, he also has the television tuned to a soccer game and his cell phone and PC are within reach.

Partway through the podcast, Kevin Rose mentions his blog on Tumblr.com: *kevinhasablogg*. Tumblr is a micromedia site—a Web site that holds small bits of quickly posted, user-generated content (www.tumblr.com). Justin looks away from the podcast and picks up his computer to find the blog. He is still listening to Rose and Albrecht but not watching them on the iPod. He is captivated by a video on the blog "Lip Dub Flagpole Sitta by Harvey Danger." This video contains a bunch of employees in hip clothes having fun by lip-synching to the song and dancing around the office doing silly stuff. While watching it, Justin picks up his cell phone to text a friend who lives in a different time zone: "You gotta see this video."

Justin wonders who created this hot video. He searches the title at Google and finds Vimeo, an online video-posting site pre-dating YouTube. The text explaining the video says, "We did this video one night after work. We are a

(continued)

(continued)

company called Connected Ventures, a group of friends who work for: Vimeo, CollegeHumor, Busted Tees, and Defunker . . . and, we're hiring: connectedventures. com/jobs.shtml." Justin follows the link to see that there are no more jobs available because the company got several hundred resumes just based on the Lip Dub video posting. Justin wasn't the first to arrive, but he really wants to work for a company like this.

During Justin's last few minutes of the 1-hour stretch, he posts a link to the video and Vimeo site to his Twitter stream. Twitter.com is another micromedia site that his friends and colleagues follow, and pretty soon other messages about the video and company appear. The buzz quickly spreads.

This is the new consumer. He is a multitasker, attending to many different electronic media simultaneously. He is difficult to catch online and won't stick around one Web site for long. His connections with friends and colleagues are enhanced by the internet, where they like to share their online treasures and conversation in a myriad of ways from e-mail, text, and micromedia sites. They don't pay much attention to traditional Web sites, preferring to connect with others and view fresh content in the social media. Justin is an important consumer because if brands can't attract the young demographic, they will eventually head into the decline stage and die. How can a marketer capture dollars from this . . . advertising online, selling music downloads and other products, fees for premium social media subscriptions? That is a problem marketers are trying to solve as you read this.

CONSUMERS IN THE TWENTY-FIRST CENTURY

This chapter is about the 71 percent of U.S. consumers who use the internet. Before we delve into understanding them and their behavior, it is important to think about the 29 percent of Americans who don't use the internet. It would not benefit a company to build a Web presence if its market were mostly in that minority percentage. The less-connected groups tend to be older, less educated, in ethnic minority groups, not have children, live in rural areas, and have a lower income (according to Pew Internet & the American Life Project). Pew suggests four segments of nonusers (Lenhart et al., 2003):

1. **Net Evaders** (8% of nonusers) don't think the internet is a good use of time, don't think they are missing out, and don't need it or want it. They have some fears about their ability to learn how to use the internet and are embarrassed about it.
2. **Net Dropouts** (17% of nonusers) tried the internet and stopped. They didn't want or like it, found it too expensive, and had content concerns or technological difficulties. They lost access due to technology problems or when they moved, changed jobs, or became ill.
3. **Truly Unconnected** (69% of all nonusers) are low income with little education. They don't go online because they may be socially unconnected, worried about the content or computer crime, can't afford it, have no computer, and think it is too complicated.
4. **Intermittent Users** are online but leave it for extended periods. They drop out because of technology problems, concern about objectionable content and potential online crime, high cost, and they just don't have time or think they need it.

The common reasons among these groups for not using the internet show clearly why internet adoption has matured, hovering at 71 percent for the past few years (Exhibit 7.1). Globally, internet use is still growing, but at a slower pace than in the past. In 2007, 1.4 billion people had access to the internet, representing 19 percent of

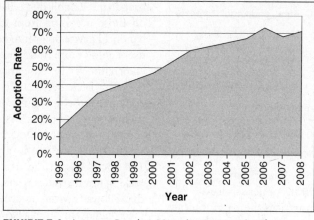

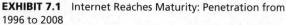

EXHIBIT 7.1 Internet Reaches Maturity: Penetration from 1996 to 2008

Source: Data from Pew Internet & American Life.

the global population (up from 16% in 2004). Recall from Chapter 4 that the top 10 countries, in terms of absolute number of users, account for nearly 763.1 million internet users (53% of all global users). In these countries, adoption rates range from 69 percent to 88 percent.

Where are the other 5.4 billion people? Not online. Chapter 4 describes many social, cultural, technological, legal, and political issues as the main reasons that consumers do not use the internet in emerging economies. Without major shifts, some countries may not ever achieve high levels of internet adoption among individual consumers, although high cell phone adoption may change this picture eventually.

Internet usage in developed nations has reached a critical mass, and marketers now ask practical questions such as whether a firm's target market is online, what these customers do online, what determines whether they'll buy from a site, and how much of the marketing effort should be devoted to online channels. This chapter addresses typical consumer behavior among internet users in the United States in order to discover the answers to some of these questions. One thing is sure: "Today, consumer behavior incorporates a lot more technology than it did 10 years ago," according to Scott Schroeder, CEO, Cohorts.

INSIDE THE INTERNET EXCHANGE PROCESS

Many stimuli, characteristics, and processes explain consumer buying behavior. Stimuli that can motivate consumers to purchase one product rather than another include marketing communication messages and cultural, political, economic, and technological factors. Individual buyer characteristics such as income level and personality also come into play, along with other psychological, social, and personal aspects. Finally, consumers move through a variety of decision processes based on situational and product attributes. Marketing knowledge about consumer behavior is quite complex, and although we make many generalizations, individual differences are also important.

To create effective marketing strategies, e-marketers need to understand what motivates people to buy goods and services, both in the short and long term (i.e., develop brand loyalty). **Exchange** is a basic marketing concept that refers to the act of obtaining a valued object from someone by offering something in return. When consumers purchase a product, they are exchanging money for desired goods or services. However, many other types of marketing exchanges can be

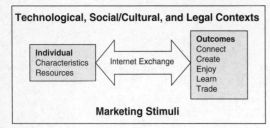

EXHIBIT 7.2   The Online Exchange Process

made, such as when a politician asks citizens to exchange their votes for his or her services.

Exhibit 7.2 summarizes the basic internet exchange process—a graphical representation to help focus this discussion. Individuals bring their own characteristics and personal resources to the process as they seek specific outcomes from an exchange. This process occurs within a technological, social/cultural, and legal context. The exchange is often motivated by marketing stimuli—the topic of Part IV of this book.

Technological Context

The internet has moved from novelty to utility in the United States and most developed nations (see Appendix A for worldwide penetration figures). Arranging for ISP services is like getting telephone services and a postal address: 71 percent of all U.S. consumers consider this activity routine. It is critical for e-marketers to understand the current state of ever-changing internet technology if they want to entice consumer exchanges. "Let's Get Technical" boxes within the text assist in this process, and the Semantic Web and other innovations mentioned in Chapter 1 bear watching. Here we focus upon two important developments affecting online consumer behavior today—home connection speeds and the changing landscape of digital receiving devices such as cell phones.

About 50 percent of online Americans connect to the internet at home with broadband (fast) internet service. Incidentally, the United States neither has the highest broadband penetration nor is it the fastest—a fact often discussed at European conferences. Consumers connecting with broadband exhibit different online behavior than do those accessing from a narrowband mobile handheld device or 56k modem in a PC. Broadband users enjoy more multimedia games, music, and entertainment because these download quickly (see the "Let's Get Technical" box). At the other extreme, those accessing with handheld devices such as personal digital assistants (PDAs) tend to access news, weather, stock quotes, and other data services that are low in graphics. For example, Travelocity has a large, user-friendly Web site for making travel arrangements, and also a mobile site that allows travelers to access a few words about their flight status from a PDA or cell phone.

The typical U.S. home has 26 different electronic devices for media and communication, according the Consumer Electronics Association. Television is still the killer medium; however, consumers spend an average of 1.5 hours online each day (Exhibit 7.3). Although DVR (Digital Video Recorder) adoption is still at less than 10 percent of all households, this technology will grow in use. The TiVo device allows owners to record digital programs and send to their PCs over the in-home wireless network. As DVR adoption grows, consumers will truly be able to watch any television program on demand while at home or on the road.

Note that the figures in Exhibit 7.3 are for all households. Among online U.S. residents, internet use is twice that of television (32.7 hours a week for internet versus 16.4 for television), according to an IDC study in late 2007. Time spent reading newspapers and magazines also declined to 3.9 hours a week, according to this study.

The key is to learn which devices a firm's customers and prospects own and prefer to use for connecting. Companies send data to customers' digital receiving devices such as the PC, electronic pager, fax machine, iTV (interactive TV), voice mail, handheld PDA, cell phone, and other devices. Users can now access stock prices, FedEx package tracking information, airline schedule changes, weather, and more over their PDAs while in a taxi on the way to a client meeting or the airport. Don't overlook **telematics**—a communication system in

LET'S GET TECHNICAL

Bandwidth and Market Opportunities

You are asked to help design a Web site with some eye-catching graphics. Your manager wants you to report on the bandwidth implications. You are not quite sure what bandwidth is and would rather not look like a fool at the meeting. You need to know about bandwidth and how it affects Web site design.

The online world is divided between those with a slow-speed and those with a high-speed connection to the internet. If you have experienced the difference then you know just how dramatic it can be. At work most people have a high-speed connection to the internet through their corporate network, which is sometimes called a broadband or high bandwidth connection. At home most people have slow-speed modem connections over their phone lines, though more and more home users are purchasing high bandwidth connections from their cable or phone companies. Many users will modify their online behavior based on the speed of the connection (e.g., shopping at work because the pages load so much faster).

The speed divide is a tremendous challenge for marketers. Rich multimedia content flows effortlessly over a high-speed connection but is almost unbearable to wait for over slow modem connection. What's a marketer to do?

Three possible strategies deal with a mixed bandwidth audience.

1. **Design for the slowest user:** The safest bet is to design content for a slow-speed connection so as to avoid alienating any group of users. This technique is adopted by some internet giants including Amazon.com and Yahoo!. Their sites tend to be light on graphics and heavy on text content that loads quickly.
2. **Design for the fastest user:** Ignore the slow-speed users and design for the higher bandwidth and generally more affluent audience. Some services (e.g., streaming music services such as rhapsody.com) are only viable over a high-speed connection.
3. **Create fast and slow versions of the site:** Customize content for the speed of the user's connection by using an auto detect feature or just asking the user what their connection speed is. News sites providing video clips will routinely adopt this approach as will sites for music downloads.

The bandwidth issue is similar to the move from broadcast to cable and satellite TV. Cable and satellite TV subscribers incur a higher cost to receive content in their homes. In return they get both more channels (more bandwidth) and a higher definition picture. In the United States, consumers opted for these alternatives. Growing evidence indicates that U.S. consumers are similarly willing to pay for high-speed internet access. In return they receive access to the following services:

- Personal selling and customer service via the computer as a videoconferencing device. Conferencing services are most important for products requiring explanation to close the sale such as the plumbing fixtures offered by FaucetDepot.com
- Phone calls delivered over the internet using Voice Over Internet Protocol (VOIP) services such as Skype.
- Delivery of music over the Web such as Apple iTunes and Rhapsody.
- Delivery of movies over the Web such as those offered by Apple TV and Netflix
- Virtual reality such as Google Earth.

Bandwidth (speed) is measured in bits per second (bps). It takes about 10 bits to code a single letter. It takes about 500,000 bits to code a photograph. With such big numbers, it is easier to speak about kilobits per second (Kbps). So the question is how long is the user willing to wait on a slow-speed connection? Research shows the maximum waiting time is about 10 seconds. Using this number as a guide, rough minimums for tolerable bandwidth to transmit different media is shown in the following table.

(continued)

(continued)

Media Type	Minimum Tolerable Bandwidth (bits per second)
Text	25 Kbps
Graphics (pictures)	50 Kbps
Sound	100 Kbps
Video	1,000 Kbps

Today's fastest phone line modems operate at 56 Kbps—fast enough for text and graphics. However, today's phone line modems are not fast enough for acceptable quality multimedia (sound and video). High-speed internet access can be purchased at a premium through cable, phone, and satellite companies. And consumers are increasingly opting for these services.

LET'S GET TECHNICAL

Broadband Options

You are trying to decide whether to get a high-speed internet connection for your apartment. You know of the different options—cable modems, DSL, and satellite—you are not quite sure how they are different and would rather not buy more than you need. You need to know about broadband connections to the home and their options.

The information channels that form the internet backbone have amazing carrying capacities and are constantly being upgraded by firms such as Cisco, Sprint, and AT&T. However, consumers pay for the last mile along the path to the internet, the connection to the consumer's home. Various wired and wireless alternatives are available.

The wired alternatives make use of two wires that are already connected to the user's home—the phone line and the cable TV line. These wires can do double duty to carry internet content on one channel while they perform their normal functions on the other channels.

Digital Subscriber Line (DSL)

Digital subscriber line (DSL) technology refers to a family of methods for transmitting at speeds up to 8 Mbps (8 million bits per second) over a standard phone line. DSL uses the phone line already installed in consumer homes, allowing users to simultaneously make phone calls and surf the Web because the data travel outside of the audible voice band. Users must install a DSL modem; some computer manufacturers offer these modems as a preinstalled item, and some phone companies supply them. The major phone companies have deployed the infrastructure to support DSL technology, but they were a bit late to the game and have been playing catch-up with cable modems. As a result, phone companies aggressively price DSL service to attract cable subscribers.

Cable Modems

The cable companies have banded together into two consortiums. In one example, Time Warner, Time Warner/Advance-Newhouse, and Media-One Group Inc. formed a consortium called Road Runner. These consortiums help to set standards and share development costs.

The consortiums attracted venture capital. As an example, Compaq Computer (now HP) and Microsoft each invested $212.5 million in Road Runner. Clearly the personal computer industry has a stake in selling computer upgrades to consumers who need beefed up machines to handle the additional bandwidth.

Cable modems allow transmission of internet traffic over the cable TV wire connected to the home. The speed of transmission over a cable modem ranges between 500 Kbps and 10 Mbps. The major problem cable companies may face is having too many subscribers! This problem arises because subscribers in a cable neighborhood share bandwidth. The more subscribers who share, the

(continued)

(continued)

less bandwidth is available to repartition. Therefore, if a neighborhood becomes saturated with subscribers, each subscriber will experience delays.

Cable companies have two big advantages—early market penetration and a much bigger information pipe. The early adopters opted for cable modems because they were the first technology available. This early usage also gives cable modems the advantage of diffusion via word of mouth. The cable companies solved their infrastructure issues early and can now focus on establishing value-added services such as the following:

- Video-on-demand
- CD-quality audio
- Online games available for download and purchase

Each value-added service provides a barrier to entry for the phone companies. Why purchase a service with fewer features? And because providing each service requires a learning curve, phone companies will experience difficulty catching up.

Cable also has a higher theoretical maximum speed than DSL. Nonetheless, phone companies such as AT&T continue to question the actual versus advertised speed of cable. However, if both networks are properly supported, cable still wins the battle.

One way the phone companies are competing is through price. DSL typically undercuts cable, though there are regional variations in price. In some cases, the companies will waive the installation fee if the user signs up for an extended period of service.

Wireless Broadband Options

Two smaller competitors in the broadband game are satellite, fixed wireless, and mobile wireless. Satellite broadband is offered through HughesNet. The major limitation is limited bandwidth that does not scale well with the increase in the number of subscribers.

Fixed wireless access is best categorized by distance and bandwidth. Some systems are designed to work over a range of miles, effectively replacing wired access to the home. Other systems operate over a range of up to hundreds of feet, providing local connectivity within the home or office. In either scenario, the bandwidth of the system determines its suitability as a broadband connection.

Mobile wireless is available over the cell phone network. With cell phone towers already in place in many areas, Web access via cell phone would seem to be a natural outgrowth. The cell phone network is reliable and in many areas the communication is already digital. The problem is bandwidth. The cell phone network was designed to handle low-bandwidth voice communications. As a result, data communication over the network is relatively slow. Third-generation (3G) cell phone networks help solve the bandwidth problem, by transferring data up to 10 times faster than traditional cell phone networks. Iphone users and laptop road warriors are leading the charge to popularize these 3G services. Ultimately, users want access to anything, anytime, anywhere, and from any device.

---

an automobile that uses a global positioning system (GPS) for interactive communication between firms and drivers. This system allows drivers to receive directions and internet content or send for emergency help. It allows marketers to send information and entertainment to automobiles.

Social and Cultural Contexts

The days of marketers holding consumers captive for the 30 seconds of a TV commercial are quickly coming to a close, and captivity in front of a display ad online is virtually nonexistent. The Web is training individuals and organizations to help themselves to information, products, and practically everything they want when and where they please. Thus, power is shifting to consumers, as mentioned in Chapter 1. For example, consumers walk into brick-and-mortar car dealerships with printed information sheets on automobile options and pricing.

One of the most important social trends is that consumers trust each other more than they trust advertising or companies online. The

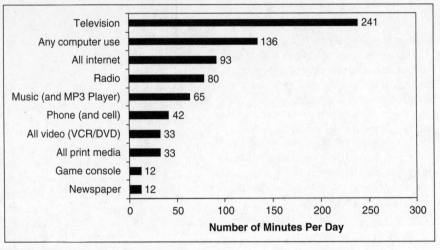

EXHIBIT 7.3 Media Use on an Average Day

Source: Data from Ball State University research (www.bsu.edu).

increase in user-generated content in special interest communities has consumers looking to each other for advice. For example, Askapatient (www.aska patient.com) hosts thousands of posts about side effects of various medicines. Consumers visit the site to see if other people experience the side effects that they experience, and what to expect for a new drug—this information seems more reliable than the corporate spin from pharmaceutical companies. PR firm, Edelman, asked this question for its 2007 Trust Barometer: "If you heard information from each of these sources, how credible would the information be?" Here's who the respondents said they trusted:

- 52 percent each: A person like yourself and a doctor or healthcare specialist.
- 47 percent: Nonprofit organization or its representative.
- 44 percent: an academic.
- 43 percent: a financial industry analyst.
- 35 percent: a regular employee of the company.
- 32 percent: the CEO or leader of your company or employer.
- 26 percent: any CEO of a company.
- 14 percent: a public relations executive.

A "person like yourself" is someone who shares your interests, such as other patients, travelers, or sports fans. Wise marketers understand this and watch Web sites and forums filled with their customers and also host these special interests groups. But it is not enough to just observe. The truly advanced marketers are joining the conversation and learning from customers, such as the Dell story in Chapter 1.

The following general social/cultural trends also have a huge affect on online exchanges:

- **Sophisticated consumers** know they are in control and have choices—they use the information at Askapatient to help their medical doctors make treatment decisions. As well, a growing number of consumers have digital video recorders (DVRs) that they have learned to use for watching 25 percent more television and skipping 70 percent of the ads (Exhibit 7.4). DVR adoption is currently at 17 percent, but expected to grow to 30 percent within three years, and because the box is free with satellite television programming delivery, we agree (Bianco, 2004).
- **Information overload** overwhelms consumers. It creates an **attention economy**—the

Product Type	Ads Ignored While Watching Television (%)	Ads Skipped Using a PVR (%)
Fast food	45	96
Mortgage financing	74	95
Upcoming program	75	94
Credit cards	63	94
Home products	42	90
Soft drinks	22	83
Pet-related	56	82
Specialty clothing	33	62
Drug	32	46
Movie trailers	12	44
Beer	5	32
Weighted average	**43**	**72**

EXHIBIT 7.4 TV Advertisers Are Losing the TV Audience

Source: Data from Anthony Bianco, "The Vanishing Mass Market," *BusinessWeek*, July 12, 2004, pp. 61–68.

idea that information may be infinite, but the demand for it is limited by human capacity. This serious problem is compounded by the internet and is one reason why consumers have little tolerance for spam (unsolicited e-mail).

- **Multitasking** speeds up normal processes and lowers attention to each task. By example, the **Millenials**, a consumer segment born between 1974 and 1994 (also called Generation Y), are great multitaskers, likely to watch several television screens with sporting events at home, talk on the cell phone, and watch sports scores on the internet at the same time—oggling to a fantasy baseball site (Baker, 2004). Notably, 102.6 million adults use the internet while watching television (Exhibit 7.5).

- **Home and work** boundaries are dissolving. Many U.S. internet users have access to the internet both at home and at work. Fourteen percent report spending more time working at home because of the internet (see www.pewinternet.org). Also, comScore Media Metrix found that many U.S. workers make travel arrangements, purchase products, and handle other personal tasks online while at work. The home has become more like a center of life and home office for many; this trend will increase as more Americans telecommute (work and live in different cities and rarely visit the physical office).

- **I want what I want when I want it.** Anywhere, anytime convenience is critical for busy people. They want to view online content, shop or pay bills anytime of the day or night from any geographic location online or not, and receive deliveries when convenient for them, not for the firm or package delivery service. Online users access the internet from mobile devices, sending e-mail, text messages, photos, and searching the Web for maps and other things. Consumers have high expectations that firms will answer e-mails within 24 hours and generally perform as expected—otherwise they will post a complaint on a blog or at Epinions.com and tell a few thousand "friends" about the underperforming company.

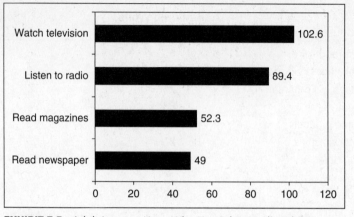

EXHIBIT 7.5   Adult Internet Users Who Use Other Media While Online (millions)

Source: eMarketer charts, January 2007 (www.emarketer.com).

- **Online oxygen**, a term coined at trend-watching.com, means that an increasing number of consumers cannot do without their internet access—they *crave* it. As an example, when Canadian internet users were asked what they would want with them if stranded on a desert island, 51 percent said the PC, 21 percent mentioned telephone, and only 12 percent said their television. Anyone who is addicted to e-mail or particular Web sites certainly understands this trend!
- **Self-service** is required. Empowered customers want to log on, find information, make purchases, track package shipments, check their accounts, and make inquiries anytime, 24/7. Furthermore, they want to do these tasks on a computer via e-mail, on the Web, or on a telephone, PDA, or fax machine—and they want all methods to produce identical information. It is an interesting contradiction: Consumers want to help themselves when they feel like it and be pampered by firms at other times.
- **Privacy and data security** are paramount, especially in Europe. Customers want marketers to keep their data confidential. They also want to safeguard children from Web sites they find objectionable. Consumers

want marketers to ask permission before sending commercial e-mail messages.
- **Online crime** worries consumers. A computer network open to 1.25 million people—and affected by frequent viruses and reports of internet fraud—makes consumers fearful. Even a signature to receive a package from United Parcel Service on the digital pad gives the company a copy for the database.

Legal Context

Chapter 5 presents a thorough discussion of legal factors affecting e-marketers, so we mention only one factor here. It wasn't until recently that ethical and legal factors had a quantifiable effect on consumers. In spite of piracy laws, illegally used software abounds. In spite of the new Can-Spam law in the United States, the number of unsolicited e-mails has actually increased. However, when the Recording Industry Association of America (RIAA) sued thousands of illegal music file downloaders, legal factors actually had a huge affect on online consumer behavior. In 2002, 37 percent of online consumers shared music files with others, dropping to 23 percent in 2004 (www.pewinternet.org). This shift is important because all digital products face this problem, and many consumers feel no hesitation about obtaining illegal copies. If the RIAA success is any indication, the law may indeed change consumer behavior such that products can be offered over the internet without losing profits— such as experienced by Apple's iTunes.

Individual Characteristics and Resources

Beyond general social and cultural trends, individuals vary in their online behavior. Some of this variance is based on differences in characteristics, such as demographics and attitudes, and some is based on the resources consumers bring to the exchange process.

INDIVIDUAL DIFFERENCES Internet users have several characteristics that differentiate them from nonusers, and similarly, users differ in their needs and desires. The first variable involves demographics. Age, income, education, ethnicity, and gender all affect internet use. For example, 92 percent of 18- to 29-year-olds use the internet, as compared with 71 percent of the general population and 37 percent of those over 65 (Pew Internet & American Life 2007 survey). As well, females and African Americans are more likely to seek religious or spiritual information online, and English-speaking Hispanics do more instant messaging than other groups (see www.pewinternet.org).

Second is a positive attitude toward technology. Internet users who purchase products online tend to hold the attitude that technology helps make their lives richer and easier. (Forrester Research created a market segmentation scheme using this variable, as described in Chapter 8.) See the "Let's Get Technical" box for differences in broadband option selection, indicating technology differences. Third, online skill and experience play an important role in the exchange process. Consumers who have been online for more than three years or have broadband connections tend to be more adept than new users at finding information and products quickly, resulting in less frustration and less shopping cart abandonment.

Next, two researchers found that online shoppers tend to be more goal oriented than experience

oriented while shopping (Wolfinbarger and Gilly, 2001). Goal-oriented behavior often includes going to a specific Web site with a purpose in mind, or searching for the lowest price for a particular product. Experience orientation relates to having fun, bargain hunting, or just surfing to find something new. Goal-oriented individuals like the idea that they don't have to deal with salespeople or crowds in the online environment, and they appreciate the online product selection, convenience, and information availability. When consumers are looking for experiential shopping, it makes sense that they would find this element more often in brick-and-mortar stores than online.

Similarly, Forrester Research found that 70 percent of online shoppers have one of two traits: convenience or price orientation (Whelan, 2001). Thirty-six percent of all online shoppers are price conscious and willing to buy from an unknown online retailer if the price is low. Another 36 percent won't turn down a bargain but won't change their favorite online retailer to find one. For these shoppers, convenience and trust are paramount, and they don't mind paying extra for these benefits.

Now that the internet has matured in terms of usage patterns, we could write an entire book on individual differences in online behavior. Instead, marketers thoroughly explore the differences in online behavior for their target markets and then design marketing mixes accordingly. It is especially important to provide options as markets continue to fragment to increasingly smaller target groups.

CONSUMER RESOURCES Chapter 2 introduced the value equation showing that consumers perceive value as benefits minus costs. These costs constitute a consumer's resources for exchange: money, time, energy, and psychic costs.

Monetary Cost Clearly, consumers need enough discretionary income to exchange for the goods and services they want—and to afford a computer and ISP connection for internet access. What makes the internet exchange different, however, is that consumers usually can't pay cash or don't write paper checks for online transactions. Instead, consumers pay by credit card, debit card, electronic check, or smart card. Most consumers in developed nations use credit cards. However, not everyone is able to acquire or wants a credit card. This problem is big for e-marketers targeting the huge teen market online and for those targeting consumers in countries with low credit card availability.

Consumers with bank accounts can use debit cards or pay by electronic check. **Electronic checks** (also called *digital money*) work this way: The consumer sets up an account and authorizes a third-party Web site (such as PayPal) to pay a specified amount and withdraw funds from the user's checking account. This method is now so popular that PayPal, the market leader (purchased by eBay in 2002), has over 164 million customer accounts, is offered at 100,000 online retailers, and operates in 190 markets in 17 different currencies. Finally, smart cards are used in many countries and becoming popular in the United Kingdom. Also called Splash Plastic, smart cards have an electronic chip that can be coded to hold a certain amount of funds, payable by the bank or a depository company. The advantages are that anyone with the cash can get one, and the limit of potential fraud is the amount of money coded into the card.

A few innovative forms of digital money appear in other countries (Farivar, 2004). In South Korea, some mobile phones include special electronic chips that allow consumers to charge vending machine purchases with their phones. In Japan, a Casio watch can be read by a retail scanner to debit the user's bank account. In Hong Kong, smart cards use radio frequency chips that store up to the equivalent of US$128 for ATM-type use. Finally, in Spain 38 important guests at a beach club had radio frequency identification (RFID) chips (the size of a grain of rice) implanted in their arms. They simply move their arms over the bar to run a tab.

Time Cost Time poverty is a problem for today's consumers, so they want to receive appropriate benefits for the time they spend online. Exhibit 7.6 shows that, worldwide, the average user went online 34 times in a month, spending 69 minutes each time, and visiting over 1,500 different Web sites (domains). Did this average user get what he or she wanted for the time invested? The burden is on internet firms to be sure their sites are well organized and easy to navigate so users can quickly find what they want.

The internet's property of time moderator, discussed in Chapter 1, helps consumers manage their scarce time. Users can shop, e-mail, or perform other activities anytime, 24/7—a big advantage for working parents who can only find the time to shop late at night after the kids are in bed.

Time resource is a critical topic because online attention from consumers is a desirable and scarce commodity. The clutter of Web sites now parallels that of other media—with some differences. Some researchers believe that consumers pay more focused attention to Web sites

Metric	December 2007
Number of sessions/visits for the month	34
Number of domains visited	69
Web pages per person per month	1,504
Page views for each session	43
PC time spent per month	32:14:51
Time spent per session	56 minutes
Duration of page viewed	44 seconds

EXHIBIT 7.6 Global Internet Usage

Source: Data from www.nielsen-netratings.com.

than to the content in any other medium. When in front of a television, consumers are easily distracted by other people or activities in the environment. The same holds true for the passivity of radio listening. Consumers seem to pay more attention to print media but may still flip pages quickly. Hoffman and Novak at Vanderbilt University applied the concept of **flow** from psychology to Web navigation behavior (see the eLab at www2000.ogsm.vanderbilt.edu). They define *flow* as:

> the state occurring during network navigation which is: (1) characterized by a seamless sequence of responses facilitated by machine interactivity, (2) intrinsically enjoyable, (3) accompanied by a loss of self-consciousness, and (4) self-reinforcing.

According to this concept, consumers are 100 percent involved and not easily distracted when they are online. Whether they are in a goal-oriented or experiential shopping trip online, they are focused. Therefore, once e-marketers can capture a pair of consumer eyeballs or earlobes, they can make a big impression in a short time as long as the Web site is enjoyable, self-reinforcing, and engaging. It was certainly the case for BMWfilms.com when it drew 30 million viewers in three years to watch 8–10 minute films online that were created by famous directors.

Energy and Psychic Costs Closely related to time are energy and psychic resources. Sometimes it is just too much trouble to turn on the computer, log on to the internet, and check e-mail, especially for dial-up users. This factor accounts for the rising popularity of short text messaging (SMS) via cell phones and handheld mobile devices. PDAs allow users to check the Web or e-mail anywhere, anytime—however, international standards are not yet consistent enough for travelers to count on this type of cell connectivity so must find a WiFi hotspot.

Consumers apply psychic resources when Web pages are hard to figure out or when facing technological glitches. Such may be the case with the 50 percent to 90 percent of all online shoppers who abandon online shopping carts, losing more than $63 billion in sales for online retailers (Janisch, 2004). At one time or another all users abandon carts due to technical problems and other issues—buying just gets to be too much trouble. Marketing Sherpa study found 59.8 percent shopping cart abandonment and concluded that consumers drop out because of marketing problems, not technology problems (as in the past) (Holland, 2006). For instance, consumers want to see a clear return policy and shipping prices before clicking that "buy" button.

Internet Exchange

Then comes the actual moment when exchange occurs. Browser favorites help consumers quickly jump to their favorite online retailer when looking for a product or making a purchase. In addition, e-mail messages from firms often contain hyperlinks to bring consumers directly to specific information, news reports, or advertised specials. The internet has the added feature of automation to facilitate exchange. For example, CNN.com sends one sentence e-mails several times a day or week with breaking news for those who sign up for the service—the full story is a click away. Also, Amazon.com sends consumers a link to a new book by a previously purchased author. These automated e-mails facilitate the exchange process.

Exchange Outcomes

Just what benefits do consumers get by exchanging all that money, time, and energy? The Pew Research Center conducts continuing research entitled *Internet and the American Life.* Along with comScore Media Metrix, Nielsen//NetRatings, the ClickZ network, and information from many other sources, we now have a rich understanding of what American consumers do online and how the internet has changed the way people behave. Using these generalizations, marketers look for differences in their target markets and then build online and off-line strategies to meet their needs.

People do only five basic things online—connect, create, enjoy, learn, and trade. Each is ripe with marketing opportunity. In the following sections, we categorize the myriad of online activities into these areas of consumer need and desire. Looking at it this way helps marketers remember that profits come from focusing on the customer.

CONNECT Unlike any other medium, the internet allows consumers to interact with individuals and organizations using multimedia in two-way communication. Nearly all internet users send e-mail (92%). E-mail is still the internet's "killer app" worldwide, in spite of spam. Consumers communicate online because it is an inexpensive way to keep in touch, and because it is usually text based so it can be easily accomplished with a slow modem or over a wireless handheld device. In addition, consumers make new connections with the people and business partners they meet online that sometimes carry over to the physical world.

Consumers also spend time instant messaging (IM), use the internet to make phone calls (Skype), and paid $449.5 million in 2003 to use online dating sites (Exhibit 7.7) ("U.S. Consumer Spending," 2004). Some of this communication takes place in communities of interest such as online dating, book reviews at Amazon, blog sites, and many more. Consumers exchange time and energy to build relationships with friends and family, and even to work out problems with companies.

E-mail popularity explains the success of Web-based e-mail services, such as Hotmail (Microsoft), Gmail (Google), AOL, and Yahoo! These sites consistently get a huge number of visitors, and the Gmail introduction serves as a reminder that many new business opportunities

still exist around online consumer needs even in crowded competitive fields.

Appliance convergence created a new form of connecting. Seventy-two percent of internet users send and receive digital pictures, some from a cell phone or PDA ("The Arrival of the Convergence," 2004). Connecting causes users to send virtual greeting cards, Monk-e-mail (www.careerbuilder.com), and much more.

CREATE This need to connect was one springboard for the Web's social networking sites, where users can create profiles, upload pictures and other content, and connect with friends and colleagues. Content creation is the highest form of user engagement because they are participating by adding to the Web's offerings, as discussed in Chapter 1. MySpace is the most popular site with 4.5 percent of all Web traffic in January 2008 (according to www.hitwise.com). Facebook is a real contender, however, due to its many new applications. For professionals, LinkedIn sets the standard, with over 19 million profiles—and increasing by 1 million a month. LinkedIn members include executives from all Fortune 500 companies.

User-content creation for uploading has grown so quickly and is so vast that we created a separate category of exchange outcome for this edition of *E-Marketing*. Exhibit 7.8 shows that 21 percent of all internet users create and post content. The biggest activity involves sharing digital photos at sites such as Flickr.com (37%). Users also create or post comments to blogs and create videos for YouTube and for a myriad of online contests for user-created television commercials (e.g., the Doritos Super Bowl Contest).

Outcome	Percentage	Outcome	Percentage
Send or read e-mail	92	Share files (P2P)	27
Support for specific situation	58	Chat in online discussion	22
Send instant message	39	Use social networking site	16
Read a blog	39	Make Internet phone call	13
Send/receive text messages from cell phone	35	Visit dating Web site	11

EXHIBIT 7.7 Proportion Connecting Online in the United States

Source: Data from 2004 to 2007 studies at www.pewinternet.org.

Outcome	Percentage	Outcome	Percentage
Upload photos to share	37	Create content and post	21
Rate a product, person, service using online rating system	32	Create a blog	12
Tag online content (photo, etc.)	28	Create avatar for virtual world	6
Post comments to blog or other site	22		

EXHIBIT 7.8   Proportion Creating and Uploading Content in the United States

Source: Data from 2004 to 2007 studies at www.pewinternet.org.

It is no wonder that users create all these videos for uploading—nearly half of all internet users enjoy watching videos on social media sites. Finally, 6 percent create avatars for virtual worlds, such as Second Life with its 11 million avatar residents. You'll find social media strategies to capitalize on this trend in later chapters.

ENJOY   Many consumers use the internet to enjoy entertainment (Exhibit 7.9). Two-thirds browse for fun, sometimes on experiential shopping trips, as previously mentioned. One of internet's big promises, however, is audio and visual entertainment. Over half of U.S. users currently watch video online, and 37 percent download music, largely due to high broadband connectivity adoption rates. We believe these numbers will increase rapidly in the future for the following reasons: First, all television content will be transmitted digitally by the time you read this (mandated by the U.S. government for 2008). Second, more devices such as the TiVo system will allow TV programs to be delivered on demand. In addition, new services such as Akimbo store programming for internet delivery to either television or PC anytime. Third, consumers will adopt broadband as part of their cable TV service. As they do, online entertainment content will grow considerably and become just one of the choices for consumers deciding how to spend time online. In the meantime, streaming media and improved compression techniques give more consumers access to online entertainment.

One way for marketers to keep their fingers on the pulse of internet users is to monitor search terms entered at Google, Yahoo!, and other search engines. Popular search items tend to change every month with breaking news events or holidays; however, a glance at the most-entered terms in 2007 validates high use of the internet for entertainment, celebrity news, and sports (Exhibit 7.10).

LEARN   Consumers access information to learn things online such as news, driving directions, travel information, jobs, weather, sports scores, and radio broadcasts over the internet (Exhibit 7.11). Thirteen percent of all users take a class online. In fact, 72 percent of respondents in a Harris Poll said the internet made them more resourceful,

Outcome	Percentage	Outcome	Percentage
Surf for fun	62	Download video files	27
Watch video on social media site	48	Download screensavers	23
Sports scores	45	Download computer games	21
Download music	37	Visit adult Web site	13
Play a game	35	Download podcast	12

EXHIBIT 7.9   Proportion Enjoying Entertainment Online in the United States

Source: Data from 2004 to 2007 studies at www.pewinternet.org.

Google		Yahoo!		Lycos	
Rank	**Term**	**Rank**	**Term**	**Rank**	**Term**
1	American Idol	1	Britney Spears	1	Poker
2	YouTube	2	WWE	2	MySpace
3	Britney Spears	3	Paris Hilton	3	Britney Spears
4	2007 cricket World Cup	4	Naruto	4	Paris Hilton
5	Chris Benoit	5	Beyonce	5	Golf
6	iPhone	6	Lindsay Lohan	6	YouTube
7	Anna Nicole Smith	7	Rune Scape	7	Naruto
8	Paris Hilton	8	Fantasy Football	8	Disney
9	Iran	9	Fergie	9	Pokemon
10	Vanessa Hudgens	10	Jessica Alba	10	WWE

Exhibit 7.10   Top 10 Search Terms for 2007

Source: Data reported by Google, Yahoo!, and Lycos.

and 46 percent said it made them smarter (see www.redefineyourworld.com).

E-marketers have known for some time that consumers only have a limited amount of time to exchange for media consumption and that the internet takes away from off-line media time. For instance, 14 percent of the U.S. population says the internet is their primary source of news, and 71 percent of online users check the news.

How do internet users find information for learning? Many are loyal to particular media sites, often prompted by breaking news e-mails. Ninety-one percent use search engines, and 36 percent use Wikipedia for information. Queries range from the vanity search ("How many times does my name come up on Google?") to the soul searching ("Who is God?") and ridiculous ("what is what") to the heartbreaking ("My mom has breast cancer—what should I do?").

TRADE Most consumers shop, buy, or conduct other transaction-oriented activities online.

Outcome	Percentage	Outcome	Percentage
Use search engine for information	91	Virtual tour of location	51
Map or driving directions	86	Research for current job	50
Hobby information	83	Political news / information	47
Check the weather	78	Info about a job	46
Travel information	73	A place to live	39
Health/medical	80	Financial	36
Get news	71	Use Wikipedia	36
Government site	66	Religious/spiritual	35
Find "how-to" or repair info.	55	Listen to live event online	29
Find phone number /address	54	Search for info about a person	28
Research for school/training	51	Take a class online for fun	13

EXHIBIT 7.11   Proportion Learning and Getting Information Online in the United States

Source: Data from 2004 to 2007 studies at www.pewinternet.org.

Outcome	Percentage	Outcome	Percentage
Research product before buying	81	Use classified ads (Craig's list)	30
Buy a product	66	Pay to access digital content	28
Buy/make travel reservation	64	Participate in online auction	26
Bank online	51	Charity donation	12
Download computer programs	39	Take class for college credit	18
Pay bills online	38	Sell something online	15
Use online classifieds (Craig's list)	32	Buy/sell stocks, bonds, mutual funds	11

EXHIBIT 7.12 Proportion Trading Online in the United States

Source: Data from 2004 to 2007 studies at www.pewinternet.org.

Estimates range from 65 percent to 87 percent of internet users in the United States who have purchased products online, and nearly a quarter pay for digital content access (such as a subscription to a dating service or *The New York Times*). Further, a majority make travel reservations online. The most dramatic new category is online classifieds, largely led by Craig's List. Online auctions are also growing, with 15 percent of internet users selling something online either via classified or auction. Consider eBay, with 276 million active, registered users in 39 global markets and $59 billion in product value sold in 2007 (see www.ebay.com fast facts). Due to its popularity, several firms offer special software to assist bidders in finding value at eBay. Conversely, online grocery shopping dropped from the list in the past few years due to its lack of viability as an online model for most U.S. grocers.

It is important to note that 81 percent of all internet users seek information online prior to buying products. Sometimes they use this information to purchase online, and sometimes they purchase at a local brick-and-mortar store—many consumers purchase outside of the internet based on information they get online.

A typical internet consumer spends an hour per day shopping online, makes 21 online purchases a year, and 57 percent of them say the internet has made them better consumers (see www.redefineyourworld.com). Exhibit 7.12 shows the e-commerce landscape for U.S. consumers.

Chapter Summary

The internet has grown more quickly than any other medium in history. In 2007, 1.2 million people had access to the internet, representing 19 percent of the global population. Yet 5.4 billion other people are not online, due to social and cultural, technological, and legal and political issues, as well as the idea that many activities cannot be replaced by the internet.

The basic marketing concept of exchange refers to the act of obtaining a desired object from someone by offering something in return. Individual consumers bring their own characteristics and personal resources to the process as they seek specific outcomes from an exchange. All of this interaction occurs within a technological, social/cultural, and legal context. Among the U.S. social/cultural trends affecting online exchanges are consumers' paramount trust in each other, consumer sophistication, information overload, multitasking, I want what I want when I want it, home and work boundary blur, online oxygen, self-service, and concerns about privacy, data security, and online crime.

Internet users tend to have a more positive attitude toward technology and be more adept and experienced with computer usage. Gender affects attitudes toward use of internet technology, and age and ethnicity can also affect internet usage. Online shoppers tend to be more goal oriented and be either convenience or price oriented. Finally, broadband connectivity means the ability to watch videos and listen to music online.

The four main costs that consumers exchange for benefits are money, time, energy,

Exercises

REVIEW QUESTIONS

1. What is an exchange?
2. What are some of the trends affecting online exchanges in the United States?
3. What individual characteristics influence online behavior?
4. What are the four costs that constitute a consumer's resources for exchange?
5. How can e-marketers facilitate internet exchange?
6. What are the five main categories of outcomes sought by internet users?
7. In what ways do consumers create content for the Web?

DISCUSSION QUESTIONS

8. Why would a consumer go to the library instead of using the internet for research?
9. Can an attention economy exist in countries where internet penetration is low? Explain your answer.
10. What might e-marketers do to accommodate consumers who are experiential shoppers?
11. Do you consider the concept of flow an explanation for what some observers call internet addiction? Explain your answer.

12. Ho̤ _____ _____ on consumer interest in relationships as an outcome of internet activity?
13. What are the reasons for the growth in social networking online?
14. Why do you think that consumers trust each other more than they trust companies? What can marketers do about this?

WEB ACTIVITIES

15. Conduct a survey in your class to determine what benefits each student looks for online. Categorize the benefits under the headings used in this chapter and then tally your answers to determine percentages.
16. Customers face many barriers when purchasing online. It has been estimated that as many as 60 percent of all purchases are abandoned midstream. Working in groups, try to develop ways that online retailers can help more site visitors be converted to buyers.
17. Visit your local newspaper classified ads online, then examine Craig's List for your local area. Why do you think that Craig's List and eBay have taken share from newspaper classifieds? What advice do you have for newspapers to regain customers?

CHAPTER 8

Segmentation and Targeting Strategies

If segmentation theorists had a god to worship, it would be the internet.

—ROGER D. BLACKWELL, CUSTOMERS.COM

Segmentation is not just about generating demographic profiles anymore. You have to know and understand the channels that you can reach them on.

—JACQUELINE ROUSSEAU-ANDERSON, FORRESTER RESEARCH, INC.

Chapter Outline

The main goal of this chapter is to examine the various bases for market segmentation, the classifications and characteristics of e-marketing segments, and two important coverage strategies for targeting selected segments. You will also gain a better understanding of the size and growth of various market segments on the internet.

After reading this chapter, you will be able to:

- Outline the characteristics of the three major markets for e-business.

- Explain why and how e-marketers use market segmentation to reach online customers.

- List the most commonly used market segmentation bases and variables.

- Outline five types of usage segments and their characteristics.

- Describe two important coverage strategies e-marketers can use to target online customers.

The 1-800-Flowers Story

Jim McCann is a guy who keeps up with technology. He started with 14 retail flower shops in New York City in 1976 and is now a multichannel retailer who understands his target customers. Ten years later he acquired the incoming toll-free number 1-800-Flowers so that customers could order flowers over the telephone from any location for New York delivery. In 1995, McCann was quick to jump onto e-commerce with an early Web site to extend the brand: 1–800-flowers.com and offer 24/7 worldwide delivery. By this point, the firm had expanded to plants, gourmet food, gift baskets, and other gift-related merchandise.

The Web site worked well and the firm generated much data about prospects and customers who registered and purchased online. How to sort it all out and use it for increasing profits? McCann used data mining software from SAS to identify customer segments for better targeting. The software sifted through clickstreams and purchasing patterns of the firm's 21 million customers and spit out some interesting findings. According to

(*continued*)

(*continued*)

McCann, "Not every customer wants the same relationship. Some want you to be more involved with them than others; some will give you different levels of permission on how to contact them. At the end of the day, you have many different customers . . . [information about] who they are and how they would like to be treated." 1-800-Flowers can respond to the segment of one person who only purchases every year on Valentine's Day, or the larger segment who wants several birthday reminders a year so they don't forget to honor their friends and family. All of this individual attention is possible at McCann's place.

As a result of identifying and serving many different usage customer segments, customer retention increased by 15 percent in 2003, and sales increased 13.8 percent to $40.9 million.

The firm's Web site attracted 13.1 million new customers and increased the annual repeat order rate to 43 percent. The bonus? Reduced cost due to less time on the phone with customers. And it seems to be working: In 2006 the Web site had 2.1 million monthly visitors and $430 million in sales. McCann is now ready to slice the data from its complementary brands, including home décor and garden merchandise under Plow & Hearth, premium popcorn and other food gifts under The Popcorn Factory, gourmet food products under GreatFood.com, and children's gifts under HearthSong and Magic Cabin Dolls. McCann is still on the cutting edge because 1-800-Flowers now has a small but growing retail presence in Second Life: "We look for all possible ways to get into a dialogue with our customers," according to McCann.

SEGMENTATION AND TARGETING OVERVIEW

1-800-Flowers clearly understands the needs and behavior of its various targets. A company must have in-depth market knowledge to devise a savvy segmentation and targeting strategy. As explained in Chapter 3, e-marketing strategic planning occurs in two highly interrelated tiers. The first involves segmentation, targeting, differentiation, and positioning, topics covered in this and the following chapter. Second-tier strategies involving the 4 Ps and customer relationship management (CRM) are discussed in Chapters 10 to 15.

Marketers make informed decisions about segmentation and targeting based on internal, secondary, and primary data sources (see Exhibit 8.1). **Marketing segmentation** is the process of aggregating individuals or businesses along similar characteristics that pertain to the use, consumption, or benefits of a product or service. The result of market segmentation is groups of customers called market segments. We use the word *groups* loosely here. A market segment can actually be any size from one

person to millions of people—an important point because the technology of internet marketing allows companies to easily tailor market mixes for targeting individuals. It is also important to note that segments are worth targeting separately only when they have bigger differences between them than within them. For example, if internet users behave differently at work than at home, marketers can capitalize on these differences by targeting each as a separate segment—otherwise why bother separating these users into two segments?

Market Targeting is the process of selecting the market segments that are most attractive to the firm. Some criteria companies use for selecting segments to target include accessibility, profitability, and growth.

THREE MARKETS

Sergio Zyman, formerly chief marketing officer of Coca-Cola, has been quoted as saying, "Marketing is supposed to sell stuff." One way information technology helps sell stuff is by facilitating

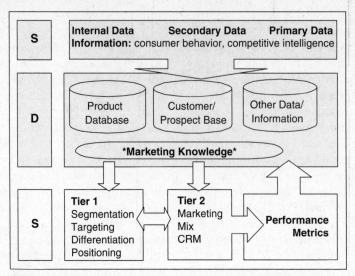

EXHIBIT 8.1 Sources, Databases, and Strategy: Tier 1 Strategies in Chapters 8 and 9

relationships before and after the transaction with prospects, customers, partners, and supply chain members. Yet all the latest technology can't help marketers sell stuff if they don't identify appropriate markets. Exhibit 8.2 highlights three important markets that both sell and buy to each other: businesses, consumers, and governments. Although this book focuses on the **business-to-consumer (B2C)** market with some coverage of **business-to-business (B2B)** activities, all three markets are briefly described next. Note that after B2C and B2B markets, the **business-to-government (B2G)** and **consumer-to-consumer (C2C)** markets are where most e-business activity occurs.

Business Market

The business market involves the marketing of products to businesses, governments, and institutions for use in the business operation, as

	To Business	To Consumer	To Government
Initiated by Business	Business-to-Business **(B2B)** *The Idea Factory* www.ideafactory.com	Business-to-Consumer **(B2C)** *Classmates.com* www.classmates.com	Business-to-Government **(B2G)** *Western Australian Government Supply* www.ssc.wa.gov.au
Initiated by Consumer	Consumer-to-Business **(C2B)** *Better Business Bureau* www.bbb.org	Consumer-to-Consumer **(C2C)** *eBay* www.ebay.com	Consumer-to-Government **(C2G)** *GovWorks* www.govworks.gov
Initiated by Government	Government-to-Business **(G2B)** *Small Business Administration* www.sba.gov	Government-to-Consumer **(G2C)** *California state* www.state.ca.us	Government-to-Government **(G2G)** *USA.gov* www.usa.gov

EXHIBIT 8.2 Three Basic Markets

Source: Updated in 2008 from Marian Wood, *Prentice Hall's Guide to E-Commerce and E-Business* (Upper Saddle River, NJ: Prentice Hall, 2001).

components in the business products, or for resale. The online B2B marketing is huge because a higher proportion of firms are connected to the internet than consumers, especially in developing countries. Much of the B2B online activity is transparent to consumers because it involves proprietary networks that allow information and database sharing. Consider FedEx, the package delivery firm. This company maintains huge databases of business customers' shipping behavior and account information. Its customers can schedule a package pickup using the Web site, track the package using a PC or PDA, and pay the shipping bill online. Sometimes the shipping order is automatically triggered when a consumer buys something online from a FedEx client; then FedEx sends e-mail notification of its delivery progress to the retailer.

Information technology created tremendous efficiencies in the B2B market, yet businesses that sell online face increasing competition due to globalization and lower market entry barriers brought about by the internet. As well, many firms are changing their entire supply chain structures, which often results in conflict between different marketing channels. This conflict is especially problematic when manufacturers sell directly to consumers online, thus taking business from retail partners. On the other hand, many firms experience greater interdependence in their value chain due to electronic collaboration practices. Many challenges and opportunities exist for firms in the B2B market.

Finally, the internet allows for strange bedfellows. Companies in unlikely industries find it relatively easy to forge partnerships that supply value to customers. Consider, for example, the joint venture that created MSNBC (Microsoft and the NBC television network). In this environment, firms compete not only for customers but also for partners and sometimes even form partnerships with rivals. As an example, the major airlines came together to form an airline reservations hub—thus undercutting online travel agents. As another example, the major U.S. auto manufacturers have a shared procurement hub to link to their suppliers.

Government Market

The U.S. government is the world's largest buyer. Add to this the purchasing power of U.S. states, counties, cities, and other municipal agencies, which makes for a huge market. The governments of other countries are also major purchasers. The state government of Western Australia, for instance, annually buys $6 billion in goods and services and authorizes more than 40,000 work contracts (Exhibit 8.3).

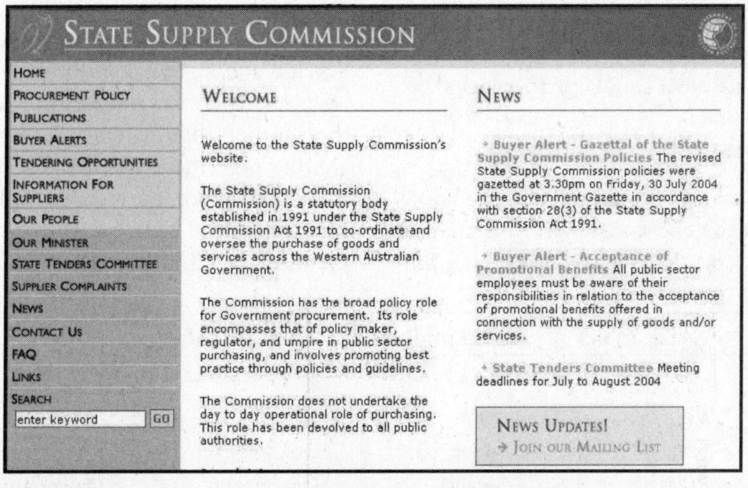

EXHIBIT 8.3 Western Australia's State Supply Commission

Source: www.ssc.wa.gov.au.

Businesses wishing to sell to governments face challenges unique to this market. Government agencies have many rules for suppliers to follow regarding qualifications, paperwork, and so on. Additionally, firms often must compete to be on the government list of approved suppliers, and then compete yet again for specific work contracts through a bidding process. Government agencies are generally particular about timely delivery of quality products at reasonable prices. The good news is that small and large businesses usually have an equal chance of selling to governments, and government Web sites announce their buying needs in advance of the bidding process. Internet technology has helped businesses to be more effective in government markets.

A debate that erupted in recent years centers on whether U.S. government agencies should accept advertising on their Web sites. Proponents suggested that advertising fees would subsidize the government costs and lower taxes; opponents worried about the ethics of mingling government and business in this way, as well as cluttering government sites with ads. The argument recently boiled down to this analogy: Is a government Web site more like a city bus or a park, with one accepting ads and the other not? In the end, the GSA (General Services Administration) made a policy that no advertising should be done on .gov Web sites because "citizens expect their government to be impartial." See www.usa.gov for the sticky details of what is approved (partner links on a Web site) and what is not (partner logos).

Consumer Market

The consumer market involves marketing goods and services to the end consumer. This chapter describes many consumer market segments, and most of this text is dedicated to e-marketing in the consumer market.

MARKET SEGMENTATION BASES AND VARIABLES

Marketers can base their segmentation of consumer markets on **demographics**, geographic location, **psychographics**, and behavior with regard to the product. Within each base, many segmentation variables come into play (see Exhibit 8.4). For example, McDonald's demographic segmentation uses the variables of age and family life cycle to target adults, children, senior citizens, and families. One way to understand segmentation bases is as a few general organizing categories, and segmentation variables as numerous subcategories.

Companies often combine bases and focus on categories such as **geodemographics** (geography and demographics). Similarly, they can build segments using any combination of variables that makes sense for their industry. The important thing to remember is that marketers create segments based on variables that can be used to identify and reach the right people at the right time.

After using any of these four bases alone or in combination, marketers profile segment members using many other variables. For example, after a Web site such as iVillage.com creates a list of mothers who register at the site (segment basis), it can use primary and secondary research to develop profiles that describe these mothers. These profiles might indicate that a certain percentage of the mothers like to cook international dishes, another percentage generally prepares traditional meals, and another percentage seldom cooks at all. Marketers need to know which variables broadly identify the target segment and which simply

Bases	Geographics	Demographics	Psychographics	Behavior
Identifying/	City	Age	Activities	Benefits sought
Profiling	County	Income	Interests	
Variable	State	Gender	Opinions	Usage level
Examples	Region	Education	Personality	Online engagement
	Country	Ethnicity	Values	User status

EXHIBIT 8.4   Segmentation Bases and Examples of Related Variables

further describe it because marketers use identification variables to enumerate and access the target. By this distinction we mean that a firm can get mailing lists of mothers and discover which magazines reach them, but it is difficult to figure out how to reach women who cook Italian food. If iVillage knows that only 5 percent of its target (mothers) cooks Italian food, and 60 percent does not cook at all, it will help them to design site products and content. Thus, marketers use profile variables to refine the marketing mix, including Web site content and advertising.

The next sections describe geographic, demographic, psychographic, and behavior segments on the internet.

Geographic Segments

Although the geographic location of online companies is not important to users accessing Web sites, it is important to organizations with an internet presence. The reason is that most firms target specific cities, regions, states, or countries with their product offerings. Even the largest multinational firms usually develop multisegment strategies based on **geographics**.

Product distribution strategy is a driving force behind geographic segmentation. A consumer goods online retailer, such as Buy.com, will want to reach only customers in countries where it distributes products. Similarly, firms offering services online will only sell to geographic areas where they can provide customer service. Before an organization decides to serve the Web community, it must examine the proportion of internet users in its selected geographic targets. Consider the Small Business Administration (SBA) (Exhibit 8.5). This government agency serves citizens speaking both Spanish and English, and like many companies and non-profits created Web site content in different languages.

Important Geographic Segments for E-Marketing

The United States boasts the largest internet usage in the world, with 186 million users (64% of population). Although it is the largest market in terms of absolute size, China is close

with 95.6 million users, and Japan with 77.9 million. In contrast, South Korea boasts the highest proportion of internet usage among its population. In total, 19 country markets have more than 50 percent internet penetration. These countries represent good markets for new technology because they are quite internet savvy. Appendix A lists all countries in the world with available statistics on internet usage, and this would be a good starting point for geographic segmentation. Bear in mind that these figures represent one point in time during 2004, and that internet usage statistics vary widely depending on who conducts the study. Marketers using geographic variables for segmentation also evaluate online markets by region, city, urban area, and so forth. For instance, the entire North American and Scandinavian regions contain attractive markets, and most urban areas, such as Mexico City, Mexico, are more wired than are rural areas.

Some research firms evaluate the quality of a country's market using additional criteria. IDC conducts an annual Information Society Index (ICI), evaluating countries on four infrastructure variables designed to predict their ability to access and absorb information technology: computer and internet adoption rates, telecom services, and social uses of and receptivity to information technology. The index seeks to quantify a nation's "ability to access and absorb information and information technology" (see www.idc.com). In 2003, Denmark, Sweden, the United States, Switzerland, and Canada gained the top five positions as the world's dominant information economies, with the United States gaining from eighth place the previous year. In part, this ranking is because the Nordic countries have quite high mobile internet access. Interestingly, two large markets, India and China, placed in the bottom five slots in 2002. Many factors indicate market viability for e-commerce and other e-business activities, as explained in Chapter 4.

LANGUAGES ON WEB PAGES English has not been the language of most Web pages and online bulletin boards for many years, and the relative decline continues. In 2007, the top internet languages included English (33%), Japanese (8%),

EXHIBIT 8.5 U.S. Small Business Administration Site in Spanish and English
Source: www.sba.gov.

Chinese (14%), French (6%), and German (5%), according to www.internetworldstats.com (Exhibit 8.6). These findings obviously have huge implications for e-marketers desiring to reach global markets via the internet; until more online text appears in local languages, users in those countries will not be able to participate in e-commerce or other online activities. Unfortunately, Web developers in many Asian and Middle Eastern countries face technical challenges because local languages require double-byte character sets (versus single byte for Romance languages) and, therefore, need more database and transaction customization and complicated search algorithms.

LOCAL MARKETING Finally, local marketing efforts work well online, thanks to Google and Yahoo! local searches. Small companies, such as the local car repair, can be listed in these searches even if they don't have Web sites. Google offers text

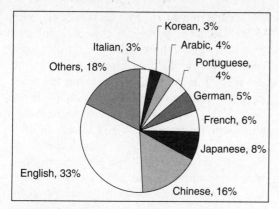

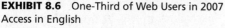

EXHIBIT 8.6   One-Third of Web Users in 2007 Access in English

Source: Data from www.internetworldstats.com.

messaging services for cell and PDA users wanting to find a local business. Simply send an SMS message to 466453 ("google" on most devices) then the item you want to find and the zip code (e.g., "movies 89557" without the quotes). Over half of internet users look for local restaurants or other services using a local search—the top Web providers were (according to comScore.com):

- Google Sites (29.8%)
- Yahoo! Sites (29.2%)
- Microsoft Sites (12.3%)
- Time Warner (7.1%)
- Verizon (6.6%)
- YellowPages.com (3.9%)
- Ask Network (2.7%)
- Local.com (1.9%)
- InfoSpace Network (1.9%)
- DexOnline.com (1.4%)

Other important local marketing efforts include eBay classifieds (with 19 million visitors in the second quarter of 2006) and the hugely popluar Craigslist. The latter operates in 450 cities worldwide and gets over 9 billion page views per month.

Demographic Segments

In the internet's early years, the typical user was a young male, college educated, with a high income—except for gender, the description of a typical innovator. This picture is generally repeated in countries with low levels of internet adoption. In developed nations, users look more like the mainstream population. From a demographic perspective, however, the heaviest internet penetration in 2008 includes 18–29-year-olds (92% use the internet) who are white (76%), live in urban or suburban areas (77% each), earn more than $50,000 in household income (over 90%), and have high education (93% of college graduates are online), according to Pew Internet & American Life research.

To reach these segments, marketers identify attractive demographic niches. The following sections describe three market segments that have recently caught the attention of e-marketers: millenials, kids, and online opinion leaders.

MILLENNIALS   In the United States, 60 million people born between 1979 and 1994 are coming of age in the twenty-first century. More than 90 percent use the internet—nearly 20 percent over the national average. They are able to handle multitasking and information overload better than older internet users because they grew up with the internet. They are the folks who can easily operate any receiving appliance, and see information, communication, and entertainment as just one data stream available on multiple devices. They know how to use pop-up ad blockers online and use the digital video recorder to watch television programming on their schedule, zapping the commercials—unless they are especially entertaining. Eighty percent of millenials carry cell phones and 36 percent use them for sending and receiving short text messages (SMS) (Baker, 2004). Most have broadband for downloading music and watching video online.

Millenials are an important market segment because they are the first generation to control information quickly, use many technology gadgets at once, and totally ignore marketers. More than half of 13-to 24-year-olds watch television and use the internet at the same time, sometimes voting online while watching *American Idol* or other television programs. They use many media channels, such as instant messaging, e-mail, chat rooms, iPods or other MP3 players, P2P networks, video games, and virtual worlds.

If marketers can get their attention and entertain them, they will listen and spread the news through online word-of-mouth (viral marketing) and social networks. This group is a real challenge, and important to e-marketers as the proving ground for the future—if brands can't capture the younger markets they eventually become obsolete. See Exhibit 8.7 for gURL.com, a great site targeting female teenagers and young adults.

KIDS The number of kids under the age of 16 online is increasing. The 2–11-year-old category jumped to over 15 million in 2007. The 8–14-year-old segment contains 29 million members with a spending power of $40 billion, according to Packaged Facts. "The number of children throughout the world using the internet will increase dramatically over the next six years and will become a huge market," according to Michael Erbschloe, Research Director of Computer Economics. What do they do online? Hang out at social networking site Webkinz.com for hours at a time, for one thing. Webkinz are the cute stuffed animals that sell for $10–$20 at brick-and-mortar retailers. Once home, kids cut

the tag and find an 8-digit code that can be used at Webkinz.com to register their new toy and receive a digital look-alike pet. Once there, children receive virtual money (KinzCash) and can spend it to build things or clothes and other items for their virtual pet unicorn, cat, or tie dye frogs. Kids can play games to earn more money and naturally, parents can add money to their children's accounts. Webkinz provides safe connections and chats with other pet owners, allows members to have virtual jobs that earn money, and also provides creative outlets, such as, allowing children to create TV shows. The average time spent on Webkinz in late 2006 was 2 hours and 8 minutes, as compared with YouTube's average time spent of 31.5 minutes.

Kids 8–12 did many other things "always or often" online in 2006, such as playing online games (70%), look up information for homework (58%), use a search engine (48%), read or send e-mail (34%), watch online videos or movie trailers (28%), use instant messenger (22%), listen to internet radio (20%), and even write blogs (6%), according to a Mindshare study.

Many parents worry about kids but they can't stop this huge potential new market. Instead, they censor Web content for children (see the "Let's Get Technical" box).

EXHIBIT 8.7   gURL.com Targets the Female Teens and Young Adults Segments

Source: www.gURL.com.

LET'S GET TECHNICAL

Content Filtering

Somehow, you were sucked into babysitting your seven-year-old cousin. He asks you if he can go online while you are making his dinner—macaroni and cheese with hot dog chunks, of course. However, you think to yourself, "How am I going to monitor him while I am downstairs cooking?" You know that you, or his parents, would never want him to experience inappropriate material online. As you pause to mull over this dilemma, your cousin says, "Don't worry! My mom and dad made the computer safe for me."

One growing segment of Web users is children under the age of 18. Children often have their own personal e-mail accounts and online nicknames. Many families are concerned that their children will be exposed to unwanted material online, such as pornography or violence, which can be considered objectionable. Even children not seeking such material may be exposed when conducting innocent searches. For example, a simple search for "girls' sites" using one of the top search engines resulted in numerous objectionable links to sex sites, such as a link titled "Naked Girls Sites Teenager Drunk and Naked".

Many solutions are available to serve the needs of user segments that do not want exposure to this type of material. One group of solutions aims to curb exposure to offensive material through education or legislation. Another group of solutions aims to limit exposure by use of technology. Education-and legislation-based solutions include:

- Educate children not to pursue offensive online material.
- Ban offensive material through legislative means.
- Require/encourage providers of offensive material to put age warnings on their sites (i.e., "if you are under 18 do not enter here").
- Require/encourage providers of offensive material to run an age verification system. Such systems require users to purchase a password using a credit card or require a valid credit card number to verify age. The presumption is that minors do not have access to credit cards.

- Require/encourage providers of offensive material to rate their material using industry-standard ratings similar to those used by the television or film industries.

Technology-based solutions include:

- Ask the internet service provider (ISP) to filter the content coming to the user.
- Filter the content right on the user's own computer using specialized software.
- Use search engines that filter the results based on user preferences.

All solutions mentioned have pros and cons, and they have been the subject of lively debates. This section focuses only on solutions that are technology based.

The internet is comprised of many different types of computers, and when users access Web pages, they are metaphorically hopping from computer to computer until the destination is reached. At any one of these hops, the content can be scanned and filtered for appropriateness. In the corporate world, employees are typically barred from objectionable sites by software running on a corporate computer that serves as the gatekeeper to the internet. This computer is called a **proxy server**. All communication between any corporate computer and the internet passes through the proxy server. It is an efficient solution and even allows employers to record attempted accesses to objectionable sites and to take disciplinary action when desired. Proxy servers have also been used to reduce employees' leisure-surfing while at work. For example, some corporations have chosen to block sports-oriented sites, such as espn.com.

The home Web user typically does not have access to a similar service; ISPs are reluctant to filter content because many users want to access this type of material. Some countries, such as China and Vietnam, filter content at the ISP level for everyone (adults as well as children). Incidentally, censorship is at the heart of the ethics debate on this issue.

Normally, the home user installs software on his or her computer to filter content. A number of products can perform this task, including

(continued)

(continued)

NetNanny, CYBERsitter, and CyberPatrol. As their names indicate, these products are intended to impede children's access to the objectionable sites. Many provide password overrides so other household members can have full internet access if they wish. Filters are also customizable, allowing users to set the strength of the filter for each user.

One way the products operate is by maintaining a "can't go" or "can go" list. Under the "can't go" scenario, the products maintain a list of banned sites—tens of thousands of sites.

Each time the child attempts to access a site, the software checks the site address against the list of banned sites. If it matches, the software can take one of the following actions:

1. Allow access to the site and silently make a record of the access for the parent to see later.
2. Allow access to the site and mask out objectionable words or images.
3. Block any access to the banned site.
4. Shut down the browser completely.

Under the "can go" scenario, the child can visit only sites that are on an approved list and nothing else. These sites might include such G-rated sites as disney.com or toysrus.com. The parents can always add to this list according to requests from the children. The same series of actions would be available should a child try to access a site not on the "can go" list.

Most products provide free updates as the list of objectionable sites grows. Updates are a major concern due to the constant production of new adult sites. However, filters that block access to sites based on words in the site name (e.g., cybersextalk.com) or the words in the Web page itself (e.g., "this site contains graphic sex") provide increased protection against the new sites. Even incoming e-mail or Microsoft Word documents can be scanned. In all cases the same list of foregoing action options is available.

The products can also monitor outgoing e-mail messages to ensure that children do not give away private information such as name, phone number, or address to a cyber pedophile. To accomplish this monitoring, the software is programmed to recognize the name, phone number, and address of household members and then scan for these keywords in any outgoing message. ISPs have also begun to offer e-mail filtering. Users are drawn to the e-mail filtering services, but still reject the idea of ISPs filtering their Web content. America Online's (AOL) filtering service is based on its customers' input. When a specific number of customers report an e-mail to be objectionable, AOL begins filtering it out of all subscribers' incoming e-mail.

Leading search engines, such as Google and AltaVista, also offer content filtering. Google has a default setting of a moderate filter, and users can permanently set their preferences to a higher or lower filter. AltaVista displays an on/off switch for its filter on every search page, which some parents have found more helpful because it is highly visible. Another type of service available is a search engine designed specifically for children, such as Ask Jeeves for Kids (www.ajkids.com) and Yahoo's Yahooligans!

Many feel that these **content filtering** products do provide the level of protection that families need. Some communities also install content filtering software in public libraries. These products are an example of a unique marketing mix that is tailored to a target market based on both demographics (age) and psychographics (beliefs). However, none of these products is completely foolproof, because Web sites change too quickly and determined kids are very clever.

ETHNIC GROUPS Hispanics, African Americans, and Asians are important online markets. English-speaking Hispanics are a huge segment with 79 percent internet adoption (www.pewinternet.org). They view 15 percent more Web pages and spend 9 percent more online than the average internet user (Vence, 2004). Hispanics who use the internet outspend those nonusers by a margin of 7 percent, a statistic that has caught the eye of marketers. In fact, in one poll, 20 percent of Hispanics said they would feel devastated if they couldn't use the Web, and they would rather give up their televisions (Greenspan, 2002). Using a geodemographic segmentation basis, marketers note that Miami–Fort Lauderdale, Florida, is the fifteenth largest market overall, but third largest for Hispanic Web users.

African Americans remain one of the largest and most quickly growing ethnic groups online, with 56 percent adoption (www.pewinter net.org). Internet users in this group tend to be younger, more highly educated, and more affluent than African Americans not using the internet. In addition, unlike other users, this group is heavy purchasers of music online and buys less clothing and travel. They are more likely than other internet users to go online from academic and public locations and are less likely to register at Web sites.

Chinese Americans living in the United States and Canada are also active online. More than half have internet access and 65 percent of those are online every day (Pastore, 2002b). Chinese Americans purchase books, computer products, and electronics online and enjoy a large purchasing power—the average income is $69,000.

INFLUENTIALS The *Washington Post* conducted research on the behavior and attitudes of opinion leaders using its Web site and discovered an important target for e-marketers ("Influentials: An Online Study," 2004). They dubbed this group *influentials*—individuals who influence others, driving change in America. They represent 10 percent of the population (and 15% of internet users) and serve as opinion leaders for the other 90 percent. Eighty-two percent of influentials have internet access (as compared with 64% of the general U.S. population). Two-thirds say they are asked for advice and forward information about products, careers, computers, Web sites, restaurants, or politics to an average of 5–20 others.

Because this segment influences others, it is important for marketers to determine how to reach them. Influentials use the internet first to research travel destinations (86%) and products (82%), and nearly all access the Web at least once a day. Recall that the sample for this study consisted of *Washington Post* Web site visitors, so these facts may not hold in the population of all online opinion leaders, but it highlights a highly attractive target market worthy of focus.

Psychographic Segments

User psychographics include personality, values, lifestyle, activities, interests, and opinions (AIO). *Personality* characteristics are traits such as other-oriented versus self-oriented and habits such as procrastination. *Values* are deeply held convictions such as religious beliefs. *Lifestyles* and *activities* as psychographics refer to non-product-related behavior such as playing sports or eating out. For example, users say that their Web surfing takes time away from these other activities: reading (39%), sleeping (23%), socializing (14%), and working (12%) (www.intelli quest.com). *Interests* and *opinions* are attitudes and beliefs people hold. As an example, some people believe that the Web is a waste of time, and others think they could not exist without e-mail.

INTEREST COMMUNITIES The internet is ideal for gathering people from all corners of the globe into communities with similar interests and tasks. Communities attract users, who then post their comments, profiles, and upload content for others to see—sometimes paying a subscription price for the benefit. Communities can form around Web sites and forums, or via e-mails to the entire group membership. We've identified 10 important types of online communities (Exhibit 8.8).

Perhaps the most important type is **Social networking**—the practice of expanding the number of one's business and social contacts by making connections through individuals online. It is based on the idea of *six degrees of separation* (that any two people are connected through contacts with no more than five others). LinkedIn is a great example of a professional network with over 19 million professionals worldwide, representing 150 industries (Exhibit 8.9). Recall that people trust others like them more than anyone else except for health care professionals, so social networking and other communities will only grow in importance.

Community Type	Description and Example
1. Entertainment communities	People join for multiplayer online gaming such as Second Life at secondlife.com or chess at Games.Yahoo.com.
2. Social networking communities	Users join and visit these communities to meet others, such as for dating (Match.com), getting a job (Monster.com), or finding a business connection (LinkedIn.com). Users are willing to pay a fee to join these communities, especially if they are large. Some sites exist purely for connecting to meet and make friends with like-minded people. These include MySpace.com, Facebook.com, and many others.
3. Trading communities	These communities exist so that users can exchange goods and services. Examples include online auctions in the consumer market (eBay.com) and business market (Guru.com), and music-sharing sites (Kazaa.com).
4. Education communities	These communities form around particular education disciplines, such as Elmar for marketing educators (marketingpower.com), educational software, or students participating in class or university discussion groups.
5. Scheduled events communities	When *American Idol*, the televised competition, invites viewers to vote and chat online, or businesses hold online conferences, they form a community for a one-time event.
6. Advocacy communities	Nonprofit communities form to influence public opinion. MoveOn.org, formed to unseat Republicans, used its community to create and pay for television ads. According to its founder, the internet is about listening to users, not talking to them.
7. Brand communities	Firms create customer relationship management communities around their brands on Web sites by allowing user posting. Examples include product reviews (Amazon.com), travel experiences (Tripadvisor.com), and tips for using your electronic gadget (engadget.com) or SAP software (Sap.com).
8. Consumer communities	Consumers post product reviews on Epinions.com and discuss their product experiences on Google Groups. What differentiates these from CRM communities is their lack of brand sponsorship, and thus, they are basically unedited opinions.
9. Employee communities	One example is the large network of former Microsoft employees who use e-mail and a private bulletin board to discuss Microsoft gossip and to network for professional purposes. LinkedIn.com and Xing.com are two important professional networks.
10. Special topics communities	In addition to the others on this list, some sites exist purely for user chat and bulletin board posting on a narrow topic of interest, such as movies, a particular automobile brand/model, various religions, and so forth. Leading this category are Google Groups (the former UseNet), Yahoo Groups, and Geocities.

EXHIBIT 8.8   Ten Important Types of Online Communities

Three ways can be used to target online communities. First, a company can build community at its own Web site through online discussion groups, bulletin boards, and online events. When folks with similar interests gather at the virtual watering hole to discuss issues, the value they receive in both information and social bonding keeps them returning. Second, companies can advertise on another firm's community site or within the e-mails to community members. Finally, many firms actually join the communities and listen and learn from others who are talking

EXHIBIT 8.9   Social Networking Community for Professionals

Source: www.linkedin.com.

about their industry. For example, Scott O'Leary, Managing Director, Customer Experience, at Continental Airlines spends several hours each day to find customer problems posted on travel sites such as Flyertalk (www.flyertalk.com). This network has nearly 135,000 members who post their air travel problems and tips for readers. O'Leary reportedly posted over 500 comments last year on Flyertalk and similar sites, answering questions and stopping rumors, according to *The Cincinnati Post*.

Several advantages and disadvantages characterize community targeting online. When an organization builds and maintains the community, it can present products and controlled messages customized to the group's interests, such as at Amazon.com. These communities are good targets for products of interest to them. For example, online gamers are always interested in hearing about the latest subscription-based game, and members of the Harley Owner's Group enjoy hearing about Harley-Davidson-branded products. Perhaps most importantly, communities are good places for companies to learn about customer problems and suggestions, such as O'Leary and Dell experienced. Conversely, online community conversation that is not moderated will gather negative product postings and offensive language. When firms sponsor a community, they must watch the content; however, if they edit it too heavily they will discourage future postings. Besides, if a

company removes negative posts, users will just post elsewhere online, so it is better to host the conversation at the company's own Web site. Finally, Web sites based on communities, such as Yahoo! Groups, experience some difficulty in drawing advertisers because of the unpredictable content and its possible effects on brand image.

ATTITUDES AND BEHAVIORS How do attitudes and behavior differ? Attitudes are internal evaluations about people, products, and other objects. They can be either positive or negative, but the evaluation process occurs inside a person's head. Behavior refers to what a person physically does, such as talking, eating, registering at a Web site, e-mailing for a free DVD, or visiting a Web site to shop or purchase a product. However, marketers do not include product-related behaviors in psychographic segmentation. Product behaviors are such a vital segment descriptor that they form an entirely separate category (see the next section). Thus, when marketers discuss psychographics, they mean the general ways that consumers spend time.

Psychographic information helps e-marketers define and describe market segments so they can better meet consumer needs. It is especially important for Web page design. For example, Japanese users do not like the flippant and irreverent tone at some U.S. sites. Japan's Web sites are more serious and do not include content such as political satire.

Baby boomers prefer earth tone colors on Web sites and the Millennials prefer more hip, bright colors. This type of attitudinal information is increasingly available about Web users.

Most marketers believe that demographics are not helpful in predicting who will purchase online or offline. Demographics help marketers find targets for communication, but other variables are more valuable for prediction, so marketers try to find a balance between both types of variables to describe segments. One such scheme is the segment's attitudes toward technology, found by Forrester Research to forecast whether or not users will buy online.

ATTITUDES TOWARD TECHNOLOGY Forrester Research measures consumer and business attitudes toward technology with a system called **Technographics**™. Since 2002, Forrester has conducted hundreds of thousands of surveys annually worldwide, with nearly one-third of those interviews held offline. Consumer Technographics discover how consumers think about, buy, and use

technology in many categories of devices and media in health care, financial services, retail, and travel industries, among others.

Technographics works by combining three specific variables (see www.forrester.com). First, the researchers ask questions to determine whether a person is optimistic or pessimistic toward technology. Next, they measure a user's income level because it is an important determinant of online shopping behavior. Finally, they query users about their primary motivation for going online. After over five years of collecting data, Forrester identified 10 consumer Technographics segments in the United States. Exhibit 8.10 displays these segments along with their descriptions. According to Forrester, the following is an example of how each segment uses technology:

- Fast Forwards are the biggest users of business software.
- New Age Nurturers are the most ignored group of technology consumers.

Motivation for Using Internet			
	Career	**Family**	**Entertainment**
Technology Optimists	<u>Early Adopters</u> **High Income**	**Fast Forwards** are time-strapped, driven, and top users of technology	**New Age Nurturers** are rarely served believers in technology for family and education	**Mouse Potatoes** are dedicated to interactive entertainment, especially on a PC
	<u>Fast Followers</u> **Low Income**	**Techno-Strivers** are up-and-coming believers in technology for career advancement	**Digital Hopefuls** are family-oriented technology lovers—a promising market for low-cost PCs	**Gadget Grabbers** are focused on low-cost, high-tech toys like Nintendo
Technology Pessimists	<u>Cautious Onlookers</u> **High Income**	**Handshakers** are successful professionals with a low technology tolerance	**Traditionalists** are small-town folks, suspicious of technology beyond basics	**Media Junkies** are visual, TV lovers and early adopters of satellite TV
	<u>Sidelined Citizens</u> **Low Income**	**Sidelined Citizens** are technophiles and technology laggards, the least receptive audience for any technology		

EXHIBIT 8.10 Consumer Technographics Segments in the United States

Source: Adapted from Mary Modahl, *Now or Never* (New York: HarperBusiness, 2000) and updated in 2008 with www.forrester.com segment descriptions.

- Mouse Potatoes love interactive entertainment on the PC.
- Of all low-income groups, Techno-Strivers have the highest proportion of PC ownership..
- Digital Hopefuls are a strong potential market for low-cost PCs.
- Gadget Grabbers buy low-cost, high-tech toys such as Nintendo.
- Handshakers aren't into technology for their business dealings.
- Traditionalists use VCRs but not anything more.
- Media Junkies love TV and are early adopters of satellite television.
- Sidelined Citizens are technology laggards.

Forrester's research revealed some interesting findings. First, technology optimism declines with age. Older users tend to have a more negative attitude toward technology. However, their attitudes may be less negative if they use a PC at work or live in one of the largest 50 U.S. cities. Men tend to be more optimistic about technology, and peer pressure can increase optimism in all demographic groups. That is, when friends discuss e-mail and Web sites, pessimists often rethink their positions. With regard to income, 40 percent of high-income citizens are optimistic, and certain low-income groups such as college students and young families are also optimistic about technology.

How do these findings translate to online purchasing? First, twice as many high-income optimists shop online compared with other groups. Only 2 percent of low-income pessimists shop online, and therefore they are not a good target for e-commerce firms. Second, combining Technographics with adopter categories, Forrester found that early adopters are high-income technology optimists, thus identifying the first consumers to shop online. Conversely, laggards are low-income pessimists who will be last to shop online. Finally, firms can use Technographics segments to profile customers who shop online and to determine where to allocate resources to attract more of the same. Starbucks used Technographics and discovered that 47 percent of its customers are early adopters (Fast Forwards, New Age Nurturers, and Mouse Potatoes). It further found that 22 percent are career-oriented, with Fast Forwards using the internet for self-advancement. These findings prompted Starbucks to begin selling merchandise online.

Forrester also maintains a database for its business Technographics. It conducts more than 2,500 interviews with senior managers of North American companies with more than $1 billion in annual revenues. In sum, Technographics survey results assist businesses with product development and launches, lead generation, cross-selling opportunities, customer service, and brand building.

Behavior Segments

Two commonly used behavioral segmentation variables are benefits sought and product usage. Marketers using **benefit segmentation** often form groups of consumers based on the benefits they desire from the product. For example, a 2007 eMarketer Survey reported on the benefits sought by adult internet users who visit travel Web sites: 55.1 percent want the "ability to check flights, hotels, and car rental availability and rates," 49.9 percent want "destination information," 49.7 percent want "travel promotion and specials," 22.0 percent want "travel bulletins and alerts," 12.7 percent want "chat/forum areas to read or post travel information," 10.8 percent want "the ability to personalize pages," and 8.6 percent want an "opt-in newsletter." These desired benefits help travel site owners, such as Expedia and Tripadvisor, design content that will appeal to various segments. Once on the site, the people looking for destination information may actually purchase as well.

Product usage is applied to segmentation in many ways. Marketers often segment by light, medium, and heavy product usage. As a hypothetical example, heavy internet users might be those who go online daily using either a PC or handheld wireless device; medium users, those who go online using a PC once every few days; and light users, those who connect only once every week or two. Companies must research to determine actual usage and decide how to split their target into appropriate user categories. Another approach is to categorize consumers as brand loyal, loyal to the competitive product, switchers (who don't care which site they use), and nonusers of the product. Next, we discuss some of these variables as they apply to the internet.

BENEFIT SEGMENTS Clearly, the internet offers something for everyone. If marketers can form segments based on the benefits sought by users, they can design products and services to meet those needs. This approach is often more practical than simply forming demographic segments and trying to figure out what, say, professional women in Peoria want from the Web. Marketers will use all segmentation bases to define, measure, and identify target markets, but "benefits sought" is the key driver of marketing mix strategy.

What better way to determine benefits sought than to look at what people actually do online? Marketers can evaluate online activities, such as those presented in Chapter 7. (Recall the five basic online activities are connect, create, learn, enjoy, and trade.) Marketers also check which Web sites are the most popular. Several sites report each month on the top online properties. Exhibit 8.11

displays the top Web site parent companies for one month in 2007. Microsoft, Google, and Yahoo! are consistently among the top sites in most countries. The exhibit demonstrates that many people search, use Web-based e-mail, use Microsoft for downloads, read news, purchase from Yahoo!, and so forth. Comparing these data with activities in Chapter 7 presents a rich picture of current and emerging benefits desired by internet users.

USAGE SEGMENTS Marketers also segment internet users according to many technology-use characteristics such as PDA or PC access and which browser they use. Following are three important internet usage segments: home and work access, access speed, and online engagement.

Home and Work Access Many companies segment by whether users access the internet from home or work. Access point is important because home and work segments tend to have different needs on the Web. In general, home users have slower connection speeds than those who enter the internet from work, making large graphics and other files undesirable on sites frequented from home. However, that distinction is changing now that 57 percent of all U.S. users have broadband connectivity at home, according to a Leichtman

Parent Name	Home Panel		Work Panel	
	Millions of Visitors	Reach of All Users (%)	Millions of Visitors	Reach of All Users (%)
Google	105.5	69.9	57.2	86.7
Microsoft	102.2	67.7	57.1	86.5
Yahoo!	94.7	62.7	50.2	76.0
Time Warner	85.4	56.6	46.2	69.9
News Corp. Online	60.3	39.9	29.4	44.5
eBay	50.4	33.4	30.2	45.6
InterActiveCorp	46.9	31.1	30.3	46.0
Amazon	40.4	26.8	29.9	45.3
Apple Computer	37.8	25.1		
Wikimedia Foundation	37.1	24.5	26.9	40.7
New York Times Co.			26.1	39.5

EXHIBIT 8.11 Top U.S. Web Properties as of January 2008 (Parent Companies)

Source: Data from www.nielsen-netratings.com.

Research survey. Another characteristic of the home market is that a small but growing number of households have more than one PC and are networking them wirelessly within the home.

Nielsen//NetRatings estimates that 69.7 million U.S. users accessed the internet from work and 217.3 million from home during January 2008. It is interesting that the top Web site properties are nearly identical for home and work access, possibly indicating that users are brand loyal to particular sites, and that the work and home boundaries are blurring (e.g., many consumers make vacation travel arrangements from work).

E-marketing strategists can use such information to target their Web site offerings or purchase online advertising. Strategies might include a higher amount of interactivity and multimedia possible for work users or advertising more heavily at *The New York Times* site to work users than home users (refer to Exhibit 8.11). It is important to monitor these trends as work and home boundaries continue to blur.

Access Speed   Clearly, the type of internet connection and the information-receiving appliance affect usage behavior. Faster connections at work allow users to receive larger data files filled with multimedia content. The same is true for broadband users accessing from home, while the reverse is true for those using 56k modems or handheld wireless devices.

Even though cost is still a barrier for many home users, broadband penetration is now high enough to reach the critical mass needed for true video and audio program delivery on demand. This high-speed capability will certainly change the face of the Web. Think about the look of CNN, the 24-hour news channel on television, which is poised for internet delivery with its mixture of text and video. In the future, users will commonly receive this type of programming on a computer and click on text boxes for more information or even delay the video delivery if desired. Already the boundaries between the online and television media are blurring.

Broadband users operate differently from narrowband users online. Nearly 80 percent of broadband online users will watch a video online at least once a month in 2008, according to an eMarketer projection—that is over 150 million Americans and this is made possible only by fast internet connectivity.

At the other extreme, handheld mobile wireless users have small screens and slow access speed. Recall from Chapter 4 that there is 90.9 percent penetration of cell phones in developed nations—a segment that is hard for marketers to resist. By comparison, 14 million PDAs (personal digital assistants) shipped in the United States in 2003 (Greenspan, 2004). PDA penetration is slowing due to convergence of the cell phone and PDA.

All these numbers add up to a market demanding attention. Wireless users do a lot more than talk on their cell phones. They send and receive data—anyplace, anytime. Exhibit 8.12 presents the kinds of applications and content used by mobile device owners in 2006. The biggest use is for text and photo messaging. It is notable that 65 percent of 18–29-year-olds use text messaging, as compared with 37 percent of 30–49-year-olds, and even fewer 50 and over. Other important uses include e-mail and purchasing ring tones. Wireless users currently track information on package shipment, stock quotes, airline schedules and changes, and news.

Notably, wireless devices cannot access typical Web pages on their tiny screens, which is why many site developers now have a mobile viewing mode and a regular viewing mode. The mobile mode is usually all text and serves precise information on demand—such as the local search using Google texting, previously mentioned. Also, Zagat, the worldwide restaurant guide, allows mobile users to search its database for restaurants by city when they are traveling, and it charges a subscription fee for the service. The mobile wireless segment creates huge opportunities for firms wanting to produce wireless portals: a customized point of entry to the internet where subscribers can access Web sites and information in text format.

Big technical problems face global e-marketers, so marketers must be clever to provide both wireless and wired users with desired services. At the same time, the wireless market is unstoppable and will grow considerably. Further, expect huge changes when consumers access the internet

Activity	Percent Using	Activity	Percent Using
Sent text message	39.2	Used mobile instant messenger	6.3
Photo messaging	14.7	Used work e-mail	5.1
Browsed news and information	10.3	Downloaded mobile game	3.6
Purchased ringtone	10.0	Purchased wallpaper or screensaver	3.5
Used personal e-mail	8.5		

EXHIBIT 8.12   2006–2007 Mobile Consumption of Content and Application

Source: M:Metrics, Inc. 2006–2007 three month survey of 30,567 U.S Mobile subscribers (www.mmetrics.com).

from their refrigerators, cars, and other appliances. At that time we think it will be about distinctly desired data, not Web pages.

Online Engagement Level   Chapter 1 introduced the concept of customer engagement online—the idea that users are actively participating by adding content for others to view. In Chapter 7, we discussed several forms of content creation, as measured by Pew Internet & The American Life: uploading photos, rating products, tagging online content, posting comments to a blog, creating a blog, and creating an avatar for a virtual world. Because this is an important new concept born from social media use, Forrester Research devised a typology for engagement

segments using its Social Technographics questionnaire (Exhibit 8.13).

Forrester asks questions that categorize social media users according to usage segments such as creators and critics—the two most highly engaged segments. If a company uses Forrester's services, it will learn which of its customers are in these, and other, segments. If the company's customers are not content creators, then a contest asking them to create a video commercial for the company will not be effective (unless they attract new customers). Conversely, if the company follows the norm and has over 50 percent of inactives in its customer base, it knows that they will read its blogs and other social media content. Watch for this system to develop in the near future. Marketers are scrambling to figure

Segment	Proportion of internet users (%)	Segment Description
Creators	13	Posted to a blog, updated a Web page, or uploaded a video within the last month
Critics	19	Commented on blogs or posted ratings and reviews. Forty percent are also creators.
Collectors	15	Save URLs on social bookmarking sites (e.g. del.icio.us.com), use RSS feeds, or create metadata to share with a community
Joiners	19	Join and use social networking sites.
Spectators	33	Blog readers, video viewers, and podcast listeners. They are the social media audience.
Inactives	52	Do not participate in social media.

EXHIBIT 8.13   Social Media Engagement Segments Based on Participation Level

Source: From Forrester Research (accessed at www.emarketer.com).

out whether or not to include social media initiatives, and how deeply to get involved. Segmentation by social media engagement level is one good way to answer this question.

Industry-Specific Usage Segments Segmenting by usage may vary from one industry or business type to the other. For example, research from Forrester and comScore indicates that visitors to car sites behave differently from visitors to other e-commerce sites (see www.forrester.com and www.comscore.com). Even serious car buyers tend to visit car sites only a few times—64 percent of all buyers complete their online research in five sessions or fewer. Further, about 25 percent buy a car within three months of visiting a car site. Forrester identified these three visitor segments for car Web sites:

- *Explorers* are the smallest group, but almost half buy their new vehicle within two months of visiting a car site. They want a convenient, explicit buying process.
- *Off-roaders* tend to do a lot of research online and, subsequently, are likely to purchase in an offline showroom.
- *Cruisers* visit car sites frequently, but only 15 percent buy a car in the short term. Still, they have a strong interest in cars and heavily influence the car purchases of others, making them important visitors.

TARGETING ONLINE CUSTOMERS

After reviewing many potential segments, marketers must select the best for targeting. For this selection, they review the market opportunity analysis (see Chapter 3), consider findings from the SWOT analysis, and generally look for the best fit between the market environment and the firm's expertise and resources. Sometimes, this task is as easy as discovering a new segment that visited the company's Web site and then experimenting with offers that might appeal to this group. Other times, it is a lengthy and thorough process. To be attractive, an online segment must be accessible through the internet, be sizable and growing (if possible), and hold great potential for profit.

Next, e-marketers select a targeting strategy. This might include deciding which targets to serve online, which in the brick-and-mortar location, and which via catalog. The internet is especially well-suited for two targeting strategies:

- **Niche marketing** occurs when a firm selects one segment and develops one or more marketing mixes to meet the needs of that segment. Amazon adopted this strategy when it targeted Web users exclusively. Cyberdialogue/findsvp (now Fulcrum) calls the internet "a niche in time," indicating its ripeness for niche marketing. This strategy has real benefits but can be risky because competitors are often drawn into lucrative markets and because markets can suddenly decline, leaving the firm with all its eggs in one falling basket.
- **Micromarketing**, also known as **individualized targeting**, occurs when a firm tailors all or part of the marketing mix to a small number of people. Taken to its extreme, it can be a target market of one person.

The internet's big promise, one that is currently being realized by many firms, is individualized targeting. Exhibit 8.14 shows a sales funnel that allows marketers to follow users as they go through the Web site registration and purchase processes. Each step creates a user segment that can be targeted with persuasive communication based on behavior, such as e-mailing those who completed registration but did not purchase. Amazon.com builds a profile of each user who browses or buys books at its site. It tracks the books that its customers read and makes recommendations based on their past purchases. Amazon also sends e-mail notifications about products that might interest particular individuals. This approach is the marketing concept at its finest: giving individual consumers exactly what they want at the right time and right place. The internet technology makes this mass customization possible in ways that were unimaginable 10 years ago.

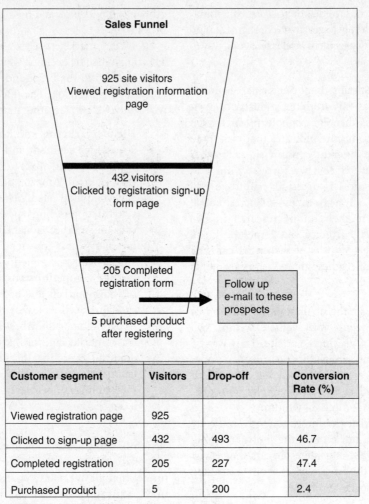

Sales Funnel

925 site visitors
Viewed registration information
page

432 visitors
Clicked to registration sign-up
form page

205 Completed
registration form

Follow up
e-mail to these
prospects

5 purchased product
after registering

Customer segment	Visitors	Drop-off	Conversion Rate (%)
Viewed registration page	925		
Clicked to sign-up page	432	493	46.7
Completed registration	205	227	47.4
Purchased product	5	200	2.4

EXHIBIT 8.14   Targeting the Right Customers

Chapter Summary

E-business occurs primarily in three markets: business-to-business (B2B), business-to-consumer (B2C), and business-to-government (B2G), although businesses also become involved in the consumer-to-consumer (C2C) market. The majority of dollars change hands in the B2B market, with many firms connected to the internet. Information technology is creating efficiencies while increasing competition. The consumer market is huge and active online. The government market consists of numerous states, cities, counties, municipal agencies, and countries buying goods and services.

Business must pay close attention to the rules for selling to this market. A number of trends are affecting the ability of marketers to tap new growth areas and become successful e-marketers.

Marketing segmentation is the process of aggregating individuals or businesses along similar characteristics that pertain to the use, consumption, or benefits of a product or service, which results in groups of customers called market segments. Targeting is the process of selecting market segments that are most attractive to the firm and choosing an appropriate segment coverage strategy.

The four bases for consumer market segmentation are demographics, geographic location, psychographics, and behavior with respect to the product. Each basis is further refined into segmentation variables—such as age and gender variables within demographics. Currently e-marketers are targeting a number of demographic niches and look forward to newly important segments: millenials, kids, ethnic groups, and influentials. Different strategies are used to target each segment.

User psychographics include personality, values, lifestyle, attitudes, interests, and opinions. The internet is an excellent way to gather people with similar interests and tasks into online communities for effective targeting. An important segmenting variable to predict online purchase behavior is attitude toward technology. Two behavioral segmentation variables commonly used by e-marketers are benefits sought (based on the benefits customers desire from the product, such as e-mail or shopping) and product usage (based on how customers behave on the internet).

User segments can be divided according to home or work access, access speed, online engagement level, and industry-specific usage segments.

Marketers use two important coverage strategies to reach the segments: (1) niche marketing and (2) micromarketing (individualized targeting). The internet holds tremendous promise, especially for effective micromarketing.

Exercises

REVIEW QUESTIONS

1. What are the three main markets of e-business, and how do they differ?
2. Define the four main segmentation bases and list at least two segmentation variables for each.
3. Why do e-marketers need to measure attitude toward technology? What measures are available?
4. What benefits do consumers seek online?
5. How do benefit segments differ from usage segments?
6. What are the two most important online engagement segmentation levels?
7. How does micromarketing differ from niche marketing?
8. Why would an e-marketer want to create or nurture a Web site for building a community?

DISCUSSION QUESTIONS

9. Underdeveloped countries tend to have sharper class divisions than those that exist in the United States. It is not uncommon for 2 percent of the population to control 80 percent of the wealth. As a marketer, how would you use this knowledge to develop a segmentation strategy for targeting consumers in these countries?
10. Many parents are upset that some Web sites specifically target children and young teens. Outline the arguments for and against a company using this segmentation and targeting strategy. Which side do you support, and why?

11. Some company managers forbid employees from using the internet for non-work-related activities. What are the implications for e-marketers that segment their markets using the variable of home and work access?
12. Forrester Research suggests a segmentation scheme for online engagement. Interview some of your classmates to see what proportion fall into each segment.

WEB ACTIVITIES

13. SRI Consulting, through the Business Intelligence Center online, features the Values and Lifestyles Program (VALS). Many marketers who wish to understand the psychographics of both existing and potential customers use this market segmentation program. Companies and advertisers on the Web can use this information to develop their sites. Visit SRI at www.sric-bi.com and follow the links to the VALS questionnaire. Take the survey to determine your type and then read all about your type. What is your VALS type? Does it describe you well? Why or why not? How can marketers use information from the VALS surveys?
14. Visit Yahoo! and Google Local searches and look for a grocer in your area. Then text Google to find all grocers in your zip code. Compare the results of these searches based on effectiveness of the results and how easy they were to use.

CHAPTER 9

Differentiation and Positioning Strategies

The only way a company can survive is to differentiate. This is true even more on the internet where business competitors are not limited by driving distance, but encompass all the similar Web sites in the site owner's country and, to a smaller degree, all the similar Web sites in the world.

—RALPH F. WILSON, DIFFERENTIATE OR DIE

Differentiation is the single most important internet marketing technique. If somebody sees a clone of YouTube they have no reason to use it since it doesn't offer anything more than YouTube. . . .

—MARKETINGHUB.INFO

Chapter Outline

The main objective of this chapter is to provide an overview of how and why e-marketers use differentiation and positioning. You will learn about the differentiation strategies used by online businesses and the bases for positioning or repositioning companies, products, and brands on the internet.

After reading this chapter, you will be able to:

- Define differentiation and positioning and explain why they are important elements of marketing strategy.

- Identify dimensions of differentiation and internet-specific differentiation strategies.

- Discuss how companies can position or reposition themselves on the basis of attributes, technology, benefits, user category, relation to competitors, integrator capabilities, or reverse positioning.

The J. Peterman Story

The J. Peterman Company is a classic example of successfully combining clever differentiation with powerful positioning. J. Peterman romances visitors to the company Web site, www.jpeterman.com, with the words of the company philosophy and proceeds to establish his company as a breed apart from its ordinary competitors:

> People want things that are hard to find. Things that have romance, but a factual romance, about them . . .

I think that giant American corporations should start asking themselves if the things they make are really, I mean really, better than the ordinary.

Clearly, people want things that make their lives the way they wish they were.

Every clothing and accessory item offered comes complete with a rambling narrative that sets the stage in the customer's mind for nostalgia and romance. For example, the preamble for the

(continued)

(*continued*)

1950s Beaded Cardigan demonstrates a unique product positioning:

THE 1950s BEADED CARDIGAN—MAY I CARRY YOUR BOOKS!

All the girls in senior high (and college, too) wore sweaters similar to this during the late '40s, '50s, and early '60s.

Similar, but rarely this good.

The girl who wore this sweater lived on the right side of the tracks. Her father was a big shot at General Motors, maybe, or ran a bank. For some reason, he had decided not to send her off to Miss Porter's.

She looked like one of the airbrushed young beauties in the Breck Shampoo ads, except she was real. She might even smile at a person like me.

That would never give me the wrong idea, though. She wasn't the kind of girl you take down to the drive-in and do feverish things with.

If she had only let me carry her books, that alone would have made my whole semester.

Or so I might have thought.

1950s Beaded Cardigan (No. 1330). Fine, soft cotton with beautifully hand-sewn faux-pearl flowers on front, near elbows, on cuffs, and back neckline (gives the fellow sitting behind you in History something to focus on). Narrow-ribbed neck, cuffs, and hems. 3/4-length sleeves. Full-fashioned construction.

Sweet, not saccharine.

Women's sizes: XS, S, M, L.

Color: Highly versatile Beige.

DIFFERENTIATION

Differentiation Dimensions

Differentiation is "the process of adding a set of meaningful and valued differences to distinguish the company's offering from competitors' offerings" (Kotler and Keller, 2006). Differentiation is what a company does to the product, as opposed to positioning, which is what it does to the mind. A firm can differentiate its offering along five dimensions: product, services, personnel, channel, and image. The following sections explain and contrast the ways in which companies capitalize on these traditional differentiation dimensions, both off-line and online.

PRODUCT DIFFERENTIATION Traditional off-line differentiation emphasized the product dimension; other differentiation bases have been used when little real difference exists between competing products. Companies still differentiate by product features online (see "Let's Get Technical" about Apple's iPod). Also, Google didn't surpass Yahoo! and MSN practically overnight by copying their product strategies (Exhibit 9.1). Instead, Google created a powerful algorithm that focused on link relevancy and displayed it in a very simple user interface. Conversely, MSN has the Microsoft business aura while Yahoo! offers more services and focuses on entertainment.

Product line differentiation is an important e-marketing strategy—the literally limitless assortment of products that companies are able to offer and the ability to capitalize on this huge assortment as a platform to customize product offerings for individual customers. The long tail concept, discussed in Chapter 1, explains how Amazon and other online retailers can offer many more products and that their revenues are much greater because of this.

Product differentiation also includes customization and bundling—offering a combination of products or services that the individual consumer needs at prices that are attractive. Consider

LET'S GET TECHNICAL

iTunes iPod

You are making a cross-country trip in your late model Mini Cooper. For 200 miles you have driven through what appears to be an unbroken string of corn fields and flat earth. Though your car has a great sound system, for the last four hours you have been listening to country stations and talk radio. Right about now you are really wishing that you had remembered to pack at least one CD. Suddenly you remember that your iPod is sitting in the glove compartment. Hooking it up to an FM transmitter you bathe the car in rock and roll. Before you know it, the hours melt away and the Rocky Mountains loom gracefully in the distance.

Apple Computer has long been the master of the simple and stylish user interface. With iTunes and iPod they continue that long tradition. iTunes is a music and video organizer and playback mechanism for the computer. iTunes can digitize an entire music and video collection—hundreds of CDs—and store and organize them on a computer. iPod loads all of that music and video into a tiny portable handheld device—with a great touch-sensitive interface.

To enable this process, we require three principal technologies: compressed music and video, high speed data transfer, and really small storage devices.

Files stored on a music CD are not compressed. Therefore they take up a lot of space—about 600 MB for an album. That's too much space for a computer. After 50 albums, your hard drive might be filled. Those same albums can be compressed into tracks one-tenth the size when digitized on a computer. You have probably heard of MP3 files, which are just compressed music files. MP3 is one compression standard; others, such as Apple Computer's Advanced Audio Coding (AAC), are also available. Compression results in a very small loss of audio quality—undetectable by many users. iTunes and iPod can play music digitized in either MP3 or AAC format.

However, even a compressed collection of music and video can be pretty large. Moving all that content from the computer to the iPod could take hours—and reduce the appeal of the product. To speed up data transfer, Apple uses a USB cable. The iPod synchronizes to a computer over the USB connection. Just a few minutes later, the contents of hundreds of CDs and videos can be transmitted to the iPod.

The final enabling technologies deal with storage. All that music and video must fit in a tiny lightweight package. Tiny hard drives up to 160 GB are used on the high-end iPods. But hard drives, even small ones, drain battery life. The iPod touch, iPod nano, and iPhone store the music instead in a flash drive—basically a large memory chip—which is the same technology used for the increasingly popular USB pen drives. Because it requires no moving parts, the battery life is enhanced.

With iTunes and iPod, Apple has a winning formula. But the game does not end there. Apple has developed a product line extension that allows iTunes to control stereo speakers located anywhere in your home using an Apple AirPort Express. The AirPort Express creates a wireless network in your home *and* pumps music to your stereo speakers using built-in AirTunes software. Want music in another room? Just buy another Airport Express. Another product line extension, Apple TV, bypasses the computer altogether and lets users download content (movies, music, and pictures) from the internet directly to a box attached to the TV. Using Apple TV, users could subscribe to their cable company's internet service and listen to music and watch movies without subscribing to even basic cable. Clever indeed!

Blue Nile, where customers can create customized diamond rings from a wide selection of stones and settings on the Web site. Such differentiation supports one-to-one relationship building with each customer—critical for a company's long-term success on the internet.

Internet marketing may have a major effect on product packaging. At present, marketers design most product packaging to appeal to consumers, be eye-catching, compete with other products on store shelves, and sell the product. Products purchased online will be

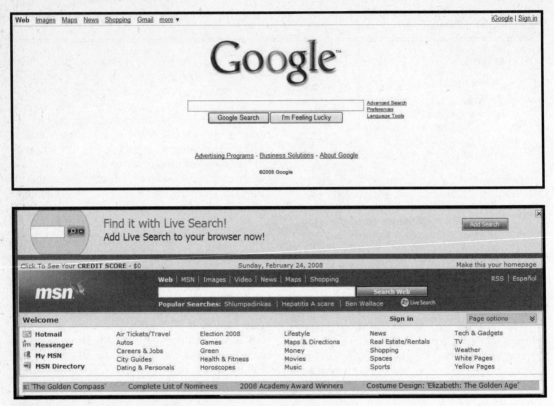

EXHIBIT 9.1   Google and MSN Differentiate for Competitive Advantage

Sources: www.google.com and www.msn.com. Microsoft product screen shot(s) reprinted with permission from Microsoft Corporation.

shipped from the distributor directly to the consumer and, thus, never appear on retailers' shelves. As a result, these products might not require the expensive, colorful packaging that is necessary for store display; nor will they require multiple layers of functional and display packaging. Conversely, packages shipped to individual households will require additional packing materials not required in bulk case shipments to wholesalers and retailers.

SERVICE DIFFERENTIATION Customer service is enhanced by the ability to receive customer feedback through e-mail 24 hours a day—even if telephone operators and customer service personnel are not available—and the ability to respond more rapidly (in real time) to customer

concerns. Another aspect of service differentiation is the distribution of products ordered online. Tesco.com in England specializes in the home delivery of products ordered online, thus differentiating their services from most traditional grocers. Tesco is the only real survivor among online grocers because it capitalized on its brick-and-mortar strengths and simply added extremely easy customer online ordering and delivery options. Other online services, such as online banking and securities trading, are very popular, differentiated both by the features they offer and the service consumption experiences. These services currently supplement traditional off-line services, but as the world becomes more inter-connected via the internet, they may one day replace the traditional off-line services.

PERSONNEL DIFFERENTIATION In the past, personalized service and one-to-one relationships between merchants and consumers required costly skilled personnel. Now, the internet allows companies to "deliver their products and services through low-cost channels that automate the process and remove the expensive human element" (Wells et al., 2000, p. 32). By reducing a company's dependence on personnel to handle business transactions, the internet leads to lower transaction cost, enabling a cost leadership advantage over off-line companies. It "also results in cost reduction for the end user and at the same time acts as a differentiation by providing higher levels of service at lower prices" (Chakravarthy, 2000, p. 2).

CHANNEL DIFFERENTIATION The internet doubles as a location-free and time-free distribution and communication channel. Customers may order a wider variety of products, at any time, day or night, for shipment to any location in the world, in contrast to the limited product assortment and limited business hours of traditional brick-and-mortar companies.

Online channel differentiation occurs on multiple levels. First, companies that provide product or service information on the Web have an advantage over companies with no Web presence by exploiting the internet as a communication channel. Second, companies that conduct commercial transactions online capitalize on the advantage of the internet's properties as a transaction and distribution channel. At a higher level is the differentiation of competitors' internet-related service offerings. For example, in the banking industry, one bank might provide free online banking if a customer will accept a virtual monthly statement (saving mailing costs), another might offer free loan quotes, and a third might provide interactive portfolio services to investment clients. Next, highly specialized personal services—"Do it yourself," Web sites— allow users to conduct activities such as transfer phone service and make international phone calls online (e.g., Skype).

Finally, the internet becomes the entire distribution channel for digital products, where brands such as iTunes and Microsoft offer digital downloads of music and software. This builds on the user desire for self-help and also saves on packaging and shipping costs. Digital products are an example of product unbundling made possible by the internet (e.g., music lovers can download one track instead of an entire CD).

IMAGE DIFFERENTIATION A company can differentiate itself by creating a unique customer experience such as superior customer service and, in turn, brand the experience. Through experience branding, "firms can greatly improve their ability to retain customers, target key customer segments and enhance network profitability" (Vincent, 2000, p. 25). Online examples of experience branding abound—Build-a-Bear extends its off-line experience online, and virtual worlds such as Second Life and Webkinz are all about the "in-world" experience.

Even the personal computer industry, which had long focused on product differentiation by computing speed, has now turned to experience branding. For example, consider perceptions of two computer industry firms, Gateway (which markets PCs) and Symantec (which markets system maintenance and protection software): "The perception is that *Gateway* is the vendor that will treat you right long term. While *Symantec* has fostered an image as the 'ambulance' . . ." (Goldberg, 1999, p. 16).

Customer engagement online is the equivalent of off-line experience marketing. In 2008 and beyond, Web sites that invite users to upload content and comments give them a competitive edge. Recall the Dell's Hell story from Chapter 1 and how its customer service image had turned sour until it began IdeaStorm and Direct2Dell blogs and joined the social media revolution. Some sites, such as Tripadvisor.com, are built entirely on this image of being customer-created.

All of these benefits help to differentiate the image and customer experience of online firms. For example, AOL and Venus Swimwear have online chat features to help customers with questions about their purchases in real time.

Differentiation Strategies

Trout and Rivkin propose a concise list of specific differentiation strategies, many of which are particularly important in e-marketing initiatives (Wilson, 2000):

1. Being the first to enter the market.
2. Owning a product attribute or quality in the consumer's mind.
3. Demonstrating product leadership.
4. Utilizing an impressive company history or heritage.
5. Supporting and demonstrating the differentiating idea.
6. Communicating the difference.

These strategies are of particular importance on the internet because the marketing strategy often revolves around the company's image and product information available on the Web. As the first internet book retailer—and one of the pioneer online retailers in any category—Amazon.com captured an early lead in online book sales. The company has grown substantially since its inception in 1995; today Amazon is recognized as a leader on the Web. If a firm is first to provide the product or services, the "brand" can potentially become synonymous with the product as the best online provider. The Amazon.com brand is known around the world and has become associated with a variety of other products in addition to books.

This asset of a strong brand image can also help a company attain "ownership" of a product. Companies with a well-known brand still have an advantage despite the low-entry barriers on the internet. Customers are drawn to brands they trust, an attraction that is enhanced by a positive company history. Monster.com has essentially gained ownership of online job searches. The company offers a wide range of job-related information including job searches and résumé posting; it also includes special pages for high-level executives as well as graduating students. Monster.com's early entry into the market and its strong brand image has allowed the firm to become synonymous with job search and career placement services.

In addition to the preceding strategies common to off-line and online business differentiation, six differentiation strategies are unique to online businesses. These strategies are summarized in Exhibit 9.2.

SITE ENVIRONMENT/ATMOSPHERICS Atmospherics refers to the in-store ambiance created by brick-and-mortar retailers. Similarly, Web sites differentiate by providing visitors with a positive environment to visit, search, purchase, and so forth. Visitors want a site that easily downloads, portrays accurate information, clearly shows the products and services offered, and is easily navigated. If customers view the homepage and like what they

1. Site Environment/ Atmospherics (Watson et al., 2000)	2. Trust	3. Efficiency and Timeliness
• Look and feel of site • User friendly • Virtual to urs	• Clearly state privacy policy • Use encryption for secure transactions	• Deliver what is promised to customers • Deliver in a timely manner
4. Pricing	5. CRM	6. User-Generated Content (UGC)
• Be aware of competitor pricing • Potential customer savings	• Customer tracking • Seamless communication • Greater relationship efficiency	• Allow site/blog visitor comments • Provide space for UGC images and videos • Trust, listen, and learn

EXHIBIT 9.2 Internet-Specific Differentiation Strategies

see, they are more likely to view additional pages and ultimately become paying customers. As well, a purely online product or service can only be seen through an image or description. Whether a company uses virtual tours, 3-D images, product image enlargements, trial downloads, or customer reviews, the goal is to make offerings seem more tangible by showing them in a realistic and customer-friendly manner.

BUILD TRUST Trust is a key issue on the internet, especially when customers are expected to pay online or their information is tracked for personalized service or supply chain management. For this reason, trust building should be an integral part of a Web site's marketing strategy. In some instances trust may appear as a by-product of strong brand recognition; however, a company site with low or no brand recognition must project a secure environment. Detmer (2002) makes the following suggestion to e-marketers:

> Take the time to clearly define your company's privacy policy, and make sure it is strictly enforced. . . . Maintaining the balance between privacy and personalization will increase the comfort level your customers feel for your business.

In addition to stating the privacy policy, e-commerce firms can reassure customers by using a safe and encrypted payment process for transactions. Trust is also important if customers should encounter problems on the Web site, require personal assistance, or need to exchange or return a purchase. Visitors may be more likely to buy from a site if they know a live person can be contacted.

Trust is an especially important issue with C2C transactions, such as on eBay. This company assists with its feedback system where buyers and sellers rate each other after transactions. Many sites follow this model and some, such as ePinions.com, allow users to rate the reviewers as well.

EFFICIENT AND TIMELY ORDER PROCESSING
One of the strongest motivators for customers who make Web-based purchases is the ease of ordering.

Organizations must market their alliances and delivery timeliness as an important benefit. If the online company follows through on its promises, it is more likely to build customer loyalty and receive referrals from satisfied customers. Customer satisfaction or dissatisfaction can spread very quickly on the internet with just a few keystrokes. One way to assure customers is to provide automated e-mails at each step of the way, such as after the order is placed and then after it is shipped, such as from auto-ship@amazon.com. The following are automated e-mails from airlines and agencies, received after buying an air ticket. Which are most descriptive, trust-generating, and effective (Beal and Strauss, 2008)?

- Member@p21.travelocity.com (Travelocity),
- pgtktg@bangkokairwaysna.com (Bangkok Airways),
- SouthwestAirlines@mail.southwest.com (Southwest Airlines),
- notify@aa.globalnotifications.com (American Airlines),
- itinerary@pcsoffice02.de (Lufthansa),
- travelercare@orbitz.com (Orbitz),
- confirmation@uasupport.com (United Airlines), or
- travel@expedia.com (Expedia).

PRICING Pricing as a method of differentiation has come under scrutiny, especially for Web marketers. When products were first offered on the Web, companies tended to offer price discounts as an incentive. Today, retailer prices are relatively comparable on the Web, although some companies, such as Buy.com, offer lower prices. The majority of firms choose to differentiate themselves using methods other than pricing because pricing is easy to imitate and nonprice differentiation is more enduring for all but the price leaders—also because shopping agents such as BizRate.com allows consumers to see competitive prices. One viable pricing strategy is to offer free content that is ad supported (e.g., CNN.com), while competitors are offering paid subscriptions (e.g., *The New York Times*).

CUSTOMER RELATIONSHIP MANAGEMENT As more firms shift away from price differentiation, customer relationship management (CRM) becomes more predominant as a means of differentiation. Netflix, for example, forges long-term relationships with consumers who want the convenience of receiving movies on DVD by mail. Customers who subscribe to one of Netflix's monthly plans can set up personal lists of the movies they want to rent. Depending on the type of subscription they choose, customers can rent three or more DVD movies at one time—with no return deadlines or late-return penalties. After viewing a movie, customers slip it into the prepaid return envelope to mail it back to Netflix; a few days later, they receive the next DVD on their list. Thus, Netflix builds customer relationships one at a time through customer-driven personalization including a personal greeting on the Web site. Most online retailers save customer purchase and credit card data in databases that make it very easy for repeat orders and future product recommendations.

INVITE USER-GENERATED CONTENT We've discussed the rapid growth of social media previously, and sites such as YouTube (videos), Del.icio.us (social bookmarking), and Flickr (photos) have differentiated by inviting customers to upload content. In the blogosphere, micromedia sites tumblr.com and twitter.com began a new product category by allowing very short blog posts. Twitter posts can also be sent via cell phone text message (SMS). Every e-marketer can invite users to post comments on their Web sites and blogs and provide space for other user-generated content. For instance, CNN.com offers iReporter so that citizen journalists can post news stories and multimedia content from the scene and Dell created blogs just for customer idea posting. The key is to trust customers, listen to them, respond, and learn—otherwise accepting user-generated content will backfire.

BASES AND STRATEGIES FOR POSITIONING

Positioning strategies help to create a desired image for a company and its products in the minds of a chosen user segment. **Positioning** is the process of creating this image, and a position is the resulting view of the firm or brand from the consumer perspective (often two distinctly different things). The concept is simple: to be successful, a company must not only differentiate itself and its products from all others, but also position itself among its competitors in the public's mind to carve out its own market niche. Firms can position brands, the company itself, the CEO, or individual products. The positioning rule of thumb is "Mediocrity deserves no praise."

When firms don't establish a position for their brands, they have little control over brand images. Ultimately a product position is in the eye of the customer, but marketing communication can help consumers see the brand in the way management wants it to be viewed. Without a company's positioning cues, customers may perform a competitive comparison using incomplete or even inaccurate information. Web sites such as www.pricescan.com and www.bizrate.com allow customer ratings and chat about products; firms do not want complaints at these sites to be the only input to influence customers' perceptions or define brand image. The rise in social media means that organizations must pay closer attention to this than ever before.

The e-marketer's goal is to build a strong and defensible position on one or more bases that are relevant and important to the consumer—and do it better than the competitors. How can a company achieve this goal?

Firms can position on the basis of product or service attributes ("the smallest cell phone"), high-tech image ("our cell phones access Web sites"), benefits ("fits in your pocket"), user categories ("best cell phone for older adults who want simplicity"), or comparison with competitors ("our phone is less expensive than the Nokia"). Also, firms can take an integrator position ("a full range of electronic products and services"). Following are examples of these positioning bases online.

Product or Service Attribute

Attributes are product or service features such as size, color, ingredients, speed, and so forth.

A patented product or process, such as Amazon's 1-Click checkout process, is an ideal basis for positioning. Other examples:

- iVillage allows users to build their own meal menus at its site using criteria such as ingredients and calorie counts (www.ivillage.com).
- Pillsbury adds value through ideas, recipes, and an advice service on its site (www.pillsbury.com).
- Kraft Foods offers *Interactive Kitchen* with tools such as *Your Recipe Box, Your Shopping List, Simple Meal Planner, Make It Now* (recipes suggestions based on what is in the fridge and cupboard), and *Party Planner.* Mothers, who are Kraft's main target, can find "real help in real time" (www.kraftfoods.com).
- Tylenol does not sell online but provides useful and entertaining one-to-one Web features such as Tylenol pain reliever and health information and Tylenol greeting cards. The site provides links to stores where customers can buy the product (www.tylenol.com).

Technology Positioning

Positioning on the basis of technology shows that a firm is on the cutting edge. This attribute is especially important for online marketers. Consider the following examples:

- At the Lands' End Web site, women can build virtual models based on their physical features such as hair color, skin tone, hair style, and face shape. Users can then see how Lands' End apparel would look on themselves by trying virtual outfits on the model. The model can be rotated for front, side, and back views (www.landsend.com).
- The American Airlines site offers various tools to allow customers to manage their flight arrangements: frequent flier account management, personalized travel planning, and personalized seat selection when booking flights. Customers can store user-profile information on preferred destinations, seating preference, companion travelers, and frequent flier rewards status and billing.

Finally, American offers flight status notification via text message, e-mail, or voice mail to any receiving device (www.aa.com).

Benefit Positioning

Benefits are the flipside of attributes—the customers' perspective of what the feature will do for them. Benefit positioning is generally a stronger basis for positioning because of its customer orientation in answering the question: *What will this product/service do for me?* Examples include the following:

- The Polo Web site focuses on how its products shape an entire lifestyle. Its products are much more than a tie or a jacket—they are designed to help customers contemplate a dream world of adventure, style, and culture (www.polo.com).
- The Miller Lite beer Web site offers a software package that can be downloaded and used as a social organizer for arranging meetings, mostly for entertainment. The Miller icon is then permanently present on the desktop, reminding the customer about the brand on a daily basis (www.millerlite.com).
- The Valvoline motor oil Web site has become a destination site for racing aficionados. It features schedules for NASCAR and other racing circuits, as well as results of recent races, driver photos, and interviews. Visitors can send racing greeting cards, buy official Valvoline racing gear, download a racing screensaver, and sign up for a weekly newsletter (www.valvoline.com).
- Kimberly-Clark's Huggies site has built a relationship with parents by offering help and advice on child care in a community format. In the "Happy Baby" section, parents can customize stories to include their child's name (www.huggies.com).

User Category

This type of positioning relies on customer segments. It is successful when the segment has some unique quality that ties product benefits more closely to the group than to other segments. Following are some Web examples:

- Kellogg's has set up an interactive Web site for children. They can register online and enter code numbers found on Kellogg's cereal packages, then use the codes as "money" on related Web sites or even earn interest in a "special" bank (www.kellogg.com).
- Yahoo! Groups hosts forums that are organized based on specific interests. Consumers can connect with others who share the same interests, from Japanese anime videos to trucks (www.groups.yahoo.com).
- Eons is a social network for baby boomers, born between 1946 and 1964. The site provides special interest groups, photo sharing, and a life path feature that allows for posting key life events in a timeline (www.eons.com).
- The U.S. Department of Commerce provides information and assistance to both English and Spanish-speaking business people (Exhibit 9.3).

Competitor Positioning

Many firms position by touting specific benefits that provide advantages over competitive offerings. Online or off-line companies often position themselves against an entire industry ("I Can't Believe It's Not Butter" margarine), against a particular firm (Amazon.com for toys), or according to relative industry position (AOL is the instant messaging leader and MSN a challenger). In the software business, Microsoft is the industry leader and lets everyone know it.

Integrator Positioning

Some companies want to be known for providing everything a consumer needs in a particular product category, industry, or even in general (e.g., Wal-Mart). This strategy is particularly important online because busy consumers want convenience and one-stop shopping. For example:

- Martha Stewart's Web site brings together a wide spectrum of business units in one place.

EXHIBIT 9.3 U.S. Department of Commerce Targets Business People

Source: www.arts.endow.gov.

The site effectively communicates the core identity of the brand—improving the quality of living in the home and encouraging do-it-yourself ingenuity. Visitors to Martha Stewart's site are linked to Kmart's site, where Martha Stewart's branded domestic products are sold.

- Microsoft has created a veritable conglomerate through its own sites plus acquisitions and affiliations, such as Microsoft Xbox, Microsoft CarPoint, MSN, PocketPC, and others.
- TheKnot.com offers everything to do with weddings, from gift registry to wedding planners and other consultants.

After the dot-com crash, online businesses positioned themselves differently from their first-round counterparts. "In the first round of internet disruption, the online players were selling commodities: books, music, or stock trades. Customers didn't need to see, squeeze, or sniff the stuff—all they cared about was price. Today's internet upstarts are pulling together more complex information and boiling it down so consumers can become smarter purchasers of a broader array of products and services" (Mullaney, 2004). This trend continues and we expect to see more integrator positioning among businesses selling online, as Mullaney demonstrates in the real estate, lending, jewelry, and hospitality industries:

- In real estate, zipRealty has learned how to use software to show potential buyers photos and floor plans for scores of potential houses. Because that reduces the agent's work, zipRealty can save consumers 20 percent to 25 percent off standard commissions. "The standard 6 percent commission is no longer standard at HomeGain," says CEO Brad Inman.

  zipRealty, Emeryville (California) based brokerage, cuts costs by having its agents work via the internet from home. Agents get online training and sales tools, which helps them sell two to three times more homes than typical realtors. In 2003, the start-up turned profitable as its home sales doubled, to $1.6 billion.

Web referral services, such as LendingTree and HomeGain.com, are taking a different tack. Their strategy is to help brokers find clients more cheaply and quickly. In exchange, brokers pay LendingTree up to 35 percent of their commission when they close a sale. In 2003, LendingTree's referrals translated into about 7,000 home sales.

- In the jewelry business, Blue Nile "packs a punch by streamlining a famously Byzantine business." It has 115 full-time staffers and a 10,000-square-foot warehouse selling an estimated $129 million worth of jewelry! A chain would need 116 stores and more than 900 workers to reach such volume. Blue Nile also bypasses the industry's tangled supply chain, where a stone might pass through five or more intermediaries before reaching the retailer. Blue Nile deals directly with major suppliers through its own network online. Larger rivals have more options. Analysts say Zales is reducing costs through more efficient purchasing. Helzberg Diamonds emphasizes the customer service it can deliver in its 265 stores. Of all the major jewelers, Tiffany may be the most insulated from the Web threat, thanks to the cachet of its coveted blue box and a flagship Fifth Avenue store that provides 9 percent of sales amid an ineffable whiff of Audrey Hepburn.
- In the hospitality business, with more people booking rooms online, Web travel agencies fill beds with a fury and are getting a bigger cut of hotel owners' revenues than the hotel chains get for the same room. Expedia gets a $106 nightly wholesale rate from the Dana Inn and Marina in San Diego for a June Sunday night, then charges the customer $132. Customers pay less than the $145 rate they would receive if they booked over the phone—a 25 percent markup for Expedia. Web travel agencies can move market share to the hotels that give the agencies the discounts they want. This capability is crucial in an industry that is chronically overbuilt. A hotel owner has two choices, either to give Web agents discounted rooms or let them sit

empty. The Snow King Resort Hotel in Jackson Hole, Wyoming, began getting up to 100 reservations a week from Travelocity after the site started promoting the 209-room hotel in January.

Repositioning Strategies

Positioning alone won't make a product successful. Marketers must also be sensitive to how the market perceives and subsequently views the company as well as the product. Based on market feedback, a company must be flexible enough to react to those opinions by enhancing or modifying a position. **Repositioning** is the process of creating a new or modified brand, company, or product position. Companies face a long-term challenge when attempting to use repositioning to change the way customers perceive their brands. Fortunately, companies can easily check on progress by tracking customers' preferences and habits on the internet.

Yahoo! is a good example of the need for repositioning along the life cycle of an online business. Yahoo! started life as a network of internet guides: Yet Another Hierarchal Officious Oracle! Soon it sought to attract new customers, keep them coming back to the site, and be perceived as the first place to go when looking for anything online. To accomplish its goal, Yahoo! repositioned from online guide to Web portal. Now, Yahoo! is making content from its site and its partners' downloadable not only on home PCs but also to PDAs and other wireless devices. Further, it invites users to set up customized Web pages through My Yahoo! Other features to draw traffic include Yahoo! chat and Yahooligans! Its brand messages, distribution arrangements, and content partnerships combine to position the site as the most reliable portal, content-information provider, and shopping spot on the internet. Yahoo! made the repositioning official in 2004 by changing its tag line from "Search Engine" to "Life Engine."

Similarly, Amazon has repositioned itself within the last few years. Originally Amazon was positioned only as the world's largest bookstore. Today, it promises the "Earth's biggest selection" of a variety of products from music to electronics and more. Finally, Facebook, which was not even a player several years ago, has already repositioned by moving away from its "social networking for college students" position. Facebook now hosts many business page profiles and offers a myriad of third-party applications: Facebook has grown up.

Chapter Summary

Differentiation is what a company does to the product. Positioning is what it does to the customer's mind. The proliferation of information, products, and services available on the internet means companies must find ways of differentiating their products and services in order to attract customers and build long-term relationships.

Many traditional differentiation strategies can be applied to an e-marketing strategy, such as product, service, personnel, channel, and image differentiation. Although these strategies are effective in both online and off-line differentiation, e-marketing requires some additional and unique differentiation strategies focusing on site/environment atmospherics, trust, efficiency,

pricing, customer relationship marketing, and inviting user-generated content.

Marketing strategies online and off-line depend on the position that the brand, company, or product holds in the minds of customers. In today's environment, where information is easily accessible and consumers hold the power of choice, positioning needs to be focused on customers' desired benefits and personalized to individuals rather than focusing on the product. Any position must answer the customer's question: "What's in it for me?"

Traditional off-line positioning strategies also apply to the internet. However, e-marketers can use internet-specific strategies such as positioning on the basis of technology, benefit, user category, competitor, or integrator. Repositioning may be required over the life cycle of the brand, company, or product. Repositioning is the process of creating a new or modified brand, company, or product position. Companies, off-line and online, face a long-term challenge when attempting to use repositioning to change the way customers perceive their brands.

Exercises

REVIEW QUESTIONS

1. How does differentiation differ from positioning?
2. What levels of online channel differentiation exist as options for companies?
3. What is the goal of experience branding?
4. How do site atmospherics affect online differentiation?
5. Why should e-marketers try to invite user-generated content?
6. Why is benefit positioning so powerful?
7. Why would an e-marketer choose to use competitor positioning? Integrator positioning?

DISCUSSION QUESTIONS

8. Why is a company able to directly control the differentiation of its brand but not its positioning?
9. The positioning rule of thumb states that "Mediocrity deserves no praise." What does this statement mean? Do you agree with this statement? Explain your answer.
10. How might an online company react if a rival embarks on competitor positioning in an unflattering way?
11. Are customers likely to be confused by an integrator positioning that suggests a Web site sells anything and everything? What are the advantages and disadvantages of this positioning?

WEB ACTIVITIES

12. Instant messaging (IM) is used by over 100 million people worldwide. Visit the industry leaders, AOL, MSN, Yahoo!, and Google, and discuss what differentiates these 4 products. Use categories from this chapter in your answer. Which service best fits your needs?
13. Amazon.com is a site trusted by millions of customers. Visit Amazon and identify what makes the site trustworthy.
14. Find one Web site that caters to kids, one to teens, one to millennials, and one to older adults. Evaluate the site atmospherics for each and report on differences.

    This chapter was originally contributed in 2003 by Adel El-Ansary, Donna L. Harper Professor of Marketing at the University of North Florida, and subsequently revised for later editions.

PART FOUR

E-Marketing Management

CHAPTER 10

Product:
The Online Offer

There are many choices for news, but the fact is, there really is only one Bugs Bunny. And when you have franchises like a Bugs Bunny or a Mickey Mouse, or the products that the networks have, there is only one place you can go to get that.

—JIM MOLOSHOK, www.warnerbros.com

Convenience for the consumer drives the digital household.

—ROBERT PITTMAN, FORMER COO FOR AOL

Give people more of what they want, and success will follow.

—SIR RICHARD BRANSON, CHAIRMAN, VIRGIN GROUP

Chapter Outline

Many Products Capitalize on Internet Properties

Creating Customer Value Online

Product Benefits
    Attributes
    Branding

Let's Get Technical: Computer Viruses and Protection
        Brand Equity
        Brand Relationships
        Branding Decisions for Web Products
            Using Existing Brand Names on the Web
            Creating New Brands for Internet Marketing

211

The primary goal of this chapter is to analyze the development of consumer and business products that capitalize on the internet's properties and technology by delivering online benefits through branding, support services, and labeling. You will become familiar with the challenges and opportunities of e-marketing enhanced product development.

After reading this chapter, you will be able to:

- Define *product* and describe how it contributes to customer value.
- Discuss how attributes, branding, support services, and labeling apply to online products.
- Outline some of the key factors in e-marketing enhanced product development.

The Google Story

What performs 7 billion searches a month, speaks 100 languages including Xhosa and Zulu, and is the most-visited U.S. Web site? The answer is Google.com, the Global Brand of the Year in 2006, according to Brandchannel.com. Google is so popular that it has changed the English language—two dictionaries recently added the verb "to google" to their dictionaries. Google's 2007 revenues were $16.6 billion, while it earned an admirable $9.9 billion in profit. The firm continues to grow in sales, new markets, number of employees, and new products offered.

  This success is particularly remarkable because Google entered the market in 1998, well after other search engines were firmly entrenched with loyal customers. How did Google do it? First, it got the technology right at a low cost. Co-founders Sergey Brin and Larry Page figured out how to pack eight times as much server power in the same amount of space as competitors by building their own system from commodity hardware parts. Second, they invented an innovative new search strategy: ranking search query page results based not only on keywords but also on popularity—as measured, in part, by the number of sites that link to each Web page. These criteria meant that users' search results were packed with relevant Web sites. Finally, the founders maintained a customer focus, used simple graphics, allowed no advertising on the home page, and allowed only text ads (without graphics) so search result pages download faster and are easier to read.

  Google continues to excel through rapid and continuous product innovation. It makes new products available on the Google Labs,

(*continued*)

(continued)

EXHIBIT 10.1 Google Labs for New Product Testing

Source: Courtesy of Google (labs.google.com).

moves them to beta testing when they seem useful to customers, and finally adds them to the suite of products—a process sometimes lasting up to a year (Exhibit 10.1). Through this process, Google learns from customers and incorporates improvements based on feedback. Google's product mix includes 15 search products (Web, blog, earth, maps, alerts, and more), three advertising products (AdSense, AdWords, and Analytics), 21 applications (e.g., Google Docs, Picassa, YouTube, Blogger), five enterprise products (e.g., Earth Enterprise, Maps for Enterprise, SketchUp Pro), and two mobile applications. All products pass Google's philosophy test: the "ten things we've found to be true:"

1. Focus on the user and all else will follow.
2. It's best to do one thing really, really well.
3. Fast is better than slow.
4. Democracy on the Web works.
5. You don't need to be at your desk to need an answer.
6. You can make money without doing evil.
7. There's always more information out there.
8. The need for information crosses all borders.
9. You can be serious without a suit.
10. Great just isn't good enough.

Google primarily uses a media e-business model, connecting users with information and selling eyeballs to advertisers. It generates revenues from several B2B markets. It licenses search services to companies, powering 54 percent of all searches worldwide; it sells enterprise services; it also sells advertising to Web advertisers, sharing risk with the advertisers by using a pay-per-click model (advertisers only pay when users click on an ad). Google's advertising revenues continue to rise at its own site and on customer sites including

(continued)

(*continued*)

Google ads because it delivers narrowly targeted relevant ads based on key word searches.

In a firm where 15 percent of employees hold a Ph.D., the innovation continues. This fact plus a monomaniacal customer focus is why the firm is always right on target with new services. The profitability is likely to continue as well, because Google pays close attention to user value, keeps costs low, and delivers eyeballs to advertisers. Google does one thing extremely well.

MANY PRODUCTS CAPITALIZE ON INTERNET PROPERTIES

The success of Google demonstrates how a new and purely online product can use the internet's properties to build a successful brand. A product is a bundle of benefits that satisfies the needs of organizations or consumers and for which they are willing to exchange money or other items of value. The term *product* includes items such as tangible goods, services, ideas, people, and places. All of these can be marketed on the internet.

Some new products such as search engines are unique to the internet, others such as music simply use the internet as a new distribution channel, and some use the internet as an electronic storefront. With the internet's unique properties, customer control, and other e-marketing trends, product developers face many challenges and enjoy a plethora of new opportunities while trying to create customer value using electronic marketing tools. This chapter focuses on both consumer and industrial products capitalizing on internet properties and does so within the rubric of time-tested, traditional product and branding strategies.

To create new products, organizations begin with research to determine what is important to customers and proceed by designing strategies to deliver more value than do competitors. In line with the sources-databases-strategy model discussed in Part III, tier 2 strategies involve the marketing mix 4 Ps and customer relationship management (CRM). Because the process of designing these strategies is closely tied to the tactics used to implement them, strategies and tactics together are presented in the chapters of Part IV. As shown in Exhibit 10.2, the marketing mix (product, price, distribution, marketing communication) and customer relationship management (CRM) work together to produce relational and transactional outcomes with consumers. Assumed

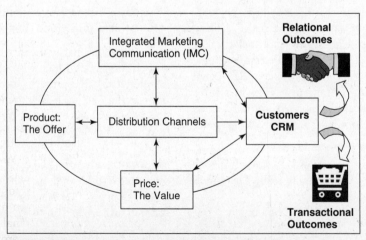

EXHIBIT 10.2 Marketing Mix and CRM Strategies and Tactics for Relational and Transactional Outcomes

in the model is the parallel idea that this activity occurs in all markets—that is, marketers want the same outcomes with government and business customers (especially those in the supply chain). The present chapter begins this discussion by describing how information technology affects product and brand name strategy and implementation.

CREATING CUSTOMER VALUE ONLINE

Never has competition for online customer attention and dollars been fiercer. To succeed, firms must employ strategies—grounded in solid marketing principles—that result in customer value. Recall from Chapter 2 that Customer Value = Benefits − Costs. But what exactly is value? First, it is the entire product experience. It starts with a customer's first awareness of a product, continues at all customer touch points (including the Web site experience and e-mail from a firm), and ends with the actual product usage and postpurchase customer service. It even includes the compliments a consumer gets from friends while whipping out that iPhone, or the fun she has bragging via e-mail to friends about her new Facebook profile page. Second, value is defined wholly by the mental beliefs and attitudes held by customers. Regardless of how favorably the firm views its own products, it is the customers' perceptions that count. Third, value involves customer expectations; if the actual product experience falls short of their expectations, customers will be disappointed. Fourth, value is applied at all price levels. Both a $0.05 micropayment for an online article in a newspaper archive and a $2 million e-commerce computer application can provide value.

The internet can increase benefits and lower costs, but it can also work in reverse. The next sections explore the value proposition online.

PRODUCT BENEFITS

Along with internet technology came a new set of desired benefits. In Chapters 7 and 8, we discussed many of the benefits customers seek online. Web users also want effective Web navigation, quick download speed, clear site organization, attractive and useful site design, secure transactions, privacy,

free information or services, and user-friendly Web browsing and e-mail reading. Thousands of new products and Web sites were quickly created to fill these and many other user needs. As internet technology evolves, user needs change, and the opportunities continue to expand. Astute marketers are ready.

To capitalize on these opportunities, marketers must make five general product decisions that comprise its bundle of benefits to meet customer needs: attributes, branding, support services, labeling, and packaging (Kotler and Keller, 2006). Except for packaging, all of these can be converted from atoms to bits for online delivery. Here we will discuss the first four in terms of the online benefits they provide to customers and their associated e-marketing strategies.

Attributes

Product attributes include overall quality and specific features. With quality, most customers know "you get what you pay for." That is, higher and consistent quality generally means higher prices, thus maintaining the value proposition. Product features include such elements as color, taste, style, size, and speed of service. Benefits, on the other hand, are the same features from a user perspective. (i.e., what will the attribute do to solve problems or meet needs and wants?) For example, MySpace hosts a lot of Web page profiles (attribute) that help users connect with old and new friends quickly online (benefit). Product benefits are key components in the value proposition.

The internet increases customer benefits in many remarkable ways that have revolutionized marketing practice. The most basic is the move from atoms to bits, one of the internet's key properties. This capability opened the door for media, music, software, and other digital products to be presented on the Web. Perhaps the most important benefit is mass customization. Tangible products such as laptop computers can be sold alone at rock-bottom prices online or bundled with many additional hardware and software items or services to provide additional benefits at a higher price. The same is true for intangible products, some offering tremendous flexibility for benefit bundling. For example, online research firms can offer many different business services in a variety of combinations; similarly, music retailers can create CDs to order, combining songs from many different artists as desired by customers. It is important to realize that information products can be reconfigured and personalized easily, quickly, and cheaply, as compared to manufactured products. Consider that changing an auto design takes years, and one model may be offered in only a few versions. In contrast, changing and customizing some software can be much easier.

Even though this type of benefit bundling occurs off-line as well as online, the internet offers users the unique opportunity to customize products automatically without leaving their keyboards. For example, Blue Nile, the profitable online jewelry retailer (www.bluenile.com), allows Web users to select from among many gemstone features (e.g., stone type, clarity, and size) and pick a ring setting to match.

User personalization is another form of customization. Through Web site registration and other techniques, Web sites can greet users by name and suggest product offerings of interest based on previous purchases. For instance, a returning customer to Amazon.com gets a tabbed menu item with his name on it: "Sam's Store." Clicking on the tab reveals a list of items that Sam might be interested in examining, based on his previous purchases from Amazon.

Branding

A brand includes a name (McDonald's), a symbol (golden arches), or other identifying information. When a firm registers that information with the U.S. Patent Office, it becomes a trademark and is legally protected from imitation. According to the U.S. government, "a **trademark** is either a word, phrase, symbol or design, or combination of words, phrases, symbols or designs, that identifies and distinguishes the source of the goods or services of one party from those of others" (www.uspto.gov). It is notable that dictionary words can't be

trademarked for Web site use—companies can own books.com or music.com but can't trademark the word "book" for its company name.

A brand is much more than its graphic and verbal representation in marketing materials, however. It is an individual's "perception of an integrated bundle of information and experiences that distinguishes a company and/or its product offerings from the competition" (Duncan, 2002). Many marketers have noted that a brand is a promise to customers. Delivering on this promise builds trust, lowers risk, and helps customers by reducing the stress of making product switching decisions. Reducing stress is especially important online because of concern over security and privacy issues and because firms and customers are often separated by large distances. Brand names such as Microsoft and Dell generate consumer trust, add to customer-perceived benefits and, thus, can command higher prices from consumers. See the Let's Get Technical box for McAfee and Symantec's Norton AntiVirus products, brands that also generate a lot of trust. Of course, some brands, such as Wal-Mart in the United States or Aldi food stores in Germany and Australia, have a brand name synonymous with low prices and fairly good quality. The value proposition is preserved in these cases because the products provide fewer benefits (e.g., a smaller set of features or fewer services).

BRAND EQUITY Brand equity is the intangible value of a brand, measured in dollars. Exhibit 10.3 displays rankings for some of the top 100 U.S. brands in 2007. Google took the Global Brand of the Year award with its 44.1 percent increase in brand value from 2006, putting it in the top 20 of all brands. Beyond its rapid value growth, Google was praised by Interbrand for its rapid product expansion beyond search while maintaining a consistent feel to everything it does. Yahoo! and AOL had the same potential but did not realize the same results (AOL fell off the list of 100, moving from $200 billion in 2001 to about $20 billion in 2006). Dell, Amazon, and eBay did not exist prior to the internet yet appear

2004 Rank	Brand	URL	Value ($ billions)
1	Coca-Cola	www.coca-cola.com	65.32
2	Microsoft	www.microsoft.com	58.71
3	IBM	www.ibm.com	57.09
4	General Electric (GE)	www.ge.com	51.57
5	Nokia	www.nokia.com	33.70
6	Toyota	www.toyota.com	32.07
7	Intel	www.intel.com	30.95
8	McDonald's	www.mcdonalds.com	29.40
9	Disney	www.disney.go.com	29.21
10	Mercedes-Benz	www3.mercedes-benz.com	23.57
Internet Companies (most business done online)			
18	Cisco	www.cisco.com	19.10
20	Google	www.google.com	17.84
31	Dell	www.dell.com	11.5
48	eBay	www.ebay.com	7.46
55	Yahoo!	www.yahoo.com	6.07
65	Amazon.com	www.amazon.com	5.41

EXHIBIT 10.3   Highest Value Global Brands in 2007

Note: To be considered, brands must have a value greater than $1 billion, have one-third of its earnings outside the United States, and have financial data publicly available. Airlines and parent companies were not included in the deliberation.

Source: Interbrand (2007). *Best Global Brands*, available at www.ourfishbowl.com.

LET'S GET TECHNICAL

Computer Viruses and Protection

The day has finally come for your presentation to the company's largest client. You have been working on the new marketing campaign for over a year, and you were at the office until 10 P.M. every night for the past week agonizing over final changes. Wearing your best suit, you walk into work, grab a cup of coffee, and turn on your computer. You notice out of the corner of your eye that the familiar screens are not flashing while your computer starts up; there is simply a message that says, "No hard disk found." You immediately call the company's helpdesk, only to learn that someone in the Human Resources Department opened a virus-infected e-mail attachment that has wiped out many computers across the company's network. After hanging up,

you calmly reach into your briefcase and pull out the CD-ROM you burned last night with the campaign and presentation on it. Not even an annoying virus can stop you from giving this presentation today.

Computer Viruses and Spam

Computer viruses are an e-marketer's worst nightmare. They reinforce consumer perceptions that the internet and computers in general are not secure. Computer viruses are intrusive pieces of computer code that secretly attach to existing files. Viruses are often self-reproducing and have the potential to wreak havoc on data. Harmful viruses can spread throughout a computer network, overwriting data files with nonsense. On the

(continued)

(continued)

other hand, prank-like viruses might be as small as making the computer beep on a certain day of the month when the user strikes a particular keyboard letter or opening the CD-ROM drive every so many minutes. In addition, some viruses, known as dormant viruses, can infect a computer and not cause problems until a specified date or time.

Four common types of viruses are macro viruses, worms, boot viruses, and Trojan horses. **Macro viruses** attach to data files and infect common desktop applications when users open the infected data file. For example, the NightShade macro virus infected Microsoft Word 97 documents. When the user closed the infected document, the Word Assistant displayed a message with the word *NightShade* in it and password-protected the file with the same word.

Worms reproduce rapidly throughout a computer's memory, destroying the stored information and eating up resources. In 2004, multiple variations of the Sasser Worm infected computers worldwide. German teenager Sven Jaschan is the alleged author, and he was arrested following the incident. Additional viruses posed as cures for the virus, causing even more chaos.

Boot viruses reside on floppy disks and destroy operating systems when users mistakenly boot the computer with a disk inserted. It is best to use antivirus software to scan all disks before using them.

Trojan horses do not replicate and often appear as legitimate programs. The virus-like program can do damage to the computer and open doors to let hackers enter the computer to do damage. The common CodeRed worm dropped a Trojan horse that facilitated remote access to computers drives, allowing hackers to run a program on the computer.

Computer viruses can appear in data, e-mail, or software from any source. In 2000, the "I Love You" virus and its variants made the rounds of the world's computers and caused billions of dollars worth of damage in a matter of days. The virus, which was transmitted via e-mail, mostly affected users of Microsoft Outlook, a common e-mail program. Old, unpatched versions of Outlook allowed small programs, called scripts, to run on the user's computer in order to automate tasks. Although this means that users can customize the program to their needs, it also means that the scripts can run almost any Windows command—including the delete command. In this case, the virus writers sent a script as a file attachment that deleted files on the user's computer. The virus also looked up addresses in the Outlook address book and sent all of the user's contacts a copy of the virus as well. The result was rapid dissemination of a destructive virus. Variants that followed were even more sophisticated and destructive. Knowing that users would be on the lookout for "I Love You" in the subject line, one variant randomly generated a new subject line on each transmittal. Also knowing that antivirus programs would be scanning messages in search of the virus script, that same variant modified the script slightly on each transmittal to escape detection. Malicious programmers often target Outlook, which is tightly integrated with Windows, and other Microsoft applications because of their popularity. However, with the release of Windows Vista, Microsoft has developed an operating system which alerts users about any pending suspicious action.

Even though viruses most commonly affect computers, they are also beginning to infect mobile devices, such as cell phones and PDAs. A worm named Cabir infected mobile phones running the Symbian OS operating system in 2004 and spread by detecting and infecting Bluetooth-enabled devices in close proximity to the infected phone.

What can e-marketers do? The best place to stop a computer virus is before it reaches the end user. All e-mail messages pass through a mail server that stores the messages on a disk drive in users' mailboxes. Software can be installed on the mail server to scan all incoming messages for known viruses and destroy them if identified as containing a virus or quarantine them if suspected. In this way, the virus never reaches the end user and infection is avoided. Antiviral software can also be installed on each individual computer. One robust antiviral program is McAfee Anti-Virus (www.mcafee.com). Also popular is Symantec's Norton AntiVirus (www.symantec.com). Virus activity is reported to and recorded by the WildList Organization International, and information about viruses is available at its Web site: www.wildlist.org.

Almost as annoying and frustrating as viruses, spam has taken over hundreds of users' e-mail

(continued)

inboxes. Spam is unwanted e-mail that is sent to many e-mail addresses at one time. Spam often have subject lines such as "Get rich quick!!!!" or "Cheap prescriptions." According to a report published by Nucleus Research in 2004, spam costs employers $1,934 a year per employee in loss of productivity. The business advisory firm did note that the figure does not include the dollars spent on software, hardware, IT personnel, and wasted bandwidth related to spam.

Although most spam messages are harmless, viruses often mask themselves as spam. Users often increase the amount of spam they receive by signing up for services online that subsequently sell user addresses. Many ISPs and e-mail providers offer spam or junk mail filters. These filters attempt to separate the spam messages from the important messages. Software similar to antivirus software scan incoming messages and either separate or delete them from the user's inbox.

Both antivirus and antispam detection are a boon for marketers because they keep the internet clear of destructive or unwanted content, helping to focus user attention on the desired content.

on this list. How did they accomplish their equity rankings? See Exhibit 10.4 for Interbrand's suggestions, gleaned from many brand experts and marketers.

We add the idea that a great brand taps into the popular culture and touches consumers, as shown in Exhibit 10.5. Popular culture trends in music, entertainment, sports, and more help the brand touch consumers and remain current. For this reason, many firms use celebrities as spokespeople and sponsor sporting events that interest their target markets. For example, Dell Computer found the branding sweet spot when it gave customers the ability to customize their computers online. This capitalized on consumer desires to have products and communication tailored to their individual needs, and popular culture trends involving increased use of the internet for 24/7 e-commerce. Skype found the sweet spot when it brought internet telephony to the global masses, and LinkedIn hit the spot for business networking.

BRAND RELATIONSHIPS Yahoo! has been so successful that individual customers actually created the Yahoo! yodel, subsequently used in the firm's commercials. This response is every brand marketer's dream—to build a following of cult-like customers who live, breathe, wear, and talk about their brand. Such is the case for Harley-Davidson motorcycle owners, Saab automobile owners, Apple computer and iPod fans, eBay auctions, Google searches, and others. Such is the case for Amazon users who vie to become a top reviewer. How does a firm go from an unknown to this high level of acceptance?

Exhibit 10.6 displays five possible levels of brand relationship intensity. The pyramid shape indicates that fewer customers are at the highest

Three Attributes	Three Observations	Five Practices
Built from a great idea	Largely American	Continuously deliver on the brand promise
Holds true to core purpose and values	Predominantly commodity businesses and industries	Possess superior products, services and technologies
Employs brand as the central organizing principle	Represents clear choices	Own a distinct position and deliver a unique customer experience
		Focus on "internal" branding
		Improve and innovate

EXHIBIT 10.4 What Makes a Great Global Brand?

Source: "What Makes Brands Great," available at www.brandchannel.com.

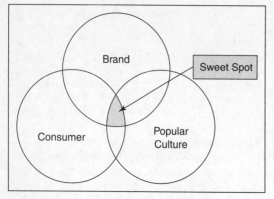

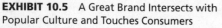

EXHIBIT 10.5 A Great Brand Intersects with Popular Culture and Touches Consumers

Source: Data from Network Wizards, available at www.isc.org.

company-initiated e-mail. Yahoo! began its Life Engine repositioning by promoting an employee contest, with 800 entries describing why Yahoo! was their life engine. This type of internal marketing helps firms communicate a consistent message at all points where customers interact with employees (refer to Exhibit 10.4 regarding the importance of internal branding).

When using the internet, a firm must be sure that its online messages and employee e-mails convey a positive brand image that is consistent with messages from all other contact points. One writer coined the term "smash test" to refer to the idea that when a Coca-Cola bottle is smashed, an individual can identify the brand from any little piece of the bottle. Web sites should pass the smash test as well—after removing logos and other identifying information, users ought to be able to identify the brand from any piece of the site. This type of identification means that the colors, font style and size, writing tone and voice, image size and appearance, and more should communicate the desired brand image.

Although the internet can assist firms in moving customers up the pyramid, it is particularly difficult to control brand images because internet users often receive brand messages about the brand from sources that the company

level, where they have become advocates who tell everyone how great *their* brand is—YouTube is fortunate to be in that spot today. Customers and prospects become aware of brands and develop beliefs and attitudes based on every brand contact. Some contacts are through one-way media such as advertising and packaging, and others are through two-way communication such as conversations with the firm's customer service or salespeople on the phone, at trade shows, on Web sites, or in

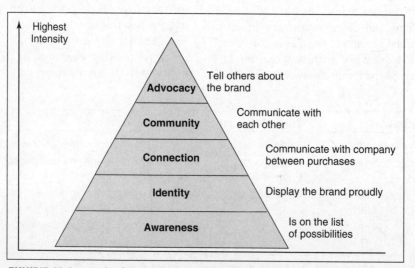

EXHIBIT 10.6 Levels of Brand Relationship Intensity

Source: Adapted from Duncan (2002).

has not planned and managed, such as blogs, consumer e-mail among friends, or a customer burning a faulty product in a home-made video posted online. The internet provides information, good, bad, and ugly about brands. Marketers must monitor the Web for brand information, as discussed in Chapter 6, and do their best to shape brand images using every available tool, including internet technology. See Chapter 13 for more details about managing brand crises online.

BRANDING DECISIONS FOR WEB PRODUCTS

Companies with products for online sale face several branding decisions: whether to apply existing brand names or create new brand names for new products; whether to lend their brand name as a co-brand with other firms; and what domain name to use for the Web site.

Using Existing Brand Names on the Web

An existing brand name can be used for any new product, and it makes sense when the brand is well known and has strong brand equity. For example, Amazon added music CDs, videos, software, electronics, and more to its product mix. It is beneficial for Amazon to use its well-established Web brand name for these other offerings rather than launch a new electronic storefront with another name. Similarly, when products with off-line sales introduce online extensions, many choose to use the same brand name (e.g., *The New York Times* became www.nytimes.com online). In fact, the dot-com crash showed that the strength of brick-and-mortar brands carried over to the internet, which is what gave many Web sites their staying power.

Some firms may not want to use the same brand name online and off-line, for several reasons. First, if the new product or channel is risky, the firm does not want to jeopardize the brand's good name by associating with a product failure. Entering the online publishing business tentatively, *Sports Illustrated* did not want to use its brand online and instead created an extension, naming it Thrive (www.thriveonline.com). The *Sports Illustrated* affiliation was not mentioned online. The thriveonline name was subsequently sold to Oxygen Media.

Also, a powerful internet success might inadvertently reposition the off-line brand. Most internet products carry a high-tech, "cool," and young image, which will carry over to off-line branded products. For example, NBC (the television network) serves an older market than does MSNBC online. Because the network hoped to bring younger viewers from MSNBC on the internet to its television network, it made a decision to stick with the brand name—thus intending to reposition the off-line brand image. In such situations, firms must ensure that online brand images will have the desired effect on the off-line versions and that overextended product lines do not create fuzzy brand images. Finally, sometimes the firm wants to change the name slightly for the new market or channel, as a way of differentiating the online brand from the off-line brand. For example, *Wired* magazine changed the name of its online version to *HotWired* to convey a high-tech image and perhaps to position the two publications differently.

Creating New Brands for Internet Marketing

If an organization wants to create a new internet brand, a good name is important. Good brand names should suggest something about the product (e.g., WebPromote.com and MySpace.com), should differentiate the product from competitors (e.g., gURL.com) and should be capable of legal protection. On the internet, a brand name should be short, memorable, easy to spell, and capable of translating well into other languages. For example, Dell Computer at www.dell.com is much easier than Hammacher Schlemmer (www.hammacher.com), the gift retailer. As another example, consider the appropriateness of these search tool names: Yahoo!, Excite, Lycos, AltaVista, InfoSeek, HotBot, WebCrawler, GoTo, Google, Technorati, and LookSmart. Which ones fit the preceding criteria?

Cobranding Cobranding occurs when two different companies form an alliance to work together and put their brand names on the same product or service. This practice is quite common on the internet and is a good way for firms to build synergy through expertise and brand recognition, as long as their target markets are similar. For example, *Sports Illustrated* now co-brands with CNN as CNNSI. Even the Web site address displays the co-brand: sportsillustrated.cnn.com. Yahoo! is a good place to look for co-branded services. In the past it has joined with *TV Guide* and then Gist to provide TV listings; it has also offered the Yahoo! Visa Shopping pages. As a second example, EarthLink, the sixth largest ISP, joined forces in early 1998 with Sprint, the telephone company, to form a co-branded business with a new Earth Link–Sprint name and logo. They used the cobrand to provide ISP services to Sprint customers and to pursue AOL customers.

Internet Domain Names Organizations spend a lot of time and money developing powerful, unique brand names for strong brand equity. Using the company trademark or one of its brand names in the Web address helps consumers find the site quickly. For example, coca-cola.com adds power to Coca-Cola brands (Exhibit 10.3). Note that most of the top global brands use their brand names in the Web site name. Disney's address is www.disney. go.com to let people know they should visit Disney, but typing www.disney.com in the browser immediately redirects to the same place. This parallel name usage is not always possible, however. Many factors must be considered when it comes to domain names.

A **URL (uniform resource locator)** is a Web site address. It is also called an **IP address (internet protocol)** and **domain name**. This categorization scheme is clever; it is similar to telephone area codes in the way it helps computer users find other computers on the internet network. URLs are actually numbers, but because users can more easily remember names, a domain name server translates back and forth. A domain name contains several levels as depicted here.

The *http://* indicates that the browser should expect data using the hypertext protocol—meaning documents that are linked together using hyperlinks. Sometimes URLs start with ftp:// (file transfer protocol), which means that an FTP server will send a data file to the user (most likely a document that is not an HTML page). The *www* is not necessary and most commercial sites register their name both with and without it. Sometimes a URL is for Web-based mail and the word "mail" will replace the "www" (e.g., http://mail.yahoo.com).

When organizations purchase a domain name, they must first decide in which top-level domain to register. Most businesses in the United States and other English-speaking countries want *.com*, because users usually type in the firm

http://www.dell.com

http://	www.	support.	dell.	com
hypertext protocol	World Wide Web	third-level domain	second-level domain	top-level domain

name.com as a best guess at the site's location. Other countries have top-level domains such as .mx for Mexico or .uk for the United Kingdom. Thus, Amazon in the United Kingdom is www.amazon.co.uk. Exhibit 10.7 displays the largest top-level domains, ranked by number of hosts. A host is a computer connected to the internet and may contain multiple IP addresses. For this and other technical reasons, these numbers represent the minimum number of possible IP addresses in each domain.

An interesting wrinkle on the country domains designation is that marketers outside those nations sometimes want the name. For example, many doctors registered in Moldavia to obtain the .md extension. Another interesting example comes from the Pacific Island nation of Tuvalu (.tv). DotTV agreed to pay Tuvalu $50 million in revenues for the right to sell .tv extensions— a big offer for a country with only $20 million gross national product. However, www.cbs.tv or www.nypdblue.tv did not materialize. Since the

Domain Designation	Top-Level Domain Name	Number of Hosts (millions)
net	Networks	193.9
com	Commercial	167.9
jp	Japan	37.0
de	Germany	20.8
it	Italy	16.8
edu	Educational	11.1

EXHIBIT 10.7   Largest Top-Level Domain Names in January 2008

Source: Data from Network Wizards, available at www.isc.org.

1998 deal, the new owner of the .tv deal, VeriSign, had spent $60 million promoting the extension to yield 400,000 registrations in 2001, with only half of that remaining by the end of 2003 ("False Hopes," 2003). So far most of the networks have chosen to brand through their .com Web sites. However, many other possible top-level domains remain as choices. The Internet Corporation for Assigned Names and Numbers (ICANN) is a nonprofit corporation that operates like a committee of experts to make decisions about protocol and names such as the latest: .biz, .info, .pro, .name, .coop, .aero, and .museum. At last count there were 40 top level names available, from .ag to .vg.

GoDaddy, along with many other sites, provides domain registering services for a mere $10 a year, including an e-mail address (www.godaddy.com). For this price, students can leave less professional yahoo.com and other Web based e-mail addresses behind and get a more professional address to impress recruiters (such as firstname.lastname@lastname.com).

One problem is that with more than 97 percent of words in the dictionary already registered as domain names, the desired online name may not be available. A dictionary name is not necessarily the best option because it already has a meaning attached to it that is generic for the product category, making it difficult to build a competitive advantage. Thus, it is more difficult to build a unique brand identity for a wine firm called wine.com than for gallo.com, a well-known brand name. Consider

the brilliance of Amazon.com when it selected a unique name and avoided the soon-to-come crowd of online booksellers using "book" in their names. The similarities in the following brand names make it very difficult to find a competitive positioning online (some now out of business, not surprisingly)

What happens if the firm name has been registered by someone else? For example, DeltaComm, a software developer and ISP in North Carolina, was the first to register www.delta.com, preempting Delta Airlines (originally www.delta-air.com) and Delta Faucet (www.deltafaucet.com). These firms were forced to come up with alternative names. Another solution is to buy the name from the currently registered holder, and that is what Delta Airlines eventually did. In another example, Grupo Posadas, the large Mexican hotel chain owner, negotiated for 18 months to buy www.posadas.com.mx

1bookstreet	BooksAMillion	gobookshopping
A1Books	BookSense	Gobookshopping
abebooks	books-forsale	HalfPriceBooks
allbooks4less	BooksNow	nwbooks
AllBookstores	Bookspot	Textbooks
Alotofbooks	Bookwire	Textbooksatcost
BestBookBuys	CheapyBook	Textbooksource
BookCloseOuts	Classbook	Textbookx
Bookland	CoolBooks	TheBookPeople
BookNetUSA	Ebooks	TrueBooks
BookPool	eSuccessBooks	VarsityBooks

from a local family with the same last name. The company paid for the name with a free condo, many nights of free hotel stays, and *mucho dinero*. Many creative internet users register lots of popular names and offer them for sale at prices of up to millions of dollars. GoDaddy offers second-level domain name auctions, and GreatDomains.com allows users to buy and sell popular domain names. If you have an extra $65,000 to spare, you can buy the name "www.prescreening.com." As you read in Chapter 5, cybersquatting—which occurs when a domain name registrant takes an already trademarked brand name—is illegal. The same is not true, however, for dictionary or personal names. A "whois" search at GoDaddy.com reveals domain name owners.

Incidentally, when registering a name, organizations would be well-advised to also purchase related names for several reasons. First, it is to keep them out of the hands of others. Many individuals publish Web sites that include criticisms and comments from disgruntled customers about a company, calling them www.companynamesucks.com. To combat this issue, some companies have begun buying their own www.companynamesucks.com to preempt their detractors.

Second, users don't always know what URL to type to find a company. Posadas, the Mexican hotel firm, purchased domain names for more than 17 different spellings of its various hotels to make things easier for customers. Coca-Cola owns cocacola.com, coca-cola.com, and coke.com; and Bently Nevada wishes that it could own both www.bently.com and www.bentley.com due to this common misspelling of its name. We recently noted that www.netmanners.com was accidentally hyphenated at the end of a line in a book to become www.net-manners.com—a site written entirely in an Asian language. Also, Compaq Computer Company paid $3 million to develop the AltaVista search engine site (www.altavista.com) only to find that www.alta-vista.com was already in operation as an adult site with sexual material. Fortunately, the search engine outlasted the adult site, and Compaq's oversight has been remedied.

Picking the right domain name can make a huge difference when trying to entice users to the site and to build consistency in the firm's marketing communications. For example, Time Warner's Pathfinder was the firm's first Web site, containing online versions of its many successful magazines: *People, Time, Fortune, Money*, and *Entertainment Weekly*. Dan Okrent, editor of *New Media* for Pathfinder, claims that the biggest error the firm initially made with the online division was selecting the name *Pathfinder* for the site. Pathfinder lacks the name recognition of its well-established magazine brands and, thus, the firm failed to capitalize on the value of its brands. Furthermore, according to Okrent, *Pathfinder* has little meaning to users. Type www.pathfinder.com today and you will be immediately presented with a page that links to all the firm's magazines.

Support Services

Customer support—during and after purchases—is a critical component in the value proposition. Customer service representatives should be knowledgeable and concerned about customer experiences. Sites that care about developing relationships with their customers, such as Amazon.com, place some of their best people in customer support. In the early days, Amazon's billionaire founder and CEO Jeff Bezos even answered some of the e-mail messages himself. Some products need extra customer support. For example, when a user purchases software such as SurveySolutions to design online questionnaires, technical support becomes important. Customer service reps help customers with installation, maintenance problems, product guarantees, and service warranties, and in general work to increase customer satisfaction with the firm's products.

CompUSA Inc., the largest U.S. computer retailer, astutely combines online and off-line channels to increase support services. At www.compusa.com, customers can enter their ZIP code to check the availability and pricing of any product at the five nearest brick-and-mortar stores. Customers can also check the status of items left for repair at the store, searching the Web site by status or product serial number. Customer service as a product benefit is an important part of customer relationship management; however, it has now become more of a necessity than competitive edge.

The topic of customer service online is so important that we dedicate much of Chapter 15 to it (as part of customer relationship management).

Labeling

Product labels identify brand names, sponsoring firms, and product ingredients, and often provide instructions for use and promotional materials. Labels on tangible products create product recognition and influence decision behavior at the point of purchase. Labeling has digital equivalents in the online world. For online services, terms of product usage, product features, and other information comprise online labeling at Web sites. For example, when users download iTunes software for organizing their iPod music, they can first read the "label" to discover how to install and use the software. In addition, many firms have extensive legal information about copyright use on their Web pages. Microsoft, for instance, allows firms to reproduce product images without permission, but any images on its former Expedia.com site must receive special permission before being copied and used in printed materials such as this

book (see Exhibit 10.8). Online labeling can serve many of the same purposes on the Web as off-line. Many brick-and-mortar businesses display the Better Business Bureau logo on their doors to give the customer a sense of confidence and trust. Similarly, the BBB offers the BBBOnLine logo to its members. Another validating label is the TRUSTe privacy shield. If firms agree to certain terms of use regarding privacy of customer information collected at their site, they may register at TRUSTe, download the TRUSTe seal, and affix it to their Web sites as part of a label.

E-MARKETING ENHANCED PRODUCT DEVELOPMENT

The move from atoms to bits adds complexity to online product offers. Developers must now combine digital text, graphics, video, and audio and use new internet delivery systems (see Chapter 12 for a discussion of how to monetize digital products). They must integrate front-end customer service operations with back-end data collection and fulfillment methods to deliver product. These requirements create steep learning curves for traditional firms. E-marketers, therefore, need to

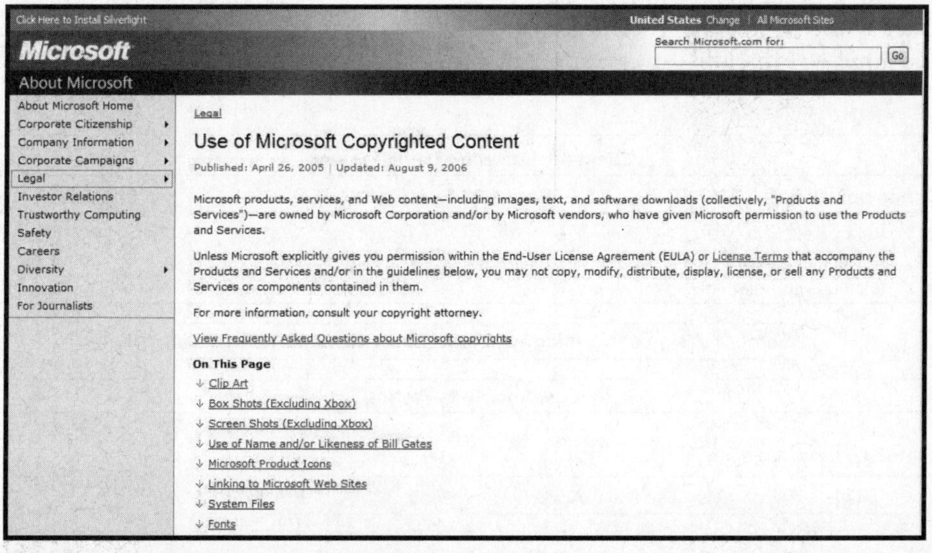

EXHIBIT 10.8 Microsoft Terms of Use Label

Source: www.microsoft.com. Microsoft product screen shot reprinted with permission from Microsoft Corporation.

consider several factors that affect product development and product mix strategies with new technologies.

Customer Codesign

The power shift to buyers, when combined with the internet's global reach, allows for many unusual business partnerships and for both business and consumer collaboration. Partners form synergistic clusters to help design customer products that deliver value. For example, after Dell Computer contractually gave one supplier 25 percent of its volume requirement for computer monitors, the supplier assigned engineers to work with Dell's product development team (Ghosh, 1998). These engineers stood beside Dell employees when new products were introduced to help answer customer questions.

Internet technology allows this type of collaboration to occur electronically among consumers across international borders as well. For example, software developers commonly seek customer input as mentioned in the Google opening story. After releasing Netscape Navigator 2.0 in 1996, the firm immediately began work on version 3.0. Netscape set objectives for improving the browser and then created Beta 0 for internal testing (Exhibit 10.9). When the browser was good enough, Netscape allowed internet users to download it at the Web site and encouraged user feedback. After five months of creating new iterations with customer input, the next version was released. This classic example is typical of the current practices of all software firms.

In another interesting example, The LEGO Group, a toy maker, allows consumers to download software for creating virtual LEGO designs (see factory.lego.com). Consumers then upload their fancy palaces and robots to the LEGO gallery online, where they are priced for those who want to order the pieces and make the design in their living rooms at home (Exhibit 10.10). We've seen designs that cost upwards of $1,000 for the parts! This is a great way for LEGO to engage customers and to learn which new kits might sell well in brick-and-mortar stores.

The Long Tail author, Chris Anderson, posted draft copies of his book on his blog as he wrote and engaged readers who posted comments about the emerging theory. This dialog helped improve the final book.

Today, many firms allow customers to create Web site content. For instance, customers write product reviews and authors write blogs at Amazon. To keep reviewers honest at Epinion.com, anyone can also rate the reviewers themselves. Two new technologies increased this co-development of Web content: blogs and RSS feeds. Bloggers invite comments to their posts, thus, increasing the content value for readers. Begun in 1997, RSS became popular for content sharing between Web

Company Software Development							
Define objectives			**Integration of user input**				**Stabilize software**
Begin product design	Beta 0 internal testing	Specs complete					Final release
	Feature design and coding with input from customers March–July						
Customer Beta Testing							
							Netscape 3.0
	Beta 1	Beta 2	Beta 3	Beta 4	Beta 5	Beta 6	
Jan	**Feb**	**Mar**	**Apr**	**May**	**Jun**	**Jul**	**Aug**

EXHIBIT 10.9 Customer Codesign of Netscape Navigator 3.0

Source: Adapted from Iansiti and MacCormack (2001).

EXHIBIT 10.10   LEGO Engages Customers with Virtual Design Software

Source: www. http://factory.lego.com.

sites. Bloggers and journalists alike use RSS to both provide and receive content that helps them to increase traffic by keeping news fresh.

Good marketers look everywhere for customer feedback to improve products, even setting up blogs for the sole purpose of gathering customer ideas and input (e.g., IdeaStorm). However, sometimes this feedback comes uninvited. With the proliferation of video posting sites and e-mail "word of mouse," the speed and reach of the internet, and the fact that consumers trust people like them more than they trust companies, customers are quick to spread the word about product strengths and weaknesses. In this environment, savvy firms monitor customer input electronically (as discussed in Chapter 6). Using an online monitoring service, Mrs. Field's Cookies caught wind of false rumors spreading on the internet that had caused off-line sales to drop 1 percent in a short time period.

Internet Properties Spawn Other Opportunities

The internet's unique properties, discussed in Chapter 1, generated unusual new products and firms. Current.com is one such example. Led by Al Gore, and Joel Hyatt, users submit 3–7 minute "pods" (videos on any topic of choice), and Current.com registered visitors' vote on their favorites. These are shown on the Current cable TV channel, which consists entirely of short programs created by both online users and the Current staff.

The AutoMall Online and Lending Tree are two companies that aggregate services for users. The Lending Tree is a firm that offers online searches for the best prices for mortgages and other types of loans. These firms provide bundles of benefits difficult to achieve before the advent of internet. Because they also represent a new type of intermediary, these firms are discussed more thoroughly in Chapter 12.

The internet is a great information equalizer, which means fierce competition, lots of product imitation, and short product life cycles. Online auctions are a perfect example. Not long after eBay came online, Amazon.com and others began offering auctions; now one restaurant in San Francisco is even auctioning meals to draw patrons during slow times. Many search engines are starting to look similar. In this environment, product differentiation is the key to keep from becoming a price-driven commodity industry.

Taking short product life cycles to an extreme, Direct Hit Technologies Inc., the firm that sells internet search engine software, has been known to launch six new product versions within a few days (King and Hoffman, 1999). In another example, when Frank Sinatra died, BMG's five-person new-product development team created a lifetime tribute and a series of product offerings for the Web site in six short hours. The firm would have needed four months to produce this in a paper catalog. CNN and other news sites refresh stories every minute, 24/7. Firms must respond quickly to new technology or lose. As one astute pundit said, "Eat lunch or be lunch." Despite the internet adoption flattening at maturity, innovation online is still rewarded.

New-Product Strategies for E-Marketing

Many new products, such as YouTube, Yahoo!, and Twitter.com, were introduced by "one-pony" firms, built around the firm's first successful product. Other firms, such as Microsoft, added internet products to an already successful product mix. This section explores product mix strategies to aid marketers in integrating off-line and online offerings.

PRODUCT MIX STRATEGIES How can marketers integrate hot product ideas into current product mixes? Companies can choose among six categories of new-product strategies (Lamb, Hair, and McDaniel, 2002). Discontinuous innovation is the highest-risk strategy, while me-too lower-cost products are the least risky ones. Firms will select one or more of these strategies based on marketing objectives and other factors such as risk appetite,

strength of current brand names, resource availability, and competitive entries.

Discontinuous innovations are new-to-the-world products never seen before. Music CDs and television were discontinuous innovations when introduced. On the internet, the first Web page creating software, shopping agent, and search engine fall into this category. Levi's Personal Pair product body scanning hardware and software is another. This idea is great for customers who can't find clothing with a proper fit and who want more influence on its design. It also helps manufacturers and retailers increase customer loyalty, lower inventory costs, and avoid seasonal cost reductions. Social networking is another discontinuous innovation—the idea that each internet user has a rich array of contacts for fun and profit when tapped. Many discontinuous innovations are yet to come on the internet. Want to keep up? Just read the most popular blog online: Engadget (www. engadget.com). Although a discontinuous innovations strategy is quite risky, the potential rewards for success are great. E-marketers planning discontinuous innovations must remember that their customers will have to learn and adopt new behaviors—things they have not done before. The company faces the risk that customers will not change unless the new behavior is easy and they perceive that the benefits are worthwhile. However, if the target is under age 35, the risk is lower because the technological savvy in this group yearn for cool new technologies.

New-product lines are introduced when firms take an existing brand name and create new products in a completely different category. For example, Microsoft created a new line when it introduced its Internet Explorer Web browser. Because the Netscape browser was already available, Microsoft's entry was not a discontinuous innovation.

Additions to existing product lines occur when organizations add a new flavor, size, or other variation to a current product line. *USA Today* (www.usatoday.com) is a slightly different version of the hard-copy edition, adapted for online delivery. It is yet another product in *USA Today*'s line. At the beginning of this chapter, we mentioned that Google has five different product lines (search, advertising, applications, enterprise, and mobile), for a total of 47 products—all leveraging the great brand name and helping to increase brand equity.

Improvements or revisions of existing products are introduced as "new and improved" and, thus, replace the old product. For example, Web-based e-mail systems improved on client-based e-mail systems such as Eudora or Outlook because users could check and send e-mail from any Web-connected computer. One provider, Web2Mail.com, allows users to pick up e-mail from any existing account—a different service from Hotmail or Yahoo! Web mail. On the internet, firms are continually improving their brands to add value and remain competitive.

Repositioned products are current products that are either targeted to different markets or promoted for new uses. As previously mentioned, Yahoo! began as a search directory on the Web and then repositioned itself as a portal (an internet entry point with many services), and then as a Life Engine. By doing so, Yahoo! first positioned itself against the early leader, America Online, and is now positioning away from prime competitor, Google. MSNBC repositioned its news organization for younger viewers.

Me-too lower-cost products are introduced to compete with existing brands by offering a price advantage. For example, eFax offers free incoming fax numbers that allow customers to receive faxes as e-mail attachments. The internet spawned a multitude of free products with the idea of building market share so the firm would have a customer base for marketing its other products. For example, Eudora Light, the e-mail reader software, and WS_FTP LE, the file transfer software, were two early entries with this strategy.

Although the B2C market gets most of the attention, many cutting-edge technology products and trends in the B2B markets are discussed in the many "Let's Get Technical" boxes throughout this book.

A WORD ABOUT ROI Part I of this book discussed the need for performance metrics as feedback so firms can assess the success of their e-marketing strategies and tactics. This type of assessment is especially important when introducing new products, online or off-line. Marketers generally forecast the expected product revenue over time, deduct marketing and other expenses, and generate a return on investment estimate for new products prior to their launch. Usually, brand managers compete for the firm's resources by showing that their products will generate either a higher ROI or payout in shorter time frame. By *payout* we mean that the R&D and other initial costs will be recovered at a particular date based on projected sales. In the process, they calculate a break-even date when the product is projected to start making a profit. How long is acceptable? In 2002, some managers were saying that internet projects had to break even within three months or they would not get funded. Of course, the exact timing varies by industry— Boeing does not expect most new aircraft to pay out for 20 years! Nonetheless, ROI and break-even point are important metrics for selling new-product ideas internally and for measuring their success in the market.

Chapter Summary

A product is a bundle of benefits that satisfies the needs of organizations or consumers and for which they are willing to exchange money or other items of value. A product can be a tangible good, a service, an idea, a person, a place, or something else. The entire product experience provides value to the customer, is defined by the customer, involves customer expectations, and applies at all price levels.

Of the five general product decisions that comprise a bundle of benefits for meeting customer needs, four (attributes, branding, support services, and labeling) apply to online products. Companies creating new products for online sale must decide whether to use existing brand names or create new brand names for new products; whether to co-brand; and what domain name to choose. Customer support—during and after purchases—is a critical component in the value proposition. Online labeling is the digital equivalent of product labeling and can serve many of the same purposes as off-line labeling.

When branding products, marketers consider popular culture, the brand, and the consumer. Firms attempt to move consumers up the pyramid from awareness to advocacy.

When developing new online products, e-marketers can turn to customer codesign and use internet properties to spark other opportunities. They can choose among six categories of new-product strategies (discontinuous innovations, new-product lines, additions to existing product lines, improvements/revisions of existing products, product repositionings, and me-too lower-cost products) and are generally required to estimate revenues, costs, and ROI or payout for management review and approval.

Exercises

REVIEW QUESTIONS

1. What are the arguments for and against using existing brand names on the Web?
2. List six new-product strategy categories and provide internet examples of each.
3. Why is value tied to the entire product experience?
4. What are some important criteria for naming internet domains?
5. How does labeling work on the internet?
6. What techniques can e-marketers employ to enhance new-product development?
7. Why do e-marketers need to forecast revenue, expenses, ROI, and payout for new products under consideration?

DISCUSSION QUESTIONS

8. Under what circumstances would it make sense to take an existing brand name online? When would it not make sense?
9. Given the list of online booksellers in this chapter, what name would you pick for a new bookstore selling both new and used books online?
10. What discontinuous innovations have you seen since this book was written? What's next, in your opinion?
11. Why do e-marketers often have difficulty estimating the revenues, costs, and payout or ROI of a new product under development?

WEB ACTIVITIES

12. Visit GreatDomains at www.greatdomains.com. Do you see any names represented there that could be interpreted as cybersquatting?
13. Visit the Country-Code Top-Level Domain database at www.icann.org. Notice how Web sites originating in the United States do not have to append the ".us" root to the end of URLs. Which root names owned by these countries could be used for commercial purposes rather than differentiating country of origin? If you wanted to register a Web site ending in one of these country root names, what requirements do you have to meet? What country root names are already being offered through registrations sites like GoDaddy.com?
14. Many companies use a new-product development process called *scenario planning*. For example, Microsoft executives wonder what it would be like if you could search your computer for phone numbers, e-mail addresses, and both file names and document content all at once with one search word. Think of five scenarios that would make your life easier while using the internet.

CHAPTER 11

Price: The Online Value

All too often, corporate strategists overlook one of their best weapons: improved pricing strategies.

—Robert Doctors, Principal, Booz Allen & Hamilton, Inc.

Price goes by many names.

—Philip Kotler

Chapter Outline

The primary goal of this chapter is to examine how internet technology is influencing pricing strategies. You will gain an understanding of both the buyer's and the seller's perspectives of pricing online, consider whether the Net is an efficient market, and learn about fixed pricing as well as the return to dynamic pricing, such as online auctions.

After reading this chapter, you will be able to:

- Identify the main fixed and dynamic pricing strategies used for selling online.
- Discuss the buyer's view of pricing online in relation to real costs and buyer control.
- Highlight the seller's view of pricing online in relation to internal and external factors.
- Outline the arguments for and against the Net as an efficient market.
- Describe several types of online payment systems and their benefits to online retailers.

The VideoEgg Story

Started in 2004 by three Yale graduate students, VideoEgg is changing the face of advertising pricing (videoegg.com). VideoEgg began as a video content company, providing internet platforms for video uploading to social media. A short 4 years later it completely changed focus, deciding to court the advertisers who want to reach the audience viewing videos. According to VideoEgg, "We connect brands to consumers with video and rich media," delivering millions of impressions to social networking sites, video sites, and gaming applications. The video content space was getting too crowded for these young entrepreneurs.

In 2006, 48 percent of online advertising was paid using a CPM model (cost per 1,000 views), and 47 percent was based on performance model, such as pay-per-click (PPC), according to the Interactive Advertising Bureau (IAB). CPM pricing closely parallels the traditional media world but PPC pricing has slowly increased online because advertisers like it better—they pay only when visitors click on their ads and visit the advertiser's site.

The increase in video posting and viewing online created a challenge for advertisers—how to place ads in videos? Without this facility, sites such as YouTube and Facebook were faced with using display ads on their Web pages and not able to monetize the deeply engaging content creating the most value for users. Enter VideoEgg. This company created AdFrames, a service that allows video viewers to roll over the

(continued)

(continued)

video with a mouse and watch entertaining ad-sponsored content. It only appears when users move the mouse over the icon, thus not interrupting the viewer experience. Engagement is defined by VideoEgg as a user-initiated rollover action that expands an ad containing a video, game, or other rich content. Users stay on the Web page and advertisers only pay when users complete a designated action.

VideoEgg's innovative pricing scheme is currently $0.75 per roll-over, which it splits 60/40 percent with the media site owner. This company has found a way to charge advertisers based on user engagement with the ad—something the CPM model ignores and all advertisers should find very attractive in the social media world (pay for engagement). Microsoft and other firms have already signed up, and VideoEgg is earning about $1 million a month from media sales. It is a good thing that VideoEgg owners are innovative and quick because Google announced the month prior to VideoEgg's launch that its AdSense program is also available for videos—using a CPM pricing model.

THE INTERNET CHANGES PRICING STRATEGIES

In the narrowest sense, **price** is the amount of money charged for a product or service. More broadly, price is the sum of all the values (such as money, time, energy, and psychic cost) that buyers exchange for the benefits of having or using a good or service. Throughout most of history, prices were set by negotiation between buyers and sellers, and that remains the dominant model in many emerging economies. Fixed price policies—setting one price for all buyers—is a relatively modern idea that arose with the development of large-scale retailing and mass production at the end of the nineteenth century. Now, one hundred years later, the internet is taking us back to an era of **dynamic pricing**—varying prices for individual customers.

Information technology complicated pricing strategies and changed the way marketers use this tool, especially in online markets. In addition, the increasing power of buyers means control over pricing in some instances—such as with online product bidding. The internet's properties, especially in the role of information equalizer, allow for **price transparency**—the idea that both buyers and sellers can view competitive prices for items sold online. This feature would tend to commoditize products sold online, making the internet an efficient market. But is it?

We explore the internet as an efficient market in this chapter, using the economist's view as a guide. We also discuss both the buyer's and seller's views of price and explain why some traditional pricing strategies are more effective online.

BUYER AND SELLER PERSPECTIVES

The meaning of *price* depends on the viewpoint of the buyer and the seller. Each party to the exchange brings different needs and objectives that help describe a *fair* price. In the end, both parties must agree or no sale takes place.

Buyer View

Recall that buyers define value as benefits minus costs. In Chapter 10, we discussed the benefit variable, explaining that the internet creates many benefits important to consumers and business buyers alike. Here we explore the cost side of the formula: money, time, energy, and psychic costs.

THE REAL COSTS Today's buyer must be quite sophisticated to understand even the simple dollar cost of a product. The seller's price may or may not include shipping, tax, and other seemingly hidden elements—hidden in the sense that these costs often are not revealed online until the last screen of a shopping experience. For example, Exhibit 11.1 displays the different prices for *The South Beach Diet Cookbook*, as displayed by shopping agent MySimon.com. These prices are fairly

Bookseller	Stars/ reviewers	Price	Tax	Shipping	Price with Shipping
DeepDiscount.com	**/19	$19.46	"Check site"	free	$19.46
Alibris	***/283	$5.00	$0.37	$3.99	$9.36
Books-A-Million	****/40	$8.99	none	$3.98	$12.97
Tower.com	**/10	$17.28	none	$3.99	$21.27
Boomj.com	Not rated	$17.19	$1.27	$6.65	$25.11
Barnes & Noble	***/253	$20.76	$1.53	$3.99	$26.28
Half.com	****/469	$7.75	none	$3.99	$11.74

EXHIBIT 11.1 MySimon Search for *The South Beach Diet Cookbook*

Source: www.mySimon.com for book by Arthur S. Agatston, M.D.

clear yet complex to understand, and the burden is on the consumer to understand his or her needs and translate those into the best price. The lowest price bookseller, Alibris, does not have the highest rating, so is it better to pay an additional few dollars to use a more highly rated store with more reviewers and a better known brand name? Why is there tax for Alibris and not for Half.com, given the same zip code? Also note how the shipping prices are so similar for most sellers. Finally, why is there a 315.2 percent price dispersion from the lowest to the highest price?

This example is what is meant by the time, energy, and psychic costs that add to a buyer's monetary costs. As well, sometimes the Net is slow, information is hard to find, and other technological problems cause users to spend more time and energy, thus becoming frustrated (psychic cost). Shopping agents will find the lowest prices online, but the search adds to the time cost. For example, when buyers search for the lowest airfare at Orbitz.com or Travelocity.com, the search time is minimal compared to the dollar savings, but the same may not be true for a book price search—it all depends on the time it takes to search, the savings as a percentage of the item cost, and how much familiarity and experience the buyer has with the search engine (making an easier search process). The internet is far from perfect, but as broadband adoption continues to increase, technology evolves, and firms develop better online strategies, some of these costs will decline.

In contrast, buyers often enjoy many online cost savings:

- **The Net is convenient.** It is open 24/7 so that users can research, shop, consume entertainment, or otherwise use the Web's offerings anytime and on any receiving appliance. E-mail allows asynchronous communication among users at any location and prevents "telephone tag" with sellers (both parties need not be online simultaneously to communicate).
- **The Net is fast.** Although it might take more time to download a Web page than dial-up users would like, they can visit a site such as iGo.com, order a laptop battery, and receive it the following day—even while on a business trip.
- **Self-service saves time.** Customers can track shipments, pay bills, trade securities, check account balances, and handle many other activities without waiting for sales reps. In addition, technology allows users to request product information at Web sites and receive it immediately. Of course, all these activities take time to perform.
- **One-stop shopping saves time.** The internet opened the door for firms to increase customer convenience through one-stop shopping. AutoMall Online has partnered with a number of firms to provide automobile price comparisons, research about various models

and manufacturers, financing and insurance information, and service options. This firm also offers instant online pricing from a large network of auto dealerships and gives customers a "purchase certificate" guaranteeing that the price quote will be honored at the dealership. AutoMall Online's track record proves that customers receive value: More than 50 percent of its users purchase a car within 45 days of using the service, and 90 percent do so within six months.

- **Integration saves time.** Web portals such as Yahoo! and Google Mobile allow users to quickly find many things they want online from any device. Some sites allow users to create individualized Web pages with news, stock quotes, weather, and other customized information. For example, one consumer purchased a unique backpack online only to find out, via e-mail, that the firm was out of business. No problem—it forwarded the order to a partner e-commerce company, which filled the order in a day.
- **Automation saves energy.** Customers value simplicity and ease; because the Net makes some activities more complex, technology can help. For example, functions that allow customer computers to keep track of passwords for Web sites and to track previous purchases at Web sites save time and energy.

Note that not everyone wants to save money in online transactions. Customer needs and their view of the value proposition vary as each individual weighs the desired and perceived benefits against all the costs. For example, some people prefer to order books from Amazon.com with overnight delivery, knowing full well that Amazon prices are often higher than other online booksellers, that the book is in stock at a local bookstore, and that overnight delivery costs quite a bit more and only shaves one or two days from the delivery time. Nevertheless, the Amazon brand name is trustworthy, these customers have had excellent previous experiences with Amazon, and they are familiar with the site, quickly finding what they need. Thus,

those benefits and time/energy-saving features overcome the higher expense.

BUYER CONTROL The shift in power from seller to buyer affects many e-marketing strategies, including pricing. For instance, in what is known as a **reverse auction**, buyers set prices for new products, and sellers decide whether to accept these prices. A good example is Priceline.com. In the B2B market, buyers bid for excess inventory at exchanges and for products at firms such as General Electric and Caterpillar. In the B2G market, government buyers put out a request for proposal for materials and labor needed for a particular project, and businesses bid for the work (see Exhibit 11.2). The government buyer selects the lowest price, in effect having control over the exchange.

Online sellers are more willing to negotiate than their off-line counterparts, thus giving power to buyers in the exchange. Perhaps it is easier for U.S. consumers to negotiate from behind an impersonal computer, as compared with standing face-to-face with the seller. Also, sellers realize that information technology can help them better manage inventories and automate frequent price changes.

Buyer power online is also based on the huge quantity of information and product availability on the Web. As a result, online buyers are becoming more sophisticated—as they must be, considering the example of the MySimon book pricing option. This was put well by Erik Brynjolfsson, codirector of the E-business Center at MIT: "We're moving toward a very sophisticated economy. It's kind of an arms race between merchant technology and consumer technology (in the form of shopbots). If consumers are not sophisticated they can be soaked. If managed intelligently, the tools are there to create a revolution."

With power comes risk. Consider what happens to a substantial number of bidders in online auctions. In what has been called "the winner's curse," some people actually pay a higher price for auctioned products than they would pay an online retailer. In the B2B market, one study found that car dealers pay significantly more for

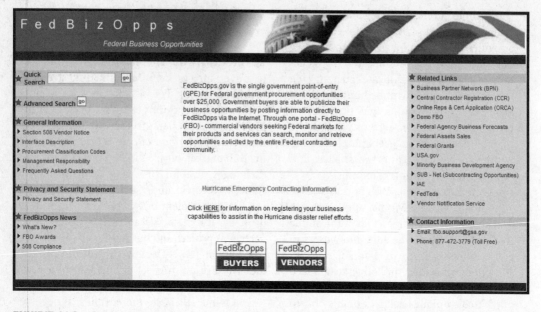

EXHIBIT 11.2 Government Portal for Vendors Seeking Government Buyers
Source: www.fedbizopps.gov/.

used automobiles online than they do off-line. In the B2C market, researchers evaluated the winning bids for new surplus computer items at Egghead.com and compared prices for the exact items sold on the retail portion of the Egghead site (Pellegrino, Amyx, and Pellegrino, 2002). They found that 20 percent of winning bidders overpaid. Perhaps the entertainment benefit of an online auction keeps the value equation in balance, but just as likely, buyers do not realize they've overpaid.

Seller View

Sellers view price as the amount of money they receive from buyers, unless they are making a barter exchange. Seller costs for producing the good or service represent the pricing floor, under which no profit is made. Above that floor, marketers have the freedom to set a price that will draw buyers from competing offers. Between cost and price is profit.

The seller's perspective on pricing includes both internal and external factors. Internal factors are the firm's strengths and weaknesses from its SWOT analysis, its overall pricing objectives, its marketing mix strategy, and the costs involved in producing and marketing the product. External factors that affect online pricing in particular include the market structure, competition, and the buyer's perspective, as discussed earlier.

INTERNAL FACTORS: PRICING OBJECTIVES

Marketers begin by setting overall pricing objectives from among those that are profit oriented, market oriented, or competition oriented. The most common profit-oriented objective for pricing is current profit maximization. Online research firms such as Forrester and Gartner Group are using a profit-oriented approach when they charge $1,500 to $4,500 and more to download current e-business research reports.

Companies can also select among various market-oriented objectives. Building a larger customer base may lead to lower costs and higher long-run profit. Low prices generally build market share. For example, Perseus Survey Solutions, a Web-based survey software program, offers its basic level software at a low price to build share (compared to competition), then upsells to annual maintenance fees and programs with more functionality. Negotiation and bidding are also market-oriented approaches. For example, at least three Oregon hotels seek bids for room nights at their Web sites (The Resort at the Mountain, The Valley River Inn, and The Salishan Lodge and Resort).

The objective of competition-based pricing is to price according to what competitors charge for similar products, paying less attention to the company's own costs or to demand. This may be why most of the shipping fees are the same in Exhibit 11.1. The internet's pricing transparency gives firms quicker access to competitive price changes and increases the number and speed of online price changes.

INTERNAL FACTORS: MARKETING MIX STRATEGY Successful companies use an integrated and consistent marketing mix strategy. For example, Volvo sells relatively high-priced automobiles through dealerships, supported by a Web site and off-line marketing communication that convey its upscale brand image. Volvo marketers know that more than 80 percent of its customers shop online (Greenberg, 2001). Highly educated men who live in urban areas are the most likely to configure a new Volvo on the firm's Web site, price it, and then talk to dealers via e-mail. Dealers say they close about 10 percent to 15 percent of these leads. Thus, Volvo uses the internet to generate sales leads, knowing that its customers are not likely to buy a high-priced item directly from the internet.

The internet is only one sales channel and must be used in concert with other marketing mix elements. Marketing managers carefully consider how to price the same product for sale in both online and off-line channels. For instance, Yale's Oxford Journals Online offers both print and online editions, giving a 10-percent discount for only online use and a 5 percent discount for only print use. No proven rules or standard practices have emerged at this point—practices vary widely by product and industry.

INTERNAL FACTORS: INFORMATION TECHNOLOGY AFFECTS COSTS Information technology can be expensive, but once it is running smoothly it can create tremendous cost efficiencies—putting both upward and downward pressure on prices.

The Internet Puts Upward Pressure on Prices Many companies fail with expensive customer relationship management or other software that does not help to generate enough new revenue to cover the sites' costs due to competitive pricing constraints. Following are some of the factors that put upward pressure on internet pricing:

- **Online customer service.** In the past, customer service online provided a competitive edge for firms such as Dell Computer and Amazon. Conversely, customers now expect firms to return e-mail promptly, provide thorough help and FAQ functions online, and give telephone and other contact information. Online customer service is no longer a competitive edge, but an expensive competitive necessity.
- **Distribution.** Online retailers face hefty distribution costs for their products: each product must be shipped separately to its destination rather than by the case to brick-and-mortar retailers or centrally-located warehouses. This is similar to the catalog marketer's cost structure. Retailers pass shipping costs on to their customers, thus, raising prices. Not surprisingly, some customers are offended by the shipping costs if higher than expected and if presented in the shopping cart only at the last minute. High shipping costs are one reason for shopping cart abandonment.
- **Affiliate programs.** Many Web sites pay a commission on referrals through affiliate programs. Affiliate sponsors reward the referring Web sites by paying a 7 percent to 15 percent commission on each reference that leads to a sale. This commission, like all channel intermediary costs, has the effect of inflating the price of the item or

lowering company profits if referral fees are absorbed.

- **Site development and maintenance.** Web site development and maintenance are not cheap. Forrester Research estimates the cost for a "conservative" site to be $10,000 to $100,000, while an "aggressive" site costs $1 million or more—and that is just to develop the site. Maintenance can be quite expensive, especially with hardware, software, and monthly internet connection costs.
- **Customer acquisition costs (CAC).** The cost of acquiring new customers online is quite high; this factor caused the downfall of many dot-com firms in 2000. For example, the average CAC for early online retailers was $82. How many orders must a firm receive to recoup that cost, and at what price? In addition, many customers are not nearly as brand loyal online as off-line.

The Internet Puts Downward Pressure on Prices The internet also allows marketers to shave costs, translating into lower prices and ultimately higher value for customers. When lower costs lead to higher prices, profit increases—a win for all stakeholders. The following are a few ways firms can save costs using internet technology for internal processes:

- **Order processing—self-service.** Because customers fill out their own order forms, firms save the expense of order entry personnel and paper processing. These expenses can be considerable. The average cost of producing and processing an invoice electronically is $10, compared with $100 in off-line transactions. An average retail banking transaction costs $0.15 to $0.20 online versus $1.50 off-line. Cisco Systems, the world's largest manufacturer of networking equipment, invites Web-based orders from customers. The paperwork reduction it reaps from its Web site saves hundreds of millions of dollars each year.
- **Just-in-time inventory.** Some manufacturers use electronic data interchange (EDI) to drive down costs in the digital channel by coordinating value chain activities and allowing for just-in-time (JIT) delivery of parts and reduced inventories. Some online and off-line retailers do not even hold inventory, saving considerably on financing costs. Instead, they acquire the inventory in response to customer orders or have partners drop-ship products directly to customers.
- **Overhead.** Online storefronts can lower their overhead costs because they do not have to rent and staff expensive retail space. Amazon's physical warehouses are considerably less expensive to rent and staff than the retail space of a trendy shopping mall. Furthermore, these warehouses can be located in areas with low rents, low wages, low taxes, and quick access to shipping hubs, such as Northern Nevada.
- **Customer service.** Although customer service can initially add to an organization's costs, companies save by automating some customer service functions that were formerly performed by employees. For instance, customer service requests average $15 to $20 in an off-line call center versus $3 to $5 when customers help themselves on the internet.
- **Printing and mailing.** Online sellers do not incur mail distribution and printing costs for their product catalogs. Once the catalog is placed online, access carries little or no incremental costs. The same holds true for e-mail promotions.
- **Digital product distribution costs.** Distribution costs for digital products are extremely low in the internet channel, such as when a customer downloads a purchased music file from iTunes. Conversely, the internet channel has high distribution costs for tangible products because they are sent to individuals in small quantities instead of in larger lots to brick-and-mortar intermediaries.

These efficiencies can result in lower prices for consumers; technology enables buyers to evaluate and demand appealing prices. With respect to price, the best-studied products online are books and CDs (among the earliest products to be marketed online). Research shows that online prices for books and CDs are indeed lower by 9 percent to 16 percent. In another study of 4,800 prices in the online video industry, researchers examined six online and six off-line retailers (Tang and Xing, 2003). They found internet-only retailers to price 6.42 percent lower than multichannel retailers (equivalent to 3% after shipping costs). In the pharmaceutical industry, 60 capsules of the prescription drug Allegra are $53.50 at retail pharmacies, $49.66 from mail-order houses, and $51.60 online. Does this mean that all prices online are lower? Further study is needed to provide solid proof, and as soon as that evidence is reported, prices will change again.

EXTERNAL FACTORS AFFECTING ONLINE PRICING The competition, market factors, price–demand relationship (i.e., elastic or inelastic), and customer behavior all affect a firm's pricing strategies online and off-line. The buyer's viewpoint was covered earlier; online behavior affecting pricing was covered in Chapter 7. In this section, we examine two important market factors in the online environment: market structure and market efficiency.

Market Structure The seller's leeway to set prices varies with different types of markets.

Economists recognize four types of markets, each presenting a different pricing challenge:

1. **Pure competition.** This market consists of many buyers and sellers trading in a uniform commodity such as corn. Product differentiation and marketing communication play little or no role, so sellers in these markets do not spend much time on marketing strategy.
2. **Monopolistic competition.** This market consists of many buyers and sellers who trade over a range of prices rather than a single market price. A range of prices occurs because sellers can differentiate their offers to buyers.
3. **Oligopolistic competition.** This market consists of a few sellers who are highly sensitive to each other's pricing and marketing strategies. If a company drops its price by 5 percent, buyers will quickly switch over to this supplier.
4. **Pure monopoly.** This market consists of one seller whose prices are usually regulated by the government.

This market structure distinction is extremely important for online sellers because if *price transparency* eventually results in a completely efficient market, sellers will have no control over online prices—the result will be pure competition as depicted in Exhibit 11.3. One example of a

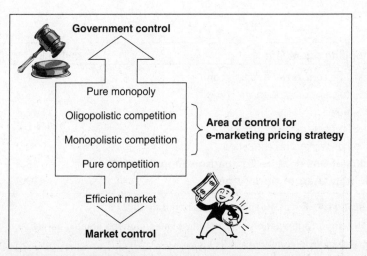

EXHIBIT 11.3 Efficient Markets Mean Loss of Pricing Control

nearly efficient market is the stock market. Note that online stock trading firms operate in a monopolistic competition because they compete based on trade commission prices, not actual security selling prices. If other products follow suit, the internet will have a profound effect on pricing strategy. This probably won't happen, however, for reasons mentioned in the next section. Next, we examine what comprises an efficient market and discuss whether the online market is approaching efficiency.

Efficient Markets Economists have long theorized about consumer behavior in **efficient markets**. Such markets would experience perfect price competition. A market is efficient when customers have equal access to information about products, prices, and distribution. In an efficient market, one would expect to find lower prices, high **price elasticity**, frequent price changes, smaller price changes, and narrow **price dispersion**—the observed spread between the highest and lowest price for a given product. As previously mentioned, the closest example of an efficient market is the stock market. Commodity markets came close to being efficient until the government intervened with controls. However, the internet is probably as close to a test ground for efficient markets as has ever existed because it exhibits so many of the appropriate characteristics. Interestingly, the behavior of consumers on the internet does not bear out all of the economists' predictions.

Is the Net an Efficient Market? Many people believe that the internet is an efficient market because of access to information through corporate Web sites, shopping agents, and distribution channels. Products sold online exhibit lower prices, high price elasticity, frequent price changes, and smaller price changes: all symptoms of efficient markets. But do these factors actually make the Net an efficient market? The following external, market factors place a downward pressure on internet prices, contributing to efficiency:

- **Shopping agents.** Shopping agents such as PriceScan (www.pricescan.com) facilitate consumer searches for low prices by displaying the results in a comparative format. Exhibit 11.4 displays the top shopping agents in 2002. Slightly more than 15 percent of internet users visited shopping agents in July 2002, an increase of 6 percent from six months earlier. In 2008, the picture is not that different. BizRate and PriceGrabber remain at the same level, MySimon declined dramatically, and DealTime doubled in use over the Christmas holiday, but then sank back, according to Alexa.com—still small usage among internet users. See Exhibit 11.5 for an example of a search for the fourth edition of this book in your hands at mySimon.com. The prices range from $63 to $101, and because the book results are listed in order

Shopping Agent Site	Millions of Visitors
DealTime.com (now Shopping.com)	7.4
BizRate.com comparison shopping	5.7
mySimon.com	2.7
PriceGrabber.com*	2.2
All other search sites combined	0.2
Users of One or More Comparison Shopping Sites	**18.2**
Monthly Users of the Internet	**119.5**

EXHIBIT 11.4   Retail Shopping Comparison, July 2002

*Represents an aggregation of commonly owned/branded domain names.

Source: Data from comScore Media Metrix.

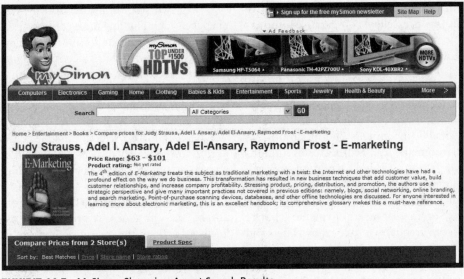

EXHIBIT 11.5   MySimon Shopping Agent Search Results

Source: Courtesy of CNET (www.mySimon.com).

with the lowest price first, outlets that are not price competitive risk being left off of the first screen and might as well be invisible.

- **High price elasticity.** Price elasticity refers to the variability of purchase behavior with changes in price. As an example, leisure travel is an especially elastic market: When the airlines engage in fare wars, consumers snap up ticket inventories creating huge demand. For many products such as books and CDs, the online market is more elastic than the off-line market, so we would expect internet users to be sensitive to price changes.
- **Reverse auctions.** Reverse auctions allow buyers to name their price and have sellers try to match that price. This format pits sellers against one another and usually drives prices down.
- **Tax-free zones.** Most online retailing takes place across state lines, so buyers often pay no sales taxes on purchases, reducing total out-of-pocket expenditures by as much as 5 percent to 8 percent per transaction. This may be the reason some of the books in

Exhibit 11.1 had no added tax. Although states and foreign governments have challenged the internet tax-free zone, the U.S. government continues to support a moratorium on taxes for internet purchases.

- **Venture capital.** Many internet companies are financed through venture capital or angel investors. Many investors take a long-term view and are willing to sustain short-term losses (up to five years, in some cases) to let those companies grow by establishing brand equity and grabbing market share. These companies can price lower because they do not have a profit-maximization pricing objective.
- **Competition.** The competition online is fierce and highly visible. Furthermore, some competitors are willing to set prices that return little or no short-term profits to gain brand equity and market share.
- **Frequent price changes.** The online market experiences more frequent price changes than the off-line market because (1) online suppliers must jockey with competitors to attract price-sensitive

consumers; (2) shopping agents give consumers excellent comparative information about prices, and vendors may frequently alter their pricing to place higher on the results; (3) sellers can easily change prices using databases to drive Web page content; (4) in a computerized environment firms can offer volume discounts in smaller increments than in an off-line environment (e.g., FedEx creates millions of different rate books based on shipping volume for posting on Web pages for individual clients); and (5) experimentation is easy online, allowing firms to change prices frequently, see how demand changes, and then adjust as competition and other factors emerge.

- **Smaller price change increments.** In one study, the smallest off-line price change was $0.35 whereas the smallest online price change was $0.01. Some of the same factors that encourage frequent price changes may play a role here as well. First, price-sensitive consumers may respond to even a small price advantage with respect to the competition. Second, shopping agents rank their results by price—even a $0.01 advantage will earn a higher ranking than the competition. Third, because it is difficult to change prices off-line, retailers may wait until the need for a price change is even greater.

Is the Net an Inefficient Market? Even though the Web exhibits many characteristics of an efficient market, it does not act like an efficient market with respect to narrow price dispersion. Prices tend to equalize in commodities markets, because sellers cannot easily differentiate one bushel of peas from another. With perfect information for all, one would expect narrow price dispersion online—for example, because buyers can search many Web sellers for iPods, we might expect the prices to gravitate to the same level. Interestingly, this expectation does not hold on the Net, due to online retailer branding and other benefits that justify price differences in the minds of customers.

In two studies, greater spread was found between high and low prices online versus high and low prices off-line for the same items. Price dispersion in the retail video industry averages 30 percent from lowest to highest, with off-line prices exhibiting much larger differences than online prices (Tang and Xing, 2003). The online price dispersion is 33 percent for books and 25 percent for CDs. One possible reason that prices are so widely dispersed may be that many buyers do not know about or use shopping agents.

However, more interesting explanations for the price dispersion relate to the strength of a firm's brand, the way goods are priced online as well as delivery options, time-sensitive shoppers, differentiation, switching costs, and second-generation shopping agents:

- **Branding.** In spite of the proliferation of Web sites, brand is still a sought-after benefit. Research shows that the top Web sites get most of the traffic. Consumers will even show a preference for brand when using shopping agents. Many consumers will pick a well-known merchant brand from the search results even if that brand does not offer the lowest price. Because of the importance of brand, the best-branded Web sites spend millions of dollars to attract customers. Amazon spends 24 percent of revenues or $29 per customer on promotion. By contrast, Barnes & Noble spends just 4 percent of revenues to promote its off-line stores. The brand-loyal customer base allows Amazon to charge 7 percent to 12 percent more than bargain online retailers.
- **How goods are priced online.** Off-line most goods are offered at fixed prices. By contrast, on the Web marketers use many more strategies. The same good is often available for a fixed, a dynamically updated, or an auction price on different sites at the same time—and the prices among them may vary widely. In addition, products are bundled with shipping and special services in different ways, confusing shoppers who want to compare like products.

- **Delivery options.** The same product delivered under differing conditions (time and place) may have considerably different value to the consumer. For example, a beer served at a bar has more value than one bought at a supermarket. Similarly, a product delivered to the door may have considerably more value for some consumers than one that is bought at the store. Online grocery shopping follows this value model. Some marketers would argue that groceries delivered to the door are not the same product as the same groceries picked up at the store. By this argument, the additional benefits actually differentiate the product. Normally, the consumer has to wait longer for a product delivered to the door, but that may be changing. Amazon offers one-hour delivery of popular books and music in some metropolitan areas and other firms may follow suit.
- **Time-sensitive shoppers.** Time-sensitive shoppers may not wish to invest the time and energy required to track down the best price. Also, some sites may be so complex that consumers need more time to navigate and complete the transaction.
- **Differentiation.** One result of strong branding is perceived or real product differentiation, which enables marketers to price their products differently (see Chapter 9).
- **Switching costs.** Customers face switching costs when they choose a different online retailer. Some customers are not willing to incur those costs and, thus, stick with a familiar online retailer. If an Amazon customer shops at another retailer he loses access to a familiar interface, personalized book recommendations, and the 1-Click ordering that Amazon has patented. Switching costs are even higher in the B2B market. Many organizations have found that it is more effective to build relationships with a limited number of suppliers rather than offer all items out for bid. These organizations readily pay a slight premium to enjoy better service and support.

- **Second-generation shopping agents.** Second-generation shopping agents guide the consumer through the process of quantifying benefits and evaluating the value equation. If a consumer ranks certain benefits highly, that consumer may be willing to pay more to receive those benefits. BizRate allows consumers to evaluate merchants based on ratings compiled from previous customers. PriceScan and DealTime allow consumers to set filters so that merchants delivering the desired benefits will rise in the rankings. See the "Let's Get Technical" box for more on shopping agents.

Is the internet an efficient market? The answer is no, not now. However, it has all the features to move toward efficiency in the future. This shift would have devastating effects for e-marketers wanting control over pricing strategies; thus, marketing planners should watch this trend closely.

PAYMENT OPTIONS

Electronic money, also called e-money or digital cash, is a system that uses the internet and computers to exchange payments electronically. It can be used in off-line or online transactions, using the internet to transfer money between buyer and seller accounts. In the United States, the only well-known off-line e-money transactions occur at toll booths when autos with transponders drive through them—and drivers receive a monthly invoice. Conversely, digital cash has widespread adoption in other countries. In Hong Kong, there are 14 million Octopus cards—twice the number of Hong Kong's population. These are smart cards, charged with up to $1,000 in cash, that can be used to pay for things, trade for cash, or recharged for reuse. Octopus cards are used in 10 million daily transactions from the ferry system to convenience stores, according to Wikipedia. Other interesting off-line e-money payment systems include:

- **Payment by smart chip.** MZOOP, created by Harex InfoTech in South Korea, is a chip

LET'S GET TECHNICAL

Unwrapping Online Shopping's Secrets

Five days before the holidays . . . and you have not even started shopping for gifts. By the time you get home from work, it is after 7 p.m. and you are tired. Because you were so busy with your new job this year, you forgot everyone's birthday, and only remembered to send a card a month late. If things weren't bad enough, you are strapped for cash because your old clunker of a car died last month, and you were forced to get a new one. Your sister wants a digital camera, and your mom wants a new TV for her bedroom. The convenience of online shopping is appealing, and you have heard that a new shopping agent from Google, aptly named Froogle, is worth a try. After a couple of hours of clicking and shipping, your holiday shopping is finished and you saved a bunch of dough. . . .Now it's time for some holiday cookies!

A majority of the large retailers in the United States and shoppers worldwide have all caught the bug—the online shopping bug, that is. While the Saturday trip to the mall used to be commonplace, many households are now doing a majority of their shopping online. Whether it is the latest consumer electronic or a new bedspread, consumers are more than happy to shop from the comfort of their homes—wearing who knows what. Most consumers say they are lured by the convenience of online shopping. Retailers are certainly used to attracting consumers to their stores using circulars, commercials, and coupons, and similar concepts are being deployed online to get consumers to their Web sites.

Since the onset of online shopping, consumers' perceptions have been that better "deals" can be found online. Of course a "deal" is based on the individual consumer's values. However, Web sites are cropping up to help frugal consumers find the best deals online. So, instead of clipping the coupons and flipping through circulars, savvy online shoppers are giving shopping agents and coupon Web sites a try. It is important for e-marketers to understand the technologies employed by consumers—and for e-marketers to properly utilize them.

A shopping agent is a Web site that collects product and price information from online retail sites and displays all of the information together. For example, many Web sites sell digital cameras. If a consumer is looking for a certain digital camera, such as the Canon PowerShot Digital Elph, he would be able to enter that information into the shopping agent's search box and receive prices from all over the Web. Many shopping agents display Web sites' advertised prices, but some also ask for the consumer's ZIP code to calculate tax and shipping costs. The final result is a list of the sites on which the item is available at the cost of the item on that site. Links are also available to go directly to the Web sites or the product pages. In addition to providing prices, some shopping agents review products and retailers. Consumers are invited to rate retailers and record comments about their buying experience on the site.

From an e-marketing standpoint, shopping agents are beneficial because they are attracting to the retailers' Web sites the consumers who are ready to buy—what more could an e-marketer ask for? The answer is that e-marketers want to attract more consumers to their sites using the shopping agents, of course. Although consumers believe that shopping agents are providing unbiased results to their queries, the truth is that most are not. Some agents list only retailers that have registered with them, and other agents list sites based on who has paid for the top spot on the results list.

Shopping agents are popular, and consumers can find hundreds of products using common search engines. When marketing products using shopping agents, it is essential to understand how to register a product and select one that is appropriate for the e-marketing campaign.

When registering a product with a shopping agent, marketers are usually required to pay a fee and give the Web site a product feed. Most agents have a pay-per-click (PPC) policy. Prices range from a few cents to more than $1.00 for each time a consumer clicks on the link to the product. Some sites also require a deposit of $100 to $200 when registering, which would be applied to the PPC account.

(continued)

(continued)

A product feed contains information about the product that is being featured, such as its name, description, category, price, and availability. Agents also ask that a URL to the product be included for linking purposes. Product feeds are fairly simple to create and give marketers an opportunity to compel consumers to purchase the product from their Web sites. Expert e-marketers recommend that clear and concise language be used when writing product feeds, and industry abbreviations should never be used. For example, the abbreviation DJ may seem reasonable when marketing a Hewlett-Packard DeskJet printer, but it is better to write out the term. Agents ask that product feeds be submitted in one of a variety of ways, such as online forms or file uploading.

When choosing which shopping agent to register with, one should definitely do one's homework. Some sites are known for their ability to provide information on a wide variety of products, while others are more specialized. Also, registering with one shopping agent can have the product listed on multiple sites due to the agent's affiliation with other agents. An example of this affiliation is Shopping.com, which shares information with DealTime and Epinions.

Shopping agents that are known for their high volume of visitors include BizRate, DealTime, mySimon, PriceScan, and shopping.yahoo.com. Each offers a slightly different service. BizRate, which like most agents lets retailers pay for top spots on results lists, is known for its high traffic rates and unique consumer survey information. BizRate's original business model included providing consumer research, and only added product comparison services in 2000. mySimon promotes its search using categories feature, and Yahoo! Shopping lets consumers search among its own online mall first instead of across of the entire internet. Even though retailers that pay the extra fees can obtain the highest spot, it is difficult for consumers to detect which retailers have paid for special listing.

PriceScan, which is also widely used, has numerous competitive advantages—it returns results from off-line retailers, ifocuses on the lowest prices, and does not allow retailers to pay for the highest spot on the list.

New to the shopping agent circuit, Google's Froogle allows consumers to search using the same technology that powers Google, a hugely popular search engine. Because Froogle is still in its testing, or beta, stage, retailers can register their product free of charge. Froogle automatically finds many retailers' information, but retailers can also submit their product information to the site. Froogle is being funded by the advertisements that appear on the right side of the results pages.

The number of consumers using shopping bots is on the rise, and e-marketers are in control of what these consumers are seeing. Consumers' use of online coupons is also increasing. Many retailers with Web sites also offer free coupons on their own sites, especially when introducing new products. For example, when Veet debuted its Bladeless Razor™ Hair Removal Kit in the summer of 2004, it offered a $2.00 off coupon on its Web site when consumers filled out a form asking for contact information.

However, coupon sites are another story. These sites offer a variety of services for the penny-pinching consumer:

- Links to company Web sites that offer free coupons
- Printable coupons for use in brick-and-mortar stores
- Coupon codes for online retailers
- Links to sites that will automatically give a percentage off an order
- Information about sale and clearance-priced items at online retailers

Some sites require consumer input to get the coupon or information listed on the site. E-marketers can submit their coupons, promotional codes, and sales to these sites usually via e-mail. Coupon sites include retailmenot.com, couponcabin.com, and couponmountain.com. Traditional paper coupon distributors, such as SmartSource and ValPak, are also offering online coupons. Industry experts say that the circulation of coupons and promotional codes online is high, and that the best way to get noticed is to offer two deals in one, such as free shipping and $10 off an order.

inserted in a cell phone that can be pointed to a vending machine or other point of purchase reader for purchasing items. The transaction is charged to the owner's debit or credit bank card. Similarly, Offica Watch, made in Japan by Casio, allows wearers to pay by e-money via the chip in the watch itself. Buyers just wave the watch near a scanner and the purchase is done. If you'd like to get rid of all gadgets, you can even have an RFID chip planted in your arm for payment at the Baja Beach Club in Barcelona!

• **Payment by cell phone.** Japan and Finland already allow off-line payments via cell phone at vending machines and elsewhere. BART in San Francisco is currently testing a system where riders can swipe their cell phones over a special reader to pay for their ticket.

Online, 51 percent of consumers pay bills with a bank's online banking service, showing the huge adoption of e-money systems. For one-time payments, PayPal has become the industry standard, with over 150 million accounts worldwide. This eBay-owned company allows users to pay for online purchases via credit card or bank debit. Exhibit 11.6 shows the various accounts and fees online merchants pay for the service—which are comparable to the fees credit card companies charge merchants. Competing with PayPal, Western Union offers MoneyZap for buying online products from merchants offering the option. Western Union targets the 80 million Americans without credit cards.

One important e-money service uses a model quite different from PayPal's. Called Bill Me Later, this model allows buyers to pay for

	E-mail Payments	Web site Payments Standard	Web site Payments Pro	Payflow Gateway	PayPal Express Checkout
Customer experience					
Where customers shop	Varies by business	Shop on your Web site	Shop on your Web site	Shop on your Web site	Shop on your Web site
Where customers check out	PayPal	PayPal	Your Web site or PayPal	Your Web site or PayPal	PayPal
Customers need PayPal account	No	No	No	No	Yes
Integration					
Internet merchant acct.	Not needed	Not needed	Included	Required	Required
Shopping cart support	Not required	Yes	Yes	Yes	Yes
Technical skills	Not required	HTML	APIs	APIs or HTML	APIs or HTML
Pricing					
Setup	Free	Free	Free	$179–$249	Free
Monthly	Free	Free	$30	$19.95–$59.95	Free
Per Transaction	1.9%–2.9% + $0.30	1.9%–2.9% + $0.30	1.9%–2.9% + $0.30	$0.10	1.9%–2.9% + $0.30
For phone, fax, mail orders	$30 per month	$30 per month	Included	Included	$30 per month

EXHIBIT 11.6   PayPal Account Options

Source: Data from www.paypal.com.

online goods and services without a credit card. They must be approved by Bill Me Later and are billed after making the purchase. This service is growing quickly, having signed up merchants such as Walmart, the Apple Store, Office Max, and Overstock.com. It is especially good for small businesses that purchase online because it costs them less than their credit card fees and interest.

Electronic money has distinct advantages for online retailers. It is more efficient, with lower transaction fees, and draws new customers without credit risk fears. Also, these services allow online merchants to sell to internet users who don't have credit cards. Finally, offering multiple payment options can actually entice more people to buy online. A Quality Research Associates study of 147 leading online retailers found that those offering only one type of payment (such as a credit card) convert 60 percent of shoppers on average, while those offering multiple payment options convert up to 72 percent of their site visitors (see www.ecommercetimes.com). Conversely, potential downsides include large economic issues involving all e-commerce, such as less taxes for states when transactions occur out of state, the possibilities of exchange rate fluctuations with high levels of international e-commerce, and the criminal use of the systems for money laundering and other fraudulent or illegal activities.

Electronic cash is an important pricing component for two reasons. First, when merchants use PayPal or other systems, their costs increase and this is reflected in the product's price. Second, when online purchasing is easier for customers, this balances the higher price—recall that the costs for consumers include money, time, energy, and psychic costs.

PRICING STRATEGIES

Price setting is full of contradictions. It has become nearly as much art as science, with lots of data needing insightful interpretation for best application. If the price is too low profits will suffer, yet if it is too high sales may decline. And that is just the short-term view. In the long run, an initial low price that builds market share can create economies of scale to lower costs and, thus, increase profits. Also, how marketers apply pricing strategy is as important as *how much* they charge. PayPal's pricing system demonstrates the skill that goes into pricing strategy.

Another contradiction is that information technology complicates pricing in some ways while making it simpler in other ways. Sellers easily change prices at a moment's notice or vary them according to each individual buyer's previous behavior. Next, buyer value perceptions vary between rational and emotional, and not everyone reacts the same way. For example, some high-income customers enjoy walking into the Volvo dealership with a printed Web page detailing what they want and how much it should cost, while others enjoy the emotional relationship with a favorite salesperson and return every three years for the latest model, trusting that "Joe will take care of me." Finally, firms using multichannel delivery systems must consider the varying costs of each channel and buyers' differing value perceptions about purchasing on the internet versus at the brick-and-mortar store. Pricing is a tricky business, guided by data, experience, and experimentation.

In general, marketers can employ all traditional pricing strategies to the online environment. Here we focus on three types of pricing strategies particularly important to online sellers: fixed pricing, dynamic pricing, and renting instead of buying.

Fixed Pricing

Fixed pricing (also called *menu pricing*) occurs when sellers set the price and buyers must take it or leave it. With fixed pricing, everyone pays the same price. Most U.S. brick-and-mortar retailers use this model. Even when wholesalers and manufacturers offer quantity discounts, the price levels apply to all businesses that purchase the required amount. The basic pricing principles every marketer uses off-line also apply online. Two common fixed pricing strategies used online are price leadership and promotional pricing:

- **Price leadership.** A **price leader** is the lowest-priced product entry in a particular category. Both online and off-line, Wal-Mart is a price leader, setting the pace for other retailers. With shopping agents on the Web, a price leader strategy is sweet indeed. To implement this strategy, however, marketers must shave costs to a minimum. Reducing costs can be done through internet marketing cost efficiencies described earlier, but a firm must do it better than the competition. Often the largest producer becomes the price leader because of economies of scale, but on the internet an entrepreneur operating out of a basement constantly challenges the large producer. This strategy is productive for the internet, although competition is fierce and price leadership is often fleeting. Of course, the second-lowest-priced item will also gain sales, especially if it offers advantages over the price leader. On the Net, Buy.com is a price leader in many different categories, selling many items below market value and recouping losses through advertising revenue from the Web site.

- **Promotional pricing.** Many online retailers have turned to **promotional pricing** to encourage a first purchase, encourage repeat business, and close a sale. Most promotions carry an expiration date that helps create a sense of urgency. For example, Amazon offered free shipping with any order over $25 with such success that it became standard. It didn't arrive at that order amount, however, without trying several other price points first to find the optimum promotional offer to motivate sales. Promotional pricing on the internet can be highly targeted through e-mail messages, and research shows high customer satisfaction with internet purchases.

Dynamic Pricing

Dynamic pricing is the strategy of offering different prices to different customers. **Yield management** is a strategy used most often by the travel industry to optimize inventory management through frequent price changes. Airlines have long used dynamic pricing software for yield management

when pricing air travel—dropping prices when traffic is light. Dynamic Web pages allow travel companies to make quick and frequent changes in order to rent cars and fill seats or hotel beds.

Dynamic pricing can be initiated by the seller or the buyer (as compared with fixed pricing, which is always initiated by sellers). Two types of dynamic pricing include **segmented pricing**, where the company sells a good or service at two or more prices, based on segment differentiation rather than cost alone. The other type is **price negotiation**, where the company negotiates prices with individual customers, who comprise segments of one. Segmented pricing involves a one-time price, which may be different for different customers; the price in negotiation may change many times before buyers and sellers agree on the final price. Also, negotiation is more often initiated by the buyer, while segmented pricing is usually set by the seller.

SEGMENTED PRICING Segmented pricing uses the internet properties for mass customization, automatically devising pricing based on order size and timing, demand and supply levels, and other preset decision factors. With segmented pricing online, the company uses decision rules to set pricing levels for segments of customers all the way to a segment of one person—that is, any customer that is X or does X gets Y price. For example, any person who books a flight within seven days of departure is quoted the full price (no discount). Segmented pricing has its roots in traditional marketing, as when theaters lower prices for consumers attending afternoon movies. Pricing according to customer behavior segments is becoming more common as firms collect an increasing amount of electronic behavioral information. See Exhibit 11.7 for an example of dynamic pricing by customer type, showing how Networksolutions.com practices segmented pricing in domain name registration.

Segmented pricing at the individual level is easier online because sophisticated software and large databases permit firms to set rules and make price changes in a *nano*second—even as a buyer is clicking on a Web page. This capability has

Launch your Web site today

Websites from ImageCafé
Put your business online! Great websites, fully customizable, hosting included. Starting at $9.95 per month.

Learn more

dot com essentials™
Our kit includes your own Web Address, a one-page website and dot com mail™ - our business e-mail service. Now 20% off!

Access your dot com mail   Learn more

Domain Name Volume Discount Program
Order 100+ domain names with the same registration information in one simple transaction and save over 50%.

Learn more

Expand you

Corporate Servi
idNames pro of domain na online.

Tools to power
Get the tools and promote

Learn more

Secure Your We
Certify your credit card pa

Current Customers
- Update your domain records
- Set up dot com mail
- Set up dot com biz card
- Set up dot com forwarding

Catalog of Services
Check out our Internet Identity services, such as:
- dot com gear™
- Free Web Mail
- Become an Affiliate

VeriSign and Network Solution
Internet Trust Service
View the e-commerce:
we provide for:
- Small Business

EXHIBIT 11.7 Network Solutions Practices Segmented Pricing for Services

Source: www.networksolutions.com. Reprinted with express permission. Copyright © 2000 Network Solutions, Inc. All rights reserved.

marketers quite excited—the internet's ability to customize prices, marketing communication, and products to the individual level. Using cookie files, online sellers recognize individuals and experiment with offers and prices to motivate transactions. Sometimes these individuals are particular customers, as when Amazon.com recognizes the customer and presents customized recommendations. Other times, individuals are part of a larger segment, such as those logging in from a particular geographic location or those exhibiting a behavior such as abandoning a shopping cart. Sellers define the segment and then customize prices following preset decision rules when an individual member of the segment visits the site. For example, an online retailer can lower the price by small increments on each subsequent visit to see whether the buyer will buy. Also, online firms can build loyalty programs, like frequent flyer programs, to offer special prices to individuals who return and purchase often.

Segmented pricing can be effective when the market is segmentable, the different prices reflect real differences in each segment's perceptions of the product's value, and the segments show different degrees of demand. It is also appropriate when the costs of segmentation and segmented pricing do not exceed the extra revenue obtained from the price difference. In addition, the company must be sure that its segmented pricing meets legal and regulatory guidelines. Finally, the firm must take care not to upset customers who learn they are getting prices different from their neighbors. Amazon.com created an uproar when customers learned of its segmented pricing for individual customers; for some reason, airline passengers have accepted this practice but not book buyers. Thus, e-marketers employing segmentation must use customer-accepted reasons such as giving discounts to new or loyal customers or adjusting shipping fees for purchases sent to outlying locations.

Internet users can be segmented using many variables, as discussed in Chapter 8. Two variables that are particularly important to online pricing strategies are geographic segmentation and value segmentation.

Geographic Segment Pricing With **geographic segment pricing**, a company sets different prices when selling a product in different geographic areas. An online seller often knows where the user resides because server logs register the user's IP address, and the top-level domain name typically indicates country of residence (e.g., a Japanese user will have a .jp designation). Geographic pricing can help a company better relate its pricing to country-by-country or regional factors such as competitive pressure, local costs, economic conditions, legal or regulatory guidelines, and distribution opportunities. For example, a Dell computer priced at $1,000 in Los Angeles may be priced at £639 in London (US$1,285 in March 2008). This difference is because the manufacturer faces price escalation and therefore must price to reflect the higher costs of transportation, tariffs, and importer margins, among other costs involved in selling in another country.

Value Segment Pricing With **value segment pricing**, the seller recognizes that not all customers

provide equal value to the firm, segmenting by high, medium, and low value—and pricing accordingly. The well-known **Pareto principle** states that 80 percent of a firm's business usually comes from the top 20 percent of customers. As represented in Exhibit 11.8, a firm's A+ customers comprise a small group that contributes disproportionately to the firm's revenues and profits (Pitt et al., 2001). These customers tend to be the most loyal and may become brand advocates to their friends and acquaintances: the frequent flyers who always go first class, the casino high rollers who return repeatedly, or the high-volume package shippers who use the FedEx Web site to automate all services. These customers are also brand-loyal frequent customers who provide significant value to the seller. When A+ or A customers appear at the Web site, they will be recognized and receive special attention. These customers may not be price sensitive because they perceive that the brand or firm offers greater benefits (e.g., free upgrades and special treatment) and has earned their loyalty.

The large group of type C customers may be price shoppers or infrequent users of the product category, not accounting for much of the seller's revenue. Type B customers are also price sensitive and probably use the product category more than do C customers.

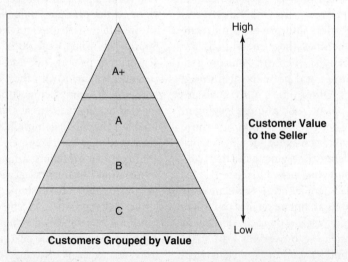

EXHIBIT 11.8   Customer Value Segments from Low (C) to High (A+)
Source: Adapted from Pitt et al. (2001).

Market factors tend to drive customers to the C level, whereas moves such as competitive offerings and price cuts attempt to lure A and B customers away. The seller's goal is to keep A customers brand loyal and to move all groups up to a higher level of value. Pricing strategies can help. For example, A customers might be allowed to bid on surplus inventory before others get a chance. Giving high-value customers the first shot at new products or promotions (e.g., Amazon's free shipping) will reinforce their loyalty. Conversely, B and C customers most often seek the lowest price, so discounts are not likely to create brand loyalty—they will continue being price-shopping brand switchers. These customers might enjoy e-mail blasts with fixed prices so they can be informed of the firm's prices and competitive benefits of the brand. The seller can use this technique to build a database for moving customers up in value. See Chapter 15 for more about value segmentation and marketing communication techniques for building customer relationships.

NEGOTIATED PRICING AND AUCTIONS Sellers usually set pricing levels when using segmented pricing, and buyers usually initiate pricing when bidding for items online. Through negotiation the price is set more than once in a back-and-forth discussion—a major difference from all other pricing strategies. Haggling over price is common in many countries; however, with a few exceptions U.S. consumers have shied away from such bargaining. The internet is changing this reluctance, as evidenced by the spectacular growth of online auctions. Many consumers enjoy the sport and community of an auction while others are just looking for a good deal.

In the C2C market, trust between buyers and sellers is an issue because the transaction happens among strangers—there is no brand name to generate trust. To assist buyers, eBay uses a feedback system consisting of one, zero, or minus one points for positive, neutral, or negative comments and ratings, respectively. Points build to the star and shooting star levels and are placed near seller profiles on eBay Web pages.

The red shooting star is reserved for a seller with 100,000 or more points. This system works: highly rated eBay sellers are more likely to make a sale and do it at a higher price. In one study of 861 golf club auctions, when sellers increased their feedback scores by zero to 25 points, they had a 3.4 percent higher probability of selling the clubs and received 5 percent higher prices (according to researcher Jeffrey Livingston).

While it seems that high levels of positive feedback mean higher prices, there are eBay scams that allow sellers to buy positive feedback. Academic researchers Jennifer Brown and John Morgan found an entire market for feedback itself at eBay, with an average value of at least $0.61 per feedback point (compiled with over 5,000 feedback market transactions) (Beal and Strauss, 2008).

Auctions in the B2B market are an effective way to unload surplus inventory at a price set by the market. For example, uBid has worked with over 7,000 businesses to sell more than $2 billion of excess inventory.

Renting Software

Companies developing software sometimes decide to rent rather than sell it to customers. Buyers want to purchase software they use on a regular basis, such as Microsoft Office, but if organizations want to use software for a short-term project or don't want to go to the expense of installing and maintaining it on their servers, renting makes sense. For example, Salesforce.com offers an incredibly complex and rich, leading CRM software system. Its customers don't want to purchase and install the system internally and watch hidden costs emerge (estimated by Salesforce.com at 90% above the purchase price of CRM software). Salesforce rents its software instead, pricing in a range from $65 per month per user to $1,200 a year for five users (based on a minimum annual commitment). Renting software is analogous to leasing cars. When leasing, the driver doesn't have to pay for maintenance and many other costs that purchasers must bear.

Chapter Summary

Price is the amount of money charged for a product or service. More broadly, it covers the sum of all the values (i.e., money, time, energy, and psychic cost) that buyers exchange for the benefits of having or using a good or service. Fixed price refers to one price set for all buyers. Dynamic pricing means varying prices for individual customers. Internet technology has prompted mass customization and a return to dynamic pricing—especially negotiation and pricing for segments as small as a single buyer. This capability is creating huge opportunities for marketers to optimize pricing strategies, including changing them daily or more often. However, the internet is also facilitating price transparency, the idea that both buyers and sellers can view all competitive prices for items sold online.

From the buyer's perspective, the cost of a product purchased online may be higher than that offline (due to seemingly hidden elements such as shipping costs and the time and effort needed to search out and compare prices). Yet buyers may also enjoy online cost savings due to the internet's convenience, speed, self-service capability, one-stop shopping, integration, and automation. Moreover, online buyers have more control through strategies such as reverse auctions, the availability of information and products, and negotiation opportunities.

From the seller's perspective, any price above the cost of producing the good or service has the potential to return profit. The seller's perspective on pricing covers internal factors such as pricing objectives, the marketing mix strategy, and information technology. Beyond the buyer's perspective, the market structure and the efficiency of the market are key external elements affecting online pricing.

A market is efficient when customers have equal access to information about products, prices, and distribution. Efficient markets are characterized by lower prices, high price elasticity, frequent and smaller price changes, and narrow price dispersion. The Web exhibits many characteristics of an efficient market except narrow price dispersion. Because the internet could become a more efficient market in the future, marketers who want to maintain control over pricing should differentiate their products on bases other than price, create unique product bundles of benefits, and consider the role of customer perceptions of value when determining pricing levels.

Exercises

REVIEW QUESTIONS

1. How does fixed pricing differ from dynamic pricing?
2. What is price transparency, and why is it an important concept for e-marketers to understand?
3. List the main factors that put downward pressure on prices in the internet channel.
4. List the main factors that put upward pressure on prices in the internet channel.
5. From the buyer's perspective, how does the internet affect costs?
6. What is an efficient market? What makes the internet an efficient market, and what indicates that it is not an efficient market?
7. How do e-marketers use geographic, value segment, and negotiated pricing online?
8. Why is PayPal a good idea for merchants?
9. What are the advantages of electronic money for online retailers?

DISCUSSION QUESTIONS

10. Near-perfect access to pricing information is a problem that airlines have faced for years. How have airlines responded to this problem? Should internet businesses adopt similar strategies?
11. Which of the online cost-saving factors do you think has the greatest effect on price? Why?

12. Which pricing strategy would you use to introduce a new product for wireless Web access? Why?

13. Internet technology allows a company to price the same product differently for different customers. What do you think would be the advantages and disadvantages of Amazon offering the same book at one price to a professor and at a different price to a student?

14. As a buyer, how do you think price transparency affects your ability to develop an appropriate bidding strategy for new products auctioned by companies through eBay?

15. As a seller, how do you think price transparency affects your ability to obtain as high a price as possible for used products you auction through eBay?

16. Would you like to use your cell phone to pay for goods and services? Why or why not?

WEB ACTIVITIES

17. Using a shopping agent such as MySimon, what is the very lowest price that you can find for a bare-bones notebook computer sold online? How is it configured? What is the highest price for the same computer?

18. Clip an ad for electronic products from the newspaper. Pick a specific electronic product and look up the product online using a shopping agent such as www.bizrate.com or www.pricegrabber.com. Create a table showing how the online prices compare with the local ad.

19. Visit PayPal, Money Zap (Western Union), and Bill Me Later. Review the prices and options for a new online bookseller and report on the pros and cons of each service. Which one(s) do you recommend?

CHAPTER 12

The Internet for Distribution

Any retailer who isn't using the online channel to promote off-line sales—as well as online sales—is missing a sizable opportunity.

—eMarketer.com

If I'm selling to you, I speak your language. If I'm buying, dann mussen Sie Deutch sprechen (then you must speak German).

—Willi Brandt, former chancellor, Germany

Chapter Outline

The key objective of this chapter is to develop an understanding of the internet as a distribution channel, identify online channel members, and analyze the functions they perform in the channel. You will learn how the internet presents opportunities to alter channel length, restructure channel intermediaries, improve the performance of channel functions, streamline channel management, and measure channel performance.

After reading this chapter, you will be able to:

- Describe the three major functions of a distribution channel.
- Explain how the internet is affecting distribution channel length.
- Discuss trends in supply chain management and power relationships among channel players.
- Outline the major models used by online channel members.
- Highlight how companies can use distribution channel metrics.

The Dell Direct Model

Michael Dell dropped out of college at age 19 to start a computer company, and it paid off big time. He owns 9 percent of Dell, Inc., a firm with more than $57 billion in annual revenues. The firm dropped the "Computer" from *Dell Computer* several years ago to reflect its growth in network servers, workstations, storage systems, and Ethernet switches for business customers, as

(continued)

(*continued*)

well as training, support, and systems integration. What does it take to be the number one notebook and desktop PC maker in the world, shipping 39 million computers in a year?

Dell sells over $50 million a day online, representing nearly half of its sales. This *direct-distribution model* offers Dell several competitive advantages. First, it eliminates wholesalers and retailers, allowing complete control over inventory levels and distribution costs. Dell turns its inventory every 10 days, minimizing costs and obsolescence. And by avoiding an extensive intermediary network, Dell can directly monitor its customers' needs.

Dell is well known for its great *customer service*—despite handling 10,000 daily customer communications from corporations, government agencies, medical and educational institutions, small businesses, and individual consumers. After the outsourcing problem (described in Chapter 1), Dell is back on track with its IdeaStorm and Direct2Dell blogs—its customer service rankings in the industry are

improving. The DellConnect diagnostic tool has delivered nearly 8 million self-help sessions with a 93 percent satisfaction rate. Dell also serves major corporate buyers by maintaining 60,000 custom Web storefronts.

Dell fully utilizes the internet's properties for *mass customization* by allowing online customers to build their own computer systems for speedy delivery. Dell offers an extensive menu of product components and lets the market decide their relative importance—the marketing concept at its best. The company analyzes what customers order and uses this information to guide new-product development.

Finally, Dell has a *tightly coordinated supply chain.* Suppliers work closely with Dell engineers to keep R&D costs low and keep products flowing to customers as ordered. Dell manages supply and demand in a way that leaves both suppliers and customers satisfied—a tricky job when selling in 140 country markets. And what does Michael Dell say about all this? "I'm having a great time. This is fun."

DISTRIBUTION CHANNEL OVERVIEW

Marketers are concerned about distribution because it involves point of purchase decisions and whether or not the customer receives a product or service satisfactorily. A **distribution channel** is a group of interdependent firms that work together to transfer product and information from the supplier to the consumer. It is composed of the following participants:

- **Producers:** Manufacturers and their suppliers, or originators of the product or service
- **Intermediaries:** Firms that match buyers and sellers and mediate the transactions among them (e.g., retailers)
- **Buyers:** Consumers or users of the product or service

A customer's experience in gaining access to the product often colors his or her satisfaction with the product, brand image, and brand loyalty. Dell maintains complete control of its distribution channel satisfaction because its customers buy directly from the manufacturer.

The structure of the distribution channel can either make or impede possible opportunities for marketing on the internet. If the transaction is automated the consumer could save money by performing some of the distribution functions. Conversely, a consumer who purchases online must perform the search function personally that is normally performed by retailers—if you've ever searched for the lowest cost flight at online travel agents, you'll realize the additional time spent versus simply calling a brick-and-mortar agent. Four major elements combine to form a company's channel structure, and all affect internet marketing strategy as shown in the sections that follow:

1. Types of online channel intermediaries
2. Length of the online channel
3. Functions performed by members of the channel
4. Physical and informational systems that link the channel members and provide for coordination and management of their collective effort to deliver the product or service.

ONLINE CHANNEL INTERMEDIARIES

A good way to understand online intermediaries is according to their business models. Many e-business models have new names, but how many of them are really new? On closer inspection, most e-business models turn out to be variations on existing marketing concepts, but technology makes them more effective or efficient. For some digital products, such as software or music, the entire distribution channel may be internet based. When a consumer buys software online, the supplier often delivers it over the internet to the buyer's computer. In most cases, however, only some of the firms in the channel are wholly or partially Web enabled. For example, nondigital products such as flowers and wine may be purchased online but must be delivered via truck. Nonetheless, the exact location of that shipment can be tracked using a Web-based interface (the informational role of distribution). Exhibit 12.1 shows the overall classification scheme for the discussion that follows.

Channel intermediaries include wholesalers, retailers, brokers, and agents.

- **Wholesalers** buy products from the manufacturer and resell them to retailers.
- Both brick-and-mortar and online **retailers** buy products from manufacturers or wholesalers and sell them to consumers.
- **Brokers** facilitate transactions between buyers and sellers without representing either party. They are market makers and typically do not take title to the goods.
- **Agents** usually represent either the buyer or seller, depending upon who hires and pays them. They facilitate transactions between buyers and sellers but do not take title to the

1. Content sponsorship	
2. Infomediary	
3. Intermediaries	
Broker:	Online exchange
	Online auction
Agent:	Agent models representing seller
	Selling agent (affiliate program)
	Manufacturer's agent (catalog aggregator)
	Agent models representing buyer (purchasing agent)
	Shopping agent
	Reverse auction
	Buyer cooperative
Online retailer (e-commerce):	Digital products
	Tangible products
	Direct distribution

EXHIBIT 12.1 E-Business Models

goods. **Manufacturer's agents** represent the seller whereas **purchasing agents** represent the buyer.

Content Sponsorship

In this model, companies create Web sites, attract a lot of traffic, and sell advertising. Some firms use a niche strategy and draw a special interest audience (e.g., iVillage.com for women), and others draw a general audience (e.g., CNN.com). Web properties using the content sponsorship model include all the major portals: Google, Yahoo!, MSN, and so on. Many online magazines and newspapers also use this model; indeed, much content on the Net is ad supported. Pandora Radio provides streaming, commercial free radio based on user preferences.

Listeners enter a song or artist they like and Pandora creates an individual radio station with similar music. Pandora monetizes its e-business model by presenting ads on the Web page that is open while users listen to music (Exhibit 12.2).

Many Web sites desire to sell advertising space, but it is difficult to get enough traffic to compete with the portals and news sites. See Exhibit 12.3 for the Web site genres delivering the most advertising impressions to advertisers (impressions are the number of times an ad can be viewed). To get an idea of how portals monetize their content, the following is the Morgan Stanley's estimate of the annualized advertising revenue per user for content sponsorship sites in 2006 (Google and Yahoo! represent 58 percent of U.S. online ad revenue):

Content Sponsor	Ad Revenue/User	Content Sponsor	Ad Revenue/User
Google	$12.28	MySpace	$1.32
Yahoo!	$8.65	YouTube	$1.00 estimate
Microsoft	$3.25	eBay	$0.33
Time Warner	$1.62		

EXHIBIT 12.2 Pandora Radio Is Sponsored Content

Note that an advertisement usually appears on the right side of the screen.

Source: www.Pandora.com.

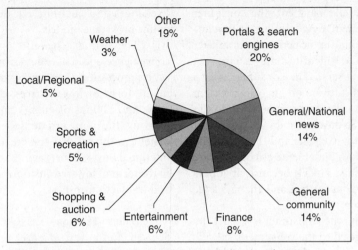

EXHIBIT 12.3 Web Site Content Sponsors Delivering the Most Impressions

Source: www.Nielsen//NetRatings.com (AdRelevance data).

The picture is a bit different if only display ads are considered because Google uses only text ads and the other search engines also rely heavily on text ads. Yahoo! sites top the display ad-sponsored content category with 18.8 percent share of all ads, followed by Fox Interactive Media with 16.3 percent and Microsoft sites at 6.7 percent (according to comScore).

We include this model in the e-commerce chapter because content sponsorship generates revenues in the B2B market. The product, of course, is ad space on a Web site, and the price for it usually increases with audience size. This model has its roots in traditional media, where television, magazines, and other media sell space and airtime. In Chapter 13 we discuss the other side: firms that buy advertising space as a way to communicate with stakeholders.

Craigslist uses the content sponsorship model because it provides free listings to the tune of 30 million ads a month that draw 9 billion page views a month. These are sponsored by paid classified ad listings for brokered apartment listings in New York City and job listings.

The **content sponsorship** model is often used in combination with other models to generate multiple revenue streams. For example, Buy.com, an online retailer, sells ads on its site to generate additional revenue, which in turn allows it to lower prices. Similarly, while most online newspapers offer their current edition for free, they often charge a small amount to retrieve an archived article.

Infomediary

An **infomediary** is an online organization that aggregates and distributes information. One form of infomediary is a market research firm. Usually, the infomediary compensates the consumer for sharing information. For example, a comScore Media Metrix panel member is paid; however, some intermediaries cull the information covertly and without compensation (e.g., DoubleClick uses cookies to track users as they surf the Web).

Another type of infomediary is a variation on the content sponsorship model. Using permission marketing, the firm pays the customer to buy space on his or her computer screen. The payment might be money, points toward shopping, or a free internet service. Here, the consumers are really selling space on their screen, but more importantly they are selling their attention—the scarcest commodity in cyberspace. The infomediary then generates revenue by reselling the screen space to advertisers. To receive payment, the consumer must sometimes share demographic or psychographic information with the permission marketer (although individual identities are usually not disclosed to advertisers). The consumer is also required to install software on his or her system that gives the infomediary a permanent window in which to run ads. So the consumer sees two sets of ads—the ads on the Web site and the ads in the infomediary window. Eudora, the e-mail software program, uses this model because it offers ad-sponsored versions for free and changes a fee for ad-free versions.

In addition, the consumer benefits by receiving ads targeted to the consumer's specific interests. Indeed, the original idea behind the infomediary model was to give consumers more control over how they receive marketing messages (Hagel and Singer, 1999). The benefit to the infomediary is that the consumer information increases the value of its ad inventory. The benefit to advertisers is that they can market to a highly targeted audience that has expressly opted into the system. Permission marketing allows advertisers to do something never before possible—advertise while the consumer is on a competitor's site!

Intermediary Models

Three main intermediary models are in common use on the internet: brokerage models, agent models, and online retailing.

BROKERAGE MODELS The broker creates a market in which buyers and sellers negotiate and complete transactions (Rappa, 2000). Brokers typically charge the seller and/or buyer a transaction fee, but they don't represent either party for providing exchange and negotiation services. Some brokers also charge listing fees. Brokers provide many value-added services to help attract customers and facilitate transactions. Brokerage models operate Web site exchanges in B2B, B2C, and C2C markets. The best example in the offline world is a stockbroker who brings buyers and sellers together at the NYSE or other exchanges.

Exchanges and auctions are the most popular online brokerage models.

The primary benefits to the buyer are convenience, speed of order execution, and transaction processing. Cost savings to the buyer come in the form of lower prices, decreased search time, and savings of energy and frustration in locating the appropriate seller. The primary benefit to the seller is the creation of a pool of interested buyers. Cost savings to the seller come in the form of lowered customer acquisition costs and transaction costs.

Online Exchange E*TRADE, Ameritrade, Schwab, and a host of other online brokerages allow customers to place trades from their computers without phoning or visiting a broker. These brokerages pass along the cost savings to the buyer in the form of lower transaction fees. They also provide the benefits of executing trades quickly, providing reference resources, and allowing for program trading. Some newer services catering to day traders bypass the Web entirely and connect traders straight to the market.

Autobytel and other online brokers allow customers to receive bids from qualified dealers on vehicles available in their area without first phoning or visiting the dealer. The dealers offer a no-hassle price quoted through the service. Thus, the customer avoids the potentially unpleasant task of negotiating price with a dealer.

The B2B market has spawned a number of successful brokerages. Converge is the leading anonymous exchange for the global electronics market (www.converge.com), aggregating supply and demand from thousands of component, original equipment and contract manufacturers, distributors, and resellers. The model is similar to a stock exchange. Customers contact a Converge trader on the floor of the exchange with their request (e.g., an order for 100,000 transistors). The trader locates a supplier, completes the purchase, and pockets the spread between the buying and selling price. Additional revenue comes from other fixed fees. The exchange is anonymous: Suppliers ship to a Converge quality control warehouse where the goods are inspected and then forwarded to the buyer. Converge guarantees the quality of the products and has a no-questions-asked return policy. Converge online services include personal buy-and-sell portfolios, chat communication with traders, and multiple methods for issuing requests including uploading a list of items or searching for items individually.

Guru.com is an exchange for talent. Employers can find freelancers in this large global marketplace with 100,000 freelancers and 30,000 employers in the database. Guru.com employers can locate consultants in 160 professional categories, including Web site design, programming, graphic design, business consulting, and administrative support. When a match is made, Guru.com collects a fee, just as do stock broker companies.

Online Auction Online auctions are challenging the fixed price model, which has been the norm for the past 100 years. Auctions are available in the B2B (uBid.com), B2C (priceline.com), and C2C (eBay.com) markets. Even though some merchants choose to host their own auctions, many more auction their surplus through auction brokers such as uBid. When merchants auction items on their own Web sites, they become direct sellers using dynamic pricing. Third-party auctioneers are broker intermediaries.

Sellers benefit by obtaining the market price for goods and unloading surplus inventory. Buyers benefit by obtaining a good deal and, in many cases, enjoying the sport of the auction. The downside is that the buyer can waste a lot of time monitoring the auction and sometimes overpay (the "winner's curse" discussed in previous chapters). Although buyers can use services to automatically proxy bid, studies show that many repeatedly visit auction sites to check on bids.

Some auction houses offer a broad range of products. uBid hosts a B2C auction for products ranging from computers to travel. Other auction houses specialize in niche markets. Industry giant eBay hosts C2C auctions in thousands of product categories. eBay has rolled out a number of innovative services to benefit the customer and facilitate the auction process, including escrow,

electronic payment via its PayPal company, and appraisal services.

AGENT MODELS Unlike brokers, agents *do* represent either the buyer or the seller depending on who pays their fee. In some cases, they are legally obligated to represent the interests of the party that hires them. In the brick-and-mortar world, real estate agents who are hired to list a property must represent the interests of the seller.

Agent Models Representing Sellers Selling agents, manufacturer's agents, metamediaries, and virtual malls are all agents that represent the seller.

Selling agents represent a single firm, helping it sell its products; these agents normally work for a commission. For example, **affiliate programs** pay commissions to Web site owners for customer referrals. Normally the referral must result in a sale in order to qualify for the commission. For example, KarstadtQuelle AG, a large holding company for European department stores, pays a commission of €2 to its more than 4,000 selling agent affiliates for referring each new customer. Some affiliates demand a share of the lifetime value of the customer as opposed to just a piece of the first sale.

Amazon.com pioneered one of the first affiliate programs in 1996, calling it Amazon Associates. Every Web site displaying an Amazon graphic that links to Amazon.com is an affiliate selling agent. It has hundreds of thousands of associates—each a point of sale for Amazon products:

> Whether you are a personal blogger, review site, product manufacturer, web portal, or price comparison search engine, the Associates Program can scale to meet your needs. Maybe you own a small site and wish to earn some money to cover your hosting costs, or represent a large corporation with a variety of web sites that you'd like to monetize. Whatever your size, the Associates Program has the tools you need to succeed.

Manufacturer's agents represent more than one seller. In traditional marketing, they generally represent only firms that sell complementary products to avoid conflicts of interest, but in the virtual world they often create Web sites to help an entire industry sell its products. In e-marketing, manufacturer's agents are often called seller aggregators because they represent many sellers on one Web site.

Almost all of the travel reservations Web sites qualify as manufacturer's agents since their commissions are paid by the airlines and hotels they represent. Expedia, Travelocity, Orbitz, and many other travel agent sites allow customers to make online travel reservations. In some cases the traveler can get a better deal online but often the greatest benefit is simply convenience.

In the B2B market, manufacturer's agents are sometimes called catalog aggregators. Each of the sellers these firms represent generally has a broad catalog of product offerings. Picture a purchasing manager in a small room surrounded by hundreds of catalogs, which suggests the origin of the term. The challenge for the aggregator is to gather the information from all of these catalogs into a database for presentation on the Web site. Normally, the catalog aggregator offers software that seamlessly interfaces with the suppliers' internal database systems. The task is made significantly easier when the suppliers use industry standard software such as Arriba, CommerceOne, Concur, or Alliance to manage their catalogs. Furthermore, the catalogs must be constantly maintained as product availability and prices change.

The more advanced manufacturer's agents support catalog customization and integration with the buyer's enterprise resource planning (ERP) systems. The customized catalogs display prenegotiated product offerings and prices. Some will even maintain spending limits for particular employees and automatically forward big-ticket orders to the appropriate officer for approval. Additional services include recommending substitutions, notifying buyers of production lead times, processing orders, and tracking orders.

With this model, the buyer gains substantial benefits, including shorter order cycles, reduced inventories, and increased control. Order processing costs are lowered through paperless transactions, automated request for proposal (RFP) and request for quote (RFQ), and integration with ERP systems.

The College Source (www.collegesource.org) is a catalog aggregator for the college market where students can search more than 40,000 catalogs at one site. Google is also testing a catalog search site (catalogs.google.com) and already has a large inventory of online versions for mail-order catalogs. Another player is Catalogs.com.

There are two other intermediaries that act like agents but defy easy categorization. One represents a cluster of manufacturers, online retailers, and content providers organized around a life event or major asset purchase. They solve four major consumer problems—reducing search times, providing quality assurance about vendors, facilitating transactions for a group of related purchases, and providing relevant and unbiased content information about the purchase. These Web site companies receive commissions for referrals or completed transactions. Edmunds.com is a good example in the car-buying market, providing information about new and used automobiles and advice on negotiating deals. It also refers interested customers to a car-buying service, financing information, aftermarket parts, and insurance alternatives. The Knot represents the bridal market, offering information about planning, fashion, beauty, grooms, bridesmaids and moms, and so forth. It also has tools such as a gown finder, registry, checklist, and guest list. In addition, The Knot provides sponsored content such as the guide to invitations by OurBeginning.com or the guide to bridal showers by GiftCertificates.com.

The other intermediary hosts multiple online merchants in a model similar to a shopping mall. Hosted merchants gain exposure from traffic coming to the virtual mall. The mall gains through a variety of fees: listing fees, transaction fees, and setup fees. Although brick-and-mortar malls provide a desirable collection of stores in one location, are easily accessible from major highways, and have ample free parking, none of these benefits apply online. Nonetheless, virtual malls may provide six customer benefits. The first is branding—consumers may be more comfortable buying from a store listed on the Yahoo! Shopping pages than buying from one that is not. The second benefit is availability of electronic money, allowing customers to register their shipping and billing information just once and retrieve that information when purchasing at any participating store, thus simplifying the order process. The third benefit is availability of frequent shopper programs that reward consumers for shopping within the mall. The fourth is a gift registry that operates across multiple stores. The fifth benefit is a search facility to locate products in mall stores. The sixth is a recommendation service such as suggestions for Mother's Day gifts.

Yahoo! Shopping hosts a number of large merchants including Best Buy and Target, as well as a number of other well-known retailers. It offers e-money that can be used to shop at many of its listed merchants; it also has a frequent shopper program, a gift registry, product recommendations, and a search facility. Amazon.com could be considered a virtual mall now that it offers such a huge variety of products and second party retailers.

Agent Models Representing Buyers Purchasing agents represent buyers. In traditional marketing, they often forge long-term relationships with one or more firms; however, on the internet they represent any number of buyers, anonymously in many cases. Shopping agents and reverse auctions help individual buyers obtain the prices they want, while buyer cooperatives pool buyers for larger volume buys and, thus, lower prices.

As discussed in Chapter 11, when shopping agents were first developed, many feared that they would drive prices on the internet down to impossible margins. That scenario has not happened because price is not the only factor consumers consider when making a purchase. Newer, second-generation shopping agents can now measure value and not just price. PriceScan and CNETs Shopper are two firms offering this service (Exhibit 12.4).

Consumers who desire a quantitative performance evaluation of a merchant can shop through Shopzilla's BizRate.com. BizRate rates over 99,000 merchants based on thousands of customer satisfaction surveys conducted after purchase at each store's Web site. BizRate rates online merchants based on customer feedback.

EXHIBIT 12.4 CNET Shopper Helps Users Find Electronic Products

Source: www.shopper.cnet.com.

BizRate posts a report card of past consumer experiences with the merchant (generated from thousands of customer surveys) and shows the merchant's stated business policies. BizRate also offers a rebate program for customers who buy from participating merchants.

A **reverse auction** occurs at a Web site serving as purchasing agent for individual buyers. In a reverse auction, the buyer specifies a price and sellers bid for the buyer's business. The buyer commits to buying at a specified price, and the seller either meets the price or tries to get close enough to make the sale. Priceline was the first major player in reverse auctions.

The benefit to the seller is in unloading excess inventory without unduly upsetting existing channels—a valuable benefit for sellers with perishable inventory such as airline seats or hotel rooms. The benefit for the buyer comes in the form of lower prices and the satisfaction of being able to name one's price. However, buyers have fewer choices of brand, suppliers, and product features. The reduced choice feature sufficiently differentiates the product in most cases to avoid conflict with the supplier's existing channel partners.

The **buyer cooperative** (also known as a buyer aggregator) pools many buyers together to drive down the price on selected items. The individual buyer, thus, receives the price benefit of volume buying. The more buyers that join the pool, the lower the price drops, usually in a step function. For example, one to five buyers pay $69 each; six to ten buyers pay $58 each, and so on. The step function encourages buyers to recruit their friends to help push the price down to the next step. Buyers can make their bid contingent on the product reaching a specified price point.

Mercata, MobShop, and other promising buyer's cooperatives closed as they were not able to build profitable business models online. The remaining online co-ops represent more traditional brick-and-mortar buyer's co-ops such as the Solar and Renewable Energy Cooperative (www.soarenergy.org). Nonetheless, we believe that the internet is capable of supporting this model as evidenced by the emergence of new co-ops on a regular basis. The latest is a homeschooling cooperative

buying program representing over 23,000 families (http://www.homeschoolbuyersco-op.org).

ONLINE RETAILING   Online retailing is one of the most visible e-business models. A huge part of e-commerce, merchants set up online storefronts and sell to businesses and consumers. Digital goods may be delivered directly over the internet while physical goods are shipped via a logistics provider such as UPS, USPS, or FedEx. Firms selling physical goods online can make any level of commitment from pure play to barely dabbling; however, most reasonably sized brick-and-mortar retailers offer at least some products online.

Although a pre-internet presence carries brand equity, it does not guarantee online success. Often the pure plays are free from the cultural constraints of the established businesses and can innovate more quickly in response to customer needs. Now some internet pure plays are establishing brick-and-mortar operations to enhance branding through additional exposure and an additional channel for customers to experience their products. Two of the more prominent examples are E*TRADE and Gateway Computer, which extended their brick-and-mortar presence in recent years.

Multichannel marketing is the use of more than one sales channel, such as online, brick and mortar, and catalog. Most large traditional retailers are multichannel marketers because they also sell products online. Most catalog retailers also use multichannel marketing, and 80 percent said they have consistent pricing, shipping, and fulfillment standards among channels (according the Direct Marketing Association). Among catalog retailers, 44 percent of their total sales were projected to come from the online channel in 2006, and 78 percent said their ROI is better when both channels are used—possibly partially because they can reach different customers through each channel. Important decisions involve product selections and appropriate pricing in each channel. The Sharper Image is an excellent example of a multichannel marketer. This specialty retailer has 186 brick-and-mortar stores (59% of sales) as well as an online store

(16% of sales) and a catalog channel (17% of sales). It sent 98 million catalogs to 19 million customers in its database in 2005—offering an average of 200–250 products in each. It also sent 64 million stand-alone direct mail pieces. Our observation is that more catalog products (than off-line store products) are Sharper Image-branded products, possibly because the profit margin is greater on store brands and catalogs are a more expensive channel due to printing, mailing, and telephone call center costs.

An advantage of online retailing is that companies can sell a wider and deeper assortment of products in smaller quantities than in off-line stores, because they are not bound by the space constraints in malls and free-standing buildings located in expensive areas. Instead, they can use warehouses on cheap land, and ship from there. Named "the long tail" by Chris Anderson, editor of *Wired* magazine, this refers to the reason it is possible to increase revenue by selling small quantities of a large number of products online. For example, in 2004 Netflix.com had 25,000 DVDs in inventory as compared to 3,000 at a typical Blockbuster brick-and-mortar store. Netflix is able to sell a large variety of hard-to-find DVDs in smaller quantities, and the product not available in off-line rental stores comprises 20 percent of Netflix's total sales.

Some of the friction consumers have regarding online shopping still need to be addressed by e-commerce firms. According to Pew Internet & the American Life, these include: 75 percent agree that they do not like using their credit cards online, and they have been frustrated (43%), confused (32%) and overwhelmed (30%) by the type and quantity (either high or low) of information online. Nonetheless, nearly all consumers have used the internet to purchase online or do research for an off-line purchase, and the numbers have grown over the years.

One of the biggest problems for online retailers is shopping cart abandonment part way through the purchasing process. In a 2006 Marketing Sherpa study of 1,100 e-commerce marketers, on average shopping carts were abandoned 59.8 percent of the time. In his paper, "20 Tips for Lowering Shopping Cart Abandonment," Bryan Eisenberg offers the following suggestions:

The number of steps in the checkout process is not related to cart abandonment.

- Show inventory availability on the product page—don't wait until the checkout page.
- Make it obvious where to click next for a smooth checkout process.
- Make it easy for shoppers to edit their shopping cart by adding or deleting items.
- Include a "progress indicator" so customers know where they are in the checkout process.
- Provide a link back to the original product page for re-checking sizes and other options.
- Add product pictures inside the shopping basket.
- Provide shipping costs as early as possible.
- Make every problem "your" fault (the online retailer).
- Let shoppers know how to contact you if problems arise.
- Give visitors an option to place the order over the telephone.
- Focus on the customer experience—it is about them, not you.
- Be careful how you handle coupon codes so it is not confusing.
- Deal with competitive pricing issues directly—perhaps offering to match lower prices.
- Get the cash by convenient means, such as PayPal.
- Offer reassurance that things are going well at critical points.
- Add third-party reassurance messages, such as security or Better Business logos.
- Develop a system to track the errors that occur, so you can fix them.
- Save shopping carts so customers can return and consummate the order.
- Try an exit survey to learn about the shopping experience.

All tangible products sold online, such as books and furniture, are distributed through conventional channels. This type of distribution is relatively inefficient: Rather than deliver 100 copies of a book to a brick-and-mortar store in a single shipment, the UPS truck must make deliveries to 100 individual customers. Consumers pay a premium for this service, which may outweigh the cost savings of purchasing online. Furthermore, local regulations sometimes impede the direct distribution of product. For example, Wine.com (the former Virtual Vineyards at www.wine.com), a wine distributor, has been forced by some state regulations to operate through local intermediaries rather than mail wine across state lines—which lengthens its distribution channel.

Digital Products One great hope for the internet is to serve as a medium for the physical distribution of digital goods and services such as news, music, software, movies, and so forth. Clearly, distribution costs are significantly lower for digital products, compared with physical distribution. *The New York Times* (www.nytimes.com) was one of the first to make the online subscription model pay off—it attracted several hundred thousands of new customers to its Web site that were not reading the printed paper. Classmates.com, iTunes, and the *Wall Street Journal Online* are also successful at selling content online.

While off to a slow start, consumers now purchase a large amount of online content—over $2 billion in 2005 (Exhibit 12.5). This does not include the digital entertainment industry, such as the estimated 2.5 billion iTunes songs, 50 million television shows, and over 1.3 million movies Apple has sold since the iPod's introduction (see www.afterdawn.com).

Direct Distribution The manufacturer sells directly to the consumer or business customer in the **direct distribution** model, as does Dell, Inc (also called direct selling). This practice is commonly used in off-line selling; however, the internet made it much easier for producers to bypass intermediaries and go directly to consumers or business customers.

Direct distribution has been successful in some B2B markets—sometimes saving millions of dollars in sales-related expenses for personnel, product configuration, and order processing. Expert systems built into some online sales systems assist the customer in configuring the product with compatible components, the way Dell's system helps customers order online.

Direct distribution also has been successful in the B2C market with sales of digital products, as previously mentioned, which require no inventory

	2003 (millions)	2005 (millions)	Percent Change
Entertainment/Lifestyles	$214.0	$573.8	168.1
Personal/Dating	449.5	503.4	12.0
Business/Investment	334.1	320.3	(−4.1)
Research	108.6	152.3	40.2
Personal growth	90.7	117.3	29.3
Games	73.0	108.4	48.5
General news	87.5	78.7	(−10.1)
Community-made directories	87.0	65.4	(−24.8)
Sports	38.2	51.3	34.3
Greeting cards	40.6	45.7	12.6
Credit help	36.6	28.4	(−22.4)

EXHIBIT 12.5 Online Content Spending Growth

Source: Data from Online Publishers Report conducted with ComScore. Available at www.online-publishers.org.

and no pick, pack, and ship logistics. Perishable products such as flowers and fresh food are also well served by direct channels. As one example, Proflowers.com delivers flowers fresh from the grower. Flowers that don't pass through an intermediary tend to be fresher, last longer, and are in many cases less expensive.

Direct distribution saves customers money by avoiding intermediaries; sometimes it leads to more rapid delivery of the product. For example, Fresh Direct processes and delivers up to 20,000 Web orders of fresh produce and meat a day to its 150,000 New York customers. By cutting out the intermediaries and using databases to keep inventory at a minimum, Fresh Direct is able to make profits unseen by other online grocers (Schonfeld, 2004).

Benefits to the manufacturer include the ability to claim a piece of the intermediary's margin, but, of course, someone has to perform the functions of those intermediaries. The major costs of direct distribution for the customer include higher search costs to locate individual manufacturers and the time costs of transacting with each manufacturer.

DISTRIBUTION CHANNEL LENGTH AND FUNCTIONS

The length of a distribution channel refers to the number of intermediaries between the supplier and the consumer. The shortest distribution channel has no intermediaries—the manufacturer deals directly with the consumer, the way Dell sells directly to customers in a direct distribution channel. Most distribution channels incorporate one or more intermediaries in an **indirect distribution channel**. A typical indirect channel includes suppliers, a manufacturer, wholesalers, retailers, and end consumers. Intermediaries help to perform important functions (described in the next section).

Originally, it was predicted that the internet would eliminate intermediaries, thereby creating disintermediation in distribution channels. **Disintermediation** describes the process of eliminating traditional intermediaries. Eliminating intermediaries can potentially reduce the costs as with Fresh Direct. Taken to its extreme, disintermediation allows the supplier to transfer goods and services directly to the consumer in a direct channel. Complete disintermediation tends to be the exception because intermediaries can often handle channel functions more efficiently than producers. An intermediary that specializes in one function, such as product promotion, tends to become more proficient in that function than a nonspecialist.

Much of the initial hype surrounding the internet focused on disintermediation and the possibility that prices would plummet as the internet eliminated costly intermediaries. This line of reasoning failed to recognize some important facts. First, the U.S. distribution system is the most efficient in the world. Second, using intermediaries allows companies to focus on what they do best. Third, many traditional intermediaries have been replaced with internet equivalents. In many cases the online intermediaries are more efficient than their brick-and-mortar counterparts. Consider the online storefront. Online retailers do not have to rent, maintain, and staff expensive retail space in desirable shopping areas. An inexpensive warehouse provides an acceptable storage location for goods sold online. On the other hand, online stores incur the costs of setting up and maintaining their e-commerce sites. Although these charges can be significant, they do not outweigh the savings realized by eliminating the physical store.

The internet has added new intermediaries that did not exist previously. For example, Yahoo! Launch aggregates multimedia content. Yahoo! and Yahoo! Launch together are like a record store, audio bookstore, radio broadcaster, and TV broadcaster all rolled into one. Other new intermediaries include shopping agents and buyer cooperatives.

Functions of a Distribution Channel

Many functions must be performed in moving products from producer to consumer, regardless of which intermediary performs them. For example, online retailers normally hold inventory and perform the pick, pack, and ship functions in response to a customer order. In an alternative

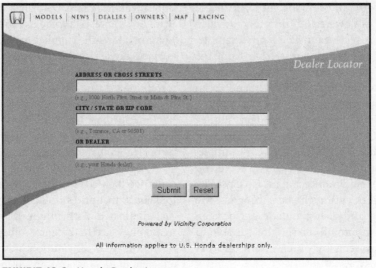

EXHIBIT 12.6 Honda Dealer Locator
Source: www.honda.com.

scenario, the retailer might outsource the pick, pack, and ship functions to a logistics provider such as UPS. Here, the retailer forwards the order to a UPS warehouse where the product waits in storage. UPS picks, packs, and ships the product to the consumer. Distributors perform many value-added functions. The functions can be broadly characterized as transactional, logistical, and facilitating (Lamb, Hair, and McDaniel, 2002).

TRANSACTIONAL FUNCTIONS Transactional functions refer to making contact with buyers and using marketing communication strategies to make buyers aware of products. They also include matching products to buyer needs, negotiating price, and processing transactions.

Contact with Buyers The internet provides a new channel for making contact with buyers. Forrester Research calls the internet the fourth channel after personal selling, mail, and the telephone; retailers see it as the third channel after brick-and-mortar stores and catalogs. The internet channel adds value to the contact process in several ways. First, contact can be customized to the buyer's needs. For example, the Honda site (www.honda.com) allows customers to find a dealer in their area where they can buy Honda vehicles (see Exhibit 12.6). Second, the internet provides a wide range of referral sources such as search engines, shopping agents, newsgroups, chat rooms, e-mail, Web pages, and affiliate programs. Third, the internet is always open for business, 24 hours a day, seven days a week.

Marketing Communications Marketing communication encompasses advertising and other types of product promotion (discussed in Chapter 13). This function is often shared among channel players. For example, a manufacturer may launch an ad campaign while its retailers offer coupons. Cooperative advertising is another example, with manufacturers sharing advertising costs with retailers. These communications are most effective when they represent a coordinated effort among channel players.

The internet adds value to the marketing communications function in several ways. First, functions that previously required manual labor can be automated. When American Airlines sends out a promotional message to millions of its registered users, it requires no papers to fold, no envelopes to stuff, no postage to imprint—its marketers simply click Send to distribute the message. As another example, promoting a Web site to the search engines can be automated by services such as Submission Pro (www.submission-pro.com) and MoreVisiblity (www.morevisibility.com). These firms study how the search engines rank Web sites and then optimize their clients' Web sites to achieve a higher ranking.

Second, communications can be closely monitored and altered minute by minute. DoubleClick, for instance, allows its clients to monitor the click-through rates of their online ads in real time and quickly make substitutions for poorly performing ads. Third, Web analytics software for tracking a user's behavior can be used to direct highly targeted communications to individuals (also available through DoubleClick).

Finally, the internet enhances promotional coordination among intermediaries. Firms e-mail ads and other material to each other, and all firms may view current promotions on a Web site at any time. It is still all-too-common for brick-and-mortar headquarter firms to run promotions that retailers don't know about until consumers begin asking for the special deals—internet communication helps prevent this kind of surprise from occurring.

Matching Product to Buyer's Needs The Web excels at matching products to buyer's needs. Given a general description of the buyer's requirements, shopping agents can produce a list of relevant products. Online retailers can also help consumers match products to needs. Gap (www.gap.com) lets consumers mix and match clothes to create outfits. Exhibit 12.7 shows the Land Rover site (www.landrover.com) where consumers can custom-configure vehicles. Of particular interest are **collaborative filtering** agents, which can predict consumer preferences based on past purchase behavior. Amazon uses a collaborative filtering agent to recommend books and music to customers. Once the system is in place, it can handle millions of users at little incremental cost. The effectiveness of the collaborative filtering agent actually increases as consumers are added to the database. Note that all of these services scale well because they are automated. By contrast, efforts to match product to buyer needs in the brick-and-mortar world can be labor intensive and are quickly overwhelmed as volume increases. Salespeople in retail outlets attempt this chore, but the internet improves on this function by being on

EXHIBIT 12.7   Land Rover Allows Customers to View Options Online
Source: www.landrover.com.

call anytime and by matching buyers with products across retailers. Of course, this capability puts a burden on electronic retailers to compete on the basis of price or to differentiate their products in a way that is meaningful to the market.

Negotiating Price True price negotiation involves offers and counteroffers between buyer and seller such as might be conducted in person, over the phone, or via e-mail—a two-way dialogue. Even so, shopping agents implicitly negotiate prices downward on behalf of the consumer by listing companies in order of best price first. Bidding, on the other hand, is a form of dynamic or flexible pricing in which the buyer gives suppliers an equal opportunity to bid (see Chapter 11). Many businesses currently conduct bidding online. Consumer market auctions include those held by eBay and Amazon. Businesses such as General Electric also solicit online bids from their suppliers. Online bidding effectively widens the supplier pool, thereby increasing competition and lowering prices. Many auction houses allow buyers to program an agent to represent them in bidding against other buyers or their agents.

Process Transactions Studies show that electronic channels lower the cost to process transactions dramatically. For instance, www. eventim.de, one of Europe's largest entertainment ticket portals, receives 6 for every ticket sold online versus €1 for off-line sales (Strobl, 2004). The National Association of Purchasing Management places the cost of manually processing an average purchase order at $79—mainly due to labor costs.

LOGISTICAL FUNCTIONS Logistical functions include physical distribution activities such as transportation and inventory storage, as well as the function of aggregating product. Logistical functions are often outsourced to third-party logistics specialists. RFID tags are an important development for tracking products through the distribution channel (see the "Let's Get Technical" box). Radio frequency identification (RFID) tags are used to transmit a signal to scanners, which detect the presence of the RFID tag in products, credit cards, or even under a person or animal's skin.

LET'S GET TECHNICAL

RFID Technology

Tired of waiting in long lines at the grocery store? Never again want to hear the phrase, "I'll have to send someone to check that price" when you just want to buy a carton of milk? Many customers become frustrated when making trips to supermarkets or large discount retailers. No matter when they choose to shop, the lines are often long, wasting valuable time. With the onset of RFID technology solutions, the supermarket of the future may not have lines at all. All customers might have to do is swipe their credit card and walk out the door.

Radio frequency identification (RFID) technology is an old technology in the field of automatic identification, but it has recently been getting lots of attention. Common forms of

automatic identification include the classic bar codes, used on millions of consumer products, and magnetic strips, commonly found on credit cards. These forms replaced manual entry, drastically decreasing error rates and saving companies millions of dollars. These forms also require manual assistance: cashiers run the UPC bar codes over the scanner and customers swipe their credit cards in the readers. However, RFIDs, which were originally developed during World War II, do not require manual intervention. As their price continues to fall, RFIDs may well revolutionize the field of automatic identification.

As the technology's name indicates, radio frequencies are used to transmit a signal to scanners, which detect the presence of the RFID tag. This technology requires three components: an RFID tag,

(continued)

(continued)

an RFID scanner, and a recording device (i.e., a computer). The RFID tag is attached to the product that is being tracked. The tag is made up of an RFID chip and a mini-antenna. The tags can cost anywhere between $0.25 and $6.00, depending on their sophistication. As the popularity of RFID tags has increased, their prices have declined.

The RFID scanner, which can also be called a reader, is connected to the computer. The RFID scanner constantly sends out a low frequency electromagnetic signal (100 kHz to 5.8 GHz). The signal powers the RFID chip and antenna to transmit data back to the scanner. When the scanner receives the information, it sends this data to the computer to store and analyze. As the technology matures, increasing amounts of information can be stored in the RFID chip and transmitted to the scanner.

The distance between the RFID tag and the scanner depends on the size of the RFID chip and mini-antenna. The more sophisticated the chip and the larger the antenna, the farther the tag and scanner can be from each other.

RFID technology has many applications in the distribution and retail industries. RFIDs are already being used to track palettes of products at large distribution centers. As shipments of products enter and exit the distribution center, the movement is automatically tracked with intense accuracy.

RFIDs are also being used at gas and toll stations. Specific gas companies have distributed a small plastic key chain to consumers, which holds the consumer's credit card information. When the consumer purchases gas, he waves the keychain in front of a small reader at the pump. The reader receives the credit card information, authorizes the pumping of the gas, and subsequently charges the credit card. The gas company's intent in providing this service was to increase customer loyalty because the key chains only work at their stations.

Many commuters pass through tollbooths each day on their way to and from work, and they painstakingly wait in lines at busy booths. Local and state governments, such as Pennsylvania and Virginia, have implemented RFID solutions. For little or no fee, commuters can purchase a small box that sits near the windshield of the vehicle. When the commuter comes to a tollbooth, he or she is allowed to enter a special lane equipped with the RFID scanner. The scanner obtains the commuters credit card or other account information and charges the toll. Some booths do not even require the traveler to drop their speed below 55 miles per hour. Another example of RFID in a similar application is with keyless entry systems.

Wal-Mart uses RFID to manage the supply chain with more than 600 of its suppliers. The benefits include a 16 percent reduction in out-of-stocks as well as 63 percent more effective restocking. RFID also ensures proof of delivery and eases reconciliation of purchase orders.

The goal is to eventually replace bar codes company-wide and to increase efficiency within the supply chain process.

Although the RFID solution will benefit Wal-Mart, the large retailer also promises benefits for its suppliers. These benefits include notifications when goods arrive at stores and when they enter the sales floor, which allow suppliers to better track demand. Wal-Mart also places RFID tags on point-of-purchase displays used as end caps and other displays for in-store promotions. These displays are often costly to produce, according to suppliers, and end up left in the back room. With the RFID tags, suppliers can track the deployment of the displays. As a result, new products reach the shelves three times faster.

With the world's largest retailer backing RFID technology, it appears poised for success. Distribution networks worldwide may need to adopt RFID standards as part of the cost of doing business.

Physical Distribution Most products sold online are still distributed through conventional channels. Yet digital content can be transmitted less expensively from producer to consumer over the internet: text, graphics, audio, and video content (see Exhibit 12.8 for a software example). Trisenx can transmit digital smells and tastes over the Web (www.trisenx.com)! The alternative step, physical distribution of digital product, is comparatively expensive.

EXHIBIT 12.8 CNET Download.com Carries Thousands of Software Titles

Source: www.download.com.

Aggregating Product In general, suppliers operate more efficiently when they produce a high volume of a narrow range of products. Consumers, on the other hand, prefer to purchase small quantities of a wide range of products. Channel intermediaries perform the essential function of aggregating product from multiple suppliers so that the consumer can have more choices in one location. Examples of this traditional form of aggregation include online category killers such as Amazon.com, with a broad product mix. In other cases the internet follows a model of virtual aggregation, bringing together products from multiple manufacturers and organizing the display on the user's computer. In the case of shopping agents, the unit of aggregation is the product page at the online store. A search for a particular product will produce a neatly arranged table with comparative product information and direct links to the vendor pages.

Third-Party Logistics—Outsourced Logistics A major logistics problem in the B2B market is reconciling the conflicting goals of timely delivery and minimal inventory. One solution for many companies is to place inventory with a **third-party logistics** provider such as UPS or FedEx.

Taking logistics one step further, third parties can also manage the company's supply chain and provide value-added services such as product configuration and subassembly. The logistics providers will even handle the order processes, replenish stock when needed, and assign tracking numbers so customers can find their orders. Alcatel, for example, uses UPS to manage orders and distribute cellular phones in Europe.

In the B2C market a major logistics problem is product returns (reverse logistics), which can run as high as 15 percent. Customers frequently complain about the difficulty and expense of returns. Some Web sites offer to pay return shipping. But even with a credit for return shipping, the customer still has to weigh the package, pay shipping fees up front, and schedule pickup (or deliver to a shipping location).

The U.S. Postal Service (USPS) has introduced a clever program to ease the return process. Merchants can install software on a site that allows them to authorize customers to download and print postage-paid return labels. The customer simply boxes the item, slaps on the label, and leaves it by the door for the letter carrier. Even if a Web site does not participate in the USPS program, customers can still weigh their packages at home and download appropriate postage onto a laser-printed label using a service from eStamps.

In the C2C market, eBay has formed a partnership with brick-and-mortar Mailboxes Etc. After auctions close, sellers take their items to Mailboxes Etc. to be packaged and shipped.

The Last Mile Problem One big problem facing online retailers and logistics managers is the added expense of delivering small quantities to individual homes and businesses. It is much less expensive to send cases of product to wholesalers and retailers and let them break the quantities into smaller units for sale. Two other problems arise: 25 percent of deliveries require multiple delivery attempts, thus increasing costs, and 30 percent of packages are left on doorsteps when no one is home, opening the way for possible theft (Laseter, Torres, and Chung, 2001). With 2.3 billion packages delivered in the United States in 2000 (an average of 13.4 packages per household), e-marketers are looking for ways to shave costs and solve this last mile problem.

Innovative firms are trying four solutions. First is a smart box. The consumer buys a small steel box that comes with a numeric keypad connected to the internet via a two-way modem. Delivery people, such as FedEx or the USPS, receive a special code for each delivery and use it to open the box and leave the shipment. This activity is sent via the internet and recorded in a database. The consumer uses his or her own code to open the box and receive the delivery—also recorded in the database. This solution is efficient and secure for consumers who are willing to pay the hefty box fee. Brivo introduced this technology but no longer offers this product.

A second solution involves a retail aggregator model. Consumers can have packages shipped to participating retailers, such as local convenience stores or service stations; then, consumers pick up the package—not as convenient as the current method. In Japan, NTT DoCoMo customers can use their Web-enabled cell phones to order goods for shipment to local 7-Eleven stores. The third solution calls for special *e-stops,* storefronts that exist solely for customer drive-through and package pickup.

Finally, many multichannel retailers allow customers to order online for off-line retail delivery. Recreational Equipment, Inc. (REI), the outdoor apparel and gear retailer, began offering this service in its 67 U.S. retail stores in mid-2003. Within one month 25 percent of Web sales were picked up in the off-line store with the added bonus of $32 of impulse buying during the same visit (Budis, 2004).

FACILITATING FUNCTIONS Facilitating functions performed by channel members include market research and financing.

Market Research Market research is a major function of the distribution channel. The benefits include an accurate assessment of the size and characteristics of the target audience. Information gathered by intermediaries helps manufacturers plan product development and marketing communications. Chapter 6 explored market research in detail, and Chapter 7 examined internet user behavior. This section will look at the costs and benefits of internet-based market research.

The internet affects the value of market research in five ways. First, some of the information on the internet, especially government reports, is available for free. Second, managers and employees can conduct research from their desks rather than making expensive trips to libraries and other resource sites. Third, information from the internet tends to be timelier, as when advertisers monitor interactions with banner ads. Fourth, Web-based information is already in digital form, so e-marketers can easily load it into a spreadsheet or other software. Finally, because so much consumer behavior data can be captured online, e-marketers can receive detailed reports. For example, comScore (www.comscore.com) produces a site interaction report that details to what extent a site shares audience with another site— showing exclusive and duplicated audience.

Nonetheless, little market research is free. Even free government reports require a significant investment of human resources to distill the material into a useful form for making decisions. Furthermore, many firms need access to costly commercial information such as comScore reports, which sell for about $50,000 each.

Financing Financing purchases is an important facilitating function in both consumer and business markets. Intermediaries want to make it easy for customers to pay in order to close the sale. Most online consumer purchases are financed through credit cards or special financing plans, similar to traditional store purchases. However, consumers are understandably concerned about divulging credit card information online—resulting in safeguards that probably make online purchasing the most secure channel for consumers.

Online merchants have a major concern as well: How do they know that they are dealing with a valid consumer using a legitimate credit card? The major credit card companies have, therefore, formed **Secure Electronic Transaction (SET)** as a vehicle for legitimizing both the merchant and the consumer as well as protecting the consumer's credit card number. Under SET, the card number goes not to the merchant but to a third party with whom the merchant and consumer communicate to validate one another as well as the transaction. The communication occurs automatically in the background and places no technical burdens on the consumer. However, SET is so technical that most consumers do not appreciate its subtleties. Furthermore, most merchants do not want to pay for costly upgrades to a SET system.

Still, SET has been successful inside the United States, in part because of legislative protections: U.S. consumers have a maximum $50 liability for purchases made with a stolen card. The card issuer usually waives the $50 in order to retain customers, and some issuers now advertise $0 liability for online purchases. However, that legal protection does not exist in some countries, and consumers may be liable for all charges on their card up to the time they report it stolen.

In the B2B market, brokers and agents often extend lines of credit to buyers to facilitate purchases. These lines of credit significantly speed the buying process and make the online channel more attractive.

Distribution System

The distribution channel is actually a system, when viewed by the flow of products, information, and finances along the channel—a unified system of interdependent organizations working together to build value as products proceed through the channel to the consumer. This perspective recognizes that a channel system is stronger when its participants compete in a unified way with other channel systems.

Defining the scope of the channel as a system can be done in three ways:

1. The first is to consider only distribution functions that are downstream from the manufacturer to the consumer, the traditional definition of the distribution channel.
2. The second is to consider only the supply chain upstream from the manufacturer working backward to the raw materials, the traditional definition of the **supply chain**.
3. The third view is to consider the supply chain, the manufacturer, and the distribution channel as an integrated system called the **value chain** (a more recent name for the value chain is *integrated logistics*). Many refer to the supply chain *as* the value chain. By this definition, the supply chain includes upstream and downstream activities as well as processes internal to the firm. See Exhibit 12.9 in which the circles represent firms in a network of suppliers, manufacturers, and intermediaries.

Redefining the supply chain to include the entire value chain is now mainstream, reflecting what a great number of practitioners mean when they talk about supply chain management. Thus, value chain, integrated logistics, and supply chain are equivalent terms.

This definition of the supply chain is used to describe the field of **supply chain management (SCM)**. SCM refers to the coordination of flows in three categories: material (e.g., physical product), information (e.g., demand forecast), and financial (e.g., credit terms) (Kalakota and Robinson, 1999). The word *flow* evokes the image of a continuous stream of products, information, and finances flowing among the channel members much as blood and nerve impulses flow through an organism. The most important flow is that of information because creation of the physical product and the financing depend on the information.

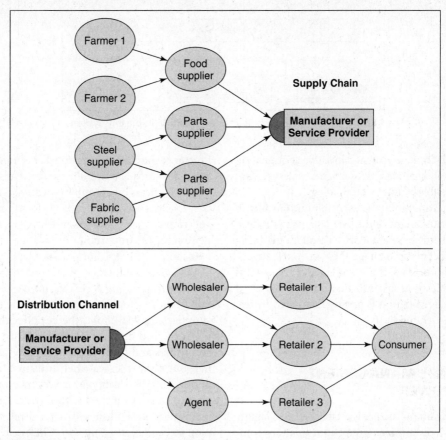

EXHIBIT 12.9 Supply Chain + Distribution Channel = New Definition of Supply Chain

The Holy Grail in supply chain management is "scan one, make one—and deliver it fast." This process is known as **continuous replenishment**. For more complex products such as computers, the goal is to build to order and deliver quickly. Both continuous replenishment and **build to order** help to eliminate inventory. In turn, this practice reduces costs because inventory is expensive to finance; it also increases profits by avoiding unsold inventory going stale and being sold at a discount. The cost savings may be passed on to the customer in the form of lower prices, which improve the value proposition for the customer. However, creating product in response to demand almost always results in some delay in delivery. The customer's value is only increased if the increased delays are acceptable. Today's customer wants it all—lower prices, quick delivery, and custom configuration. The only way to provide these benefits is to tightly coordinate the activities of upstream suppliers, the inner workings of the firm, and the downstream distribution channel—a formidable task that would have been impossible before the information age.

A difficult problem in SCM is deciding which participant should manage a channel composed of many firms. For example, Sun Microsystems designs computers but doesn't build any of them—yet Sun manages the entire supply chain, even the suppliers, of its contract manufacturers. The coordination is made possible by sophisticated SCM software from i2, which operates over the Web. Interestingly, the coordination is cooperative rather than dictatorial. Sun makes customer demand information visible to the suppliers, who then indicate what portion of the demand they can handle.

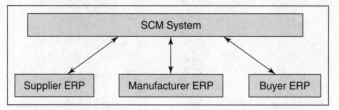

EXHIBIT 12.10   SCM System Interfaces with Multiple ERP Systems

Supply chain management allows for coordination of all supply chain functions into a seamless system, made possible by internet technology.

Interoperability is especially important in SCM because many of the participants in modern supply chains have **enterprise resource planning (ERP)** systems to manage their in-house inventory and processes. If the individual ERP systems can seamlessly share information with the SCM system, coordination is greatly facilitated in real time. See Exhibit 12.10.

CHANNEL MANAGEMENT AND POWER

Once a channel structure is established, its viability requires a certain measure of coordination, communication, and control to avoid conflict among its members. A powerful channel member must emerge to assume the leadership and institute these required measures, the way Sun coordinates its supply chain participants. Increasingly, market competition is between entire supply chains, which is why e-marketers need to understand power relationships among channel players.

Whenever new information technology is introduced into a distribution channel, it can potentially alter the power relationships among existing channel players. Nowhere has this effect been more evident than with the internet. In many cases, buyer power significantly increased at the expense of the supplier. In other cases, the power of the supplier has come out on top. Wal-Mart gained power over its channels when it introduced electronic systems to notify suppliers of needed product. This shift caused a major power upheaval in channels where giant manufacturers such as

Procter & Gamble had previously been in control. A classic source of power for retailers and distributors has been geographic location. Retailers have built power on the place (location) utility and restricted access to manufacturers. The Web neutralizes the importance of location and offers new sources of supply for purchasing.

Just as the internet increased the power of buyers by providing access to more information and to more suppliers, it increased the power of suppliers, as well. First, the supplier that takes the early lead online will receive business from consumers and firms eager to shop in this channel. But even in cases when multiple firms are online, suppliers can gain power by establishing structural relationships with buyers. For example, Amazon establishes structural relationships with its customers using its 1-Click ordering and collaborative filtering technologies. Amazon customers switching to another site would have to reenter their billing information and, more important, they would lose access to Amazon's recommendations.

A type of business-to-business commerce known as **electronic data interchange (EDI)** is particularly effective for establishing structural relationships between businesses. Electronic data interchange is the computerized exchange of information between organizations, typically used to eliminate paperwork. A buyer logs onto the supplier's computer system and types in an order. The order is electronically conveyed to the supplier and the buyer receives an electronic bill.

The internet puts a new face on EDI with the advent of open standards and interoperable systems. First, the internet replaces expensive proprietary networks, yielding tremendous cost savings. Second, business can use the same

Openness	Transport	Technology
Proprietary	Non-Internet	Traditional EDI
Open system	Non-Internet	Standards-based EDI (X.12)
Proprietary	Internet	Application Program Interface (API)
Open system	Internet	Open Buying on the Internet (OBI)
Open system	Internet	Extensible Markup Language (XML)

EXHIBIT 12.11   Flavors of EDI

computer to interface with multiple suppliers. Third, networks of suppliers and buyers can more easily exchange data using a Web-based interface.

Thus, EDI is based on three key variables: the openness of the system, the transport method (internet or non-internet), and the type of technology used for implementation. Combining these variables in different ways shows the five flavors of EDI most commonly used today (see Exhibit 12.11).

The goal is to create a standards-based open system that runs over the internet so all suppliers and buyers can seamlessly integrate their systems. The technology with the greatest promise to meet this goal is Extensible Markup Language (XML).

DISTRIBUTION CHANNEL METRICS

Does online commerce work? To answer this question, a company must consider its effectiveness in terms of reaching target market segments efficiently and enticing them to purchase online.

B2C Market

U.S. consumers spent $136 billion online during 2007, according to eMarketer. The U.S. Department of Commerce also measures online retailing, estimating it at 136.4 billion, a 19-percent growth from 2006. This is 3.5 percent of all retailing in the fourth quarter of 2007—putting it at about 14 percent for the entire year. Online retailing continues to grow, as shown in Exhibit 12.12. Online research about products resulted in $471 billion of off-line purchases (i.e., for every $1 of online sales, the internet influences $3.45 in off-line sales), according to eMarketer. This company concludes

that e-commerce sales and influences on off-line sales accounted for 27 percent of all retail sales in 2007.

These statistics show general spending levels; however, individual retailer sales vary based on how well their online strategies work. Companies track sales from all channels (online, retail, and catalog) on a daily basis to determine whether they are meeting their objectives and to refine Web sites, cross-channel promotion, and both online and off-line communication to achieve better results.

In one global study of online retailers, McKinsey and Company researchers found that two strategies are particularly effective online:

- A high-reach strategy of accumulating large numbers of customers with cost-effective conversion rates (visit the site and buy) for high-frequency purchases of low-margin products and services such as CDs and books (i.e., Amazon.com).
- A niche strategy with narrow focus on a particular product or service category, such as luxury items or apparel (i.e., Dell.com).

For all others, the best use of online retailing is as a complement to off-line channels. As Daryle Scott of Venus Swimwear says, "When your customers have the opportunity to purchase your products through *any* channel *they* choose— bricks and mortar, the internet, or traditional catalogs—that's true customer service."

Chapter 2 presented many performance metrics to aid e-marketers in evaluating online retailing and supply chain management. A few of the more important include revenues (as just mentioned), ROI, customer satisfaction levels,

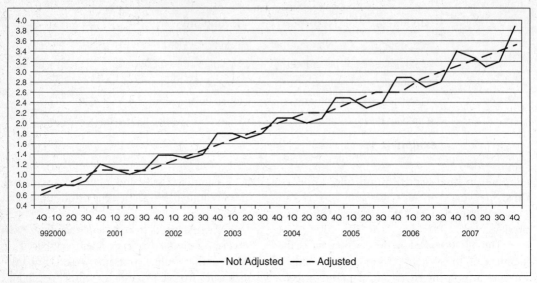

EXHIBIT 12.12 Estimated Quarterly U.S. Retail E-commerce Sales as a Percent of Total Quarterly Retail Sales: 4th Quarter 1999–4th Quarter 2007

Note: Adjusted for seasonal variation and holiday and trading-day differences, but not for price changes.

Source: www.census.gov.

customer acquisition costs, conversion rates, and average order values. Conversion refers to the proportion of all Web site visitors who actually purchase on that visit. Exhibit 12.13 displays average conversion rates, indicating a decline to 2.5 percent over time. This is a good benchmark metric for e-commerce companies.

The following are additional measures recommended by NetGenesis, an e-metrics firm:

- Which affiliations deliver the most users? (This measure assesses affiliate program effectiveness.)
- What is happening to users referred from an affiliate site?
- When and how do customers arrive at a Web site?
- How long do users stay at a Web site?
- How is buyer behavior different from other users who do not buy?
- How frequently are visitors converted to customers?
- Which channel partners deliver the most profitable customers? The most loyal ones?

B2B Market

The B2B market is big business. Although it is impossible to measure the amount of dollars that exchange hands in supply chains, one estimate puts U.S. B2B e-commerce at $624 billion ("Marketing Fact Book," 2004). The internet has proven to be a much more efficient way for firms to order from each other, spurring growth in e-procurement. Businesses use the Web to search for suppliers, but more often they simply facilitate current relationships throughout online ordering, shipment tracking, and more.

In the B2B market, as in B2C, e-marketers should select metrics that relate to their e-marketing goals. It is critical to understand how e-commerce fits into the overall marketing strategy, what the firm expects to accomplish through it, and whether it is working. For B2B, metrics may look at time from order to delivery, order fill levels, and other activities that reflect functions performed by channel participants.

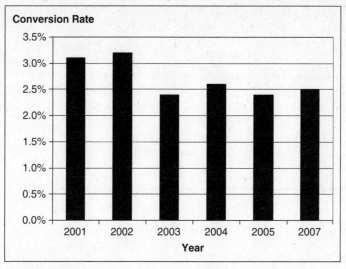

EXHIBIT 12.13 E-Commerce Conversion Rates, 2001–2007
Source: Data from eMarketer.com.

Chapter Summary

The internet increased the power of buyers and suppliers. It also changed the way electronic data interchange is used to establish structural relationships between suppliers and buyers. The major business models used by online intermediaries can be categorized as content sponsorship, direct distribution, infomediary, brokerage models (online exchange and online auction), and agent models (selling agents, manufacturer's agents, shopping agents, buyer's cooperative). Online retailing (e-commerce) is another important model including online sales of digital or tangible products and is done by direct distribution, with intermediaries, or by using multichannel marketing.

A distribution channel is a group of interdependent firms that work together to transfer product and information from the supplier to the consumer. The transfer may be either direct or through a number of intermediaries that perform certain marketing functions in the channel between suppliers and customers. By specializing, intermediaries are able to perform functions more efficiently than a supplier could.

Channel intermediaries include wholesalers, retailers, brokers, and agents. The length of a distribution channel refers to the number of intermediaries between the supplier and the consumer. The shortest distribution channel has no intermediaries; the producer deals directly with customers. Indirect channels include one or more intermediaries. Disintermediation describes the process of eliminating traditional intermediaries. Eliminating intermediaries can potentially reduce costs but functions must be performed by someone. Although the internet was expected to lead to disintermediation and lower prices, new intermediaries are emerging instead.

Three broad types of value-added functions performed in the channel are transactional, logistical, and facilitating functions. Transactional functions refer to making contact with buyers, using marketing communication strategies to raise awareness of products, matching product to buyer needs, negotiating price, and processing transactions. Logistical functions include physical distribution such as transportation and storing inventory and aggregating product; e-marketers often outsource these to third-party logistics providers. Facilitating functions include providing marketing research about buyers and providing financing. The last mile problem is the added expense of delivering small quantities to individual homes or businesses.

The distribution channel is a unified system of interdependent organizations working together to build value as products proceed through the channel from producer to consumer. This perspective recognizes that channels are stronger when they compete in a unified way with other channels. Supply chain management is the coordination of flow of material (e.g., physical product), information (e.g., demand forecast), and financial (e.g., credit terms).

Exercises

REVIEW QUESTIONS

1. What is a distribution channel?
2. What are the types of intermediaries in a distribution channel?
3. What are the three major functions of a distribution channel?
4. What is supply chain management (SCM) and why is it important?
5. Why are e-marketers concerned with the last mile problem?
6. What is disintermediation? Give an example.
7. What is an infomediary? Give an example.
8. What is multichannel marketing? Give an example.
9. How do brokers and agents differ?
10. What types of distribution channel metrics are used in the B2C market?
11. Name five ways to keep consumers from abandoning online shopping carts.

DISCUSSION QUESTIONS

12. How does the value of distribution channel functions change when they become internet based?
13. Do you agree with the more inclusive definition of the supply chain to include the entire value chain? Support your position.
14. Although direct distribution often results in lower prices, does it have disadvantages for buyers?
15. Each intermediary in the channel has to mark up a product's price to make a profit. Some retailers sell products for almost double the wholesale cost. What would a retailer have to do to add enough value to justify such a markup?
16. How would you suggest e-marketers solve the last mile problem?
17. What is the future of e-commerce, in your opinion? Will it continue to increase? Will it ever become larger in terms of sales than off-line retailing? Explain your answers.

WEB ACTIVITIES

18. Survey 20 people. Ask them to rate their online purchase experience on a scale of 1 to 10, with 10 as the best. If they have never purchased online, try to find out what stops them. Summarize the results.
19. Working in small groups, discuss online shopping experiences and what companies did to meet group members' needs, including follow-up e-mail.
20. Survey 10 people. Ask them to recall a time when they abandoned a shopping cart online while in the middle of a purchase. Query them about what the online retailer could have done to prevent that from happening. Summarize the results.

CHAPTER 13

E-Marketing Communication Tools

Interactive Advertising continues to experience tremendous growth as marketers experience its overall effectiveness in building brands and delivering online and off-line sales.

—GREG STUART, INTERACTIVE ADVERTISING BUREAU CEO

Firms that are truly customer driven will build 1-to-1 technologies into every corner of their firm and will link their networks to many other networks.

—BRUCE KASANOFF, ACCELERATING 1 TO 1

Chapter Outline

The primary goal of this chapter is to understand the internet as a tool for efficiently and effectively exchanging marketing communication messages between marketers and their audiences. You will learn how each marketing communication tool can carry messages over the internet and which are the most effective.

After reading this chapter, you will be able to:

- Define integrated marketing communication (IMC) and explain the importance of the hierarchy of effects model.

- Discuss how marketers use the internet for advertising, marketing public relations, sales promotions, direct marketing, and personal selling.

- Identify several emerging IMC tools.

- Describe the most effective online IMC tactics.

Will it Blend?

"Will it Blend? That is the question." Thus opens a video starring Blendtec's CEO, Tom Dickson. Wearing a white lab coat and safety glasses, and appearing very scientific yet amused, Dickson stands next to an ordinary-looking blender on a table. The things he blends are anything but ordinary—a wood handled garden rake, a golf club, light bulbs, glow sticks, marbles, and even the sacred iPhone. The latter received 3.9 million views on YouTube in an eight-month period. This was only surpassed by an iPod blending video, which received over 5 million views in a year. Watching the destruction of these is like watching a train wreck—irresistible. Sending the links to friends is also irresistible. This is viral marketing at its best.

Blendtec is well known in the business market for supplying commercial blenders to Starbucks and others. The goal of the hilarious videos was to build awareness for a new high quality blender for the consumer market. Retail sales

for the $400 blender increased 500 percent in the first year after the video series began, and total annual sales were projected to be over $40 million in 2008. Not bad for an initial $1000 investment in the videos. Blendtec posts videos both on YouTube and on its microsite WillItBlend.com, and the latter has prompted ancillary revenue streams. Visitors can purchase "Tom Dickson is My Homeboy" T-shirts and the videos themselves.

The brainchild of Dickson, the *Will it Blend?* campaign clearly shows the product benefits in a relevant, humorous, and engaging way. This campaign shows the value of connecting with consumers versus interrupting them with unwanted advertising. It also shows the strength of consumer conversation because over 12,000 viewers posted responses to the iPhone-blending YouTube video, including five video responses. The video was marked as a favorite by nearly 10,000 registered YouTube visitors. Brilliant job, Blendtec.

E-MARKETING COMMUNICATION

As the opening example of *Will it Blend?* demonstrates, internet marketing is a powerful way to start and strengthen relationships with customers. However, online marketers must be increasingly clever to design and deliver brand messages that capture and hold audience attention—because on the internet, users are in control. They can delete unwanted incoming e-mail and impatiently click away when Web sites don't quickly deliver desired information. Also, the internet allows consumers to widely disseminate their own views and brand experiences via e-mail and Web postings, shifting the balance of control over brand images from companies to consumers. In this environment, the keys to success include (1) providing relevant, interesting messages when and where target customers want them and (2) engaging internet users by enticing them to upload content, make comments, or simply play with the game or other fun content.

Marketing communication (MarCom) tools that use technology to build brands, in conjunction with value-added product experiences, are important in capturing attention and winning long-term customer relationships. Advertising online still works for building brands, but there are many other innovative techniques that are often more successful—discussed here and in Chapter 14. And as a bonus, technology lowers the costs of communicating with customers and prospects. For example, companies spend about $33 to serve a customer over the phone, $9.99 through e-mail, and $1.17 using automated Web-based support, according to Forrester Research.

Integrated Marketing Communication (IMC)

Integrated marketing communication (IMC) is a cross-functional process for planning, executing, and monitoring brand communications designed to profitably acquire, retain, and grow customers. IMC is cross-functional because every contact that a customer has with a firm or its agents helps to form brand images. For example, a Sharper Image retail customer might buy and use a product from the Web site, then e-mail or call 1-800 to complain about a problem, and finally return the product to the brick-and-mortar retail store. Every contact with an employee, a Web site, a blog comment about the product, a YouTube video, a magazine ad, a catalog, the physical store facilities, and so forth helps the customer form an image of the firm. In addition, the product experience, its pricing level, and its distribution channels enhance the firm's marketing communication in a variety of online and off-line media to present a strong brand image. The best advertising can be undermined if these online and off-line contact experiences do not communicate in a unified way to create and support positive brand relationships with customers.

Profitable customer relationships are key to a firm's existence. Successful firms recognize that not all customers are equally valuable—some, such as frequent flyers or buyers, are more important than others. Using technology, firms can monitor profits customer-by-customer and, based on this analysis, pay more attention to high-value customers both online and off-line. Databases and the analysis techniques described in Chapter 6 allow firms to differentiate customers by value, send them appropriate e-mail offers and Web site landing pages, and track the results of company MarCom campaigns. You'll find more about online customer relationship management in Chapter 15.

IMC strategy begins with a thorough understanding of target markets, the brand, its competition, and many other internal and external factors. Then marketers select specific MarCom tools to achieve their communication objectives and media for reaching target markets. After implementation, they measure execution effectiveness, make needed adjustments, and re-evaluate the results. Many IMC experts agree that it should "(1) be more strategic than executional (i.e., more than just about 'one voice, one look'), (2) be about more than just advertising and sales promotion

messages, (3) include two-way as well as one-way communication, and (4) be results driven" (Duncan and Mulhern, 2004, p. 9).

Although strategic IMC entails a coordinated marketing mix and cross-functional participation, this chapter focuses on the promotion mix elements (also called marketing communication tools), the core of a firm's marketing communication plan. Chapter 14 discusses online media, including the newest way to communicate online—via the social media.

Marketing Communication Tools

MarCom consists of both planned and unplanned messages between firms and customers, as well as those among customers. Companies use planned messages when trying to inform or persuade their target stakeholders. Unplanned messages include things such as word-of-mouth among consumers and publicity in media. However, because consumers have more control over communication on the internet, it is nearly impossible for companies to directly manage unplanned messages. Thus, firms should concentrate on creating positive product experiences and two-way brand communication so that unplanned messages will be positive. In fact, some firms have experienced tremendous growth almost entirely based on unplanned e-mail (e.g., Hotmail and Blendtec).

Using innovative technologies, e-marketers can enhance the effectiveness and efficiency of traditional MarCom in many interesting ways. Important technologies include text and multimedia messages carried via Web pages and e-mail; databases to store information; new ways of connecting with customers online (such as blogs); and a plethora of digital-receiving devices from PCs to cell phones for viewing multimedia messages. For example, Mitsubishi Motors North America began an IMC campaign with two goals: to register prospective buyers at the Web site and urge them to make test drive appointments. Tactics included running a TV ad in the 2003 Super Bowl that drove 31 million visitors to its Web site. This advertising was combined with e-mail targeted to 10 major geographic markets and a microsite with a dealer locator (Barnako, 2004). A **microsite** is a Web page or small site with specialized information and its own URL that is promoted separately from the main site (such as the *Will it Blend?* site).

In this chapter, we approach internet MarCom from the perspective of the traditional promotion mix, discussing advertising, sales promotions, marketing public relations (MPR), direct marketing, and personal selling.

IMC Goals and Strategies

Marketers create marketing communication objectives based on overall marketing goals and the desired effects within selected target markets. For instance, Mitsubishi Motors desired to sell more automobiles, so it identified marketing communication goals of (1) driving prospects to the Web site, (2) increasing Web site registrations, and (3) increasing test drive appointments. Sales are the primary goal, and the three communications objectives helped Mitsubishi reach it.

The traditional **AIDA model** (awareness, interest, desire, and action) or the "think, feel, do" **hierarchy of effects** model is part of what guides marketers' selection of online and off-line MarCom tools to meet their goals. Both the AIDA and hierarchy of effects models suggest that consumers first become aware of and learn about a new product (think), then develop a positive or negative attitude about it (feel), and ultimately move to purchasing it (do) (Ray, 1973). The thinking, or cognitive, steps are awareness and knowledge. The feeling, or attitude, steps are liking and preference. Consequently, e-marketers must select the appropriate IMC tools—which may vary from one stage to the other, depending on the desired results. For example, e-marketers may opt to use traditional IMC tools of sales promotion, such as giving away free T-shirts or mouse pads, to create awareness; television advertising to create interest and desire; and direct selling by telephone to get the desired action (buying). They might combine these with online tools of sales promotion (free music sampling at iTunes), advertising on search engines, or direct selling via e-commerce at the online store.

The **think, feel, do** model is well accepted for high-involvement product decisions (those that are perceived as being high financial, emotional, or social risk). This model works because consumers spend some amount of time gathering information and considering alternatives prior to buying such products. The internet is especially well-suited for this because of the abundance of product information online. Conversely, for low-involvement decisions, consumers often just hear about a product, give it a try, and then decide whether they like it. Exhibit 13.1 presents this classic model and its low-involvement adaptation.

If an organization wants to build its brands and inform customers, it will operate at the cognitive and attitude levels of the hierarchy of effects, perhaps utilizing blogs, white papers (as PDF files) on Web sites, Web advertising, e-mail campaigns, and other promotional techniques. When Ourbeginnings.com spent more than $4 million on Super Bowl XXXIV TV ads, it was trying to build awareness of the Web site—and it was so eager to achieve this goal that it spent four times its annual revenue on the campaign. This strategy turned out to be a poor one, which is why now only the strongest firms purchase Super Bowl advertising, such as E*TRADE in 2002 and 2008, and Apple's iTunes in 2004. If a firm wants to encourage online transactions (behavior), it needs more persuasive communication messages that tell how to complete the transaction on the Web site, over the telephone, and so forth. Postpurchase behavior doesn't appear

High Involvement		Low Involvement	
Awareness Knowledge	Cognitive (think)	Awareness Knowledge	Cognitive (think)
Liking Preference	Attitude (feel)	Purchase Conviction	Behavior (do)
Conviction Purchase	Behavior (do)	Liking Preference	Attitude (feel)

EXHIBIT 13.1   Hierarchy of Effects for High- and Low-Involvement Product Decisions

on the commonly accepted hierarchy, yet many MarCom strategies seek to build customer satisfaction after the purchase. E-mail is especially well suited for this goal.

The hierarchy of effects model is important because it helps marketers understand where consumers stand in relation to the purchase cycle so the company can select appropriate communication objectives and strategies that will move consumers closer to purchase and loyalty. Bear in mind that some MarCom tools are more appropriate for building awareness and brand attitudes (advertising, public relations) and others are more suited for encouraging transactional behavior (direct marketing, sales promotions, personal selling). Nevertheless, all can be used at each level. Understanding the desired effects in each target market is the first step to building an effective IMC plan and establishing benchmarks for applying performance metrics to measure the plan's success.

Branding Versus Direct Response

Online marketing communication can be used to build brand equity or to elicit a direct response in the form of a transaction or some other behavior (such as Web site registration, blog comment post, or e-mail inquiry). The goal of **brand advertising**

online is to put the brand name and product benefits in front of users: "Brand advertising creates a distinct favorable image that customers associate with a product at the moment they make buying decisions" (Doyle et al., 1997). Marketing public relations also aims to build brands, while sales promotion, direct marketing, and personal selling primarily attempt to solicit a direct response. **Direct-response advertising** seeks to motivate action. Brand communication works at the awareness and attitude levels of the hierarchy of effects model (heads and hearts), while direct-response communication primarily works at the behavioral level (do something).

See Exhibit 13.2 for a listing of online tactics by the desired hierarchy of effects goal. E-marketers rely on keyword search (see Chapter 14), display ads, branded sponsorships, and video ads for brand building and on e-mail, keyword search, and referral programs for direct response, according to McKinsey research.

INTERNET ADVERTISING

Advertising is non-personal communication of information through various media, usually persuasive in nature about products (goods and services) or ideas and usually paid for by an identified

Tactic	Brand Building (%)	Consideration (%)	Direct Response (%)	Retention (%)
E-mail (*n* = 231)	5	20	33	37
Paid keyword search (*n* = 175)	27	29	29	7
Display ads (*n* = 206)	36	18	27	10
Branded sponsorship (*n* = 135)	55	11	7	24
Referrals (*n* = 109) (e.g., Affiliate programs)	13	28	27	11
Video ads (*n* = 94)	33	30	17	12
Podcasts (*n* = 70)	22	25	5	33
Overall (*n* = 149)	25	21	22	21

EXHIBIT 13.2   E-Marketing Tactics for Hierarchy of Effects Goals

Source: eMarketer.com from McKinsey Research Study.

sponsor. All paid space on a Web site or in an e-mail is considered advertising. Internet advertising parallels traditional media advertising, in which companies create content and then sell space to outside advertisers. This can be confusing, especially when a house banner appears on a firm's own Web site. The key is exchange—if a firm pays money or barters with goods for space in which to put the content it creates, the content is considered advertising. In Chapter 12, we discussed how firms create revenue streams from selling advertising space, but this and later sections discuss the flipside: buying advertising space from someone else to reach a firm's stakeholders. These specific definitions are meaningless to consumers (who view all commercial messages as advertising), but they are important to marketers because various MarCom tools help to accomplish various specific goals.

Trends in Internet Advertising

Internet advertising in the United States began with the first series of banner ads on Hot wired.com on October 27, 1994. Exhibit 13.3 is a representation of one of these types of ads, sponsored by AT&T (others included IBM, Sprint, MCI, Volvo, Zima, and Club Med). The ad ran for 12 weeks, cost $30,000, and received an amazing 30 percent click-through. Compare this ratio to the 0.04 percent click-through rates on similar ads in July 2007, according to eMarketer. Interestingly, 6 percent of internet users represent one half of all ad clicks. Dubbed "heavy clickers" by eMarketer, on average they are 25–44 years of age, online four times as much as other users, and have annual household incomes under $40,000—not the optimum profile for online retailers.

Online advertising reached $1 billion in 1998, grew quickly to $8.2 billion in 2000, dropped 12.3 percent in 2001 and again in 2002 (due to the economic recession), and has finally reached a tipping point when it jumped to over $21.1 billion in 2007 (Exhibit 13.4). Most advertisers now believe the internet to be an important medium for reaching their target markets.

To understand the context of advertiser spending on the internet, consider that total advertising expenditures in the United States alone during 2007 were expected to reach $237.8 billion. In other words, in 2007, internet firms with space to sell captured only 8.9 percent of advertiser dollars (see Chapter 14 for more details). Yet averages can be misleading—the internet is actually an important advertising medium for particular industries and firms but not for all. This figure may not increase much in the future as marketers increase their use of blogs, videos, social networks, and other non-paid forms of social media communication with their target markets.

Which industries are advertising online? According to the Internet Advertising Bureau (IAB), most ad spending came from the following product categories in 2006:

> Consumer related (52%)
>
> Financial services (16%)
>
> Computing (10%)
>
> Telecom (8%)
>
> Media (6%)

Consumer-related advertising includes retailing (37%), automotive (22%), leisure (13%), entertainment (8%), and packaged goods (8%).

An important online advertising trend involves user-generated advertising. Frito Lay offered internet users $10,000 and a free trip to the 2007 Super Bowl for creating winning 30-second television commercials. The winning

EXHIBIT 13.3   The First Banner Ad in 1994

Note: This is a graphic representation—actual was in colored font.

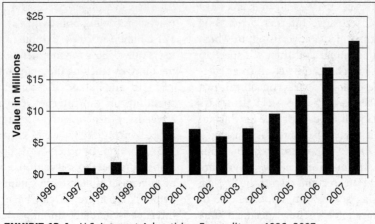

EXHIBIT 13.4 U.S. Internet Advertising Expenditure, 1996–2007

Source: PricewaterhouseCoopers LLP/IAB Internet Advertising Revenue Reports.

spot was aired at the game. There were 1100 entries and nearly 700,000 internet users logged on to see the commercials and vote for their favorites. Frito Lay paid $2.5 million for the Super Bowl TV spot plus prize money, while the ad only cost winner Dale Backus $12.79 to produce. General Motors tried the same strategy, providing consumers video, audio, and images to use in constructing commercials. It worked well for GM, too; however, there was a negative backlash—approximately 20 percent of the entries had superimposed text mentioning the Chevy Tahoe's part in using up the world's oil and causing global warming. These videos were posted as ad parodies on YouTube and received lots of press. The moral: in an online environment where everyone is a journalist, expect your underbelly to be exposed. Regardless, GM felt the campaign was a huge success.

Advertisers continue to experiment with user-created ads for good reason—one study found that consumers believe companies with customer-created ads are more friendly (68%), creative (56%), and innovative (55%) than those which use only professional advertising (according to AMA and Opinion Research Corporation research). Also, recall from Chapter 1 that consumers trust each other more than they trust companies, so consumer-created advertising is an appropriate tactic.

Internet Advertising Formats

Anything goes with internet advertising: text—from a sentence to pages of story—graphics, sound, hyperlinks, or the Energizer Bunny hopping through a page. Keyword search is the fastest growing and most important technique (see Exhibit 13.5). Keyword search is part of a larger strategy called **search marketing**: the act of marketing a Web site via search engines, whether to improve rank in listings, purchase paid listings, or combine these and other search engine–related activities (see Chapter 14 for more on this tactic).

Classified ads are the second largest spending category, and then display ads (www.iab.net). It is interesting to note how ad formats have changed over the past five years, reflecting the intense competition for audience attention in an environment where consumers are in charge. The following section discusses several interesting or commonly used advertising formats.

DISPLAY ADS Note that the banner ad is not listed as an advertising format in Exhibit 13.5. The Interactive Advertising Bureau no longer reports on banner ad use due to its rapid decline in use and effectiveness for direct response goals, and the growth of larger and different ad sizes. The industry now uses the traditional ad nomenclature to

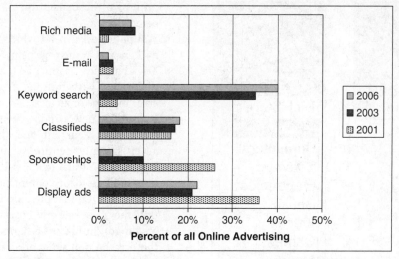

EXHIBIT 13.5   Proportion of Advertising Dollars by Format in 2001–2006
Source: PricewaterhouseCoopers LLP/IAB Internet Advertising Revenue Reports.

describe both banners and other sizes—**display ads**. These ads contain more graphics and white space than text, and include traditional banners and many additional sizes. Looking at Exhibits 13.2 and 13.5, one wonders why so many advertisers still use display ads for direct response when the click-through rates are so low. The answer is that display ads do help build brand awareness when viewed by site visitors.

The Interactive Advertising Bureau (IAB) and the Coalition for Advertising Supported Information and Entertainment (CASIE) have proposed standard dimensions for what they call *interactive formats*—to see them, visit www.iab.net. Rectangles, pop-ups, banners, buttons, and skyscraper display ads occupy various amounts of pixels of designated space for rent on Web pages (recall that one pixel is one dot of light). For instance, banners are rectangular at 468 pixels wide ¥ 60 pixels tall (Exhibit 13.3), skyscrapers are 160 ¥ 600 pixels, and medium rectangles are 300 ¥ 250 pixels. Pop-ups usually appear in a separate window that overlays the current browser window. Many people are irritated by pop-ups because users must close them, but many users now use pop-up blocking software, so this format is slowly disappearing. Although similar to the print advertising model used by magazines and newspapers, on the

internet these ads involve video and audio capabilities in that few square inches of space.

Some observers thought that the industry would eventually standardize online ad sizes, as in traditional media, to smooth the way for Web sites selling space and agencies designing ads. That standardization hasn't happened because newer sizes and formats break through the online clutter and grab user attention better than do standard banners. In fact, DoubleClick (recently acquired by Google) reported serving more than 8,000 different ad sizes in May 2002 alone ("DoubleClick Ad Serving," 2002). Nonetheless, the IAB now suggests the following ad sizes in its attempt to create industry standards:

- Seven differently sized rectangles and pop-ups
- Eight banners and buttons
- Three skyscrapers

RICH MEDIA ADS All ads in this category are interactive, at least offering click-through. By clicking on the ad, the user is transported to the advertiser's Web site, where the transaction or any other objective is actually achieved. Some display ads enhance the interactivity by sensing the position of the mouse on the Web page and animating

EXHIBIT 13.6 BuyComp Interactive Display Ad

Source: www.buycomp.com.

faster as the user approaches. Other ads have built-in games. Still others have drop-down menus, check boxes, and search boxes to engage and empower the user. Exhibit 13.6 displays a banner ad that allows users to interact by selecting items from a drop-down menu. According to Wikipedia editors, rich media ads often use Flash animation and many other elements to attract attention. All of the following formats can be rich media (see www.wikipedia.com):

- **Banner ad**: An advertising graphic image or animation displayed on a Web site, in an application (such as Eudora), or in an HTML e-mail.
- **Interstitial ad**: The display of a page of ads before the requested content.
- **Floating ad**: An ad which moves across the user's screen or floats above the content.
- **Expanding ad**: An ad which changes size and which may alter the contents of the Web page.
- **Polite ad**: A method by which a large ad will be downloaded in smaller pieces to

minimize the disruption of the content being viewed.
- **Wallpaper ad**: An ad which changes the background of the page being viewed.
- **Trick banner**: A banner ad that looks like a dialog box with buttons. It simulates an error message or an alert.
- **Pop-up**: A new window which opens in front of the current one, displaying an advertisement, or entire Web page.
- **Pop-under**: Similar to a Pop-Up except that the window is loaded or sent behind the current window so that the user does not see it until they close one or more active windows.
- **Video ad**: Similar to a banner ad, except that instead of a static or animated image, actual moving video clips are displayed.
- **Map ad**: Text or graphics linked from, and appearing in or over, a location on an electronic map such as on Google Maps.
- **Mobile ad**: An SMS text or multi-media message sent to a cell phone.

One downside of animated and highly interactive display ads is that they tend to require more bandwidth. Keeping banner file sizes small reduces the time that they take to load. Small ads often appear before most content on a given Web page. Therefore, the ad is spotlighted on the user's screen if only for a split second. Users may not wait for large display ads to download, but instead follow a hyperlink to leave the page before the ad loads—effectively making the ad invisible. With increased bandwidth and high-speed Net delivery to most homes, these interactive banners will become more important in the future.

TRANSITION AND FLOATER ADS Transition ads appear while other content is loading (between pages). **Interstitials** are Java-based ads that appear while the publisher's content is loading. They represent only 2 percent of all Web advertising expenditures. Interstitials held great promise when they were first introduced, but their number has not increased. One reason is that they are hard to execute properly; another is that they give the impression of lengthening user waiting time, which is not good. However, user response is good to interstitials if they are entertaining.

The next iteration of interstitials is called superstitials. Created by Unicast, superstitials feature videolike ads timed to appear when a user moves the mouse from one part of a Web site to another (www.unicast.com). Superstitials look like mini videos, using Flash technology and Java to make them entertaining and fast. The advantage of superstitials over interstitials is that the former loads behind the scenes and doesn't appear until it is fully loaded on the user's computer. Thus, a superstitial doesn't slow page download time, nor does the user have the impression that it does. Agency.com, a dot-com ad agency, designed a superstitial for British Airways that created an amazing 20 percent click-through. Of course, anything new on the Web draws attention.

The **Shoshkele**, created by United Virtualities, is a five-to-eight second Flash animation that runs through a Web page to capture user attention. The Energizer Bunny was among the first Shoshkeles, creating a lot of excitement as it hopped through and interrupted the page text. A recent Shoshkele appeared at Speedvision.com. After arriving at the page, the screen slowly darkened to the point of making the text unreadable, and then a hand emerged at the lower left corner and sparked up a Zippo lighter to illuminate the page again before disappearing. These ads are enjoyable to some and invasive to others because they can't be stopped. Web technology allows for many interesting multimedia advertising formats. The novelty of new formats such as screen interrupts captures consumer attention, but the traditional rules persist: Marketing communication success is about reaching the right audience with the right message at the right time.

E-MAIL ADVERTISING By far the least expensive type of online advertising, **e-mail advertising**, is generally just a few sentences of text embedded in another firm's content. Advertisers purchase space in the e-mail sponsored by others (e.g., Hotmail). Exhibit 13.7 displays an e-mail ad that CDW purchased to accompany e-mail discussion among community members using the former Listbot service (now Microsoft List Builder). E-mail newsletters sponsored by firms is another example. Exhibit 13.8 displays an ad for the *E-Mail Marketing Handbook* that helps to sponsor an interesting newsletter about marketing communication online from WordBiz.com. Despite a trend toward more HTML and rich media e-mail such as this ad, many users still prefer text-based e-mail due to its faster download time. As a result, before purchasing e-mail advertising, firms must be sure that their recipients closely match their own target markets. However, based on the definition of advertising, note that HTML and multimedia e-mail messages sent from a firm directly to internet users are direct marketing, not advertising.

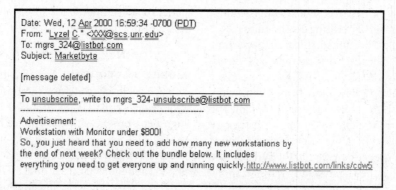

EXHIBIT 13.7 Embedded Text Advertisement in E-Mail Message

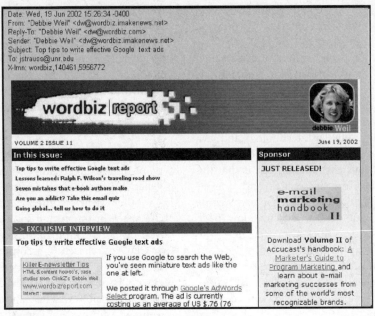

EXHIBIT 13.8   Advertisement in E-Mail Newsletter

SPONSORSHIPS **Sponsorships**, also called advertorials, integrate editorial content and advertising—something traditional publishers abhor. Most traditional media clearly separate content from advertising; women's magazines are an exception. Food advertisers usually barter for recipes that include their products in these magazines, and fashion advertisers get mentions of their clothing in articles. This practice pleases advertisers because it gives them additional exposure and creates the impression that the publication endorses their products. This blending of content by two firms is declining in use by Web sites: It now comprises only 3 percent of all Web advertising expenditures.

We think that sponsorships are important on the Web because display ads are easily overlooked by users, sponsorships allow great interactivity, and because more firms build synergistic partnerships to provide useful content. For instance, Astrology.com sponsors an astrology quiz on iVillage.com, a site for women. This adds value for site users and revenue for iVillage. See Exhibit 13.9 for the Candystand Web site, sponsored by Life Savers candy. Each link at the site leads to a game sponsored by one of the Life Savers candies.

Note that the sponsor in this ad is clearly identified. Consumers know that this content is brought to them by Life Savers in conjunction with Candystand. Some people worry about the ethics of sponsorships when consumers cannot easily identify the content author(s). Perhaps this problem is not significant because many users view the entire Web as one giant advertisement. However, when advertising is passed off as locally generated content, it can potentially lower user trust in the Web site and hurt brand image. To address this important issue, the IAB established a panel to set standards for sponsor disclosure in this type of advertising.

MOBILE ADVERTISING Forward-thinking marketers are closely watching developments in the mobile device market. PDAs and cell phones have high penetration, with cell phones being the primary internet device in many countries (see Chapter 4). While mobile advertisers spent only $871 million in 2006, according to *The Economist*, "Marketers hail the mobile phone as advertising's promised land." Four promising marketing communication techniques for mobile devices are

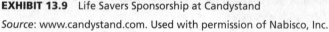

EXHIBIT 13.9 Life Savers Sponsorship at Candystand

Source: www.candystand.com. Used with permission of Nabisco, Inc.

discussed in this chapter: free mobile content delivery (marketing public relations), content-sponsored advertising, and two direct marketing techniques—location marketing and short message services (SMS). In practice, the line between these techniques is blurred.

Content-sponsored advertising for mobile devices is the wireless version of display and other ads that sponsor Web content. Some mobile ads employ the *pull* model of advertising: Users pull content from mobile Web sites and ads come along for the ride. Companies such as Microsoft and AvantGo offer free news and other content to mobile users, sponsored by a third-party advertiser (Exhibit 13.10). America's Virgin Mobile and a few others have been successful with opt-in *push* model ad-sponsored content, as well. In Virgin Mobile's "Sugar Mama" campaign, it offered cell phone owners free minutes in exchange for viewing ads. For example, viewing a 45-second ad while on the Web got them one free minute of cell talk time, and receiving text message ads or completing online questionnaires got them more free minutes. According to Ultramercial, the company running the campaign, Virgin Mobile

EXHIBIT 13.10 Content-Sponsored Advertising on Visor PDA

Source: AvantGo, Inc: AvantGo Mobile Internet (www.avantgo.com).

had given away over 10 million free minutes by mid-campaign.

Mobile ads are a new area with great promise and many unanswered questions. An important current debate involves whether mobile users would rather pay for content or receive advertising-sponsored content. This is analogous to television—the audience can pay for cable TV programming with no commercials or receive advertising-sponsored programming from stations. One survey of 3,300 mobile users in 11 global markets found users receptive to mobile ads, although 86 percent said wanted a clear benefit to them (Pastore, 2002a). In a study by Cahners In-Stat Group, 64 percent of the respondents said they would not embrace mobile advertising unless they could decide whether to receive messages.

Several major issues may affect the future of mobile advertising. First, wireless bandwidth is currently small, so additional advertising content interferes with quick download of the requested information. Second, the smaller screen size of cell phones and PDAs greatly limits ad size. Third, it requires different techniques to track advertising effectiveness, although AvantGo does track page views and advertising click-throughs for content partners. Finally, many mobile users must pay their service provider by the minute while accessing the internet—and many do not want to pay for the time it takes to receive ads. In spite of these issues, content-sponsored advertising on mobile devices is likely to increase in the future.

EMERGING FORMATS On the internet, anything goes. This is a fertile ground for the creative advertiser, who constantly devises new ways to reach target markets with online advertising. Downloadable widget ads are one of the latest trends. Kraft Foods offers a widget that once installed on a consumer's desktop will automatically send a different recipe every day. Yahoo! has nearly 5,000 widgets, some of which offer shopping assistance—such as one that searches for Amazon.com deals or finds products at Sears.com. Another new frontier is

video advertising due to high video viewership numbers, with four new ad formats emerging in early 2008:

- Yahoo! announced a three-second splash ad that will show right before a video launches and then become a banner ad above the video window after it starts. When users click on the ad, banner interactivity starts and the original video pauses.
- Yahoo! also announced a semi-transparent video overlay, shown either before or after the video plays. The user sees a cue to mouse over the video, prompting the ad to emerge. The user can click through to the advertiser's site.
- Google offers "gadget ads" with interactive, rich media capabilities allowing users to interact in ways not done before. For example, gadget ads look more like interesting content (such as the Honda Civic concert tour) and users can post them anywhere online and share them with others in social networks.
- VideoEgg allows users to click on a video and interact with a small pop-up animated banner, new video, or game. Over 100 brands on YouTube and other video sharing sites have used this technology.

MARKETING PUBLIC RELATIONS (MPR)

Public relations (PR) consists of activities that influence public opinion and create goodwill for an organization. PR is used to create goodwill among a number of different publics including company shareholders and employees, the media, suppliers, and the local community, as well as consumers, business buyers, and other stakeholder groups. **Marketing public relations** (MPR) includes brand-related activities and nonpaid, third-party media coverage to positively influence target markets. Thus, MPR is the marketing department's portion of PR directed to the firm's customers and prospects in order to build awareness and positive attitudes about its brands. For example, traffic spikes of 25 percent to 35 percent are common for online retailers during the holiday shopping season, and GoDaddy.com saw 1564 percent more Sunday visitors at its site on the Sunday of the 2006 Super Bowl, in which it advertised.

MPR activities using internet technology include the Web site content itself, online events, and many ways to build a buzz online. In this chapter we discuss MPR using traditional online techniques, and in Chapter 14 we discuss blogs, communities, and other social media used for creating an online buzz.

Web Site

Every organization, company, individual, or brand Web site is an MPR tool because it serves as electronic brochure, including current product and company information. In Chapter 7, you learned that 65 percent to 87 percent of internet users purchase online and 81 percent use the internet to gather information before shopping either online or off-line. In fact, the company Web site is the largest influence for online consumers in all shopping decisions, according to Double Click

research (Exhibit 13.11). Eighteen percent said the Web influenced their product/service purchase the most, compared to less than 4 percent for any type of advertising.

According to the Direct Marketing Association, "As marketers gain a better understanding of their ROI, they have begun to allocate more resources to online site development than to promoting their Web sites as the way to increase their profitability. Improving the customers' experience online is now a priority" (see www.the-dma.org). For example, Butterball's site (www.butterball.com), which features cooking and carving tips, received 550,000 visitors in one day during Thanksgiving week. Although it costs the firm money to create such a Web site, it is not considered advertising (paid-for space on another firm's site).

Several advantages come with using the Web for publishing product information. First, the Web is a low-cost alternative to paper brochures or press releases sent in overnight mail. Second,

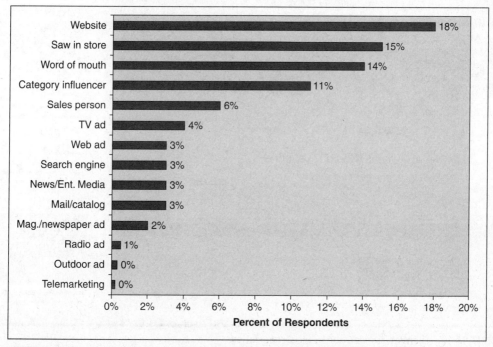

EXHIBIT 13.11 Greatest Influence for Online Consumers Making Shopping Decisions

Source: DoubleClick, November 2006 Research (www.doubleclick.com).

product information is often updated in company databases, so Web page content is always current. Finally, the Web can reach new prospects who are searching for particular products. Many books discuss how to create effective Web sites—thus, the topic is beyond the scope of this book. The most important point is to create a site that satisfies the firm's target audiences better than the competition. Web sites can entertain (games and electronic postcards), build communities (online events, chat rooms, and e-mail discussion groups), provide a communication channel with the customer (customer feedback and customer service), provide information (product selection and purchase, product recommendation, retailer referrals), and assist in many other ways.

The Web site is a door into a company, and must provide inviting, organized, and relevant content. Exhibit 13.12 shows the Microsoft door with a full list of all the Microsoft sub sites, its

mother lode product (Microsoft Office) and operating system (download Vista now), and links by market (business, consumer). Finally, it shouts customer orientation: "Connect and share anywhere" and "Your Potential. Our Passion." It is difficult to make a simple Web doorway when there is such an abundance of products and information and tens of thousands of Web pages, and we think Microsoft did well.

Online Events

Online events are designed to generate user interest and draw traffic to a site. In a highly publicized event, Amazon let users contribute to a story started by author John Updike. Each year Land Rover sponsors the Camel Trophy race through exotic regions of the world. Land Rover allows users to receive updates from the race at its Web site. Perhaps the most memorable commercial

EXHIBIT 13.12   The Web Site as Door to the Organization

Source: www.microsoft.com. Microsoft product screen shot(s) reprinted with permission from Microsoft Corporation.

online event occurred in 1999 when Victoria Secret held a Web-based fashion show. The firm announced it in advertisements in the *New York Times,* Super Bowl football game, and other traditional media. The event drew 1.2 million visitors, an 82 percent increase in Web traffic and the firm's Web servers could not handle all the traffic.

Companies and organizations can hold seminars, workshops, and discussions online. In the 2008 U.S. Presidential race, CNN held a debate online and invited video questions from citizens. A publisher might encourage people interested in a new book to chat with the author at an online forum. Companies use forthcoming events as legitimate reasons to e-mail potential as well as existing clients. Holding online events in which clients get to "talk to" senior or prestigious people may be seen as one more valuable reason for being a client of a particular organization. It also saves considerable time and cost compared to holding or attending a physical seminar.

CVENT is an online firm that provides clients with a Web interface for inviting and registering potential attendees to either online or off-line special events (www.cvent.com). It is particularly strong because it also allows for registrant online payment and travel arrangements, and gives client firms business intelligence to improve event participation in the future (such as conversion rates and post-event surveys). Using CVENT, the Marketing Director for Nasdaq (stock exchange) doubled the response rate and reduced marketing costs by 92 percent. Likewise, WebEx provides a space for online meetings and Webinars, and Meetup.org users form special interest groups by location and then arrange off-line meetings.

Podcasts

"A podcast is a digital media file, or a series of such files, that is distributed over the Internet using syndication (Web feed(s)) for playback on portable media players and personal computers," according to Wikipedia. Podcasts began with purely audio files for the iPod and other MP3 players, but now users can download video podcasts ("vidcasts" or "videocasts") for use on many types of receiving appliances. The line between video podcasts and other online video is quite fuzzy. Twelve percent of all internet users have downloaded a podcast (according Pew Internet & American Life research), and nearly 18 percent of companies offer them (according to digital agency cScape's customer engagement research).

It seems that podcasts are in limited use as an IMC tool, especially in light of the growing popularity of online video; however, some companies are using them quite successfully. For example, the Eastman Kodak Company records interviews with professional photographers and offers them as podcasts on iTunes. Kodak notes that many other professionals like to listen to the podcasts during their long commute to work. Other companies offering podcasts to build their brands include media (e.g., Comedy Central, ESPN, and The New York Times), music (e.g., MTV, Quincy Jones), sports (e.g., HBO, the NBA), and technology firms (e.g., Diggnation, CNET).

Build a Buzz Online

The news has moved online, and this includes information and announcements about a company and its brands. "The top fifty newspapers in the U.S. have a combined daily circulation of around twenty-one million readers," according to Beal and Strauss (2008). However, the top five general news Web sites in 2007 attracted 131.4 million monthly visitors (Yahoo! News, CNN Digital Network, MSNBC Digital Network, AOL News, and NYTimes.com), according to Nielsen//NetRatings. For this reason, companies usually include a press room with releases about brands on their Web sites and also send them electronically via e-mail or the Web to media firms for publishing. The resulting brand publicity is the result of most company MPR strategies.

Increasingly, journalists don't publish information from the thousands of daily press releases arriving in their e-mail, but instead go searching for information on stories of interest. Even when a big story breaks, such as the iPhone introduction, the first place journalists go is to the Web site for more details. This makes the company online press room and "About Us" pages critical assets. It also means that online press releases should be loaded with key words to help journalists find them when searching for a story on a particular topic. For example, Google has outstanding pages for the press. As shown in Exhibit 13.13, the "About Google" Web page is well organized, simple, and offers all the information a visitor needs. It is one click to the press center, where journalists can get images, information, and contact data if more is needed for any story.

The social media has added another interesting dimension to online MPR. Citizen journalists post photos of just about anything, including a product malfunction. Social media journalists, such as influential bloggers, write on a topic and it often spreads around the Web within hours, with links and conversation on many blogs and Web sites. For example, JetBlue had a PR crisis on Valentine's Day 2007 when bad weather hit the U.S. east coast and resulted in passengers sitting in airplanes on airport tarmacs for up to 11 hours. Passengers sent video from the airplane to YouTube as events occurred. Within one day a new blog appeared: JetBlueHostage.com, with posts about the event and the airline's responses to it all the way until August that year. JetBlue's CEO posted an apology video on YouTube that was viewed by 300,000 visitors, and received comments such as: "I'll pass on the Kool-Aid, thanks. This airline is a joke and anyone who buys this B.S. from this moron deserves to be stranded for 10 hours w/no food, water or toilets! Boycott JetBlew!!" Companies need to proactively manage their brand images online and become an authentic and transparent part of the online conversation about them.

There are many positive ways to build a buzz online using MPR. Viral marketing, customer-created ads, and other ideas in this chapter will help companies build a buzz. Below are more ideas:

- Provide engaging, fresh content on Web sites to draw traffic and repeat visits.
- Offer RSS feeds so that both traditional and social media journalists can monitor content.

About **Google**		Search our site
Google Content Network Reach the right audiences through our extensive network of partner sites.	**Our Products** Help Help with Google Search, Services and Products... Google Web Search Features Translation, I'm Feeling Lucky, Cached... Google Services & Tools Toolbar, Google Web APIs, Buttons... Google Labs Ideas, Demos, Experiments...	**For Site Owners** Advertising AdWords, AdSense... Business Solutions Google Search Appliance, Google Mini, WebSearch... Webmaster Central One-stop shop for comprehensive info about how Google crawls and indexes websites. Submit your content to Google Add your site, Google Base, Google Sitemaps...
Google Clean Energy Learn about Google's new Renewable Energy Group.		
AdSense Earn money by placing relevant ads on your website.	**Our Company** Press Center News, Images, Zeitgeist... Jobs at Google Openings, Perks, Culture... Corporate Info Company overview, Philosophy, Addresses... Investor Relations Financial info, Corporate governance...	**More Google** Contact Us FAQs, Feedback, Newsletter... Logos and Photos Logos, Doodles, Googlers at work and play... Google Blog Insights to Google products and culture... Google Store Pens, Shirts, Lava lamps...
Google AdWords Create your ad See your ad on Google and our partner sites. Your ads can appear when people search Google and our advertising network.		
	©2008 Google Privacy Policy · Terms of Service	

EXHIBIT 13.13 About Google Page at Google.com

Source: www.google.com/about.html.

- Use online news wires to disseminate press releases online (such as Business Wire, PR Newswire and PRWeb).
- Consider using the new social media press release that improves on the traditional format because it offers easy links, images, quotes, and more (available at Shift Communications: www.shiftcomm.com).
- Find influential bloggers in the appropriate industry, such as Seth Godin in the marketing profession. Comment on their blogs when they write about things in your area of expertise.

SALES PROMOTION OFFERS

Sales promotions are short-term incentives of gifts or money that facilitate the movement of products from producer to end user. Sales promotion activities include coupons, discounts, rebates, product sampling, contests, sweepstakes, and premiums (free or low-cost gifts). Of these promotion types, only sampling, discounts, and contests/sweepstakes are widely used on the internet. Online coupons had great promise in the internet's early days; however,

only 5.7 percent of internet users seek coupons online—as compared with 58.4 percent who find them in newspapers or magazines, and 4.4 percent who print them from e-mail (see Exhibit 13.14 for a Web site that distributes coupons online).

Online sales promotion works, especially to entice consumers to change their behavior in the short term (e.g., visit a Web site, register online, purchase in the next week). Marketers report three to five times higher response rates with online promotions than with direct mail. Whereas most off-line sales promotion tactics are directed to businesses in the distribution channel, online tactics are directed primarily at consumers. As with off-line consumer sales promotions, many are used in combination with advertising. Sales promotions are popular display ad content and are also good for drawing users to a Web site, enticing them to stay, and compelling them to return. Online sales promotion tactics can build brands, build databases, and support increased online or off-line sales, but like off-line promotions, they do not help to build customer relationships in the long term.

EXHIBIT 13.14 H.O.T.! Coupons Distributes Coupons in Most Local Areas

Source: www.hotcoupons.com.

Sampling

Some sites allow users to sample digital product prior to purchase. Many software companies provide free download of fully functional demo versions of their software (Exhibit 13.15). The demo normally expires in 30 to 60 days, after which time users can choose to purchase the software or remove it from their system. Online music stores allow customers to sample 30-second clips of music before downloading the song or ordering the CD. Market research firms often offer survey results as a sampling to entice businesses to purchase reports. For example, comScore Media Metrix posts the results of its monthly survey of top Web sites for prospects to see, use, and, thus, perhaps discover a need for more in-depth data.

Reflecting the growth in computer virus attacks, Symantec offers free product sampling online. Users can run a security scan or virus detection on their PC directly at the Symantec Web site. More than 20,000 Web sites now link to Symantec's site and this as well as other IMC techniques resulted in an annual 20 percent growth rate for the firm from 1998 to 2003 (see www.symantec.com).

Contests, Sweepstakes, and Games

Many sites hold contests and sweepstakes to draw traffic and keep users returning. Contests require skill (e.g., trivia answer) whereas sweepstakes involve only a pure chance drawing for the winners. Just as in the brick-and-mortar world, these sales promotion activities create excitement about brands and entice customers to visit a retailer. They persuade users to move from page to page on a Web site, thus increasing site engagement. If sweepstake offers are changed regularly, users will return to the site to check out the latest chance to win.

ContestHound.com, a sweepstakes and contest directory originating in 1999, does an excellent job of consolidating promotions from many Web sites (see Exhibit 13.16). This site gets nearly 200,000 visitors a year, and 10 percent are double opt-in newsletter subscribers. Its three key sites also offer other entertainment and personalization tactics to engage customers such as games, a newsletter, and an affiliate program. ContestHound uses both e-commerce and media models—the revenue comes from paid ads and affiliate programs to which they belong.

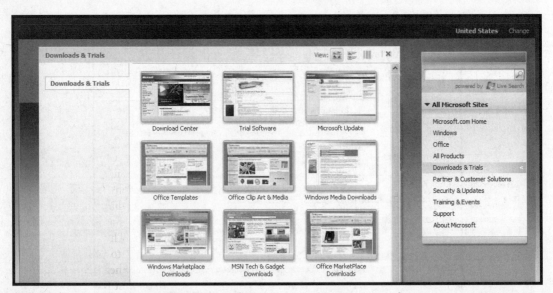

EXHIBIT 13.15   Software Sampling at Microsoft.com

Source: www.microsoft.com/downloads/.

EXHIBIT 13.16   ContestHound.com Consolidates Sales Promotions from Many Web Sites

Source: www.contesthound.com.

It posts about 20 new contests a day. According to co-owner Kathleen Gunther:

> Contests range from the stay-at-home mom giving away hand made soaps and soy candles every month, to cars, vacations and home makeovers. Other really popular prizes are electronics, DVDs, gift cards, and concert tickets with VIP passes and once-in-a-lifetime prizes (like awarding the Fans Choice Award at the Junos in Calgary, Canada). We have a few criteria a contest must meet before we'll list it: the prize must be worth at least $15; both the prize and the site must be family-friendly; there must be full rules listed on the site; it must be free to enter. I think the craziest contest we came across was "Win Free Toilet Paper." Every month

there was a new winner of 24 rolls and, believe it or not, it was very popular. We were paid by unique lead for that contest and ran it for a long, long time!

In one popular promotion, Wendy's restaurants and the Canadian TSN sports TV network offered the 2006 Wendy's "Kick for a Million" sweepstakes and contest. Contestants entered online and TSN drew 5 winners from the 200,000 entries (sweepstake portion). One finalist had a chance at $1 million Canadian by kicking a field goal during the halftime of a Wendy's Canadian Football League game. This kicking contest attracted 829,000 viewers to the football game, but unfortunately the winner did not make the field goal—he did get a Best Buy shopping spree and some cash, however (see Wendys.com and "Popular Wendy's Kick . . .," 2007).

Orbitz.com entered the online travel agent market in mid-June 2001 after competitors Travelocity.com and Expedia.com were well established. Nonetheless, the site drew 1.9 million customers in its first month, partly because of a huge sweepstakes featured in radio advertising. Every visitor who registered on the site was eligible for a free round-trip ticket given away every hour, 24/7, for six weeks (Orbitz, 2001). ePrize, an interactive promotion agency, reports good results for its client firms using recent online promotions: Verizon increased conversion rates by 800 percent; Kimberly Clark saw 11 percent of customers return more than 10 times to its Web site; and Petsmart increased revenue by $450,000 by cross-promoting from the retail store to the online site (Linkner, 2004).

Advergames are growing in popularity online. They combine online advertising and gaming; the user sees products and services in the game itself. They are used to draw site traffic and build brands in both B2B and B2C markets. For instance, consumers can test drive a Toyota online or play any number of exciting games at the Nickelodeon Web site, such as SpongeBob's Pizza Toss (www.nick.com). The advergame is an important tactic that acknowledges the consumer's increasing power by engaging users with entertaining product-related content.

Sales Promotion Metrics

In addition to the IMC metrics presented at the end of the chapter, marketers want to know how their sales promotions contribute to the overall communication goals. For example, if the firm desires increased Web site traffic, how much came from the display ad and how much from the online contest? Which group of users had a higher conversion rate to sales at the site? Obviously the selected metric depends on campaign goals. Symantec will want to measure the number of users who sampled its free online virus scan, and how many subsequently purchased the software.

As an example, Russell Athletics teamed with ESPN in 2003 to draw traffic to ESPN.com and build a database of prospects for Russell Athletics (Linkner, 2004). The athletic apparel company created an online contest based on its sponsorship of college football's Bowl Championship Series (BCS). Russell ran television spots on the ESPN Motion video channel that encouraged viewers to visit ESPN.com to pick 10 winners in the BCS. The highest-scoring winners each week received Russell Athletic jerseys and the top entry over a longer time period received a trip to the BCS Championship game. To measure the campaign's success, Russell Athletics and ESPN gathered the following metrics:

- 500,000 viewed the Russell Athletics television spot (traffic to ESPN.com objective).
- 21 million visited ESPN.com (number of impressions on the site).
- 85,000 men in the target age group visited the game site.
- 20,000 of the target group entered the game.
- 34 percent of contest participants asked for ongoing communication from Russell Athletics (database objective).

Obviously marketers must plan to collect this information prior to beginning the sales promotion campaign, and continuously monitor the results. Online technologies make it easy.

DIRECT MARKETING

According to the Direct Marketing Association, **direct marketing** is "any direct communication to a consumer or business recipient that is designed to generate a response in the form of an order (*direct order*), a request for further information (*lead generation*), and/or a visit to a store or other place of business for purchase of specific a product(s) or service(s) (*traffic generation*)" (www.the-dma.org). It includes such techniques as telemarketing, outgoing e-mail, and postal mail—of which catalog marketing is a big part. Targeted online ads and other forms of advertising and sales promotions that solicit a direct response are also considered direct marketing. For simplicity, and because e-mail is the internet's "killer app," we focus our discussion of direct marketing communication on this application and its wireless offspring, **text messaging**—also called **short message services (SMS)**. In addition, we touch upon multimedia message services (MMS) and instant messaging (IM) because of their potential to become valuable marketing tactics (see the "Let's Get Technical" box). In Chapter 15 we discuss e-mail's customer relationship–building implications.

E-Mail

With 2.4 trillion e-mails a year flying over the internet in the U.S. alone, it is still the internet's killer application—used by 92 percent of internet users (according to Pew Internet & the American Life).

E-mail remains the most important communication technique for building customer relationships, as evidenced by the 94 percent of marketers investing in e-mail campaigns (according to Forrester Research). E-mail marketing is second only to search marketing in marketing spend. E-mail is the most often used marketing tactic in the B2B market, used by 84 percent of the business respondents according to a survey conducted by MarketingProfs and Forrester Research (search marketing and Webinars were the only other digital tactics used by over half of the respondents).

LET'S GET TECHNICAL

Instant Messaging

Your company has two offices: one in the United States and one in India. As the director of marketing and public relations, it is your responsibility to facilitate communication between the product development team in India and the marketing and sales teams in the United States. Due to budget limitations, you need a low-cost, reliable solution, and the phone company has been unwilling to negotiate beyond its corporate packages. The teams are currently communicating via e-mail, but they are disappointed with the lag time—it often takes 45 minutes to get a simple questioned answered. An old technology—instant messaging—is now being reapplied in the business world, and it is changing the way businesspeople communicate worldwide.

Instant messaging (IM) has taken internet users by storm. Even though e-mail was the most rapidly adopted form of communication to date, instant messaging beats the speed of e-mail and maintains all of its other handy features.

Once the user is logged on, he or she views a list of contacts, which is often referred to as a buddy list or contact list. The list indicates each contact's status: online, off-line, away, or idle. The list updates dynamically as friends and associates enter and exit the online world.

Sometimes instant messaging user names are exchanged instead of e-mail addresses, especially among students of all ages. Students are known for

displaying their entire days' schedules in an away message, thereby apprising friends of their whereabouts. To send an instant message to another user, the user has to be online. Double-clicking a name on the buddy list initiates a conversation in most clients. A separate window opens, in which one types a message: "hi, how are you?" Only the two users can see the message and subsequent text.

In addition to instant messages, most clients offer a variety of features:

- *Chat rooms.* Multiple users can all engage in one conversation.
- *Hyperlinks.* Users can send each other active links to Web sites.
- *Files.* Users instant messaging each other can send files (i.e., Microsoft Word documents) to one another.
- *Talk.* With a microphone and speakers attached to the PC, users can talk to each other over the internet.
- *Videoconference.* With a Web camera connected to the PC, users can engage in videoconferencing.
- *Streaming information.* Up-to-date news, stock quotes, and other information can be displayed in the client application.

ICQ ("I Seek You") is considered to be the first instant messaging client. In November 1996, four Israeli entrepreneurs founded Mirabilis, Ltd., the company that developed ICQ. The thought

(*continued*)

(continued)

behind the instant messaging concept was to create interpersonal communication online. The four noticed that the world was quickly adopting surfing and browsing online and wanted to create a simple solution for people to find and talk to each other. Just six months after its release, ICQ had 850,000 registered users and was considered the "World's Largest Internet Online Communication Network." By May 2002, ICQ had been downloaded more than 200 million times from CNET.com, and ICQ claimed to have 150 million registered users in 2004. ICQ believes that its success is due to viral marketing, for the software was never formally marketed. Emanuel Rosen, expert author on word-of-mouth marketing, discusses the ICQ phenomenon in his book titled *The Anatomy of Buzz*. According to Rosen, the "marketing" occurs when the ICQ client asks users if it can scan the user's e-mail address book to send friends and family an invitation to join the ICQ community.

Shortly after ICQ took off, other Web providers developed instant messaging clients. Today, AOL's Instant Messenger rivals ICQ. Microsoft's Windows Messenger and Yahoo! Messenger also offer similar features free of charge. Windows Messenger is popular among businesspersons because it is preinstalled in Microsoft Windows.

As the number of clients available increased, avid users faced a dilemma—friends they wanted to talk to were all using different clients. Rival firms attempted to retain market share by refusing to allow their clients to interoperate. The Internet Engineering Task Force (IETF) has not been able to gain agreement on a standard protocol for instant messaging. As a result, utilities were developed to allow users to communicate with users of different clients all at once. Examples include Pidgin, Trillian, Adium, and Miranda.

After the success of instant messaging using stand-alone clients, large software developers took note and began adding the feature to corporate communication packages. Microsoft's Office Communication Server allows companies to run their own instant messaging network. This approach addresses security and privacy issues that companies often face. Office Communication Server interfaces with Microsoft Office and SharePoint, which is a file-sharing and team-collaboration package. Microsoft developers claim that instant messaging fits better with these programs so that the conversation is discussed in context.

Although corporate instant messaging solutions have been on the market for a few years, they have not been widely adopted. Most companies use one of two tactics: use free clients to communicate within the company or block instant messaging completely.

E-mail has not been replaced by RSS feeds, blogs, and social networking. In fact, e-mail is how people communicate with others they meet online in the social media. E-mail is a word-of-mouse tool when consumers communicate about products with each other. It is the way companies send promotional offers or company announcements to customers. E-mail is used to build a buzz about products. Perhaps this will change when blog and RSS feed adoption increases to 90 percent, but that is unlikely in the near future.

E-mail has several advantages over postal direct mail (Exhibit 13.17). First, it requires no postage or printing charges. The average cost of an e-mail message is less than $0.01, compared to $0.50 to $2.00 for direct mail. Second, e-mail offers an immediate and convenient avenue for direct response; in fact, e-mail often directs users to Web sites using hyperlinks. Third, and perhaps most important, e-mail can be automatically individualized to meet the needs of specific users. For example, Exhibit 13.18 displays a monthly e-mail from MCI regarding American Airlines frequent flyer miles earned via long-distance calls. Similarly, marketers use e-mail for behavioral targeting. For example, an Expedia customer receives an e-mail about a particular travel destination after she searched flights on the Web site. Finally, e-mail is quicker than postal mail.

	E-Mail	Postal Mail
Delivery cost per thousand	$30	$500
Creative costs to develop	$1,000	$17,000
Click-through rate	10%	N/A
Customer conversion rate	5%	3%
Execution time	3 weeks	3 months
Response time	48 hours	3 weeks

EXHIBIT 13.17 Metrics for Electronic and Postal Mail

Source: Jupiter Communications as cited in "E-Mail and the Different Levels of ROI," available at www.boldfish.com (accessed on November 17, 2001).

Conversely, e-mail must be delivered, opened, and acted upon in order to work. E-mail's disadvantages include the difficulty of making it though an ISP's spam filters (in 2004 AOL became famous for blocking nearly 80 percent of incoming e-mail, and it still blocks 75 percent of the 2 billion e-mails coming to members each day). E-mail software, such as Microsoft Outlook, also use spam filtering at the user's computer. Jupiter Research estimates that 17 percent of all e-mail that users agree to receive is erroneously blocked, which costs firms $230 million a year. Consumers are much more upset about spam than they are about unsolicited postal mail and might not open anything looking like spam.

Then there is the difficulty in finding appropriate e-mail lists. While many highly targeted and accurate direct-mail lists exist for postal addresses, e-mail lists are hard to obtain and maintain. Lists can be built any of three ways: (1) generated through Web site registrations, subscription registrations, or purchase records (the most responsive

---

Date: Mon, 14 Feb 2002 09:13:14 -0500
To: Judy Strauss <jstrauss@unr.edu>
From: MCI WorldCom <statement@email.mciworld.com>
Subject: Monthly Mileage Statement

Dear Judy Strauss,

Your monthly statement helps you keep track of the AAdvantage miles you're earning with the MCI/AAdvantage program.

MCI WorldCom Account Number: XXX
American Airlines Frequent Flyer Number: XXX

MCI AADVANTAGE MILES EARNED

ON YOUR LAST BILL:
PROGRAM TO DATE:

160
44785

See your miles online anytime. Go to Online Account Manager at www.mci.com/service.

AAdvantage miles represented in this statement reflect your prior month's balance. These AAdvantage miles have been sent for posting to your American Airlines AAdvantage account. Please allow 6–8 weeks for AAdvantage miles earned to appear on your account.

EXHIBIT 13.18 Individualized E-Mail to Account Holder

list members); (2) rented from a list broker; or (3) harvested from newsgroup postings or online e-mail directories—though this practice is questionable for reasons to be mentioned shortly. Only 15 percent of the 150 million U.S. postal addresses can be associated with e-mail addresses that identify particular individuals (as compared with about 75 million phone numbers connected to postal addresses). ("The Value of a Corporate E-Mail Address," 2001.) Thus, even though nearly 70 percent of the U.S. population has one or more e-mail addresses, at this time it is difficult to match a list of these e-mail addresses with individual customers and prospects in a firm's database. And as soon as a good list exists, individuals change their e-mail addresses—a problem because no forwarding system for e-mail addresses exists like the ones for telephone and postal addresses.

E-marketers must remember that e-mail is not simply postal mail minus the paper and postage. E-mail offers the chance for real dialogue with individual customers, as well as a way to develop broad and deep customer relationships instead of merely using it to acquire customers. Companies can use outgoing e-mail to make announcements, to send promotional offers, or to communicate anything important and relevant to stakeholders. When Pendleton Mills e-mailed customers in 2006 with an offer of 20 percent off already discounted items, 33 percent clicked on the mail—the majority within three hours of the mailing's start. When Amazon tested free shipping on orders over $49 in 2001 and over $25 in 2003, CEO Jeff Bezos sent a message to Amazon's customers informing them of the new offering. Microsoft e-mails registered users when new software patches were available for download. Many firms send out periodic e-mail newsletters, an excellent tool for communicating with clients; small wonder that 80 percent of U.S. online customers enjoy receiving them. E-mail newsletters are a growth area because they provide many benefits. They:

- Regularly and legitimately promote the company name to clients.
- Personalize the communication with tailored content.

- Position the company as an expert in a subject.
- Point recipients back to the company Web site.
- Make it easy for clients to pass along the information to others.
- Pay for themselves by carrying small advertisements.

Virtual postcards are another alternative. Firms send e-mail to users informing them of a Web site address and claim number for viewing a digital postcard. Usually the firm uses its own site or a special fulfillment site because commercial sites such as Blue Mountain Arts do not allow postcards to be sent in bulk. IKEA sent e-mail postcards to promote its San Francisco store opening; Johnson & Johnson sent postcards to its target market for the adolescent skin care brand, Clean & Clear. The postcards included audio, and kids could even record their own voices and send additional postcards to friends, all with the Clean & Clear message, of course (thus initiating viral marketing).

Permission Marketing: Opt-In, Opt-Out

When renting e-mail address lists from list brokers, marketers should search for lists that are guaranteed to be 100 percent opt-in. The opt-in qualification means that users have voluntarily given permission to receive commercial e-mail about topics of interest to them. NetCreations' PostMaster Direct is such a list broker, with more than 50 million opt-in names and e-mail addresses, 13 million of which are segmented by 235 countries outside of the United States (www.netcreations.com). Brokers rent lists rather than sell them because they prefer to charge a fee for each mailing. The cost to rent from Net Creations is about $0.15 per name ($150 CPM—cost per thousand) for B2C market lists, and $250 CPM for the B2B market. Compare this rate to a typical B2C postal mail list rental at $20 CPM.

Web users have many opportunities to opt-in to mailing lists at Web sites, often by simply checking a box and entering an e-mail address. Research shows that lists with opt-in members get much higher response than do lists without. Marketing messages to opt-in lists can generate response rates of up to 90 percent, quite good when compared to 0.15 percent click-through rates on banner ads. For instance, Ticketmaster reported a 90 percent click-through on a mailing offering additional merchandise to Bruce Springsteen fans who had already bought a ticket for an upcoming concert. Opt-in lists may be successful, in large part, because users often receive coupons, cash, or products for responding. With this technique, marketers are shifting marketing dollars directly to consumers for rewards in lieu of purchasing advertising space.

Opt-out is similar to opt-in; however, users have to uncheck the box on a Web page to prevent being put on the e-mail list. Some marketers question this practice because users do not always read a Web page thoroughly enough to evaluate the meaning of checked boxes and, therefore, may be surprised and upset at receiving e-mail later. Some U.S. legislators have proposed laws banning opt-out e-mail.

Opt-in techniques are part of a bigger traditional marketing strategy called **permission marketing**. According to Seth Godin (1999), permission marketing is about turning strangers into customers. How to make this conversion? Ask people what they are interested in, ask permission to send them information, and then do it in an entertaining, educational, or interesting manner. We expect opt-in techniques to evolve and grow considerably over the next few years.

Rules for Successful E-Mail Marketing

Knowing how to use e-mail that gets through spam filters, is opened by recipients, and is acted upon, is as much science as art. The Direct Marketing Association, among others, constantly reports on the most effective techniques. Obviously, tactics vary by industry, but the following are some general guidelines:

- Use opt-in to build your lists because your reputation for being customer oriented is more important than having a large list.
- Check your e-mail reputation to see if it will make it through ISP filters. Check e-mail blacklists and use a service such as Return Path's Sender Score Reputation Manager, that screens for 60 reputation variables.

- Use an e-mail address that is professional. Senders from Yahoo, Hotmail, and even GMail are more likely to be blocked than company or education e-mail addresses. For example, the best e-mail address is Firstname.Lastname@companyname.com or Firstname.Lastname@university.edu.
- Make it easy for users to unsubscribe. This builds trust.
- Use microsegmentation, sending offers to smaller lists of relevant customers and personalize them. The Expedia e-mail just mentioned is a perfect example, as are automated shipping confirmation e-mails.
- A small improvement in creative layout and multimedia use in e-mail can raise response rates up to 75 percent, according to MailerMailer.com. Test HTML e-mail approaches to see which pulls best for various offers.
- Give recipients plenty of opportunities to engage with the e-mail and act on the offer. High performing e-mails offer an average of 27 links per message, according to the Peppers and Rogers Group (www.1to1.com).
- Use metrics to track the open rates, response rates, and ROI. Also, consider the cost of non-responses which may contribute to lower brand equity if your mail is perceived as spam (and narrow the list afterward).

As previously mentioned, many organizations study effective e-mail marketing. They provide lots of advice about what works, considering everything from how to build the best opt-in list, to the creative look and subject lines, and to the unsubscribe Web page and how it might be used to build relationships. The previous list was just a sampling—much more information is available online for e-mail marketers.

Viral Marketing

Viral marketing is a bad name for a great technique. When individuals forward e-mail to friends, coworkers, family, and others on their e-mail lists, they are using what we like to call *word-of-mouse.* More commonly known as **viral marketing**, it is the online equivalent of word-of-mouth—and it is free. Viral marketing works well as long as the recipient's friends are in the firm's target market. Hotmail started with only a $50,000 promotion budget (as compared with the $50 to $100 million needed to launch a brand off-line). The firm simply sent some e-mail telling folks about its Web-based e-mail service, and within six months the firm had 1 million registered users (Ransdell, 1999). Eighteen months after the launch, it had 12 million subscribers and Microsoft acquired the firm for $400 million in Microsoft stock.

Every marketer wants a campaign that goes viral, yet few achieve it. *Will it Blend?*, the Doritos Super Bowl consumer-created TV commercials, and many YouTube videos achieve this status, but it is unpredictable and there is lots of competition online for entertaining and engaging video and contests. Oftentimes the huge success of a viral video is a surprise—and more often it is a disappointment that the great video that caused everyone at work to laugh their heads off didn't go viral. Much can be learned by studying the successes, but beware because cultural tastes change quickly.

Other viral marketing success stories include Dell, the six-month 0 to 50 percent MP3 adoption rate, JibJab.com's animated political cartoon featuring President Bush and Sen. John Kerry that got 4.5 million visitors with no advertising, and the *Blair Witch Project* film. Lions Gate films sent 16,000 people e-mail for 30 days prior to the 1999 opening of *American Psycho.* The twist that made it work as viral marketing is that the e-mails were from the film's main character, a serial killer. Recipients got a kick out of passing these notes to others.

In Europe, Red Zac, an electronics retailer, offered an online "quiz duel" game that consumers played by challenging a friend via e-mail (Valerius, 2004). Both participants then answered five questions whenever convenient, but the Web site presented it as a live quiz show for the last participant by matching the two sets of player responses. During the game, participants saw ads for Hewlett-Packard notebook computers. Within four weeks of the campaign start, 60,000 duels were played and notebook sales at Red Zac increased by 35 percent.

Perhaps the most famous recent campaign to go viral was Burger King's Subservient Chicken (Exhibit 13.19). At www.subservientchicken.com, users type commands into the box and the chicken, an actor in a chicken suit, performs as commanded. This Web site drew 14 million visitors in the first year.

Text Messaging

Short message services (SMS) are up to 160 characters of text sent by one user to another over the internet, usually with a cell phone or PDA. In the United States, SMS is usually commonly known as **text messaging**, and is used by 35 percent of internet users (according to Pew Internet & the American Life). It is different from **instant messaging (IM)**, short messages sent among users who are online at the same time (used by 39 percent of internet users). IM is used both by consumers and employees (who have a quick question needing attention). Most commercial use of IM today involves the ads delivered to IM screens as users send messages to one another (such as movie ads presented to AOL's 30 million subscribers using its AIM product). Multimedia message service (MMS) involves multimedia content, but is not commonly in use yet because handheld receiving appliances are generally not MMS capable.

SMS differs from e-mail because users can receive the messages much more easily and instantly, on cell phones or pop-up browser windows on the PC. SMS, which uses a store-and-send technology that only holds messages for a few days, is particularly attractive to cell phone users because they can communicate quickly and inexpensively. When users send short text messages, they are either charged cell phone minutes or by the message, but the cost is minimal compared to using the cell phone for a conversation. In addition, accessing SMS is easy because users do not have to open e-mail or

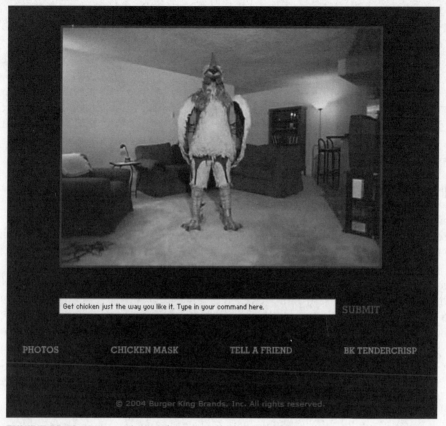

Get chicken just the way you like it. Type in your command here.   SUBMIT

PHOTOS   CHICKEN MASK   TELL A FRIEND   BK TENDERCRISP

EXHIBIT 13.19   Burger King's Subservient Chicken Goes Viral
Source: www.subservientchicken.com.

other software to send or receive. Instead, they simply type the message on the phone keyboard. In Japan, consumers are reportedly so adept at this they have created what is called the "thumb culture" (because they rapidly type out messages using their thumbs).

By one estimate, 200 billion short text messages a month were flying between mobile phones worldwide by the end of 2002 (Silk, 2001). European text message penetration is approximately 71 percent (Mandel, 2004). U.S. penetration depends on age group: 18–24 (76%), 25–34 (58%), 35–44 (43%), 45–64 (28%), and over 64 (19%) (according to Forrester Research in 2006). Japanese use is even higher than that of Europe. SMS use continues to grow in all industrialized nations.

How can marketers capitalize on SMS use? Most experts agree that marketers can build relationships by sending permission-based information to customers when and where they want to receive it. To be successful, the messages should be short, personalized, interactive, and relevant. Some customers might want to receive an SMS warning about pending natural disasters from their insurance firm, an SMS notification of an upcoming flight delay, or notification of an overnight shipment. In Germany, opt-in customers of local clubs receive text messages each week that announce the band playing during the upcoming weekend.

In one interesting example, Heineken, the global beer brand, used an SMS sales promotion to capitalize on the British pub tradition of quiz nights. Typically a quiz night consists of a loyal pub customer shouting out a series of questions to which other customers answer on paper score sheets. Winners receive free pints or meals. Using a combination of online and off-line promotion, Heineken placed point-of-purchase signs in pubs inviting customers to call a phone number from cell phones or other mobile devices, and type in the word "play" as a text message (SMS). In response, the customer received a series of three multiple-choice questions to answer. Correctly answering all the questions scored a food or beverage prize to be redeemed by giving a special verifiable number to the bartender—and 20 percent of all players won. "Feedback was that it was a great promotion . . . consumers found it fun and sellers found it to be a hook," said Iain Newell, marketing controller at Interbrew, which owns the Heineken brand.

Location-Based Marketing

A few marketers have experimented with **location-based marketing**: promotional offers that are pushed to mobile devices and customized based on the user's physical location. This is different from the huge local online marketing discussed in Chapter 1—including classifieds, Craigslist, eBay, and other local e-commerce. The technology behind location-based marketing is either a global positioning system (GPS) in a handheld device or automobile (telematics) or the cell phone system. Lycos spent $1.2 million in 2001 turning some Boston and New York taxicabs into animated billboards by sending relevant ads based on the cab's physical location. The GPS device sent physical coordinates to the ad server, which then returned financial ads when the cab was in the financial district, and so forth.

Google is on the leading edge with its local text messing service. Simply send a text to Google (466453) and put a query in it, such as "weather NYC," "pizza san francisco," or "define SMS," and Google immediately returns a text message with the weather, pizza restaurant locations, or

definition (Exhibit 13.20). The service is free, but Google will certainly use advertising to support it.

In one study of 3,300 people in 11 countries, 88 percent said they would be receptive to getting coupons on their mobile devices for redeeming at a store near their physical location (Pastore, 2002a). Imagine receiving a short text message on your cell phone offering a free beverage while driving by your favorite restaurant!

Direct Marketing Metrics

Response rate is the most appropriate metric for any direct marketing campaign. Additionally, many firms use direct tactics to build databases and measure success in terms of customer record growth. E-mail marketers collect metrics on every mouse click, desiring to know which offers pull best, which message content brings the greatest response, when is the best time to send e-mail for maximum response (by the way, it is Monday between 6 A.M. and 10 A.M. Eastern time), and so forth. Many of these metrics are presented later in the chapter.

E-mail receives a 3 percent to 10 percent click-through to the sponsor's Web site and an average 5 percent conversion rate (Pricewater houseCoopers, 2002; Saunders, 2001); however, as we've already said, the right list and offer can yield much higher click-throughs. Catalog companies and retailers both realize more than 9 percent click-throughs on e-mail campaigns run through Google's DoubleClick ("DoubleClick Ad Serving," 2002). SMS marketers also study response rates (see Exhibit 13.21). In a study of more than 200 SMS campaigns, the response performance was outstanding (www.enpocket.com):

- 94 percent of messages were read by recipients.
- 23 percent showed or forwarded messages to a friend.
- 15 percent to 27 percent of recipients responded to SMS campaigns.
- Cost per response was $1.92, returning a better ROI than direct postal mail.

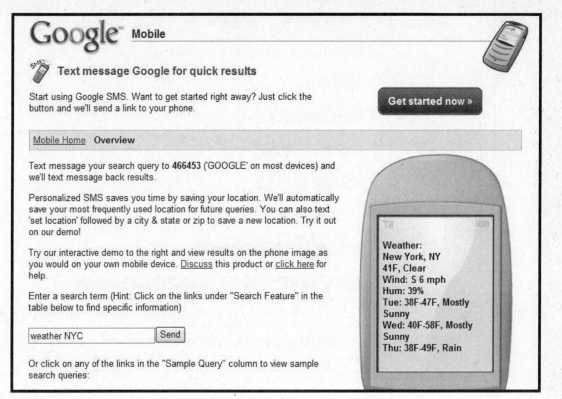

EXHIBIT 13.20   Google Local Text Messaging Service
Source: www.google.com/mobile.

Spam

Now for the dirty side of e-mail marketing. Internet users do not like unsolicited e-mail because it shifts the burden of selectivity from sender to recipient. Users developed the term *spam* as a pejorative reference to this type of e-mail. It was made illegal in the United States with the CAN-SPAM Act; however, thus far it appears to have little ability to stop spam (see Chapter 5). Marketers must be careful because viral marketing can work in reverse as well. Recipients of e-mail perceived as spam can vent their opposition to thousands of users in blogs and to friends on e-mail lists, thereby quickly generating negative publicity for the organization. The Nike Corporation is so sensitive to spam that it published an antispam policy that reads as follows:

Nike does not sell, trade, or otherwise transfer outside the company personally identifiable information that visitors voluntarily provide in any registration or contest submission. This information is used to better understand visitors' use of Nike's site and to support related transactions made on the site.

However, this data in an aggregate form may be provided to other parties for marketing, advertising, or other uses. For example, the majority of visitors to Nike.com are boys age 8 to 18. Nike may also use e-mail addresses and other personally identifiable information to contact visitors who communicate with us. For example, we direct e-mail to visitors who provide us with their e-mail addresses for specific purposes such as receiving our e-mail newsletters or being notified if they have won one of our contests. Each e-mail newsletter always

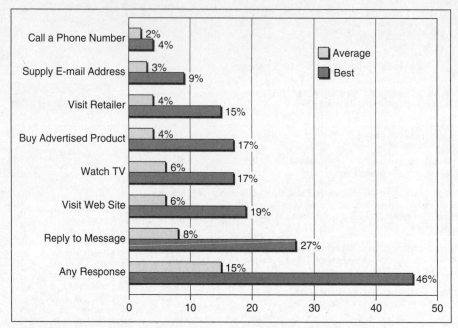

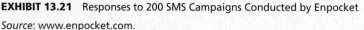

EXHIBIT 13.21   Responses to 200 SMS Campaigns Conducted by Enpocket

Source: www.enpocket.com.

contains instructions on how to discontinue receipt of the newsletter. However, if a visitor at anytime chooses to no longer receive such information and opt-out from any future mailings, they should simply reply to any Nike e-mail sent to them and type UNSUBSCRIBE as the subject of their reply.

Spammers routinely harvest e-mail addresses from newsgroup postings (e.g., Google Groups) and then spam all the newsgroup members. Spam lists can also be generated from public directories such as those provided by many universities to look up student e-mail addresses. Spammers often hide their return e-mail addresses so that the recipients cannot reply. Other unscrupulous tactics include spamming through a legitimate organization's e-mail server so that the message appears to come from an employee of that organization.

Incidentally, spam is a problem in the B2B market as well as the B2C market. Editorial staffs

from the media complain about getting spam from public relations personnel at firms. James Fallows, a journalist from *The Industry Standard*, gave an example of the typical note he receives from folks he has never met nor heard of:

> Subject: New Company Meeting
> From: Frankie@AcmePR.com
>
> Hi Jim,
>
> My client will be in the area on Wednesday, April 12, is there any way you could take a quick meeting? [Blah, blah, blah about the company.] Please let me know ASAP for a meeting, thanks!
> Best, Frankie

Some measures have been put in place to limit spam. Many moderated groups filter spam, and most e-mail programs offer users the option to filter spam as well. Also, a number of suits filed by ISPs seek to recover costs from spammers for the strain on their systems from the tremendous number of spam messages. Remember that all unsolicited e-mail is considered spam; still, as with direct mail, when the e-mail is appropriate and useful to the recipient, it is welcomed, unsolicited or not.

It is increasingly common for opt-in lists to remind users that they are not being spammed. Usually a disclaimer appears right at the beginning of the message, "You are receiving this message because you requested to be notified about. . . ." The message also advises users how they can easily unsubscribe from the list. This notification is important because many users do not realize that they opted-in—especially if they did so far in the past or in an unrelated context.

Privacy

Databases drive e-mail marketing. Such a database requires collecting personal information, both online and off-line, and using it to send commercial e-mail, customized Web pages, display ads, and more. Astute marketers have found that consumers will readily give personal information to firms that use it to provide value and that do not share it with others unless given permission. For example, Amazon.com has implicit permission to collect customers' purchase information in the database and serve it

collectively to others looking for book recommendations. Users don't mind this service because they receive valuable information and their privacy is guarded on an individual level. Amazon also has permission to send customers e-mail notification of books that might interest each individual. When Amazon announced that it would share customer databases with partners, it faced a huge media backlash. This reaction proves, once again, that firms that desire to build customer relationships must guard the privacy of customer data (see the "Let's Get Technical" box). This topic is discussed more thoroughly in Chapters 5 and 14.

PERSONAL SELLING

The fifth traditional tool, personal selling, involves real time conversation between a salesperson and customer, either face-to-face or with some technology mediator, such as the telephone or computer. It is not used much online because when a salesperson is involved, it is simply more effective to use the telephone or to visit the prospect in person. However, some companies provide real time sales assistance online. Land's End has a live chat feature. Users can open it and ask questions about products in a real time chat with a customer service representative. The rep

LET'S GET TECHNICAL

Spyware

A goofy-looking purple gorilla keeps popping up on your screen, and you do not know where it came from. Its prevalence and persistence is getting on your nerves. However, it is potentially performing much more damage behind the scenes. The purple gorilla is part of a spyware program, known as Bonzi Buddy, which can broadcast your personal information onto the internet. But just how do you get rid of the pesky guy?

As far too many internet users have experienced, spyware is everywhere on the net. Any type of

program that is downloaded to your computer that collects information about you can be considered spyware. Spyware can be downloaded and installed on your computer without you ever knowing, and it can also transmit the information it collects about you to a third party without being detected. For example, common spyware programs send a list of the MP3s on your computer or a list of the Web sites you recently visited. They can also send the contents of your address book or password and banking information.

Spyware programs that collect information about your surfing habits to feed you with focused

(continued)

(continued)

advertisements are often considered adware. Spyware programs that perform malicious activity, such as retrieving your bank account number, are called malware. The information that is collected is stored in large databases. Adware is extremely common online, and a Web site owner can distribute it to visitors in order to track their viewing habits and preferences. Although Web site owners and developers can use this information to make sites more in-tune with customer preferences, they are more interested in this information because of its ability to sell advertising space.

Web site owners can obtain the adware software from media networks. The purpose of media network companies is to track and record the behavior of online consumers. The information is stored in large databases and is used to target consumers. When you visit a site that is associated with the media network, the adware is downloaded and starts monitoring your internet usage. As it records your usage, it can determine certain demographic information about you. For example, if you visit babystyle.com, it might infer that you are a new parent or grandparent. Media networks lease the advertising space on Web sites and, in turn, sell it to advertisers. The media network then uses your profile to provide targeted advertisements the next time you visit a site in its association, such as a banner ad sold to a diaper company. When advertisers purchase ads from the media network, they are guaranteed a certain number of impressions, or the number of times their ad is displayed on a user's page.

In order for spyware to infect a computer, the computer user must visit a Web site that has the spyware program embedded in the programming code for the Web site. Spyware can also be triggered accidentally by the user when installing a regular program which is infested with spyware.

The origin of spyware is actually cookies, which are small files downloaded to and stored on the user's computer. Cookies were used by Web developers to collect usability information and were generally harmless. For example, sites that recognize who you are when you visit them most likely stored a cookie on your computer and read it upon your return to the site. The user could use his or her browser's settings to accept or reject cookies.

Today's spyware can be extremely dangerous because the information collected can end up anywhere. Spyware can also do any of the following:

- Flood your computer with pop-up advertisements
- Send spam to your e-mail inbox
- Slow down your internet connection speed
- Slow down your computer's performance
- Crash your computer

Thousands of different spyware programs exist online. Names of software to watch out for include: CoolWebSearch, Internet Optimizer aka DyFuCa, Zango, HuntBar aka WinTools or Adware, Websearch, Movieland aka Moviepass.tv or Popcorn.net, and Zlob Trojan.

Software that specifically finds and removes spyware should be installed on all computers that are connected to the internet. Some antivirus software companies have developed product line extensions to handle spyware. Popular and reliable anti-spyware programs include AdAware, Spybot, and Pest Patrol. Microsoft even includes a free anti-spyware program, Windows Defender, with its Vista operating system. Nonetheless, the easiest way to reduce spyware instances on your computer is to not download something unless you know it is from a reliable source.

can also push Web pages directly to the customer so she can view the product and take the order during the chat session.

The internet can also effectively generate leads for salespeople. It is common for companies to request e-mail and other contact information when a user downloads a white paper (special report on a topic, usually in a PDF file). Also, when business people attend online webinars, they register. The companies serving white papers or hosting webinars collect contact information and follow-up with a sales contact. There are many other ways of generating leads in the B2B market using online approaches.

IMC METRICS

Savvy marketers set specific objectives for their IMC campaigns and then track progress toward those goals by monitoring appropriate metrics. Exhibit 13.22 displays many of the commonly used measurements along with industry averages. Note that individual results vary widely; however, the following generalizations are based on research studies. As you review these comments, remember that the purpose of marketing is to create exchanges. The most important metrics are the number and dollar amount of sales, and all the rest help improve those numbers in either the short or long term.

Effectiveness Evidence

When viewed as a direct-response medium, display ads are generally ineffective: Only 0.15 percent of all users click on them. However, many individual firms have received stunning click-through results, as seen in this chapter.

Metric	Definition/formula	Online Averages
CPM	Cost per thousand impressions CPM = [Total Cost/(Impressions)]/1000	$7 to $15 for banners[1] $75 and $200 for e-mail ads[2] $20 and $40 for e-mail newsletter[2]
Cost per message	Cost to send an e-mail Cost = Number of E-mails/Total Cost	Less than $0.01[3]
Opt-out rate	Percent who opt-out of an e-mail list Rate = Opt-Out Number/Total Number	Ranges between 0.2% and 0.5%[4]
Opt-out rate		Average 0.5% in Q4 2005
Response time	Time between sending e-mail and click-through response	85% within 48 hours[3]
Site stickiness	Length of stay as tracked on Web site log	Varies 44 seconds per page[5]
Click-Through Rate (CTR)	Number of clicks as percent of total impressions CTR = Clicks/Impressions	0.3% – 0.8% for banners[3,6] 2.4% rich media ads[6] 3.2% – 10% opt-in e-mail[3,7]
Click-Through Rate—Acquisition rate	Click-Through — Acquisition rate	Average 6.23% in Q4 2005
Click-Through Rate—Retention rate	Click-Through Rate — Retention rate	Average 10.46% in Q4 2005
Visitors resulting from click-through	A pageview(s) on Web site resulting from a click Visitors = Impressions/Click-Through %	Varies widely
Cost per Click (CPC)	Cost for each visitor from ad click CPC = Total Ad Cost/Clicks	Varies widely Google.com ranges from a $0.15 to $15.00 per click

(continued)

Metric	Definition/formula	Online Averages
Cost per lead (CPL)	Pay only for delivered leads from special offer CPL = Cost / Number of Leads	25 cents to $2.50, B2B prices at the high end[1] $12.97 for internet gambling.[8]
Conversion Rate	Percent of people who purchased from total number of visitors Conversion Rate = Orders / Visitors	1.8% for Web sites[9] 5% for e-mail[7]
Cost per order equation (CPO)	Cost of each order resulting from click-through visit CPO = Total Ad Cost/Orders	Varies widely
Customer Acquisition Cost (CAC)	Total marketing costs to acquire a customer	Varies by industry $82 for online retail pure plays; $31 for multi-channel brick and mortar retailers[10]
E-mails sent per ESP (E-mail service provider)		19.27 m 0.5% in Q4 2005
Customer drop-off rates	shopping cart abandonment	66% of consumers[11]

EXHIBIT 13.22 IMC Metrics and Industry Averages

Sources: [1]Hallerman (2002); [2]data from www.eMarketer.com; [3]Saunders (2001); [4]Gallogly and Rolls (2002); [5]data from www.nielsen-netratings.com; [6]"DoubleClick Ad Serving . . ." (2002); [7]PricewaterhouseCoopers, LLP (2002); [8]"Gambling Lawsuit Filed . . ." (2004) (www.computerworld.com); [9]data from shop.org; [10]data from www.computerworld.com; [11]Web site Traffic Analysis (www.computerworld.com).

According to research, when display ads are viewed as branding media, they increase brand awareness and message association, and they build brand favorability and purchase intent (see www.iab.net). In three studies, online ads that were bigger, were placed as interstitials, or contained rich multimedia delivered an even greater impact. For example, skyscrapers and large rectangles were found to be three to six times more effective than standard size banners in increasing brand awareness (Pastore, 2001). These findings hold today—bigger and more novel ads are noticed more frequently.

Increasing evidence indicates that online and off-line advertising work well together, such as with the 2006 Wendy's "Kick for a Million" sweepstakes and contest, the large number of people who research online and shop off-line, and the huge Web site visitations experienced by GoDaddy after advertising in the Super Bowl.

The best online IMC tactic depends on the target, competition, company, offer, and how novel, engaging, relevant and creative the tactic is. A January 2007 MarketingSherpa study asked online marketers to name the best and worst performing online tactics based on ROI in comparison with other tactics. Paid search and e-mail came out on top, but note that some respondents found these tactics to be the worst (see Exhibit 13.23). Paid search and e-mail are validated in many other studies as being effective tactics, but don't forget that it all depends—a creative and scientific e-marketer can make the lowly banner ad a stellar tactic if used adroitly.

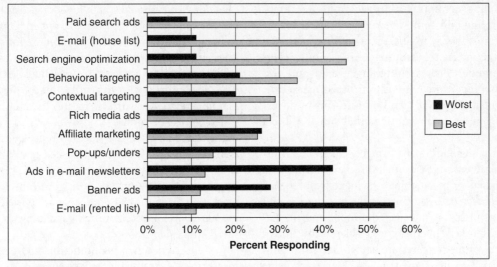

EXHIBIT 13.23 Best and Worst Performing Online IMC Tactics According to U.S. Online Marketers

Source: MarketingSherpa, Inc., January 2007 (as found at www.emarketer.com).

Chapter Summary

Integrated marketing communication (IMC) is a cross-functional process for planning, executing, and monitoring brand communications designed to profitably acquire, retain, and grow customers. Marketers use specific MarCom tools (advertising, sales promotions, marketing public relations, direct marketing, and personal selling) to achieve their communication objectives. After implementation, they measure effectiveness, make any adjustments required, and evaluate results. Marketers' use of the internet for MarCom can be understood in light of the AIDA (awareness, interest, desire, and action) model or the "think, feel, do" hierarchy of effects model. These models suggest that consumers first become aware of and learn about a new product (think), develop a positive or negative attitude about it (feel), and then move to purchasing it (do). Each online tool is more or less effective at particular levels of these models.

Advertising is nonpersonal communication of information through various media, usually persuasive in nature about products and usually paid for by an identified sponsor. Display ads (rectangles, banners, buttons, pop-ups, and sky-scrapers), rich media ads, e-mail advertising, sponsorships (integrating editorial content and advertising), and mobile advertising are the major vehicles for internet advertising. The least expensive type of online advertising is e-mail ads. Content-sponsored advertising for mobile devices is the wireless version of display and other ads that sponsor Web content, similar to commercials that typically support broadcast television programming.

Marketing public relations (MPR) includes brand-related activities and nonpaid, third-party media coverage to positively influence target markets. MPR activities using internet technology include Web site content and online events. Companies build a buzz online by using an online press room, RSS feeds, and providing engaging content online. Sales promotion activities include coupons, rebates, product sampling, contests, sweepstakes, and premiums. Sampling and contests/sweepstakes are among the most widely used sales promotion activities on the internet. Direct marketing online covers techniques such as outgoing e-mail and text messaging, as well as location-based marketing, targeted display ads, and other forms of advertising and sales promotions that solicit a direct response.

Outgoing e-mail is a highly efficient and customizable form of internet direct marketing with potential for maintaining a dialogue with targeted customers. Its disadvantages include the negative image of spam (unsolicited e-mail) and the ISP spam blockers. Internet users dislike spam and, as a result, some measures are being enacted to limit it—such as the CanSpam Act. Marketers using outgoing e-mail should search for address lists that are guaranteed to be 100 percent opt-in. Opt-in techniques are part of a strategy called permission marketing, which offers consumers incentives to willingly accept information in e-mail messages.

Individuals who forward e-mail to other people are using word-of-mouth (sometimes called "word-of-mouse"), also known as viral marketing. Marketers are starting to use permission marketing to send short text messages (SMS) over the internet to cell phones and PDAs. Another emerging technique is location-based marketing, promotional offers that are pushed to mobile devices and customized depending on the user's physical location.

Marketers can apply numerous metrics for measuring IMC campaign effectiveness.

Exercises

REVIEW QUESTIONS

1. What is integrated marketing communication and why is it important?
2. What is the hierarchy of effects model and how does it apply to high- and low-involvement product decisions?
3. What is the difference between brand advertising and direct-response advertising?
4. What are the main vehicles for advertising on the internet?
5. What are the advantages and disadvantages of using the advertising formats of display ads, buttons, skyscrapers, interstitials, and superstititals?
6. In what ways do companies use the internet for marketing public relations, sales promotion, and direct marketing?
7. How does permission marketing differ from viral marketing?
8. Name five rules for effective e-mail marketing.
9. How can a company build a buzz online?
10. What is a microsite? How do e-marketers use it?

12. How effective is online display advertising compared to other media?
13. What danger lies in letting sponsorship blend with content? Defend your position.
14. If you were running an online ad campaign for Nike, how would you allocate your ad budget? Why?
15. Why would manufacturers invite consumers to search for and print coupons from the Web? Could this approach encourage customers who were prepared to pay full price to simply use the Net to lower their costs?
16. Some U.S. sites draw one-third of their visitors from overseas. Do these users dilute the value of advertising at these sites? Why or why not?
17. "You should aim to be consultative not persuasive in the way you use the internet for marketing communication." What does this statement mean? What is the reasoning behind it?
18. Why do you think that text messaging is used so often among employees at work?

DISCUSSION QUESTIONS

11. "The more successful list brokers are in renting their lists, the more they dilute the value of those lists." Do you agree or disagree—and why?

WEB ACTIVITIES

19. Visit Yahoo! and evaluate its advertising widgets. Do you want to use any of them? Do you think they will be successful or not?

20. You have been given the difficult task of researching online marketing communication practices in the soft-drink industry. Do some online searching and list sources that you discover to help with this problem.

21. Find three display ads that you think are particularly effective and three more that are ineffective. Explain your reasons, telling how you might improve the ineffective ads.

22. Identify a company, such as Microsoft, that advertises on TV, the Web, and a print medium. Make copies of ads from that firm and discuss the similarities and differences among them. Is the firm following the IMC concept? Why or why not?

23. Go to www.hotcoupons.com and print a coupon for a retailer in your area. Visit the retailer and interview him or her about the effectiveness of the electronic coupons. How many are redeemed? How long has the offer been running? How often does the retailer change the offer?

24. Flip through a magazine, looking at the ads. Write down each mention of a Web site and in what context the mention appeared. In what percentage of the ads were Web sites mentioned?

CHAPTER 14

New Digital Media

You can't just buy people's attention anymore. You must engage them.

—DAVID LUBARS, BBDO CHAIRMAN

Humans like humans. They hate organizations.

—SETH GODIN, AUTHOR OF PERMISSION MARKETING

74% of Americans are online; 50% of them are part of a social network; 25% of them have joined online communities; 100% of companies need to join the conversation.

—EMARKETER

The primary goal of this chapter is to understand the internet as a medium for efficiently and effectively exchanging marketing communication messages between marketers and their audiences. You will learn how marketers use the social media for both paid and unpaid messages, and how marketers buy and use space on the internet as a communication medium.

After reading this chapter, you will be able to:

- Describe the characteristics of the major physical (off-line) and digital (online) media.
- Differentiate among broadcast, print, narrowcast, and pointcast electronic media.
- Explain how marketers use reputation aggregators for natural, paid, and vertical search.
- Compare and contrast social media communities, blogs, and social networks.
- Outline the main methods for buying media and for evaluating an integrated marketing communication (IMC) campaign's effectiveness.

Halo 3 Launch

Halo 3 is the final chapter in the wildly popular trilogy that includes both video and online versions. The first-person shooter game was created by Bungie Studios and promoted by Microsoft for the Xbox 360 game and entertainment system. Halo 3 went on sale worldwide on September 25, 2007, with a backlog of over a million pre-orders and first-week sales of 3.3 million units. Obviously, Halo 2 players were primed for Halo 3 so they could participate in the battle of Master Chief as he tried to save humankind. Such is the benefit of delivering a great product and gaining loyal customers. Beyond that, Microsoft brilliantly combined physical and digital media using IMC tools to announce the new game and create a buzz.

Off-line, Microsoft formed partnership deals with Burger King (Halo Whopper wrappers and plastic cups), Mountain Dew (a new high-caffeine "game fuel" beverage), Doritos (Halo 3 packaging), 7–11 stores (Halo Slurpee cups and contest with the winner's voice being put into the Halo Wars game), and Pontiac (limited edition Halo 3 G6 GXP street car).

(continued)

(continued)

These co-branded products, licensed merchandising (action figures and toys), and a sponsored race car painted with Halo images helped to spread the word. Microsoft also created cinematic trailers that it showed at off-line electronic product shows and in television ads—such as ESPN and the Discovery Channel. To round out the physical media promotion, Microsoft and Bungie PR efforts resulted in coverage in many publications: "The release of *Halo 3* this week was an event that stretched far beyond our little gaming world. Everyone from the *New York Times* to *Mother Jones* wanted to cover it," according to *Wired* magazine.

Digital media added to the buzz. Bungie Studios slowly released plot teasers and game features using online video documentaries. Developer-created video documentaries, explaining the game's making and ideas behind some of the characters, were available for download and play on the Xbox. Near the launch date, Microsoft posted a "Believe" Web site where users could take unique screen images in a massive visual diorama and use as personal wallpaper with the Halo 3 logo. The story of the Believe site spawned more off-line television ads. Microsoft made the one-month beta testing a competitive event online. Halo 3 invited the first 13,333 Halo 2 players to sign up on the Halo3.com Web site for beta testing. There were other requirements for the beta-testing privilege and some spots were allocated to European community Web sites important for buzz-building. The blogosphere was abuzz with discussions about the game details, newly revealed images, and strategies for being the first to get the new game.

Bridging the physical and digital worlds, launch parties were held on September 24 in selected cities. Microsoft invited fans, bloggers, and journalists to a San Francisco launch party using online meeting invite site Upcoming.com (as well as Microsoft's private invitation site). Honored enthusiasts got to play the game and as predicted spread the buzz online. Some took pictures at the event and uploaded them to their blogs or Tumblr.com and other micro content sites from the party itself, thus, showing how cool they were. The result of all this? First-day sales of Halo 3 topped $170 million and the first 24-hour sales beat many big movie blockbusters. (Note: Much of this information is from Wikipedia and related sources.)

MARKETING COMMUNICATION MEDIA

Microsoft and Bungie Studios used physical (off-line) and digital (online) media in an integrated effort to create this huge success. **Communications media** are tools for disseminating information, such as an online video, the newspaper, and e-mail. For disseminating information, all of these can be either paid or free (such as a paid ad in a newspaper or free brand publicity from a press release). By "free," we mean that marketers do not have to pay for the space to run their message, but they do have costs related to producing the communication piece. **Digital media** are electronic tools used to store, transmit, and receive digitized information, according to Wikipedia. These can also be either paid or free, such as a company's own blog as PR or someone else's Web site that holds a paid display ad. Microsoft used both paid media, such as television ads, and unpaid media—the Believe Web site, online videos, and publicity in off-line media.

The line between these physical (also called traditional or off-line) and digital platforms (often called non-traditional or online) and paid and unpaid media space is blurring more every day. For example, Current.com allows users to submit video "pods," with the highest voted videos being played on Current's cable television programming. When television becomes completely digital in February 2009 and as more sites like iTunes, Hulu.com, and Akimbo.com offer television and movie viewing on computers and MP3 players, the meaning of the terms *off-line* and *online* will continue to lose their distinction—the same fate awaits the terms *traditional media* (newspapers, magazines, TV, radio, outdoors) and *non-traditional media* (everything else, including digital media). Already, newspaper ads and articles are often accessible in either location. Recall also that the medium is not the appliance: TV programming can carry ads that are seen on television and the PC; radio audio transmission can come into many devices, and so forth. Exhibit 14.1 displays many media, categorized as paid/unpaid and physical/digital. We put television programming in the digital category and note that it can be received on a TV set, PC, or elsewhere.

In this environment, the most effective tactics will be those that integrate IMC tools to reach their target markets effectively and efficiently (lowest cost)—regardless of communication channel (as with the Halo 3 introduction). This is especially important because of the high level of multitasking among consumers, as mentioned in previous chapters.

To do this, marketers must know the capabilities, strengths, and weaknesses of each medium. As a frame of reference, recall that only 8.2 percent of paid media is for internet advertising (Exhibit 14.2). Of course, much non-paid marketing communications are not included in this figure. This chapter focuses on digital media used to carry marketing communication messages.

Media Characteristics

Marketers need to understand the characteristics of the major physical media(often called traditional media) as well as the internet's digital media characteristics so they can make appropriate choices when buying promotional space—as did Microsoft for Halo 3. Span of coverage is one important criterion. Electronic media such as network television, radio, cable television, the internet, facsimile (fax) transmission, and cellular phones can be classified as broadcast, narrowcast, and pointcast on the basis of their capability to reach mass audiences, smaller audiences, or even individuals with different messages, respectively. Marketing communication can be sent to an individual (e.g., postal mail or e-mail) or the masses (e.g., newspapers), and can range from broadcast (e.g., television) to pointcast (e.g., e-mail) (Exhibit 14.2). Differences among these and other media allow marketers to select the best combination to achieve their goals. For instance, e-marketers might

	Paid Media Space	Free Media Space (production costs only)
Physical Media	Newspapers Magazines Outdoor (e.g., billboards, busses, sporting events) Other (e.g., bathroom ads)	Postal mail Flyers, posters, brochures, and so on Street buzz activities Other (e.g., publicity and promotions)
Digital Media	Web page/blog ads Paid search (e.g., keyword buys) Paid search site listing Television program ads Ads in e-mail Sponsored mobile content Video game placement	Web site/blog E-mail to list Natural search Free vertical search inclusion Social network profile Online community Virtual world

EXHIBIT 14.1   Media Classification

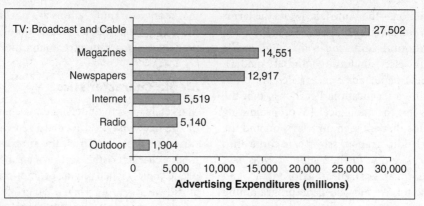

EXHIBIT 14.2 Proportion of Spending for Various Media of $67.5 Billion in the First Half of 2007

Source: Data from TNS Media Intelligence, available at www.tns-mi.com/.

select e-mail if they want to customize an offer to one individual and request an interactive response via clicking on a hyperlink. Exhibit 14.3 compares traditional, physical media with the digital, online media.

BROADCAST MEDIA Broadcast media (TV and radio) have a number of strengths and weaknesses, as reflected in Exhibit 14.3. TV penetration is 98 percent in U.S. households, with one-third owning three or more sets. TV remains the only medium for advertisers wanting to reach large numbers of consumers at one time, but it is costly ($100,000 to $550,000 for 30 seconds of prime

time in the United States). Radio's penetration is also ubiquitous. Almost every household and car has a radio. Radio advertising time is inexpensive ($20 to $200 for 60 seconds) and has excellent local market coverage.

PRINT MEDIA Print media include newspapers (local and national) and magazines. The internet was often compared to print media because its content is text and graphic heavy, and because many traditional print media publishers maintain online versions. However, the increase in broadband use and online video content has changed that image. Unlike television and radio, but like the

Criterion	TV	Radio	Magazine	Newspaper	Direct Mail	Internet
Involvement	passive	passive	active	active	active	interactive
Media Richness	multimedia	audio	text and graphic	text and graphic	text and graphic	multimedia
Geographic Coverage	global	local	global	local	varies	global
CPM	low	lowest	high	medium	high	medium
Reach	high	medium	low	medium	varies	medium
Targeting	good	good	excellent	good	excellent	excellent
Track Effectiveness	fair	fair	fair	fair	excellent	excellent
Message Flexibility	poor	good	poor	good	excellent	excellent

EXHIBIT 14.3 Strengths and Weaknesses of Major Media

internet, print media allow for active viewing: Readers can stop and look at an ad that interests them, sometimes spending quite a bit of time reading the details. In general, magazine advertising space is much more expensive than newspaper space because, like the internet, magazines can reach very specialized audiences (e.g., tennis players or chemical purchasing agents).

NARROWCAST MEDIA Cable TV (CATV) is a narrowcast medium. It is called *narrowcast* because cable channels contain focused electronic content appealing to special-interest markets—as does the internet. For example, cable channels such as CNN or ESPN are networks in that they reach extremely large audiences worldwide, but they still have specialized programming. CATV advertising tends to be less expensive than broadcast advertising, although some exceptions apply.

POINTCAST MEDIA The folks at pointcast.com, who brought individualized news service to every computer desktop (and do not exist today), coined the term *pointcast*. **Pointcast media** are electronic media with the capability of transmitting to an audience of just one person, such as e-mail, personalized Web pages on the internet, and the cell phone networks. Pointcast media can transmit either personalized or standardized messages in bulk to the entire audience of those who have the equipment to receive them, and these individuals can transmit a single message back to the sender using the same equipment. Receiving devices include pagers, cell phones, PDAs, computers, TV, fax machines, and more. Fax machines are the only pointcast receiving device where unsolicited marketing communications are illegal, due to the cost of receiving messages.

DIRECT POSTAL MAIL Finally, like e-mail, postal mail allows for more selective targeting than any other mass medium, can be personalized, gives good message length and timing flexibility, and is excellent for measuring effectiveness because of its response-tracking capability. However, direct mail has a poor image (junk mail and spam) and postal mail has high costs for production and postage.

DIGITAL MEDIA

From a media buyer's perspective, the strengths of the internet include selective targeting with e-mail and Web content by using databases, ability to track advertising effectiveness, flexibility of message length and delivery timing, ability to reach global markets with one message, and interactivity. The internet is the first electronic medium to allow active, self-paced viewing (similar to print media), and it is the first and best medium for interactivity. Users can create their own marketing communication content for uploading to the internet, as mentioned many times in this book. The internet's weaknesses include the inability to reach mass audiences, inability to reach up to 30 percent of the population not online, slow video delivery to individuals without a broadband connection, and problematic audience measurement systems. Many of the weaknesses of the internet are in the process of being remedied. Audience measurement was initially a weakness, though companies such as comScore Media Metrix and Nielsen//NetRatings have made major improvements in this area.

IMC tools can be used to communicate with target markets via many types of digital media. In Chapter 13 we discussed two key digital media—it might help to review the formats and details at this point:

- **E-mail** is a direct marketing digital medium. Companies can send their own e-mail as digital communication, or purchase text or display ad space in e-mail sent by others. E-mail has low costs but limited market coverage as compared with postal mail.
- **Web sites** are digital communication vehicles for an organization's own PR efforts; an organization can also purchase advertising space on other people's Web sites.

We add to these the newest digital media—the social media, which are discussed in this chapter. **Social media** are online tools and platforms that allow internet users to collaborate on content, share insights and experiences, and connect for business or pleasure (see Appendix B for a list of 50 social media). As a group, most advertisers and PR practitioners are still trying to understand how to use these for effective marketing communication; however, the reasons to do so are compelling—iProspect research found that 34 percent of internet users take advantage of a site with user-generated content to help make a purchase decision. We group the internet's social media into four categories: search engines, blogs, online communities, and social networks (Exhibit 14.4) . All provide engagement opportunities, interactivity, and great access to target markets via advertising, PR, and other IMC tools. Like all categorization schemes, there are some areas of overlap, but this way of examining social media helps companies because each type has unique properties that inform their use as media.

Search Engines as Reputation Aggregators

Search engines are **reputation aggregators**—Web sites that rank Web sites, products, retailers, or other content according to some rating system. Reputation is pure perception, involving what others say about the brand, site, individual, and so forth. An aggregator gathers these perceptions and displays them in some organized fashion. These sites are social media because they rely heavily on user input for their rankings. These social media are critical to a company's brand image and sales, because a poor reputation will not gather many click-throughs. Companies learn how to manage their reputations online and how to show well in reputation aggregator rankings.

General search engines are the most important general reputation aggregators in terms of traffic. Among the giants is Google, which ranks search engine results page links partially based on popularity—the number of quality sites linking to each Web site. For example, type "books" into Google and the top four links are books.google.com, nytimes.com/pages/books, barnesandnoble.com, and amazon.com—the four sites with the highest reputation for relevance to the keyword "books." Many authors are now calling Google a "reputation engine" instead of a search engine because of the way it determines these rankings. Users visit Google because the search engine results pages are so relevant and not just an unordered list of pages with just the keyword in it, with no regard to importance.

Other reputation aggregators include social media niche sites with search capability, such as YouTube for video and Tripadvisor for hotel ratings. We discuss these in the vertical search and online community sections that follow.

Marketers are keen to implement the newest search marketing techniques for natural, paid and **vertical search**. The latter is an emerging area

Social Media	What is it?	Examples
Reputation aggregators	Databases allowing users to search for content	Google, Yahoo!, MSN, Tripadvisor.com, ePinions.com
Blogs	Online multimedia journals with frequent updating	Technology: TypePad, Blogger, Wordpress. Site: Marketingpilgrim.com
Online communities	Sites offering professional or user content and allowing members to upload content	CNN, Slate, YouTube, Google Groups, Flickr, Del.icio.us, Wikipedia, Second Life
Social networks	Associations of internet users for social connection	Myspace, Facebook, Xing, LinkedIn

EXHIBIT 14.4   Social Media Types

involving reputation aggregators on very specialized topics, such as Amazon.com with its searchable database of books rated by reviewers. **Search marketing** is an umbrella term that refers to the act of marketing a Web site via search engines, whether through improving rank in listings, purchasing paid listings, or a combination of these and other search engine-related activities. Thus, search marketing as social media is an important way to reach target markets for brand- and sales-building IMC activities. According to the search marketing company iProspect, there are three components to search marketing, as discussed in the following sections:

> Search engine marketing (SEM) is a complex art and science that combines the intricacies of human behavior, linguistic preferences, marketing techniques, analytics, website usability and technology to drive qualified visitors to your website and convert them into customers. An integrated, thorough SEM campaign, that thoughtfully and effectively utilizes these disciplines, provides the best results. This involves:

- Utilizing **natural search engine optimization** techniques to create a foundation for the campaign
- Incorporating the practical advantages of **paid inclusion**
- Establishing the appropriate mix of **pay per click advertising**

Recall from Chapter 1 that paid search yields 35 percent of new customers for online retailers, while 29 percent comes from natural search. It is no wonder that search marketing is a much used and valuable tactic.

NATURAL SEARCH Also called organic search, **natural search** is a search marketing strategy involving optimizing a Web site so it will appear as close to the first search engine results page as possible. **Search engine optimization (SEO)** is the act of altering a Web site and incoming links so that it does well in the organic, crawler-based listings of search engines. Natural search is critical because with more than 2 billion search engine queries each

day, 62 percent of searchers will click on a link in the first page of search engine results pages (SERP), and 90 percent click on links within the first three pages ("iProspect Search Engine User . . .," 2006). As well, natural search listings are perceived as more relevant than paid search ad listings by 61 percent of users, according to iProspect.

There are many ways for a Web site or blog to inch its way to page one, but first it is important to understand that every reputation aggregator uses somewhat different criteria for ranking content. Among general search engines, Google is the key player, with 58 percent market share, as shown in Exhibit 14.5. Google uses an ever-changing algorithm with over 200 variables, one of the most important of which is popularity as measured partially by relevant incoming links to a site (thus, its nickname as reputation engine). Thus, companies wanting to optimize their site for Google will seek as many relevant and high quality incoming links as possible (e.g., a link from a .edu site is seen as being of higher quality than one from a .com).

Another important tactic involves **keywords**—the words users type into the search query box to find what they seek. When Web sites are optimized in both their content and HTML meta tags that hold keywords, it will make it easy for search engines to know how to categorize the site and to provide a relevant match when users

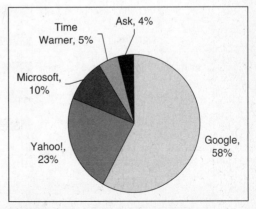

EXHIBIT 14.5   Search Engine Market Share, December 2007

Source: Burns (2008), available at www.searchenginewatch.com.

actually type in those keywords. These and other meta tags are not seen by visitors unless they choose to view the page source code. For example, these are the actual keywords used by eBay.com: "ebay, electronics, cars, clothing, apparel, collectibles, sporting goods, ebay, digital cameras, antiques, tickets, jewelry, online shopping, auction, online auction." When someone types in those words at Google, the search engine will consider the match as one of the 200 variables. Meta tags include a title tag, description tag, and a keywords tag. Following are the actual HTML meta tags for YouTube.com:

YouTube — Broadcast Yourself.

- (appears at the top of the browser window and on the SERP link)
- <meta name="**description**" content= "Share your videos with friends and family"> (appears as a description under the title on the SERP link at Google and other search engine)
- <meta name="**keywords**" content="video, sharing, camera phone, video phone">

To discover the best keywords, companies (1) use Web logs to see what words their visitors type into search engines before arriving at their sites, (2) use Web tools, such as Google's AdSense keyword auctions, to discover the keywords used in their industy so they can find unique words for their site (e.g., "vintage jewelry" instead of "jewelry"), and (3) by polling customers and prospects to see what words they actually use when looking for firms in the industry. Organizations also carefully craft the text on their pages to reflect this content, including even purposefully using different spellings of keywords that searchers might use (e.g., *email* and *e-mail*). According to an SEOmoz.com study of 3,000 search marketers in 2008, title tags were the most often used; however, each of these meta tag keyword tactics was used by over three-quarters of the responsents (Exhibit 14.6). Oftentimes, experimentation is the best way to see which words actually produce the highest click-throughs to a Web site.

Exhibit 14.7 shows a search for "email marketing" at Google. On the left side, Constant Comment grabbed the number one natural result spot for these keywords—quite a feat in a crowded field of vendors.

Following are just a few of the other important guidelines that Google offers to Webmasters.

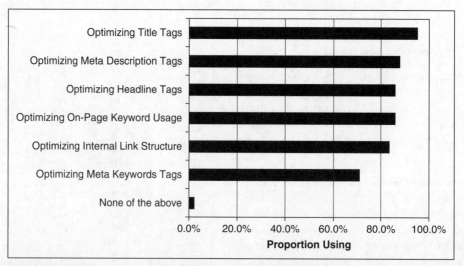

EXHIBIT 14.6 SEO Tactics Used to Help Achieve Greater Rankings

Source: Data from SEOmoz.com 2008 industry survey (www.seomoz.org).

EXHIBIT 14.7 Natural and Paid Search for Keywords "Email Marketing"

Source: Courtesy of www.google.com.

Visit the Google Webmaster pages for more (www.google.com/support/webmasters).

- **Design and content.** Create a site for users, not search engines. It should be useful, information rich, and include content that accurately describes the site. For example, if the site is about great golf courses, those terms should appear in the page title (top of the Internet Explorer window), headlines, and in the content. This makes it easy for search engines to categorize the site. Be sure that the words selected are the ones users would type into the search engine to find the site. Be sure that there aren't broken links and that important text isn't embedded in images that can't be read by search engines.

- **Technical factors.** Be sure the site is search bot ready. Search robots, also called spiders, are the automated programs that crawl the Web in search of new and revised pages for including in search engine indexes. Many technical features that can't be read by robots will result in poor search rankings, such as fancy JavaScript, cookies, Flash, and

frames. See Exhibit 6.17 for an example of how search spiders work.

- **Register the Web site.** Instead of waiting for robots to find a site, firms can register online at the search engine itself.

- **Site quality.** Maintain a site that is high quality, content rich, and constantly updated. Don't use any content to "trick" the search engines because Google is very adept at catching these and banning sites from the index. For example, "cloaking" or "doorway pages" are those instances where sites create different content for the search engines, hoping to gain higher rankings. Hidden links, irrelevant content, and link spam schemes all lower site quality and will be discovered.

Finally, a company, brand, or individual name will rise in the SERP if it has more than one Web site. Some possibilities include (1) subdomains with lots of unique, quality content, such as support.dell.com, (2) frequently updated blogs, and (3) content on highly visited sites such as Facebook, YouTube, Flickr, and Amazon (e.g., many book reviews). All of this content, linked to each other, presents a picture of a highly relevant expert on a particular topic. This is one of the keys to using the social media to build an online presence that gets noticed by search engines.

PAID SEARCH Paid search occurs when an advertiser pays a reputation aggregator a fee for directory submission, inclusion in a search engine index, or to display their ad when users type in particular keywords. A MarketingSherpa study found that paid search was the best-performing method of online advertising, according to 49 percent of U.S. online marketers. Three tactics currently prevail when it comes to paid search marketing: keyword advertising, paid inclusion, and directory listings.

Keyword advertising at search engine sites prompts sponsored text or display ads to appear on the SERP. For example, advertisers can buy the word *automobile,* and when users search using that word, the advertiser's banner or message will appear on the resulting page. Exhibit 14.7 shows the advertisers who bought the term *email marketing* as sponsored links on the top and right of the natural SERP links. Google.com orders the ads by price paid in a keyword bidding process, the landing page URL, and the click-through rate. Thus, the most relevant ad tops the list of sponsored links on the page. Google also sends contextual ads for display on other Web sites in its AdSense program (site owners get paid whenever a user clicks on the ad).

Paid inclusion occurs when sites receive guaranteed indexing in a search engine. For example, Yahoo! offers "Search Basic Submit," a service allowing Web site owners to submit their URLs and be guaranteed of appearing in the index within four days. The fee is $49 annually. Paid inclusion doesn't guarantee position in the SERP, however—other factors used for ranking determine position there. Google does not offer paid inclusion, preferring to keep the natural search results purely based on its algorithm. Sites can submit URLs to Google for free.

Directory submission is when an organization pays to be included in a searchable directory. For example, Yahoo! includes products in its shopping pages at a cost-per-click fee and includes local business listings in its local directory ($299 for most businesses and $600 for adult content sites). Directory submission is important for many other reputation aggregators in vertical markets, such as job listing fees in Craigslist or business listings in Business.com. Note that some directory listings are free.

Paid search is commonly called pay-per-click (PPC) because advertisers pay whenever users click on the ads. Google charges between $0.15 and $15 per click; however, depending on the popularity of keywords the monthly bill can range from $100 to millions of dollars. Click-through rates can vary from 0% to 50 percent, so picking the best keywords is key if advertisers don't want to be surprised with a huge bill. Google and other search engines greatly increased revenues for advertisers and their own firms by selling keyword ads because the user is more open to messages that relate to the context of their online activity.

VERTICAL SEARCH Vertical search is site-specific search on very specialized topics, such as travel, online retailers, or books. As compared with general search engines, such as Google and Yahoo!, vertical sites are desintations for fewer users seeking very specific content. For example, Tripadvisor.com attracts 25 million visitors a month, has five million registered members, and features 10 million reviews and opinions about various hotels worldwide (Exhibit 14.8). Someone seeking a hotel in New York City or Bangkok can search the Tripadvisor site and get a listing of hotels ranked by popularity, with hundreds of reviews and several traveler photos per hotel. This social media site capitalizes on the fact that people trust others like themselves more than they trust the company Web sites.

Other vertical search site examples include ZoomInfo and LinkedIn (people search), Guru.com (vendor search in B2B market), Autobytel (automobile search), CareerBuilder (jobs), Retrevo (consumer electronics), YouTube (video), and iTunes (music). The B2B Infomat fashion engine provides access to over 350,000 fashion designers, showrooms, retailers, manufacturers, and more, and DPRWorld helps dentists find everything from whitening agents to anesthesia. As

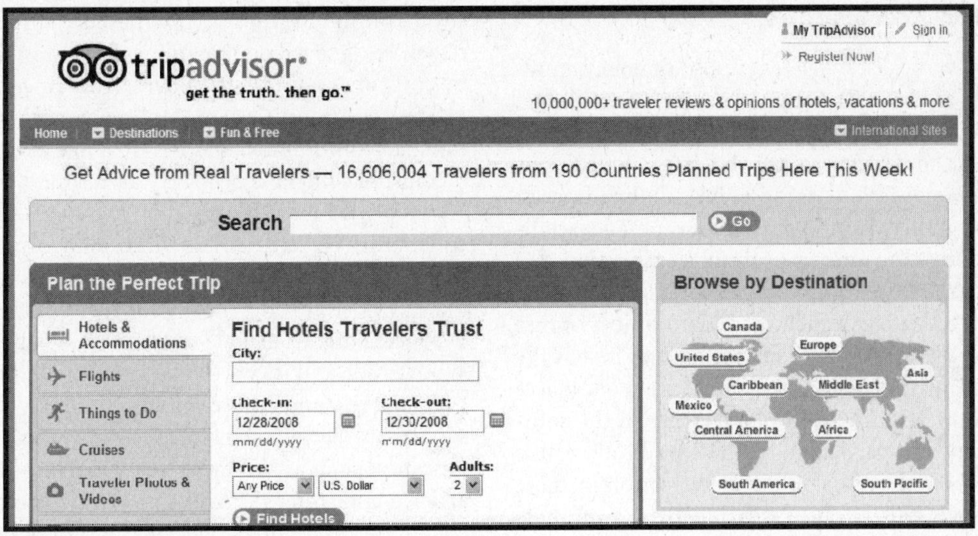

EXHIBIT 14.8 Find Hotels Travelers Trust at Tripadvisor.com

Source: Courtesy of Tripadvisor.com.

a comparison, ComScore measured the number of general and vertical searches in January 2008:

- Google (7.5 million)
- Yahoo! sites (2.5 million)
- YouTube and other Google searches (1.6 million)
- Microsoft sites (1.1 million)
- eBay (0.5 million)
- MySpace (0.4 million)
- Craigslist (0.3 million)
- Amazon sites (0.2 million)
- Facebook (0.2 million)

Companies need to learn whether or not there are vertical sites for their industries, and then to see if they are also indexed by the general search engines. For example, MySpace and Facebook pages are also indexed on Google, potentially necessating search engine optimization (SEO) tactics for both the general and vertical search engines. Marmite, the English food spread, has a Facebook page with over 67,000 connected friends—its Facebook link appears fourth in a Google search.

Vertical search is a growing area because it helps users find what they are looking for quickly—20 percent of online users search at vertical sites, according to iProspect. A consumer seeking a local pizza restaurant might do better at a yellow page vertical search site than at a general search engine, where the local entries will be buried among thousands of similar businesses nationwide. According to iProspect research, users search on vertical sites for both branding and e-commerce reasons. Survey respondents searched to find entertainment on YouTube (72% search for this reason), and to connect with others on Facebook (49%) and MySpace (35%). Visitors search to research a product on Tripadvisor (56% search for this reason), Yahoo! Answers (39%), Craigslist (39%), and iVillage (32%). On Amazon, 41 percent search for product information (branding) and 46 percent search to purchase something (e-commerce).

The pricing models on vertical search sites include directory submission fee, cost-per-click and cost-per-action, as well as the traditional cost-per-thousand (CPM) impressions. When the directory content is user-generated, such as with Tripadvisor.com, advertisers can pay for display ads on the site or can enter comments in response to reviews for free.

Online Communities

Many vertical search sites are also online communities, such as Tripadvisor for travelers. When Web sites gather folks with similar interests, users will keep returning to see what like-minded users are discussing and doing online. Online interest communities from diverse geographic locations are one of the internet's advantages for users and it is capitalized upon by marketers. Good marketers either create their own communities or find those whose audience characteristics match the company target markets. Once target audiences are found, marketers can advertise on the community and participate in the conversation. It is critical to monitor online conversation in these communities because this is where customers discuss a company's brands, activities, CEO, and customer service. Community chatter online can make or break a reputation within hours.

TYPES OF ONLINE COMMUNITIES Online communities gather businesses and consumers, who create content on every imaginable topic. A few important types of communities include wikis, news aggregators, video and photo sharing sites, online forums (text-based), product review sites, social bookmarking sites, consumer-to-consumer (C2C) commerce, other special interest communities, and online gaming. One thing all communities share is that, like all social media, the content is primarily user-created.

A **wiki** is software that allows users to collaboratively create, edit, link, and organize the content of a Web site, usually for reference material, according to leader Wikipedia. Wikipedia brands include Wiktionary, Wikibooks, Wikiversity, Wikinews, Wikispecies, Wikiquote, Wikisource, and more (Exhibit 14.9). Wiki software is the engine that drives many wiki communities, such as Wikihow (over 35,000 how-to articles and videos). Wiki software is used for collaboration among colleagues and on Google docs (docs.google.com).

News aggregators use client or Web software to bring news from many sources to one place for easy reading. When users (clients) install Google Reader, Yahoo! Widgets, or any other news aggregator software, they can bring headlines onto their desktops via RSS feeds. These are individually based and not based on online communities—such as when news

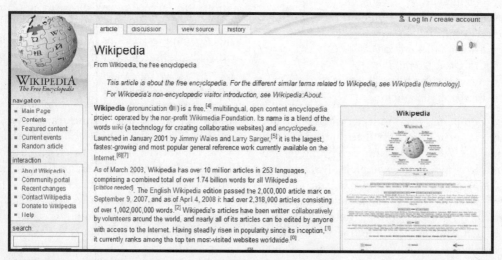

EXHIBIT 14.9   Wikipedia.com Defines Everything, Including Itself

Source: www.wikipedia.com.

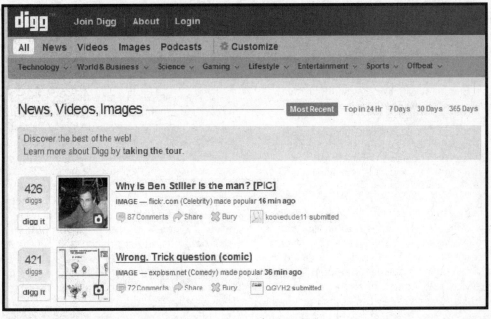

EXHIBIT 14.10   Digg.com Wants Visitors to Vote on the Best Story

Source: Courtesy of www.digg.com.

aggregators feed content to a blog or Web site for community viewing and comment. Digg.com is one of the most popular general-headline Web site–based news aggregators (Exhibit 14.10). When internet users see stories they like, they submit those stories to Digg.com by clicking on a button at the original media site: "Digg it." The headline and link are transmitted to Digg.com, where visitors can read and vote on the story. The top stories make it to Digg's home page and get discussed in the weekly Diggnation podcast by founders Kevin Rose and Alex Albrecht (also available at iTunes).

Video and photo sharing sites host user-generated content. YouTube and Google Video are two popular social media sites for video. They are also communities because visitors can upload or view video, post comments in response, link to videos, and even embed them in Web sites. Flickr.com holds nearly 500 million registered user photos—not surprising since 37 percent of internet users upload photos.

Some companies also follow this trend; for example, instant message firm Meebo.com has placed nearly 1,500 of its office photos, Web log statistics, and more on Flickr as a way to increase its content all over the Web and, thus, its ranking on Google's SERPs. See the "Let's Get Technical" box about a digital photo receiver that downloads photos from the internet.

In previous chapters we discussed the idea of image tagging—attaching meta data to video, photos, or text to help users find the desired content. This practice makes multimedia searchable at the sites hosting this video or photo content, so it is helpful that 28 percent of internet users tag internet content and that search engine Technorati.com tracks 250 million pieces of tagged social media. Because nearly 60 percent of internet users view online videos, advertisers are coming up with clever ways to embed advertising. For example, VideoEgg offers ads that pop up when a user moves her mouse over a video. Not wanting to

LET'S GET TECHNICAL

Ceiva Digital Photo Receiver

It's Christmas Day. Grandma couldn't make Christmas this year because she isn't feeling so well. You call her on the phone and try to describe the lovely family scene all around you. You wish you could send her a picture but she's not very technical. You both feel a little sad that she can't be more a part of the action. If only you could put a new picture in that frame on her mantle . . . now you can.

Imagine a computer screen that looks like a picture frame, whose only function is to receive and display a picture slide show without *any* intervention on the part of the user. That is the Ceiva digital photo receiver in a nutshell. One popular use of the service is for nontechnical grandparents. The children or grandchildren can upload pictures to the Ceiva service. The grandparent's picture frame then pulls those pictures off the service each day and runs a continuous slide show for grandma.

Ceiva represents the convergence of three technologies: flat screen displays, modems, and file servers. The flat screen display is what helps Ceiva look like, well, a picture frame. This capability allows for easy and unobtrusive placement around the house. Ceiva's built-in modem dials the Internet to connect to the Ceiva server and download the pictures daily. The modem operates on a timer to dial in once a day without any user intervention.

The file server contains the repository of pictures. Pictures are uploaded to the file server (say, by the children and grandchildren) and then downloaded by the Ceiva frame. Thousands of pictures can be placed on the file server and those are downloaded in daily chunks of up to 30 pictures.

Ceiva models come in different sizes and have additional built-in features. The user can freeze the slide show on a particular picture, delete a picture with the touch of a button, and even have one-button printing (the print is delivered by mail). When new pictures are downloaded to the unit, a "You've got Smiles" light glows. One frame in the slide show can even be set to the local weather report.

Product line extensions include the ability to bypass the modem and use the home's Wi-Fi network instead. Another product line extension with Whirlpool has a Ceiva frame mounted on the door of a refrigerator. That would certainly clean up the refrigerator door.

Technologically, Ceiva is not particularly complex. However, what is being sold is hassle-free access to memories—and for many users the yearly subscription fee is worth it.

upset users, VideoEgg ads are fun-animated games or videos themselves.

Text-based communities abound online. Many sites build community through online chat rooms and discussion groups. Online forums, also called bulletin boards, are areas where users can post e-mail messages on selected topics for other users to read. The largest public newsgroup forum is the Usenet, which has 35,000 groups (accessed at groups.google.com) and contains community discussion about product experiences, among other topics. The Usenet has over 1 billion messages, beginning in 1981 (far pre-dating the Web in 1993). When the Web began, Deja.com archived the Usenet, and then Google took it over when Deja quit business. Although the Usenet is no longer the most-used forum, it holds a special place in the hearts of all geeks who have been online since the beginning. For us, it seems that the internet has come back to its Usenet roots with the advent of the social media—an internet for, by, and about users. Google and Yahoo! Groups carry on the Usenet tradition with private and public text-based groups for collaboration and sharing common interests (Exhibit 14.11). In addition to text-based message posting, Google's new groups include file posting, wikis, image posting, and many other capabilities important for social media collaboration.

A LISTSERV is an e-mail discussion group with regular subscribers—another old, yet persisting special interest community. Each message

EXHIBIT 14.11   Google Hosts the Usenet and News Group Formats with Many Capabilities

Source: Courtesy of www.groups.google.com.

that members send to the LISTSERV is forwarded to all subscribed members. LISTSERVs push content to the e-mailboxes of subscribed users, whereas bulletin boards require users to visit the page and pull content. E-mail newsletters use LISTSERV technology.

Product review sites, such as Amazon.com, allow users to write book reviews and read and rate the reviews of others. Other important review sites are BizRate (with nearly 20 million users a month) and Epinions.com (millions of products in 30 categories). These sites are social media e-commerce communities because consumers create the product and online retailer ratings.

Consumer-to-consumer (C2C) commerce spawned e-commerce communities around buying and selling goods. Two of the most well-known types are auctions (e.g., eBay) and classifieds (e.g., Craigslist and Oodle.com). Both rely on

users selling products to other users, filling the site with user content, and thus qualifying as social media. eBay auctions also allow for feedback on both buyer and seller actions, as mentioned in previous chapters. These transactions among strangers call for special security features and rating systems that help both parties determine whether or not they can trust each other to complete transactions satisfactorily.

Social bookmarking sites allow users to share their favorite Web sites and comments on them online, such as StumbleUpon.com. Del.ic.ious.com provides free software as a Web browser plug-in so that users can simply click on a button to bookmark a Web site. Once done, a Del.ic.ious window opens and asks for text tags, which are used to categorize the bookmark. Exhibit 14.12 displays a list of tagged sites and articles. Plaxo tops the list, with 3,108 other

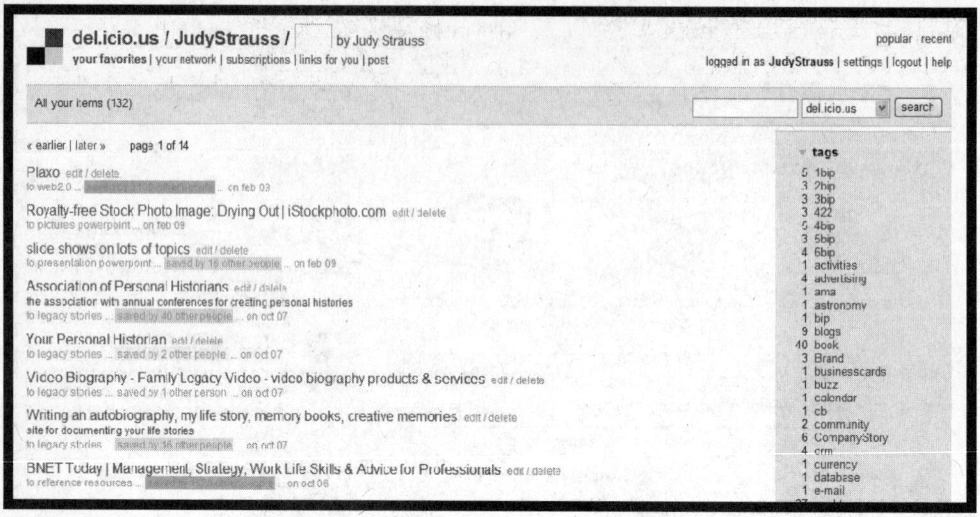

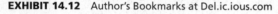

EXHIBIT 14.12   Author's Bookmarks at Del.ic.ious.com

Source: www.del.ic.ious.com, Courtesy of yahoo.com.

people also bookmarking it. Social bookmarking is powerful because users can click through to other users who have bookmarked the same articles to see what else they are reading on the same topic. It is a great resource for individual or collaborative research, and one we've used to indicate assigned class reading lists. It is even better for marketers wanting to create a buzz about a white paper, blog post, or other online article.

There are many other special interest communities with lots of user-generated content, such as **iVillage for women,** RateMyProfessors **for college students,** RateMDs **for patients,** Monster and CareerBuilder for job posters and seekers, and many more. Yahoo! Answers and other answer sites offer space for users to post questions that the community answers, and then others rate the response effectiveness. Some professionals have built a knowledge leadership niche by answering questions in their areas of expertise. Three other general communities are worthy of mention: (1) Squidoo, where users create a single free Web page on something of interest (called a "lens"), (2) 43Things, where users share their goals, such as what they are interested in learning, and then can connect for support with those mentioning the same goals, and

(3) Meetup.org, where users register in groups by special interest in their hometowns and then arrange to meet in the physical world.

Note that even the news sites have gotten into the social media business. CNN introduced iReport, inviting citizens to post video and photos depicting breaking news. By early 2008, over 80,000 users had posted content from worldwide locations, and from those 1,100 were selected for the iReport site in March 2008—an honor that keeps the citizen journalists going.

Finally, online gaming creates huge special interest communities. There are many types of online games with social interaction, from two-player chess to Massive Multiplayer Online Role Playing Games (MMORPG)—sporting thousands of players moving about as avatars at the same time. Some games have storylines or plots with players accomplishing goals and developing in skill and power, and others are completely non-structured, with players designing the action. MMORPGs were estimated to have 15 million global players that generated over 1 billion in USD revenues in 2006. World of Warcraft may be the most popular MMORPG, with 8 million monthly subscribers worldwide. Advertisers are keenly interested in online games because the players actually like to see product placement in the games because it makes them more real and also because games reach a broad spectrum of demographics.

Virtual worlds, such as Second Life and Webkinz (for children), are growing in popularity. Although only 6 percent of internet users have created an avatar to play in a virtual world, the Gartner Group predicts that 80 percent of active online users (an estimated 50 to 60 million people) will join a virtual world by 2010. Many businesses have set up shop in Second Life—IBM, Adidas, Pontiac, etc.—and so have many musicians and professors. Google is rumored to be thinking about combining Google Earth with its 3D Sketch software and creating a virtual world, or metaverse, for business users. This would be the tipping point for business use of virtual worlds. However, many new virtual worlds have gone out of business, so the future for this business model is uncertain.

COMMUNITY BUILDING PRINCIPLES Building a successful online community is not as simple as putting a link on a Web site and hoping folks will drop by. As with most e-business strategies, research and planning precede success. Larry Weber (2007) suggests a seven-step program:

1. **Observe**. Visit social media hangouts for Web users on the topics of interest in the industry of the company that wants to start a social media community. For example, the Saturn automobile brand managers would track conversations among users and industry analysts at blogs and Web sites to find the largest and most active communities.
2. **Recruit**. Find internet users who want to talk about the industry and recruit them for joining the new social media property.
3. **Evaluate platforms**. Decide whether the format should be a blog, vertical search site (reputation aggregator), pure online community, or social network.
4. **Engage**. Plan ways to get the community members to talk and upload content.
5. **Measure**. Identify metrics that will measure the success of the effort. For example, number of comments posted to the blog (more on this later in the chapter).
6. **Promote**: Plan ways to advertise and build a buzz in the social media and with reputation aggregators so the new community will attract users.
7. **Improve**. Use the metrics to continuously improve the community.

A book by Amy Jo Kim (2000) on this topic offers nine critical success factors (Exhibit 14.13); note how many follow good CRM principles (see Chapter 15). For example, community members are more loyal because of the social bond they form with the company or the salesperson (such as Dell's IdeaStorm blog).

Blogs

Blogs are online diaries, or journals, frequently updated and presented in chronological order on Web pages (from the term *Web log*). In 2007, 12 percent of internet users had created a blog, and 22 percent had posted comments to one. Technorati.com, the killer blog search engine, tracks over 112 million blogs. It estimates that over 175,000 new blogs appear every day, with over 1.6 million posts to the blogosphere a day. When blogs first emerged in 1999, it appeared that they contained irrelevant scribbling about miscellaneous personal topics and would probably not work their way into marketing strategy. How did their image change? Marketers began paying attention to blogs because many people writing them had valuable things to say. For instance, Robert Scoble in the Microsoft marketing department wrote about his views on Microsoft's role in the industry—and competitors surely read his musings.

Blogs are social media because of all the commenting done by blog readers. Some blogs allow posts by multiple authors as well. For instance, Engadget, a technology blog, offers many daily posts about new technologies, most by different authors. This blog is always listed in the

Define the community's purpose

Construct a mission statement, identify the target market, and create a strong site personality.

Create extensible gathering places

Provide a good system overview or map, include rich communications features, and allow members to extend-the environment.

Create evolving member profiles

Communicate the benefits of membership, make profile creation as easy and fun as possible, and keep the profiles up-to-date and evolving.

Promote effective leadership and hosting

Set up your program to grow, build some flexibility into the house rules, and set reasonable expectations for online support.

Define a clear yet flexible code of conduct

Create and enforce your code of conduct and don't try to stifle all conflict.

Organize and promote cyclic events

Hold regular, hosted, themed events, conduct community surveys, and hold contests that reinforce the purpose.

Provide a range of roles

Offer newcomers a controlled experience, offer increased privileges to regulars, and recruit leaders and mentors from within.

Facilitate member-created subgroups

Provide features that facilitate small groups and create events and contests for groups.

Integrate with the real world

Celebrate events that reinforce social identity, acknowledge important personal events, and encourage real-life meetings (when appropriate).

EXHIBIT 14.13   Community-Building Design Principles

Source: Adapted from Kim (2000), available at www.naima.com.

top three of all blogs on Technorati because of its high readership and activity (with each post generating lots of comments), and high confidence ratings by users. It is helpful to have multiple blog authors to keep the posts frequent, as long as they all follow the goals and style of the blog.

There are many types of blogs. Chief among them are personal and company; however, blogs differ widely by topic. Many CEOs blog to put a personal face on their companies. When JetBlue had a huge crisis in February 2007 (with 1,100 planes grounded and people stuck for up to 14 hours on airport tarmacs), its CEO David Neeleman posted blog apologies and introduced the new company Bill of Rights. The Eastman Kodak Company produces a brilliant company blog that is populated by employee stories and photos (1000words.kodak.com).

Many consultants and thought leaders create blogs to disseminate their views and gain clients, promote books, and more. Exhibit 14.14 displays the personal profile of Andy Beal on his blog. Note the user-friendly format for an online resume. Also note the RSS, Del.ic.ious, and other buttons that invite users to subscribe to or bookmark the blog. Beal has been quite successful with his MarketingPilgrim.com blog, gaining over 3,000 subscribers who follow his fresh commentary on SEO, reputation management, and all things related to e-marketing. Why does he blog? Besides being fun, it keeps him current on his industry and helps him gain paid speaking and consulting jobs.

Marketers also use blogs to draw users to their sites. For example, in 2004 Dr. Pepper/Seven-Up introduced the new flavored milk product with a blog written by a cow: Raging Cow Blog. Ghostwritten by six teenagers under the supervision of marketing staff, it sounded like a cow discussing her adventures as she traveled across country. It reads like a travelogue written with a Generation Y attitude based on the product positioning: ". . . a milk-based drink 'gone wild' because there are outrageous, intriguing and

EXHIBIT 14.14 Andy Beal's Business Blog
Source: Courtesy of Andy Beal at www.andybeal.com.

delicious flavor combinations." Within three weeks of the launch, 20,800 users logged on each day to read the crazy cow ramblings such as (Arnold, 2004):

> Ho hee, we did it! Fate was on our side that night—the moon was in its final quarter (I hear a number of you asking, 'How would a cow know diddly about the phases of the moon?' Good question, but ever since that whole jumping over the moon incident, we cows and yonder moon have been TIGHT . . .).

This type of strategy can backfire, however. When Jim and Laura took their RV across country and camped in Wal-Mart parking lots, they wrote a blog about it (any RV or trailer owner can spend the night for free at any Wal-Mart). The blog gained many readers, but then a few questioned why all the reports of interactions with Wal-Mart employees were so glowing—where were the criticisms? Finally, Laura was exposed as a freelance writer hired with Wal-Mart funds to do the blog. This hurt the Wal-Mart reputation. Online, transparency, authenticity, and consistency rule the day because if other bloggers discover corporate dishonesty, the entire blogosphere will be buzzing about it. Laura and Jim ended up returning the money they were paid and making a public apology.

The Wall Street Journal helps bloggers by sending an e-mail each day offering a link to a free online article (versus the normal subscription rate). It encourages bloggers to write their reactions to the article and link the blog to the WSJ Web site. The newspaper reports that the number of visits from blog sites is often as high as those from search engines. Also, this high number of incoming links raises the paper's "Google juice" (ranking in SERPs).

A new trend is blogs that hold micro content—very small posts, such as a hyperlink, image, or sentence comment. Tumblr.com offers free micro content blogs: "To make a simple analogy: If blogs are journals, tumblelogs are scrapbooks," according to Tumblr. Users can form groups or follow each other's frequently updated posts. Twitter is an even smaller mini blog, formed around the question: "What are you doing right now?" Members send text messages of up to 140 characters that post to their Twitter space. Friends follow

each other's "tweets" either on computers or via incoming text messages to cell phones or PDAs.

There are many things to consider when companies want to start blogging, such as which platform to use, who will do the writing, how often will they post, and what is the purpose of the blog. Companies should follow the online community guidelines previously mentioned for deciding how to promote the blog, draw a following, and engage them in conversation. For more details on starting a blog, we recommend *The Corporate Blogging Book* by Debbie Weil (Exhibit 14.15).

Finally, companies can become involved in blogs without starting their own. It is important to find influential bloggers in one's industry, follow their posts using RSS feeds, and add occasional comments. This keeps companies engaged in

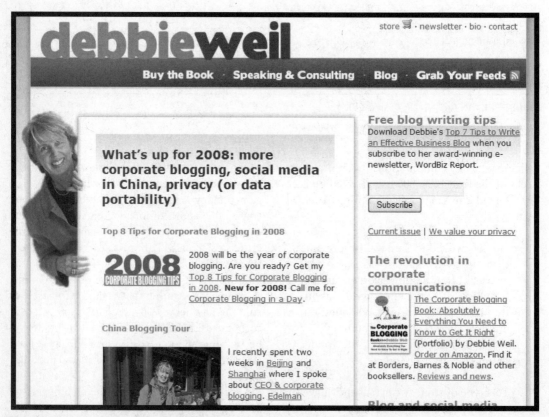

EXHIBIT 14.15 Debbie Weil's Blog about Corporate Blogging
Source: Courtesy of www.wordbiz.com.

important conversations and projects them as experts in the industry. It is equally important because when they follow blogs through some automated monitoring system, they will discover potentially reputation-damaging discussion when it breaks and can become involved in the discussion by telling their side of the story.

Social Networks

Social networks are "social structures made of nodes (which are generally individuals or organizations) that are tied by one or more specific types of interdependency, such as values, visions, idea, financial exchange, friends, kinship, dislike, conflict, trade, web links . . . disease transmission (epidemiology), or airline routes," according to Wikipedia. They are based on the idea of six degrees of separation—that each individual is connected to every other individual in the network by up to six other people. As shown in Exhibit 14.16, if you join LinkedIn, a business network, you might be only six contacts away from the CEO of a Fortune 100 company. All it takes is introductions from the individuals between you and him.

There are over 200 million people worldwide in online networks, and 16 percent of internet users say they use a social networking site (according to Pew Internet & the American Life). As seen in Exhibit 14.17, MySpace remains the top share site, with 65.7 million visitors a month who return many times, for a total of 955.1 million visits a month (in February 2008). Several sites are growing quickly in this rapidly changing field.

Social networks help individuals connect deeply with others for many different purposes, depending on the network. Purely social networks are for meeting people, sharing interests, and having fun. Professional networks are for working the contacts to get a job, venture capital, or to find employees. Job recruiters use LinkedIn by working their own personal networks to get introductions to others suitable for the positions.

According to Lewis PR, 33 percent of companies will implement a social networking initiative by 2008, and 70 percent will include social networking in their marketing strategy. Marketers use social networks by advertising on them or providing applications to network users—such as games and virtual postcards. More importantly, marketers create pages for their own brands. Pepsi-cola's Aquafina water brand has a MySpace page with games, other interesting things, and 10,825 "friends" who've connected to the brand and discuss its merits. This is good for brand-building, learning about customer opinions, and it is more content that builds credibility and stature on Google.

Social networks were unknown prior to 2006. In 2007, Ben Willis educated marketers with his article *The Five Pillars of Social Media Marketing* (available at www.marketingpilgrim.com). In it, he

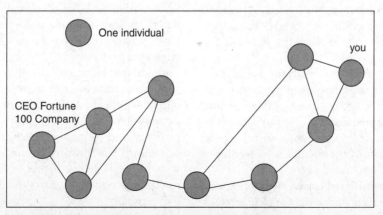

EXHIBIT 14.16 Social Networks are About Connections

Site	Monthly Visitors	Monthly Visits	Percent Change from February 2007
MySpace	65.7	955.1	−1
Facebook	28.6	326.4	77
Classmates.com	12.0	22.5	11
myyearbook.com	3.0	20.0	284
Bebo.com (purchased by AOL)	3.5	19/3	3
LiVEJOURNAL.com	3.3	16.5	10
BlackPlanet.com	2.1	13.7	9
hi5.com	2.4	11.8	1
LinkedIn.com	3.8	11/2	729
tagged.com	2/4	10.6	11

EXHIBIT 14.17   Most Popular Social Networks in February 2008

Source: Compete Analytics (www.compete.com).

suggested the following important social network components:

1. **Declaration of identity.** This refers to the network profile—a carefully crafted set of images and facts to help the member achieve desired goals in the network. For instance, if a MySpace member wants a job, she should build a professional profile and delete all the college party pictures and references.

2. **Identity through association.** Members "friend" others by creating connections in the network. Part of their identity comes from the people they friend. For example, some people get many more requests for connections than they accept, because they only want to connect with those they know and trust (many strangers ask for connections).

3. **User-initiated conversation.** Social networks provide the opportunity to listen and learn from customers, such as doe Marmite and Aquafina. Conversations in social networks occur in many ways, from posting messages to other members to feeding a blog post into friend pages.

4. **Provider-initiated conversation.** Social networks offer companies the chance to ask questions to customers connected to the brand or executive. This is a bit like a huge focus group with no cost.

5. **In-person interaction.** Network connections spill over to the off-line world. Job opportunities and future business await those who invite online contacts to meet them in real life. As previously mentioned, some social networks, such as Meetup.org, exist to facilitate off-line member meetings.

BRANDING GOALS IN DIGITAL AND PHYSICAL MEDIA

In this chapter we have suggested that all traditional off-line and digital online media are useful for engaging and communicating with customers. It is up to marketers to figure out where their targets hang out online and become a part of those communities. Many media will successfully build awareness, create positive branding, and motivate purchase—the best depends on a number of factors, such as the product, campaign goals, competition, and company's technological savvy. Combining the tools mentioned in Chapter 13 with the media in this chapter will be successful at motivating online consumers and business buyers if done well.

One difficulty now facing marketers is how to retain control over brand images in light of the social media, the amount of user control online, and the degree of trust consumers have in one another (and not in companies). The answer is that they can't. Instead, companies can use the brand Web site and blogs to tell the company story; then they must monitor the internet for conversations about their brands, responding when appropriate. See Exhibit 14.18 for the varying degrees of control marketers have over messages in different media. With social media, astute marketers not only listen to conversations, but also join them—such as Dell Computer did with its IdeaStorm blog (Chapter 1).

Everyone knows that no one is perfect, so when companies make mistakes they need to admit fault, apologize, make reparation, and report back about what they did—all the while communicating online with bloggers and others who are discussing the crisis. It is now about authenticity, transparency, consistency, and two-way dialog with customers.

WHICH MEDIA TO BUY?

Advertisers pay for space on Web sites, blogs, and in e-mail, as previously mentioned. In this section, we focus on paid media and how to determine which are the best buys. Marketers spent more of their 2007 media budgets on the internet than on radio and outdoor, but much less than on television, magazines, or newspapers (refer to Exhibit 14.1). This generalization is interesting but not especially useful for media buyers who plan a combination of media to achieve marketing communication goals for a particular campaign and brand. Media planners want both effective and efficient media buys. *Effectiveness* means reaching and gaining the attention of the target market, and *efficiency* means doing so at the lowest cost.

Effective Internet Buys

Once a firm decides to buy online advertising (medium), it faces the question of which vehicle

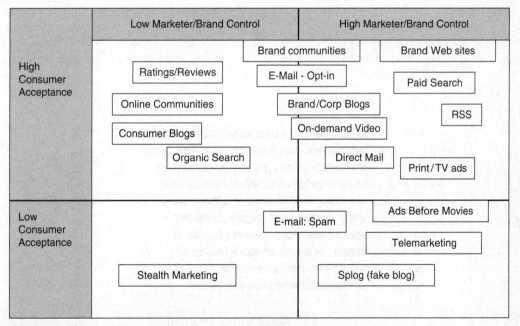

EXHIBIT 14.18 Marketers' Control Over Media Messages

Source: Adapted from Nielsen Online "The Internet in Transition." Available at www.nielsen-netratings.com.

(individual site) to use. As noted earlier, media planners look for the media with audiences that closely match the brand's target markets. Beyond that important principle, marketers use many innovative digital strategies to reach narrowly targeted markets, including proprietary databases and social media.

Advertisers trying to reach the largest number of users will buy space at reputation aggregators (search engines) such as the big three—Google, Yahoo! and Microsoft. Regardless of these large sites, the Web is less effective at reaching the masses than some network television, but is better at reaching niche markets. This reason explains the huge growth in vertical search marketing and keyword advertising.

It is difficult to generalize about the most effective media because it varies widely based on many factors. In a study of 297 marketing and public relations "social media power users," online video and blogs topped the list of effective media; however, all were very effective at reaching campaign goals (Exhibit 14.19). Note that these are all social media, not purely purchased advertising space.

Weather.com used search marketing effectively in 2006 to drive traffic to its lifestyle content pages (weather considerations for golf, skiing, weddings, allergies, and so forth). Its goals were to increase page views by 45 percent a year, maintain leadership in the weather category (with 30 percent of all weather category search clicks coming to Weather.com), and to drive lifestyle page visits because they have the highest revenue value. To do this, they planned a keyword advertising campaign. Weather.com marketers tested two key phrases for its wedding pages—for people planning outdoor weddings away from home. The phrase "wedding planner" brought 1.5 visits to Weather.com per unique visitor, 3.6 Web pages per visit, and 5.2 pages per unique visitor. The term "outdoor wedding" did better, with 1.8 visits per unique visitor, 6.6 pages per visit, and 12.0 pages per unique visitor. Thus they settled on "outdoor wedding" for their keyword ad buy. "Our analytics data drives 95 percent of our decisions. We want to make sure what we changed worked and have data to back up our decisions," according to Marketing Director Derek Van Nostran.

Efficient Internet Buys

If the audience for certain media vehicles matches the firm's target (*effective* buy), CPM calculations will determine the most efficient buy. To measure efficiency before buying advertising space, media buyers use a metric called CPM (cost per thousand). This metric is calculated by taking the ad's cost,

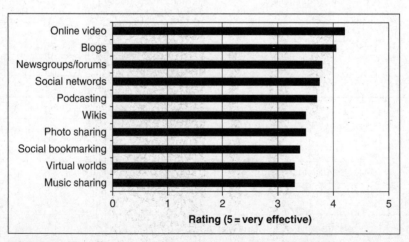

EXHIBIT 14.19 Effectiveness of Each Social Media Tool at Reaching Campaign Goals

Source: Gillin, Paul (2008).

dividing it by the audience size, and then multiplying by 1,000 (Cost ÷ Audience ¥ 1,000). Internet audience size is counted using **impressions**: the number of times an ad was served to unique site visitors. For example, in June 2002, a full banner ad at MediaPost.com, an advertising and media internet portal, received 2.4 million impressions and cost $168,000 a month for a CPM of $70. CPM is used because it allows for efficiency comparisons among various media and *vehicles* within the media (e.g., a particular magazine or Web site). Magazines are usually the most expensive media to reach 1,000 readers; radio is often the least expensive.

Typical Web CPM prices are $7 to $15 CPM (Hallerman, 2002) or $0.15 to $15.00 at Google. The CPM of MediaPost is higher because it reaches a select target in the B2B market. According to eMarketer in March 2002, the CPM ranged between $75 and $200 for e-mail ads (see Exhibit 13.22), and between $20 and $40 for e-mail newsletter sponsorship.

It is interesting to note that in 2006, only 48 percent of Web site advertising was purchased using the CPM model (see www.iab.net). Unlike most traditional media, 47 percent of online advertisers pay based on performance (nearly doubling from the previous two years), and the remainder use some combination of the two models.

Performance-based payment, often called pay per click (PPC) or cost per action (CPA), includes schemes such as payment for each click on the ad, payment for each conversion (sale), or payment for each sales lead or new registered user. This type of pricing is beneficial to advertisers but risky for Web sites, which must depend partially on the power of the client's ad and product for revenues. As an example, the following are average CPC costs from multiple advertisers, according to SearchEngine Watch.com (data from Efficient Frontier):

- Total finance $2.43
- Credit $2.65
- Mortgage $2.05
- Auto finance $1.47
- Travel $0.72
- Automotive $0.50
- Insurance $7.87
- Retail $0.37
- Dating $0.37

CPM, PPC, CPA, and other online advertising pricing models are only part of the measurement picture. Marketers use many other metrics to evaluate the efficiency of their advertising while it is running, as mentioned in Chapter 13. Adding social media measures to this, Exhibit 14.20 displays the most important measures used by social media

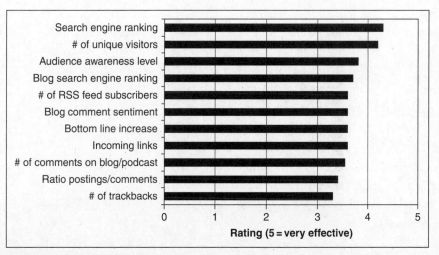

EXHIBIT 14.20 Most Important Social Media Efficiency Measures
Source: Gillin, Paul (2008).

power users in Gillin's study. Obviously, it all depends on which tactics a marketer uses. For instance, Weather.com measured visitors that clicked through to its wedding pages based on keyword buys. Pharmaceutical companies will measure the sentiment of comments to their blogs (percent positive and negative). If companies are working on SEO initiatives, they will measure incoming links to their Web sites because this raises their rankings on SERP pages. Bloggers also want to know how many RSS feed subscribers they have because this indicates the number following their writing. Refer also to Chapter 2, where we discussed engagement metrics of time spent on a page, social bookmarking, uploading content, and so forth.

Metrics Example

To see how a firm evaluates the effectiveness of its internet advertising buy, consider the actual internet buy made by iGo, an online retailer selling batteries and small electronic devices by catalog and online (Exhibit 14.21). Many different forms of online advertising are represented in this buy, from a simple text link to buttons, banners, and content sponsorships at major portals (names removed to protect confidentiality). This spreadsheet shows estimated click-through percentage, conversion to people who might order, number of visitors that might visit the iGo site from the ad, number of orders expected, and

Type	Yearly Impressions	Est. Click %	Est. Conv.	# Visitors	# Orders	Cost @ $4.64 CPM
E-commerce text link	400,000,000	0.20%	0.60%	800,000	4,800	$1,856,000
Shopping Channel						
Computing - anchor	8,500,000	3.00%	2.00%	255,000	5,100	39,440
Computing - sponsor	1,700,000	3.00%	2.00%	51,000	1,020	7,888
Homepage	10,000,000	1.10%	1.50%	110,000	1,650	46,400
Computing Channel						
ROS	40,000,000	1.10%	1.50%	440,000	6,600	185,600
Section front pages	3,500,000	1.10%	1.50%	38,500	578	16,240
Homepage	2,100,000	0.75%	1.00%	15,750	158	9,744
Homepage text link	7,200,000	0.75%	1.00%	54,000	540	33,408
News Portal						
Selected sections	10,000,000	1.10%	1.50%	110,000	1,650	46,400
Technology	5,000,000	1.10%	1.50%	55,000	825	23,200
Shopping section	200,000	1.10%	1.50%	2,200	33	928
ROS sticky ads	5,000,000	0.75%	1.00%	37,500	375	23,200
ROS banners	11,000,000	0.75%	1.00%	82,500	825	51,040
Portal (6.5 months)						
Homepage - button	6,000,000	0.75%	1.00%	45,000	450	27,840
Homepage - text link	6,000,000	0.75%	1.00%	45,000	450	27,840
Office computing	50,000	0.75%	1.00%	375	4	232
Office computing	300,000	0.75%	1.00%	2,250	23	1,392
BCentral ROS	6,000,000	0.75%	1.00%	45,000	450	27,840
Link exchange	20,000,000	0.75%	1.00%	150,000	1,500	92,800
Portal Co-Promotion						
Promo main page	75,000,000	1.10%	1.50%	825,000	12,375	348,000

(continued)

Type	Yearly Impressions	Est. Click %	Est. Conv.	# Visitors	# Orders	Cost @ $4.64 CPM
Sweepstakes						
Banners linkedsweeps	4,000,000	1.10%	1.50%	44,000	660	18,560
Promo button	6,000,000	1.10%	1.50%	66,000	990	27,840
Button on sweeps site	1,000,000	1.10%	1.50%	11,000	165	4,640
Portal Package						
Transition Ads-1	2,000,000	1.10%	1.50%	22,000	330	9,280
Mid page Ads-2	1,000,000	1.10%	1.50%	11,000	165	4,640
Mid page Ads-3	5,000,000	1.10%	1.50%	55,000	825	23,200
Mid page Ads-4	5,000,000	1.10%	1.50%	55,000	825	23,200
A-column Ads-5	5,400,000	1.10%	1.50%	59,400	891	25,056
	646,950,000	**0.54%**	**1.27%**	**3,487,475**	**44,255**	**$3,001,848**

EXHIBIT 14.21 iGo.com $3 Million Dollar Advertising Buy

Source: Adapted from information provided by Brian Casey, iGo.

cost of the ad. Exhibit 14.22 displays several effectiveness measures: average order value and more. Based on the annual profit and loss estimate from this campaign, it appears to generate more than half a million dollars in profits as well as drawing nearly 3.5 million visitors to iGo.com—folks who may develop into long-term customers.

Variables	
AOV	$140
Incremental order (annual)	0.60
Gross margin	0.36
Click rate	0.54%
Conversion	1.27%
Annual P&L	
Revenue	$ 6,195,735
Incremental revenue	3,717,441
Total Revenue	**$ 9,913,176**
COGS	(6,344,433)
Advertising cost	(3,001,848)
Total	**$ 566,895**
CPM	**$ 4.24**
Cost per Order (CPO)	**67.83**
Cost per Click (CPC)	**0.86**
Total Visitors	**3,487,475**

EXHIBIT 14.22 iGo Effectiveness Measures

Source: Adapted from information provided by Brian Casey, iGo.

Chapter Summary

As the internet is often compared to traditional media, marketers need to understand the major media's characteristics as well as digital media characteristics so they can make appropriate choices when buying or freely using promotional space. Electronic media include network television, radio, cable television, the internet, fax, cellular phone, and more. It is helpful to view these media as broadcast, narrowcast, and pointcast based on their ability to reach mass audiences, smaller audiences, or even individuals, and the information they disseminate as uniquely addressable or sent to the masses. The internet is often compared to print media because of its text and graphics content; print media allow for active viewing. Direct mail allows for selective targeting, can be personalized, offers good message length and timing flexibility, and is excellent for measuring effectiveness; however, it has a poor image and is costly (although e-mail is low cost yet riddled with spam).

Digital media include Web sites, e-mail, and the newer social media. Reputation aggregators gather searchable content from the Web and are important to marketers for advertising and communicating with users. General search engines Google, Yahoo! and MSN are the biggest reputation aggregators, ordering search results partially by popularity and relevancy. These engines offer natural and paid search tactics for achieving marketing goals. Vertical search occurs at niche reputation aggregators, such as Tripadvisor.com. Online communities are another type of social media, based around any type of special interest: wikis, news aggregators, video and photo sharing sites, online text-based communities (e.g., Usenet bulletin boards), product review sites, C2C commerce (e.g., auction and classified sites), social bookmarking, online games, virtual worlds, and many other types of special interest communities.

Blogs and social networks are also important social media for carrying either paid or free marketing communication messages. Social networks, such as MySpace and LinkedIn, offer marketers the opportunity to create profiles and build pages for connecting with consumers, colleagues, or job recruiters. Marketers use the social media for marketing communication to manage their brand images and increase sales.

When selecting advertising media and vehicles, media buyers look at CPM (cost per thousand) and performance-based payment methods such as PPC (pay-per-click) or CPA (cost per action). Media planners look for Web sites, social media, and e-mail lists that match the brand's target markets; they also use ad targeting techniques such as keyword advertising. Marketers use a number of metrics to track communication campaign effectiveness, such as mentioned in Chapter 13 (e.g., click-through rate) and Chapter 2 (engagement metrics).

Exercises

REVIEW QUESTIONS

1. List examples of broadcast, print, narrowcast, and pointcast media.
2. What are the advantages and disadvantages of digital media for marketing communication messages?
3. Compare and contrast digital and physical media.
4. How is e-mail different from postal mail as a medium?
5. Compare and contrast natural and paid search.
6. Name two ways that Web sites can use general search engines for increasing traffic.
7. Why is Google called a reputation engine?
8. Why are keywords important?
9. What are meta tags? Name three important types.
10. Name five types of online communities.
11. Name the top three social networks.
12. Why are blogs important to marketers?
13. What is the difference between an effective and an efficient media buy?

DISCUSSION QUESTIONS

14. The text made a statement that social media should still be considered media even though they often carry free marketing communication messages. How would you justify this to an agendy media buyer whose only task is to buy paid media?

15. Do you think that virtual worlds, such as Second Life, will grow to reach 80 percent of all internet users as predicted? Why or why not?

16. Do you think that off-line and online media will become a meaningless distinction in the near future? Why or why not?

17. Is it better to start a community on a company's own Web site or use an already established online community for engaging customers? Explain your answer.

18. Do you think the internet will ever surpass television advertising in terms of dollars spent by marketers? Why or why not?

19. Do you think that marketers are losing control of brand images because of the social media? What should marketers do to gain more control?

20. Which is better for a private university wanting to place ads on Web sites: CPM or PPC advertising? Defend your answer.

21. Which would be more important to a company selling hotel rooms: a general search engine or a vertical engine? Explain your answer.

WEB ACTIVITIES

22. Visit www.google.com and do a search for your favorite car. What sponsored ad appeared on the results page? Now do a search for your favorite music group. What sponsored links appeared on the results page? What conclusion can you draw about targeted advertising?

23. Visit Amazon.com and then go to a spider site to see what the search engine sees (such as www.feedthebot.com/tools/spider/). What are the differences?

24. Visit your favorite Web site and "view source" by clicking on the appropriate menu item in your browser. Find the meta tags. Report back on whether or not they reflect the site well.

25. The Gartner Group predicts that 80 percent of active online users will join a virtual world by 2010 (an estimated 50 to 60 million people). Do you agree with this estimate? Why or why not?

26. LinkedIn is growing at a fantastic pace. Visit LinkedIn.com and read about it. Do you think business networks like this will ever draw more traffic than social networks, such as MySpace? Why or why not?

CHAPTER 15

Customer Relationship Management

CRM is a business strategy, not a suite of software, and employees may find it difficult to adopt a CRM orientation.

—EDNA RAGINS AND ALAN GRECO,
NORTH CAROLINA STATE A & T UNIVERSITY

If you have an unhappy customer on the internet, he doesn't tell his six friends, he tells his 6,000 friends.

—JEFF BEZOS, PRESIDENT, AMAZON.COM

The main objective of this chapter is to provide an overview of the purpose and process of building a company's relationship capital through customer relationship management (CRM). You will learn about CRM's benefits, its three facets, and the eight building blocks needed for effective and efficient e-marketing CRM.

After reading this chapter, you will be able to:

- Define customer relationship management and identify the major benefits to e-marketers.
- Outline the three legs of CRM for e-marketing.

- Discuss the eight major components needed for effective and efficient CRM in e-marketing.
- Differentiate between relationship intensity and relationship levels.
- Highlight some of the company-side and client-side tools that e-marketers use to enhance their CRM processes.

The Cisco Story

Cisco Systems, Inc., is a company that practices what it preaches. Cisco primarily provides internet networking systems for corporate, government, and education clients worldwide, ringing up $34.9 billion in annual revenues for fiscal 2007. Operating in the B2B market, Cisco turned a hefty $7.3. billion in net income in 2007 by solving its own networking problems and turning those solutions into products for customers. It offers 10 product families for transporting data, voice, and video within buildings and around the world. Cisco boasts that its solutions increase clients' revenue, decrease costs, increase productivity, empower employees, transform corporate cultures, and integrate core processes. What better way to prove it than to use its products to build relationships with its own clients?

At Cisco, the internet plays a major role in acquiring, retaining, and growing customer business. With over 3 million users logging onto the Cisco site each month, Cisco has become quite adept at online customer relationship management (CRM). The following demonstrates Cisco's success, using CRM metrics.

Relationship Task	Metric (2007–2008)
Acquire/grow	Order growth 10%.
	60% of the business is from outside the U.S.
customers	92.2% of orders come through the internet.
	3.5 million registered users at the Cisco Web site.
Retain customers	81% of all customer technical issues solved online.
	Over 250,000 issues solved online each month U.S. registered site user satisfaction is 4.7 on a 5.0-point scale.

Cisco set a goal to migrate customers to the online channel, and it has: In early 1996 a mere 5 percent placed orders on the Web site. Further, Cisco was able to increase customer satisfaction from 3.4 in 1996 to 4.3 (2001) and 4.6 (2003) and 4.7 (2008). Such gains do not occur without a vision from the top and careful planning, focus, and execution throughout the company. Cisco's close attention to customer care includes a Web-to-live-agent contact center and a collaborative whiteboard so that customers and Cisco employees can work together on problems as visually displayed on their computers. Customer care agents operate several customer live chats simultaneously to help customers find what they need on the Web. Additionally, customers can contact the company via e-mail or even telephone for help.

Cisco's attention to CRM and monitoring of performance metrics have paid off. The firm saved $340 million in 2001 in customer service costs due to automation. More important, Cisco gains considerable repeat business and sells products to customers who want to follow Cisco's lead by using technology to solve their own problems.

BUILDING CUSTOMER RELATIONSHIPS, 1:1

Cisco develops long-term customer relationships one at a time (1:1), not unlike those developed by neighborhood retailers in the early 1900s—except that information technology allows Cisco to handle millions of these close relationships. A Cisco customer with an investment in software and high satisfaction is brand loyal and will not easily be enticed by competition. This customer will slowly spend an increasing amount of money on additional products and services and also refer others. According to *Harvard Business Review* authors Thomas Jones and Earl Sasser, "Increased customer loyalty is the *single most* important driver of long-term performance." *Business 2.0* calls **relationship capital** the most important asset a firm can have ("Relationships Rule," 2000). In an environment of customer control, where attention is a scarce commodity, a firm's ability to build and maintain relationships with customers, suppliers, and partners may be more important than a firm's land, property, and financial assets. It is this relationship capital that provides the foundation of future business.

This approach represents a major shift in marketing practice: from mass marketing to individualized marketing, and from focusing on acquiring lots of new customers to retaining and building more business from a smaller base of loyal high-value customers. Although many industrial firms have practiced customer relationship management for a long time, now firms in the consumer services market (e.g., Google.com) and even marketers of consumer packaged goods work to build long-term customer relationships, 1:1. How can the maker of canned dog food profitably build relationships with each consumer? Internet technologies can facilitate relationship marketing in many new ways, yet many firms that purchase and install relationship management technologies are losing money on them. This chapter explains the process, identifies key internet tools, and presents the case for a consumer centric customer relationship management focus throughout the entire supply chain.

RELATIONSHIP MARKETING DEFINED

Marketers named this customer focus *relationship marketing* (also *1:1 marketing*). As originally defined, **relationship marketing** is about establishing, maintaining, enhancing, and commercializing customer relationships through promise fulfillment (Grönroos, 1990). Usually firms try to build profitable, mutually beneficial relationships in the long term (versus the short term). Promise fulfillment means that when firms make offers in their marketing communications programs, customer expectations will be met through actual brand experiences. For example, an offer on the Stash Tea Web site homepage promises a free box with the purchase of three but the order page does not confirm this offer, and the total quantity shown on the final order is only three. If four do not arrive, the customer will likely consider buying tea from competitor Twinings next time. Even when the four boxes arrive, the suspense may erode some of the customer's trust in the firm. Similarly, good relationships are built when company personnel meet the promises made by salespeople and promotional messages.

Today relationship marketing involves much more than promise fulfillment. It means two-way communication with individual stakeholders, one at a time (1:1). How can a firm understand an individual customer's needs without asking what they are? Fortunately, the internet's social media allow companies to listen much better than ever before (recall the Dell story in Chapter 1).

An organization using relationship marketing focuses on wallet share more than market share. **Wallet share** is the amount of sales a firm can generate from one customer and, thus, reflects a focus on retention and growth rather than an acquisition focus (market share). For instance, Amazon wants to sell books, music, household appliances, and more to each customer. Relationship marketing differentiates individual customers based on need rather than differentiating products for target groups—such as buyers of novels by a particular author. It will be more profitable for

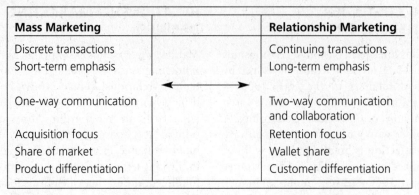

Mass Marketing		Relationship Marketing
Discrete transactions		Continuing transactions
Short-term emphasis		Long-term emphasis
	←———————→	
One-way communication		Two-way communication and collaboration
Acquisition focus		Retention focus
Share of market		Wallet share
Product differentiation		Customer differentiation

EXHIBIT 15.1   Continuum from Mass Marketing to Relationship Marketing

Cisco to identify its best customers, get to know them individually, and suggest additional products based on their needs than to spend all its efforts acquiring new customers. If Cisco is successful, clients will eventually buy all their networking products and services from the firm (greater wallet share). Cisco saves on promotion and price discounting expenditures by spending time on customer retention versus customer acquisition. Exhibit 15.1 displays a summary of these ideas, comparing mass marketing to relationship marketing.

Few firms fall on either end of the continuum but instead use varying strategies for different products and markets. For example, Procter & Gamble must differentiate its brands of laundry detergent for sale to the masses; however, it tries to build relationships with mothers who will buy increasing numbers of P&G products over the years, from Ivory powder for washing baby clothes and Pampers diapers to Crest toothpaste for the family and Olay cosmetics for themselves.

STAKEHOLDERS

Most companies also use relationship marketing techniques to build mutually supportive bonds with stakeholders other than consumers, such as employees and suppliers. Organizations can establish and maintain relationships with many different stakeholder groups. The four most affected by internet technologies are the following:

1. **Employees.** It is difficult for a firm to persuade buyers when employees are not happy. When Yahoo! introduced its new position, "The Life Engine," it gave away a Harley-Davidson motorcycle to one of 800 employees who wrote the best reason that Yahoo! was their life engine. This prize generated excitement among employees for the new positioning strategy. As many employees are instrumental in building relationships with customers, it is critical for them to have training and access to data and systems used for relationship management. In fact, some observers say that many relationship management programs fail due to lack of employee training and commitment.

2. **Business customers in the supply chain.** Firms build and maintain relationships with other businesses for the purpose of buying and selling both upstream and downstream. First are business customers: the B2B market. Procter & Gamble works with numerous wholesale and retail intermediaries, using internet technologies to facilitate these relationships. Second are a company's suppliers. General Electric uses the internet to receive bids from its suppliers, a system that not only lowers transaction costs but also enhances competition and speeds order fulfillment.

3. **Lateral partners.** Other businesses, not-for-profit organizations, or governments join with the firm for some common goal but not for transactions with each other. CargoNet Transportation Community Network, a consortium of 200,000 shippers, handled 250 million trade-related

documents a year in its peak for Hong Kong shippers at the world's busiest port. The internet facilitates document tracking and customer service for manufacturers, ocean, rail, truck, and air carriers as well as banks, insurance companies, and governments associated with CargoNet (www.eds.com).

4. **Consumers.** These individuals are the end users of products and services. Marketers must differentiate between business customers and final consumers because different tactics are usually employed in the B2C and B2B markets.

CUSTOMER RELATIONSHIP MANAGEMENT (CRM)

Customer relationship management (CRM) is the process of targeting, acquiring, transacting, servicing, retaining, and building long-term relationships with customers. CRM is an oft misused term that many companies use to refer to the software and other technology used to implement CRM solutions. As you'll see, CRM is much more—it is a philosophy, strategy, and process. It includes all the tenets of relationship marketing, and is grounded in customer data and facilitated by technology. Increasingly, organizations recognize that if they don't keep their customers happy, someone else will.

CRM Benefits

The benefits of CRM include increased revenue from better prospect targeting, increased wallet share with current customers, and retaining customers for longer periods of time. These benefits are realized through databases that help firms understand their customers better and use this knowledge to build loyalty and optimize lifetime value. CRM tactics can also decrease costs, resulting in greater profitability.

In a study of 45 companies, 68 percent used prospect and customer data to build mathematical models that helped them perform more effective customer segmentation ("Managing Customer Data," 2003). Effective segmentation allowed them to define prospect and customer profiles that were most likely to respond favorably to particular promotional offers, or simply to identify the best segment of prospects for current or new products.

Most businesses spend more money acquiring new customers than they spend keeping current customers—but this approach is usually a mistake. The cost of acquiring a new customer is typically five times higher than the cost of retaining a current one, as shown in Exhibit 15.2. In this example, if a firm budgets $3,000 to acquire six customers, the cost of acquiring each will be $500. Because retaining customers costs one-fifth less (on average), that same $500 could be spent enticing five customers to stay at a cost of $100 each. If instead of spending $3,000 on gaining six customers, a firm spent $1,500 on three new customers and $1,500 on customer retention, it would be 12 customers ahead.

One reason that retention is less costly than acquisition is reduced promotion costs, both for advertising and discounts. Additionally, higher response rates to promotional efforts yield more profits. Sales teams can be more effective when they get to know individual customers well.

Acquisition Emphasis		Retention Emphasis	
Gain 6 new customers ($500 each)	$3,000	Gain 3 new customers ($500 each)	$1,500
Retain 5 current customers ($100 each)	$ 500	Retain 20 current customers ($100 each)	$2,000
Total cost	$3,500	Total cost	$3,500
Total number of customers	11	Total number of customers	23

EXHIBIT 15.2 Maximizing Number of Customers

Source: Adapted from Don Peppers and Martha Rogers, The One to One Future (New York: Doubleday, 1996).

Another reason CRM makes sense is that loyal customers are experienced customers. They know the products well, and they know who to call in the firm when they have questions. Loyal customers cost less to service.

Having more customers leads to more sales. However, acquiring and retaining customers is only part of the equation. A firm must also attempt to increase the amount purchased by each customer. For example, Southwest Airlines and most online travel agents send e-mails to customers when the airfare to a destination of interest to them drops.

In addition to buying more, satisfied customers recommend Web sites, stores, and products to their friends. Word-of-mouth communication among customers has been called the heart of CRM. Positive word-of-mouth can attract many new customers, but negative word-of-mouth can drive them away. One study reported that each dissatisfied customer tells 10 people about the unhappy experience; of 13 percent of dissatisfied customers each tells 20 people how bad the company and its products were (Sonnenberg, 1993). The internet outdates this off-line statistic because now each dissatisfied customer can tell thousands with one keystroke. For example, MSN.com featured an online article, "Is Home Depot Shafting Shoppers?" That same day 14,000 readers commented in the story's talk back section at the Web site or sent an e-mail to share their bad customer service stories (Beal and Strauss 2008). This extensive word-of-mouth is accomplished through e-mail, newsgroups, blogs, social networks, and personal Web pages.

One key CRM benefit is its cost saving advantage, as seen in the Cisco example. Consider the following:

- One study estimated that U.S. businesses saved $155 billion between 1998 and 2000 by using internet technology for both CRM and supply chain management (interactive.wsj.com).
- A 5 percent increase in customer retention translates to 25 percent to 125 percent profitability in the B2B market.

CRM's Facets

Many e-marketers, especially those focusing on CRM software capabilities, suggest that CRM has three facets: sales force automation, marketing automation, and customer service. The first occurs primarily in the B2B market, while the second and third are important in all markets.

SALES FORCE AUTOMATION (SFA) "Increase your sales, not your sales force," proclaims SFA software. Used primarily in the B2B market, SFA allows salespeople to build, maintain, and access customer records; manage leads and accounts; manage their schedules; and more. In relation to e-marketing, SFA helps the sales force acquire, retain, and grow customers by accessing customer and product data from the company's data warehouses, both while in the office and on the road. Salespeople can also send the results of sales calls and activity reports to the data warehouse for access by others. Up-to-date customer and prospect records help customer service representatives and others build customer relationships. As an example, SFA leader Salesforce.com's software boasts the following benefits:

- **Sales.** Salesforce SFA enables companies to drive sales productivity, increase visibility, and expand revenues with an affordable, easy-to-deploy service that delivers success to companies of all sizes.
- **Service & Support.** The Salesforce solution for customer service gets companies up and running in a matter of weeks with a call center application that is loved by agents and a customer self-service application—powered by Web 2.0—that generates new levels of customer loyalty.
- **Partner Relationship Management.** Salesforce Partners makes it easy for partners to access leads, collaborate on deals, and locate all the information they need in order to be successful. The Salesforce Partners is seamlessly integrated with Salesforce SFA to

deliver unparalleled visibility to your company's entire sales pipeline for direct and indirect channels.

- **Marketing** Salesforce Marketing enables closed-loop marketing to execute, manage, and analyze the results of multichannel campaigns. Marketing executives can measure the ROI of their budgets, tie revenue back to specific marketing programs, and make adjustments in real time.
- **Content.** Salesforce Content brings Web 2.0 usability to your business content so you can share it more effectively and enhance collaboration within your organization. Empower employees to find the exact documents they need, right from the business applications they use on a daily basis.
- **Analytics.** Salesforce Analytics empowers business users at every level to gain relevant insight and analysis. With real-time reporting, calculations, and dashboards, businesses can optimize performance, decision making, and resource allocation (*source:* www.salesforce.com).

MARKETING AUTOMATION Marketing automation activities aid marketers with effective targeting, efficient marketing communication, and real-time monitoring of customer and market trends. It is "a disciplined approach to the capture, integration, and analysis of customer data [that] is needed to identify and leverage customer relationships and opportunities to their fullest. This emerging space, called marketing automation, forms the core of the knowledge engine which drives customer relationship management (CRM)" (Distefano, 2000). Marketing automation software usually takes data from Web sites and databases and turns it into reports for fine-tuning CRM efforts. Software solutions include e-mail campaign management, database marketing, market segmentation, Web site log analysis, and more.

In 2008, marketing automation is no longer emerging, but a powerful marketing solution for CRM. SAS, business intelligence and predictive analytics software provider, offers the following marketing automation benefits with its software (www.sas.com):

- **Maintain an integrated customer view.** SAS provides a unified view of customers across your enterprise that incorporates information from all touch points and channels, ensuring that customer information is consistent, secure, accurate and comprehensible to users.
- **Manage customer life cycles.** Customer segmentation and profiling capabilities consolidate insight at a customer level to build and monitor critical strategic segments over time.
- **Improve effectiveness through better targeting, measurements and analytics.** Through advanced analytic techniques such as data mining, market basket analysis, link analysis, forecasting and optimization, as well as segmentation, profiling and behavior analysis, SAS Marketing Automation helps you understand customers' past behavior and predict future opportunities.
- **Drive complex communication strategies.** Through an intuitive graphical interface and in-depth campaign management functions, business users can easily deploy the results of advanced analytics and drive multichannel, multistage communications using reliable customer intelligence.
- **Understand the results of marketing activities.** SAS Marketing Automation allows users to fully understand campaign responses, whether those responses involve direct communication or subtle changes in behavior. Reports on campaign effectiveness combine this response analysis with budget expectations to deliver a full picture of the financial return achieved by each marketing initiative.
- **Provide integrated support for all business units.** SAS Marketing Automation fully supports the activities of your key marketing campaign participants, including business users, database marketers, quantitative analysts and IT.

- **Manage your IT infrastructure.** Allowing companies to take advantage of their existing IT infrastructure, SAS Marketing Automation is built on technology that can be deployed across the enterprise in a scalable, multitier architecture.

CUSTOMER SERVICE Customer service permeates every stage of customer acquisition, retention, and development practices, although most service occurs postpurchase when customers have questions or complaints. Key tools include e-mail, online live chat, and Web self-service through frequently asked questions and more. Mercedes-Benz takes customer service to a new level with its "teleweb" technology. The consumer types a question into a form on the Web site and receives an immediate phone call from a Mercedes representative. The consumer and representative can then discuss the question while viewing the same Web pages. In fact, software now allows customer service reps on the telephone with a customer to take control of the user's mouse and guide the customer around the company Web site. E-mail, customized Web pages, live Web chat, and package tracking using PDAs are just a few of the customer service techniques described throughout this chapter.

Regardless of technique, online or off-line, customer service is critical to building long-term customer relationships.

CRM BUILDING BLOCKS

Although companies understand CRM's benefits and are investing heavily in CRM software, as many as 70 percent lose money on this investment. Thus, businesses are trying to determine what works and what doesn't, knowing that they have to get it right to win. This section focuses on the eight important CRM components used for e-marketing, based on a Gartner Group CRM model (see Exhibit 15.3).

1. CRM Vision

Many organizations purchase expensive CRM software just because it is becoming a necessary component of successful competition. It is no wonder that so many projects fail. Exhibit 15.4 shows some of the differences in successful and unsuccessful CRM efforts in the insurance industry. It shows that more than twice as many firms with successful CRM strategies spent time working with employees before and while implementing CRM systems.

---

1. CRM Vision: Leadership, value proposition
2. CRM Strategy: Objectives, target markets

---

3. Valued Customer Experience
Understand requirements
Monitor expectations
Maintain satisfaction
Collaboration and feedback
Customer interaction

4. Organizational Collaboration
Culture and structure
People, skills, competencies
Incentives and compensation
Employee communication
Partners and suppliers

---

5. CRM Processes: Customer life cycle, knowledge management
6. CRM Information: Data, analysis, one view across channels
7. CRM Technology: Applications, architecture, infrastructure
8. CRM Metrics: Value, retention, satisfaction, loyalty, cost to serve

---

EXHIBIT 15.3   Eight Building Blocks for Successful CRM

Source: Adapted from Gartner Group, available at www.gartner.com.

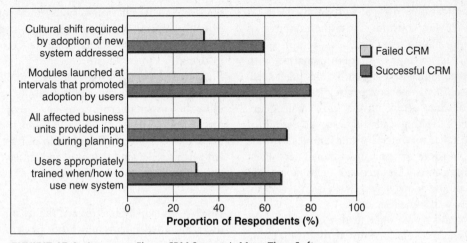

EXHIBIT 15.4 Insurance Firms: CRM Success Is More Than Software

Source: Agarwal, Anupam, Harding, and Schumacker (2004).

Management must start with a vision that fits the company culture and makes sense for the firm's brands and value propositions. Some say that the main reason CRM projects fail is because firms do not realize how pervasive they are and underestimate the costs. For example, when a company installs CRM software to integrate data from the Web site and brick-and-mortar retail operations, customer service reps need training and must be committed to the initiative. Some customer service reps bypass CRM software because it is easier to do it the old way. To be successful, the CRM vision must start at the top and filter throughout the company to keep the firm completely customer focused.

The privacy policy also needs a vision supported by key executives. Marketers have access to lots of information about every customer and prospect, and that information is stored in databases and used for direct-marketing communications. One key aspect of this vision is how to guard customer privacy.

GUARDING CUSTOMER PRIVACY Use of customer data is very important to marketers, yet the temptation to overuse it must be balanced by the need to satisfy customers and not anger them. The burden is on marketers to use customer and prospect information responsibly, both for their own business health and for the image of the profession. In one study of 1,000 adult internet users, 92 percent said they were concerned about online privacy, and this concern remains high on consumer lists today ("Consumers Wary," 1999). Two-thirds said they were very concerned about misuse of personal information and did not want it shared with others unless they gave permission. Consumers are unaware of the extent to which real-time profiling and other techniques monitor their online behavior—and marketers must address this issue before regulators make them do it. For instance, Facebook made a huge mistake in late 2007 when it published customer purchasing behavior on profile pages. One Facebook user purchased an item at Overstock.com using her personal e-mail address, and then saw the following on her Facebook Profile news feed: "Charlene bought a basin square table and one other item at Overstock.com" (see Charlene's Blog at blogs.forrester.com).

CRM is based on trust. Customers must believe that the information they give companies when they purchase online, in e-mail, or in other ways will be used responsibly. It means using the information to improve the relationship by tailoring goods, services, and marketing communications to meet individual needs. It means allowing consumers to request removal of their information from databases, to opt-out of e-mail lists, and not to share information with other companies unless permission is granted.

Another important privacy issue concerns intrusions into people's lives. "Junk" mail, spam, repeated telephone calls requesting a switch of long-distance provider are all examples of marketing messages that can upset consumers. Even the community classified ad newspaper that arrives on the doorstep each week is an assault on the privacy of some residents.

What's a marketer to do? The answer is twofold: build relationships through dialogue and through better target profiling. Companies must listen to customers and prospects and give them what they want. If a consumer wants to receive e-mail from American Airlines, great. If not, the firm should remove that customer from the list, perhaps checking once a year to see whether the status has changed. Why? Organizations know that retention and development of customer relationships are more profitable than one-time customer transactions, and that relationship capital is one of the firm's strongest assets. Second, marketers can use consumer information to build more precise target profiles. Instead of sending a mass e-mailing to everyone who visits the site, how about sending individual or small group e-mails to people who might really need a car for the flight they just booked at the site? Individuals do not get upset with firms who send valuable and timely information to them.

TRUSTe To help Web sites earn the trust of their users, an independent, non-profit privacy initiative named TRUSTe was created. TRUSTe provides its seal and logo to any Web site meeting its philosophies, as stated on the site (Exhibit 15.5). Note how well these and the following information requirements fit with good CRM practices.

• Adopting and implementing a privacy policy that factors in the goals of your individual Web site as well as consumer anxiety over sharing personal information online.

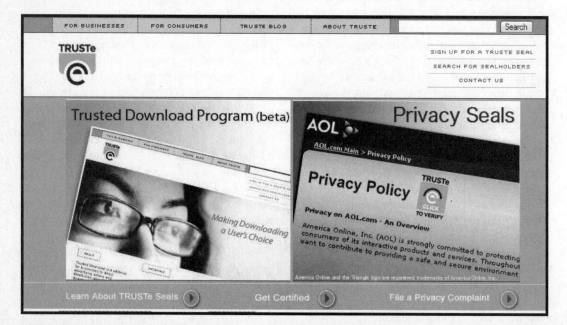

EXHIBIT 15.5   TRUSTe Builds User Trust

Source: www.truste.org.

- Posting notice and disclosure of collection and use practices regarding personally identifiable information (data used to identify, contact, or locate a person) via a posted privacy statement.
- Giving users choice and consent over how their personal information is used and shared.
- Putting data security and quality, and access measures in place to safeguard, update, and correct personally identifiable information.

In addition, sites must publish the following information on their sites to gain the TRUSTe seal (www.truste.org):

1. What personal information is being gathered by your site
2. Who is collecting the information
3. How the information will be used
4. With whom the information will be shared
5. The choices available to users regarding collection, use, and distribution of their information (You must offer users an opportunity to opt-out of internal secondary uses as well as third-party distribution for secondary uses.)
6. The security procedures in place to protect users' collected information from loss, misuse, or alteration (If your site collects, uses, or distributes personally identifiable information such as credit card or social security numbers, accepted transmission protocols, including encryption, must be in place.)
7. How users can update or correct inaccuracies in their pertinent information (Appropriate measures shall be taken to ensure that personal information collected online is accurate, complete, and timely, and that easy-to-use mechanisms are in place for users to verify that inaccuracies have been corrected.)

Other organizations also provide guidelines for internet privacy. The American Marketing Association has a code of ethics for internet marketing, dealing primarily with privacy and intellectual property. See Chapter 5 for more about the legal aspects of privacy.

2. CRM Strategy

E-marketers must determine their objectives and strategies before buying CRM technology. These objectives may involve any stakeholders (employees, business customers, partners, or consumers) and will likely entail targeting, acquiring, retaining, and growing specified relationships. The B2B market is different from the B2C market due to its CRM focus on lead generation and follow-up for salespeople (often using the previously discussed Sales Force Automation software).

Many of these CRM goals refer to customer loyalty. Most firms would be delighted if they had customers who proudly wore their brand name on clothing and tried to talk others into buying the brand—like customers of Harley-Davidson and Apple Computer. Chapter 10 discussed five levels of relationship intensity (awareness, identity, connection, community, and advocacy). Thus, an important CRM strategy is trying to move customers upward in this pyramid.

Another CRM goal involves building bonds with customers that transcend the product experience itself. Some experts suggest that relationship marketing is practiced on three levels (see Exhibit 15.6). The strongest relationships are formed if all three levels are used and if the product itself actually satisfies buyers. At level one, marketers build a financial bond with customers by using pricing strategies. At this lowest level of relationship, price promotions are easily imitated. Southwest Airlines sends periodic e-mail notification of price discounts to individual users. These discounts can be timed and priced to build wallet share.

At level two, marketers stimulate social interaction between customers and the company, and among customers themselves. According to eMarketer, 9 out of 10 interactions with customers are nontransactional communication, thus demonstrating this strategy. Community-building is an important way to forge level-two relationships and strengthen loyalty (see Chapter 14).

At level three, relationship marketing relies on creating structural solutions to customer problems. Structural bonds form when firms add value by making structural changes that facilitate

Level	Primary Bond	Potential for Sustained Competitive Advantage	Main Element of Marketing Mix	Web Example
One	Financial	Low	Price	www.southwest.com
Two	Social Build 1:1 relationships Build community	Medium	Personal communications	www.MySpace.com
Three	Structural	High	Service delivery	my.yahoo.com

EXHIBIT 15.6   Three Levels of Relationship Marketing
Source: Adapted from Berry and Parasuraman (1991).

the relationship. For example, the Google toolbar for Internet Explorer assures Google search use by customers installing it (Exhibit 15.7). All of the major Web portals work to create structural bonds with their users. Services such as My Yahoo! allow consumers to customize their interface to Yahoo! so it lists local weather and movies, personal stock portfolios, and news of interest to

them. Once consumers invest the time and effort to customize this interface, they will be reluctant to switch to another portal.

Social networks combine levels two and three: they create community and structural bonds. When customers create profiles on MySpace or LinkedIn, they spend time learning how to use the sites and they invest by uploading content. Thus,

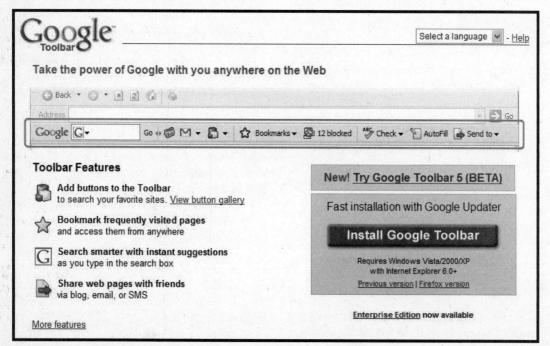

EXHIBIT 15.7   Google Downloadable Toolbar
Source: www.google.com.

customers are likely to stick with the few social networking sites they use. Even Tripadvisor has this structural bond because customers have to register in order to log on and rate hotels.

3. Valued Customer Experience

Most customers want brand loyalty as much as the firms they patronize want it. Being a consumer can be difficult because of constant bombardment by marketing communications and unlimited product choices. Jagdish Sheth (1995) wrote that from a consumer's perspective, the basic tenet of CRM is choice reduction. This notion suggests that consumers want to patronize the same Web site, social network, and online booksellers because doing so is efficient. That is, consumers do not want to spend their days contemplating which brand of toothpaste to buy or how to find a good search engine. Many consumers are "loyalty prone," searching for the right product or service and then sticking with it as long as the promises are more or less fulfilled. For example, many customers buy from Amazon.com because of good previous experiences, the convenience of having personal preferences on file, one-click ordering, and the familiar interface, regardless of price.

Customers generally like to patronize stores, services, and Web sites where they are treated like individuals with important needs and where they know those needs will be met, "satisfaction guaranteed." Users believe the company cares when they get an e-mail about upgrades to their PDA, addressed to them by name that refers to the exact product purchased. They feel more brand loyalty when Amazon sends an e-mail announcing a new book by an author they enjoy. Of course, firms must learn to answer e-mails sent from customers as well. Listening to hundreds of thousands of customers one at a time can be difficult and expensive, but it satisfies customers.

Customers' preferences for communicating with each company vary by individual as well as by situation and product type. Customers might want to call and speak with a live rep about an account problem, go to a Web site to research product information, use e-mail to complain about a service problem, and so forth. Exhibit 15.8 displays these options covering many technologies, using both automated and human intervention for both synchronous (simultaneous) and asynchronous communication. This exhibit reinforces the importance of the internet in creating valued customer experiences and the idea that firms must be adept with many different technologies and processes, putting the focus on customers and their preferences, not the company's capabilities.

4. Organizational Collaboration

Marketers collaborate both within and outside the organization. Within the firm, cross-functional teams join forces to focus on customer satisfaction to create a CRM culture. Outside the firm, when two or more companies join forces, the results often exceed what each firm might have accomplished alone—whether it is in the distribution channel or a nontransactional-type collaboration. In fact, some marketers believe that today's marketplace consists of supply chain competition,

	Automated	**Human**
Synchronous	Web 1:1 self-service	Telephone
	Online transactions	Online chat
	Telephone routing	Collaboration tools
Asynchronous	Automated e-mail	E-mail response
	Short message services (SMS)	Postal mail
	Web forms	Blog posts/comments
	Fax on demand	Micromedia sites (e.g., twitter.com)

EXHIBIT 15.8 Relationships Over Multiple Communication Channels

not individual firm competition. For instance, Amazon and Toys "R" Us teamed up to form the online baby retail site BabiesRUs (at www.toysrus.com).. Amazon's online retail expertise combined with the toy merchandising expertise of Toys "R" Us benefits both partners as well as the site's customers.

In the following sections, we discuss two important collaboration techniques that capitalize on internet properties: CRM–SCM integration and extranets.

CRM–SCM INTEGRATION   CRM usually refers to "front-end" operations, meaning that firms work to create satisfying experiences at all customer touch points: telephone calls to customer service reps, e-commerce purchases at online stores, e-mail contact, and so forth. This challenge is substantial because different employees and computer systems collect various information, which somehow must be integrated into appropriate customer records. In one study sponsored by Jupiter Communications, three phone calls were made to *Forbes* magazine asking why two renewal offers were different. The interviewer got three different explanations. Fortunately several firms now provide software to address this issue. For example, the Aspect Relationship Portal assists CRM staff by integrating all customer contact media—phone, fax, e-mail, and Web—with front- and back-office operations (www.aspect.com).

In the online environment of customer control, however, even consistently good customer service is not enough. With technological advances and interoperability, online retailers can seamlessly link the "back-end" (e.g., inventory and payment) with the "front-end" CRM system and the entire supply chain management system (SCM). The entire supply chain can work together to single-mindedly focus on meeting consumer needs and make higher profits in the process. It all centers, of course, on information (Exhibit 15.9).

Imagine that a customer orders a particular shirt from a clothing retailer's Web site. In the past, if the shirt was out of stock, the customer might see a Web screen with that message, but more likely she would receive a postcard or an e-mail after some time. With an integrated CRM–SCM system, however, the system can instantly check inventory levels at the retailer and notify the customer that it is not available—usually this information appears right on the product page. The next generation of CRM–SCM integration would allow immediate inventory checking at the wholesaler or manufacturer to determine availability. Then the system could notify the customer during the ordering process and offer options: Wait two weeks for delivery from the manufacturer or consider a similar shirt currently in stock, for example. This option message could even be done with a pop-up window featuring a live customer service rep helping the customer. Lands' End, Toyota, and Intuit are three of many sites using LivePerson software, which offers Web site integration with live customer service reps in real time (www.liveperson.com).

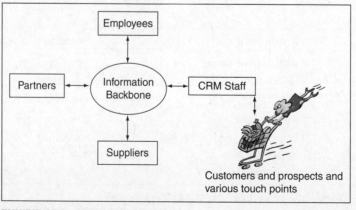

EXHIBIT 15.9   CRM-SCM Integration

Connecting customers with supply chain businesses provides several advantages. First, all firms will share transaction data so that inventories can be kept low. If producers and wholesalers constantly receive data about consumer orders, they can produce goods in a timely manner. Second, upstream firms can use the data to design products that better meet consumer needs (see the co-designing discussion in Chapter 10). Third, if customer service reps have up-to-the-minute information about product inventories, they will be able to better help consumers immediately. Catalog firms are already fairly accomplished at this task but the process breaks down when supplier firms are several levels upstream from the retailer.

As more firms integrate CRM and SCM activities, they will become more responsive to individual customer needs. For example, Levi's Personal Pair program used electronic scanners to send precise measurements directly to the factory for individualized jeans, and Dell produces and ships customized computers within days. Conversely, this type of integration is quite difficult when a firm has many different channels for its brands and when each firm uses different software and hardware to manage its internal systems. Nevertheless, the systems for integration are currently available and are helping firms become market winners.

EXTRANET Extranets are two or more intranet networks that are joined for the purpose of sharing information. If two companies link their intranets, they would have an extranet. By definition, extranets are proprietary to the organizations involved. Companies participating in an extranet have formed a structural bond, the third and strongest level of relationship marketing. It is the use of extranets that allows CRM–SCM integration.

Electronic Data Systems (EDS) is a Dallas-based firm that provides enterprise-wide computer desktop services from procurement to network management for large clients. The word *enterprise* means that EDS focuses on all the computer desktops in an entire company, bringing them together in a network. In 1998, the firm managed more than 736,000 desktops, both internally and externally, in 19 countries. EDS created an innovative extranet called the Renascence Channel,

which links desktops of its suppliers, clients, and employees into an electronic marketplace. Forty suppliers selling more than 2,000 software products fund the private network, paying $25,000 to $100,000 each to display their products and services in a catalog-type format. Suppliers benefit because they have access to and can build relationships with lots of potential buyers. The buyers trust the suppliers because EDS selected them and they pay lower prices because suppliers' costs are lower in this channel: One vendor reported a drop in order-processing expenses from $150 to $25 per item. Buyers benefit by having desktop access to convenient product information, click-of-a-mouse purchasing, product delivery tracking, online training, and expedited delivery. The Renascence Channel both creates a barrier to entry for suppliers not part of the network and presents switching costs for companies using the channel's services. The Renascence Channel is a good example of relationship building in the B2B market using internet technology.

5. CRM Processes

CRM involves an understanding of the customer care life cycle, as presented in Exhibit 15.10. Firms monitor and attract customers, both online and off-line, as they progress through the stages: target, acquire, transact, service, retain, and grow. This process begins with the e-marketing plan when companies select target markets. However, opportunities often arise when a new target group

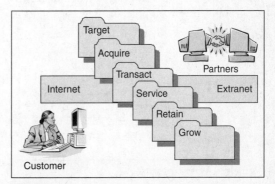

EXHIBIT 15.10   Customer Care Life Cycle

Source: Adapted from speech by Tod Famous, Cisco Systems.

appears at the Web site—such as when Brooks Brothers noted a large number of Japanese users at the site. Thus, the cycle is circular in nature: for example, while servicing customers a new target may emerge. This important cycle is based on one central tenet of CRM—it is better to attract, retain, and grow customers than to focus only on customer acquisition. Of course, not all customers go through this process—some do less business with the firm or leave to transact with a competitor. Sometimes companies try to reacquire these customers, as when AOL sends CDs to customers who have cancelled their accounts, with the line "We want you back" and an offer of free service for a certain period.

Digging deeper into CRM techniques reveals that firms use the process shown in Exhibit 15.11 to focus on moving specific individual customers through the customer care life cycle.

IDENTIFYING CUSTOMERS Firms obtain information about prospects, business customers, and end consumers through personal disclosure, automated tracking through the sales force, customer service encounters, bar code scanners at retailers, and Web site activity. Every piece of user information goes into a database that helps firms identify the best customers. *Best* is described in many different ways, such as highest value, longest loyalty, highest frequency of purchase, and so on, as described next.

DIFFERENTIATING CUSTOMERS Customers have different needs. The internet allows firms to collect information to identify various demographic, geographic, psychographic, or usage segments as

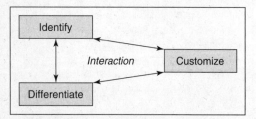

EXHIBIT 15.11 CRM Process

Source: Formulated from the ideas of Moon (2000), NS Kasanoff and Thompson (1999).

well as individual similarities and differences, and use this information to increase profits.

One important way to differentiate is by customer value: Not all customers have equal value to a firm. One rule of thumb states that 20 percent of the customers provide 80 percent of the business's profits (recall the Pareto principle pyramid from Chapter 11). Although this ratio varies widely by industry and firm, CRM allows marketers to leverage their resources by investing more in the most lucrative customers. The idea is not new but what is new is that technology allows firms to identify high-value customers and respond with offers in real time over the internet. Value differentiation pays off: When a plastics firm focused on its most profitable customers, it cut its customer base from 800 to 90 and increased its revenues by 400 percent (Renner, 2000). However, not all firms have high- and low-value customers. According to the Rogers and Peppers Group, differentiation by valuation is not profitable unless a firm can say that at least half of its profits come from 20 percent or fewer of its customers (the A and A+ customers in Chapter 11).

How can organizations identify their high-value customers? By mining and profiling in customer databases and using real-time and real-space data collection techniques. Many firms use RFM analysis (recency, frequency, and monetary value) to mine databases for customers who spend the most money and buy frequently and recently. They also evaluate sales growth per customer over time and determine service costs for individual customers.

Some customers call more often with questions and inquiries; some return products more frequently. Some customers are clearly not profitable and, thus, should be "fired" so that the firm can allocate resources profitably. For example, Continental Airlines identified 35,000 tier A+ customers and 400,000 A level customers. These customers get extra services, such as being put on a competitor's flight immediately when the customer's Continental flight is cancelled (Kupper, 2004). This attention has resulted in an extra $200 in annual revenue from each A customer and $800 each for A+ customers. Continental doesn't exactly fire low-value customers, but simply does not give them the same high level of service as it does with those of high value. Casinos operate the same way—high rollers get anything they want, and low spenders might get only a buffet discount. They know the difference because customers use player cards in slot machines that are networked and always collecting data on spending patterns.

Tripadvisor.com has 5 million registered users at its travel Web site. In 2007 it sent a special reward to those who had posted hotel reviews, thus differentiating and rewarding the customers who engage by uploading content (Exhibit 15.12).

CUSTOMIZING THE MARKETING MIX Once a firm identifies prospects and differentiates customers according to characteristics, behavior, needs, or value, it can consider customizing offerings to various segments or individuals. **Customization** occurs when firms tailor their marketing mixes to meet the needs of small target segments, even to the individual level, using electronic marketing tools. Products, marketing communication messages, and dynamic pricing can all be tailored to individuals and delivered over the internet in a timely manner. These approaches were not possible before the internet except with very high-priced products such as manufacturing

EXHIBIT 15.12 Tripadvisor.com Rewards Customers Who Add Content to the Site

Source: Author's E-Mail (Used with Permission of Tripadvisor.com).

equipment. Through customization firms can zero in on the precise needs of each prospect and customer and build long-term, profitable relationships. The mission statement for MatchLogic, Inc., puts the communication customization goal quite succinctly:

> To deliver the right marketing message, to the right person, with the right offer, at the right time, and know within seconds if that message was effective.

Some writers use the term *personalize* when referring to customization. **Personalization** involves ways that marketers individualize in an impersonal computer networked environment. For example, Web sites may greet users by name or automatically send e-mail to individuals with personal account information (see Exhibit 15.13) . We use the term *customization* because it refers to much more than automated personalization.

INTERACTION Implicit in the MatchLogic statement is a feedback loop. Interaction with customers is what allows firms to collect the data necessary for identification and differentiation and to evaluate the resulting customization

effectiveness on a continuous basis. Peppers and Rogers (1997, p. 15) call this interaction a "learning relationship."

> A **learning relationship** between a customer and an enterprise gets smarter and smarter with each individual interaction, defining in ever more detail the customer's own individual needs and tastes.

The idea here is that both the firm and the customer learn from each experience and interaction. In a perfect relationship, this ongoing experience equates to increased trust, loyalty, and an increasing share of business for the firm, with peace of mind for the customer. The internet is uniquely positioned to deliver on this promise. When a company adopts this philosophy, it is a learning organization.

6. CRM Information

Information is the lubricant of CRM. The more information a firm has, the better value it can provide to each customer and prospect in terms of more accurate, timely, and relevant offerings. Many firms entice customers to provide additional

EXHIBIT 15.13 Amazon.com Uses Customization to Personalize Web Pages

Source: www.amazon.com. Amazon.com is a registered trademark or trademark of Amazon.com, Inc. in the United States and/or other countries. © 2000 by Amazon.com. All rights reserved.

information over time by engaging them in blogs, product reviews, or through e-commerce transactions. For example, Orbitz.com first requests a simple e-mail address from those who want information about discount offers and subsequently asks about vacation preferences so as to provide more relevant e-mailings. A customer who provides increasingly more personal information shows enough trust in the firm to invest in the relationship.

Sometimes firms gather this type of information under the guise of entertainment. For example, the Mini Cooper automobile gains valuable information about the preferences of site visitors by allowing them to configure the perfect car online, using 10 million possible option combinations (www.miniusa.com).

Companies gain much information from customers less intrusively by tracking their behavior electronically. Information technology allows companies to move beyond the traditional segment profiling (e.g., Generation X) to detailed profiles of individuals. For example, when product bar code scanner data collected at the checkout is combined with a store shopping card, the company can identify individual customer purchases over time. On the internet, software tracks a user's movement from page to page, indicating how much time was spent on each page, whether the user made a purchase, the type of computer and operating system, and more. Firms can track which sites users visited before and after theirs, and use this information to guess which competitive products are under consideration and to learn about users' interests. Tracking user behavior is valuable to both users and companies but it has its critics because of privacy considerations, as previously mentioned.

Retailers face the daunting task of gathering information from each channel and filtering it into a common database. The Sharper Image does this task brilliantly. Now a customer can telephone the customer service representative to discuss a product purchased in the brick-and-mortar store last week, and refer to an e-mail sent yesterday, because the data are all in the database under one customer record. This approach is known as having a 360-degree customer view, or one view across channels. In her book, *Customers.com*, Patricia Seybold (1998) identified eight critical success factors for building successful e-business relationships with customers. Even a decade later, these factors remain a good springboard to understanding how internet technologies facilitate customer relationship management using e-marketing.

1. *Target the right customers.* Identify the best prospects and customers and learn as much about them as possible.
2. *Own the customer's total experience.* This factor refers to the customer share of mind or share of wallet previously discussed.
3. *Streamline business processes that impact the customer.* This task can be accomplished through CRM–SCM integration and monomaniacal customer focus.
4. *Provide a 360-degree view of the customer relationship.* Everyone in the firm who touches the customer should understand all aspects of that customer's relationship with the company. For example, customer service reps should know all customer activity over time and understand which products and services might benefit that particular customer.
5. *Let customers help themselves.* Provide Web sites and other electronic means for customers to find things they need quickly and conveniently, 24/7.
6. *Help customers do their jobs.* Especially in the B2B market, if a firm provides products and services to help customers perform well in their businesses, they will be loyal and pay a premium for the help. Many supply chain management electronic processes facilitate this factor.
7. *Deliver personalized service.* Customer profiling, privacy safekeeping, and marketing mix customization all aid in delivering personalized services electronically.
8. *Foster community.* Enticing customers to join in communities of interest that relate to a firm's products is one important way to build loyalty.

7. CRM Technology

Technology greatly enhances CRM processes. Incoming toll-free numbers, electronic kiosks, fax-on-demand, voice mail, and automated telephone routing are examples of technology that assist in moving customers through the life cycle. The internet, however, is the first fully interactive and individually addressable low-cost multimedia channel—it forms the centerpiece of a firm's CRM abilities. Cookies, Web site logs, bar code scanners, automated Web monitoring (such as Google Alerts), and other tools help to collect information about consumer behavior and characteristics. Databases and data warehouses store and distribute these data from online and off-line touch points, thus allowing employees to develop marketing mixes that better meet individual needs.

We describe CRM software packages in a subsequent section—here we discuss do-it-yourself tools that aid organizations in customizing products to groups of customers or individuals.

These include "push" strategies that reside on the company's Web and e-mail servers, and "pull" strategies that are initiated by internet users. The difference is important, because firms have more control over push techniques.

COMPANY-SIDE TOOLS Exhibit 15.14 displays important tools used to push customized information to users. Visitors are generally unaware that marketers are collecting data and using these technologies to customize offerings.

Cookies Cookie files are the reason that customers returning to Amazon.com get a greeting by name, and that users don't have to remember passwords to every site for which they are registered. Cookie files allow ad-server firms to see the path users take from site to site and thus serve display advertising relevant to user interests. Finally, cookies keep track of shopping baskets and other tasks so that users can quit in the middle and return to the task later.

Company-Side Tools (push)	Description
Cookies	Cookies are small files written to the user's hard drive after visiting a Web site. When the user returns to the site, the company's server looks for the cookie file and uses it to personalize the site.
Web log analysis	Every time a user accesses a Web site, the visit is recorded in the Web server's log file. This file keeps track of which pages the user visits, how long the user stays, and whether the user purchases.
Data mining	Data mining involves the extraction of hidden predictive information in large databases through statistical analysis.
Behavioral targeting	Behavioral targeting occurs when software tracks a user's movements through a Web site, then sends appropriate Web content at a moment's notice.
Collaborative filtering	Collaborative filtering software gathers opinions of like minded users and returns those opinions to the individual in real time.
Outgoing e-mail / Distributed e-mail	Marketers use e-mail databases to build relationships by keeping in touch with useful and timely information. E-mail can be sent to individuals or sent *en masse* using a distributed e-mail list.
Chats Bulletin boards	A firm may listen to users and build community by providing a space for user conversation on the Web site.
iPOS terminals	Interactive point-of-sale terminals are located on a retailer's counter and used to capture data and present targeted communication.

EXHIBIT 15.14   Selected E-Marketing "Push" Customization Tools

Web analytics By performing **Web analytics**, firms can do many things, not the least of which is to customize Web pages based on visitor behavior. Web analytics are tools that collect and display information about user behavior on a Web site. Software, such as WebTrends, also tells which sites the users visited immediately before arriving, what keywords they typed in at search engines to find the site, user domains, and much more.

AutoTrader.com uses Web analytics to transform 25 million rows of daily Web log data into marketing knowledge. This firm is an automotive marketplace offering more than 2 million new and used vehicles with price comparisons, performance reviews, and financing and insurance resources. More than 6 million monthly visitors view more than 200 million pages, including pages where advertisers sell cars. To make sense of it all, AutoTrader created the *Management Dashboard,* a marketing tool powered by SAS statistical data analysis software. The dashboard reports on the following:

- Visitor demographics and customer behavior online—analyzed by U.S. region
- Analytics about the advertisements served on the site Web pages
- Key site metrics such as number of visitors and the makes and models of cars viewed

As an example, SAS software evaluates 30 million monthly vehicle searches, categorizing them by city, state, and zip code, as well as make, model, year, and price. The regional sales force can then quickly answer inquiries about Web traffic in different localities. The firm also uses an Oracle database, extracting e-mails, leads, and other information to generate more than 100 month-to-date reports for marketing managers. AutoTrader learns many things from these analyses. First, it knows which vehicles are in demand in various regions, which helps participating car dealers and individual sellers. Second, it can fine-tune the Web site based on traffic patterns. Third, and most importantly, AutoTrader can demonstrate the value of advertising on its site. Advertisers receive automatically generated reports about how many times their cars were viewed, how many visitors asked for a map to the brick-and-mortar location, and how many e-mail inquiries were received about the cars. Finally, these reports help AutoTrader bill its e-commerce partners.

Data Mining Marketers don't need *a priori* hypotheses to find value in databases but use software to find patterns of interest. For example, Nissan used E.piphany software to increase its sophistication with up-selling and cross-selling. Prior to using the software, Nissan would simply attempt to sell the same model of automobile as previously owned to a repeat customer. Using E.piphany data mining software, Nissan identified a group of affluent, loyal customers with children ages 19 to 24 living at home who purchased the Sentra model. Nissan used this information to cross-sell Sentras to other customers fitting the same profile. Even though Nissan did not use the Web, it is a great e-marketing application.

Behavioral Targeting **Behavioral targeting** occurs when software tracks a user's movements through a Web site, then sends appropriate Web content at a moment's notice. Amazon uses it when it presents recently viewed products on its home page when a return customer visits. Double Click uses it when sending ads as users click through several different Web sites. This targeting uses data warehouse information to help marketers understand the characteristics and behavior of specific target groups.

American Express has used behavioral targeting for years: It sends bill inserts to groups of customers based on their previous purchasing behavior. What's new is that this type of targeting can be done online inexpensively via e-mail and customized Web pages. For example, the software could be set to use the following rule: If a customer orders a Dave Matthews Band CD, display a Web page offering a concert T-shirt. TokyoPop.com, a site targeted at Generation Y, carries behavioral targeting over to all its affiliate sites. Every time a TokyoPop registered member visits an affiliate site, it serves rule-based content, advertising, or offers. This targeting builds relationships because members are presented with relevant and timely offers, which increases their business with TokyoPop.

Consumers visiting Greatcoffee.com are greeted with personalized Web content on their *first visit*! The site doesn't know who the users are because they have never entered information at the site nor been given a cookie file from GreatCoffee (Peppers, 2000). So how is it done? The site uses behavioral profiling to match a database of anonymous cookie files from Angara. This firm's e-commerce targeting service purchased more than 20 million anonymous cookie files with demographic and geographic data from firms such as Dell (all personal information is removed first). When users surf to the Web sites at Angara's clients, such as Greatcoffee.com, this database is accessed and relevant Web page content served. For example, if Angara matches a new user's IP address and other easily obtained information and the database shows that the user lives in California, the site might display the greeting, "Drink our coffee, win free San Francisco Giants tickets." This directed ad happens in less than a half a second and has increased surfer-to-buyer conversion to twice the normal amount in some segments. In addition, the reorder rate at Greatcoffee.com is 60 percent versus 5 percent before using Angara's service.

Collaborative Filtering In the off-line world, individuals often seek the advice of others before making decisions. Similarly, collaborative filtering software gathers the recommendations of an entire group of people and presents the results to a like-minded individual.

BOL.com, an international media and entertainment store (owned by Germany's Direct Group Bertelsmann), uses Net Perceptions collaborative filtering software to observe how users browse and buy music, software, games, and more at its site. The more time a user spends at the site, the more BOL.com will learn about user behavior and preferences, and the better able it will be to present relevant products ("learning relationship"). BOL.com notes that it realized increased revenues from using this software, and achieved a positive ROI within months. In its brochure, Net

Perceptions makes the following claims about its "recommendation engines":

> Harness the collective knowledge of all your customers to make predictions for an individual. It is based on collaborative filtering technology, which automates word-of-mouth recommendations. . . . The recommendation engine lets you generate online recommendations in real-time, and dynamically tailor content and advertising to [the user's] preferences. With every visit, the recommendation engine learns more and gets smarter.

Outgoing E-Mail As discussed in earlier chapters, outgoing e-mail from firm to customer is the internet's "killer app." E-mail is used to communicate with individuals or lists of individuals in an effort to increase their purchases, satisfaction, and loyalty. E-mail sent to distribution lists is redistributed to the entire subscription list. Many companies maintain e-mail distribution lists for customers and other stakeholders.

Permission marketing dictates that customers will be pleased to receive e-mail for which they have opted-in. MyPoints rewards consumers with points and gift certificates, all for reading targeted e-mail ads and shopping at selected sites (Exhibit 15.15). MyPoints client companies pay a fee for these e-mails, part of which goes directly to customers as points. MyPoints advertises "responsible" e-mail messaging, meaning that consumers agree to receive commercial messages within their e-mails. Conversely, spam does not build relationships but instead focuses on customer acquisition. The internet provides the technology for marketers to send 500,000 or more e-mails at the click of a mouse, and all for less than the cost of one postage stamp. Relationship-building e-mail requires sending e-mails that are valuable to users, sending them as often as users require, and offering users the chance to be taken off the list at any time. It means talking and listening to consumers as if they were friends.

Chat and Bulletin Boards Companies build community and learn about customers and products through real-time chat and bulletin

EXHIBIT 15.15   MyPoints Rewards Members for Time Spent Online

Source: www.mypoints.com.

board/newsgroup e-mail postings at its Web site (for government examples, see Exhibit 15.16). Analysis of these exchanges is used in the aggregate to design marketing mixes that meet user needs. For example, if many consumers log onto a Caribbean Chat at Expedia, it might feature special tours of Caribbean islands during the next week (www.expedia.com). Expedia can also send e-mail notes to users who participate in the chats with offers of special tours. Lively and useful chat and bulletin boards increase repeat visits and time spent on the site.

iPOS Terminals iPOS terminals are small customer-facing machines near the brick-and-mortar cash register, used to record a buyer's signature for a credit card transaction. They are important because they can gather survey and other data as well as present individually targeted advertising and promotions. Federated Department Stores installed 34,000 of these Web-enabled machines in 2001. The retailer used signature data to see whether women are buying their own clothing, as well as clothing for male family members, and it plans to use the terminals to send images and personalized messages—all generated from a database and sent over the internet.

CLIENT-SIDE TOOLS Client-side tools come into play based on a user's action at a computer or handheld device. Although the tools generally reside on a Web server, it is the customer "pull" that initiates the customized response. See Exhibit 15.17.

Agents Software agents such as shopping agents and search engines match user input to databases and return customized information. Agent software, such as Inference's k-Commerce products, often relies on more than one interaction. For example, a user might type in "computer" on the Dell site and then be presented with either laptop or desktop options. This process continues until the search is narrowed. Similarly, when visitors to Yahoo! use a keyword search, they often receive a banner or other ad based on the word they entered along with a customized Web page of Web site links. For example, if a user types "automobile" into the search box, an ad for Toyota might be returned along with the list of relevant sites. Agents are the basis of all shopping comparison sites, such as BizRate.com.

Individualized Web Portals *The Wall Street Journal*'s online edition allows individual customers to create a personalized Web page based on

The Bureau of Land Management

INFORMATION

Information Menu (Graphics)   Information Menu (Text)   Home Page

Last updated: 01/12/01

Conversations with AMERICA is a White House initiative to engage customers in conversations about improving Government service. The initiative is part of the National Partnership for Reinventing Government (NPR). It builds on the steps to improve customer service outlined in the President's Executive Order of September 11, 1993 entitled "Setting Customer Service Standards." You can read more about this national initiative by clicking here.

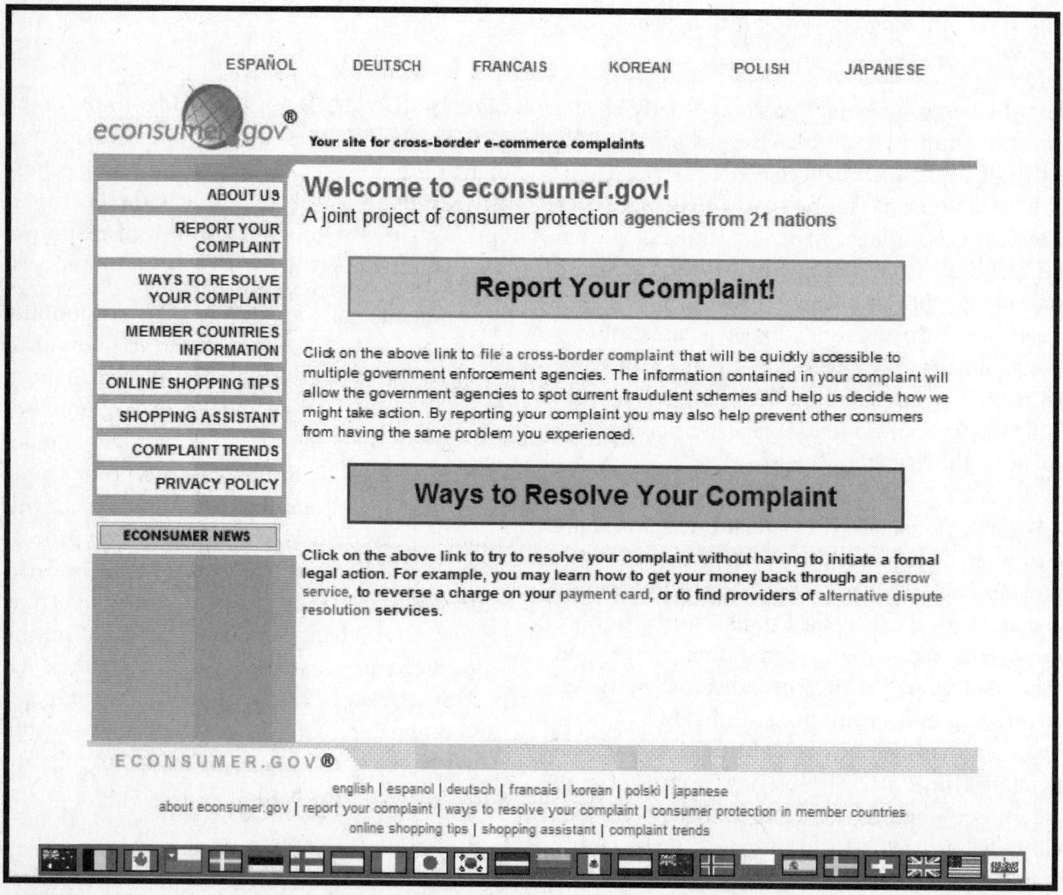

My Government Listens

ESPAÑOL   DEUTSCH   FRANCAIS   KOREAN   POLISH   JAPANESE

econsumer.gov®   Your site for cross-border e-commerce complaints

ABOUT US
REPORT YOUR COMPLAINT
WAYS TO RESOLVE YOUR COMPLAINT
MEMBER COUNTRIES INFORMATION
ONLINE SHOPPING TIPS
SHOPPING ASSISTANT
COMPLAINT TRENDS
PRIVACY POLICY

ECONSUMER NEWS

Welcome to econsumer.gov!
A joint project of consumer protection agencies from 21 nations

Report Your Complaint!

Click on the above link to file a cross-border complaint that will be quickly accessible to multiple government enforcement agencies. The information contained in your complaint will allow the government agencies to spot current fraudulent schemes and help us decide how we might take action. By reporting your complaint you may also help prevent other consumers from having the same problem you experienced.

Ways to Resolve Your Complaint

Click on the above link to try to resolve your complaint without having to initiate a formal legal action. For example, you may learn how to get your money back through an escrow service, to reverse a charge on your payment card, or to find providers of alternative dispute resolution services.

ECONSUMER.GOV®

english | espanol | deutsch | francais | korean | polski | japanese
about econsumer.gov | report your complaint | ways to resolve your complaint | consumer protection in member countries
online shopping tips | shopping assistant | complaint trends

EXHIBIT 15.16   Chat Opportunities with the U.S. Government and Its Citizens
Sources: www.blm.gov and econsumer.gov.

Client-Side Tools (pull)	Description
Agents	Agents are programs that perform functions on behalf of the user, such as search engines and shopping agents.
Individualized Web portals	Personalized Web pages users easily configure at Web sites such as MyYahoo! and many others.
Wireless data services	Wireless Web portals send data to customer cell phones, pagers, and PDAs, such as the Palm Treo.
Web forms	Web form (or HTML form) is the technical term for a form on a Web page that has designated places for the user to type information for submission.
Fax-on-demand	With fax-on-demand, customers telephone a firm, listen to an automated voice menu, and select options to request a fax be sent on a particular topic.
Incoming e-mail	E-mail queries, complaints, or compliments initiated by customers or prospects comprise incoming e-mail, and is the fodder for customer service.
RSS Feeds	Really Simple Syndication feeds are an XML format designed for sharing headlines and other Web content.

EXHIBIT 15.17   Selected E-Marketing "Pull" Customization Tools

keywords of interest. This capability is particularly helpful for business readers who want to monitor stories about their competitors. *The Wall Street Journal* creates a structural bond with individual customers, thereby boosting loyalty—something that was unheard of prior to the internet.

Individualized Web portals are more often used to build relationships in the B2B market than the B2C market. It is through these portals that supply chains access inventory and account information and track various operations. Webridge sells partner and customer relationship management software (PRM/CRM) that allows businesses to access all the data they need on demand. This resource represents a huge improvement over the previous method, where buyers searched through piles of brochures, catalogs, and price lists that included many products not carried by channel partners and were constantly out-of-date. InFocus Systems used Webridge software to send offers of interest via e-mail to partners and then serve Web pages customized to display those featured products and prices when partners visited the site. Primedia, a health care training company, used Webridge software to create a site for hospitals, doctors, and other partners using its services. Differentiating customers, it offers four layers of

entry to the site: visitor, registered user, member, and premier partner. B2B Web portals use extranets to access partner information.

Wireless Data Services Wireless data services are included as a separate tool because of their rapid growth and distinctive features. These portals are remarkable because wireless users only want text data due to the screen size of wireless devices and download time for graphics. Services such as AvantGo.com offer users ad-sponsored news headlines, sports scores, stock quotes, weather in selected cities, and more to users on pagers. Microsoft's wireless services even notify users when they've received a new e-mail in their Hotmail account (mobile.msn.com). As users customize this information, they give companies a better idea of how to better serve them and, thus, build the relationship. In the future, watch for mobile data aggregators. Firms such as Yodlee.com allow mobile or desktop access to Web sites, online accounts, and user data anywhere, anytime. See the "Let's Get Technical" box about these "third screens."

Web Forms Many corporate Web sites sport Web forms, using them for a multitude of purposes from site registration, communication, and survey research to product purchase. In fact, many

LET'S GET TECHNICAL

Mobile Trends

As you stroll through the supermarket on Sunday afternoon, you suddenly realize that you have forgotten to buy peanut butter. In what aisle do they stock the 20 different varieties of peanut butter? And how are you going to know which size is the best price? Then you remember . . . the supermarket is now offering a wireless access in the store to a searchable floor plan, weekly specials, and unit price calculator for every item. You are once again relaxed as you pull out your iPhone.

Are Your Web Sites Ready?

Many classic marketing strategies hinged on the concept of giving potential customers information about a product or service right when they are likely to need it, such as an advertising billboard stating "McDonald's, Exit 11, Turn Left" or automatic coupon dispensers attached to the shelves at the grocery store. The interesting part of these strategies is that the information was in a form that the potential customers could use: a large billboard readable from the highway and a pocket-sized coupon for use at checkout.

These days, potential customers are hungry for information on their smart devices, which include iPhones, PDAs, Pocket PCs, Tablet PCs, and any combination of these products. Today's customers want their smart device to be just that—smart. Just as the classic marketing strategies did, today's e-marketer must also provide information for potential customers in a form that is easy to use for the customer. In other words, Web sites and online services should be developed specially for smart devices, using industry standards. Specially designed Web sites and online services should also be tested before distribution to the public. For example, frozen Web pages (fixed height and width) are difficult for Pocket PC users to view. To view the information, they must scroll both down and to the right. A better solution is liquid Web pages that allow the information to be resized to the width of the device's screen.

The Third Screen

Information technology visionaries are nicknaming the screen of mobile devices the "third screen." The first was television, the second was the personal computer, and the third includes a variety of mobile devices. The unique aspect of these screens is that users take them just about everywhere, especially the iPhone. The iPhone works off of both regular phone networks and the faster 3G networks. The iPhone is a fully functioning internet device with a very intuitive and easy to use interface. Interestingly, the iPhone also cannibalizes Apple's iPod market since the iPhone duplicates iPod functionality and then some.

Although mobile devices are convenient for users because of their size, portability, and organizer functions, they are even more convenient when they are able to access wireless networks. Popular mobile devices can access one or more of the available wireless networks: wireless phone signals, WiFi Internet hotspots, and Bluetooth wireless networks. The type of network that the mobile device can access depends on the hardware it possesses.

As the ability to access wireless networks and the speed of data transfer on the networks increase, services for mobile devices are becoming more prevalent. MobiTV converts the content of such stations as MSNBC, Fox, ABC, and the Discovery Channel. The speed needed for streaming content should be at least 10 frames per second and ideally 24 or 30.

Advertisers have long used the "first screen" to reach their target market, and the question of whether advertising dollars will support the "third screen" is being asked. Most current content converters have not included advertisements, except for MobiTV. The company feels that it should provide genuine television programming to their customers, and that includes the commercials. MobiTV sells advertisements in the same spaces where cable operators insert their ads. And due to the nature of the mobile phone, viewers have bonus interactive features, such as clicking a button to get more information on a product.

sites strive to build the number of registered users as a prelude to transactions. For example, the U.S. Federal Trade Commission (FTC) allows consumers to complain about questionable business practices and advertising via its Web site form. Regardless of purpose, the information gathered serves to help the firm build relationships and move users through the customer life cycle.

Fax-on-Demand In the B2B market, firms sometimes want information sent via fax. Services such as eFax.com allow internet users to send and receive fax transmissions at the eFax Web site. Why would a user use this service as opposed to an e-mail attachment? This service is appropriate when the document is not in digital form, a signature is needed, or internet access is not available so the document cannot be sent as an e-mail attachment. Also, eFax is handy for users who do not want to leave their fax machines online constantly. eFax will notify users by e-mail if a fax is waiting and they can download it when convenient. Adobe's Acrobat has become very sophisticated with digital signature capabilities, perhaps signaling the eventual demise of the fax machine.

Incoming E-Mail Posttransaction customer service is an important part of the customer care life cycle. Automated e-mail confirming purchase or shipping activities assured customers that the company is taking care of them. Normally the Web sites include a feedback button or form that delivers an e-mail message to the corporation. Often an automated customer service program acknowledges the message via e-mail and indicates that a representative will be responding shortly. Research shows that firms are getting much better at responding to incoming e-mail. In one study, 100 percent of customer service departments responded to e-mail inquiries within one week: 26 percent responded within a day, and 51 percent responded the same day ("Vast Improvements," 2001). Companies should include feedback options online only if they have staff in place to respond: E-mail addresses on a Web site imply a promise to reply. Some firms, such as Apple

Computer, decide not to provide e-mail feedback from their Web sites, opting instead for automated telephone routing.

RSS Feeds Really Simple Syndication allows users to subscribe to blogs and Web sites. Subscribers will receive notification as soon as there is new information posted. This technology creates a structural bond tying user to content originator in a way that enhances the relationship. For instance, subscribers to CNN feeds will receive breaking news headlines, which increases their loyalty to CNN.

CRM SOFTWARE As previously mentioned, CRM success depends on all eight building blocks, not simply technology. Nonetheless, technology and software are what grease the CRM wheel, allowing firms to gather, interpret, and use masses of customer and prospect data. The leading software firms in the large enterprise B2B market are displayed in Exhibit 15.18. To be ranked a leader, a firm must meet the following set of requirements (from Gartner Group):

- They must set the pace for the market, enabling a competitive advantage for their customers.
- They must offer CRM functionality for all business models (B2B, B2C, and so on).
- Their solutions must be highly scalable.
- Their solutions must support cross-application business processes.
- They must have an established ecosystem of implementation partners.
- They must have a proven track record of successful deployments, evidenced by satisfied customers who report real ROI.

What exactly do CRM software firms offer? As in any market, firms differentiate their products to assist with the three facets previously discussed (sales force automation, marketing automation, and customer service). The best way to understand how software can assist firms is to visit the company Web sites and read about the products and successful client

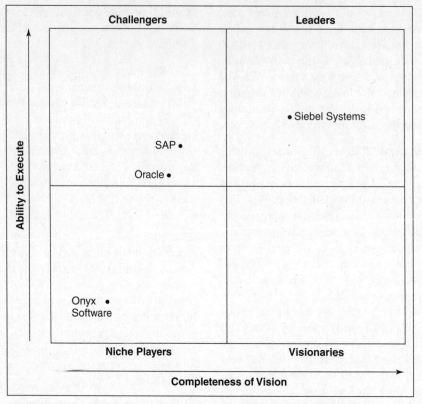

EXHIBIT 15.18 CRM Software Firm Positions for B2B Large Enterprise Market

Source: Speech by Jeff Pulver, Vice President, Worldwide Marketing, Siebel Software (data from Gartner Group, 2004).

solutions. In summary and taken directly from the Web sites:

- **"Siebel Systems** is the world's leading provider of customer relationship management (CRM) solutions and a leading provider of applications for business intelligence and standards-based integration (www.siebel.com). Through its 'CRM for Everyone' strategy, Siebel provides CRM solutions for any kind of organization, any type of user, and any budget."

- **"Sap** is the world's largest inter-enterprise software company and the world's third-largest independent software supplier overall (www.sap.com). mySAP CRM enables real-time availability checks, contract management, billing management, fulfillment visibility, and order tracking. And it gives you the features and functions necessary for marketing planning, campaign management, telemarketing, lead generation, and customer segmentation. Plus, mySAP CRM allows you to offer ongoing customer care across all channels—with a customer interaction center, Web-based customer self-service capabilities, service and claims management, field service and dispatch, and installed-base management."

- "With Oracle CRM you know more about your customers, products and results using real-time information across your business (www.oracle.com). Your organization can do more because Oracle CRM focuses on driving profitable customer relationships, not just automation of activities. Only Oracle offers breakthrough opportunities for savings on software implementations and maintenance to ensure that you spend less for better results."

- "With Onyx Enterprise CRM you can manage the complexity of customer and partner relationships through a single unified CRM suite (www.onyx.com). Onyx Enterprise CRM provides web-based solutions for organizations to power CRM strategies across sales, marketing and service organizations. By combining critical customer data with information from other business systems and the internet, Onyx Enterprise CRM effectively manages key prospect, customer and partner relationships, helping you build more profitable business networks and deliver real value."

Ready to purchase CRM software based on these descriptions? Before you do, look at other important CRM software providers: SAS (www.sas.com), Infor (go.infor.com), Salesforce (www.sales force.com), and many others. It is a complex group of products, which is another reason that marketers must heed the eight building blocks, setting objectives and strategies first, and being sure

that CRM is a top-down management philosophy. Remember that most CRM software installations fail because the firm did not take steps to gain buy-in and feedback from employees at every step.

8. CRM Metrics

E-marketers use numerous metrics to assess the internet's value in delivering CRM performance—among them are ROI, cost savings, revenues, customer satisfaction, and especially the contribution of each CRM tactic to these measures. Recall that all e-marketing performance measures assess specific tactics from different perspectives, and that the metrics of choice depend on the firm's goals and strategies. Refer to the balanced scorecard in Chapter 2 and note the metric dashboard generated for customers of Salesforce.com (Exhibit 15.19). Here we present a few of the common metrics used to track customers' progress through the customer life cycle in Exhibit 15.20. One current study named the three most important to be customer retention rates (89% using the metric), ROI (89% using), and **customer lift**—increased response or transaction rates (93%).

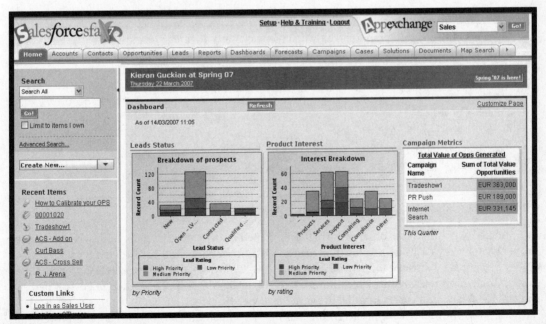

EXHIBIT 15.19 Metrics Scoreboard Generated by Salesforce.com Software

Source: www.salesforce.com.

Target

- Recency, frequency, monetary analysis (RFM)—identifies high-value customers
- Share of customer spending—proportion of revenues from high-value customers as compared to low-value customers

Acquire

- New customer acquisition cost (CAC)
- Number of new customers referred from partner sites
- Campaign response—click-throughs, conversions, and more from Chapter 13
- Rate of customer recovery—proportion of customers who drop away that the firm can lure back using various offers

Transact

- Prospect conversion rate—percent of visitors to site that buy
- Customer cross-sell rate from online to offline, and the reverse
- Services sold to partners
- Sales of a firm's products on partner Web sites
- Average order value (AOV)—dollar sales divided by the number of orders for any given period
- Referral revenue—dollars in sales from customers referred to the firm by current customers
- Sales leads from Internet to closure ratio

Service

- Customer satisfaction ratings over time (see Cisco opening story)
- Time to answer incoming e-mail from customers
- Number of complaints

Retain

- Customer attrition rate—proportion who don't repurchase in a set time period
- Percentage of customer retention—proportion of customers who repeat purchase

Grow

- Lifetime value (LTV)—net present value of the revenue stream for any particular customer over a number of years
- AOV over time—increase or decrease
- Average annual sales growth for repeat customers over time
- Loyalty program effectiveness—sales increase over time
- Number of low-value customers moved to high value

EXHIBIT 15.20 CRM Metrics by Customer Life Cycle Stage

Armed with this and other information about what makes customers value the firm's products, companies attempt to increase conversion and retention rates, reduce defection rates, and build AOV and profits per customer over time (acquire, retain, grow). For example, FTD.com, the florist, worked hard in 2001 to improve its CRM metrics over those in 2000. In the second quarter, it successfully increased orders year-to-year from 514,000 to 624,000, increased AOV from $57.00 to $58.93, and reduced marketing costs 8 percent, from $8.30 to $7.67 (Cox, 2002).

In addition to performance improvements, many firms use some of these methods to identify

Year	Total Customers	Retention Rate	Total Revenue	Net Profit	NPV at 15%	10-Year LTV
1	1,000	60%	$35,900	$ 5,900	$ 5,900	$ 66.94
2	600	65%	45,540	27,540	23,948	118.12
3	390	70%	29,601	17,901	13,536	129.15
4	273	75%	20,721	12,531	8,239	138.35
5	205	78%	15,541	9,398	5,373	143.45
6	160	79%	12,122	7,330	3,645	145.55
7	126	80%	9,576	5,791	2,504	146.81
8	101	80%	7,661	4,633	1,742	146.81
9	81	80%	6,129	3,706	1,212	146.81
10	65	80%	4,903	2,965	843	146.81

EXHIBIT 15.21 Customer Lifetime Value (LTV)

Source: Adapted from Peppers and Rogers Group, available at www.1to1.com.

the least profitable customers and minimize interactions with them. The point is not to treat some customers poorly but to try to minimize the time invested in servicing low-profit customers.

One important CRM metric deserves more discussion—customer **lifetime value (LTV)**, shown in Exhibit 15.21, is an adaptation of an LTV calculation from the Peppers and Rogers Group. This calculation assumes that the firm has 1,000 customers in the first year, each spending an average of $35.90. In the second year, 60 percent of the customers are retained, and due to clever cross- and up-selling, they each spend $75.90 in that and subsequent years. The second-to-last column includes the net present value of each year's net profits, calculated at 15 percent. Finally, the 10-year LTV of each customer is displayed. The numbers may look smaller than expected because this calculation realistically discounts revenue to its present value. Note that the LTV increases after the fifth year due to a higher retention rate in later years. Even with this high retention rate assumption (60 percent to 80 percent), notice how few customers are left in year 10. This calculation demonstrates the benefits of retaining customers over time and the need for building wallet share. It also shows that no matter how good a firm is at retaining customers, new customer acquisition is still an important activity.

TEN RULES FOR CRM SUCCESS

Many organizations lose money with their CRM efforts. This prompted Chris Selland, Managing Director of Reservoir Partners, to write a white paper about how to succeed with CRM applications for e-marketing. Following are his ten rules, along with explanations from material in this chapter (see www.frontrange.com for more).

1. **Recognize the customer's role.** It is all about the customer, as evidenced by the rise in social media and the balance of control shifting from companies to customers. Customer relationship management may be a misnomer because successful firms don't "manage customers" but provide technology so that customers can manage their relationships with the company.
2. **Build a business case.** Before investing in CRM technology or processes, it is important to examine the cost versus predicted benefits. Don't forget, costs such as employee training and staff impact. Put the metrics in place, as discussed in building block 8.
3. **Gain buy-in from end users to executives.** Many CRM installations fail because no one uses them. SFA from companies such as Sales force.com provides tremendous benefits but only if the sales force is trained and ready.

4. **Make every contact count.** CRM means integrating data from all customer touch points, and it is likely that much of these data already exist in databases. Before starting, a company should determine how it can integrate all customer or partner data into the system.

5. **Drive sales effectiveness.** If the CRM application involves a sales force, companies should ensure that the system helps salespeople close more deals, and is not simply used to manage the metrics such as sales costs and close ratios.

6. **Measure and manage the marketing return.** Marketing is different from sales, and often responsible for generating sales leads. Good CRM solutions will monitor the marketing expenditures and their role in revenues—things such as mailing list management and how leads flow through an organization.

7. **Leverage the loyalty effect.** Customer service is one of the three CRM facets, and although most companies consider it a cost, it plays a huge part in retaining customers and building wallet share. CRM initiatives can monitor customer service efforts to see how they help increase customer loyalty, and thus, add to profitability.

8. **Choose the right tools and approach.** This chapter covered many types of technology solutions for CRM from enterprise-wide tools to smaller tactics focusing on individual aspects of CRM. It is important that marketers evaluate these tools and not leave it to information technology personnel alone. As well, CRM application can be purchased and installed on the company servers or "leased" on a contract basis, such as with the Salesforce.com solution. Which fits the problem most adequately?

9. **Build the team.** Although an effective CRM solution begins with vision from the top, it is critical to build the right team before purchasing the software and beginning the training. The team might include members from marketing, IT, sales, and finance.

10. **Seek outside help.** It is often worthwhile to hire a consultant to assist, especially if the company has little experience with CRM.

Chapter Summary

Marketers have practiced relationship marketing for some time; however, internet technologies made it possible to manage many relationships one at a time. In the move from mass marketing to relationship marketing, the emphasis has become long-term customer retention rather than many discrete transactions with new customers.

Customer relationship management is used to create and maintain relationships with employees, business customers in the supply chain, lateral partners, and final consumers. CRM's benefits include cost-effective acquisition, retention, and growth of current customers as well as word-of-mouth referrals. The three legs of CRM are sales force automation, marketing automation, and customer service. The Gartner Group model of CRM covers eight building blocks: CRM vision, CRM strategy, valued customer experience, organizational collaboration, CRM processes, CRM information, CRM technology, and CRM metrics.

The CRM vision must include guarding of customer privacy and building user trust. CRM strategy starts by defining what the company wants to accomplish with CRM technology. Relationship intensity ranges from awareness (the lowest intensity) to advocacy (the highest intensity). Three relationship levels mark the bonds that e-marketers build with customers. The highest level of CRM involves creating structural bonds that raise switching costs and build loyalty. E-marketers need to think about the experience of their valued customers, how customers prefer to interact with companies, and how they can forge ties through community building.

An important trend in CRM is the integration with supply chain management (SCM). When the firm's front end, back end, and supply chain all focus on the consumer, value is delivered, satisfaction is increased, and the firm has a competitive edge. The customer care life cycle covers the stages of targeting, acquiring, transaction, servicing, retaining, and growing customers by identifying customers, differentiating customers, and customizing the marketing mix for targeted segments or individuals—customization. CRM depends on information and on technology using company-side tools (including cookies, Web site logs, data mining, behavioral targeting, collaborative filtering, outgoing e-mail, chat and bulletin boards, and iPOS terminals) and client-side tools (including agents, experiential marketing, individuals' Web portals, wireless data services, Web forms, fax-on-demand, incoming e-mail, and RSS feeds). Then e-marketers use a variety of software for implementation and metrics to assess the performance and value of using the internet for CRM. The chapter concludes with ten rules for successful CRM.

Exercises

REVIEW QUESTIONS

1. Explain why relationship capital is the foundation of future business.
2. Define relationship marketing and contrast it with mass marketing.
3. What are the main benefits of CRM?
4. Why do companies use sales force automation and marketing automation?
5. What are the eight building blocks of CRM?
6. What are the five levels of relationship intensity, and why do e-marketers strive to move customers to the top level?
7. Why do e-marketers see community building as an important aspect of CRM?
8. What are the advantages to CRM–SCM integration? Give an example.
9. What are the six stages in the customer care life cycle?
10. Explain how data mining, real-time profiling, collaborative filtering, and outgoing e-mail help firms customize offerings.
11. How are company-side and client-side customization tools different? Explain your answer.
12. What are the ten rules of CRM success, according to Reservoir Partners?

DISCUSSION QUESTIONS

13. Explain the difference between wallet share and share of market.
14. If good relationship marketing means firing a company's least profitable or most costly customers, suggest how it might be accomplished without causing them to criticize the company to their friends.
15. Explain how the customer benefits from SCM-CRM integration.
16. Do you agree with the statement that the customer's goal in relationship marketing is choice reduction? Are consumers really such creatures of habit? Why or why not?
17. Which tools do you think are more powerful for building relationships—company-side tools or client-side tools? Why?
18. Compare and contrast the concept of differentiating customers with that of differentiating products.
19. As a consumer, would you be more likely to buy from a Web site displaying the TRUSTe and logo than from a competing Web site without the TRUSTe affiliation? Explain your answer.

WEB ACTIVITIES

20. Register at two Web sites and see if you get e-mail. Identify the ways in which those sites attempt to build relationship with you: Evaluate the sites as well as the incoming e-mail.
21. Find a company online that you think does a poor job with relationship marketing. Suggest a strategy by which it could build in phases toward a structural relationship with its customers.
22. Visit Amazon.com and list all of the ways they personalize and customize the site to retain and increase your business.

APPENDIX A

Internet Penetration Worldwide in 2007

Nation	Population	Internet Users	Internet Penetration (%)
Afghanistan	31,889,923	535,000	1.7
Albania	3,600,523	471,200	13.1
Algeria	33,333,216	2,460,000	7.4
Andorra	71,822	23,200	32.3
Angola	12,263,596	172,000	1.4
Anguilla	13,487	3,000	22.2
Antigua and Barbuda	72,377	29,000	40.1
Argentina	40,301,927	16,000,000	39.7
Armenia	2,971,650	172,800	5.8
Aruba	70,322	24,000	34.1
Australia	20,984,595	15,300,000	72.9
Austria	8,199,783	4,650,000	56.7
Azerbaijan	8,120,247	829,100	10.2
Bahamas	335,142	103,000	30.7
Bahrain	708,573	157,300	22.2
Bangladesh	150,448,339	450,000	0.3
Barbados	267,353	160,000	59.8
Belarus	9,724,723	5,477,500	56.3
Belgium	10,392,226	5,100,000	49.1
Belize	312,233	38,000	12.2
Benin	8,078,314	700,000	8.7
Bermuda	66,163	42,000	63.5
Bhutan	671,887	30,000	4.5
Bolivia	9,119,152	580,000	6.4
Bosnia and Herzegovina	4,552,198	950,000	20.9
Botswana	1,815,508	60,000	3.3
Brazil	190,010,647	42,600,000	22.4
Brunei Darussalem	374,577	176,029	47.0
Bulgaria	7,322,858	2,200,000	30.0
Burkina Faso	14,326,203	80,000	0.6
Burma	47,373,470	300,000	0.6
Burundi	8,390,505	60,000	0.7

Nation	Population	Internet Users	Internet Penetration (%)
Cayman Islands	50,348	9,909	19.7
Cambodia	13,995,904	44,000	0.3
Cameroon	18,060,382	370,000	2.0
Canada	33,390,141	22,000,000	65.9
Cape Verde	423,613	29,000	6.8
Central African Republic	4,369,038	13,000	0.3
Chad	8,915,381	60,000	0.7
Chile	16,284,741	7,035,000	43.2
China	1,321,851,888	162,000,000	12.3
Colombia	44,379,598	6,705,000	15.1
Cook Islands	18,723	3,600	19.2
Comoros	681,800	21,000	3.1
Congo, Democratic Republic	60,226,717	180,000	0.3
Congo, Republic	3,774,537	70,000	1.9
Costa Rica	4,133,884	1,214,400	29.4
Cote d'Ivoire	20,169,352	300,000	1.5
Croatia	4,493,312	1,576,400	35.1
Cuba	11,394,043	240,000	2.1
Cyprus	788,457	356,600	45.2
Czech Republic	10,228,744	5,100,000	49.9
Denmark	5,468,120	3,762,500	68.8
Djibouti	790,709	11,000	1.4
Dominica	71,388	26,000	36.4
Dominican Republic	9,365,818	2,100,000	22.4
East Timor	1,084,971	1,000	0.1
Ecuador	13,755,680	1,549,000	11.3
Egypt	72,478,498	6,000,000	8.3
El Salvador	6,948,073	637,000	9.2
Equatorial Guinea	1,120,061	8,000	0.7
Eritrea	4,254,498	100,000	2.4
Estonia	1,315,912	760,000	57.8
Ethiopia	73,872,056	164,000	0.2
Faroe Islands	47,511	34,000	71.6
Fiji	0867,655	080,000	09.2
Finland	5,238,460	3,286,000	62.7
France	63,718,187	34,851,835	54.7
French Guiana	204,932	42,000	20.5
French Polynesia	267,028	65,000	24.4
Gabon	1,461,679	81,000	5.5

Nation	Population	Internet Users	Internet Penetration (%)
Gambia	1,508,727	58,000	3.8
Georgia	4,646,003	332,000	7.1
Germany	82,400,996	53,240,115	64.6
Ghana	21,801,662	609,800	2.8
Gibraltar	27,967	6,200	22.2
Greece	10,706,290	3,800,000	35.5
Greenland	56,344	38,000	67.4
Grenada	101,008	19,000	18.8
Guadeloupe	458,174	85,000	18.6
Guam	169,879	79,000	46.5
Guatemala	12,728,111	1,320,000	10.4
Guernsey & Alderney	65,573	36,000	54.9
Guinea	8,171,096	50,000	0.6
Guinea-Bissau	1,492,189	37,000	2.5
Guyana	886,113	160,000	18.1
Haiti	8,429,006	600,000	7.1
Honduras	7,483,763	337,300	4.5
Hong Kong	6,980,412	4,878,713	69.9
Hungary	9,956,108	3,500,000	35.2
Iceland	301,931	258,000	85.4
India	1,129,866,154	60,000,000	5.3
Indonesia	234,693,997	20,000,000	8.5
Iran	65,397,521	18,000,000	27.5
Iraq	27,499,638	36,000	0.1
Ireland	4,109,086	2,060,000	50.1
Israel	6,426,679	3,700,000	57.6
Italy	58,147,733	33,143,152	57.0
Jamaica	2,710,063	1,067,000	39.4
Japan	127,433,494	87,540,000	68.7
Jersey	91,321	27,000	29.6
Jordan	6,053,193	796,900	13.2
Kazakhstan	15,284,929	1,247,000	8.2
Kenya	35,062,192	2,770,300	7.9
Kiribati	93,565	2,000	2.1
Kuwait	2,505,559	816,700	32.6
Kyrgyzstan	5,284,149	298,100	5.6
Laos	6,521,998	25,000	0.4
Latvia	2,259,810	1,070,800	47.4
Lebanon	3,925,502	950,000	24.2
Lesotho	2,513,076	51,500	2.0

Nation	Population	Internet Users	Internet Penetration (%)
Liberia	3,146,406	1,000	0.03
Libya	6,293,910	232,000	3.7
Liechtenstein	34,247	22,000	64.2
Lithuania	3,575,439	1,221,700	34.2
Luxembourg	480,222	339,000	70.6
Macao	456,989	201,000	44.0
Macedonia	2,055,915	392,671	19.1
Madagascar	18,996,075	110,000	0.6
Malawi	11,553,163	59,700	0.5
Malaysia	24,821,286	14,904,000	60.0
Maldives	369,031	20,100	5.4
Mali	10,914,989	70,000	0.6
Malta	401,880	127,200	31.7
Marshall Islands	55,449	2,200	4.0
Martinique	400,229	130,000	32.5
Mauritania	2,959,592	100,000	3.4
Mauritius	1,292,309	300,000	23.2
Mexico	108,700,891	23,700,000	21.8
Micronesia	110,064	16,000	14.5
Moldova	4,328,816	727,700	16.8
Monaco	32,671	20,000	61.2
Mongolia	2,951,786	268,300	9.1
Montenegro	684,736	266,000	38.8
Morocco	30,534,870	6,100,000	20.0
Mozambique	20,356,242	178,000	0.9
Myanmar	47,373,470	300,000	0.6
Namibia	2,083,405	80,600	3.9
Nauru	11,424	300	2.6
Nepal	28,901,790	249,400	0.9
The Netherlands	16,570,613	14,544,400	87.8
Netherlands Antilles	186,026	2,000	1.1
New Caledonia	243,233	80,000	32.9
New Zealand	04,274,588	03,200,000	074.9
Nicaragua	5,675,356	155,000	2.7
Niger	12,533,242	40,000	0.3
Nigeria	162,082,868	8,000,000	4.9
Niue	1,722	450	26.1
Norfolk Island	1,673	700	41.8
Northern Marianas	84,228	10,000	11.9
Norway	4,627,926	4,074,100	88.0
Oman	3,204,897	319,200	10.0

Nation	Population	Internet Users	Internet Penetration (%)
Pakistan	164,741,924	12,000,000	7.3
Palestine (West Bk.)	2,535,927	266,000	10.5
Panama	3,242,173	264,316	8.2
Papua New Guinea	6,157,888	170,000	2.8
Paraguay	6,669,086	260,000	3.9
Peru	28,674,757	7,324,300	25.5
Philippines	91,077,287	14,000,000	15.4
Poland	38,518,241	11,400,000	29.6
Portugal	10,642,836	7,782,760	73.1
Puerto Rico	3,992,545	1,000,000	25.0
Qatar	907,229	289,900	32.0
Reunion	802,911	220,000	27.4
Romania	22,276,056	7,000,000	31.4
Russia	141,377,752	28,000,000	19.8
Rwanda	8,959,095	65,000	0.7
Saint Helena (UK)	4,662	1,000	21.5
St. Kitts and Nevis	39,382	10,000	25.4
Saint Lucia	169,576	55,000	32.4
St. Vincent and the Grenadines	125,882	10,000	7.9
Samoa	184,633	8,000	4.3
San Marino	29,615	15,400	52.0
Sao Tome and Principe	173,942	23,000	13.2
Saudi Arabia	27,601,038	4,700,000	17.0
Senegal	11,069,755	650,000	5.9
Serbia	10,150,265	1,400,000	13.8
Seychelles	84,927	29,000	34.1
Sierra Leone	5,159,619	10,000	0.2
Singapore	4,553,009	2,421,800	53.2
Slovakia	5,447,502	2,500,000	45.9
Slovenia	2,009,245	1,250,600	62.2
Solomon Islands	492,170	8,400	1.7
Somalia	12,448,179	94,000	0.8
South Africa	49,660,502	5,100,000	10.3
South Korea	49,044,790	34,430,000	70.2
Spain	40,448,191	22,843,915	56.5
Sri Lanka	20,926,315	428,000	2.0
Sudan	36,618,745	3,500,000	9.6
Suriname	505,973	32,000	6.3
Swaziland	1,173,758	41,600	3.5

Nation	Population	Internet Users	Internet Penetration (%)
Sweden	9,031,088	6,981,200	77.3
Switzerland	7,554,661	5,230,351	69.2
Syria	19,314,747	1,500,000	7.8
Taiwan	22,858,872	15,400,000	67.4
Tajilistan	7,076,598	19,500	0.3
Tanzania	38,870,348	384,300	1.0
Thailand	65,068,149	8,465,800	13.0
Togo	5,527,332	320,000	5.8
Tokelau	1,394	540	38.7
Tonga	104,057	3,100	3.0
Trinidad and Tobago	1,330,164	160,000	12.0
Tunisia	10,342,253	1,294,900	12.5
Turkey	71,158,647	16,000,000	22.5
Turkmenistan	5,097,028	64,800	1.3
Tuvalu	9,860	1,700	17.2
Uganda	28,574,909	750,000	2.6
Ukraine	46,299,862	5,545,000	12.0
United Arab Emirates	4,444,011	1,708,500	38.4
United Kingdom	60,776,238	40,362,842	66.4
United States	301,139,947	215,088,545	71.4
Uruguay	3,460,607	1,100,000	31.8
Uzbekistan	27,780,059	1,745,000	6.3
Vanuatu	222,606	7,500	3.4
Vatican City State	767	93	12.1
Venezuela	26,023,528	5,297,798	20.4
Vietnam	85,262,356	18,226,701	21.4
Wallis & Futuna	15,352	900	5.9
Yemen	22,230,531	270,000	1.2
Zambia	11,486,812	500,000	4.4
Zimbabwe	12,398,897	1,220,000	9.8

Sources: Internet World Stats: Usage and Population Statistics, available at: http://www.internetworldstats.com/stats.htm. Internet Usage and World Population Statistics are for November 30, 2007.

APPENDIX B

50 Social Media Sites Every Marketer Needs

INSIDE CRM ANNOTATED LIST

Social-Media/Social-Bookmarking Sites

"Share your favorite sites on the Web with potential clients and business partners by commenting on, uploading and ranking different newsworthy articles. You can also create a member profile that directs traffic back to your company's Web site.

1. **Reddit**: Upload stories and articles on reddit to drive traffic to your site or blog. Submit items often so that you'll gain a more loyal following and increase your presence on the site.

2. **Digg**: Digg has a huge following online because of its optimum usability. Visitors can submit and browse articles in categories like technology, business, entertainment, sports and more.

3. **Del.icio.us**: Social bookmark your way to better business with sites like del.icio.us, which invite users to organize and publicize interesting items through tagging and networking.

4. **StumbleUpon**: You'll open your online presence up to a whole new audience just by adding the StumbleUpon toolbar to your browser and "channel surf[ing] the Web. You'll "connect with friends and share your discoveries," as well as "meet people that have similar interests."

5. **Technorati**: If you want to increase your blog's readership, consider registering it with Technorati, a network of blogs and writers that lists top stories in categories like Business, Entertainment and Technology.

6. **Ning**: After hanging around the same social networks for a while, you may feel inspired to create your own, where you can bring together clients, vendors, customers and co-workers in a confidential, secure corner of the Web. Ning lets users design free social networks that they can share with anyone.

7. **Squidoo**: According to Squidoo, "everyone's an expert on something. Share your knowledge!" Share your industry's secrets by answering questions and designing a profile page to help other members.

8. **Furl**: Make Furl "your personal Web file" by bookmarking great sites and sharing them with other users by recommending links, commenting on articles and utilizing other fantastic features.

9. **Tubearoo**: This video network works like other social-bookmarking sites, except that it focuses on uploaded videos. Businesses can create and upload tutorials, commentaries and interviews with industry insiders to promote their own services.

10. **WikiHow**: Create a how-to guide or tutorial on wikiHow to share your company's services with the public for free.

11. **YouTube**: From the fashion industry to Capitol Hill, everyone has a video floating around on YouTube. Shoot a behind-the-scenes video from your company's latest commercial or event to give customers and clients an idea of what you do each day.

12. **Ma.gnolia**: Share your favorite sites with friends, colleagues and clients by organizing your bookmarks with Ma.gnolia. Clients will appreciate both your Internet-savviness and your ability to stay current and organized.

Professional-Networking Sites

Sign up with these online networking communities as a company or as an individual to take advantage of recruiting opportunities, cross-promotional events and more.

13. **LinkedIn**: LinkedIn is a popular networking site where alumni, business associates, recent graduates and other professionals connect online.

14. **Ecademy**: Ecademy prides itself on "connecting business people" through its online network, blog and message-board chats, as well as its premier BlackStar membership program, which awards exclusive benefits.

15. **Ryze**: Ryze lets members organize contacts and friends; upcoming events; and even job, real-estate and roommate classifieds.

16. **YorZ**: This networking site doubles as a job site. Members can post openings for free to attract quality candidates.

17. **Xing**: An account with networking site Xing can "open doors to thousands of companies." Use the professional contact manager to organize your new friends and colleagues, and take advantage of the Business Accelerator application to "find experts at the click of a button, market yourself in a professional context [and] open up new sales channels."

18. **Facebook**: Facebook is no longer just for college kids who want to post their party pics. Businesses vie for advertising opportunities, event promotion and more on this social-networking site.

19. **Care2**: Care2 isn't just a networking community for professionals: It's touted as "the global network for organizations and people who Care2 make a difference." If your business is making efforts to go green, let others know by becoming a presence on this site.

20. **Gather**: This networking community is made up of members who think. Browse categories concerning books, health, money, news and more to ignite discussions on politics, business and entertainment.

This will help your company tap into its target audience and find out what they want.

21. **MEETin.org**: Once you've acquired a group of contacts in your city by networking on MEETin.org, organize an event so that you can meet face-to-face.

22. **Tribe**: Cities like Philadelphia, Boston, San Francisco, New York and Chicago have unique online communities on tribe. Users can search for favorite restaurants, events, clubs and more.

23. **Ziggs**: Ziggs is "organizing and connecting people in a professional way." Join groups and make contacts through your Ziggs account to increase your company's presence online and further your own personal career.

24. **Plaxo**: Join Plaxo to organize your contacts and stay updated with feeds from Digg, Amazon.com, del.icio.us and more.

25. **NetParty**: If you want to attract young professionals in cities like Boston, Dallas, Phoenix, Las Vegas and Orlando Fla., create an account with the networking site NetParty. You'll be able to connect with qualified, up-and-coming professionals online, then meet them at a real-life happy-hour event where you can pass out business cards, pitch new job openings and more.

26. **Networking For Professionals**: Networking For Professionals is another online community that combines the Internet with special events in the real world. Post photos, videos, résumés and clips on your online profile while you meet new business contacts.

Niche Social-Media Sites

Consider linking up with one of these social-media sites to narrow down your business's target audience. You'll find other professionals, enthusiasts and consumers who are most likely already interested in what your company has to offer.

27. **Pixel Groovy**: Web workers will love Pixel Groovy, an open-source site that lets members submit and rate tutorials for Web 2.0, email and online-marketing issues.

28. **Mixx**: Mixx prides itself on being "your link to the Web content that really matters." Submit and rate stories, photos and news to drive traffic to your own site. You'll also meet others with similar interests.

29. **Tweako**: Gadget-minded computer geeks can network with each other on Tweako, a site that promotes information sharing for the technologically savvy.

30. **Small Business Brief**: When members post entrepreneur-related articles, a photo and a link to their profile appear, gaining you valuable exposure and legitimacy online.

31. **Sphinn**: Sphinn is an online forum and networking site for the Internet marketing crowd. Upload articles and guides from your blog to create interest in your own company or connect with other professionals for form new contacts.

32. **BuzzFlash.net**: This one-stop news resource is great for businesses that want to contribute articles on a variety of subjects, from the environment to politics to health.

33. **HubSpot**: HubSpot is another news site aimed at connecting business professionals.

34. **SEO TAGG**: Stay on top of news from the Web marketing and SEO (search-engine optimization) industries by becoming an active member of this online community.

General Social-Media Sites

The following social-media sites provide excellent opportunities for businesses to advertise; promote specials, events or services; and feature published, knowledgeable employees.

35. **Wikipedia**: Besides creating your own business reference page on Wikipedia, you can connect with other users on Wikipedia's Community Portal and at the village pump, where you'll find conscientious professionals enthusiastic about news, business, research and more.

36. **Newsvine**: Feature top employees by uploading their articles, studies or other news-related items to this site. A free account will also get you your own column and access to the Newsvine community.

37. **43 Things**: This site bills itself as "the world's most popular online goal setting community." By publicizing your company's goals and ambitions, you'll gain a following of customers, investors and promoters who cheer you on as you achieve success.

38. **Wetpaint**: If you're tired of blogs and generic Web sites, create your own wiki with Wetpaint to reach your audience and increase your company's presence online. You can easily organize articles, contact information, photos and other information to promote your business.

39. **Frappr**: Embed a Frappr map and guestbook into your company's Web page so that you can pinpoint exactly how users find your site, discover in real-time what they have to say about your company profile and services, and create an "interactive, fun and engaging" spot for visitors.

40. **Yahoo! Answers**: Start fielding Yahoo! users' questions with this social-media Q&A service. Search for questions in your particular areas of expertise by clicking categories like Business & Finance, Health, News & Events and more. If you continue to dole out useful advice and link your answer to your company's Web page, you'll quickly gain a new following of curious customers.

Job Sites

If you want to secure high-quality talent during your company's next hiring spree, you'll need to maintain a strong presence on popular job sites like the ones listed below.

41. **CareerBuilder.com**: Reach millions of candidates by posting jobs on this must-visit site.

42. **The Wall Street Journal's CareerJournal**: The Wall Street Journal's CareerJournal attracts well-educated professionals who are at the top of their game. Post a job or search résumés here.

43. **CollegeRecruiter.com**: If your firm wants to hire promising entry-level employees, check CollegeRecuriter.com for candidates with college degrees.

44. **Monster**: Post often to separate your business from all the other big companies that use this site to advertise job openings.

45. **Sologig**: Top freelancers and contractors post résumés and look for work on this popular site.

46. **AllFreelance.com**: This site "offers self-employed small business owners links to freelance & work at home job boards, self-promotion tips" and more.

47. **Freelance Switch Job Listings**: Freelance Switch is the freelancer's online mecca and boasts articles, resource toolboxes, valuable tips and a job board.

48. **GoFreelance**: Employers looking to boost their vendor base should check GoFreelance for professionals in the writing, design, editing and Web industries.

49. **Yahoo! Hot Jobs**: This site is often one of the first places that job seekers visit. Post open opportunities and check out informative articles and guides to gain insight on the hiring and interviewing process.

50. **Guru.com**: Build your company's repertoire with top freelancing professionals by advertising projects on this site, otherwise known as "the world's largest online service marketplace."

Source: "50 Social Sites That Every Business Needs a Presence on." *Inside CRM*. Written by the site editors on January 28, 2008. Accessed at www.insidecrm.com on February 15, 2008. Used with permission.

APPENDIX C

Glossary

access Users' ability to see their data and correct them if erroneous.

access control Laws and standards that enable persons to reasonably regulate the information that they are giving up.

action plan One of the phases of the internet marketing plan in which the marketer identifies specific tactics to implement selected strategies.

ad clicks The number of times a user "clicks" on an online ad, often measured as a function of time ("ad clicks per day").**

advergame A combination of online advertising and gaming, where the user sees products and services in the game itself.

Advertising Non-personal communication of information through various media, usually persuasive in nature about products (goods and services) or ideas and usually paid for by an identified sponsor.

advertorial A print advertisement styled to resemble the editorial format and typeface of the publication in which it runs.**

ad views On the internet, the number of times an online ad was downloaded by users, often measured as a function of time ("ad views per day"). The actual number of times the ad was seen by users may differ because of caching (which increases the real number of ad views) and browsers that view documents as text only (which decreases the number of ad views).**

affiliate program A link to an e-tailer's Web site, put in by firms to make a commission on all purchases by referred customers.

agent An intermediary who represents either the buyer or the seller, does not take title to the goods, and makes a commission for work completed.

aggregation The gathering of products from multiple suppliers so that the consumer can have more choices in one location.

AIDA model Stands for awareness, interest, desire, and action and is one of the **hierarchy of effects** models.

AIO Activities, interests, and opinions of consumers.

animated GIF (Graphic Interchange Format) Files that consist of a series of frames each containing a separate picture; used to provide the animation for banner ads.

Application Service Provider (ASP) Organization that develops software, which resides at the ASP's site, to allow businesses to outsource value chain functions to separate providers.

assistive technologies Help people with disabilities use their computers to communicate over the Net; includes voice-activated computers, large-type screen displays, type-to-speech or braille, speech-to-text telephony, and eye gaze-to-type.

atmospherics The in-store ambiance created by retailers.

attention economy The idea that infinite information is available but the demand for it is limited by human capacity.

attitudes Individuals' internal thoughts—either positive or negative—about people, products, and other objects.

audience composition The demographic profile of a media audience.**

automatic customization Tailoring of the content presented to the user based on information known about the user and the user's historical surfing behavior. See *mass customization*.

average order value (AOV) A calculation that reflects dollar sales divided by the number of orders.

bandwidth The data-transferring capacity of a system—how much information can be sent from one place to another in a given period of time (can be measured in a number of ways—i.e., the number of megabytes transferred per second).

Balanced Scorecard An enterprise performance management system that links strategy to measurement by asking firms to set goals and subsequent performance metrics in four areas: customer, internal, innovation and learning, and financial.

banner ad A rectangular space appearing on a Web site, paid for by an advertiser, which allows the user to click-through to the advertiser's Web site.

bar code scanner A real-space primary data collection technique by which information is gathered off-line at brick-and-mortar retail stores and is subsequently stored and used in marketing databases.

barter The exchange of goods and services without the use of cash (i.e., the acquisition of media time or space by a media company in exchange for similar time/space in return).**

basic cable A "basic" service agreement in which a subscriber pays a cable TV operator or system a monthly fee. Does not include "pay" services that might be offered by the cable operator.**

Behavioral targeting Occurring when software tracks a user's movements through a Web site, then sends appropriate Web content at a moment's notice.

benefit segmentation A variable in behavioral segmentation where marketers form groups of consumers based on the benefits they desire from the product.

Blogs or Web logs, Web sites where entries are listed in reverse chronological order

brand advertising Advertising that creates a distinctly favorable image that customers associate with a product at the moment they make buying decisions.†

brand equity The intangible value of a brand, measured in dollars.

brand loyalty Level of commitment customers feel toward a certain brand, expressed by their continued purchase of that brand.

brick-and-mortar An off-line firm.

broadband High bandwidth required for the delivery of multimedia content over the Web.

brochureware A site that provides information about the company's products and services; offers an excellent opportunity to brand as well as to develop a relationship with the consumer and other stakeholders.

broker An intermediary that brings buyers and sellers together but doesn't represent either side. Like agents, brokers are paid by either the buyer or the seller.

build to order A complex product that is created as it is ordered, which helps to eliminate inventory and reduce cost.

business intelligence The gathering of secondary and primary information about competitors, markets, customers, and more.

business model A method by which the organization sustains itself in the long term, which includes its value proposition for partners and customers as well as its revenue streams.

business-to-business (B2B) The marketing of products to businesses, governments, and institutions for use in the business operation, as components in the business products, or for resale.

business-to-consumer (B2C) The marketing of products to the end consumer.

button Similar to banners ads, a space paid for by an advertiser that is square or round instead of rectangular.

buyer cooperative (buyer aggregator) A type of online purchasing agent that brings buyers together for the purpose of buying in larger quantities and, thus, reducing prices.

cable modem Allowing transmission of internet traffic over the cable TV wire connected to the home, with a speed of transmission over a cable modem ranging between 500 Kbps and 2.5 Mbps.

cable TV Reception of TV signals via cable (wires) rather than over the air (i.e., via a TV antenna).**

caching Phenomenon that occurs when access providers or browsers store or buffer Web page data in a temporary location on their networks or in their disk space to speed access and reduce traffic. Reduces the number of measured page views at the original content site.**

catalog aggregator Brings together many catalog companies, creating a new searchable database of products for buyers.

CDA (Computer Decency Act) Legislation added, in 1996, to the federal Telecommunications Act of 1934 making it a criminal act to send an obscene or indecent communication to a recipient who was known to the sender to be under 18 years of age.

chat room Virtual space where internet users can communicate in real time using special software.

circulation In print media, the number of copies sold or distributed by a publication. In broadcast, the number of homes owning a TV/radio set within a station's coverage area. Or, in cable TV, the number of households that subscribe to cable services for a given network. In out-of-home media, the number of people passing an advertisement who have an opportunity to see it.**

citizen journalists Internet users who contribute their perspectives by posting content to online blogs, forums, and Web sites, usually without editorial review.

click-and-mortar Stores with both off-line and online selling.

clickstream A user's Web surfing patterns.

click-through Determined when a Web surfer clicks on a banner or other ad that is hyperlinked to the advertiser's site.

client-side Refers to activities that occur on the user's computer, such as writing and sending e-mail.

client-side data collection Information about consumer surfing is gathered right at the user's PC (e.g., the cookie file).

co-branding Occuring when two different companies form an alliance to work together and put their brand names on the same product or service.

collaborative filtering This software gathers opinions of like-minded users online and returns those opinions to the individual in real time.

common law Decisions, presumptions, and practices traditionally embraced by Anglo-American courts.

Communications media Tools for disseminating information.

community building Firms build Web sites to draw groups of special interest users.

competitive intelligence (CI) The analysis of the industries in which a firm operates as input to the firm's strategic positioning and to understand competitor vulnerabilities.

consent When users are allowed to choose participation or exclusion.

Consumer centric A Web audience measurement model similar to the Nielsen ratings for TV; occurs when a panel representative of the population is formed, its Web viewing actions are recorded, and the results are generalized to the population.

consumer-to-consumer (C2C) Business transaction from one consumer to another. Once limited to classified advertising and garage sales, C2C has now grown due to the popularity of online auctions.

content filtering A process by which Web users may block unwanted material.

content publishing (brochureware) Used by every firm that has a Web site. Content refers to any text, graphics, audio, or video online that informs or persuades.

content sponsorship An e-commerce business model that involves companies selling online Website space or e-mail space to advertisers.

continuous replenishment The concept of "scan one, make one—and deliver it fast"; helps to eliminate inventory and reduce cost.

Content sponsorship A form of e-commerce in which companies sell advertising either on their Web sites or through their e-mail.

Conversion The proportion of all Web site visitors who actually purchase on that visit.

cookie A persistent piece of information stored on the user's local hard drive, which is keyed to a specific server (and even a file pathway or directory location at the server), and is passed back to the server as part of the transaction that takes place when the user's browser again crosses the specific server/path combination.**

cookie file See *cookie*.

COPPA (Children's Online Protection Act) Requires that Web sites and other online media that knowingly collect information from children 12 years of age or under (1) provide notice to parents; (2) obtain verifiable parental consent prior to the collection, use, or disclosure of most information; (3) allow parents to view and correct this information; (4) enable parents to prevent further use or collection of data; (5) limit personal information collection for a child's participation in games, prize offers, or related activities; and (6) establish procedures that protect the confidentiality, security, and integrity of the personal information collected.

copyright A protection of the right to publish or duplicate the expressions of ideas.

corporate portal A second-generation intranet with a goal of merging all of the employee's information and communication needs into a single interface, accessing internal documents, data warehouses, groupware, e-mail, and calendars, in addition to the Web.

cost per click Total advertisement cost divided by number of clicks on an ad or hyperlink.

cost per order Total ad cost divided by the number of orders.

cost per thousand (CPM) The cost to deliver 1,000 impressions (associated with delivery of ad views on the internet, and delivery to people or homes in traditional media).**

coverage The percentage of a population group covered by a medium; commonly used with print media to describe an average issue's audience within defined demographic or purchasing groups; akin to rating.**

CPM Cost of advertising per thousand people reached.

creative The name given the art/design within an advertisement.**

customer lift Increasing the response rates from promotions; increasing transaction rates.

customer profiling Use of data warehouse information to help marketers understand the characteristics and behavior of specific target groups.

customer relationship management (CRM) The process of targeting, acquiring, transacting, servicing, retaining, and building long-term relationships with customers.

customization The third step in the CRM process (identify, differentiate, and customize) in which firms tailor their marketing mixes to meet the needs of small target segments, even to the individual level, using electronic marketing tools; sometimes refers to technology that allows consumers to cater the Web site to suit their own needs.

cybersquatting A type of trademark violation that involves the registration of domains that resemble or duplicate the names of existing corporations or other entities.

database management For e-marketing, the collecting, analyzing, and disseminating of electronic information about customers, prospects, and products in order to increase profits.

database marketing Collecting, analyzing, and disseminating electronic information about customers, prospects, and products in order to increase profits.

data mining Extraction of hidden predictive information from the warehouse via statistical analysis in order to find patterns and other information in databases.

data warehouse Repository for an entire organization's historical data (not just marketing data), designed specifically to support analyses necessary for decision making.

demographics The characteristics of populations.

Diaspora communities When a large number of people leave their home country and live together in a common neighborhood or city abroad, they become part of a diaspora community, often wanting to maintain a relationship with their homeland.

differentiation "The process of adding a set of meaningful and valued differences to distinguish the company's offering from competitors' offerings."*

digital audio, video, graphics Visual materials stored in a digital format for inclusion on Web pages and other electronic transmission over the internet.

digital divide The distinction between countries and between different groups of people within countries between those who have real access to information and communications technology and are using it effectively, and those who don't.

Digital media Electronic tools used to store, transmit, and receive digitized information, according to Wikipedia.

dilution The diminishment of the ability to identify or distinguish a good or service.

Direct distribution Refers to a type of e-commerce in which manufacturers sell directly to consumers, eliminating intermediaries such as retailers (the Dell model). Also called direct selling.

direct marketing Any direct communication to a consumer or business recipient that is designed to generate a response in the form of an order (direct order), a request for further information (lead generation), and/or a visit to a store or other place of business for purchase of specific product(s) or service(s) (traffic generation) (*source*: www.the-dma.org).

direct-response advertising Seeking to create action such as inquiry or purchase from consumers as a result of seeing the ad.

discontinuous innovations New-to-the-world products never seen before, such as music CDs and the television at their introductions.

disintermediation The process of eliminating traditional intermediaries. Eliminating intermediaries has the potential to reduce costs because each intermediary must add to the price of the product in order to make a living.

display ads Ads that contain more graphics and white space than text and include traditional banners and many additional sizes.

distributed e-mail E-mail sent to distribution lists that is redistributed to the entire subscription list.

distribution channel A group of interdependent firms that work together to transfer product from the supplier to the consumer. The transfer may either be direct or employ a number of intermediaries.

DMCA (Digital Millennium Copyright Act) A complex piece of legislation that contains several provisions, among granting internet service providers (ISPs) protection from acts of user infringement as long as certain procedures are followed, including the prompt reporting and disabling of infringing material, and criminalizing the circumvention of software protections and the development or distribution of circumvention products.

domain name The unique name that identifies an internet site, such as microsoft.com. A domain name always has two or more parts, separated by periods. A given server may have more than one domain name, but a given domain name points to only one machine.**

dot-com A firm engaging in e-commerce activities.

DSL (Digital Subscriber Line) Technology that refers to a family of methods (nine variations) for transmitting at speeds up to 8 Mbps (8 million bits per second) over a standard phone line.

dynamic pricing The strategy of offering different prices to different customers.

early adopters The next 13.5 percent to purchase the product, after the innovators, who comprise the first 2.5 percent. Early adopters are eager to buy new products, but they are more community minded than innovators and tend to communicate with others about new products.

e-business See *electronic business.*

e-business model A method by which the organization sustains itself in the long term using information technology, which includes its value proposition for partners and customers as well as its revenue streams.

e-business strategy The deployment of enterprise resources for capitalizing on technologies to reach specified objectives and ultimately improve performance and create sustainable competitive advantage.

e-commerce Use of digital technologies such as the internet and bar code scanners to enable the buying and selling process. E-commerce is about transactions through distribution channels and e-tailing.

e-coupons Like traditional coupons, but internet users "point and clip" these electronic coupons.

ECPA (Electronic Communication Privacy Act) Legislation, similar to the Fair Credit Reporting Act, that provides sanctions for misuse of consumer data.

EDI (electronic data interchange) The computerized exchange of information between organizations in order to avoid paper forms. The classic use of EDI is to eliminate purchase requisitions between firms.

effectiveness The extent to which choices made maximize a company's competitive advantage.

efficiency Generally referring to the relative costs of delivering media audiences.** See *cost per rating point* and *cost per thousand.*

efficient market A market in which customers have equal access to information about products, prices, and distribution.

electronic business (e-business) The continuous optimization of a firm's business activities through digital technology. This term and *e-commerce* are often used interchangeably.

electronic check A consumer's authorization for a third-party Web site to pay a specific amount in a transaction and withdraw funds from the user's checking account.

electronic commerce (e-commerce) The subset of e-business focused on transactions that includes buying/selling online, digital value creation, virtual marketplaces and storefronts, and new distribution channel intermediaries. This term and *e-business* are often used interchangeably.

electronic marketing (e-marketing) The use of information technology in the processes of creating, communicating, and delivering value to customers, and for managing customer relationships in ways that benefit the organization and its stakeholders.

electronic money Also called e-money or digital cash, a system that uses the internet and computers to exchange payments electronically.

e-mail advertising The least expensive type of online advertising, generally consisting of a few sentences of text embedded in another firm's e-mail content.

e-marketing strategy A marketing strategy using information technology.

emerging economies Those with low levels of gross domestic product (GDP) per capita that are experiencing rapid growth.

enabling technology Electronic marketing products unique to the internet that operate behind the scenes and assist in the creation of customer value.

enforcement The process through which users have effective means to hold data collectors to their policies.

engagement Involving turning on a prospect to a brand idea enhanced by the surrounding context

enterprise knowledge management (EKM) A combination of the database contents and the technology used to create the system: the marketing information system (MIS) at a company-wide level. Marketing knowledge contributes to the EKM system through the MIS.

enterprise resource planning (ERP) Back-office operations such as order entry, purchasing, invoicing, and inventory control that allow organizations to optimize business processes while lowering costs.

environmental factors The online legal, political, and technological environments that can greatly influence marketing strategies, alter the composition of the internet audience, and affect the quality of material that can be delivered to them. These factors also affect laws regarding taxation, access, copyright, and encryption on the internet.

environmental scan Continual task of observing factors that affect a firm's operations; includes economic analysis as well as social and demographic trends.

e-tailer An intermediary firm that buys products and resells them online, just as traditional retailers do off-line.

ethical code A statement outlining proper behaviors of participants as developed by trade associations, commercial standards groups, and the professions.

ethics A general endeavor that takes into account the concerns and values of society as a whole.

evaluation plan System of tracking effectiveness, put in place before the site is launched, whereby the site is continually assessed after it is created and published.

exchange A basic concept in marketing that refers to the act of obtaining a desired object from someone else by offering something in return.

experiential marketing A technique that gets the consumer involved in the product to create a memorable experience.

Extensible Markup Language (XML) The next generation of HTML that allows Web browsers to pull information from databases on-the-fly and display in Web pages.

extranet Two or more proprietary networks that are joined for the purpose of sharing information. If two companies link their intranets, they would have an extranet. Extranets are proprietary to the organizations involved.

fax-on-demand Customers telephone a firm, listen to an automated voice menu, and through selecting options request that a fax be sent on a topic of interest.

fixed pricing A price set by sellers, which buyers must take or leave. Also called *menu pricing*.

flow The state occurring during network navigation that is (1) characterized by a seamless sequence of responses facilitated by machine interactivity, (2) intrinsically enjoyable, (3) accompanied by a loss of self-consciousness, and (4) self-reinforcing.‡

focus group A qualitative methodology that attempts to collect in-depth information from a small number of participants.

framing A process in which a Web browser is instructed to divide itself into two or more partitions and load within a section material obtained from another Web site through the execution of an automatic link.

fraud The use of deception and false claims to obtain profit.

frequency The number of times people (or homes) are exposed to an advertising message, an advertising campaign, or a specific media vehicle. Also, the period of issuance of a publication (e.g., daily, monthly).**

frequency distribution The array of reach according to the level of frequency delivered to each group.**

FTC (Federal Trade Commission) Administrative agency concerned with making laws responsive to particular situations by promulgating rules and opinions within the sectors of its expertise.

FTP (File Transfer Protocol) The procedure whereby files are transferred from the designer's computer to the Web server; used in the publication of Web pages.

geodemographics Combination of geography and demographics of consumer market segmentation designed to identify and reach the right people at the right time.

geographic segment pricing A company sets different prices when selling a product in different geographic areas

geographics Separation of large markets into smaller groupings according to country, region, state, city, community, or block divisions.

GPRS (General Packet Radio Service) Also known as 3G (third generation) mobile phone technology, supporting a wide range of bandwidths for receiving and sending e-mail and large amounts of data, and for Web browsing in many different countries.

GUI (graphical user interface) Software that allows users to interact with their computer via icons and a pointer instead of by typing in text at a command line.

hierarchy of effects model Device that attempts to explain the impact of marketing communication. It assumes that consumers go through a series of stages when making product decisions and that communication messages are designed to assist that movement.

high bandwidth See *broadband*.

hit Web-speak for any request for data from a Web page or file; often used to compare popularity/traffic of a site in the context of getting so many "hits" during a given period. A common mistake is to equate hits with visits or page views. A single visit or page view is usually recorded as several hits and, depending on the browser, the page size, and other factors, the number of hits per page can vary widely.**

hostile applets Programs that can be used to surreptitiously access and transmit data on hard drives, including e-mail addresses, credit card records, and other account information.

HTML (Hypertext Markup Language) A simple coding system used to format documents for viewing by Web clients. Web pages are written in this standard specification.**

hyperlink See *link.*

hypertext Generally, any text on a Web page that contains links to other documents—words or phrases in a document that can be chosen by a user and that cause another document to be retrieved or displayed.**

ICANN (Internet Corporation for Assigned Names and Numbers) The organization responsible for the administration of the internet name and address system and for resolving conflicts that surround the assignment and possession of domains.

IMC (integrated marketing communication) See *integrated marketing communication.*

impressions The gross sum of all media exposures (number of people or homes) without regard to duplication.**

in-depth interviews (IDI) A semistructured conversation with a small number of subjects.

indirect distribution channel A typical indirect channel includes suppliers, a manufacturer, wholesalers, retailers, and end consumers

individualized targeting See *micromarketing.*

infomediary An online organization that aggregates and distributes information.

information architecture The design of Web site organization, indexing, labeling, and navigation systems to support browsing and searching.

infrastructure The equipment and communication lines that allow data to travel through a network.

integrated marketing communication (IMC) A comprehensive plan of communication that includes advertising, sales promotion, public relations, direct marketing, personal selling, and the rest of the marketing mix to provide maximum communication impact with stakeholders.

interactive advertising All forms of online, wireless, and interactive television advertising, including banners, sponsorships, e-mail, keyword searches, referrals, slotting fees, classified ads, and interactive television commercials (*source*: IAB Glossary of Interactive Advertising terms at www.iab.net).

interactive banner The most advanced stage of the banner; a banner that may sense the position of the mouse on the Web page and begin to animate faster as the user approaches; have built-in games, or have drop-down menus, check boxes, and search boxes to engage and empower the user.

interactive point of sale terminals A device located on a retailer's counter and used to capture consumer data and present targeted communication to customers.

intermediary A firm that appears in the channel between the supplier and the consumer, and specializes in performing functions more efficiently than the supplier could.

internal efficiencies Reductions in marketing and operations costs. A company going online usually realizes internal efficiencies.

internet As relates to marketing strategy, the internet is a global network of interconnected networks (technology), a medium for communication with stakeholders, and a distribution channel for digital products.

internet business models A subset of e-business models that uses the internet to add value and generate a revenue stream.

internet marketing Use of the internet and other network systems for marketing a firm's products; a term soon to be replaced by *e-marketing* because it includes a broader range of technologies.

internet telephony Use of the internet to carry simultaneous digitized voice transmission.

interstitials Java-based ads that appear while the publisher's content is loading.

intranet A network that runs internally in a corporation but that uses internet standards such as HTML and browsers; can be thought of as a mini-internet but only for internal corporate consumption.

instant messaging Short messages sent among users who are online at the same time.

inventory Normally defined as the quantity of goods or materials on hand. On the internet, a site's inventory is the number of page views it will deliver in a given period of time and is, thus, the amount of product that can be sold to advertisers.**

IP address (internet protocol) See URL and domain name. All three terms are used interchangeably.

iPOS terminals Small customer-facing machines near the brick-and-mortar cash register, used to record a buyer's signature for a credit card transaction.

ISP (internet service provider) Company that has a network of servers (mail, news, Web, and the like), routers, and modems attached to a permanent, high-speed internet "backbone" connection to which subscribers can then dial in, via a local network, to gain internet access.

jurisdiction The legal term that describes the ability of a court or other authority to gain control over a party; traditionally based on physical presence, but now less certain within the online world commonality of physical location.

just-in-time inventory/delivery (JIT) A goal of value chain management in which carrying excessive amounts of inventory is avoided. Some retailers do not even hold inventory but rather acquire and ship it at the time of the order.

keyword advertising Banner ads or links on a search query return page based on the keywords entered by the user at a search engine.

knowledge management The process of managing the creation, use, and dissemination of knowledge.

laggards The last 16 percent of buyers of new products, who are traditional, generally of lower socioeconomic status, and who often adopt a product when newer products have already been introduced.

Lanham Act Legislation that protects trademarks registered with the government and some not registered with the government.

law An expression of values, normally created for broader purposes, with the goal of addressing national or sometimes international populations, and made by legislatures such as Congress or Parliament, enforced by executives or agencies, and interpreted by the courts.

learning relationship A learning relationship between a customer and an enterprise that gets smarter and smarter with each individual interaction, defining in ever more detail the customer's own individual needs and tastes.

Least developed countries (LDCs) These are those countries with the world's poorest economies.

license Contractual agreement made between consumers and software vendors that allows the buyer to use the product but restricts duplication or distribution.

lifetime value (LTV) Net present value of the revenue stream for any particular customer over a number of years.

line extensions A lower-risk strategy for marketers introducing a new-product line.

link The path between two documents that associates an object, such as a button or hypertext, on a Web page with another Web address. The hyperlink allows a user to point and click on an object and thereby move to the location associated with that object by loading the Web page at that address.**

list broker A firm that sells lists, not usually by handing over the list but by sending a company's e-mail message to massive distribution lists.

LISTSERV A program that provides automatic processing of many functions involved with mailing lists. E-mailing appropriate messages to it will automatically subscribe the e-mailer to a discussion list or unsubscribe the person. A LISTSERV will also answer requests for indexes, FAQs, archives of the previous discussions, and other files.

location-based marketing Promotional offers that are pushed to mobile devices and customized based on the user's physical location.

Logistics This includes physical distribution activities such as transportation and inventory storage, as well as the function of aggregating product.

log file In internet server software, a feature that records every file sent by the server along with the destination address and time sent.

lower-cost products Products introduced to compete with existing brands by offering a price advantage. The internet spawned a series of free products with the idea of building market share so the firm would have a customer base for marketing other products owned by the firm. For example, Eudora Light, the e-mail reader software, was an early entry with this strategy.

macroenvironment All stakeholders, organizations, and forces external to the organization.

manufacturer's agents (seller aggregators) An entity that represents more than one seller, and in the virtual world generally creates Web sites to help an entire industry sell product.

market deconstruction The removal of distribution channel or other functions from the players that normally perform them.

marketing concept The idea that an organization exists to satisfy customer wants and needs while meeting organizational objectives.

marketing intelligence The procedure in which marketers continually scan the firm's macroenvironment for threats and opportunities.

marketing public relations (MPR) Brand-related activities and nonpaid, third-party media coverage to positively influence target markets.

market opportunity analysis Analysis conducted by a firm upon reviewing the marketing environment, focusing on finding and selecting among market opportunities. A traditional market opportunity analysis includes both demand and supply analyses. The demand portion reviews various market segments in terms of their potential profitability. Conversely, the supply analysis reviews competition in selected segments that are under consideration.

marketing concept The social and economic justification for an organization's existence as it seeks the satisfaction of customer wants and needs while meeting organizational objectives.

market differences Ways in which two country markets exhibit dissimilar characteristics, such as different languages, cultural behaviors, buying behaviors, and so forth.

market similarity Ways in which two country markets exhibit similar characteristics, such as different languages, cultural behaviors, buying behaviors, and so forth.

marketing segmentation The process of aggregating individuals or businesses along similar characteristics that pertain to the use, consumption, or benefits derived from a product or service.

market skimming pricing Introduction of new products at a high price that will only attract the innovators and early adopters, after which time the company then steadily drops the price as it introduces newer high-end models.

market targeting The process of selecting the market segments that are most attractive to the firm.

mass customization The internet's unique ability to individualize marketing mixes electronically and automatically to the individual level.

mass marketing See *undifferentiated targeting*.

metatags HTML statements, which describe a Web site's contents, that allow search engines to identify sites relevant to topics of their inquiries.

metric Another word for a measurement number.

microenvironment Stakeholders and forces internal to the organization.

micromarketing Individualized targeting. A **microsite** is a Web page or small site with specialized information and its own URL that is promoted separately from the main site.

Microsite is a Web page or small site with specialized information and its own URL that is promoted separately from the main site.

Millenials A consumer segment born between 1974 and 1994 (also called Generation Y).

MIS (marketing information system) The system of assessing information needs, gathering information, analyzing it, and disseminating it to marketing decision makers. In a separate context MIS also refers to management information systems—a field of study in many business schools.

MP3 Technology for the compression of audio multimedia, which can reduce CD recordings to one-tenth their original size and helps to alleviate the problem of low bandwidth.

multimedia The audio and video experience that is not prevalent yet on the internet due primarily to lack of sufficient bandwidth for its transmittal.

multichannel marketing The use of more than one sales channel, such as online, brick and mortar, and catalog.

multisegment targeting See *differentiated targeting*.

narrowcast An electronic media term referring primarily to cable channels because they contain focused electronic content that appeals to special-interest markets.

natural search An SEO strategy involving optimizing a Web site so it will appear as close to the first search engine results page as possible.

NET (No Electronic Theft) Act Legislation that confers copyright protection for computer content and imposes sanctions when infringement is committed for commercial or private financial gain or by the reproduction or distribution of one or more copies of copyrighted works having $1,000 or more in retail value.

network A broadcast entity that provides programming and sells commercial time in programs aired nationally via affiliated or licensed local stations (e.g., ABC television network, ESPN cable network). On the internet, an aggregator/broker of advertising inventory from many sites.**

new-product lines Lines introduced when firms take an existing brand name and create new products in a completely different category. For example, General Foods applied the Jell-O brand name to pudding pops and other frozen delights.

News aggregators Using client or Web software (such as RSS) to bring news from many sources to one place for easy reading.

newsgroup Communities of interest that post e-mails on electronic bulletin boards (e.g., Usenet, which is organized around topics or products).

niche marketing A firm's selection of one segment and development of one or more marketing mixes to meet the needs of that segment.

notice A statement to users to make them aware of a site's information policy before data are collected.

online agents Represent either the buyer or the seller and earn a commission for their work.

online auctions The auction-style sale of merchandise via the internet.

Online brokers Intermediaries who assist in purchase negotiations without actually representing either buyers or sellers.

online community Users who are widely dispersed geographically but come together in cyberspace based on similar interests.

online exchange Electronic forum in which buyers and sellers meet to make transactions.

online observation The monitoring of people's behavior in relevant situations, such as consumer chatting and e-mail posting through chat rooms, bulletin boards, or mailing lists.

online panel A panel of people who are paid to be the subject of marketing research. Also called *single-source data systems* or *opt-in communities*.

open buying on the internet (OBI) An electronic data interchange (EDI) that supports the sharing of internal information with value chain partners.

opt-in Occurs when users voluntarily agree to receive commercial e-mail about topics that might be of interest to them by simply checking a box and entering an e-mail address. Also called permission marketing.

opt-out Similar to opt-in; however, users have to uncheck the box on a Web page to prevent being put on the e-mail list.

out-of-home media Those media meant to be consumed only outside of one's home (e.g., outdoor, transit, in-store media).**

outsource To contract services from external firms in order to accomplish internal tasks.

page An HTML (Hypertext Markup Language) document that may contain text, images, and other online elements, such as Java applets and multimedia files. It may be statically or dynamically generated.**

page interactivity Ability of a user to submit information to an organization from a browser and receive either standard or tailored responses including search tools, forms, purchase options, and e-mail.

Page tags One pixel on a page that is invisible to users (a pixel is one dot of light on a computer screen).

page view The number of times a page was downloaded by users, often measured as a function of time ("page views per day"); the actual number of times the page was seen by users may be higher because of caching.**

Paid inclusion Occuring when sites receive guaranteed indexing in a search engine.

Paid search Occuring when an advertiser pays a reputation aggregator a fee for listing, directory submission, inclusion in a search engine index, or to display their ad when users type in particular keywords.

Pareto principle The generalization that 80 percent of a firm's business usually comes from the top 20 percent of customers.

patent The registered protection of inventions and the ability to reproduce or manufacture an inventor's product.

penetration The percentage of people (or homes) within a defined universe that are physically able to be exposed to a medium.

pay per click advertising Sometimes called cost per action (CPA), this is an advertising model whereby the adve rtiser pays a predetermined amount to the website for each visitor that clicks on the ad. Advertisers may also pay the for each conversion (sale), or each sales lead or new registered user.

penetration pricing The practice of charging a low price for a new product for the purpose of gaining market share.

performance metrics Specific measures designed to evaluate the effectiveness and efficiency of an organization's operations.

permission marketing An opt-in form of marketing in which advertisers present marketing communication messages to consumers who agree to receive them.

personal digital assistant (PDA) Handheld personal organizer that sometimes allows for wireless Web access.

personal video recorder (PVR) Hard drives that can let viewers pause live shows or record up to 160 hours of television programming. Also knows as digital video recorders (DVR).

personalization Methods of individualizing an impersonal computer networked environment (e.g., Web sites that greet users by name, providing personalized information).

personalized Web page Web page created with cookies that were put on the user's hard disk by the Web site, which helps companies to personalize Web pages by greeting the user by name or by listing previous purchases, thus building relationship with users.

PICS (Platform for Internet Content Selection Rules) An application that allows for the filtering of sites deemed inappropriate for minors.

piracy Installing computer software or other copyrighted intellectual property (such as music or movies) that the individual did not purchase.

pixel One dot of light on a computer or television screen.

pointcast Electronic media with the capability of transmitting to an audience of just one person.

portal A point of entry to the internet such as Yahoo!, Lycos, and Excite.

positioning A strategy to create a desired image for a company and its products in the minds of a chosen user segment.

price The amount of money charged for a product or service. More broadly, price is the sum of all the values (such as money, time, energy, and psychic cost) that buyers exchange for the benefits of having or using a good or service.

price dispersion The observed spread between the highest and lowest price for a given product.

price elasticity The variability of purchase behavior with changes in price.

price leadership The lowest-priced product entry in a particular category.

price negotiation A company negotiates prices with individual customers, who can comprise segments of one online.

price transparency The idea that both buyers and sellers can view all competitive prices for items sold online.

primary data Information gathered for the first time to solve a particular problem. It is usually more expensive and time-consuming to gather than secondary data, but conversely, the data are current and generally more relevant to the marketer's specific problem. In addition, primary data have the benefit of being proprietary and, thus, unavailable to competitors.

privacy Topic of much debate, including issues of the Warren and Brandeis concept of a right to be left alone, often referred to as the seclusion theory; access control, which places its emphasis on laws and standards that enable persons to reasonably regulate the information that they are giving up; and autonomy that identifies private matters such as those necessary for a person to make life decisions.

probability sample A sample selected in such a way that each item or person in the population being studied has an equal likelihood of being included in the sample.

product life cycle (PLC) A model that describes the stages a product or a product category passes through from its production to its removal from the market.

product line Products grouped for sale in a specific market category.

product usage A variable in behavioral segmentation in which marketers group consumers based on how or when they use a product.

promotional pricing Special deals in price that retailers use to encourage a first purchase, to encourage repeat business, or to close a sale.

protocol A formal, standardized set of operating rules governing the format, timing, and error control of data transmissions and other activities on a network.

proxy server A system that stores frequently used information closer to the end user to provide faster access or to reduce the load on another server; also serves as the gateway to the internet.

proxy server caching The process that occurs when users access copies of Web sites rather than the site itself. Users accessing Web sites from proxy servers are not counted as new visitors.

psychographics The identification of personality characteristics and attitudes that affect a person's lifestyle and purchasing behavior.**

Purchasing agents Represent buyers. In traditional marketing, they often forge long-term relationships with one or more firms; on the internet, however, they represent any number of buyers, often anonymously.

pure play A business that began only on the internet, even if it subsequently added a brick-and-mortar presence.

radio frequency identification (RFID) Tags used to transmit a signal to scanners, which detect the presence of the RFID tag in products, credit cards, or even under a person or animal's skin.

random digit dialing Telephone survey technique of calling people at random and asking specific questions.

rating The percentage of a given population group consuming a medium at a particular moment. Generally used for broadcast media but can by applied to any medium. One rating point equals 1 percent of the potential viewing population.**

reach The number of different homes/people exposed at least once to an impression (ad view, program, commercial, print page, etc.) across a stated period of time. Also called the cumulative or unduplicated audience.**

real-space data collection Information gathering off-line at points of purchase such as smart card and credit card readers and bar code scanners.

real-time chat Interactive communication in which Web users type messages to each other in real time at a Web site.

real-time multimedia Technology that offers opportunities such as distance learning and education, virtual reality, entertainment, and video/audio conferencing through live broadcasting from radio stations or online chatting and other real-time broadcasts.

real-time profiling The use of special software to track a user's movements through a Web site, and then compile and report on the data at a moment's notice.

referral revenue Dollars in sales from customers referred to the firm by current customers.

relationship capital A firm's ability to build and maintain relationships with customers, suppliers, and partners: The total value of these relationships to a firm in the long term is its relationship capital.

relationship marketing The process of establishing, maintaining, enhancing, and commercializing customer relationships; its long-term customer orientation involves ongoing interactive communication between a firm and selected stakeholders, and focuses on individual customers 1:1.

repositioned products Current products that are either targeted to different markets or promoted for new uses.

repositioning The process of creating a new or modified brand, company, or product position.

reputation aggregator A Web site that ranks Web sites, products, retailers, or other content according to some rating system.

respondent authenticity A disadvantage of online research in which it is difficult to determine whether respondents are who they say they are.

retailers Buy products from manufacturers or wholesalers and sell them to consumers. Retailers can operate either off-line or online.

Return on investment (ROI) A measure of investment success. It is calculated by dividing net profit by total assets (fixed plus current).

revenue streams Cash flows that may come from Web site product sales, advertising sales, and agent commissions.

reverse auction An exchange arrangement in which individual buyers enter the price they will pay for particular items at the purchasing agent's Web site, and sellers can agree or not.

revisions of existing products Products that are introduced as "new and improved" and, thus, replace the old product. On the internet, firms are continually improving their brands to add value and remain competitive.

RFM analysis A scan of the database for three criteria: recency, frequency, and monetary value. This process allows firms to target offers to the customers who are most responsive, thus saving promotional costs and increasing sales.

RSS (Really Simple Syndication) An easy XML format designed for sharing headlines and other Web content.

safe harbor Provisions for the protection of EU citizen data.

sampling An arrangement in which users are allowed to sample a digital product prior to purchase. For example, software companies provide a free 30- to 60-day trial and online music stores give 30-second sound clips to customers.

search engine A Web site that scans the Web, searching for matches for the user's keywords, and returns a list of Web sites that might have the desired information.

Search Engine Optimization (SEO) The act of altering a Web site and incoming links so that it does well in the organic, crawler-based listings of search engines.

search marketing The act of marketing a Web site via search engines, whether through improving rank in listings, purchasing paid listings, or a combination of these and other search engine-related activities.

seclusion Warren and Brandeis theory outlining the concept of the right to be left alone.

secondary data Information that has been gathered for some other purpose but is useful for the current problem; can be collected more quickly and less expensively than primary data.

second-generation shopping agents Shopping agents that measure value and not just price.

security Policies that ensure the integrity of data and the prevention of misuse should be in place.

segmentation basis Dividing the market by the general categories of demographics, geographic location, psychographics, and behavior, each of which has a number of variables.

segmentation variables Variables used by marketers to identify and profile groups of customers.

segmented pricing Setting the price of a good or service at two or more levels, based on segment differentiation rather than cost alone.

self-regulation The private sector's ability to rapidly identify and resolve problems specific to its areas of competence.

selling agent An entity that represents a single firm to help it move product and normally works for a commission.

semantic Web An extension of the current Web in which information is given well-defined meaning.

server-side Activities that take place on an organization's Web server such as processing forms, streaming video, and accessing product databases for sending product Web pages to users.

server-side data collection Information about consumer surfing that is gathered and recorded on the Web server.

session A series of consecutive visits made by a visitor to a series of Web sites.**

SET (Secure Electronic Transaction) A vehicle for legitimizing both the merchant and the consumer as well as protecting the consumer's credit card number. Under SET the card number is never directly sent to the merchant. Rather a third party is introduced to the transaction with whom both the merchant and consumer communicate to validate one another as well as the transaction.

share The audience or percentage of homes using TV (HUT) tuned to a particular program or station. Share of market is the percentage of total category volume (dollars, unit, etc.) accounted for by a brand. Share of voice is the percentage of advertising impressions generated by all brands in a category accounted for by a particular brand but often also refers to share of media spending.**

share of mind Refers to relationship marketing focusing on customer development in the long term: maintaining and enhancing. A firm using this kind of relationship marketing differentiates individual customers based on need rather than differentiating products for target groups.

shopping agents Programs that allow the consumer to rapidly compare prices and features within product categories. Shopping agents implicitly negotiate prices downward on behalf of the consumer by listing companies in order of best price first.

short message services (SMS) 160 characters of text, using a store-and-delivery technology, sent by one user to another over the internet, usually with a cell phone or PDA. Also called *text messaging*.

Shoshkeles Browser-driven, platform-agnostic, sound-enabled, free-moving forms that interrupt Web page content; a technology that does not require plug-ins, with no discernable download time for users (*source*: www.unitedvirtualities.com).

site stickiness A measure of length of time spent at a site.

situation analysis Review of the existing marketing plan and any other information that can be obtained about the company and its brands, examination of environmental factors related to online marketing, and development of a market opportunity analysis.

slotting fee A fee charged to advertisers by media companies to get premium positioning on their site, category exclusivity, or some other special treatment; similar to slotting allowances charged by retailers (*source*: www.iab.net).

social bonding Stimulated social interaction between companies and customers resulting in a more personalized communication and brand loyalty.

social media Online tools and platforms that allow internet users to collaborate on content, share insights and experiences, and connect for business or pleasure.

social networking The practice of expanding the number of one's business and social contacts by making connections through individuals online.

Social networkss "Social structures made of nodes (which are generally individuals or organizations) that are tied by one or more specific types of interdependency, such as values, visions, idea, financial exchange, friends, kinship, dislike, conflict, trade, web links . . . disease transmission (epidemiology), or airline routes," according to Wikipedia.

spam Unsolicited e-mail, either sent to users or posted on an electronic bulletin board.

spam filter A program that has the capability of blocking unsolicited e-mails.

spider Automatic programs in search engines that search the Web from site to site, page by page, and word by word in order to build up a massive index or database of all the words found, where they were found, how many times they appear on each page, and so on. It is this database that is actually queried when you type in a search term.

sponsorship Integration of editorial content and advertising on a Web site. The sponsor pays for space and creates content that appeals to the publisher's audience.

spoofing A manipulation of the average person's lack of knowledge—and understanding of exactly how information is displayed, transferred or store—which provides opportunities for novel deceptions and is often used to extract sensitive information by leading a user to believe that a request is coming from a reputable source, such as an ISP or credit card company.

spot TV or radio commercial time purchased on a market-by-market basis as opposed to network (national) purchases; the term commonly used in lieu of *commercial announcement*.**

stakeholder Entity with a specific interest in a company (e.g., an employee, stockholder, supplier, lateral partnership, and customer).

stakeholder communication Interaction with a stakeholder involving strategies, such as advertising, public relations, sales promotion incentives, and lead generation, that can help marketers to accomplish cognitive and attitude objectives, often at substantial cost savings over traditional methods.

strategic e-marketing The design of marketing strategy that capitalizes on the organization's electronic or information technology capabilities to reach specified objectives.

strategic planning The "managerial process of developing and maintaining a viable fit between the organization's objectives, skills, and resources and its changing market opportunities" (Kotler, 2003, p. 64).

strategy The means to achieve a goal.

stealth marketing A type of guerilla marketing in which the consumer is unaware of being the target of a marketing tactic.

streaming audio/video Content sent to the user's computer as it is viewed versus sending an entire file before the user can view it.

structural bonds Relationships created when firms add value by making structural changes that facilitate the relationship with customers and suppliers.

supply chain management (SCM) The behind-the-scenes coordination of the distribution channel to deliver products effectively and efficiently to customers. Also called *integrated logistics*.

switchers Consumers who do not show any specific brand loyalty but generally go for the best price.

SWOT Strengths, weaknesses, opportunities, and threats analysis. SWOT analysis objectively evaluates the company's strengths and weaknesses with respect to the environment and the competition.

syndicated research Data collected regularly using a systematic process, such as the Nielsen television Ratings. This is secondary data for the companies who purchase it.

syndication In broadcasting, a program carried on selected stations that may or may not air at the same time in all markets; in newspapers, an independently written column or feature carried by many newspapers (e.g., "Dear Abby"); in magazines, a centrally written or published section being carried by newspapers, generally in the Sunday edition (e.g., *Parade*).**

synergy Result that occurs when two or more firms join in a business relationship in which the results often exceed what each firm might have accomplished alone.

TCP/IP Transmission Control Protocol/Internet Protocol, the most widely used protocol on the internet, consisting of a set of rules that each computer follows in order to enable communication. Only computers using the same protocol are able to communicate.

technographics Segments of online shoppers as identified by Forrester Research. Consumers fall into one of 10 groups based upon their attitude toward technology, income as an indicator of shopping behavior, and primary motivation to go online.

Telecenters Small shops with three to ten computers that offer internet connections to the general public in simply furnished settings.

Telematics A communication system in an automobile that uses a global positioning system (GPS) for interactive communication between firms and drivers.

third-party logistics The outsourcing of logistics such that a third party manages the company's supply chain and provides value-added services such as product configuration and subassembly.

trademark Any image, symbol, word, or other indicator positively associated with a product's identity in the market and registered with the government.

transactional functions The process of matching product to buyer needs, negotiating price, and carrying out the transaction.

TRIPs (Trade Related Intellectual Property Rights) A 1995 agreement that is part of the World Trade Organization's (WTO) program of international treaties.

ubiquitous application An application that is able to function in the course of nearly any online session without a user's knowledge or control.

UCITA (Uniform Computer Information Transactions Act) A model that, if adopted by the states, would govern all legal agreements pertaining to software transactions, including sales.

UNCITRAL (United Nations Commission of International Trade Law) The governing body that established the Model Law on Electronic Commerce to provide for global uniformity in digital commerce.

unique users The number of individuals—without repetition—who visit a site within a specific period of time. With today's technology, this number can be calculated only with some form of user registration or identification.**

unique visitors See *unique users*.

universal product code (UPC) Also called the bar code, a symbol scanned by retailers, wholesalers, and manufacturers for the purpose of inventory management.

universe The total population within a defined demographic, psychographic, or product consumption segment against which media audiences are calculated to determine ratings, coverage, reach, and so on.

URL (uniform [or universal] resource locator) Information on the protocol, the system, and the file name that enables the user's system to find a particular document on the internet. An example of a URL is http://www.sholink.com, which indicates that "Hypertext Transfer Protocol" is the protocol and that the information is located on a system named "www.sholink.com," which is the Sholink Corporation's Web server. This example does not show a particular file name (such as index.htm), because most Web servers are set up to point to a homepage if no file name is used.**

Usenet Worldwide network of thousands of computer systems with a decentralized administration. The Usenet systems exist to transmit postings to special-interest newsgroups.

value Benefits minus costs.

value chain (integrated logistics) The supply chain, the manufacturer, and the distribution channel viewed as an integrated system.

Vertical search Is site-specific search on very specialized topics, such as travel, online retailers, or books.

Value segment pricing The seller recognizes that not all customers provide equal value to the firm, and segments by high, medium, and low value—and pricing accordingly.

viral marketing The online equivalent of word-of-mouth and referred to as word-of-mouse, which occurs when individuals forward e-mail to friends, coworkers, family, and others on their e-mail lists.

virtual Magistrate Mediation-oriented program developed to resolve online disputes.

virtual mall A model similar to a shopping mall in which multiple online merchants are hosted at a Web site.

virtual worlds Sites where users can take the form of avatars and socialize in an online space of their own making.

visitor A user who visits a site, but does not distinguish between one-time and repeat visitors.

Voice over Internet Protocol (VoIP) The term used to refer to internet telephony that relies on the Web to transmit phone calls, thus eliminating long-distance charges.

volume discount The price discount offered advertisers who purchase a certain amount of volume from the medium (e.g., pages or dollar amount in magazines).**

wallet share The amount of sales a firm can generate from one customer, which reflects the focus on customer retention versus acquisition (market share).

wearout A level of frequency, or a point in time, when an advertising message loses its ability to effectively communicate.**

Web analytics Tools that collect and display information about user behavior on a Web site.

Web form Technical term for a Web page that has designated places for the user to type information. Many corporate Web sites sport Web forms, using them for a multitude of purposes from site registration and survey research to product purchase.

Web log See *Blog.*

Web page An HTML (Hypertext Markup Language) document on the Web, usually one of many that together make up a Web site.**

Web server A system capable of continuous access to the internet (or an internal network) through retrieving and displaying documents and files via Hypertext Transfer Protocol (HTTP).**

Web site The virtual location for an organization's presence on the World Wide Web, usually made up of several Web pages and a single homepage designated by a unique URL.**

Web site content The text, graphics, video, and audio that are displayed on a Web page, which can also include interactive features such as search tools, forms, purchase options, and e-mail.

Web site log Data about how long users spend on each page, how long they are at the site, and what path they take through the site, among other things.

Webisode An episode of a TV-like program where the viewer takes a more active role. The BrilliantDigital product captures the user on video in the studio, performs voice-overs, and then places the user in the program.

wireless The transmission of communication signals that relies on towers to relay the signals in a mode similar to that of cell phones.

WiFi Abbreviation for Wireless Fidelity, the popular name for 802.11b wireless networking.

wiki Software that allows users to collaboratively create, edit, link, and organize the content of a Web site, usually for reference material, according to Wikipedia.

word-of-mouse See *viral marketing.*

World Wide Web The mechanism originally developed by Tim Berners-Lee for CERN physicists to be able to share documents via the internet. The Web allows computer users to access information across systems around the world using URLs (uniform resource locators) to identify files and systems and hypertext links to move between files on the same or different systems.**

yield management A strategy used most often by the travel industry to optimize inventory management through frequent price changes.

Notes

* Kotler and Keller, 2006.
** Reprinted with permission from Dean Witter Morgan Stanley.
‡ Quoted from Hoffman/Novak Project 2000.
† Quoted from Forrester Research.

APPENDIX D

References

Note: References for Chapter 5 are displayed at the end of this list.

"50 Social Sites That Every Business Needs a Presence on." Inside CRM Editors on January 28, 2008. Available at www.insidecrm.com on February 15, 2008.

Afuah, Allan, and Christopher Tucci (2001). *Internet Business Models and Strategies.* New York: McGraw-Hill/Irwin.

Agarwal, Anupam, Harding, and Schumacher (2004). "Organizing for CRM," *The McKinsey Quarterly* (November 3). Available at www.mckinsey quarterly.com.

"American Chamber of Commerce in Egypt" (2007). *Information and Communications Technology Developments in Egypt.* Available at http://www.amcham.org.eg/bsac/studiesseries/report50.asp.

Arnold, Catherine (2004). "Marketers Discover Weblogs' Power to Sell—Minus the Pitch," *Marketing News* (March 15).

Baez, Gabriela (2004). "Identifying the Main Areas of Growth in Latin America's Communications Market." Available at www.abranet.org.br/BrazilBreakfast04.pdf.

Baker, Stephen (2004). "Channeling the Future," *BusinessWeek* (July 12), pp. 70–72.

Barnako, Frank (2004). "Internet Daily." Available at CBS.MarketWatch.com (August 6).

Beal, Andy and Judy Strauss (2008). Radically Transparent: Monitoring and Managing Reputations Online. Indianapolis, Indiana: Wiley and Sons, Inc.

Berners-Lee, Tim, James Hendler, and Ora Lassila (2001). "The Semantic Web," *Scientific American* (May). Available at www.scientificamerican.com.

Berry, Leonard and A. L. Parasuraman (1991). *Marketing Services—Competing Through Quality.* New York: Free Press.

Bianco, Anthony (2004). "The Vanishing Mass Market," *BusinessWeek* (July 12), pp. 61–68.

Bolande, H. Asher (2002). "Shanghai Start-up Hopes Deal with McDonald's Scores Victory," *The Wall Street Journal* (May 22), p. B7A.

Brown, Eryn (2002). "Slow Road to Fast Data," *Fortune* (March 18), pp. 170–172.

Bruner, Rick and Kathryn Koegel (2005). "Target Demographics, Before and After," *DoubleClick Report.* Available at www.doubleclick.com.

Budis, Christian (2004). "Recreational Equipment Inc. (REI)," Working paper.

Burns, Enid (2008). U.S. Search Engine Rankings, December 2007. Available at: searchenginewatch.com (accessed on March 30, 2008).

Case, K.E. and R.C. Fair (2001). *Principles of Economics.* Upper Saddle River, NJ: Prentice Hall.

Cateora, P.R. and G.R. Graham (2007). *International Marketing.* 13th ed. Boston: McGraw Hill.

Chakravarthy, Srinivas (2000). "E-Strategy: Different Strokes," *Businessline* (October 4), pp. 1–2.

Chandrasekaran, Rajiv (2001). "Life in Cambodian Village Transformed by Internet," *Seattle Times* (June 17). Available at archives.seattletimes.nwsource.com/cgibin/texis.cgi/web/vortex/display?slug=wired villagesub17&date=20010617.

Chon, Gina (2001). "Bernard Krisher: Healing the Killing Field," *Asia Week* (June 29).

CNNIC. (2007). "20th Statistical Survey of Internet Use in China." Available at www.usatoday.com.

"Consumers Wary of Online Profiling" (1999). *USA Today* (November 5). Available at www.usatoday.com.

Cox, Beth (2002). "The Little Flower Company That Could" (January 22). Available at www.internetnews.com.

Curioso, Walter et al. (2007). "Opportunities for Providing Web-based Interventions to Prevent

Sexually Transmitted Infections in Peru," *PloS Medicine Online Journal*. Available at http://medicine.plosjournals.org/perlserv/?request=get-document&doi=10.1371%2Fjournal.pmed.0040011&ct=1.

Cutler, Matt (2001). Forrester Research Study as Cited in "NetGenesis Spotlight on ROI." Presentation at Internet World (December 9).

Detmer, Tom (2002). "Seeking the Complete Customer Experience: The Web as a Marketing Tool," *Customer Inter@Ction Solutions*, vol. 20, no. 11, p. 45.

Distefano, John (2000). "The Decisioning Frontier: Get Ready for Marketing Automation," *DM Review* (March). Available at www.dmreview.com.

"DoubleClick Ad Serving Data Shows Rich Media Click-Through Rates Six Times Higher Than Standard Ads" (2002). Press release available at www.doubleclick.com.

Doyle, Bill, Bill Bass, Ben Abbott, and Kerry Moyer (1997). "Branding on the Web," Forrester Report: Media & Technology Strategies (August).

Duncan, Tom (2002). *Using Advertising and Promotion to Build Brands*. New York: McGraw Hill-Irwin.

Duncan, Tom, and Frank Mulhern (eds.) (2004). "A White Paper on the Status, Scope, and Future of IMC," The IMC Symposium (March).

"E-Biz Strikes Again!" (2004). *BusinessWeek Online* (May 10). Available at www.businessweek.com.

"E-Mail and the Different Levels of ROI" (date unknown). Available at www.boldfish.com (accessed on November 17, 2001).

"Egyptians Flock to New Net Plan" (2002). *Wired* (June 25). Available at www.wired.com.

Esmat, B. (n.d.). "Internet Evolution in Egypt: Success Stories and Lessons Learned." Available at http://www. authorstream. com/Presentation/Ming-29973-Baher-Esmat-Egypt-Internet-Evolution-Success-Stories-Lessons-Learned-Egyptian-Information-Society-Initiat-as-Entertainment-ppt-powerpoint/

"False Hopes on Fantasy Island" (2003). *Business 2.0* (December), p. 38.

Farivar, Cyrus (2004). "New Ways to Pay," *Business 2.0* (August), p. 26.

"Gambling lawsuit filed against top Web content sites" (2004). Available at www.computerworld.com (August 4).

Gemius SA. (2007a). "E-commerce in the Countries of Central and Eastern Europe: Ukraine." Available at http://files.gemius.pl/Reports/2007/Short&free_version_of_report_E_commerce_Ukraine.pdf.

Gemius SA. (2007b). "E-commerce in the Countries of Central and Eastern Europe: Lithuania." Available at http://files.gemius.pl/Case_Studies/gemiusAdHoc/Short_free_version_report_Lithuania.pdf.

Ghosh, Shikhar (1998). "Making Business Sense of the Internet," *Harvard Business Review* (March–April), pp. 126–135.

Gillin, Paul (2008). "New Media, New Influencers and Implications for the Public Relations Profession," *Journal of New Communications Research*, vol II, no. 2.

Godin, Seth (1999). *Permission Marketing*. New York: Simon and Schuster.

Goldberg, Aaron (1999). "Speed Kills," *MC Technology Marketing Intelligence*, vol. 19, no. 6, p. 16.

Greenberg, Karl (2001). "Automakers Rev Up Online Efforts, But Some Dealers Are Skeptical," *BrandWeek* (December 10), p. 10.

Greenspan, Robyn (2002). "In Any Language, Hispanics Enjoy Surfing." Available at www.cyberatlas.internet.com.

Greenspan, Robyn (2004). "PDA Penetration Flattens" (January 4). Available at www.clickz.com.

Grönroos, Christian (1990). "Relationship Approach to Marketing in Service Contexts: The Marketing and Organizational Behavior Interface," *Journal of Business Research*, 20 (January), pp. 3–11.

Gruener, Jamie (2001). "How to Measure Storage ROI," *Network Connections*, pp. 8–10.

Hagel, John, and Marc Singer (1999). *Net Worth: Shaping Markets When Customers Make the Rules*. Boston: Harvard Business School Press.

"Haier's Purpose" (2004). *The Economist* (May 18). Available at www.economist.com/business/displayStory.cfm?story_id=2524347.

Hallerman, David (2002). "Online Ad Pricing: Count Heads or Count Results." Available at www.emarketer.com (accessed on April 25, 2002).

Hill, C.W.L. (2008). *Global Business Today.* Boston: McGraw-Hill Irwin.

Holland, Anne (2006). "Study Data: 1,120 Online Shoppers Say Why They Abandon Ecommerce Sites," (May 29). Available at www.marketingsherpa.com.

Iansiti, Marco, and Alan MacCormack (2001). "Developing Products on Internet Time," in *Internet Marketing,* J. Sheth, A. Eshghi, and B. Krishnan (eds.) Orlando, FL: Harcourt Inc., pp. 239–251.

"Influentials: An Online Study" (2004). RoperASW and WashingtonPost.com report.

"Internet Usage Statistics—The Big Picture." Available at www.internetworldstats.com/stats.htm.

iProspect Search Engine User Behavior Study (2006). Available at www.iprospect.com (accessed on January 5, 2008).

ITU (2000). "The Internet in the Andes: Bolivia Case Study." Available at www.itu.int/ITU-D/ict/cs/bolivia/material/bolivia.pdf.

ITU (2002). "Kretek Internet: Indonesia Case Study." Available at www.itu.int/ITUD/ict/cs/indonesia/index.html.

ITU (2006a). "The World Telecommunication/ICT Development Report 2006." Available at http://foss.org.my/projects/us-my-free-trade-agreement-issues/resources/wtdr2006-e.pdf.

ITU (2006b). "ITU Internet Report 2006: Digital.Life." Available at http://www.itu.int/osg/spu/publications/digitalife.

ITU (2007). "World Information Society Report." Available at http://www.itu.int/osg/spu/publications/worldinformationsociety/2007/WISR07_full-free.pdf.

Janisch, Troy (2004). "Checking Out or Getting Out? Reasons for Shopping Cart Abandonment," *Wisconsin Technology Network* (March 8). Available at www.wistechnology.com.

Jarvis, Steve (2001). "Follow the Money: Web Analytics Help Marketers Fix Sites, Revise Strategies," *Marketing News* (October 8), pp. 1, 10.

Jeanette, J.-P., and H.D. Hennessy (2002). *Global Marketing Strategies.* Boston: Houghton Mifflin Company.

Johnson, Bradley (2006). "Forget Phone and Mail: Online's the Best Place to Administer Surveys," *Advertising Age* (July 17).

Kalakota, Ravi, and Marcia Robinson (1999). *E-Business: Roadmap for Success.* Reading, MA: Addison-Wesley.

Kasanoff, Bruce, and Toria Thompson (1999). Advanced Strategies for Differentiating Customers and Partners: Software That Enables 1 to 1 Relationships. Stamford CT: Rogers and Peppers Group Report: Accelerating 1 to 1. Available at www.1to1.com.

Kim, Amy Jo (2000). "Secrets of Successful Web Communities," *Naima* (May). Available at www.naima.com/articles/webtechniques.html.

King, Julia, and Thomas Hoffman (1999). "Pace of Change Fuels Web Plans; Sites Must Shift Offering Every 60 Days to Thrive," *ComputerWorld* (July 5), p. 1.

Kotler, Philip, and Kevin Keller (2006). *Marketing Management,* 12th ed. Upper Saddle River, NJ: Prentice Hall.

Kupper, Phillip (2004). "How Continental Airlines Interprets and Uses CRM." Working paper.

Laseter, Tim, David Torres, and Anne Chung (2001). "Oasis in the Dot-Com Delivery Desert," *Strategy+Business,* no. 24, pp. 28–33.

Charles W. Lamb, Joseph F. Hair, and Carl D. McDaniel (2002). *Principles of Marketing,* 6th ed. Cincinnati, OH: South Western Publishing.

Lenhart, Amanda et al. (2003). "The Ever-Shifting Internet Population," Pew Internet & American Life. Available at www.pewinternet.org.

Linkner, Josh (2004). "Interactive Promos Engage Buyers," *Marketing News* (June 15), p. 13.

Long, Geoff (2000). "Bhutan Goes Online: A Modern Folktale," *Reports from Developing Worlds.* Available at www.icrc.ca/reports/read_article_englihs.cfm?article_num=611 Note: Accessed in 2002 but not currently available.

Malik, Om (2003). "The Rise of the Instant Company," *Business 2.0* (December), pp. 99–102.

"Managing Customer Data for Strategic Advantage" (2003). Conference Board Report.

Mandel, Maria (2004). "Sizing the U.S. Mobile Messaging Market." Available at www.forrester.com.

"Marketing Fact Book" (2004). *Marketing News* (July 15).

Melymuka, Kathleen (2001). "The Balanced E Scorecard," *ITWorld* (March 12). Available at www.itworld.com.

Miller, Thomas (2001). "Can We Trust the Data of Online Research?" *Marketing Research* (Summer), pp. 26–32.

Minges, Michael (2000). "E-Commerce in Three Land locked Nations." Available at www.itu.int/ITU-D/ict/cs/material/e-commerce%20in%203R.ppt.

Minges, Michael (2001). "Measuring the Internet in South East Asia." Available at www.itu.int/asean2001/documents/pdf/Document-25.pdf.

Modahl, Mary (2000). *Now or Never.* New York: HarperBusiness.

Moon, Youngme (2000). "Interactive Technologies and Relationship Marketing Strategies," Harvard Business School Article 9–599–101 (January 19).

Mullaney, Timothy J. (2004). "E-Biz Strikes Again!" BusinessWeek Online (May 10).

"National Pew Global Attitude Survey" (2007). Available at pewglobal.org/reports/pdf/258.pdf.

"New eGlobal Report" (2000). *Business Wire.* Available at www.lexis-nexus.com/ universe (accessed on March 28, 2000).

Newman, Eric (2007). "For LVMH, China is Fashion Retail's Future" (October 24). Available at www.brandweek.com.

Nickols, Fred (2000). "Strategies: Definitions and Meaning" (February 16). Available at home.att.net/~nickols/strategy_definition.htm.

Nielsen//NetRatings press release. Available at www.nielsen-netratings.com.

Orbitz (2001). Press release. Available at 212.133.71.16/hsmai/news (accessed on April 26, 2002).

Palacios, Ivan (2002). "Transforming the Digital Divide into a Digital Opportunity." Workshop presentation at APEC Workshop on e-Business and Supply Chain Management, Bangkok, Thailand. Available at www.ecommerce.or.th/APEC/eei/presentation/day3/peru.ppt.

Pastore, Michael (2001). "SMS Continues to Take Messaging World by Storm," CyberAtlas (April 4). Available at http://cyberatlas.Internet.com/

Pastore, Michael (2002a). "Incentives Still Key to Mobile Advertising," *Cyberatlas* (April 15). Available at cyberatlas.internet.com.

Pastore, Michael (2002b). "Chinese-Americans Have High PC, Internet Penetration Rates" (February). Available at cyberatlas.internet.com.

Pellegrino, Robert, Doug Amyx, and Kimberly Pellegrino (2002). "A Methodology for Assessing Buyer Behavior: Price Sensitivity and Value Awareness in Internet Auctions." Working paper.

Pennings, J. and P. Puranam (2000). *Market Convergence & Firm Strategies: Towards a Systematic Analysis.* Paper presented at Organization Science Winter Conference.

Peppers, Don (2000). "Getting to Know You Without Knowing You," *Peppers and Rodgers Newsletter* (Spring). Available at www.1to1.com.

Peppers, Don, and Martha Rogers (1996). *The One to One Future.* New York: Doubleday.

Peppers, Don, and Martha Rogers (1997). *Enterprise One to One.* New York: Doubleday.

Pitt, Leyland, Pierre Berthon, Richard Watson, and Michael Ewing (2001). "Pricing Strategy and the Net," *Business Horizons* (March), p. 45.

Ponder, Jaroslaw (2006). "ICTs for Economic Growth: Theory, Policy Implications, Case Studies," *Briefing Session on Economics, UNDP, Geneva, Switzerland* (May 22). Available at www.itu.int/osg/ spu/presentations/2006/ponder-ICTsEconGrowth.ppt.

Ponnaiya, Elzaurdia, and Sanjay Ponnaiya (1999). "The Distribution of Survey Contact and Participation in the United States: Construction a Survey Based Estimate," *Journal of Marketing Research*, no. 36, pp. 286–294.

"Popular Wendy's Kick for a Million CFL Contest Returns to Tsn for Second Season" (2007). Available at http://www.bce.ca.

PricewaterhouseCoopers, LLP (2002). *IAB Internet Advertising Revenue Report: Third Quarter 2001 Results.* New York: PricewaterhouseCoopers New Media Group. Available at www.iab.net (accessed on April 10, 2002).

Radding, Alan (2001). "A Tale of Two Users," *Network Connections*, p. 20.

Ransdell, Eric (1999). "Network Effects," *Fast Company* (September), pp. 210–216.

Rappa, Michael (2000). "Business Models on the Web," (April 29). Available at ecommerce.ncsu.edu/business_models.html.

Ray, Michael L. (1973). "Communication and the Hierarchy of Effects," in *New Models for Mass Communication Research*, P. Clarke (ed.). Beverly Hills, CA: Sage Publications, pp. 147–175.

"Relationships Rule" (2000). *Business 2.0* (May), pp. 303–319.

Renner, Dale (2000). "Closer to the Customer: Customer Relationship Management and the Supply Chain," Andersen Consulting. Available at renner.ascet.com.

Rhoads, C. (2007). What's the Hindi word for dot.com? *Wall Street Journal* (October 11).

Ridley, Kirstin (2007). "Global Mobile Phone Use to Pass Record 3 Billion" (2007). *Reuters News* (June 27). Available at http://www.reuters.com/article/technologyNews/idUSL2712199720070627.

Saunders, Christopher (2001). "E-Mail Marketing Revenue to Top $2 Billion in 2001." Available at www.internetnews.com.

Schonfeld, Erick (2004). "The Big Cheese of Online Grocers," *Business 2.0* (January–February), pp. 60–61.

Seybold, Patricia (1998). *Customers.com.* New York: Random House.

Sheth, Jagdish N. (1995). "Relationship Marketing in Consumer Markets: Antecedents and Consequences," *Journal of the Academy of Marketing Science*, vol. 23, no. 4, pp. 255–271.

Silk, Jon (2001). "SMS Marketing Finds Its Voice," *Internet World Show Daily* (December 13), pp. 7, 32.

Sonnenberg, Frank (1993). "If I Had Only One Client," *Sales and Marketing Management*, vol. 56 (November), p. 4.

Spector, Robert (2000). *Amazon.com: Get Big Fast.* New York: HarperBusiness.

Strobl, Verena (2004). "CTS: Sales Via Internet Doubled by Investing in IT Projects." Working paper.

"Super Buzz or Super Blues?" (2008). *Nielsen Media Company webcast* (January 3). Available at http://www.netratings.com/emc/0801_buzzwebcast/Super_Bowl_Webinar_1_08.pdf.

Tang, Fang-Fang, and Xiaolin Xing (2003). "Pricing Differences Between Dotcoms and Multi-Channel Retailers in the Online Video Market," *Journal of the Academy of Business and Economics* (March). Available at www.findarticles.com/p/articles/mi_m0OGT/is_1_2/ai_113563641.

Taylor Nelson Sofres (2001). "Global eCommerce Report." Available at www.tnsofres.com/ger2001/download/index.cfm.

Terdiman, Daniel (2005). "Study: Wikipedia as Accurate as Britannica," *CNET News.* Available at www.news.com.

"The Arrival of the Convergence Generation" (2004). Ipos Press Release (April 1). Available at www.ipsos-na.com.

"The Benefits of e-Business and Marketing" (2006). *biz/ed* (April 3). Available at www.bized.co.uk.

"The ICT Picture in Africa" (2007). *ITU News* (November). Available at http://www.itu.int/itunews/manager/display.asp?lang=en&year=2007&issue=09&ipage=ICT-Africa&ext=html.

"The Value of a Corporate E-Mail Address" (2001). eContacts Media Kit.

"U.S. Consumer Spending for Online Content Totals Nearly $1.6 Billion in 2003, According to Online Publishers Association Report" (2004). ComScore Press Release (May 11). Available at www.comscore.com.

U.S. State Department (1998). "The Global Landmine Crisis," *Hidden Killers.* Available at www.state.gov/www/global/arms/rpt_9809_demine_ch3h.html.

"Vast Improvements in Prompt Email Response" (2001). *1to1 Magazine* (November–December), p. 11.

Valerius, Tina (2004). "Success Factor Internet Big Sales with Low Budget." Working paper.

Vence, Deborah (2004). "You Talkin' To Me?" *Marketing News* (March 1), pp. 1–11.

Vincent, Lynn (2000). "The Brand That Binds," *Bank Marketing*, vol. 32, no. 11, pp. 24–29.

Watson, Richard, Pierre Berthon, Leyland Pitt, and George Zinkhan (2000). *Electronic Commerce.* Orlando, FL: The Dryden Press.

Weber, Larry (2007). *Marketing to the Social Web.* Hoboken, NJ: John Wiley & Sons, Inc.

Wells, Nigel, Jeff Wolfers, and Richard C. Riecken (2000). "Finance with a Personalized Touch," *Association for Computing Machinery. Communications of the ACM*, vol. 43, no. 8, pp. 31–34.

Whelan, David (2001). "A Tale of Two Consumers," *American Demographics* (September), pp. 54–57.

Wilson, Ralph (2000). Review of Trout & Rivkin's "Differentiate or Die: Survival in Our Era of Killer Competition," *Web Marketing Today*, p. 1.

Wolfinbarger, Mary, and Mary Gilly (2001). "Shopping Online for Freedom, Control and Fun," *California Management Review*, vol. 43, p. 39.

Wood, Marian (2001). *Prentice Hall's Guide to E-Commerce and E-Business.* Upper Saddle River, NJ: Prentice Hall.

World Bank (2007). *World Development Report.* Washington, DC: World Bank. Available at http://www-wds.worldbank.org/external/default/WDSContentServer/WDSP/IB/2006/09/13/000112742_20060913111024/Rendered/PDF/359990WDR0complete.pdf.

Notes for Chapter 5

1. American Marketing Association, *Code of Ethics* (Chicago, IL: American Marketing Association, 1996).
2. S. Warren and L. Brandeis, "The Right to Privacy," 4 *Harvard Law Review* 193 (1890).
3. 381 U.S. 479 (1965).
4. 410 U.S. 113 (1973).
5. Restatement [Second] of Torts, § 652 (1977).
6. W. Adkinson, J. Eisenach, and T. Lenard, "Privacy Online: A Report on the Information Practices and Policies of Commercial Web Sites," The Progress & Freedom Foundation, March 2002, Available at www.pff.org.
7. *Timothy R. McVeigh v. William Cohen, et al.*, 983 F. Supp. 215 (D.D.C., January 26, 1998).
8. "Privacy Online: A Report to Congress," p. 12, Federal Trade Commission, June 1998, Available at www.ftc.gov/reports/privacy3/toc.htm.
9. Children's Online Privacy Protection Act of 1998, 15 U.S.C. 6501 et seq.
10. Federal Trade Commission Children's Online Privacy Protection Rule, Final Rule, 16 CFR Part 312, November 3, 1999, Available at www.ftc.gov/os/1999/9910/64fr59888. htm.
11. Fair Credit Reporting Act, 15 USC 1681 (1992).
12. Electronic Communications Protection Act (ECPA) 18 USC §2510–21, 2701–11 (1994).
13. The Direct Marketing Association guidelines are available at www.the dma.org/library/guidelines/onlineguidelines.shtml.
14. In re Northwest Airlines Privacy Litigation, No. 04–126 (D. Minn. June 6, 2004).
15. Directive 95/46/EC of the European Parliament and of the Council of 24 October 1995 in the protection of individuals with regard to the processing of personal data and on the free movement of such data. Article 25.
16. Updated Safe Harbor Principles are available at www.ecommerce.gov.
17. "Commission Staff Working Paper: The Application of Commission Decision 520/2000/EC of July 2000 to Directive 95/46 of the European Parliament and of the Council on the Adequate Protection of Personal Data Provided by the Safe Harbor Privacy Principles and Related Frequently Asked Questions Issued by the U.S. Department of Commerce," Commission of the European Communities, February 13, 2002, available at www.europa.eu.int/comm/internal_market/en/dataprot/news/02–196_en.pdf.
18. "Privacy Online: A Report to Congress," p. 12, Federal Trade Commission, June 1998, available at www.ftc.gov/reports/privacy3/toc.htm.
19. 35 U.S.C. §101, et seq.
20. *Amazon.com v. Barnesandnoble.com* (W.D. Wash., filed October 21, 1999).
21. 17 U.S.C. §§107 and 109 (1998).
22. 17 U.S.C. §506(a) (as amended 1997).
23. 17 U.S.C. §512 et seq. (1998).
24. 17 U.S.C. §1201et seq. (1998).
25. See, "Unintended Consequences: Three Years Under the DMCA," Electronic Frontier Foundation, May 3, 2002, available at www.eff.org.

26. WIPO Copyright Treaty, adopted by the Diplomatic Conference on December 20, 1996, WIPO Doc. CRNR/DC/94 (December 23, 1996), and WIPO Performances and Phonograms Treaty, adopted by the Diplomatic Conference on December 20, 1996, WIPO Doc. CRNR/DC/95 (December 23, 1996).

27. 15 U.S.C. §1051 et seq.

28. 15 U.S.C. §1125.

29. *Playboy Enterprises, Inc. v. Calvin Designer Label,* 985 F. Supp. 1220 (N.D. Cal. 1997).

30. *Playboy Enterprises, Inc. v. Welles,* 279 F.3d 796 (9th Cir. 2002).

31. *Estee Lauder Inc. v. The Fragrance Counter and Excite, Inc.* (S.D.N.Y. complaint filed March 5, 1999).

32. *Ticketmaster Corp. v. Microsoft Corp.,* No. 97–3055 DDP (D. Cal. filed April 28, 1997).

33. *Washington Post v. TotalNEWS, Inc.,* 97 Civ. 1190 (PKL) (S.D.N.Y., filed February 28, 1997).

34. *M. A. Mortenson Co. v. Timberline Software,* 998 P.2d 305 (Wash. 2000).

35. *Groff v. America Online,* 1998 WL 307001 (R.I. Super. Ct., May 27, 1998).

36. 18 USC §1831 et seq.

37. *New England Circuit Sales v. Randall,* No. 96–10840-EFH (D.Mass., June 4, 1996).

38. *eBay, Inc. v. Bidder's Edge, Inc.,* 100 F.Supp. 2d 1058 (N.D. Cal. 2000).

39. Directive 96/9/EC of the European Parliament and of the Council of 11 March 1996 on the legal protection of databases.

40. 948 F.Supp. 436 (E.D. Pa., 1996).

41. *America Online v. Christian Brothers,* No. 98 Civ. 8959 (DAB) (HBP) (S.D. N.Y., December 14, 1999).

42. 15 U.S.C. §7701, et seq.

43. *Intel Corp. v. Hamidi,* 1 Cal Rptr. 3d 32 (Cal. 2003).

44. *267623 Ontario Inc. v. Nexx Online,* No. C20546/99 (Ontario Super. Ct., June 14, 1999).

45. 47 U.S.C. §230(c)(1) [Communications Decency Act of 1996].

46. *Zeran v. America Online,* 129 F.3d 327 (4th Cir. Va. 1997), cert. denied, 524 U.S. 937 (1998).

47. 117 S.Ct. 2329 (1997).

48. *United States et al. v. American Library Association, Inc., et al.,* 539 US 194 (2003).

49. *Zippo Manufacturing Company v. Zippo Dot Com, Inc.,* 952 F. Supp. 1119 (W.D.Pa. January 16, 1997).

50. *Digital Control Inc. v. Boretronics, Inc.,* 161 F. Supp. 2d 1183 (W.D. Wash. 2001).

51. *ALS Scan, Inc. v. Robert Wilkins,* 142 F. Supp. 2d 793 (D.Md. 2001).

52. *Net2Phone, Inc. v. Superior Court,* 109 Cal. App. 4th 583 (Cal. Ct. App. 2003.

53. vmag.cilp.org.

54. www.arbiter.wipo.int/center/index.html.

55. "Combating Internet Fraud and Deception," Federal Trade Commission, May 2001, available at www.ftc.gov/bcp/internet/cases-internet.pdf.

INDEX